Center for Digital Economy, Nankai University
School of Economics, Nankai University
Center for Transnationals' Studies, Nankai University

数字经济与中国
（Digital Economy and China）

南开大学数字经济研究中心编写组　著
Editorial Committee of Center for Digital Economy, Nankai University

南开大学出版社
天津

图书在版编目(CIP)数据

数字经济与中国 ＝ Digital Economy and China：英文 / 南开大学数字经济研究中心编写组著. －天津：南开大学出版社，2021.12(2025.6 重印)
ISBN 978-7-310-06199-0

Ⅰ.①数… Ⅱ.①南… Ⅲ.①信息经济－研究－中国－英文 Ⅳ.①F492

中国版本图书馆 CIP 数据核字(2021)第 242781 号

版权所有　侵权必究

数字经济与中国
SHUZI JINGJI YU ZHONGGUO

南开大学出版社出版发行
出版人：王　康
地址：天津市南开区卫津路 94 号　　邮政编码：300071
营销部电话：(022)23508339　　营销部传真：(022)23508542
https://nkup.nankai.edu.cn

河北文曲印刷有限公司印刷　全国各地新华书店经销
2021 年 12 月第 1 版　　2025 年 6 月第 2 次印刷
260×185 毫米　16 开本　26.75 印张　2 插页　615 千字
定价：108.00 元

如遇图书印装质量问题，请与本社营销部联系调换，电话：(022)23508339

Editorial Committee of Center for Digital Economy, Nankai University

Consultant: Xian Guoming

Director: Sheng Bin

Deputy Directors: Yan Bing   Shi Bingzhan   Li Lei

Members of Editorial Committee:

Sheng Bin	Shi Bingzhan	Li Lei
Yan Bing	Huang Jiuli	Sun Puyang
Jiang Dianchun	Liu Cheng	Zhou Xing
Liu Chenyang	Luo Wei	

Special Thanks to the World Economic Forum for Its Support

Introduction

Digital economy emerges with the gradual development of Information and Communications Technology (hereinafter referred to as "ICT"). It has experienced a gestation period (1940s to 1960s), a growing period (mid-1970s to early 1990s), a rapid developing period (mid-1990s to early 21st century), a comprehensive coverage period (2001 to 2015), and a transformation and adjustment period (2016 to present). In recent years, with the emergence and development of new-generation ICTs such as artificial intelligence/mobile Internet, the Internet of Things, big data, and blockchains, digital economy also shows a trend of rapid growth. Its contribution to overall economic growth is increasing. Digital economy has produced profound and extensive influences on economy, society, culture and other sectors. Digitalization has increasingly become the focus of economic development strategies of all countries.

Although starting late, China's digital economy has enjoyed a significant late-mover advantage. After entering the 21st century, especially during the last 10 years, the rapid development of China's digital economy has gradually become an important driving force for China to promote supply-side reform and realized high-quality economic development by replacing old growth drivers with new ones. With the rapid development of the global digital economy, China's domestic and international environment has changed significantly, which puts forward new requirements for the economic work in the new era. The report of the 19th National Congress pointed out that the supply-side reform shall be deepened: "promote the deep integration of Internet, big data, artificial intelligence, and real economy"; strengthen the construction of an innovative country, vigorously develop science and technology, and support the "improvement of China's strength in Internet, digitalization, and the effort of building a smart society". According to the "White Paper on China's Digital Economy Development (2020)" by the China Academy of Information and Communications Technology, the scale of China's digital economy reached 35.8 trillion yuan in 2019, accounting for 36.2% of the GDP, a 1.4 percent year-on-year increase. Calculated on a comparable basis, China's digital economy grew by 15.6% in nominal terms in 2019, about 7.85 percent higher than the nominal GDP growth rate over the same period. The status of digital economy in the national economy is further underlined. General Secretary Xi Jinping proposed to vigorously develop digital economy on many important occasions. On November 8, 2018, the World Internet Conference was held, to which Xi Jinping sent a congratulatory letter stating that "the Internet, big data, artificial intelligence, and other modern information technologies have continuously made breakthroughs, digital economy is booming, and the interests of all countries are more closely linked." During the 2018 G20 Summit, Xi Jinping pointed out that "the digitalized transformation of the world economy is the general trend, and the new industrial revolution will profoundly reshape human society. We must not only encourage innovation and promote the deep integration of digital economy and real economy, but also be aware of the risks and challenges brought about by the application of new technologies, strengthen the construction of institutional and legal systems, and put emphasis on education and vocational training."

As the development of China's digital economy continues to deepen, analyzing the development of digital economy in related fields bears significance and value. Specifically, from aspect of industry upgrading, as an integrating economy, digital economy has a huge enabling effect. The rapid development of digital economy will help promote the optimization of resource allocation in real economy, adjust the industrial structure, achieve transformation and upgrading, and improve the overall competitiveness; from the aspect of digital trade, digital economy promotes the development of China's international trade of information products and services, gradually improves China's trade structure, offers new development opportunities for China's underdeveloped regions, promotes regional economic development, expands China's access to the international market, and promotes the growth of China's trade economy; from the aspect of international investment, investigating the development trend and limits of global digital investment will not only help identify the developing direction of the digital age, but will also help to avoid obstacles and further release the growth potential of digital investment, which is important for promoting China's development of innovation and supply-side reform under the new normal; from the aspect of digital finance, digital finance reduces the cost of China's credit system, improves the accuracy of the anti-fraud system, and promotes the tailored development of financial products. Research on the development of digital finance in China is conducive to improving the operation and management level of Chinese financial institutions and promoting the innovation of China's financial model; from the aspect of the labor market, digital economy, featuring digitalization and network, has changed the approaches and means of combining production tools and labor force, enabling the labor market to function under digital technology, which not only creates many employment opportunities, but also makes the job market more flexible. Researching the relationship between digital economy and the labor market is important for solving the employment problem for China's huge workforce population, optimizing the employment structure, allowing the general public to share the fruits of the development of digital economy, and avoiding the impact of digital economy on the labor market; from the aspect of global governance, while leading the globalization of economy, digital economy promotes revolutionary changes for global economic and trade models and promotes the revolutionary transformation of global economy toward a more inclusive direction. Research on digital economy and global governance will help form and improve the global digital economy supervision and governance system, and establish a multilateral, democratic, and transparent global governance system of digital economy. In summary, systematically summarizing the typical facts of the emergence and development of digital economy, and studying the causes, current status, and impact of the development of China's digital economy bear practical significance for the sustained and stable development of China's economy.

This research report is comprised of 9 parts: the development of global digital economy; the development of China's digital economy; digital economy and industrial upgrading; digital economy and trade; digital economy and investment; digital economy and finance; digital economy and the labor market; digital economy and global governance; and policy recommendations for the development of China's digital economy. A detailed introduction is as follows:

Chapter 1 is about the development of the global digital economy. A new round of innovation of ICT has cultivated big data, the Internet of Things, artificial intelligence, blockchains, cloud computing, and other digital technologies. The commercialized application of digital technology has made data an important factor of production. Qualitative changes in the economic form take place in aspects of technology and factors, which generates digital economy. The narrowly defined digital economy only refers to the ICT sector, including ICT manufacturing and ICT service industries. The broadly defined digital economy includes digital industrialization and industrial digitization; the former involves emerging industries, and the latter refers to the digital transformation of traditional industries. At the macro level, the proportion of digital economy in the total economy increases year by year, becoming an important force that drives economic growth. Industrial digitization and ICT services constitute the major aspects of the broadly defined and narrowly defined digital economy, respectively. The structural features of digital economy are determined by the scale of each component and the difference in the degree of digitization. The scale, structure, and output scale of employment of digital economy show similar characteristics. At the micro level, digitalized companies have gradually grown into large multinational companies; the level of digitalization generally increases but differences remain, leading to the re-allocation of resources among micro subjects, which can increase efficiency and improve welfare but can also cause digital divide and expand inequality. This is the micro foundation formed by the scale and structural characteristics of digital economy. As a new type of economy, digital economy has influence on a wide range of fields, including international trade, the labor market, the financial market, government affairs, etc.; the potential problems brought about by digital economy are data security and digital economy security, which require important changes in economic governance models.

Chapter 2 is about the development of China's digital economy. Firstly, it explains the development process of China's digital technology. As a representative of the industrialization of digital economy, ICT has gradually evolved into an independent industry in China, promoting the development and application of big data, the Internet of Things, artificial intelligence, blockchains, and cloud computing, which further promotes the steady development of digital economy and provides new momentum for China's economic growth. Secondly, it describes the current status of China's digital economy. The large scale of Internet users and the improvement of new infrastructure lay a sound foundation for the development of digital economy, allowing China's digital industrialization to continue to improve. The digitalization of industries enjoys an energetic drive, and the overall level of China's Internet administrative services also continues to improve; in addition, the relationship between China's digital economy development and the world is discussed, including the global status and influence of China's digital economy, and China's cooperation with the world in the field of digital economy; finally, the policy system for the development of China's digital economy is elaborated on, including the opportunities and challenges faced by China's digital economy. China must grasp the opportunities of digital transformation and make full use of digitalized development. At the same time, China must always pay attention to a series of challenges brought about by the application of digital technology. This chapter also explains the policy guarantees in the process of the integration of the existing digital economy and real economy, as well as relevant incentive policies for the development of digital economy. The analysis of this chapter shows that China's digital economy is showing a trend of rapid development. On the one hand, it is constantly changing China's traditional forms of organization of industries; on the other hand, it is reconstructing China's market form. The rapid growth of multiple indicators indicates the rapid advancement of digital economy in China and the continuous advancement of cooperation between China and the world. The introduction of relevant policies has also laid a solid foundation for the development of China's digital economy.

Chapter 3 is about digital economy and industrial upgrading. The industrialization of digital technology and the digitization of traditional industries proceed along parallel paths, while the commercialized application of digital technology affects each level of the industrial structure, bringing new sources of drivers for industrial transformation and upgrading. This chapter focuses on the internal connection between digital economy and China's industrial upgrading. First, it clarifies the impacting mechanism of digital economy on industrial upgrading, including the fact that digital technology can optimize the R&D, production, circulation, and sales processes for companies; platformization gradually replaces the trend of vertical integration, becoming the main mode of value acquisition in the industry; integration and development between industries provide a new approach to increase the value chain. Next, the latest development trend of digital economy and its integration with traditional industries are introduced: the industrial technology and business model of the fundamental digital economy are relatively mature; the integrating digital economy presents an imbalance across industries and regions. Based on the above analysis, this chapter compares the different effects of digital economy on the transformation and upgrading of various key industries. It shows that the digitalized development of each industry has its own focus, which develops into different transformation paths such as "digital agriculture", "smart manufacturing", and "digital logistics". Finally, digital transformation strategies are discussed with representatives of "Fanmi Technology", "Rootcloud", "SF Express", and "Pinduoduo". With the constant deepening of the integration of digital technology and real economy, digital economy will become an important driving force for industrial transformation and upgrading in the future. Therefore, it is worth the attention of all sectors of society to create a sound environment for the development of digital economy from the aspects of talent training, infrastructure construction, and business environment.

Chapter 4 is about digital economy and trade. Driven by digital economy, trade activities go through profound changes, and the era of digital trade has arrived. The research topic of this chapter is digital economy and trade, which focuses on the analysis of the development of China's digital trade, possible changes to China's trade under the influence of digital economy, and the prospects and possible challenges of digital economy in China. Firstly, it analyzes the changes in the concept of trade and methods of statistics, as well as the impact and significance of digital trade while we embrace the digital trade era. Secondly, this chapter conducts a comprehensive and detailed mechanism analysis on the impact of digital economy on trade from the perspectives of trade products, the number of trading companies, international trade networks, transition and upgrading of processing trade, the involvement in global value chains, the status in international trade, etc. Next, two exemplary business cases of China's digital trade are studied: the construction of Tmall's international digital trade value chain and the innovation of Huawei's trade form of mobile phones in digital economy. Finally, based on the analysis of the current status of China's digital product trade and digital service trade, the problems, challenges, and prospects of China's digital trade are discussed. It is believed that global trade has entered a new stage of digital trade. The impact of digital economy on China's trade activities is reflected in promoting changes in trade products, increasing the number of service trade companies and goods trading companies, increasing the diversification of the international trade market, promoting the transformation and upgrading of processing trade, facilitating China's participation in the global value chain, and improving China's status in international trade; in recent years, the scale and growth rate of China's digital product trade and digital service trade have increased rapidly, and ICT product trade, cross-border e-commerce, and ICT service trade have gradually become the core of China's development of digital trade; although problems and challenges in China's digital trade development remain, including unbalanced development and weak innovation capabilities, digital trade will lead the future development of

China's trade by increasing the level of companies' involvement in trade, continuously extending the industrial value chain, and promoting the reconstruction of the order of global trade.

Chapter 5 is about digital economy and international investment. The rapid development of information technology and the ever-increasing market demand for digital products and services have spawned a boom of investment in digital economy. Investment hotspots continue to emerge in cloud computing, cloud storage, virtual reality, artificial intelligence, blockchain, online medicine and health, and shared travel. Therefore, it is understandable that despite the lack of momentum of economic growth, the hindrance of globalization, and the overall decline in international investment in recent years, international investment in the field of digital economy still grows steadily. As the world's second-largest digital economy power, China has a pivotal position both as an investment destination and as a capital-exporting country. The rapid development of digital technology is closely related to the strong support of national policies that help create a sound market environment for international investment in digital economy. The research perspective of this chapter extends from the macro level to the micro level, presenting readers with an overview of the international investment in digital economy (including mergers and acquisitions, private equity investment, and venture capital investment), especially the history and development of international investment in China's digital economy. The first two sections describe the development of global investment in digital economy, foreign investment in China's digital economy, and China's outbound investment in digital economy from several dimensions, such as the total volume of investment, types of transactions, industries, host countries, and source countries, with the number of transactions and the transaction amount as two quantitative standards. This chapter also takes three typical Chinese digital investment companies (Baidu, Tencent, and JD) as examples to show the structure and philosophy, scale and type, investment fields, and internationalization strategies of Chinese companies' digital investment from a micro perspective.

Chapter 6 is about digital economy and finance. Digital finance is the product of the evolution of the combination of finance and technology. After more than 10 years of rapid development, the global digital financial ecosystem has begun to take shape. At present, digital finance incorporates almost all areas of global financial businesses, including credit, lending, foreign exchange, deposits, investment, and other sectors, and has become an indispensable part of the financial system, representing the direction of the development of the finance industry. Artificial intelligence and online business collaboration based on big data will become the mainstream of the development of financial technology for the foreseeable future. In the field of financial technology, traditional financial institutions are actively embracing financial technology, and digital technology is being incorporated with financial application scenarios more closely. Asia and the Americas are in a leading position in the global landscape of financial technology, while Europe is less developed. China's Yangtze River Delta region, the San

Francisco Bay Area (Silicon Valley), the Beijing-Tianjin-Hebei area, the Greater London area, the Guangdong-Hong Kong-Macao Greater Bay Area, and the New York Bay Area are key areas for the development of global financial technology. Fintech companies in the US are mainly start-ups. Although their scale is much smaller than China's start-ups, their innovation capabilities are stronger. Chinese financial technology companies are primarily Internet giants, which not only have advantages in technology and data but also in talents and capital. The application of digital technology has brought both opportunities and challenges to the development of China's financial industry. Digital finance reduces the cost of the credit system, improves the accuracy of anti-fraud activities, promotes the personalized development of financial products, improves the operation and management level of financial institutions, and promotes the innovation of financial models. As a result, digital currency and blockchain technology arise, which greatly improves the efficiency of financial activities and increases the inclusiveness of finance. Meanwhile, the operation of digital currency outside the banking system challenges the effectiveness of traditional monetary policies. The fast and wide nature of digital finance risk transmission challenges the traditional financial supervision model. Risk prevention and control have become a very important part of the development of digital finance.

Chapter 7 is about digital economy and the labor market. The rapid development of digital economy has caused a huge impact on the traditional labor market. This chapter first summarizes the typical characteristics of the labor market under the background of digital economy from the aspects of the scale, structure, and form of employment. From the perspective of the scale of employment, the scale of employment in digital economy across all countries in the world is growing rapidly, be it in absolute number or relative number. From the perspective of the structure of employment, digital economy in the tertiary industry is the main source to attract employees. There is great potential for the secondary industry to attract labor if digitalized. The rapid development of digital economy leads to a structural contradiction between the supply and demand of highly skilled digital talents, and the structure of skills for employment opportunities is polarized. With the development and application of digital technology, flexible employment forms such as self-employment, freelance, and part-time employment are emerging. Then, by analyzing research literature, a deep theoretical discussion of the multiple impacts and impacting mechanisms of the development of digital economy on the scale of supply and demand, the structure and forms of employment is conducted. Finally, focusing on the development of China's digital economy, the employment situation under digital economy from the aspects of scale, structure, forms, and industrial and regional differences is discussed. With the rapid expansion of China's digital economy, the ability of digital economy to attract jobs has increased significantly, and its share in employment has increased rapidly. Digital economy fully plays its role as a "stabilizer" and "multiplier" for employment. The employment structure is also rapidly adjusting with the development of digital economy. Many repetitive and low-value job opportunities in traditional industries will be replaced by highly skilled job opportunities. The rapid development of China's platform economy, sharing economy, "crowdsourcing", "crowd innovation", and other new digital economic models and new business forms have spawned new flexible employment models such as self-employment, freelance, and part-time employment. This chapter uses three cases, i.e., "Meituan Dianping", "5G mobile communication technology", and "Didi Sharing Platform Economy", to illustrate the innovation of employment forms brought about by digital economy.

Chapter 8 is about digital economy and global governance. Digital economy is becoming the source of further global economic growth and the core driving force of globalization. While leading the new development of economic globalization, failure to carry out efficient cooperation on regulations and governance at the international level may threaten the global economic growth. Therefore, as the status of digital economy in the development of global economy improves rapidly, it is urgent to improve the relevant global governance system and the construction of specific institutions. The global governance of digital economy should not only include the supervision of governments, but also introduce digital economy participants such as platforms, third parties, companies, consumers, etc., to jointly explore how to create a sustainable and healthy ecosystem, and to better leverage the role of digital economy in shifting the economic growth model and replacing old growth drivers with new ones. This chapter first outlines the background and significance of building a global governance system for digital economy. While digital economy gradually becomes an important driving force for global economic growth, it has also brought about new challenges to the global trade and investment ecosystem, and issues such as the "digital divide" and information security have become increasingly prominent. At present, the WTO, the G20 Group, the Asia-Pacific Economic Cooperation (APEC), the "Comprehensive and Progressive Trans-Pacific Partnership Agreement" (CPTPP), the "Data Circulation Circle" of the US, Japan, and Europe, and other international institutions and economic and trade agreements are committed to building a multilateral digital trade system. The European Union, the US, China, Japan, ASEAN, Australia, and other important global economies haven't reached a consensus on national development strategies and policies in debated fields such as the leadership in the global governance of digital economy, cross-border data flow, personal privacy protection, server localization, and protection of digital intellectual property. Looking forward, challenges remain in the global governance of digital economy. Not only is it difficult for major economies to reconcile, but it is also difficult to achieve a global free flow of data, the core resource for the development of digital economy, in the short term. A global governance system that lacks an overall plan will restrict the sustainable development of digital economy.

Chapter 9 offers policy recommendations for the development of China's digital economy. As the last chapter of this report, it elaborates on policy recommendations related to digital economy and provides policy references for the future development of digital economy in China.

This report is an important product of the international cooperation between Nankai University and the World Economic Forum. Professor Klaus Schwab, the founder and chairman of the World Economic Forum and an honorary doctor of Nankai University, visited Nankai University on September 18, 2018. Professor Yang Qingshan, Secretary of the Party Committee of Nankai University, received Professor Schwab with a warm welcome. The two sides achieved the intention of deepening cooperation and conducting joint research. Subsequently, under the leadership of Professor Wang Lei, vice president of Nankai University, School of Economics and the Center for Transnationals' Studies of Nankai University organized a team of experts to go to the Beijing Representative Office of the World Economic Forum for specific discussions. Both sides agreed that digital economy is a very important topic in China. The World Economic Forum Provided Support to this project following the discussion.

The composition of this report started in May 2019 and ended in October 2020, lasting 1.5 years. Nankai University attaches great importance to this cooperation and has provided essential financial support for the preparation of the report. Secretary Yang Qingshan has been personally following the progress of the research report closely. School of Economics and the Center for Transnationals' Studies of Nankai University organized a strong research team consisting of Professor Xian Guoming (Director of the Center for Transnationals' Studies of Nankai University) and David Aikman (Chief Representative of the World Economic Forum Greater China) as consultants, and Professor Sheng Bin (Dean of School of Economics and Director of the Digital Economy Research Center) as the chief coordinator. Professor Shi Bingzhan (Chapter 1), Professor Li Lei (Chapter 2 and Chapter 9), Professor Yan Bing and Professor Huang Jiuli(Chapter 3), Professor Sun Puyang (Chapter 4), Professor Jiang Dianchun (Chapter 5), Associate Professor Liu Cheng (Chapter 6), Associate Professor Zhou Xing (Chapter 7), Professor Liu Chenyang and Associate Professor Luo Wei (Chapter 8) composed each chapter of the report respectively. Professor Li Lei is responsible for coordinating the Chinese version of this report, and Professor Yan Bing is responsible for coordinating the English translation and publication of this report.

Contents

Chapter 1　Development of Global Digital Economy ·································· 1
　　Section 1　Development of Digital Technology and the Emergence of Digital Economy ··· 1
　　Section 2　The Concept and Features of Digital Economy ··················· 8
　　Section 3　An Overview of the Development of Global Digital Economy ········ 19
Chapter 2　The Development of China's Digital Economy ························ 48
　　Section 1　The Development Process of China's Digital Technologies ········ 48
　　Section 2　Current Status of the Development of China's Digital Economy ······ 57
　　Section 3　The Relationship between China's Digital Economic Development and the World ··· 83
　　Section 4　The Policy System of China's Digital Economic Development ········ 90
Chapter 3　Digital Economy and Industrial Upgrading ·························· 106
　　Section 1　Impact of Digital Economy on Industrial Upgrading ·············· 106
　　Section 2　Digital Economy and China's Industrial Upgrading: An Overview ······ 110
　　Section 3　Digital Economy and Industrial Upgrading: Development of Key Industries ··· 144
　　Section 4　Representative Digital Enterprises in China ······················ 168
Chapter 4　Digital Economy and Trade ·· 180
　　Section 1　The Advent of the Digital Trade Era ······························ 180
　　Section 2　The Impact of Digital Economy on Trade ·························· 188
　　Section 3　Typical Enterprise Case Studies of China's Digital Trade ········ 205
　　Section 4　Trade Development in the Digital Economy Era ·················· 211
Chapter 5　Digital Economy and International Investment ······················ 226
　　Section 1　The Development of Global Digital Economy Investment ········ 226
　　Section 2　International Investment in China's Digital Economy ············ 235
　　Section 3　Typical Enterprise Case Studies of China's Digital Investment ······ 249
Chapter 6　Digital Economy and Finance ·· 262
　　Section 1　An Overview of Digital Finance ····································· 262
　　Section 2　Effect of Digital Finance ·· 267

Section 3	Digital Financial Innovation	281
Section 4	Risks of Digital Finance and Risk Prevention and Control	296

Chapter 7　Digital Economy and the Labor Market ········· 307
　　Section 1　Typical Characteristics of the Labor Market in the Digital Economy Era ····· 308
　　Section 2　The Impact of Digital Economy on the Labor Market ········· 316
　　Section 3　Development and Changes of China's Labor Market in the Context of
　　　　　　　Digital Economy ········· 329
　　Section 4　The Impact of the Development of Digital Economy on the Labor Market ··· 344

Chapter 8　Digital Economy and Global Governance ········· 353
　　Section 1　The Significance of a Global Governance System for Digital Economy ····· 354
　　Section 2　The Evolution and Development of a Global Governance System for
　　　　　　　Digital Economy ········· 357
　　Section 3　Key Issues in Global Governance of Digital Economy ········· 366
　　Section 4　Prospects for Global Governance of Digital Economy ········· 387

Chapter 9　Policy Recommendations for the Development of China's Digital Economy ····· 389
　　Section 1　Policy Recommendations for the Development of Digital Technology
　　　　　　　and Economy ········· 389
　　Section 2　Policy Recommendations for the Development of Digital Economy
　　　　　　　Industries ········· 391
　　Section 3　Policy Recommendations for the Development of China's Digital Trade ····· 393
　　Section 4　Policy Recommendations for the Development of International
　　　　　　　Investment in Digital Economy ········· 396
　　Section 5　Policy Recommendations for the Development of Digital Finance ········· 398
　　Section 6　Policy Recommendations for Digital Economy and the Labor Market ········· 400
　　Section 7　Policy Recommendations for Digital Economy and Global Governance ······ 403

Chapter 1　Development of Global Digital Economy

A new round of innovation of Information and Communications Technology (ICT) cultivates big data, the Internet of Things, artificial intelligence, blockchains, cloud computing, and other digital technologies. The commercialized application of digital technology makes data an important factor of production, which then generates digital economy. The narrowly defined digital economy only refers to the ICT sector, including ICT manufacturing and ICT service industries. The broadly defined digital economy includes digital industrialization and industrial digitization. At the macro level, the proportion of digital economy in the total economy increases year by year, becoming an important force that drives economic growth. Industrial digitization and ICT services constitute the major aspects of the broadly and narrowly defined digital economy, respectively. The structure and characteristics of digital economy are determined by the scale of each component and the differences in the degrees of digitization. In terms of digital economy, its employment scale and structure, and output scale and structure show similar characteristics. At the micro level, digitized enterprises have gradually grown into large multinational enterprises; the level of digitization generally increases but differences remain, leading to the re-allocation of resources among micro-subjects, which can increase efficiency and improve welfare but also cause digital divide and expand inequality. This is the micro foundation formed by the scale and structural characteristics of digital economy. As a new type of economy, digital economy has a wide range of influence, including international trade, the labor market, the financial market, and the model of governance, etc.; potential problems brought by digital economy are data security and digital economy security, which require important changes in models of economic governance.

Section 1　Development of Digital Technology and the Emergence of Digital Economy

1.1 Development and economic influence of ICT

After the Second World War, ICT developed rapidly and promoted rapid economic growth, generating new concepts such as information economy, Internet economy, new economy, and knowledge economy. In 2000, the "Okinawa Charter for the Global Information Society" issued by the G8 mentioned for the first time the concept of "information and communications technology", referring to the organic combination of communications technology, information technology, and their applications, but there was no official definition.

Important inventions such as general computers, transistors, optical fiber communications, the Internet, and mobile communications illustrate the rapid development of ICT. They are also the precondition for the emergence of digital technology and digital economy. Since the first general electronic computer was invented by the University of Pennsylvania in 1946, ICT has been advancing with a series of new products, which greatly promote economic growth and social progress. Table 1.1 shows milestones in the development of ICT.

Table 1.1 Development of ICT after WWII

Year	Milestone
1946	The world's first electronic computer, ENIAC, was invented
1947	The transistor was introduced
1948	The world's first stored-program computer was born
1950	The world's first commercial computer was born
1959	Integrated circuit technology was introduced
1965	The US launched the first communications satellite
1966	The concept of optical fiber communications was first introduced
1967	Large-scale integrated circuit technology was introduced
1969	The predecessor of the Internet, ARPENET, was launched
1970	Optical fiber communications technology evolved from theory to practical application
1977	VLSI (very-large-scale integration) technology was introduced; optical fiber communications was commercially applied for the first time
1978	Mobile communications network technology (1G) was introduced
1989	The World Wide Web was introduced
1994	The Internet was commercially used for the first time

Source: Information from the Internet.

With the improvement of ICT, its impact on economic development has gradually taken shape. In particular, in the 1990s, the economic growth of the US and some developed countries showed the following characteristics: the growth rate of the ICT sector exceeded the growth rate of the total economy, and the proportion of ICT sectors increased year by year; the macroeconomic growth rate increased while the unemployment rate and the inflation rate decreased. This new phenomenon was described by the economists' community with new terms such as "information economy", "Internet economy", "new economy", or "knowledge economy" from diverse perspectives. Although the expressions are different, their substantive contents all reflect the influence of ICT on economic growth, which is consistent with the theory of economics, emphasizing the importance of technology.

1.2 Emergence and development of digital technology

Digital technology is the latest development of ICT. On the one hand, the emergence of digital technology is based on communications technology and computer technology. Digital technology relies on the close integration of communications technology and computer technology, and is the heritage and development of ICT. On the other hand, digital technology is characterized by high precision, a high level of fault tolerance, and a sound versatility that distinguishes it from traditional ICT. Digital technology is an emerging technology accompanying the development of electronic computer technology. Initially, digital technology refers to the technology that converts information (including pictures, texts, audio, images, etc.) into assemble language that can be recognized by electronic computers and then performs calculations, processing, storage, transmission, distribution, and restoration with certain equipment. According to Ronnie J. Phillips, any method of transmitting information using the two statuses of the circuit (i.e., the binary method) can be defined as digital technology. Under this definition, the telegraph is the first piece of digital technology.[1] Later, with the development of the Internet, the definition of digital technology got broader and more complex, such as digitization of resources, digitization of equipment, and digitization of information. At present, digital technology is represented by big data, the Internet of Things, artificial intelligence, blockchain, cloud computing, etc., which will be introduced below.

Data is the foundation and constituent of big data. It is generally believed that data is a logical induction of objective matters and the expressive carrier and form of information. As is defined in "Xin Ci Yu Da Ci Dian" (*New Vocabulary Dictionary*), data is a system of symbols that uses digits to reflect the content and is internally coherent. In computer language, it is expressed primarily as binary language. Data has two important characteristics: it relies on a carrier, that is, it has to rely on communications equipment (including servers, terminals, mobile storage devices, etc.), without which data cannot exist; the other characteristic is that it displays information through an application code or program, but the generation, transmission, and storage of information must be reflected by the physical data.[2] The development of Internet technology has broken the rule that information must exist prior to the carrier. Data produced by individual actions on the Internet can generate synchronous information through the network, which is the technical basis of the emergence of big data. According to the "Action Outline for Promoting the Development of Big Data", "Big data refers to data sets characterized by high volume, more varieties, high velocity, and high application value, and is rapidly developing into a new generation of information technology and service type for collection, storage, and

---

[1] Ronnie, P. (2000). Digital Technology and Institution Change from Gilded Age to Modern Times: The Impact of the Telegraph and the Internet. *Journal of Economic Issues*, 34(2): 267-289.

[2] Mei Xiaying (2016). The Legal Properties of Data and the Position of Date in Civil Law. *Social Science in China*, 9: 164-183.

correlation analysis of huge amounts of data from disparate sources in various formats whereby we can discover new knowledge, create new value, and improve the capabilities." Big data is not simply piling up large amounts of data; it has many dimensions, including quantity, speed, diversity, value increment, etc. Quantity is the fundamental dimension of big data. Relying on the huge quantity of data, big data increases the value of data that bears low value when considered individually. Speed refers to the speed of generation and processing of data. Timely and rapid processing of data could maximize the value of data. Diversity refers to the diversified types and sources of data. If data is diversified, it is more objective. Narrowly defined, big data is regarded as a computer technology for mining and analyzing data, and a computer technology that uses cloud computing, machine learning, and other computer methods to collect, process, and recreate the information left by users on the Internet. A more broadly defined big data emphasizes the way of thinking, and emphasizes the use of extensive, diverse, and rapidly updated data to predict the trend, so as to find the correlation between various phenomena. Currently, the understanding of big data is limited to the narrowly defined technical level, instead of seeing it as a commodity, a service, or an industry.

Artificial intelligence (AI) is an important branch of computer science, which refers to technology that can react in a way like human intelligence. It is a new technological science that researches and develops theories, methods, technology, and application systems used for stimulating, extending, and expanding human intelligence. In short, it is "a machine with intelligence".[1] AI uses computers to simulate certain thinking processes and intelligent behaviors of human beings (such as learning, reasoning, thinking, planning, etc.), creating computers similar to human intelligence and enabling computers to achieve higher-level applications. AI involves computer science and branches of natural sciences and social sciences such as philosophy, logic, and psychology. Its scope has reached beyond that of computer science. In the summer of 1956, a group of young scientists gathered to discuss issues related to machine simulation intelligence and proposed the term "artificial intelligence" for the first time. The development of AI has experienced three stages: The first stage was from the late 1950s to the 1960s. This period was characterized by translating programs with natural language to achieve the effects of searching and reasoning. Machine theorem proofs and a checkers program were both important fruits in this period. The second stage was in the 1980s when AI gradually moved from theory to practice. The sign was when a large number of expert systems were produced and successfully applied in the medical, chemical, geological, and other fields. The third stage is from the beginning of the 21st century to the present. The main feature is that AI is gradually realizing machine learning, active learning, and deep learning on the basis of big

---

[1] Qiao Xiaonan and Xi Yanping (2018). Artificial Intelligence and the Construction of a Modern Economy. *Economic Review*, 6: 81-91.

data.[①] The role of AI in economic development is becoming increasingly prominent. It has a huge impact on the labor market, driving the development of an "unmanned economy", and is also promoting the upgrading of traditional industries.

Blockchains are a new application of computer technologies such as distributed data storage, peer-to-peer transmission, consensus mechanism, and encryption algorithm. The concept of blockchains was first proposed by Satoshi Nakamoto in 2008[②], who described how to establish a brand-new, decentralized, point-to-point transaction methodological system that does not require a foundation of trust. The core of blockchain technology is decentralization, which uses encryption algorithms, timestamps, tree structures, consensus mechanisms, and reward mechanisms to realize point-to-point transactions in a distributed network where nodes do not need to be trusted. Compared with the centralized model, it solves problems such as poor reliability, low level of security, high cost, and low efficiency.[③] Although blockchains were originally a derivative product of Bitcoin, it quickly attracted the attention of academia with its unique advantages. A large number of blockchain-related research and applications appeared. Some scholars believe that blockchain technology is the fifth revolutionary computing paradigm (after the public-access computer, microcomputer, Internet, and mobile social interaction) and that it will lead to tremendous changes in human production and life. The scope of application of blockchains is divided into three levels[④]: blockchain 1.0 (programmable money), 2.0 (programmable finance), and 3.0 (programmable society). When blockchains enters level 3.0, its application will not be limited to the financial field. The decentralization and collective maintenance of blockchains will be integrated into all sectors of social production and life, and the combination of blockchains and the Internet of Things will completely overturn the underlying protocols of the Internet, and a truly intelligent and programmable society will be constructed.

Cloud computing is a way of distributed parallel computing, public computing, and network computing. As early as the 1960s, the concepts of public computing and distributed computing came into being as the predecessors of cloud computing. It was not until 2006 that the words "Cloud Computing" appeared in English for the first time. Professor Michael Armbrust of the University of California, Berkeley and others believe that cloud computing consists of two parts: One is application services on the Internet, the so-called "Software-as-a-Service (SaaS)"; the other is facilities that provide these application services in the data center, that is the so-called

---

① Qiao Xiaonan and Xi Yanping (2018). Artificial Intelligence and the Construction of a Modern Economy. *Economic Review*, 6: 81-91.

② Satoshi, N. (2008). Bitcoin: A Peer-to-Peer Electronic Cash System. Retrieved from https://bitcoin.org/bitcoin.pdf.

③ Shen Xin, Pei Qingqi and Liu Xuefeng (2016). Survey of Blockchain. *Chinese Journal of Network and Information Security*, 11: 11-20.

④ Swan, M. (2015). *Blockchain: Blueprint for A New Economy*. Sebastopol, CA: O'Reilly Media Inc.

"cloud"[1]. Cloud computing has brought tremendous changes to people's work- and lifestyle. In the cloud environment, a powerful and scalable data and service center could be established through virtualized technology to provide users with sufficient computing capability and storage space[2]. With just an Internet terminal, users can achieve expected functions through cloud access free from the restrictions of time and location. As a result, the emergence of cloud computing has accelerated the demand shift from hardware to services.

The English name of the Internet of Things means "a network where everything is connected" or "networked things". The concept of the Internet of Things was first proposed by the Auto-ID Center of the Massachusetts Institute of Technology in 1999, but the definition at that time was limited to making things identifiable and manageable by the Internet. The European Technology Platform on Smart Systems Integration (EPoSS) defines the Internet of Things as a network comprising objects with marks and virtual personalities. These marks and personalities communicate with users, society, and the environment through smart interfaces in intelligent space.[3] When the Internet of Things reaches a certain scale, it will realize the interactive feedback and real-time communications between humans and things, and between things and things, thereby changing the mode of production and lifestyle.

The development and maturity of digital technology is the prerequisite and foundation for the emergence of digital economy. The commercial application of digital technology is also the development process of digital economy, such as the digitization of manufacturing, management, and circulation; the information revolution brought about by digital technology improves human brainpower; digital tools, production, and products reduce the resistance to information flow and improve the efficiency of economic entities matching with one another. In summary, digital technology is the prerequisite for the development of digital economy and provides new momentum for economic development.

1.3 Emergence of data and digital economy

The development of digital technology enhances data functions in quantity, dimension, transmission speed, processing capacity, etc.; data is used as a new factor to generate value in economic activities, and in turn promotes innovation of digital technology. The interaction between digital technology and data has caused a qualitative change in the form of economy. Digital technology and data become new factors of economic activities, and thence digital

---

[1] Michael, A. *et al.* (2009). Above the Clouds: A Berkeley View of Cloud Computing. Retrieved from https://www2.eecs.berkeley.edu/Pubs/TechRpts/2009/EECS-2009-28.pdf.

[2] Xu Baomin and Ni Xuguang (2015). Development Trend and Key Technical Progress of Cloud Computing. *Bulletin of Chinese Academy of Sciences*, 2: 170-180.

[3] EPOSS (the European Technology Platform on Smart System Integration) (2008). Internet of Things in 2020: Roadmap for the Future. Retrieved from https://docbox.etsi.org/erm/Open/CERP%2020080609-10/Internet-of-Things_in_2020_EC-EPoSS_Workshop_Report_2008_v1-1.pdf.

economy comes into being.

The development of digital technology complements with the expansion of data. First, the revolution in communications technology increases data transmission speed, improves transmission quality, and reduces transmission costs. In particular, the development and application of optical fiber communications and wireless communications make it possible to transmit large amounts of data instantly, quickly, and conveniently. Second, the maturity of Internet technology and widespread access make it easier to obtain data. As a result, massive data generates big data technology; the storage and processing of such large-scale data generate cloud computing technology. Third, the miniaturization of electronic computers and the improvement of computing capabilities have popularized personal computers and Internet, extending data sources and diversifying data types; meanwhile, the strong computing power of supercomputers provides a technical basis of massive data processing.

As a brand-new factor of production, data has generated a series of changes in economic activities, which makes the form of economy show a series of new characteristics, thereby becoming a recognizable feature of digital economy. Specifically, data may affect economic entities from the following aspects:

First, the information contained in data can optimize decision-making, facilitate production, accelerate resource circulation, and improve the efficiency of resource allocation. For enterprises, a large amount of data improves the availability of information from the external market. Enterprises can make more accurate market positioning based on this information, then create greater benefits. Companies have access to other enterprises' information of suppliers, and this information enables them to be better placed in dislocation competition. They can also gain spillover effects by learning about products and technical information from other enterprises more quickly.

Second, the information contained in data can reflect consumers' personalized needs, which can stimulate consumption, and encourage producers to refine the division of labor and increase the industry entry barriers. In the traditional form of economy, the large-scale production, together with the delay of message delivery, leads to limited choices of consumers and generalization of consumption. In the era of big data, the clustering of information enables precise identification of the different needs of consumers, which will be responded to by refined division of labor. Previously limited demand due to unsatisfied individual needs is released, thereby stimulating consumption. On the other hand, the refinement of labor division will increase the categories of products, which will increase the elasticity of substitution of products within the industry. A small drop in the price of a product will cause a greater impact on the demand for related products. The natural barriers to the industry will rise.[1]

---

[1] Yang Rudai (2018). Big Data and Economic Growth. *Research on Economic and Financial Issuers*, 2: 10-13.

Third, data will improve the government's ability to regulate macro economy and achieve better governance. The driving force for sustained economic growth lies in the continuous flow of resources to more efficient producers to maximize output. When the "invisible hand" cannot or does not fully perform its role, it requires the government to intervene in the resource allocation to make it more reasonable. In traditional economic activities, the difficulty of the government's macro-control lies in the inability to fully and comprehensively obtain market information; therefore, the regulatory measures taken do not always conform to the reality or even backfire. When data, as an important factor, participates in the government's macroeconomic control activities, a large amount of data can help the government understand market information more comprehensively; on the other hand, targeted analyses of large amounts of data can help the government identify the problems in the operation of the current economic system faster, more precisely, and at a deeper level.

To sum up, the development of digital technology generates numerous data. Information value contained in mining data generates demand for digital technology. The interaction between these two gives birth to digital economy and digital technology. Data becomes an identified factor of digital economy.

Section 2   The Concept and Features of Digital Economy

2.1 The concept of digital economy

The concept of digital economy was first used by American economist Don Tapscott in his book *The Digital Economy: Promise and Peril in the Age of Networked Intelligence* in 1996. In the following 20 years, scholars and institutions have continued to supplement the concept of digital economy. A large part of the reason is that, in the development of digital economy, new technologies, new organizational forms, new business models, and new industries continue to emerge, and the connotation and extension of digital economy continue to expand. Table 1.2 summarizes the evolution of the concept of digital economy from 1997 to 2016.

Table 1.2   Evolution of the concept of digital economy

Source	Concept
Tapscott 1997[1]	No clear definition, but it is proposed that digital economy benefits from technologies such as the Internet and artificial intelligence. Humans can use these technologies to create wealth and promote economic development.

---

[1] Tapscott, D. (1997). *The Digital Economy: Promise and Peril in the Age of Networked Intelligence*. New York, NY: McGraw-Hill Companies.

Continued

Source	Concept
US Commerce Department 1999[①]	No clear definition, but four factors driving the development of digital economy were proposed: development of the Internet, e-commerce, digital transformation of goods and services, and retail of tangible goods[②].
Mesenbourg 2001[③]	The definition of digital economy is divided into three parts: "infrastructure of e-commerce, meaning the share in the economic aggregate that is used to support the infrastructure of e-commerce and e-trade[④]; e-commerce, meaning any business activities conducted by enterprises through computer networks; and e-trade, meaning the value of goods and services sold through computer networks".
G20 Hangzhou Summit 2016: Development of Digital Economy and Cooperation Initiative	"Digital economy refers to a series of economic activities with digital knowledge and information as key production factors, modern information network as an important carrier, and the effective utilization of ICT as an important driving force for efficiency improvement and economic structure optimization."
Dahlman et al. 2016[⑤]	"The digital economy is a collection of multiple general-purpose technologies (GPTs), people's economic and social activities through the Internet or related technologies. The digital economy includes the infrastructure (broadband lines, routers), access equipment (computers, smartphones), and applications provided (Google, Salesforce) and their functions (Internet of Things, data analysis, cloud computing), upon which digital technology depends."

Source: based on the author's literature research.

A summary of the information in the table shows that earlier definitions of digital economy focused on Internet technology. Later, computer technology and communications technology were included. Recently, with the rise of big data and cloud computing, scholars adopt "digital technology", a broader concept, to define and describe digital economy. The definition of digital economy begins to shift from the technical aspect to the application aspect. The later and more mature definitions of digital economy share one common feature, that is, digital economy is divided into the technical side and the application side. The former refers to the fundamental

---

① US Commerce Department (1999). The Emerging Digital Economy. Retrieved from https://www.commerce.gov/news/reports/1998/07/emerging-digital-economy.

② Original English text: building out the internet, electronic commerce among business, digital delivery of goods and services, retail sale of tangible goods.

③ Mesenbourg, T. (2001). Measuring the Digital Economy. Retrieved from https://www.census.gov/content/dam/Census/library/working-papers/2001/econ/umdigital.pdf.

④ E-business and E-commerce are both translated into 电子商务, meaning "E-commerce" in Chinese. In the original text, the former refers to commercial activities and the latter refers to trade. Therefore, the author translates "e-commerce" as 电子贸易, meaning "e-trade".

⑤ Dahlman, C. Mealy, S. Wermelinger, M. (2016). Harnessing the Digital Economy for Developing Countries. Retrieved from https://www.oecd-ilibrary.org/development/harnessing-the-digital-economy-for-developing-countries_4adffb24-en.

sector that is directly related to digital technology, such as the communications industry, computer industry, etc., briefly known as "digital industrialization"; the latter refers to the additional economic output brought by the use of digital technology, briefly known as "industrial digitization". Many institutions adopt this classification when assessing the contribution of digital economy to the overall national economy.

With the 2016 G20 Hangzhou Summit as a reference, this report defines and restates digital economy as follows: "Digital economy refers to a series of economic activities with digital knowledge and information as key production factors, modern information network as an important carrier, and the effective utilization of ICT as an important driving force for efficiency improvement and economic structure optimization."[①] This definition is generally recognized in China. For example, China Academy of Information and Communications Technology used this definition in the white papers on China's digital economy development published in 2017 and 2018.

As mentioned above, many institutions divide digital economy into two aspects: "digitized industry" and "industrial digitalization"; however, digital economy is increasingly intertwined with traditional economy, making the differences between them unclear. As digital technology penetrates increasingly deep into industries, the boundary between digital economy and traditional economy becomes increasingly blurred. What parts of economic activities should be absorbed in the scope of digital economy? Bukht and Heeks (2017) pointed out: "Economic activities in which a part of economic output comes solely or mainly from digital technology and their business model is based on digital goods or services belonging to the category of digital economy"[②]. Different from the previous definitions of digital economy, they divided digital economy into three scopes: the first scope is the infrastructure of digital economy, also known as the "core" sector, that is, the sector that directly uses ICT technology to conduct production activities, such as the information and communications industry, R&D, and manufacturing of computer-related hardware and software; the second scope is the industries with data as the core factor, also known as the narrowly defined digital economy, that is, the new forms of businesses due to digital technology's participation in economic activities, such as the Internet industry, cloud services, e-commerce, etc.; the third scope is the digitization of traditional industries, which is referred to as the broadly defined digital economy, that is, increased output of traditional industries due to the use of digital technology or digital tools. For example, farmers' additional income derived from the sale of crops by the futures trading system based on big data, industry 4.0, precision agriculture, and blockchain all belong to this scope. Compared with the aforementioned classification of digital industrialization and industrial digitalization, this

---

① *G20 Digital Economy Development and Cooperation Initiative.* 2016-01-10.
② Bukht, R. and Heeks, R. (2017). Defining, Conceptualizing, and Measuring the Digital Economy. Development Information Working Paper No.68. Retrieved from SSRN, https://papers.ssrn.com/sol3/papers.cfm?abstract_id=3431732.

concept is more specific.

2.2 Features of digital economy

2.2.1 Data becomes an important factor of production

Every major change in the economic form is accompanied by the emergence of new factors of production. Just like labor and land to agricultural economy and capital and technology to industrial economy, data has become the most critical factor of production in digital economy. With the development of the mobile Internet and the Internet of Things, the connectivity among people, connectivity between people and things, and connectivity among things have generated explosive growth of data. The growth of global data is in line with Moore's Law regarding big data, which doubles every two years. According to the "Digital Economy Report 2019" released by UNCTAD, it is estimated that by 2022, the world's Internet traffic will reach 150,700 gigabytes per second. Since the 1990s, more than 95% of new information has been stored, transmitted, and used in digital format. Human production and lifestyle become inseparable from data. The data carried by the network, the information extracted from the data, and the knowledge evolved from information are becoming a new driving force for business decision-making, a new content of trade in goods and services, and a new means of comprehensive social governance, bringing new increments of value. This process is called the Data Value Chain. The huge amount of data and application requirements give rise to the concept of "big data". Data becomes the most important strategic asset. American big data expert Andreas Weigend pointed out: "The most important raw material in the 21st century is data. Data is oil. There is less and less remaining oil, but data is increasing exponentially. Whoever has data has advantages, not only at the corporate level, but also at the national level."[①] Figure 1.1 shows the changes in the scale of data globally.

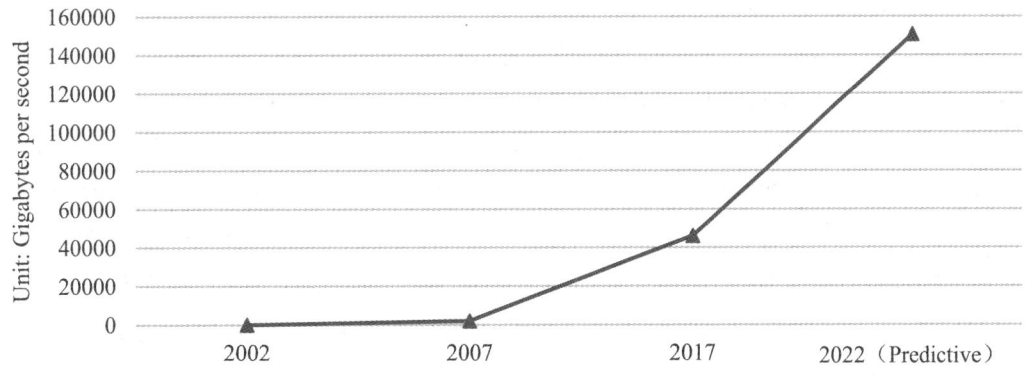

Figure 1.1 Development of global Internet data traffic

Source: UNCTAD, "Digital Economy Report 2019".

---

① Weigend, A. (2017). *Data for the People: How to Make Our Post-Privacy Economy Work for You*. New York, NY: Basic Books.

The rapid expansion of the scale of global data benefits from the substantial reduction in data storage costs. In the early 20th century, the excessively high cost of data storage was an important obstacle for enterprises to create value; in recent years, cloud storage and flash memory technologies have developed rapidly, and the cost of data storage decreases significantly. According to "Data Age 2025: The Evolution of Data to Life-Critical"[①], the cost to store 1TB data has dropped from nearly USD 0.09 in 2010 to about USD 0.003, as shown in Figure 1.2. With the continuous introduction of emerging digital technologies such as the Internet, the Internet of Things, and artificial intelligence to other industries, enterprises have generated many demands for instant storage of data, and the increasingly powerful capability of data storage and decreasing data storage costs help enterprises better counter the challenges of speedy data processing brought by digital economy.

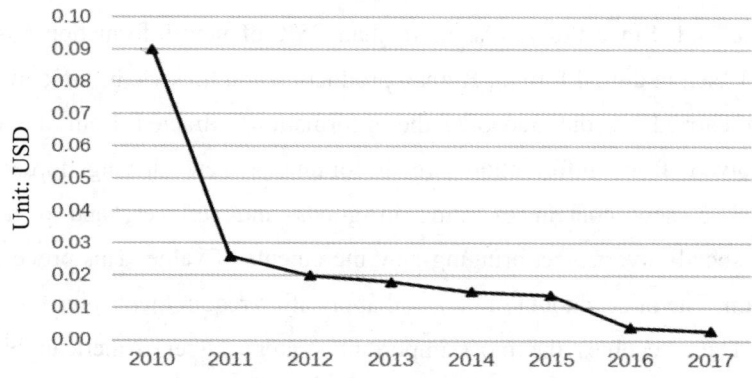

Figure 1.2   Costs of storing 1TB data

Source: IDC "Data Age 2025: The Evolution of Data to Life-Critical".

2.2.2 Innovation and progress of digital technology becomes the main driving force of economic development

The advancement of technology is the sustainable driving force of economic growth, while the advancement of digital technology is the core driving force of today's economic and social development. Figure 1.3 shows patent applications received by the European Patent Office in 2018, in which the number of applications of digital communications technology and computer technology ranked the second and third respectively. Unlike previous general-purpose technologies, digital technology shows an exponential growth. Moore's Law states that when the price remains stable, the number of components that can be accommodated on an integrated circuit will double in about every 18-24 months, and the performance will also double. The continuous progress of technologies such as big data, cloud computing, the Internet of Things, and machine learning promotes the continuous improvement of the efficiency of industries and

---

① IDC (International Data Corporation) (2017). Data Age 2025: The Evolution of Data to Life-Critical. Retrieved from https://itupdate.com.au/page/data-age-2025-the-evolution-of-data-to-life-critical.

promotes product quality; in addition, the rapid development of digital technology is deeply integrated with the fields of manufacturing, biology, and energy, leading to group breakthroughs and comprehensive expansion of the growth space for human knowledge and categories of products. The upgrading product quality and the expansion of product categories constitute the core of innovation and promote sustainable economic growth.

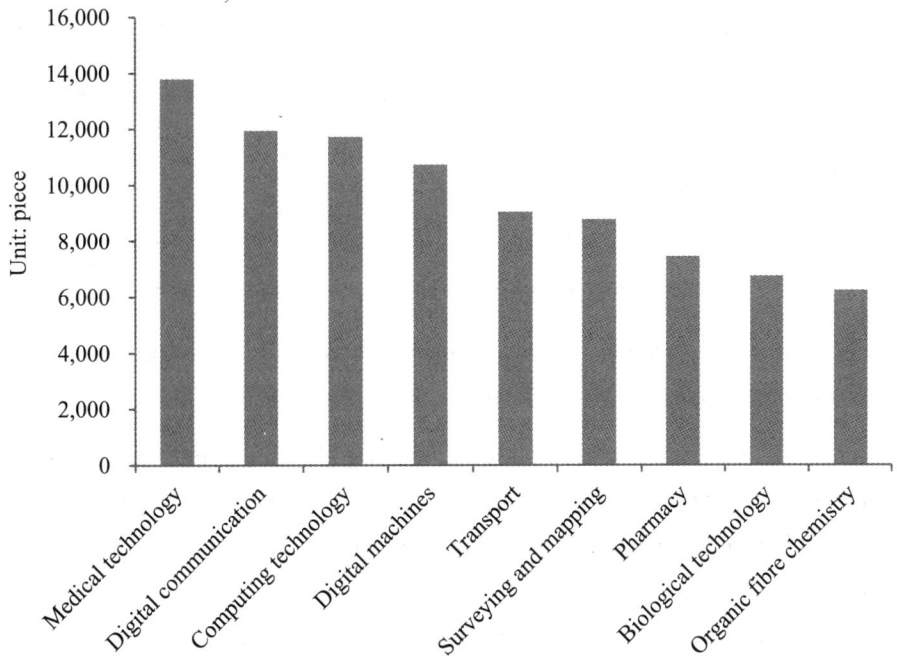

Figure 1.3   Patent applications received by the European Patent Office in 2018

Source: "EPO'S Annual Report 2018".

2.2.3 Digital information infrastructure becomes the most important infrastructure

In the era of traditional industrial economy, all economic activities were built on the physical infrastructure represented by "railroads, highways, and airports". Entering the era of digital economy, with the development of new technologies such as 5G, MEC (mobile edge computing), and AI (artificial intelligence), the Internet, the Internet of Things, and cloud computing have become essential information infrastructure. As the media for digital signal propagation, the rapid increase in the number of signal base stations also reflects the rapid transformation of infrastructure in the era of digital economy. Figure 1.4 shows that the number of mobile communications base stations in China in 2017 increased fourfold compared with 2010, while the number of 3G/4G base stations was 25 times that of 2010.

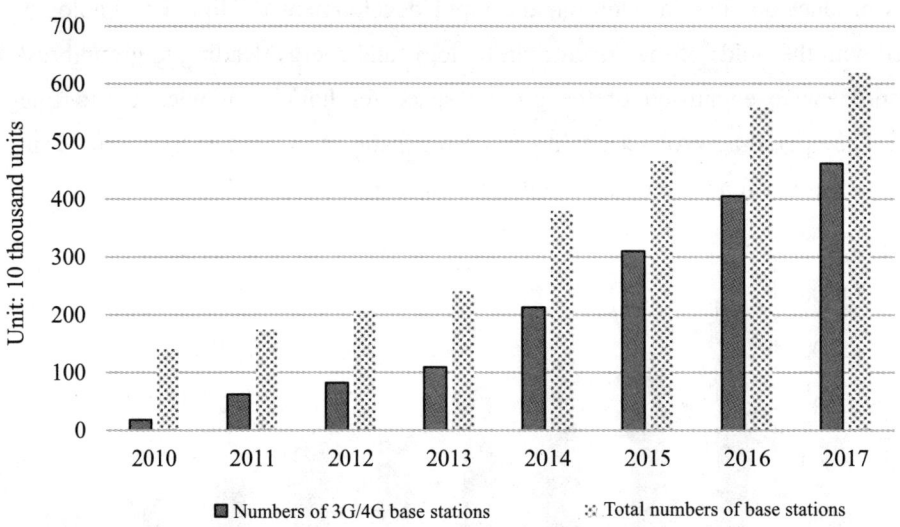

Figure 1.4 Numbers of mobile communications base stations in China
Source: China Industry Information Network.

The concept of the infrastructure of digital economy becomes more and more extensive, including information infrastructure such as the Internet, the Internet of Things, and cloud processing, as well as the digitalized transformation of traditional physical infrastructure, such as digitalized transportation systems, fire-fighting facilities embedded with sensors and monitoring devices, agricultural irrigation systems equipped with drones, etc. These two types of infrastructure play a very important role in promoting the development of digital economy, and significantly promote the change of infrastructure in the industrial era represented by "brick and mortar" to digital infrastructure represented by "light and chips".

2.2.4 Online and offline integrated development becomes a new direction of industrial development

In the era of digital economy, cyberspace continues to expand its boundaries to physical space; traditional industries are also moving towards digitalization. The integration of online and offline becomes a new direction. On the one hand, Internet giants continue to grow their strength offline and expand their operations toward real economy. Since 2017 when Jingdong established its own logistics business, it has promoted the transformation of consumption patterns and the increased efficiency of social supply chains through open and smart strategic measures. It organically combines logistics, business flow, capital flow, and information flow to achieve mutual trust with customers and a win-win situation. Alibaba also cooperates with the Bailian Group and Ririshun and other entity enterprises to jointly create a new retail system integrating online and offline services. On the other hand, traditional enterprises are also actively exploring and developing online services, looking for new development space in the digital age. Large state-owned enterprises such as PetroChina and Sinopec established their own e-commerce platforms, which reduces procurement costs and optimizes the supply chain significantly; Volvo has also continuously increased its R&D investment in digital information technology in recent years, using digital virtual technology to replace real physical experiments and cancel the prototype car testing, reducing the design and development cycle of new cars from 42 months to 20 months, responding to changes in market demand more quickly.

The joint development of online and offline businesses integrates the advantages of virtual economy and real economy. In the traditional economic system, enterprises create value and compete on the market in physical space, which is easily limited by time and space. In virtual economy, the development of digital economy creates a new space: cyberspace, which opens up new dimensions for market competition and value creation. More and more manufacturers are establishing virtual production lines and virtual workshops. The development, design, simulation, and manufacturing of products are all conducted in the digital space through building virtual production lines and virtual workshops. In the retail area, the online and offline integration improves online retailing efficiency: online transactions are free from time and space constraints and release long-tail demand; offline transactions enhance and enrich the customer experience. This new model of online and offline interaction satisfies customers' diverse needs.

It is worth noting that both developed and developing countries have presented an imbalance between virtual economy and real economy in the process of digitalization over recent years. Take China as an example: while the e-commerce industry witnesses the vigorous development, the desolation of the traditional real economy comes about. The steel industry, the coal industry, and other traditional real economies are faced with overcapacity. Offline stores are on the verge of bankruptcy, and the financial services industry is overleveraged and faces huge risks. These are all huge problems in digital economy. Therefore, there is no priority in the integration of online and offline development; what is more important is to identify the balance point and promote the stable development of national economy.

2.2.5 Inclusive development

The characteristics of "general participating, building and sharing" in digital economy realize inclusive technology, inclusive finance and inclusive trade. In the field of science and technology, thanks to the rapid development of cloud computing and the Internet of Things, individuals and enterprises can obtain the computing, storage, and network resources they need without having to purchase expensive software and hardware products and network equipment, which greatly reduces costs. According to AliResearch, the use of cloud computing has reduced the cost for enterprises for using network data by nearly 70%, and the efficiency has increased by three times.

In finance, the credit rating model based on Internet credit enables individuals to obtain accurate risk assessments, thus enabling them to be matched to differentiated financial products and financial services, which greatly promotes the development of inclusive finance. The

"Digital Economy 2.0" issued by AliResearch introduces the advantages of the new risk-assessment system introduced by the e-commerce and banking business team: if the total amount of non-performing loans remains unchanged, this new type of credit rating model will increase the number of creditable corporate customers by 360%, 4.6 times higher than the original number; the number of creditable individual customers will increase by 1600%, 17 times higher than the original number.

The development of digital economy also unfolds a new chapter for inclusive trade, which enables various trading entities to benefit from trade, and the order of trade will also be improved. Inclusive trade includes the following aspects: more convenient trade processes; more symmetrical trading information; consumers are able to obtain higher-quality products at more favorable prices. The rapid development of the cross-border e-commerce industry over recent years has well illustrated the great driving force of digital economy to boost the inclusive trade.

2.3 Operating system of digital economy

Synchronized with the concept of digital economy, the operating system of digital economy can be divided into four levels: 1. Infrastructure level, including digital infrastructure and the digitalized transformation of traditional physical infrastructure; 2. Technical level, including a series of emerging digital technologies applied in digital infrastructure; 3. Industrial and corporate level, including the digitization of industry, agriculture, the service industry, the public service industry, and a large number of digital enterprises that emerge during the digital age; 4. Assurance level, including market and legal guarantees required for the regular operation of the economic system.

2.3.1 Infrastructure level

In the age of traditional industry, value creation is difficult because of the limitation of time and space. Therefore, physical transportation channels such as railways, highways, and airports had to be used as infrastructure. In the era of digital economy, data, as the core factor in the value creation process, promotes the transformation of infrastructure from railways, highways, and airports to information infrastructure represented by "cloud network terminals" (cloud computing, the Internet, the Internet of Things, and smart terminals).

2.3.2 Technical level

In recent years, with the improvement of information infrastructure, a series of new technologies has emerged. These new technologies merge with different industries to form new development trends, such as artificial intelligence, blockchains, big data, cloud computing, and other emerging digital technologies.

Augmented Reality (AR) refers to the use of cameras and image processing technology to realize the seamless connection between the information of the real world and the information of the virtual world, so as to realize the interaction between the virtual world and the real world on the screen. The AR glasses Moverio BT-300 launched by Epson are able to present all kinds of information encountered by the user in front of the user's eyes. Walking on the streets of foreign countries with these glasses on, users can easily recognize road signs even if they don't understand the foreign language, with the glasses working as an instant translator; in the field of industrial manufacturing, AR technology can provide workers with more detailed information on key steps in the production line, thereby minimizing errors and improving the efficiency of production. The real-time interaction changes modes of production and lifestyles significantly and attracts many technology giants to invest funds and talents in this field.

With the continuous development of digital economy, the nature of the "Internet of Everything" in the digital world allows all individual information to be uploaded to the cloud, which means that the risk and damage of information leakage continue to increase. Biometrics refers to technologies that use human biological characteristics for verification of identification, including fingerprint recognition, retina recognition and facial recognition. The emergence and application of biometric technology not only makes the storage and use of cloud data more secure but also has important applications in national security and other fields. After the "9.11" events, countries such as the UK, the US, and France issued biometric electronic passports for their citizens and biometric visas for foreign citizens. The application of these technologies not only improves the anti-counterfeiting of visas, but also reduces the probability of terrorist attacks. It also improves the working efficiency of cross-border departments of customs and airports.

2.3.3 Industrial and corporate level

In response to the wave of the development of digital economy, industries are using existing information infrastructure and emerging digital technologies to carry out digital transformation. Industry, agriculture, the service industry, and public service industries are all developing in the process of digitalization, adding new impetus to the development of national economy.

Industrial digitization. Traditional industries are powered by conventional energy sources and featured by machine technology. In the digital economy era, the industrial system is undergoing a major transformation. For example, China's shipbuilding industry has been plagued by overcapacity over recent years. Common problems such as high costs and obsolete production lines put most shipyards to bankruptcy. In this situation, digitalized transformation becomes a way out for the shipbuilding industry. The TRIBON software, independently developed by Jiangnan Shipyard, realizes the transformation of shipbuilding design from 2D to 3D, realizes the whole-process ship design, integrates information flow throughout the manufacturing process, and greatly improves the efficiency of design and manufacturing. The delivery cycle is shortened. A new path is blazed in the context of slack shipbuilding industry.

Digitalization of agriculture. As the population continues to grow, food supply has become one of the major problems shared by the whole world. Internet of Things technology helps farmers operate their farmland remotely with the help of sensors; robots in agriculture help farmers increase yield and reduce costs. The spraying and cleaning robots introduced by John Deere can effectively help farmers reduce the usage of pesticides by 90%. Additionally, the application of drones helps farmers monitor crops in real time. The application of a series of digital technologies has helped agriculture quickly move toward digitalization.

Digitalization of the service industry. The service industry is still pivotal in the era of digital economy. In recent years, the digitalized transformation of the financial service industry is the most prominent, with the emergence of new services such as mobile banking, mobile payment, and smart investment consultation. As one of the largest securities enterprises in China, Guosen Securities has always regarded digitization as an important strategy for future development. During the rapid development of digital economy, Guosen Securities trading system is facing challenges in all aspects. Guosen Securities invests a large amount of money in Microsoft SQL Server 2014 to fully upgrade its trading system, which satisfies customer needs and reduces system risks.

Digitization of the public service industry. The public service industry covers the basic needs of the general public. As the level of economic development continues to improve, the needs for public services become more diverse. Ma Huateng, Chairman of Tencent's board, pointed out at the China "Internet +" Digital Economy Summit in 2018 that China's public service agencies were becoming the protagonists in the process of digitalization. At present, provincial and municipal governments are promoting the development of "e-taxation offices" where enterprises and individuals can pay taxes online, making it more convenient for the general public; the application of smart transportation systems has also effectively improved the capabilities of the urban transportation system, reduced the occurrence of traffic accidents, and avoided the waste of resources.

Digitalized enterprises. In the operating system of digital economy, digitalized enterprises that rely on digital infrastructure and position digital technology as their core competitive competence are the most important part. Companies are the main participants in market economic activities and the main carriers of value creation in modern society. Typical digitalized enterprises include Alibaba, Jingdong, Google, Facebook, etc.

2.3.4 Assurance level

Market guarantee. In any economic system, as an "invisible hand", the market plays a fundamental role in resource allocation. Market trading systems and order of competition are facing challenges in the era of digital economy when enterprises with the most powerful digital technology in the industry can monopoly the entire market, thus disrupting the order of market competition. The causes of the monopoly problem in the digital economy era are as follows: First, the network effect is more pronounced. Take Facebook as an example: the more users Facebook has, the higher the value of Facebook is. Therefore, Facebook can attract more funds to improve based on customer needs, and then attract more customers. Second, digitalized enterprises can use their digitalized platforms to analyze user data and improve precision marketing capabilities, thereby reducing costs and squeezing competitors out of the market. Fewer competitors mean more customers and more data. This forms a virtuous circle. In response to this trend, how the market manages and controls monopolistic enterprises becomes an urgent problem that needs to be resolved. For example, according to the United Nations "Digital Economy Report 2019", Google occupies 90% of the share of global Internet search, Facebook occupies 66% of the social media market, and Amazon occupies 66% of the global online retail market.

Legal guarantee. The modernization of digital economy governance is the core of advancing the modernization of national governance, and it also plays an important role in building a network and digital power. Legal guarantee includes governmental supervision, legislative protection and risk control. When the market mechanism dysfunctions, legal guarantee can play its role. In June 2018, a series of collapses occurred in the P2P industry. Part of the reasons were untransparent information and poor supervision, which led to a situation where some ill-rated enterprises could obtain P2P business licenses. This incident had a very bad effect on China's financial industry. After the crisis, the central government issued the "Provisions on the Functions, Structure, and Staffing of the China Banking and Insurance Regulatory Commission", which strengthened the supervision to P2P enterprises and clarified the relevant responsibilities, thereby effectively avoiding similar incidents. This indicated the necessity of legal protection and governmental supervision in the digital economy era.

Section 3   An Overview of the Development of Global Digital Economy

3.1 The scale of global digital economy

As mentioned earlier, the narrowly defined "digital economy" refers to ICT; the broadly defined "digital economy" includes digital industrialization and industrial digitalization. According to the 2019 United Nations Digital Economy Report, covering both narrowly and broadly defined concepts of digital economy, the proportion of digital economy in global GDP was 4.5%-15.5% in 2017. In the US, digital economy accounted for 6.9%-21.6% of its GDP, while in China it accounted for 6%-30%. According to "A New Landscape of the Global Digital Economy" issued by China Academy of Information and Communications Technology in 2019, in the US, the UK, and Germany, digital economy accounted for more than 60% of the GDP in 2018, reaching 60.2%, 61.2%, and 60.0% respectively; in Korea, Japan, France, and Ireland, digital economy accounted for more than 40% of the GDP; in Singapore, China, Finland, and

Mexico, digital economy accounted for more than 30% of the GDP. Although the calculation results of different institutions vary, they show that the scale of digital economy is getting larger and it will occupy an increasingly important position in the economic system.

3.1.1 The scale of the broadly defined digital economy

AliResearch conducts weighted analysis based on 16 indicators in five categories: digital technology facilities, consumers of digital economy, digital business ecology, digital public services, and digital education and scientific research, involving 150 countries. All original data is processed in a standardized approach to obtain the digital economy index of each country.

Table 1.3 Top 10 and bottom 10 countries of the world by digital economy index in 2018

Ranking	Country	Overall index	Ranking	Country	Overall index
1	the US	0.837	141	Mauritania	0.15
2	China	0.718	142	Malawi	0.148
3	the UK	0.694	143	Liberia	0.145
4	Korea	0.621	144	Yemen	0.134
5	Sweden	0.618	145	Angola	0.128
6	Norway	0.617	146	Burundi	0.126
7	Japan	0.615	147	Chad	0.124
8	Denmark	0.612	148	Sierra Leone	0.107
9	Singapore	0.609	149	Burkina Faso	0.106
10	the Netherlands	0.606	150	Syria	0.103

Source: AliResearch, "2018 Global Digital Economy Development Index".

Table 1.3 shows that among the top 10 countries by digital economy index, China is the only developing country, and the rest are all developed countries. Among them, digital economy index of the US is 0.837, the highest; digital economy index of China is 0.718; those of all other countries are all below 0.7. On the other hand, among the bottom 10 countries, which are all developing countries, the digital economy indexes are between 0.103 and 0.15, which is a huge gap from those of the top 10 countries. Therefore, on the one hand, the level of the development of digital economy is positively correlated with the level of the country's per capita income; on the other hand, there are huge differences in the development of digital economy in various countries, i.e. "digital divide". The digital economy development indexes show the development of digital economy worldwide. Table 1.4 further reports the scale of digital economy of various countries calculated by China Academy of Information and Communications Technology.

Table 1.4 Scales of digital economy in major countries in 2018 (100 million USD)

Country	Scale	Country	Scale	Country	Scale
the US	123,408	Italy	3,828	Indonesia	1,186
China	47,290	Mexico	3,670	Belgium	1,055
Germany	23,994	Russia	2,942	Poland	1,045
Japan	22,901	Australia	2,664	Finland	945
the UK	17,287	Spain	2,391	Denmark	910
France	11,550	Ireland	1,618	Norway	888
Korea	7,636	Singapore	1,348	Malaysia	780
India	5,415	Sweden	1,296	South Africa	635
Canada	5,342	Switzerland	1,277	Thailand	580
Brazil	3,832	the Netherlands	1,239	Turkey	542

Source: China Academy of Information and Communications Technology, "A New Landscape of Global Digital Economy (2019)".

In Table 1.4, the scale of digital economy in the US stands out, exceeding 10 trillion dollars; the scale of China's digital economy is close to 5 trillion dollars; the scales of other countries are all below 2 trillion dollars, which means the difference of scale is huge. The scale of digital economy of the US, which ranks first, is 227 times that of Turkey, which ranks 30th. This, once again, confirms the existence of the "digital divide".

3.1.2 Scale of the narrowly defined digital economy

Table 1.3 and Table 1.4 show the scale of the broadly defined digital economy in various countries. The ICT sector is the infrastructure of digital economy, belonging to the narrowly defined digital economy. Additionally, the statistics of ICT bear more legitimacy. Therefore, learning from the practices of international organizations such as the United Nations, the World Bank, and OECD, this report further focuses on the ICT sector in various countries. Table 1.5 shows the top 10 countries/regions of ICT product manufacturing in 2014.

Table 1.5 Top 10 countries/regions by ICT product manufacturing scale in 2014

Country / region	Scale (100 million USD)		Percentage (%)	
	Value added	Output value	Value added	Output value
China	5,580	13,720	32.3	34.1
the US	2,670	6,190	15.5	15.4
European Union	1,350	3,860	7.8	9.6
Korea	1,070	2,330	6.2	5.8
Japan	210	820	1.2	2.0
Taiwan, China	170	250	1.0	0.6
Malaysia	170	100	1.0	0.2
Singapore	160	660	0.9	1.6
Mexico	90	90	0.5	0.2
Brazil	70	370	0.4	0.9
Total	11,540	28,390	66.9	70.6

Source: UNCTAD, Information Economy Report, 2017.

In terms of the scale of ICT manufacturing, China's digital economy ranks first in the world, both in added value and output value. The proportion of China in the world is about 1/3. The total amount of added value of the top 10 economies of ICT manufacturing is 1,154 billion dollars, accounting for 66.9% of the world; the output value is 2,839 billion dollars, accounting for 70.6% of the world. Therefore, from the perspective of the narrowly defined digital economy, the scale of digital economy varies among countries. Table 1.6 further reports the scale and proportion of the top 10 ICT service-and-production economies in the world in 2015.

Table 1.6 Top 10 economies by ICT service production in 2015

Economy	Value added (100 million USD)	Percentage (%)	Percentage in GDP (%)
the US	11,060	42.0	6.2
European Union	6,970	26.5	4.3
China	2,840	10.8	2.6
Japan	2,230	8.5	5.4
India	920	3.5	4.5
Canada	650	2.5	4.2
Brazil	540	2.1	3
Korea	480	1.8	3.5
Australia	320	1.2	2.4
Indonesia	300	1.1	3.5
Total	26,310	100	

Source: UNCTAD, Information Economy Report, 2017.

Table 1.5 and Table 1.6 show that ICT manufacturing and ICT services are highly correlated, which is shown as a high level of overlap among the top 10 economies. When considering scales, the scale of ICT services in the top 10 economies is 2,631 billion dollars, far exceeding the scale of ICT manufacturing, 1,154 billion dollars. It indicates that the percentage of services in the narrowly defined digital economy is higher.

Table 1.5 and Table 1.6 use year-round data to show the cross-sectional characteristics of the scale of the narrowly defined digital economy. Using data of OECD countries, Table 1.7 conducts a trend analysis to show the changes in the percentage of ICT value added in GDP of major OECD economies from 2008 to 2015. It is used to analyze the development trend of the narrowly defined digital economy.

Table 1.7 Percentages of ICT value added in GDP and growth rates (%) of OECD countries

Economy	2008	2012	2015	Average value	Growth rate
OECD as a whole	5.38	5.28	5.41	5.36	0.5
Korea	9.94	10.15	10.35	10.14	4.1
Finland	9.85	5.49	6.90	7.41	-29.9
Sweden	6.80	6.82	7.31	6.97	7.4
Japan	6.65	5.99	5.96	6.20	-10.4

Continued

Economy	2008	2012	2015	Average value	Growth rate
Ireland	6.46	6.48	5.36	6.10	-17.1
the US	5.78	5.84	6.04	5.89	4.5
Hungary	5.92	5.77	5.80	5.83	-2.1
Czech Republic	5.58	5.89	5.88	5.78	5.4
Estonia	4.99	5.43	6.00	5.47	20.2
the UK	5.12	5.18	5.36	5.22	4.8
Luxembourg	5.50	5.13	4.89	5.17	-11.0
Germany	4.98	4.83	5.04	4.95	1.2
France	5.03	4.71	4.63	4.79	-7.9
the Netherlands	4.95	4.59	4.66	4.73	-5.8
Slovakia	4.63	4.97	4.46	4.69	-3.8
Switzerland	4.44	4.35	4.49	4.43	1.1
Denmark	4.31	4.29	4.24	4.28	-1.6
Slovenia	4.08	4.23	4.29	4.20	4.9
Canada	3.97	4.13	4.04	4.05	1.7
Latvia	3.40	4.05	4.18	3.87	22.9
Spain	3.82	3.94	3.85	3.87	0.8
Italy	4.05	3.94	3.57	3.85	-11.8
Belgium	3.83	3.84	3.64	3.77	-4.8
Austria	3.63	3.63	3.92	3.73	8.0
Iceland	3.08	3.31	3.96	3.45	28.5
Poland	3.42	3.36	3.55	3.44	3.8
Portugal	3.65	3.42	3.18	3.42	-12.7
Norway	3.00	3.33	3.55	3.29	18.1
Greece	3.00	2.83	3.10	2.97	3.3
Mexico	3.22	2.76	2.75	2.91	-14.5
Turkey		2.60	2.69	2.64	3.5

Source: OECD Digital Economy Outlook, 2017.

As shown in Table 1.7, as a whole, the OECD's ICT added value as a percentage of GDP increased from 5.38% to 5.41% in 2015, a small change; specifically, US ranked the 1st of the world by the scale of digital economy, whose scale as a percentage of world scale increased from 5.78% to 6.04%. As the US scale of digital economy accounts for a higher percentage in the world scale, while OECD as a whole accounts for a higher percentage in the world's economic scale, we have reason to believe that the overall scale of digital economy is growing, and its growth rate has exceeded that of traditional sectors. The contribution of digital economy to global economic growth is significant.

Based on the above analysis, as far as the global digital economy is concerned, the US is in a leading position with the largest digital economy; the data related to digital economy released by the US is comprehensive and consistent. Therefore, we will take the US as an example to show the scale of digital economy development and its significance to the macro-economy. The data in this part is from the official website of the Bureau of Economic Analysis (BEA). For the scope of the statistics of digital economy, the BEA provides the following criteria: (1) The digital-enabling infrastructure needed for Internet to exist and operate, that is, the "core digital technology sector" mentioned above; (2) Digital transactions using digital tools or digitalized platforms, referred to as e-commerce transactions; (3) Digital media, which is the content that digital economy users create and access. This method of measurement primarily covers the first two aspects of digital economy and part of the third aspect. The BEA does not attempt to estimate the digitalized part of the aggregate economy but chooses to focus on completely or mainly digitalized commodities and services.[①] From this perspective, the scale of digital economy the BEA shows is mainly that of the narrowly defined one.

Figure 1.5 shows the US digital economy volume from 2008 to 2017. The data was all current year data, without consideration of inflation. In 2017, the US digital economy volume was 1,351.278 billion dollars, an increase of more than 50% over the past 10 years from 891.119 billion dollars in 2008. Despite the 2008 US financial crisis, the US digital economy still achieved a decade-long continuous growth. With the economic recovery, the growth of US digital economy volume is accelerating.

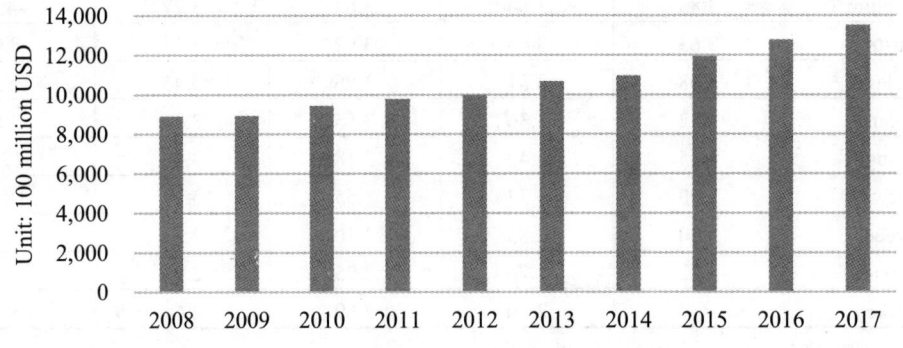

Figure 1.5 US digital economy volume (2008-2017)

Source: based on the author's BEA literature research.

Figure 1.6 shows the percentage of US digital economy volume in its GDP from 2008 to 2017. In 2017, the US digital economy volume was 1,351.278 billion dollars, accounting for 6.93% of its GDP. This percentage was slightly lower than 7.1%, the percentage of the financial and insurance industry. Excluding government expenditures, the contribution of digital economy to the US economy is only less than that of the real estate, manufacturing, and financial and insurance industries. From 2008 to 2017, the average of the US digital economy volume as a percentage of its GDP was 6.39%. This average fluctuated slightly in the past 10 years but

---

① BEA (US Bureau of Economic Analysis) (2018). Defining and Measuring the Digital Economy. Retrieved from https://www.bea.gov/research/papers/2018/defining-and-measuring-digital-economy.

generally grew steadily.

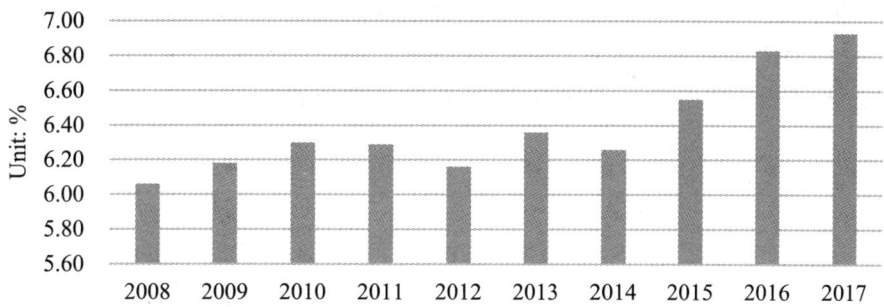

Figure 1.6　Percentages of the digital economy volume in US GDP

Source: based on the author's BEA literature research.

Figure 1.7 shows the growth rate of US digital economy volume and that of US GDP from 2012 to 2018. From 2012 to 2018, the average growth rate of the US digital economy was 5.56%, higher than that of the GDP, 3.84%. During the seven years, the growth rate of the US digital economy in 2012 and 2014 was lower than that of the GDP, the differences being 2.17% and 1.69%, respectively. The growth rate of US digital economy was greater than that of US GDP in 2013, 2015, 2016, 2017, and 2018. The largest difference occurred in 2015 when the growth rate of digital economy was 4.87 percentage points higher than that of the GDP. Therefore, the growth of digital economy is a strong driver of the growth of the GDP in the US, which was particularly significant in 2015 and 2016.

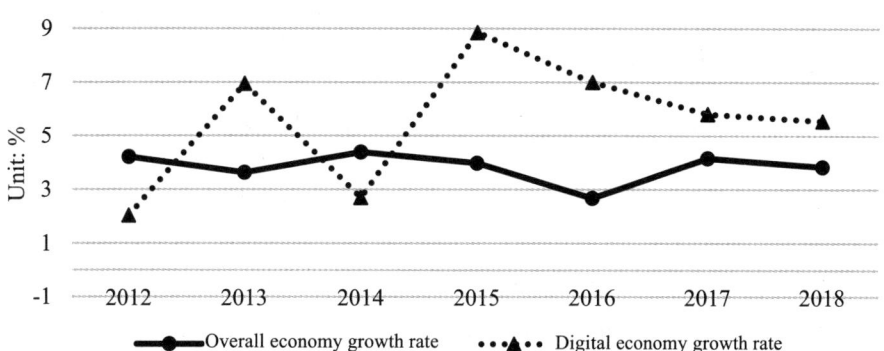

Figure 1.7　Growth rates of US digital economy and GDP from 2012 to 2018

Source: based on the author's BEA literature research.

Figure 1.8 shows the number of new jobs created in US digital economy in recent years. From 2010 to 2016, the number of new jobs in digital economy in the US continued to increase, from 4.28 million jobs in 2010 to 4.98 million jobs in 2016, with an AGR of 2.7%. In 2016, there were 4.98 new jobs in the US digital economy industry, accounting for about 3.3% of the total jobs. In the same year, there were totally 150 million new jobs in the US. Among them, computer system design and related services, broadcasting and telecommunications industries, and manufacturing of computers and electronics created most new jobs, that is, 1,880,000, 860,000, and 500,000 respectively. In 2016, the average annual salary of employees in US digital economy was USD 114,275, much higher than the US average salary, USD 66,498. Therefore, the development of US digital economy has a positive impact on the quantity and quality of employment.

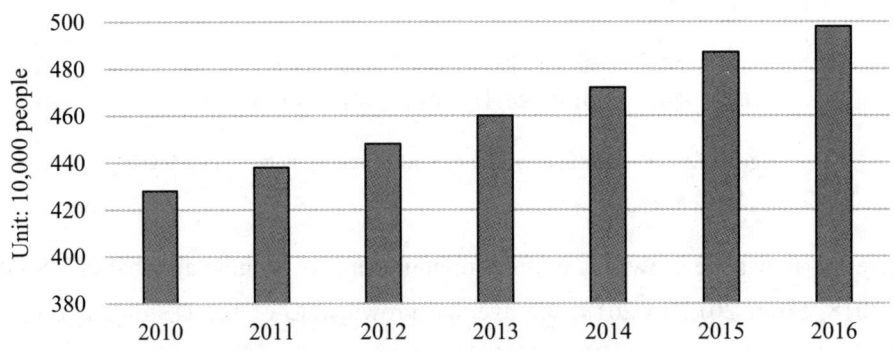

Figure 1.8　New jobs in the US digital economy industry

Source: based on the author's BEA literature research.

In summary, vertically, the scale of the global digital economy grows rapidly, and the growth rate exceeds that of traditional economic sectors and digital economy becomes an important emerging force driving the growth of world economy and employment; horizontally, the scale and degree of the development of digital economy in the world are uneven, and the digital divide is widespread at the macro level, which will have an adverse impact on the balanced and sustainable development of the world.

3.2 The structure of global digital economy development

3.2.1 Structural characteristics of the broadly defined digital economy

According to Table 1.4, the broadly defined digital economy is divided into two parts: digital industrialization and industrial digitization. Digital industrialization is reflected in the incremental characteristics of digital economy, that is, emerging business forms, such as Internet search and video websites; industrial digitization is reflected in the stock adjustment of digital economy, that is, the digital transformation and upgrading of traditional industries, such as e-commerce and secondary industry digitalization. Table 1.8 reports the scale and proportion of the two types of digital economy. Industrial digitization is the main component of the general digital economy; in other words, the digital transformation and upgrading of traditional business forms constitute the main part of the general digital economy, which is manifested in the proportion of industrial digitization: higher than 70%.

Table 1.8 Analysis of the structure of the broadly defined digital economy: digital industrialization and industrial digitalization

Economy	Total (100 million USD)	Digital industrialization		Industrial digitization	
		Scale (100 million USD)	Proportion	Scale (100 million USD)	Proportion
the US	123,408	15,236	12.3	108,172	87.7
China	47,290	9,686	20.5	37,604	79.5
Germany	23,994	2,410	10.0	21,584	90.0
Japan	22,901	3,548	15.5	19,353	84.5
the UK	17,287	2,038	11.8	15,249	88.2
France	11,550	1,728	15.0	9,822	85.0
Korea	7,636	2,253	29.5	5,383	70.5
India	5,415	1,511	27.9	3,904	72.1
Canada	5,342	819	15.3	4,523	84.7
Brazil	3,832	711	18.6	3,121	81.4
Average	26,866	3,994	17.6	22,872	82.4

Source: China Academy of Information and Communications Technology, "A New Landscape of Global Digital Economy (2019)".

3.2.2 Structural characteristics of the narrowly defined digital economy

Table 1.9 reports the changes of the value-added structure of the ICT sector in OECD countries. The ICT sector can be divided into ICT manufacturing and ICT service sectors. Generally speaking, the ICT service sector includes software publishing, telecommunications, and information service industries. Table 1.9 shows a visible "servicing" trend during the development of digital economy in OECD countries, which is presented by a decline in the ICT manufacturing index, from 100 to 93.1. ICT services show a trend of growth, increasing from 100 to 111.9, whereas information services increased from 100 to 115.9.

Table 1.9 Changes of structure and departments in the ICT sector in OECD countries: 2008-2015

Year	Overall	ICT manufacturing	Software publishing	Telecommunications	Information service
2008	100	100	100	100	100
2009	94.3	89.6	96.1	95.4	96.3
2010	97.4	98.7	95.8	94.9	99.1
2011	103.0	99.8	104.0	98.1	109.6
2012	101.5	95.1	106.7	95.5	110.7
2013	102.1	93.6	109.9	94.7	113.7
2014	103.8	94.7	109.4	93.7	118.7
2015	101.3	93.1	111.9	90.0	115.9
Growth rate	5.3	-2.4	13.5	-4.1	17.9

Note: The ICT sector includes the last four columns. In the 4th edition of the International Standard Industrial Classification (ISIC Rev.4), the manufacturing sector is no. 26 (Computer Electronic and Optical Products); software publishing is no. 582 (Software Publishing); telecommunications is no. 61 (Telecommunications); information service is no. 62-63 (IT and other Information Services).

Source: OECD Digital Economy Outlook, 2017.

Table 1.10 reports the structural characteristics of the ICT sector in some OECD countries and divides ICT into manufacturing and service. OECD countries as a whole account for 18.4% of manufacturing, while services account for 81.6%. Among the countries shown, the proportion of ICT manufacturing in only four countries—Korea, Switzerland, China, and Mexico—is higher than 40%. Therefore, in the structure of the narrowly defined digital economy, digital economy is presented with a highly service-oriented feature.

Table 1.10 Added value structure of ICT sectors in some countries in 2016 (%)

Economy	Overall	ICT manufacturing	ICT service	Proportion of manufacturing	Proportion of service
OECD	5.88	1.08	4.79	18.4	81.6
Ireland	11.53	1.77	9.76	15.4	84.6
Korea	10.27	6.47	3.80	63.0	37.0
Sweden	8.42	0.74	7.68	8.8	91.2
the US	7.93	1.59	6.34	20.1	79.9
Finland	7.81	2.04	5.77	26.1	73.9
Luxembourg	7.27	0.35	6.92	4.9	95.1
Switzerland	7.26	3.14	4.12	43.3	56.7
Hungary	6.84	1.84	5.00	26.9	73.1
Czech Republic	6.72	1.58	5.14	23.5	76.5
Japan	6.68	1.66	5.02	24.8	75.2
the UK	6.56	0.45	6.11	6.9	93.1
Estonia	6.36	0.84	5.51	13.3	86.7
India	6.27	0.39	5.87	6.3	93.7
Germany	6.16	1.42	4.74	23.0	77.0
France	5.77	0.59	5.18	10.2	89.8
Denmark	5.52	0.94	4.58	17.1	82.9
the Netherlands	5.40	0.61	4.79	11.3	88.7
Latvia	5.20	0.63	4.57	12.1	87.9
Slovakia	5.04	0.84	4.21	16.6	83.4
China	4.99	2.36	2.62	47.4	52.6
Iceland	4.95	0.05	4.90	0.9	99.1
Australia	4.92	0.36	4.57	7.3	92.7
Slovenia	4.89	0.77	4.12	15.7	84.3
Costa Rica	4.84	0.10	4.74	2.1	97.9
Canada	4.76	0.33	4.42	7.0	93.0
Norway	4.62	0.36	4.27	7.7	92.3
Indonesia	4.61	1.01	3.61	21.9	78.1
Austria	4.52	1.00	3.51	22.2	77.8
Belgium	4.50	0.36	4.14	7.9	92.1
Poland	4.47	0.43	4.04	9.5	90.5
Italy	4.22	0.58	3.65	13.7	86.3
Lithuania	4.22	0.50	3.71	12.0	88.0

Continued

Economy	Overall	ICT manufacturing	ICT service	Proportion of manufacturing	Proportion of service
Spain	4.18	0.28	3.89	6.8	93.2
Brazil	3.68	0.27	3.41	7.2	92.8
Portugal	3.66	0.27	3.39	7.3	92.7
Greece	3.55	0.12	3.42	3.5	96.5
Mexico	3.52	1.64	1.88	46.7	53.3
Colombia	3.44	0.27	3.17	7.8	92.2
Chile	3.31	0.24	3.07	7.4	92.6
Russia	3.09	0.76	2.34	24.5	75.5
New Zealand	3.08	0.23	2.85	7.5	92.5
Turkey	3.00	0.28	2.72	9.3	90.7
South Africa	2.23	0.20	2.03	9.1	90.9

Source: OECD, 2019, Measuring the Digital Transformation: A Roadmap for the Future.

To further discuss the reasons for the formation of the structural characteristics of digital economy, Table 1.11 reveals the proportion of three major industries of digital economy. These indicators can describe the level of digitalization in the three major industries. A clear conclusion is that the service industry has the highest level of digitization, followed by the digitalization of industry, and the digitization of agriculture. The differences in the level and scale of digitalization of different industries are important factors in forming the structural characteristics of digital economy.

Table 1.11 Levels of digitalization in the three major industries (%)

Service industry		Industry		Agriculture	
Country	Proportion	Country	Proportion	Country	Proportion
the UK	57.2	Korea	44.5	the UK	27.1
Germany	57.1	Germany	42.5	Germany	21.9
the US	55.1	the US	37.7	Korea	13.7
Japan	41.0	Ireland	34.6	the US	13.7
France	36.7	the UK	31.5	Finland	13.4
China	35.9	Japan	30.8	New Zealand	13.4
Finland	29.8	Singapore	28.9	Japan	12.7
Mexico	27.7	France	24.8	France	12.3
Ireland	27.3	Finland	20.9	Singapore	11.3
Korea	25.3	Denmark	19.3	Ireland	10.9
Singapore	23.6	China	18.3	Denmark	10.1
Average	37.9	Average	30.3	Average	14.6

Source: China Academy of Information and Communications, 2019, New Prospect of Global Digital Economy.

Based on the above analysis of the structural characteristics of digital economy, the following conclusions could be drawn: First, in terms of the structure of the broadly defined digital economy, industrial digitization is the major component of digital economy, accounting for more than 70% in all major countries. Second, in terms of the structure of the narrowly defined digital economy, ICT services are more important than ICT manufacturing, and digital services are more important than digital products.

The above structural features can be attributed to two aspects. One is the scale and structure of industries. The proportion of service industry, industry, and agriculture vary in the world economy, and the proportion in each country is different. This is the reason for temporal and cross-sectional differences in digital economy. The second is the levels of digitalization in various industries. The service industry has the highest level of digitalization, and the agricultural industry has the lowest level of digitalization. The transition from agriculture and industry to the service industry is a shared feature of the economic structure transformation of all countries. It is expected that the digitalization of the world economy will continue to increase in the future, and digital economy will occupy an increasingly important position. Looking deeper, the advancement of digital technology is the source and prerequisite for the improvement of digitalization, and the empowerment of factors determines the industrial structure of each country. The overlap of these two factors will form horizontal differences and the vertical trend of the scale and structure of digital economy. This explanation actually echoes the relationship between digital technology and digital economy described in the previous two sections.

3.3 Analysis of micro-subjects in the operation of global digital economy

3.3.1 Digitalized enterprises

In the wave of global digitization, many digital enterprises have sprung up. They are the epitome of the development of digital economy. In 2009, among the top 10 enterprises with the biggest market value in the world, only Microsoft was a digital enterprise; by 2019, seven out of the top 10 enterprises in the world were digital enterprises. This change in the ranking of micro-enterprises profoundly demonstrates the digitalized trend of micro entities in the world economy. Digitalized enterprises have become important micro entities in economic operations. Table 1.12 lists the top 10 enterprises in the world by market value.

Table 1.12 Changes in the top 10 enterprises by market value

Ranking	2009	2019
1	Exxon Mobil	Apple
2	China National Petroleum Corporation	Microsoft
3	Walmart	Google
4	ICBC	Amazon
5	China Mobile	Facebook
6	Microsoft	Alibaba
7	AT&T	Tencent

Continued

Ranking	2009	2019
8	Johnson & Johnson	JPMorgan
9	Shell	Johnson & Johnson
10	Procter & Gamble	Walmart

Source: Compiled by the author based on Forbes' annual report.

There are three points worth noting in Table 1.12. First, by 2019, there were seven digital enterprises (out of 10), and most of them were information service-oriented enterprises. This is the micro foundation for the aforementioned expansion of digital economy and the service-oriented structure of digital economy. Second, it took only 10 years for digital enterprises to occupy the major part of the market, which shows that the development and application of digital technology are advancing significantly, and the digital trend of the world economy will be further accelerated. Third, from the perspective of the distribution of enterprises, most digital enterprises are in developed countries, which is the micro foundation of the digital divide at a macro level.

Further, Table 1.13 reports the application of websites in the world's top 10 enterprises. First, from the description of functions, these websites involve knowledge research, video and information provision, sales, and purchase, etc. This means that they will have a profound and extensive influence on the behavior of enterprises, consumers, and researchers. This serves as the micro foundation for the multi-level impact of digital economy. Second, login times and browsing history show users browsing extensively on various websites, which means that digital life has become a daily part of the behavior of economic subjects. Third, in terms of the number of users, the number of users on all the websites exceed 200 million, and some of them have more than one billion users. This means that more than one-fifth of the world's population are invisible customers of these enterprises, indicating the widespread influence of digitalized enterprises and digital economy. This will have a profound impact on the survival and development modes of enterprises.

Table 1.13 Application of the world's top 10 websites in 2016

Website	Description	Average daily login time (minutes: seconds)	Number of pages viewed per person	Number of links	Number of users (100 million)
Google	Web portal	8:45	8.63	3011003	10
YouTube	Video website	9:23	5.4	2347245	10
Facebook	Social media	13:56	5.32	7278321	18.60
Baidu	Search Engine	7:43	6.68	118000	6.57
Wikipedia	Encyclopedia	4:26	3.31	1287362	3.74
Yahoo	Web portal	4:28	3.9	529800	6.5
Tencent	Instant messaging	5:05	4.52	211248	8.77

Website	Description	Average daily login time (minutes: seconds)	Number of pages viewed per person	Number of links	Number of users (100 million)
Taobao	E-commerce	8:33	4.48	48973	4.07
Reddit	News links	13:31	9.28	416267	2.34
Tmall	E-commerce	5:51	3.45	8642	4.07

Note: The numbers of users of Google and YouTube are estimated; the numbers of users of Baidu, Wikipedia, Taobao, and Tmall are from 2015 data.

Source: World Bank, 2018, Information and Communications for Development: Data Driven Development.

It is worth noting that in the digital economy era, the space for the survival and development of digital enterprises continues to expand in the international market, thereby promoting the digitization of international trade and investment. Table 1.14 reports the international operations of Facebook and Google. It shows that the share of foreign capital in revenue and profit of the two enterprises far exceeds that of domestic enterprises. They live up to the title of "multinational enterprises". This indicates that these emerging digitalized multinational enterprises will have a profound impact on the international market. Of course, from the perspective of the taxation structure, about 90% of the tax revenue is obtained by the local government. This means that in the digital economy era, the digital divide is not only manifested by the difference in scale of digital economy at a macro level, but also manifested by the uneven distribution of the benefits of digital economy.

Table 1.14 International operation of typical digital enterprises in 2017

Firm	Index	Scale (100 million USD)			Proportion (%)	
		Foreign	the US	Overall	Foreign	the US
Facebook	Revenue	229.19	177.34	406.53	56.4	43.6
	Profit	135.15	70.79	205.94	65.6	34.4
	Tax	3.89	46.45	50.34	7.7	92.3
Google	Revenue	584.06	524.49	1108.55	52.7	47.3
	Profit	165	107	272	60.7	39.3
	Tax	17.46	126.08	143.54	12.2	87.8

Source: UNCTAD, Digital Economy Report 2019.

Table 1.12 and Table 1.14 reflect the business of new digital enterprises and Internet enterprises in the digital economy era. It shows that these new enterprises have an extensive influence on economic growth, income distribution, investment, and consumption.

3.3.2 Digitalization of enterprises and its impact

In the digital economy era, traditional enterprises may adopt digital technology to enhance their operating capabilities and improve business performance. This digitalization is precisely the micro foundation of industrial digitization. Table 1.15 shows the adoption of digital technology by enterprises in OECD countries from 2010 to 2018. From the level of performance, most enterprises in OECD countries have adopted broadband technology; however, the adoption of high-end or advanced digital technologies remains uncommon, such as big data, radio frequency identification systems (RFID), etc., the adoption rates of which are no higher than 20%. This means there is room for improvement for traditional enterprises to go digitalized. Secondly, in terms of growth rate, excluding supply chain management technology, these enterprises all witness an increase in the application of other digital technologies, especially in enterprise resource planning systems, cloud computing, high-speed networks, and RFIDs, the growth rates of which are higher than 50%. Therefore, the fast development and great potential of the digitalized development of traditional enterprises may constitute a large growth rate as a contribution to the future development of digital economy.

Table 1.15 Changes of dynamism in the use of digital technology by enterprises in OECD countries (%)

Technology	Early stage		Final stage		Growth rate	
	Median	Mean	Median	Mean	Median	Mean
Broadband	85.0	84.0	92.8	91.9	9.1	9.3
Electronic purchase	42.5	41.7	49.7	48.0	17.0	15.1
Enterprise resource planning system	21.2	21.4	30.6	32.3	44.5	51.0
Cloud computing	14.5	19.7	24.6	30.3	70.0	53.8
Customer relation management system	23.4	25.3	30.9	29.5	32.2	16.7
E-sales	18.9	18.9	20.1	22.1	6.0	17.1
High-speed network	7.1	7.9	19.2	21.9	168.5	176.3
Supply chain management	18.0	19.9	15.1	15.5	-16.1	-22.2
RFID	3.1	4.1	10.9	12.9	255.6	215.7
Big data	11.3	11.2	12.6	12.4	11.2	11.0

Note: "High-speed network" refers to a network with a speed higher than 100M. The timespan is 2010-2018; due to the difference in data availability, differences between the initial and final years of various technologies may occur.

Source: OECD, 2019, Measuring the Digital Transformation: A Roadmap for the Future.

Table 1.16 shows the penetration rates of the application of big data technology by enterprises of different sizes in different countries. Looking at the overall average, about 11% of enterprises adopt big data technology, a low penetration rate; from the differences of penetration rates among enterprises of various sizes, the lowest adoption rate of big data technology in small enterprises is only 9.5%, and that in big enterprises is 27.8%; the difference in adoption rates of big data technology by enterprises of different sizes exists in almost all countries. Therefore, the adoption of digital technologies does not only have differences in time dimension, as shown in Table 1.15, but also have large differences in firm dimension. Large enterprises have generally higher adoption rates of new digital technologies. It is believed that compared with small enterprises, large enterprises are larger in scale, have higher production efficiency and better technological inventions, etc. Therefore, the application of big data technology may cause resources to flow from small enterprises to large enterprises, which is a possible channel for digital technology to promote the optimal allocation of resources.

Table 1.16 Differences among enterprises using big data technology in 2016 (%)

Country	All enterprises	Small enterprises	Medium-sized enterprises	Large enterprises
the Netherlands	19.1	16.7	25.7	43.1
Belgium	17.0	14.6	26.1	41.8
the UK	15.4	13.3	23.6	35.4
Finland	14.8	12.3	24.4	40.0
Portugal	13.4	12.5	17.1	23.9
Estonia	12.7	11.3	17.0	32.5
Luxembourg	12.5	10.4	18.7	33.8
Lithuania	12.0	11.4	13.4	20.4
Denmark	11.7	9.8	16.9	39.6
Greece	11.4	10.3	18.0	24.4
France	11.3	10.0	17.6	24.4
Slovenia	11.0	8.0	21.9	38.0
Slovakia	10.8	8.8	16.5	24.3
Sweden	9.9	8.5	14.9	30.4
Italy	9.0	7.7	17.0	29.8
Czech Republic	8.5	6.8	13.5	21.9
Spain	8.3	7.1	13.2	20.9
Hungary	7.0	6.7	7.9	11.7
Poland	5.9	4.9	8.4	17.6
Germany	5.7	4.6	9.3	16.9
Korea	3.6	3.1	5.7	13.4
Average	11.0	9.5	16.5	27.8

Note: "Small enterprises" refers to enterprises with 10-49 employees; "medium-sized enterprises" refers to enterprises with 50-249 employees; "large enterprises" refers to enterprises with over 250 employees.

Source: OECD Digital Economy Outlook, 2017.

In fact, not only are there differences in the utilization of digital technology among enterprises, but the utilization of digital technology among industries also sustains, which shows the differences in the level of digitalization in different industries. Table 1.17 shows that in all industries, the utilization of enterprise resource planning and customer relationship management systems is relatively high, with an average value exceeding 30%; however, the utilization of big data and cloud computing is low, both less than 30%. In terms of the differences among industries, the adoption rate of digital technology in the information and communications industry and technical service industry is relatively high and that in traditional industries such as the construction industry and transportation and storage industry is relatively low. The difference in the adoption of digital technology in different industries also indicates the difference in the growth space and development potential of different industries in the future, which will further affect the adjustment of industrial structure and the allocation of resources among industries.

Table 1.17 Differences in the utilization of digital technology in OECD countries (%)

Industry	Cloud computing	Big data	Enterprise resource planning	Customer relationship management
Information and communications industry	64	24	49	62
Technical services	44	11	34	41
Real estate	33	9	33	36
Wholesale	30	10	54	48
Administrative services	29	11	26	33
Manufacturing	22	7	45	33
Transportation and storage	21	15	25	24
Construction	21	8	21	20
Retail	20	9	28	30
Hospitality and catering services	17	10	15	20
All industries	26	10	34	33

Source: OECD, 2019, Measuring the Digital Transformation: A Roadmap for the Future.

In fact, the impact of digital technology on the development of industries is reflected in Table 1.18. In digital intensive industries, the entry and exit rates of enterprises are higher than those of other industries, which means the levels of competition and liberalization are higher. The intense competition will bring elimination and subsequently lead to the optimized allocation of industry resources. This illustrates the importance of digital technology to production efficiency and resource allocation at the industry level.

Table 1.18 Entry and exit rates of digital technology and enterprises (%)

Year	Entry		Exit	
	Digital intensive industry	Other industries	Digital intensive industry	Other industries
1998	10.3	7.8	6.5	6.3
1999	10.4	7.0	6.6	6.4
2000	10.5	7.0	6.7	6.2
2001	10.6	7.2	7.3	6.8
2002	9.3	6.4	7.2	6.1
2003	8.8	6.1	7.0	5.9
2004	8.6	6.1	6.2	5.9
2005	8.5	6.1	6.4	5.9
2006	8.8	6.1	6.2	5.9
2007	8.6	6.4	6.5	5.9
2008	8.5	6.1	7.0	6.0
2009	7.4	5.3	7.4	6.4
2010	7.5	5.5	6.6	5.8
2011	7.1	5.4	6.5	5.8
2012	6.6	5.2	6.7	6.1
2013	6.5	5.0	6.6	6.2

Year	Entry		Exit	
	Digital intensive industry	Other industries	Digital intensive industry	Other industries
2014	6.3	4.8	7.0	6.3
2015	5.4	4.3	6.9	6.4
Average	8.3	6.0	6.7	6.1

Source: OECD, 2019, Measuring the Digital Transformation: A Roadmap for the Future.

Table 1.19 introduces the number of robots in OECD countries and BRICS countries, revealing the differences in the utilization of digital technology among countries. The data is presented in descending order according to the number of robots owned by every 10,000 people in 2016.

Table 1.19 Number of robots in OECD members and BRICS countries

Economy	Stock		Number owned per 10,000 people	
	2007	2016	2007	2016
Korea	52,086	180,027	129	398
Japan	307,739	311,290	270	306
Singapore	2,882	9,420	51	189
Germany	89,715	139,441	123	185
Sweden	6,226	9,353	91	171
Denmark	2,170	3,709	60	130
Belgium	4,372	6,229	74	125
the US	114,161	183,463	70	119
Taiwan, China	15,126	35,772	53	118
Italy	35,549	45,190	77	117
Spain	17,172	22,824	62	110
Austria	3,401	6,542	53	104
France	21,591	24,911	71	97
Slovakia	583	4,573	11	90
the Netherlands	2,812	6,837	34	90
Finland	2,504	2,960	60	88
Slovenia	545	1,678	24	85
Switzerland	2,805	4,580	42	70
Canada	-	11,012	-	66
Czech Republic	2,491	9,250	18	66
the UK	9,576	13,984	34	56
Hungary	598	3,503	7	44
Portugal	1,139	2,679	14	37
Norway	706	691	27	30
Mexico		17,223		29
China	17,880	253,306	1	20
South Africa	987	2,891	5	17

Economy	Stock		Number owned per 10,000 people	
	2007	2016	2007	2016
Brazil	2,334	7,908	2	7
Russia	5,558	3,884	5	4
India	2,097	8,830	0	2

Source: OECD, 2019, Measuring the Digital Transformation: A Roadmap for the Future.

Table 1.19 shows that the number of robots per capita in developed countries is above 29. Among them, Mexico has the fewest robots per capita, 29, and Korea has the most, 398; while the number of robots per capita in BRICS countries is very low, with China having 20 and India only 2; therefore, there are huge differences in the application of digital technology, represented by robots, among countries. This may be the root cause in the scale and structure of digital economy among countries, and it also reflects the digital divide in the application of digital technology. Of course, vertically speaking, the number of robots per capita in all countries increases.

Based on all the analyses from Table 1.12 to Table 1.19, important changes have taken place on the supply side of the market, i.e. enterprises, in the digital economy era. On the one hand, a large number of digital enterprises have become market entities and an important driving force for economic development in the new era; on the other hand, the application of digital technology has also improved the level of digitalization of traditional enterprises, but substantial differences remain in the utilization of digital technology among different enterprises, industries, and countries. This may be a supply-side reason that causes the digital divide.

3.3.3 Digitalization of consumer behavior

In the digital economy era, not only is the behavior of producers experiencing important changes, but the behavior of consumers is also changing. Table 1.20 shows the changes in purchasing and spending behavior in OECD countries. Obviously, online shopping and spending increase year by year, exceeding 50% in 2015. Changes in consumer behavior, in turn, have a profound impact on the development of digital finance and digital trade, and increase the level of economic digitalization.

Table 1.20 Proportion of consumers choosing online banking and online purchases in some countries (%)

Behavior type	2010	2011	2012	2013	2014	2015	2016	2017
Online banking	36.5	38.3	42.7	46.0	48.0	51.2	53.6	57.0
Online purchasing	35.6	40.2	44.9	44.8	48.5	52.0	56.2	57.6

Source: OECD, 2019, Measuring the Digital Transformation: A Roadmap for the Future.

Similarly, different types of consumers embrace digital consumption at different levels. An approximate indicator is the difference in average daily online duration for all types of consumers, as shown in Table 1.21.

Table 1.21 Average daily online duration of residents in some countries in 2016 (hours: minutes)

Country	14-24 years old	Overall population	14-24, male	14-24, female
the Netherlands	6:02	3:42	5:43	6:16
Portugal	5:40	4:06	5:53	5:29
Sweden	5:31	3:45	5:44	5:17
Iceland	5:20	4:09	5:55	4:40
Estonia	5:17	4:12	5:21	5:13
Spain	5:15	3:28	4:54	5:35
the UK	5:09	3:37	5:27	4:54
Norway	4:55	3:35	4:54	4:57
Germany	4:30	3:07	4:44	4:16
Russia	4:29	3:39	4:16	4:44
Israel	4:25	3:38	4:09	4:43
France	4:03	2:54	3:59	4:08
Czech Republic	4:02	3:12	4:24	3:42
Lithuania	3:58	3:13	4:07	3:51
Belgium	3:57	3:05	3:57	3:57
Finland	3:52	2:50	4:02	3:42
Hungary	3:49	3:26	3:36	4:01
Ireland	3:44	3:00	3:45	3:44
Italy	3:40	2:46	3:31	3:51
Switzerland	3:36	2:43	3:27	3:48
Poland	3:28	2:57	3:22	3:36
Austria	2:55	2:18	2:41	3:07
Slovenia	2:45	2:53	2:35	2:56

Source: OECD, 2019, Measuring the Digital Transformation: A Roadmap for the Future.

There are large differences in the time spent online among consumers in various countries. Among samples, consumers between the ages of 14 and 24 in the Netherlands spend six hours online, while in Slovenia it is less than three hours, which reflects the national differences in digital behavior; similarly, younger people between the ages of 14-24 spend significantly more time online than others, indicating that there are structural differences related to age in consumers' digital behavior; in most countries, there are also differences in online duration between men and women.

Based on the above analysis of the digital behavior of enterprises and consumers, it can be concluded that in the digital economy era, the digital behavior of micro-entities shows a significant increase, which is reflected in the adoption of digital technology by enterprises and the increasing proportion of digital consumption by consumers; on the other hand, the level of digitalization of economic subjects also varies, which is reflected in the differences in the popularity of digital technology among enterprises, industries, and countries, as well as the differences in the duration online among consumers. To sum up, the intertemporal differences in the digital behavior of economic subjects promotes the development of digital economy and forms the micro foundation for the increasing importance of digital economy; individual differences in the digital behavior of economic entities contribute to the differences in the scale and structure of digital economy in various countries, forming the micro foundation of the digital divide. In this way, we can understand the scale, the structural difference, and the characteristics of digital economy, from the perspective of the digital behavior of microeconomic subjects.

3.3.4 Comparative analysis of typical digital enterprises

In order to conduct a detailed analysis, this report selects Chinese company Tencent and America company Facebook for comparative analysis, focusing on showing the development trend of digital enterprises and the differences between digital enterprises, so as to provide a specific case study for the above analysis. In the digital economy era, the boundary between digital and non-digital enterprises is no longer distinctive. Every enterprise is more or less digitalized. With reference to the definition of digital economy in the previous section, "digital enterprise" mentioned in this section refers to an enterprise that wholly or mainly uses digital technology or data factors in the production and operation process. Facebook (US) and Tencent (China) are typical representatives of digital enterprises. In 2019, Facebook ranked 5th with a global market value of 554 billion dollars, and Tencent ranked 7th with a market value of 442 billion dollars. The two are of similar size, and both are based on social networking platforms, which are their main business.[1] Therefore, the two enterprises are compared and analyzed as typical representatives of digital enterprises in developed and developing countries.

In terms of scale, Facebook's total revenue in 2018 was 55.838 billion dollars, and that of Tencent was 45.561 billion dollars. In 2014, Tencent's revenue was 12.899 billion dollars, slightly higher than Facebook's 12.466 billion dollars. The growth rate of the revenue of the two enterprises is also accelerating. The growth rate of revenue of Tencent averages 63% in the past five years, and that of Facebook averages 87%. In the early days, Tencent's revenue was larger than that of Facebook. This is because, first, Tencent was established earlier, and accumulated capital earlier; second, Tencent gained the dividends of China, a populous country. Later, this advantage gradually disappears as the level the internationalization of the two enterprises got higher. The rapid growth of these two enterprises reflects the development and growth of digital enterprises from a micro aspect, and also reveals the micro foundation of the large-scale digital economy in China and the US in a macro aspect.

---

[1] The analysis data of Tencent and Facebook is from Wind Financial Terminal and the annual reports of the two enterprises. This report will not repeat the source in the following figures.

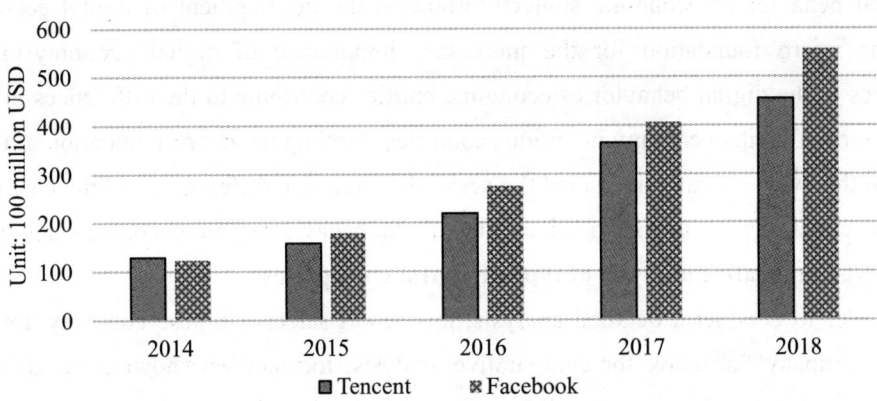

Figure 1.9 Comparison of total revenues of Tencent and Facebook from 2014-2018

From the structure of revenue, it can be concluded that the composition of the revenues of Tencent and Facebook is different. In 2018, Facebook's advertising revenue was 54.85 billion dollars, accounting for 98.2% of the total revenue, whereas other revenues only accounted for 1.8%, mainly coming from the hardware sales revenue of the company's VR brand, Calibra. Tencent's main revenue comes from games rather than advertising. In 2018, Tencent's revenue consisted of three parts: value-added services, online advertising, and other products, which accounted for 56.5%, 24.9%, and 18.6% of the revenue respectively. Value-added services include revenue from PC games, online games, and social network services (such as virtual items in games, virtual products on social platforms, etc.); online advertising revenue includes media advertising (Tencent News, Tencent Video, etc.) and advertising revenue from social networking platforms; other services include revenue from financial technology services, cloud services, revenue from the production of TV series and film, etc. Looking at the structure of revenue, on the one hand, the profit model of the two enterprises is completely different from that of traditional manufacturing enterprises. The profit is based on platforms, and customer data is the key resource of factor, and digital technology is the guarantee for operation. This reflects the difference between digital enterprises and traditional enterprises. It is a micro reflection of the difference between digital economy and the traditional economy. On the other hand, the digital economy structure of different countries is different. Facebook relies on the connection between its data and traditional industries to obtain advertising revenue, which is reflected in the characteristics of industry and scientific research; Tencent relies on its customer groups to sell services, which is reflected in the number of consumers. This reflects the micro foundation of the difference in the structure of digital economy between developed and developing countries.

Although the two enterprises are both Internet giants, Facebook is much more internationalized than Tencent. Tencent's revenue still comes from China. In 2018, 44.244 billion dollars of Tencent's revenue came from China's mainland, accounting for 97.1%. In comparison, in 2018, 25.727 billion dollars of Facebook's revenue came from the US and Canada, accounting for 46.1%; 13.631 billion dollars came from Europe, accounting for 24.4%; 11.733 billion dollars came from the Asia-Pacific region, accounting for 21%; income from other regions was 4.747 billion dollars, accounting for 8.5%. For large digital enterprises in the digital economy era, there is still a huge gap in the competitiveness between developed and developing countries. The root cause may be that scientific research takes a big part in the structure of digital economy in developed countries; while developing countries only have the advantage of the scale of the domestic market. The advantage of scientific research can be transformed into a monopoly advantage for international operations, while the domestic market has not formed effective home market effects, nor can it be transformed into a digital technology advantage for international expansion.

In terms of users, in 2018, Facebook's average MAU (monthly active users) was 2.330 billion; WeChat's MAU was 1.098 billion; QQ's MAU was 807 million. The average MAP (monthly active people) on Facebook's full-fledged social network platforms (including Facebook, Instagram, WhatsApp, Messenger)① was 2.64 billion. In addition, affected by the difference in GDP per capita between China and the US, the average spending power of active Facebook users is stronger than that of Tencent, which further affects the value of advertisements of the platform.

The following can be concluded: Although Tencent and Facebook are both typical representatives of digital enterprises, both Internet giants in China and the US, both started from social network platforms and use it to support the corporate ecosystem, and both focus on advertising, their organization structure and business strategies are different. First, Facebook's revenue is highly dependent on the online advertising business, while Tencent uses games as its main source of income, and online advertising is an important part of its comprehensive development, and it develops in multiple areas. The root of this difference is that although both Tencent and Facebook operate social networking platforms, Tencent's WeChat, QQ, and other platforms have strong social attributes, which are typical social platforms for acquaintances with close relationship circles; Facebook and Instagram are media-oriented platforms. Users of these platforms have a higher tolerance and acceptance of advertisements than the former. In addition, Tencent's involvement in games, entertainment, music, search engines, finance, cloud services, and many other fields immediately reduces the advertising value of the company's social network platform in many industries. Second, the development strategies of the two are very different. Facebook chose to deepen its social networking platforms. Facebook positions itself as a free media platform. Instagram positions itself as a dating platform with photos and short videos. WhatsApp and Messenger position themselves as acquaintance social platforms with communication functions and use a rich product portfolio to satisfy the different needs of users.

---

① The difference between MAP and MAU is that the former measures the number of active users, which excludes the situation where one natural person uses multiple accounts.

Tencent uses game services as its main source of revenue. It regards WeChat and QQ as tools to generate traffic and extensively expand other businesses as a means of monetizing traffic. Thanks to the huge user base and traffic brought by WeChat and QQ, Tencent is China's industry leader in many areas. For example, with QQ Music, Kuwo Music, and Kugou Music, Tencent has a market share of nearly 80%; Tencent Video is China's second-largest online video-streaming platform, and it is not far behind the leader iQiyi; Tencent owns the PC online game "League of Legends" and the mobile online game "PUGB MOBILE" with the highest average MAU in the world. These are all derived from the traffic dividends brought by QQ and WeChat. To sum up, although the two enterprises reflect the huge differences in profit-generating models and operating mechanisms between microeconomic subjects and traditional enterprises in the digital economy era, the differences in the technological advantages of the two enterprises make the core of competitiveness and operation strategy significantly different, which reflects that, despite the fact that the scales of digital economy of both China and the US are huge, the structures of their digital economy are completely different.

In summary of all the analyses on microeconomic subjects, we believe that the behavior of all microeconomic entities in the digital economy era is digitalized; however, due to the limits of technology, factors, and market size, differences of digitalization of micro entities in different countries remain. This explains the fact that digital economy is developing rapidly in all countries, and shows the differences in the structure of digital economy in various countries. This may give us an insight into the cause and resolution of the digital divide.

3.4 The influence of the global development of digital economy

3.4.1 International trade

Digital technology changes not only the production of enterprises and consumers, but also the sales behaviors of producers and the flow of goods. One important sign is the rapid development of global e-commerce. Table 1.22 shows the scale, ratio, structure, and other characteristics of e-commerce in major countries.

Table 1.22 Top 10 countries in the scale of development of e-commerce in 2018

Country	Total value (billion dollars)	Proportion in GDP (%)	B2B	B2C	Per capita value of purchase (USD)
the US	8,883	46	8,129	754	3,851
Japan	2,975	61	2,828	147	3,248
China	1,931	16	869	1,062	2,574
Germany	1,503	41	1,414	89	1,668
Korea	1,290	84	1,220	70	2,983
the UK	755	29	548	207	4,658
France	734	28	642	92	2,577
Canada	512	31	452	60	3,130

Continued

Country	Total value (billion dollars)	Proportion in GDP (%)	B2B	B2C	Per capita value of purchase (USD)
India	400	15	369	31	1,130
Italy	333	17	310	23	1,493
Overall	19,315	36	16,782	2,533	2,904

Source: UNCTAD, Digital Economy Report 2019.

Table 1.22 shows that the proportions of e-commerce in the GDP in the US, Japan, and Korea are 46%, 61%, and 84%, respectively, indicating the important influence of e-technology on commodity circulation; in terms of distribution, among the top 10 countries with the largest scale of e-commerce, only China is a developing country, suggesting the existence of a digital divide in e-commerce; in terms of structure, most developed countries are dominated by B2B. China, as a developing country, is dominated by B2C. This suggests that the structure of e-commerce in countries with different development levels varies. This is consistent with the overall structure of digital economy. Table 1.22 does not distinguish the domestic market from the international market. If the international market is taken into account, the impact of digital technology is reflected in the growth and changes in digitalized service trade. Table 1.23 shows the development and changes of service trade in the digital economy era.

Table 1.23 Volume of digitalized services and trade (million dollars)

Region	2005	2018	growth rate (%)
World	1,179,430	2,931,400	7
Developed countries	989,320	2,232,100	6
Developing countries	178,030	659,870	11
Economies in transition	12,080	39,430	10
Least developed regions	2,100	7,460	10

Source: UNCTAD, Digital Economy Report 2019.

Two things are worth noting in Table 1.23. First, global digitalized service trade is growing rapidly, with an overall global growth rate of 7%. The growth rate of developed countries is 6%, and that of developing countries is 11%. This shows that the development of digital technology is changing the content of and approaches of international trade. Second, developed countries are still in dominance in terms of the scale of digitalized trade, accounting for about 84%, which is consistent with the overall distribution of digital economy.

3.4.2 Labor market

The application of digital technology and the development of digital economy have an extensive influence on the labor market. The adoption of new digital technologies by enterprises leads to changes in work processes. Workers need to learn how to use software and equipment, as well as get additional training. This reflects the influence of digital economy on the demand side of the labor market. Table 1.24 reports the impact of the development of digital economy in

EU countries on job assignments and demands for labor in different industries.

Table 1.24 Demand-side changes in the labor market in EU countries (%)

Industry	Changes in job assignments	Demand for learning software	Demand for training
All industries	21	39	11
Information and communications	26	52	9
Finance	27	45	10
Manufacturing and mining	22	39	12
Commercial services	19	39	9
Public service, education, and health care	20	35	12
Real estate	19	34	9
Other service industries	17	33	15
Trade, transport, warehouse, accommodation and catering	19	32	11
Architecture	18	28	14
Agriculture	12	24	17

Source: OECD, 2019, Measuring the Digital Transformation: A Roadmap for the Future.

According to Table 1.24, on average, across all industries, 21% of jobs witness changes of the nature of job assignments due to the adoption of digital technology. Among them, information and communications, and finance industries have the highest percentage; agriculture has the lowest percentage. In terms of labor demand, 39% of workers need to learn how to use software and improve skills; 52% of workers in the information and communications industry have such needs. Therefore, the development of digital economy has an important impact on the demand for labor skills, which will further affect the scale of employment, the structure of employment, and the wage gap between laborers with different skills, thereby affecting the labor market at multiple levels.

3.4.3 Financial market

The development of digital economy not only affects the labor market, but also has an important impact on the financial market. In particular, the development of digital technologies such as blockchains may have a revolutionary impact on the financial industry. From a practical perspective, inclusive finance and digital finance have become important forces driving economic development. According to the "2019 White Paper on Inclusive Development of Digital Finance" released by China Academy of Information and Communications Technology, between 2015 and 2018, the amount of online payment of non-bank payment institutions was 49.48, 99.27, 143.26, and 208.07 trillion yuan, respectively. The development is fast and the scale expands. This reflects an important breakthrough in digital economy in the field of finance. This emerging online payment has expanded the scope of financial services. However, due to regulations and other factors, it also leads to online fraud and financial risks. Table 1.25 shows the proportion of property losses of consumers caused by online payment fraud in some countries.

Table 1.25 Proportion of property losses in online payment caused by Internet fraud in some countries (%)

Country	2010	2015	Average	Growth rate
the UK	4.29	2.37	3.33	-44.8
Luxembourg	2.14	2.92	2.53	36.6
Denmark	1.58	3.40	2.49	114.4
France	1.24	2.35	1.80	90.1
Norway	1.34	1.88	1.61	40.4
Sweden	1.26	1.64	1.45	29.6
Switzerland	1.10	1.65	1.37	49.9
Ireland	1.36	1.24	1.30	-8.6
Spain	1.36	1.13	1.24	-17.0
Belgium	1.21	1.23	1.22	1.5
the Netherlands	1.14	1.25	1.20	9.8
Italy	1.45	0.74	1.09	-49.2
Germany	1.22	0.57	0.90	-52.9
Austria	1.07	0.52	0.80	-51.3
Finland	0.61	0.95	0.78	54.4
Hungary	0.73	0.52	0.62	-28.8
Latvia	0.94	0.27	0.61	-70.6
Estonia	0.64	0.40	0.52	-37.6
Turkey	0.47	0.52	0.49	10.7
Greece	0.53	0.23	0.38	-56.1
Slovakia	0.49	0.27	0.38	-45.1
Slovenia	0.28	0.42	0.35	52.2
Czech Republic	0.23	0.29	0.26	26.6
Lithuania	0.29	0.11	0.20	-63.0
Poland	0.20	0.12	0.16	-38.6
Average	1.09	1.08	1.08	-1.90

Source: OECD Digital Economy Outlook, 2017.

Table 1.25 shows that, on the whole, the probability of online financial fraud is not high, less than 2%, but from the perspective of development trends, the situation is not showing any significant improvement. It is worth noting that Table 1.25 reflects the situation in developed countries where there is a higher level of financial supervision. Therefore, it can be deduced that online fraud caused by digital finance in developing countries is likely to be higher.

3.4.4 Economic security and model of governance

The security issue of digital finance is only one aspect of the security of digital economy. In the digital economy era, data has become an important factor of production, and data security becomes a matter of concern to enterprises, individuals, governments, and countries. Table 1.26 shows the proportion of enterprises in some countries that encountered digital security incidents since 2010.

Table 1.26 Proportion of digital security incidents encountered by enterprises in some countries since 2010

Country	All enterprises	Small enterprises	Medium-sized enterprises	Large enterprises
Portugal	40.3	39.3	47.1	42.6
Japan	37.5	-	31.8	54.1
Switzerland	30.1	29.3	32.1	45.8
Greece	28.8	27.9	33.2	35.1
Denmark	28.7	27.2	34.5	43.4
Finland	28.3	25.5	40.9	46.9
Portugal	26.2	25.4	30.9	34.1
Czech Republic	25.8	23.0	34.9	43.5
the Netherlands	22.3	19.8	30.4	42.9
Lithuania	21.8	19.5	29.8	43.4
Norway	20.9	19.3	27.8	43.7
Slovakia	20.2	18.7	24.6	31.4
Ireland	19.8	18.9	23.3	25.9
Sweden	19.5	18.4	23.8	32.4
Iceland	19.2	18.0	21.0	35.7
Italy	18.9	17.8	26.7	34.0
Belgium	15.3	14.0	21.0	24.4
New Zealand	13.6	12.8	16.3	27.9
Luxembourg	11.5	9.9	17.0	25.6
Latvia	10.0	8.7	14.8	25.5
Poland	10.0	8.5	13.9	21.5
Austria	9.5	8.5	13.4	19.0
Canada	9.4	8.4	9.8	19.4
Germany	9.2	7.3	15.2	19.5
Slovenia	8.7	6.9	15.2	21.5
France	8.6	7.5	12.8	19.6
Turkey	8.1	7.0	12.6	20.0
the UK	5.7	5.2	7.9	10.3
Hungary	4.9	4.0	8.5	14.3
Korea	4.2	4.0	4.9	7.3
Average	17.9	15.9	22.5	30.4

Source: OECD Digital Economy Outlook, 2017.

Table 1.26 shows that, on average, 17.9% of enterprises have encountered digital security incidents, among which large enterprises have a higher percentage of 30.4%. This suggests that data security is an important issue in the digital economy era. Government supervision and public governance systems are facing new challenges, and the governance system of digital economy becomes an important topic of research. Admittedly, despite the government's responsibility for data security and digital economy security, the development of digital technology also has an important impact on the approaches of the government. On the one hand, the government is digitalized, which is reflected as the level of e-government. This index is interpreted in the following three aspects: online service index, telecommunications infrastructure index, and human capital index, each accounting for 1/3. The development level of digitalization of each government is shown in Table 1.27.

Table 1.27 Digitalized government: level of e-government in various countries

Country	2008	2010	2012	2014	Average
US	0.864	0.851	0.869	0.875	0.865
UK	0.787	0.815	0.896	0.870	0.842
Canada	0.817	0.845	0.843	0.842	0.837
France	0.804	0.751	0.864	0.894	0.828
Japan	0.770	0.715	0.802	0.887	0.794
Germany	0.714	0.731	0.808	0.786	0.760
Italy	0.668	0.580	0.719	0.759	0.682
Russia	0.512	0.514	0.735	0.730	0.622
Brazil	0.568	0.501	0.617	0.601	0.572
China	0.502	0.470	0.536	0.545	0.513
South Africa	0.512	0.431	0.487	0.487	0.479
India	0.381	0.357	0.383	0.383	0.376

Source: UN E-Government Survey.

Two points are worth noting in Table 1.27. First, the level of e-government in G7 and BRICS countries increases year by year, indicating the impact of the development of digital technology and digital economy on governance. Second, there is still a big gap in e-government levels between developing countries and developed countries. India's index is 0.376, while that of the US is 0.865. This reflects the digital divide at the level of government behavior.

Chapter 2 The Development of China's Digital Economy

This chapter mainly depicts the development of China's digital technologies and digital economy. The first section mainly describes the development process of digital technologies in China and how ICT, as the representative of the industrialization of China's digital economy, has continuously promoted the rapid development of China's economy. At the same time, it also pushed the digital transformation and development of other industries. This section also elaborates on the development and application of digital technologies in China, such as big data, the Internet of Things, artificial intelligence, blockchains, and cloud computing. The second section shows the current situation of China's digital economic development. The rapid growth of various indicators shows the fast development of China's digital economy. The third section discusses the relation between China's digital economy development and the world, including its position and impact on the global scale, as well its global cooperation in the digital economy aspect. The fourth section describes the policy systems of China's digital economic development, including the opportunities and challenges it faces, and expounds the policy orientation of the integration of both the digital and real economy. Then, it lists the relevant incentive policies of China's digital economic development. Next, the above will be discussed in detail.

Section 1 The Development Process of China's Digital Technologies

With the impetus of a new round of technological revolution across the world, China's digital economy has shown to be thriving. The application of digital technology in the economic field has continuously changed the form of traditional industries in China, restructuring the supply and demand form of the market, creating new growth drivers and new forms for economic development, expanding our consumer market, and continually promoting digital transformation. With the gradual maturity and application of technologies such as ICT, big data, the Internet of Things, artificial intelligence, and blockchains, China's digital age is about to arrive. As mobile communications technologies continue to infiltrate the economic society, in the future, digital technology will be widely used in commercial, industrial, and enterprise activities. The technical scalability of digital technology in the economic society has been continuously strengthening, and digital economy will gradually grow stronger as a new ecosystem.

1.1 The development of ICT in China and its impact on the economy

ICT is the representative of digital economy's industrialization and it is also an independent industry in China. It continually promotes the rapid development of China's economy. At the same time, it also pushes forward the digital transformation and development of other industries. The basic industries of traditional ICT mainly include electronic information manufacturing, information communications, software services, broadcasting and television, as well as the Internet. According to a study by China Academy of Information and Communications Technology (CAICT), the proportion of the electronic information manufacturing industry has been declining continuously since 2008 while software and the Internet industries have been soaring to significant proportions in the basic ICT industry. This shows that in the future, ICT will constantly develop toward the digital technology field. At the same time, some emerging basic ICT industries are coming to form, with cloud computing, mobile applications and services, mobile Internet, as well as data analysis and services being the four hottest emerging ICT industries at present. On the whole, China's basic ICT industries are moving toward two main directions. The first is to promote the construction of informatization infrastructure and the development of communications technologies for broadband, mobile Internet, etc., as well as continuously realize the extensive spreading of digital infrastructure and provide a physical basis for the development of digital economy. The second direction is to promote the expansion and upgrading of ICT technology, vigorously developing the Internet of Things, mobile Internet, big data, cloud computing, and artificial intelligence as the core of emerging technologies, and to promote the deep integration and application of emerging ICT technologies in different fields.

In recent years, ICT has also continuously accelerated integration and penetration into traditional industries. It has also continuously promoted the digital transformation of the ICT, manufacturing, finance, and retail industries. Among these, the digital transformation of the manufacturing industry is the core of digital economy's strategic layout. In 2016, China proposed the "Made in China 2025" plan, which made a great push for the deep integration of ICT with the traditional manufacturing industry. The digital transformation of China's manufacturing industry mainly concentrates on the formation of an intelligent ecological system with the Internet of Things as its technological foundation. It aims to continuously launch applications of digital technology such as intelligent perception processing, industrial Internet, big data service platform, etc., thus pushing the manufacturing industry to become more intelligent, digitalized, and open.

In the process of the financial industry's digital transformation, ICT mainly promotes industrial transformation on the supply and demand sides at the same time. On the one hand, digital technologies that center around the Internet, artificial intelligence, and big data continuously promote the innovation and transformation of the financial industry, especially in the field of Internet payment, as well as constantly promote the realization of an intellectualized financial industry. On the other hand, digital technologies such as big data, cloud computing, and the Internet have provided a large amount of loan information for the financial industry, thus lowering the bar in the traditional industry for online loans as well as investment and financial management. This has stimulated the vitality of investments and financial management in the financial market and continuously promoted the realization of an inclusive financial industry. At the same time, the digital transformation of the financial industry has also continuously influenced other industries to do the same, including digital integration in fields like e-commerce, thus constantly promoting the formation and development of new systems such as consumer finance.

As one of the first industries to begin digital transformation, retail trade has undergone continuous reform. Now, it is not just limited to online e-commerce platforms. Instead, it also integrated online and offline trading platforms and realized the implementation and sharing of scenarios, data, and resources. This results in maximizing the satisfaction of consumers' needs and providing them with a more diversified user experience and a demand-oriented service system. In addition, the rapid development of online retailing has also continuously promoted the intellectualization development of the logistics industry and boosted the industry's digital transformation and upgrading.

The new generation of ICT represented by the 5G network is an important driving force for China's economic development today. It also played an indispensable role in the prevention and control of the COVID-19 outbreak. At the same time, 5G network construction is also being continually commercialized, thus effectively supporting the digital transformation of various industries. Compared with previous mobile communications technologies, the 5G network has an exponential growth in system performance. It can provide bandwidths at a peak of more than 10Gbps, limit delays to a millisecond, and provide ultra-high dense connectivity. This serves as a fundamental support for related industries' digital transformation and upgrade. Other than improvements in system performance, user experience rate of 5G technology can reach 100Mbps and up to 1Gbp, supporting mobile virtual reality and other ultimate business experiences. Connection density can reach 1 million/square kilometer, supporting massive access from the Internet of Things devices. Traffic density can reach 10Mbps/square meter, supporting a more than 1,000-fold growth in mobile business traffic in the future. Transmission delays can be limited to just a millisecond, thus meeting the relevant needs of the Internet of Vehicles (IoV) and industrial control. In the future, 5G technology will be deeply integrated with technologies like cloud computing, big data, artificial intelligence, and virtual augmented reality to connect people to everything. It will be the key infrastructure for the digital transformation of all industries.

The International Telecommunication Union (ITU) has defined three application scenarios of the fifth-generation mobile communications technology (5G), including enhanced Mobile Broadband (eMBB), massive Machine Type Communications (mMTC), and Ultra Reliable Low Latency Communications (uRLLC). Features of the 5G network such as high speed, low latency, and high reliability can provide a higher experience rate and greater bandwidth access capacity in enhanced mobile broadband application scenarios. In the case of a massive connection to IoT application scenarios, 5G provides an optimized signaling control capability in high-density connection. It supports high-efficiency access and management for big scale, low-cost, and low-consumption IoT equipment. When facing minimal delay and highly reliable communications application scenarios, including the IoV, crisis communications, industrial Internet, and other vertical industry application scenarios, 5G provides higher indicator standards for time delay and reliability. It also supports highly real-time, highly precise, and highly secure business collaboration between the physical space and the Internet. This has become an important basis for the rapid development of the new generation of information technology and the gradual advancement of digital economy. 5G drives the digitalization, networking, and intellectualization of traditional fields and enhances national core competitiveness. In this way, 5G technology has made the Internet of Everything and human-computer interaction become possible.

The commercialized application of 5G technology will induce a new round of investment boom in China, fostering emerging information products and services, reshaping the development models of traditional industries, and becoming a key driver for China's economic and social development. The application of 5G technology has promoted digitalized investments in China, boosted capital deepening of China's ICTs, driven an increase in China's demands, stimulated the market vitality, increased effective supply and demand of digital consumption, and uplifted China's competitiveness in the international market, thus leading to the rapid growth of China's domestic economy.

The CAICT pointed out in the report that the impact of 5G on China's economic society was measured by the production method of national economic accounting. The measurement scope mainly considered the income growth of telecom operators, Internet enterprises, and equipment manufacturers. It was then divided into direct and indirect economic society contributions. The results showed that in 2030, in terms of direct contribution, 5G would bring about a total output and economic growth value of 6.3 trillion and 2.9 trillion yuan respectively, as well as 8 million employment opportunities. In terms of indirect contribution, total output and economic growth value would be 10.6 trillion and 3.6 trillion yuan respectively, with 11.5 million employment opportunities.

Currently, 5G technology is in the standard formation stage. China has actively developed relevant policies to realize 5G technology R&D and industrialization. In the future, 5G technology will act as the network infrastructure. Combined with traditional paths and other infrastructure, it will boost the digital transformation of China's economic society, create a new ecological environment for the development of digital economy, and promote deep integration with China's traditional industries.

1.2 Current stage of China's digital technology development

With the continuous formation of large data ecologies, the application of digital technology has gradually begun to emerge and mature. On the basis of the new generation of 5G network's mobile network infrastructure, new forms of infrastructure such as cloud (cloud computing), network (Internet, Internet of Things (IoT), server (IoS), and other new platforms), and terminals (smart terminals (unmanned vehicles, etc.)) have been created. This has led to the emergence of digital technology systems that are represented by their technologies such as big data, artificial intelligence (AI), and blockchains.

1.2.1 Big data

Big data is a product of information technology development. With the widespread application of information technology in human society and the establishment of platforms such as the Internet and Internet of Things, data around the world has shown an explosive growth. This has an important impact on the development of economic societies and social governance. In the digital economy era, data is a new form of production factor. Although it is constantly impacting the traditional economic system, as an important strategic resource in the information society, it is able to improve the shareability of data by reducing the cost of data traffic. This becomes an important driving force in pushing forward data processing in the future real economy, promoting the implementation of the China's Big Data Strategy, and speeding up the construction of digital China.

The integrated application of big data in the digital economy era is mainly reflected in the use of information flow to drive the flow of technology, capital, and talents to constantly release the digital dividend. Through combining with real economy, big data technologies have promoted the realization of the intellectualization of the manufacturing industry, the digitization of the agriculture industry, and the transformation of the service industry. Through promoting the formation of scientific decision-making and social governance systems, big data technologies have continuously promoted the innovation of the government's management models and boosted the government to realize the rationalization of their decision-making, the precision of governance, and the effectiveness of its services.

At present, China's big data development is rapidly growing. On the one hand, thanks to the construction of a digital technology ecology, in which the 5G network, artificial intelligence, blockchains, and other digital technologies act as pillars, big data technologies are continuously empowered. This improves the data processing capacity of big data technologies. Through the integration of technologies, this has continually promoted the deep integration of big data and real economy, including driving forward the continuous expansion of the ICT industry, thereby constantly strengthening the market competitiveness of ICT enterprises. On the other hand, infrastructure constructions are constantly improved, including various multilevel platform systems such as the Internet Data Center (IDC) terminal, Content Distribution Network (CDN), and the industrial Internet. The devoted application from data transaction platforms across the country has pushed for the continuous refinement of the data traffic mechanism. All these infrastructure constructions brought about the extensive integration of big data technologies with physical industries. At the same time, enterprises have actively responded to the development of information technology. They continuously improve their own informatization level, data application capacity, etc. This improves the overall data demand from enterprises and accelerates the digital transformation of society. The government's policy environment is also continuously optimized and constantly provides legal assurance for integration of big data and real economy.

1.2.2 The Internet of Things

As the focus of digital technology development, the Internet of Things has shown a rapidly growing trend in recent years. The scale of China's Internet of Things data has been expanding continuously, and industry ecosystems are also constantly improving. According to statistics from the Ministry of Industry and Information Technology, up to 2018, the number of end-users of the Internet of Things in China has reached 460 million. With giant market size and the development of related industries in China, the application range will gradually expand, thus bringing in a new round of industrial technology changes.

With the continuous development of technology, the core part of the Internet of Things, the semiconductor chip, shows a trend of increasing demand. In terms of computing, the Internet of Things microcontrollers continue to develop in the direction of high performance, low power consumption, and high integration. In the field of sensors, the Internet of Things is evolving toward becoming smaller, smarter, and lower consumption. In addition to the development of artificial intelligence and the development and application of 5G network infrastructure, the deployment and construction of the government's network infrastructure have provided strong support for the development of China's Internet of Things. In the future, the deployment of the Internet of Things in China will gradually improve and gradually move toward application scenarios.

1.2.3 Artificial intelligence

Artificial intelligence is "the ability of agents to achieve the goal in complex environments". It is the research and development of "intelligent (machine) agents", including machines, software, or algorithms, which can respond intelligently to the surrounding environment through identification and response. Artificial intelligence is a branch of computer science and technology. It refers to the various sciences, technologies, methods, and engineering that use computers to simulate human intelligence behavior and realize the automation of work. With the rapid development of information technology and the fast popularization of the Internet, analysis predicted that the artificial intelligence market in China would reach 76 billion yuan in 2019, at a growth rate of 34.8%. The five core technologies of artificial intelligence include machine learning and depth learning, computer vision, natural language processing, knowledge mapping, and voice technology.

The three main pillars to promote AI technology development and application are big data, algorithms, and computing power. The foundation of artificial intelligence development lies in data and scenarios. On the one hand, China has a giant data consumer group that promotes the rapid development of China's artificial intelligence. On the other hand, digital technology platforms such as the Internet have rapidly popularized and accumulated a large data source that serves as a rich database for the application of artificial intelligence. The application of new technologies such as artificial intelligence has significantly increased the width, depth, and speed of data mining. As data mining continuously deepens, artificial intelligence constantly subverts the existing business models and builds a new business ecology. In terms of algorithms, machine learning and deep learning mature increasingly, so will the application of AI. The rapid progress of algorithms has also increased the demand for computing power, thus promoting the development of fields like chips and cloud computing. It is noted that Moore's Law① reveals the development pattern of the integrated circuit industry. However, AI's computing power has a faster development speed. In the future, AI computing power will be the core computing power. Artificial intelligence has a powerful empowering effect that forces us to rethink the development speed of the economic society.

The application of artificial intelligence mainly refers to the application of intelligent voice, natural voice processing, knowledge graph, and intelligent recommendation, as well as in other fields such as finance, transportation, security, home, retail, manufacturing, medicine, education, and entertainment. China's artificial intelligence technology is constantly integrating with the transformation of traditional industries and constantly penetrating into various application scenarios in society, thus forming a relatively comprehensive industrial chain and becoming an important driving force to promote the rapid development of China's economy. At present, China has an abundant array of end-point products of artificial intelligence applications. Computer vision, natural language processing, robots, and other technologies are undergoing in-depth integration with traditional fields such as security, transportation, medical care, and education. Among these, products in the security, retail, and education fields continue to mature. However, the intellectualization of the medical, manufacturing, and agriculture fields are still relatively low.

In the process of deep integration with real economy, artificial intelligence has continuously

---

① Moore's Law refers to the number of components that can be accommodated on the integrated circuit while the price remains unchanged. The number will double every 18-24 months, as will its performance.

improved the intelligence of the manufacturing industry. At the same time, artificial intelligence can also continuously empower industrial scenarios, increase production efficiency, improve quality stability, reduce consumption costs, improve equipment stability, and improve the safety of dangerous industrial scenarios. In addition, the application of artificial intelligence at the industrial level is mainly concentrated on assisting human work. Hence, it is not possible to break through mankind's innate cognitive scope in the short run.

In China, the development of artificial intelligence has the advantages of policy promotion and investment pull. After "Smart+" was proposed in the 2019 Government Work Report, many technologies that were entering maturity have been applied and developed more rapidly. At the same time, the value of artificial intelligence on economic and social development has also received great support from the public. Large amounts of social funds are constantly pouring into the application field of artificial intelligence.

In the future, chip, computing power, and data sharing will remain an important focus of artificial intelligence development. At the same time, the manufacturing industry is still the main target of artificial intelligence's deep integration. However, it should be pointed out that there are obvious regional differences in the industrial application of China's artificial intelligence. The eastern coastal areas are developing faster with their relatively more comprehensive digital infrastructure, while the development of the western regions is relatively lagging behind. However, different development advantages can be proposed to target such regional differences to form a differentiated development layout. At the same time, since the development of artificial intelligence will involve the application of big data, the main obstacle to overcome in the future development of artificial intelligence would be how to plan for the safety and standard of artificial intelligence.

1.2.4 Blockchains

On October 24, 2019, the Political Bureau of the CPC Central Committee held a collective study on the development status and trends of blockchain technology. While hosting the collective study, President Xi Jinping, General Secretary of the Central Committee of the CPC, stressed that the integrated application of blockchain technology played a vital role in new technological innovation and industrial transformation. It is necessary to treat blockchains as an important breakthrough point in the innovation of core technologies. The target must be clear and China need to greatly increase investments, focus on targeting a bunch of key core technologies, and accelerate the development of blockchain technology and its R&D.

The development of China's blockchain technology has an advantage in its good foundation and can promote the development of the China's real economy. Now, the application of blockchain technology has gradually extended to fields such as digital finance, the Internet of Things, and intelligent manufacturing. It has accelerated the deep integration of blockchains with digital technologies such as artificial intelligence, big data, and the Internet of Things. This leads to benefits such as realizing the open sharing of data resources, improving operational efficiency, and lowering operating costs. The open sharing of data will solve challenges that SMEs are facing, such as loan financing. At the same time, it can realize the application of blockchain technology in livelihood-related fields such as education, employment, pension, targeted poverty alleviation, medicine, and health. Besides, blockchain technology can advance the construction of Smart City and the flow of the factors of production between cities. Additionally, it can also improve the management standard of government affairs through data sharing, realize cross-department open use of government data, improve efficiency and decision-making standards, and simplify relevant government affairs processes.

The application of blockchains in the economic field can create a convenient, highly-efficient, fairly competitive, stable, and transparent new business form for enterprises. It can also act as an important guarantee for promoting the supply-side structural reform, realizing the sharing and utilization of data from various industries, promoting the digital transformation of the traditional economy, and pushing the high-quality development of economy.

Blockchains have the characteristics of decentralization, trustlessness, accrual maintenance, and a reliable database. All these guarantee the authenticity and confidentiality of data transmission. They have gradually been applied in financial fields such as digital currency, supply chain finance, and cross-border payment. They also continuously extends into the field of real economy and are an important push in realizing data sharing for real economy and promoting the rapid development of SMEs.

1.2.5 Cloud computing

In 2008, cloud computing was reintroduced to Chinese market as a brand-new ICT application model. Founded in 2009, Aliyun is the leading cloud computing and artificial intelligence technology company in the world. It was followed by the rapid development of cloud service platforms such as Baidu and Tencent. In 2011, with the strong support of the government and the join efforts of operators, vendors, and service providers, China's cloud computing applications were finalized with a market size of more than 30 billion yuan. In 2014, the National Development and Reform Commission, the Ministry of Finance, the Ministry of Industry and Information Technology, and the Ministry of Science and Technology jointly organized the implementation of cloud computing projects. They provided great support for areas such as the construction of public cloud computing service platforms and big data services based on cloud computing platforms, as well as solution development and project expansion for cloud computing and big data. In order to further activate the development of cloud computing, the State Council issued the "Opinions of the State Council on Promoting the Innovative Development of Cloud Computing and Cultivating New Business Forms of the Information Industry" on January 6, 2015. The document pointed out that "developing cloud computing is beneficial for information sharing, resource innovation, lowering the cost for societal entrepreneurship, and nurturing and forming new industries and new consumer hotspots. It is extremely important for stable growth, structure readjustment, benefiting people's livelihood, and the building of an innovative country." In March of 2017, SVM Software Technologies Co., Ltd. released a new generation of cloud-computing operating system customized for Chinese users, Cloudview SVM Edition V3 Cloud Computing Operating System, which is more stable, safe, and reliable. In July 2019, the Cyberspace Administration of China, the National Development and Reform Commission, the Ministry of Industry and Information Technology, and the Ministry of Finance issued the "Cloud Computing Services Security Assessment Measures".

Hence, it can be seen that under the dual impetus of both the government and the industry, cloud computing technology has developed rapidly since its birth in China. According to the "White Paper on the Development of China's Cloud Computing Industry" released by the Development Research Center of the State Council, the scale of the cloud-computing industry is expected to exceed 160 billion yuan by 2020 and 200 billion yuan by 2021. Cloud computing has gradually become an important driving force of China's digital economic development. It constantly pushes the development of China's software and information technology, deepens the supply-side structural reform, promotes the continuous realization of deep integration between relevant fields of technologies and real economy, and accelerates China's digitalization process.

Section 2　Current Status of the Development of China's Digital Economy

Digital economy is an economic activity system that integrates with information technology and is built on a series of information technology development. It is not meant to overthrow the existing traditional economic system. On the contrary, it is to complement, transform, and upgrade the existing system to shape a new economic ecological system. Since the beginning of the 21st century, especially in the last 10 years, China's digital science and technology have continued to permeate politics, economy, culture, and other fields. Digital economy, which is nurtured by the deep integration of real economy and digital technology, has promoted the continuous emergence of new models and new formats. It has greatly reduced economic costs and significantly improved efficiency. Digital economy is a new form of information revolution in the economic field. The Chinese government has seized this development opportunity, continued to implement the National Big Data Strategy, and pushed forward the deep integration of the Internet, big data, artificial intelligence, and real economy in full force.

2.1 Current development status of China's Internet

2.1.1 Size of Internet users

According to statistics from the China Internet Network Information Center, as of June

2019, the number of China's netizens, 854 million, was about triple that in 2007; Internet penetration rate was 61.2%, 1.6% higher than that at the end of 2018; the number of mobile netizens was 847 million, accounting for 99.1% of the total number of Internet users. As compared with the same period in 2007, the proportion increased by 75.1%.

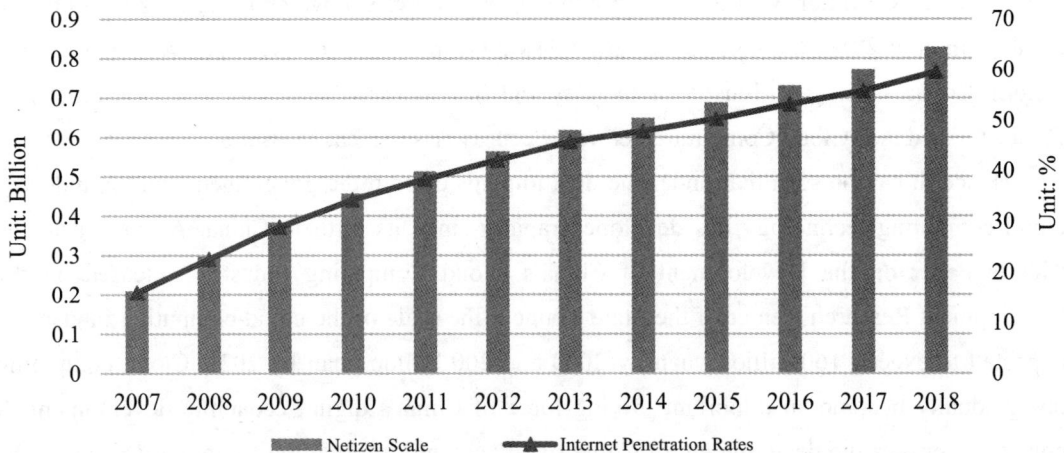

Figure 2.1　China's netizen scales and Internet penetration rates (2007-2018)

Source: China Internet Network Information Center, "Statistical Reports on Internet Development in China (2019)".

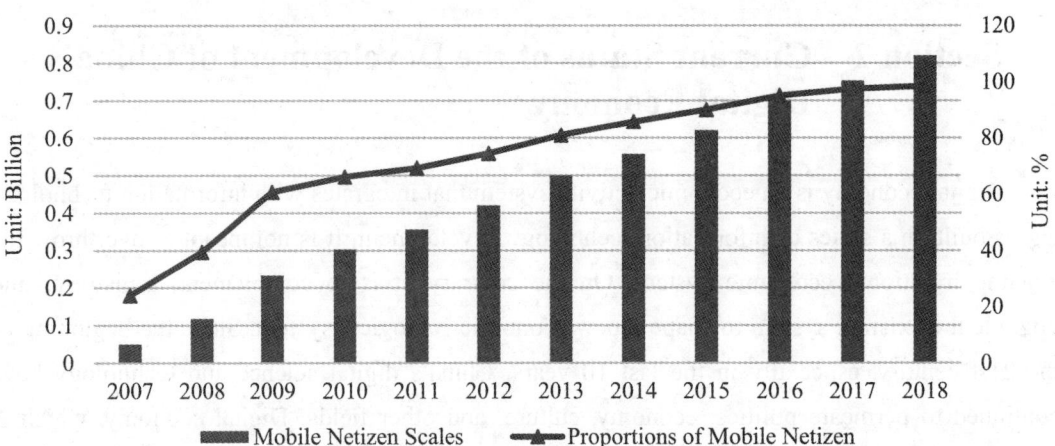

Figure 2.2　Numbers of mobile netizens in China and their proportion among total Internet users (2007-2018)

Source: China Internet Network Information Center, "Statistical Reports on Internet Development in China (2019)".

2.1.2 Internet infrastructure

According to statistics from the Asia-Pacific Network Information Center and the China Internet Network Information Center, as of June 2019, the total number of IPv4 addresses in China was 385,979,136, of which 338,991,360 were in China's mainland, 35,678,976 in the Taiwan Region, 10,972,672 in Hong Kong SAR, and 336,128 in Macao SAR. China's total number of IPv6 addresses was 50,286, of which 47,315 were in China's mainland, 2,515 in the

Taiwan Region, 449 in Hong Kong SAR, and 7 in Macao SAR.

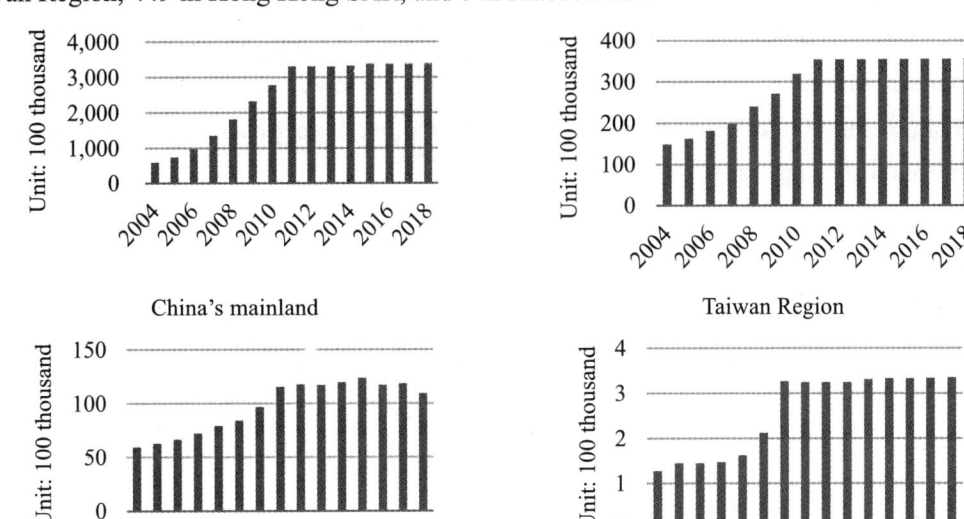

Figure 2.3   Changes in IPv4 numbers in China (2004-2018)

Source: China Internet Network Information Center, "Statistical Reports on Internet Development in China (2019)".

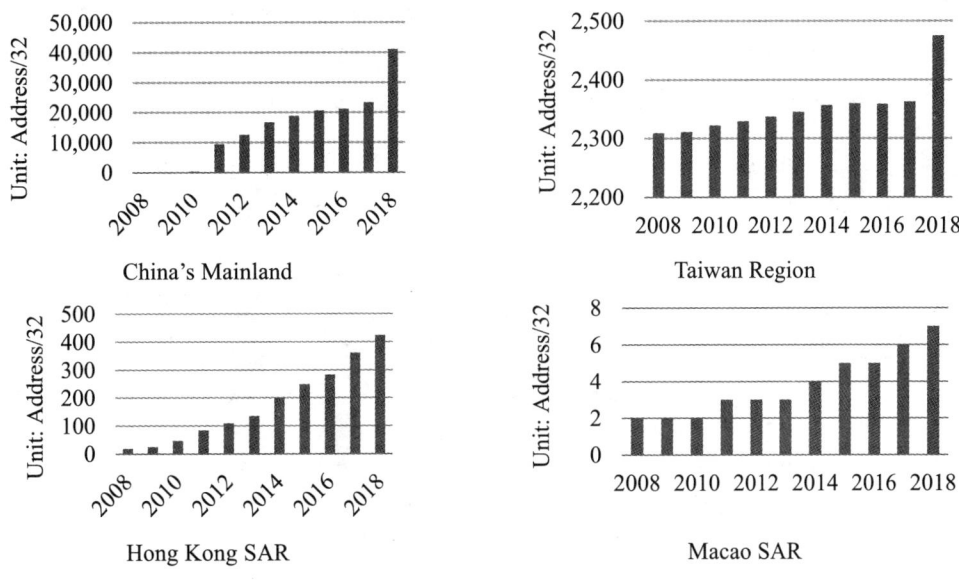

Figure 2.4   Changes in IPv6 numbers in China (2008-2018)

Source: China Internet Network Information Center, "Statistical Reports on Internet Development in China (2019)".

In December 2019, the total length of China's optical cable route was 47.5 million kilometers, of which 4.34 million kilometers were newly built in 2019[①]. At the same time,

---

[①] Source: China Internet Network Information Center, "Statistical Reports on Internet Development in China (2019)".

according to statistics from the China Internet Network Information Center, by the end of 2017, China's mobile broadband network had basically realized the continuous coverage across cities and counties, as well as hot spot coverage across developed towns and rural areas. The coverage and depth of the 4G network coverage, as well as the user experience, performed better than many developed countries.

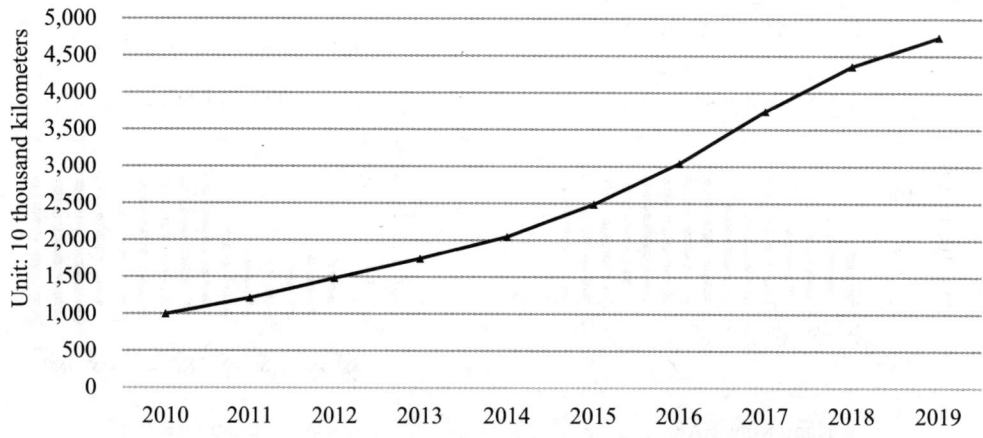

Figure 2.5   Total mileage of China's construction of optical cables (2010-2019)

Source: China Internet Network Information Center, "Statistical Reports on Internet Development in China (2019)".

As of December 2019, optical fiber access (FTTH/0) ports increased by 64.79 million compared with the end of the previous year, reaching 836 million. It accounts for 91.3% of Internet access ports, up from 88.9% at the end of the previous year[①].

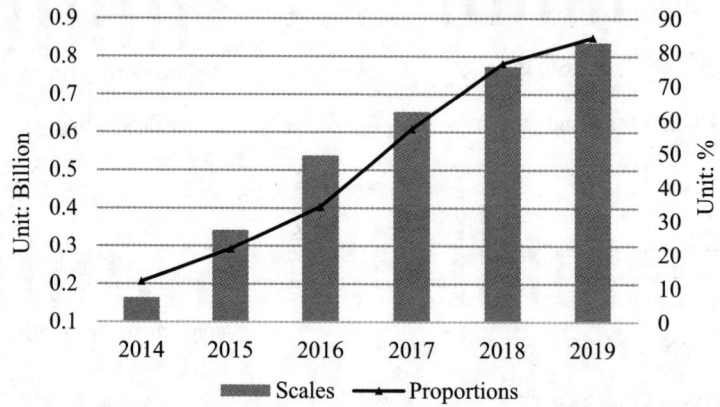

Figure 2.6   Sizes and proportions of China's fiber broadband users (2012-2019)

Source: "Annual Report of China's Communications Industry Statistics (2017)", "Indicator Completion of the Communications Industry (2018)".

---

① Source: "Annual Report of China's Communications Industry Statistics (2017)", "Indicator Completion of the Communications Industry (2018)".

2.2 Current status of China's digital economy

China's economy has evolved from a stage of high-speed growth to high-quality development. In recent years, China has insisted on being the first in quality, prioritizing efficiency, and pushing for changes in the quality, efficiency, and dynamics of economic development. Digital economy has achieved rapid development with characteristics such as high growth, wide coverage, and strong permeability.

In 2018, the momentum of China's digital economic development remained strong, achieving a total scale of 31.3 trillion yuan. Calculated in comparable terms, nominal growth was 20.9%, accounting for 34.8% of the GDP, a 1.9% year-on-year increase. At the same time, the booming digital economy promoted the transformation and upgrading of traditional industries, thus adding new growth drivers for economic development. In 2018, the contribution rate of digital economic development toward GDP growth reached 67.9%, an increase by 12.9% year-on-year[①], surpassing some developed countries and becoming a core essential force in driving China's national economic development.

Compared with the traditional economy, digital economy has more obvious economies of scale and scope. This gives it a unique advantage in reducing operating costs for enterprises and improving overall economic efficiency. Therefore, the contribution of digital economy toward China's economic growth has become increasingly important. According to statistics from China Academy of Information and Communications Technology, in terms of scale, the overall scale of China's digital economy has shown a constantly increasing trend. It had grown 24 times from 1.22 trillion yuan in 2002 to 31.3 trillion yuan in 2018. In terms of proportion, the proportion of China's digital economy in economic aggregate has also increased year-on-year from 10.14% in 2002 to 34.8% in 2018. As for nominal growth rate, the growth rate of China's digital economy each year is higher than the economic aggregate growth rate on average.

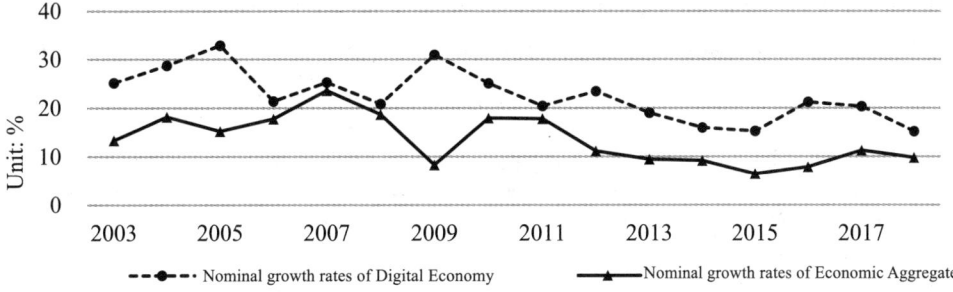

Figure 2.7 Growth rate comparison between China's digital economy and economic aggregate (2003-2018)

Source: China Academy of Information and Communications Technology, "White Paper on China's Digital Economic Development and Employment (2019)".

---

① Source: China Academy of Information and Communications Technology, "White Paper on China's Digital Economic Development and Employment (2019)".

From the province dimension[①], digital economy in all areas continued to grow steadily. In terms of scale, in 2018, Guangdong Province had the largest digital economy, as it exceeded 4 trillion yuan. Jiangsu Province followed closely behind with over 3 trillion yuan. In addition, digital economy in Shandong and Zhejiang Provinces exceeded 2 trillion yuan. Shanghai, Beijing, Fujian, Hubei, Sichuan, Henan, and Hebei Provinces all exceeded 1 trillion yuan[②].

In terms of growth rates, the digital economic growth rates of the provinces and cities ranged between 10% to 25%, which is 3% to 10% higher than the GDP growth rates in the same period. Among them, Guizhou and Fujian Provinces had the fastest growth of over 20%. In addition, the growth rate figures in Jiangxi, Zhejiang, and Jiangsu Provinces exceeded 19%; Xinjiang Uygur Autonomous Region, Shanghai, Shaanxi, Guangdong, Shanxi, Anhui, Shandong, Sichuan, and other provinces exceeded 15%; the remaining provinces and cities exceeded 10%. The status of digital economy in China's national economy has increased significantly[③].

In terms of proportion, in 2018, digital economy of all provinces and cities accounted for more than 20% of the total GDP on average. Among them, digital economy development in Beijing and Shanghai accounted for more than 50%. Digital economy of Tianjin, Guangdong, Zhejiang, and Jiangsu Provinces accounted for more than 40% of the GDP. Fujian, Shandong, Hubei, Chongqing, Liaoning, and Sichuan accounted for more than 30%, and the remaining provinces and cities accounted for more than 20%[④].

In terms of key regions[⑤], the Yangtze River Economic Belt had the largest digital economy. At the end of 2017, the total digital economic scale of the Yangtze River Economic Belt was 12.2 trillion yuan, followed by the Pearl River Delta region with 3.67 trillion yuan, the Beijing-Tianjin-Hebei region with 3.03 trillion, the northeast region with 1.44 trillion yuan, and the lowest was 1.08 trillion yuan from the northwest region. In terms of the proportion in GDP at the end of 2017, the Pearl River Delta region's digital economy accounted for 40.8% of the GDP, putting it in first place. This was followed by 36.7% from the Beijing-Tianjin-Hebei region, 32.6% from the Yangtze River Economic Belt, 26.0% from the northeast region, and the lowest was 23.1% from the northwest region. In terms of growth rate, the region with the fastest digital

---

① Excluding Hainan, Tibet, Hong Kong SAR, Macao SAR, and Taiwan; the same below.

② Source: China Academy of Information and Communications Technology, "White Paper on China's Digital Economic Development and Employment (2019)".

③ Source: China Academy of Information and Communications Technology, "White Paper on China's Digital Economic Development and Employment (2019)".

④ Source: China Academy of Information and Communications Technology, "White Paper on China's Digital Economic Development and Employment (2019)".

⑤ The Yangtze River Economic Belt includes Sichuan Province, Chongqing City, Guizhou Province, Yunnan Province, Anhui Province, Jiangxi Province, Hubei Province, Hunan Province, Shanghai City, Jiangsu Province, and Zhejiang Province; the Pearl River Delta region includes Guangdong Province; the Beijing-Tianjin-Hebei region includes Beijing City, Tianjin City, and Hebei Province; the northeast region includes Heilongjiang Province, Jilin Province, and Liaoning Province; the northwest region includes Shaanxi Province, Gansu Province, Qinghai Province, the Ningxia Hui Autonomous Region, and the Xinjiang Uygur Autonomous Region.

economy growth rate was the Pearl River Delta region with 21.7% year-on-year growth. This was closely followed by the northwest region and the Yangtze River Economic Belt with 21.6% each on average. The Beijing-Tianjin-Hebei region comes in next with 17.4%, and the Old Industrial Base Area with 12.7%[①].

In terms of vertical comparison, from 2002 to 2017, the region with the largest increase in the proportion of digital economy in GDP was the Pearl River Delta region, with an increase of 27.1%, followed by 24.3% from the Beijing-Tianjin-Hebei region, 21.2% from the Yangtze River Economic Belt, 14.7% from the northeast region, and the lowest was 13.8% from the northwest region[②].

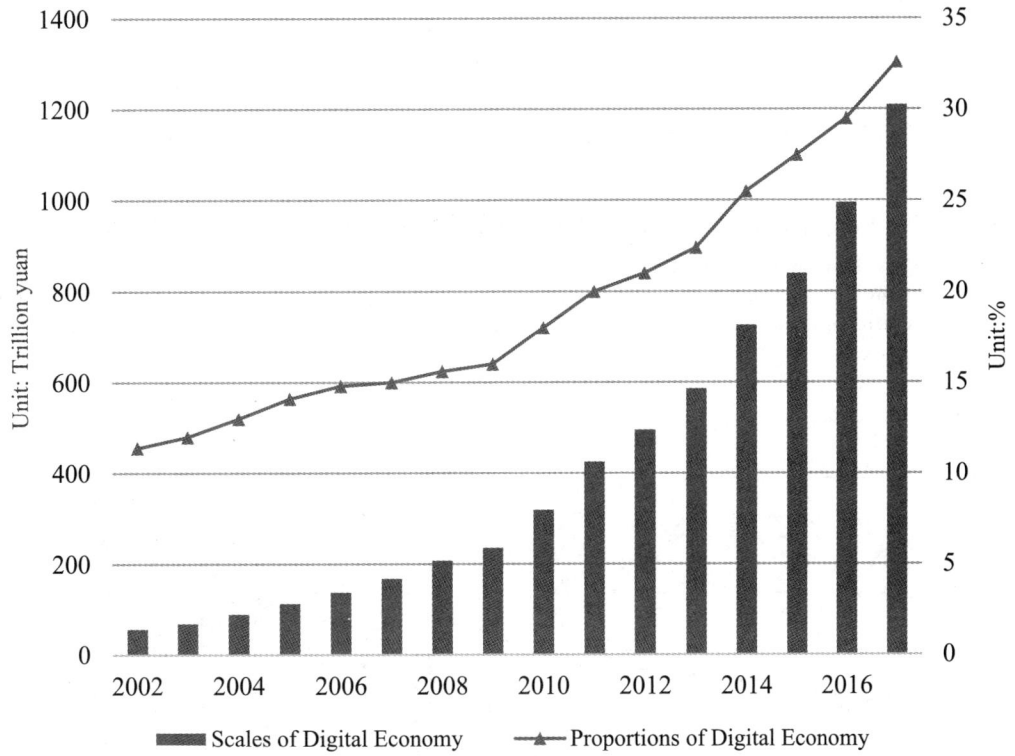

Figure 2.8 Development status of the Yangtze River Economic Belt's digital economy (2002-2017)

Source: China Academy of Information and Communications Technology, "White Paper on the Development of China's Information Economy (2016)", "White Paper on the Development of China's Digital Economy (2017)", "White Paper on Chinese Digital Economic Development and Employment (2018)", "White Paper on China's Digital Economic Development and Employment (2019)".

---

① Source: China Academy of Information and Communications Technology, "White Paper on Chinese Digital Economic Development and Employment (2018)".

② Source: China Academy of Information and Communications Technology, "White Paper on the Development of China's Information Economy (2016)", "White Paper on the Development of China's Digital Economy (2017)", "White Paper on Chinese Digital Economic Development and Employment (2018)", "White Paper on Chinese Digital Economic Development and Employment (2019)".

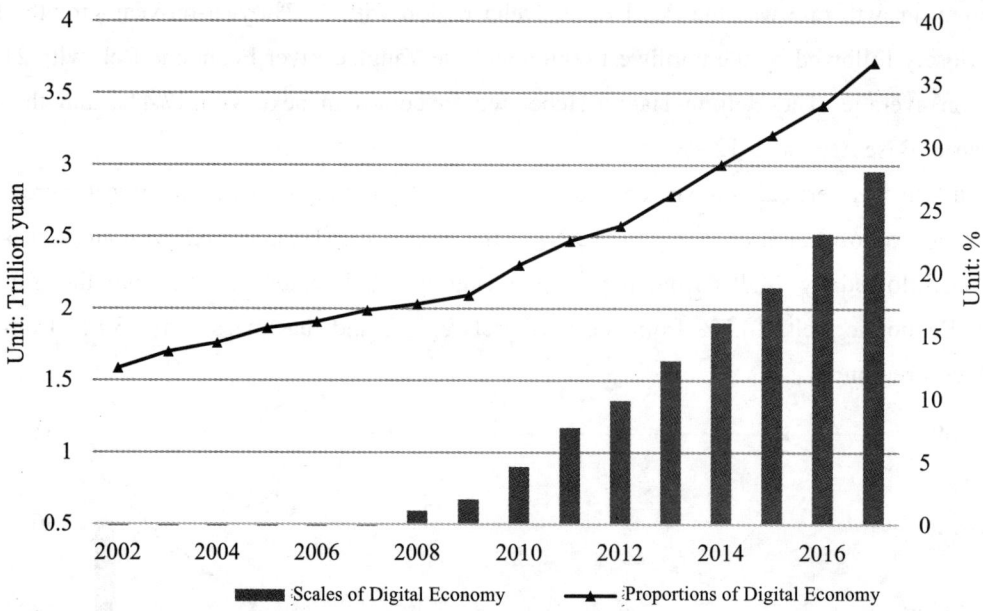

Figure 2.9 Development status of the Beijing-Tianjin-Hebei region's digital economy (2002-2017)

Source: China Academy of Information and Communications Technology, "White Paper on the Development of China's Information Economy (2016)", "White Paper on the Development of China's Digital Economy (2017)", "White Paper on Chinese Digital Economic Development and Employment (2018)", "White Paper on Chinese Digital Economic Development and Employment (2019)".

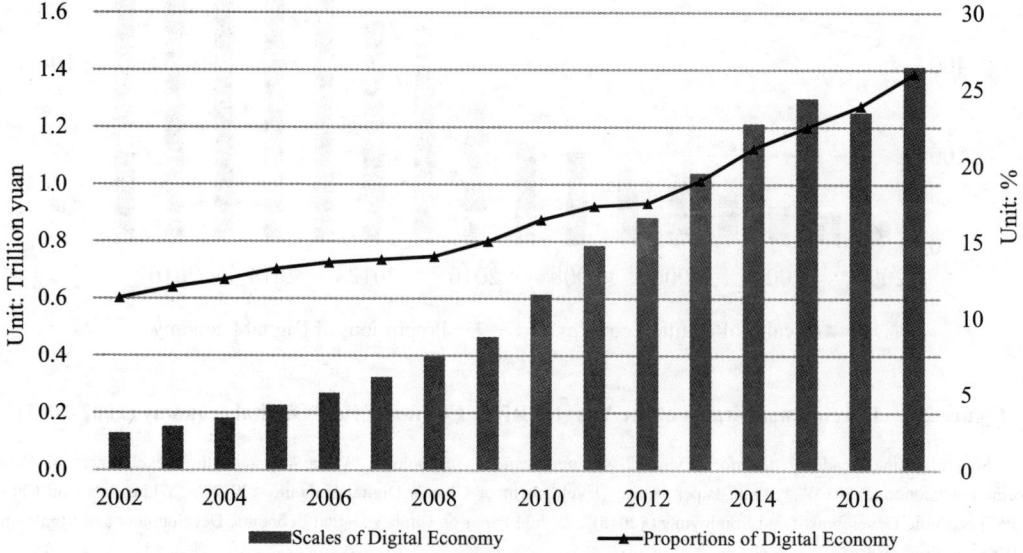

Figure 2.10 Development status of the northeast region's digital economy (2002-2017)

Source: China Academy of Information and Communications Technology, "White Paper on the Development of China's Information Economy (2016)", "White Paper on the Development of China's Digital Economy (2017)", "White Paper on Chinese Digital Economic Development and Employment (2018)", "White Paper on Chinese Digital Economic Development and Employment (2019)".

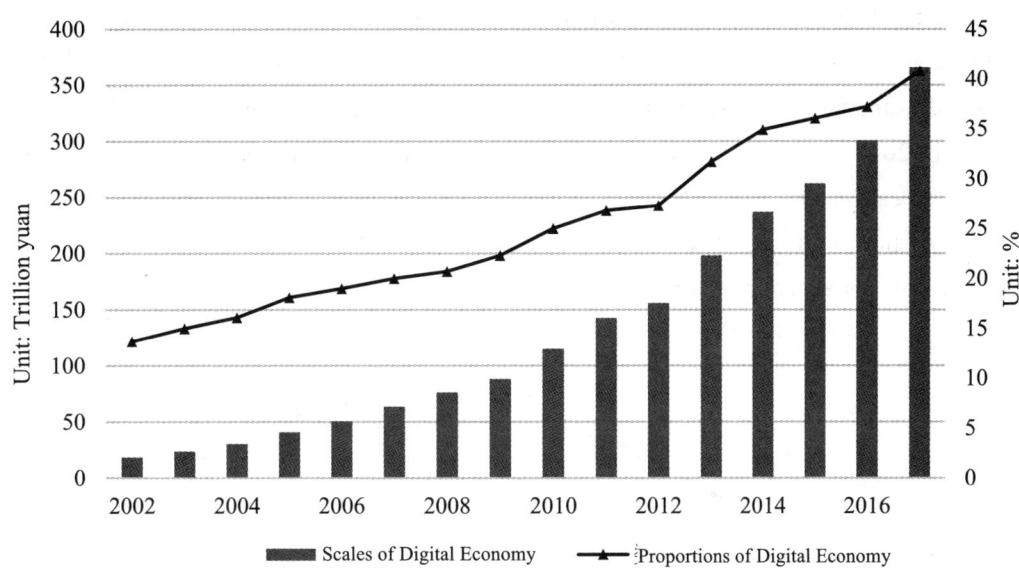

Figure 2.11　Development status of the Pearl River Delta's digital economy (2002-2017)

Source: China Academy of Information and Communications Technology, "White Paper on the Development of China's Information Economy (2016)", "White Paper on the Development of China's Digital Economy (2017)", "White Paper on Chinese Digital Economic Development and Employment (2018)", "White Paper on Chinese Digital Economic Development and Employment (2019)".

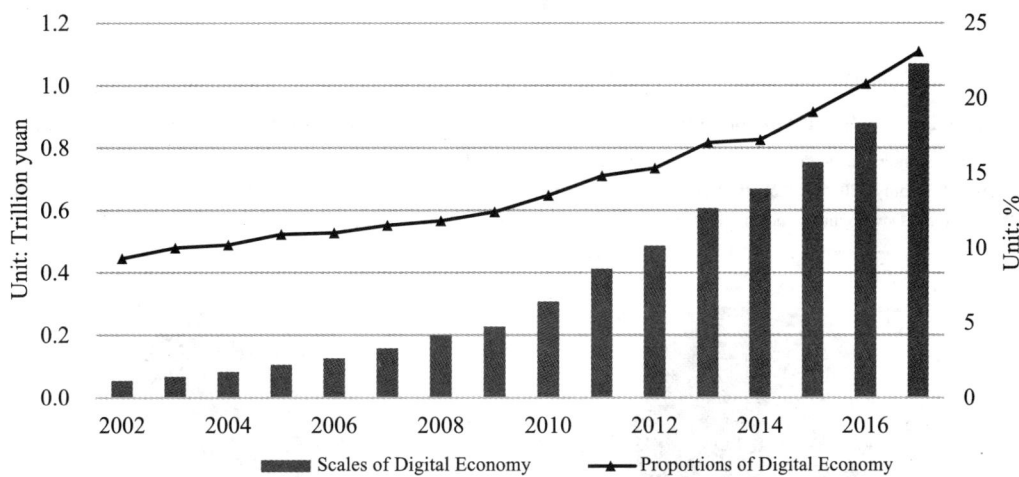

Figure 2.12　Development status of the northwest region's digital economy (2002-2017)

Source: China Academy of Information and Communications Technology, "White Paper on the Development of China's Information Economy (2016)", "White Paper on the Development of China's Digital Economy (2017)", "White Paper on Chinese Digital Economic Development and Employment (2018)", "White Paper on Chinese Digital Economic Development and Employment (2019)".

2.3 Current status of China's digital economy structure

In recent years, the internal structure of China's digital economy has been continuously optimized. On the one hand, digital industrialization has strengthened unceasingly. The economic scale has reached 6.4 trillion yuan, accounting for 20.5% of digital economy. The continuous development of digital industrialization provides sufficient digital technology, as well as product and service support for all industries, thus laying a solid foundation for digital economic development. On the other hand, industrial digitization continues to dominate digital economy. In 2018, its economic scale was 24.9 trillion yuan, an increase of 23.1% in nominal growth on a year-on-year basis. Its contribution to digital economic growth amounted to 86.4%, and its proportion in the digital economy increased from 49% in 2005 to 79.5%, becoming the main engine of digital economic growth.

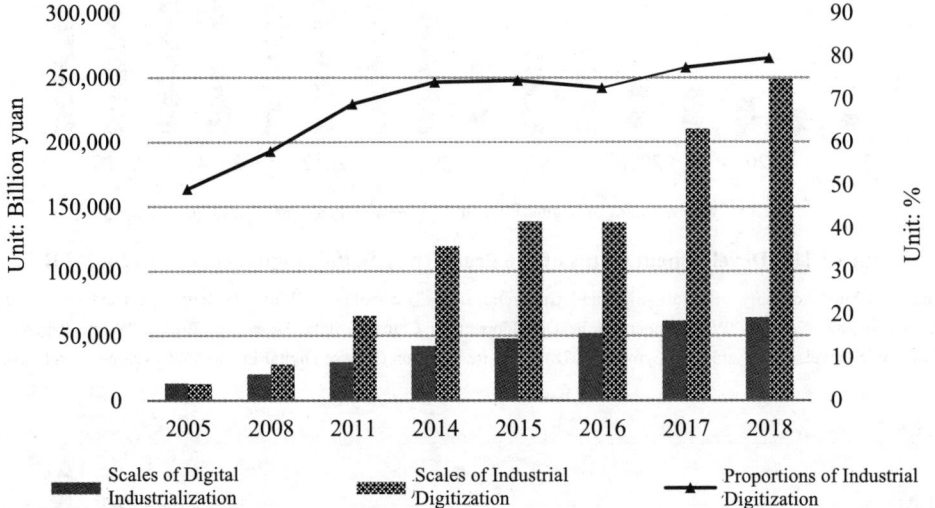

Figure 2.13 Scales and proportions of digital industrialization and industrial digitization (2005-2018)

Source: China Academy of Information and Communications Technology, "White Paper on the Development of China's Information Economy (2016)", "White Paper on the Development of China's Digital Economy (2017)", "White Paper on Chinese Digital Economic Development and Employment (2018)", "White Paper on Chinese Digital Economic Development and Employment (2019)".

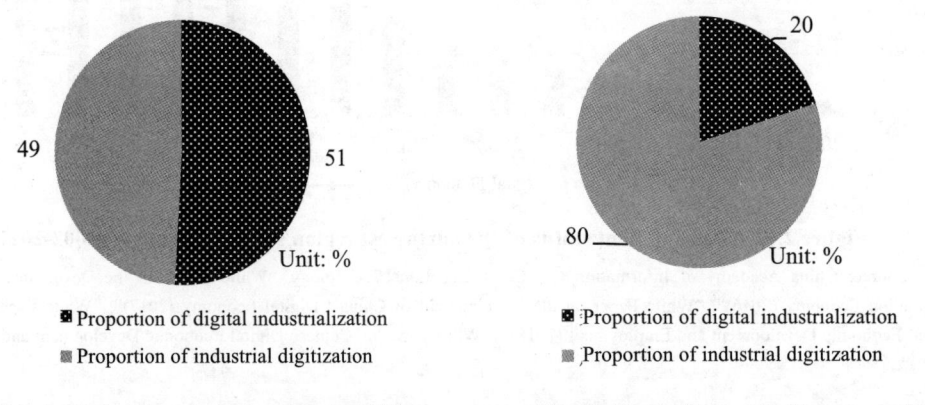

Figure 2.14 China's digital economic structural changes in 2005 and 2018

Source: China Academy of Information and Communications Technology, "White Paper on the Development of China's Information Economy (2016)", "White Paper on Chinese Digital Economic Development and Employment (2019)".

In terms of the subdivision of main regions, the digital economic structures show an inverse correlation between the proportion of industrial digitization and the degree of regional prosperity. The proportion of industrial digitization reaches 90.8% in the northwest region, 88.8% in the northeast region, and 79.7% in the Beijing-Tianjin-Hebei region. Meanwhile, in the relatively more economically-developed Yangtze River Delta and Pearl River Delta regions, the proportions of industrial digitization are relatively low at 71.3% and 62.6% respectively.

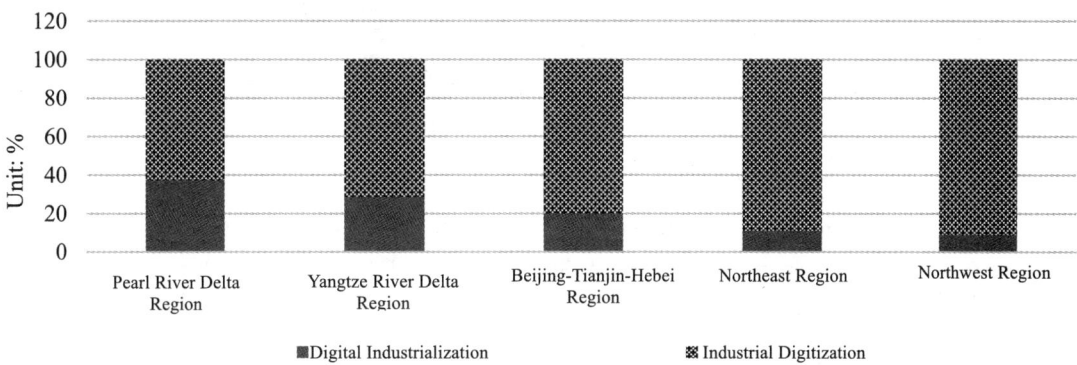

Figure 2.15　The digital economic structure of certain key regions in 2018

Source: China Academy of Information and Communications Technology, "White Paper on Chinese Digital Economic Development and Employment (2019)".

2.3.1 Digital industrialization

As of December 2018, China had 281.6 billion web pages[①]. The rapidly growth of the scale of 4G mobile phone users and the enrichment of mobile Internet applications pushed the Internet traffic increase rapidly and continuously. In 2019, mobile Internet access traffic consumption amounted up to 122 billion GB, a 71.57% year-on-year increase[②].

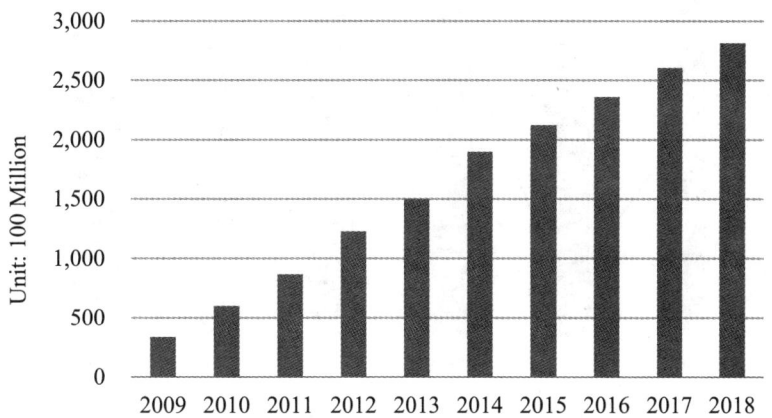

Figure 2.16　Numbers of Chinese web pages (2009-2018)

Source: China Internet Network Information Center, "Statistical Reports on Internet Development in China".

---

① Source: China Internet Network Information Center, "Statistical Reports on Internet Development in China".

② Source: Ministry of Industry and Information Technology of the People's Republic of China, http://www.miit.gov.cn/n1146312/n1146904/n1648355/index.html.

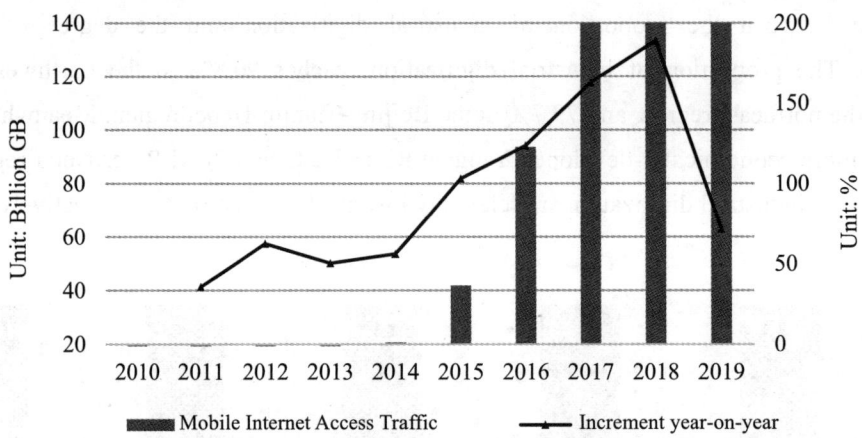

Figure 2.17 Mobile Internet access traffic in China (2010-2019)

Source: Ministry of Industry and Information Technology of the People's Republic of China, http://www.miit.gov.cn/n1146312/n1146904/n1648355/index.html.

(1) The telecommunications industry

In 2019, the total amount of services offered and total revenue earned by China's telecommunications businesses continued to grow rapidly. Among them, the total amount of telecommunications services calculated with last year's prices amounted to 1.74 trillion yuan, an increase of 18.5% as compared to the previous year. The total revenue earned by completed telecommunications businesses was 1.31 trillion yuan, an increase of 0.8% on a year-on-year basis.[①]

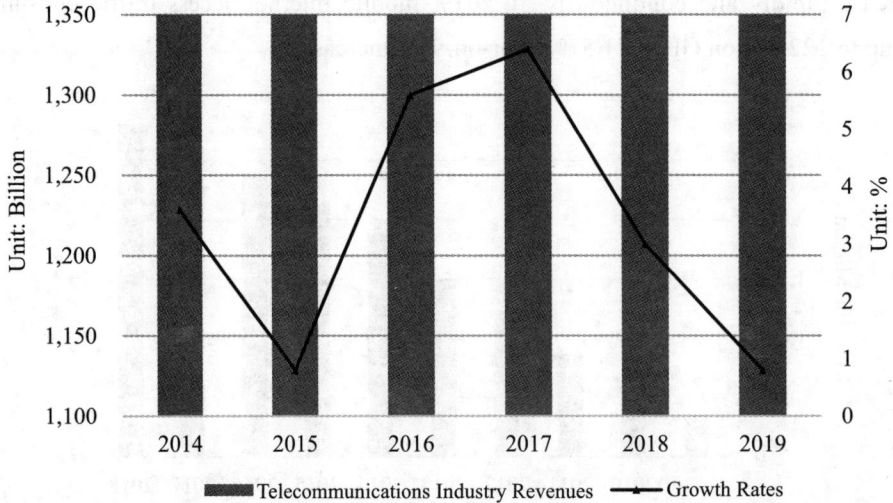

Figure 2.18 China's telecommunications businesses' revenue and growth in (2014-2019)

Source: Ministry of Industry and Information Technology of the People's Republic of China, http://www.miit.gov.cn/n1146312/n1146904/n1648355/index.html.

---

① Source: Ministry of Industry and Information Technology of the People's Republic of China, http://www.miit.gov.cn/n1146312/n1146904/n1648355/index.html.

Looking at regions, in 2019, the revenue from telecommunications businesses in the eastern region still had an absolute advantage, accounting for 50.9% of the entire country's telecommunications revenue. The central region accounted for 19.6%, and the western and northeast regions accounted for 23.7% and 5.8% respectively.

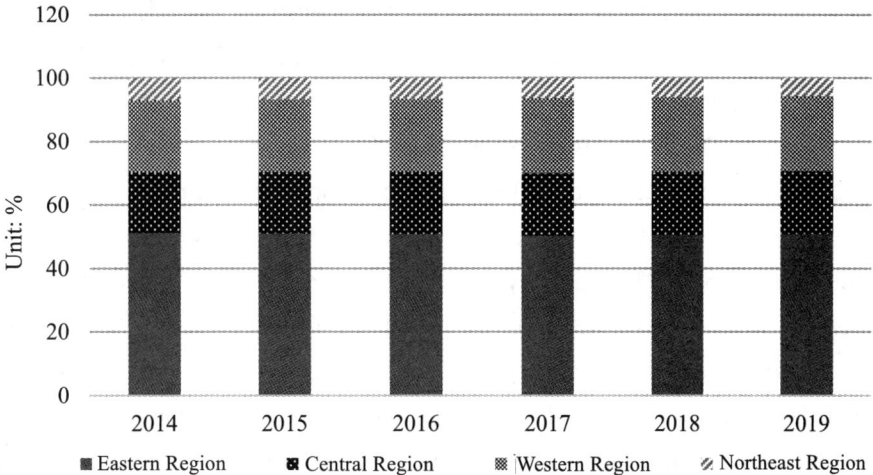

Figure 2.19 **Proportions of revenue from telecommunications businesses in various regions of China (2014-2019)**

Source: Ministry of Industry and Information Technology of the People's Republic of China, http://www.miit.gov.cn/n1 146312/n1146904/n1648355/index.html.

(2) The electronic information manufacturing industry

According to statistics from the Ministry of Industry and Information Technology, China's electronic information manufacturing industry continued its growing trend in 2019. Among all, the added value from electronic information manufacturers with annual revenue of more than 20 million yuan increased by 9.3% compared with the previous year, with a fall in growth rate by 3.8%. The operating revenue of electronic information manufacturers[①] increased by 4.5% year-on-year, total profit increased by 3.1% year-on-year, the operating profit margin was 4.41%, and operating costs increased by 4.2% year-on-year. The output delivery value of electronic information manufacturers[②] was up 1.7% year-on-year. Breaking this down into more specific industries, the added value of industrial communication device manufacturers grew by 9.4% year-on-year, while export delivery value fell by 2.4% year-on-year. Added value from manufacturers of electronic components and materials for electronic use increased by 20.7% year-on-year, while export delivery value decreased by 2.3% year-on-year. The added value of electronic equipment manufacturers increased by 8.3% year-on-year, and export delivery value increased by 5.4% year-on-year. The added value of computer manufacturers increased by 9.2% year-on-year, and export delivery value increased by 5.6% year-on-year.

---

① Large-scale enterprises with annual revenue more than 20 million yuan.

② Large-scale enterprises with annual revenue more than 20 million yuan.

(3) The software and information technology service industry[①]

In 2019, China's software and information technology service industry continued to maintain high-quality development and gradually evolved as an important driving force for digital industrialization development. Overall, in 2019, the total number of Chinese enterprises in the software and information technology service industry[②] exceeded 40,000. The total revenue generated from completed software businesses was 7.1768 trillion yuan, a 13.81% year-on-year increase in comparable terms. The total profit was 936.2 billion yuan, a 9.9% year-on-year increase. Breaking this down into specific fields, the software industry generated a revenue of 2.0067 trillion yuan from software products, up 12.5% year-on-year, accounting for 28% of the whole industry. The information technology service industry generated a revenue of 4.2574 trillion yuan, up 18.4% year-on-year. Its growth rate was 3% higher than the industry average, and the revenue generated was 59.3% of the whole industry. Information security products and services generated 130.8 billion yuan in revenue, a 12.4% year-on-year increase. The embedded system software industry generated 782 billion yuan in revenue, a 7.8% year-on-year increase, accounting for 10.9% of the whole industry[③].

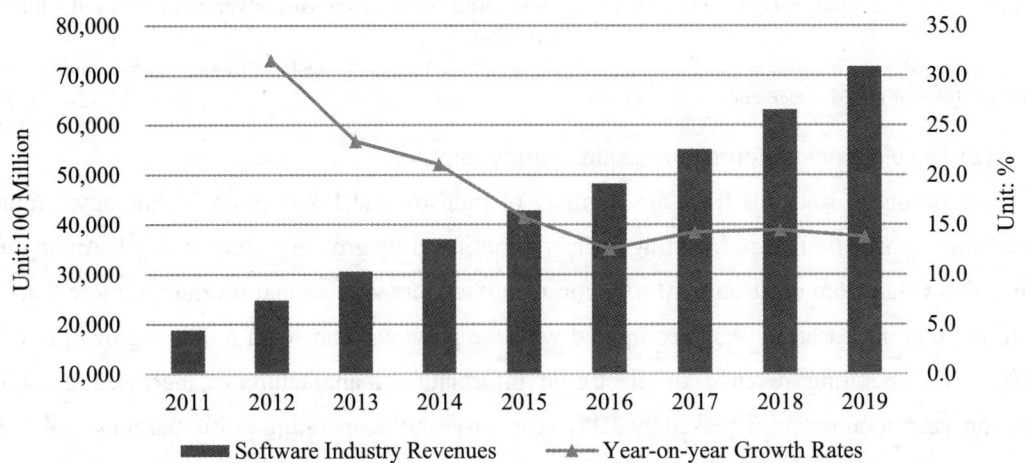

Figure 2.20 Revenue and growth of China's software businesses (2011-2019)

Source: Ministry of Industry and Information Technology of the People's Republic of China, http://www.miit.gov.cn/n1146312/n1146904/n1648355/index.html.

---

① Statistics range: 1. Software enterprises registered in China (excluding Hong Kong SAR, Macao SAR, and Taiwan) that mainly engage in software R&D, system integration, and relevant information technology service businesses, have annual revenue of more than 5 million yuan in primary business, and possess the status of an independent legal person; 2. Independent legal entities registered in China, with annual revenue of more than 10 million yuan in primary business, that have revenues from software R&D, system integration, and related information technology services that account for more than 30% of the enterprises' main business revenue; 3. Enterprises registered in China that mainly design integrated circuits or independent legal entities registered in China with revenue generated from designing and testing integrated circuits accounting for more than 60% of the enterprises' main business revenue and annual revenue from main business exceeding 5 million yuan.

② Large-scale enterprises with annual revenue of more than 20 million yuan.

③ Source: Ministry of Industry and Information Technology of the People's Republic of China, http://www.miit.gov.cn/n1146312/n1146904/n1648355/index.html.

According to statistics from the Ministry of Industry and Information Technology, looking at the data by provinces①, the total revenue generated from Chinese software was higher in the east than the central and west areas, while the growth rate was higher in the central and west areas than the east. Specifically, as of November 2019, the top 10 provinces and cities with the most number of enterprises in China's software and information technology service industry included 7,409 in Jiangsu Province, 4,889 in Guangdong Province, 4,439 in Shandong Province, 3,324 in Fujian Province, 3,200 in Beijing City, 2,476 in Hubei Province, 1,892 in Zhejiang Province, 1,831 in Sichuan Province, 1,700 in Shanghai City, and 1,521 in Liaoning Province. As of November 2019, the top 10 provinces and cities with the highest revenue in China's software and information technology service industry were: 1150.1378 billion yuan from Guangdong Province, 999.18093 billion yuan from Beijing City, 885.2781 billion yuan from Jiangsu Province, 550.21298 billion yuan from Shanghai City, 546.04163 billion yuan from Zhejiang Province, 514.74787 billion yuan from Shandong Province, 317.15658 billion yuan from Sichuan Province, 292.03027 billion yuan from Fujian Province, 209.167 billion yuan from Shaanxi Province, and 202.53508 billion yuan from Hubei Province. As of November 2019, the top 10 provinces and cities with the fastest revenue growth in China's software and information technology service industry were: 90.6% from the Guangxi Zhuang Autonomous Region, 55.4% from Hainan Province, 30.6% from Anhui Province, 22.1% from Hunan Province, 21.7% from Shaanxi Province, 21.5% from the Ningxia Hui Autonomous Region, 20.5% from Hubei Province, 20.4% from Guizhou Province, 19% from Yunnan Province, and 18.6% from Chongqing City.

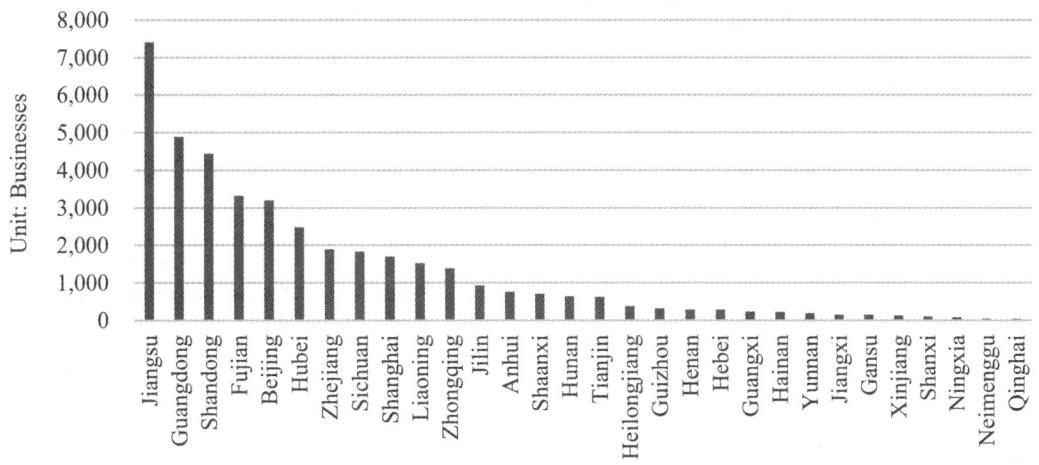

Figure 2.21 Numbers of software and electronic information technology service enterprises in certain Chinese provinces and cities from January 2019 to November 2019

Source: Ministry of Industry and Information Technology of the People's Republic of China, http://www.miit.gov.cn/n1146312/n1146904/n1648355/index.html②.

---

① The Data does not include Tibet, Taiwan, Hong Kong SAR, and Macao SAR.

② There is currently no statistical data of enterprises with annual revenue of more than 20 million yuan from Tibet.

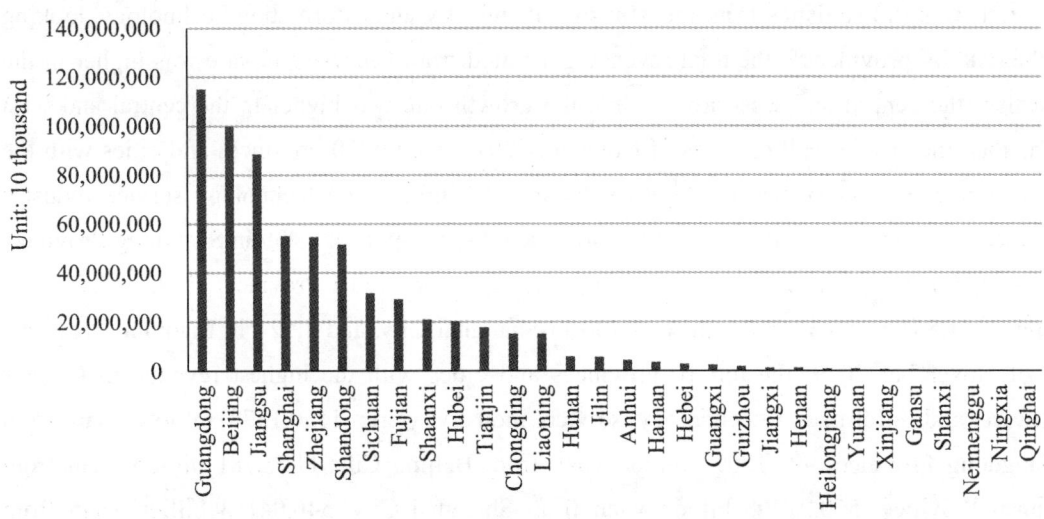

Figure 2.22 Total revenue from the software and electronic information technology service industry in certain Chinese provinces and cities from January 2019 to November 2019

Source: Ministry of Industry and Information Technology of the People's Republic of China, http://www.miit.gov.cn/n1 146312/n1146904/n1648355/index.html①.

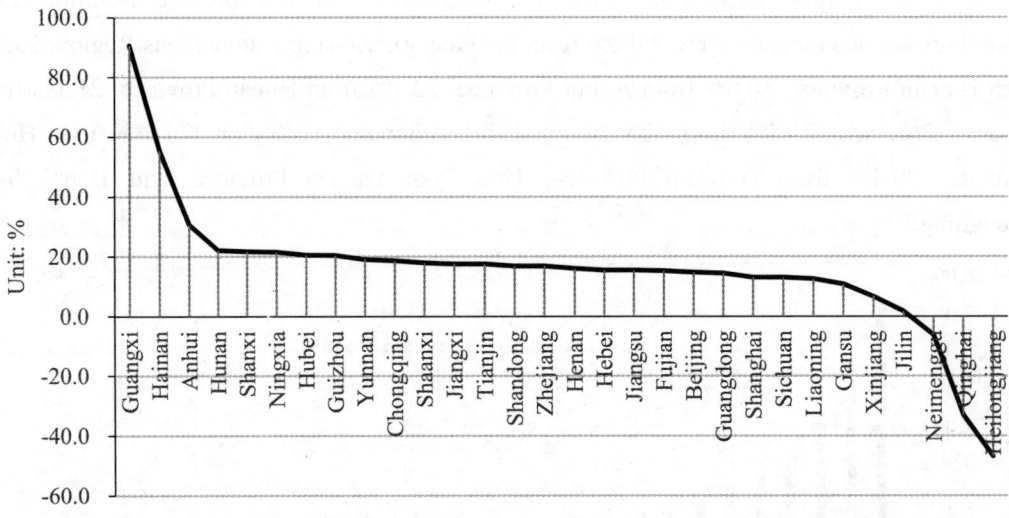

Figure 2.23 Growth rates of total revenue of the software and electronic information technology service industry in certain Chinese provinces and cities from January 2019 to November 2019

Source: Ministry of Industry and Information Technology of the People's Republic of China, http://www.miit.gov.cn/n1 146312/n1146904/n1648355/index.html②.

(4) The Internet and Internet-related service industry

In 2019, China's Internet and its related service industry continued to maintain good development. The Internet and its related service industry generated 1.2061 trillion income in 2019, a year-on-year increase of 21.4%.

---

① There is currently no statistical data of enterprises with annual revenue of more than 20 million yuan from Tibet.
② There is currently no statistical data of enterprises with annual revenue of more than 20 million yuan from Tibet.

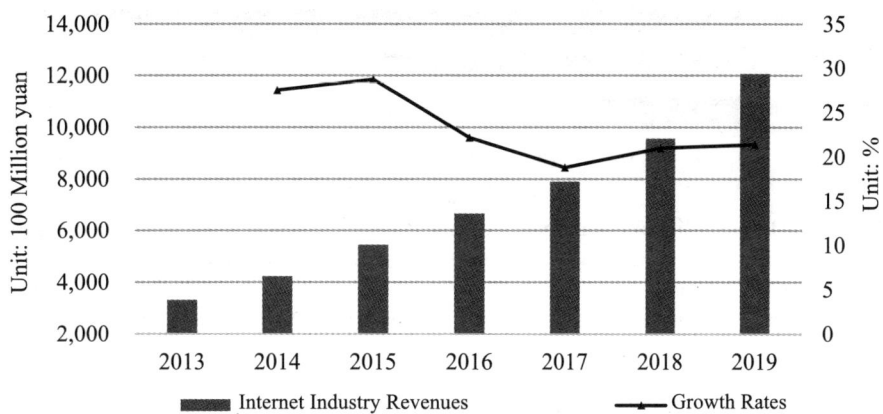

Figure 2.24 Revenue and growth of China's Internet businesses (2013-2019)

Source: Ministry of Industry and Information Technology of the People's Republic of China, http://www.miit.gov.cn/n1146312/n1146904/n1648355/index.html.

2.3.2 Industrial Digitization

In 2018, the digitization of Chinese industries remained the main driving force for the growth of China's digital economy, with the total scale amounting to 79.5% of digital economy. At the same time, there was a significant difference in the level of digital economic development between industries, and this was mainly shown through the tendency of the gradual decline in the development level from tertiary industries to primary industries. More specifically, in the service industry (excluding the information and communications service industry, and the software and information technology service industry), industrial businesses (excluding the electronic information manufacturing industry), and the agricultural industry, digital economy takes up 35.9%, 18.3%, and 7.3% of the value-added in the respective industries. This is a 0.7% year-on-year increase for industrial businesses and around a 0.3% year-on-year increase for the agriculture and service industries[1]. Overall, the digitization of industrial businesses is growing at a faster rate than the digital economies of the agriculture and service industries. Digital economy lowers costs for real economy, increases efficiency, and pushes for a more precise match in supply and demand. This lowers the cost of existing economic activities even further, thus inspiring new business formats and models, pushing the economy to evolve toward a higher phase that has a more precise labor division, more reasonable structure, and a much bigger space to evolve. In the future, the digital transformation of the three industries will continue to grow, thus increasing output efficiency, reducing production costs, and promoting the economic development of the whole industry.

---

[1] Source: China Academy of Information and Communications Technology, "White Paper on the Development of China's Information Economy (2016)", "White Paper on the Development of China's Digital Economy (2017)", "White Paper on Chinese Digital Economic Development and Employment (2018)", "White Paper on Chinese Digital Economic Development and Employment (2019)".

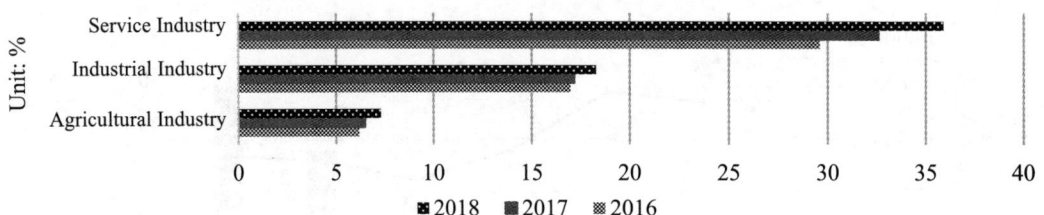

Figure 2.25 Proportions of digital economy in the added values of China's tertiary industries (2016-2018)

Source: China Academy of Information and Communications Technology, "White Paper on the Development of China's Information Economy (2016)", "White Paper on the Development of China's Digital Economy (2017)", "White Paper on Chinese Digital Economic Development and Employment (2018)", "White Paper on Chinese Digital Economic Development and Employment (2019)".

The standard of digitalization in industrial businesses has accelerated. Among typical industrial businesses, the 2018 year-on-year increase in the proportion of digital economy is as follows: household appliances 1.4%, ferrous metal mining & dressing products 1.3%, petroleum and natural gas extraction products 1.0%, pharmaceutical products 1.0%, steel and casting 0.9%, automobiles 0.9%, textile and clothing 0.8%, and furniture 0.8%. These increments have gone up by 0.4, 0.6, 0.4, 0.5, 0.4, 0.4, 0.4 and 0.4 percentage points respectively as compared to the previous year[①].

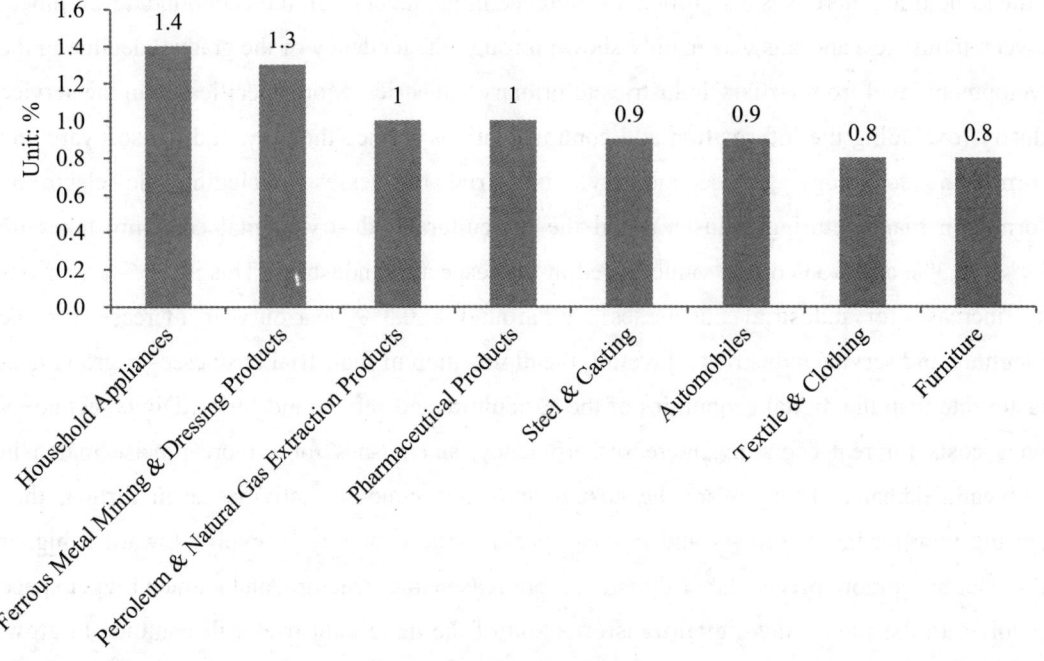

Figure 2.26 Changes in typical industrial businesses' proportion in digital economy in 2018

Source: China Academy of Information and Communications Technology, "White Paper on China's Digital Economic Development and Employment (2019)".

---

① Source: China Academy of Information and Communications Technology, "White Paper on China's Digital Economic Development and Employment (2019)".

The digitalization standard of the service industry continues to be in the lead. In 2018, the proportion of each sector in digital economy was as follows: 56.4% in insurance, 55.5% in radio, television, film, video, and sound productions, 48.7% in capital market services, 48.6% in monetary and other financial services, 46.0% in public administration and social organizations, 44.6% in professional technical services, 42.7% in postal services, 40.0% in education, 39.1% in social security, and 35.5% in leases①.

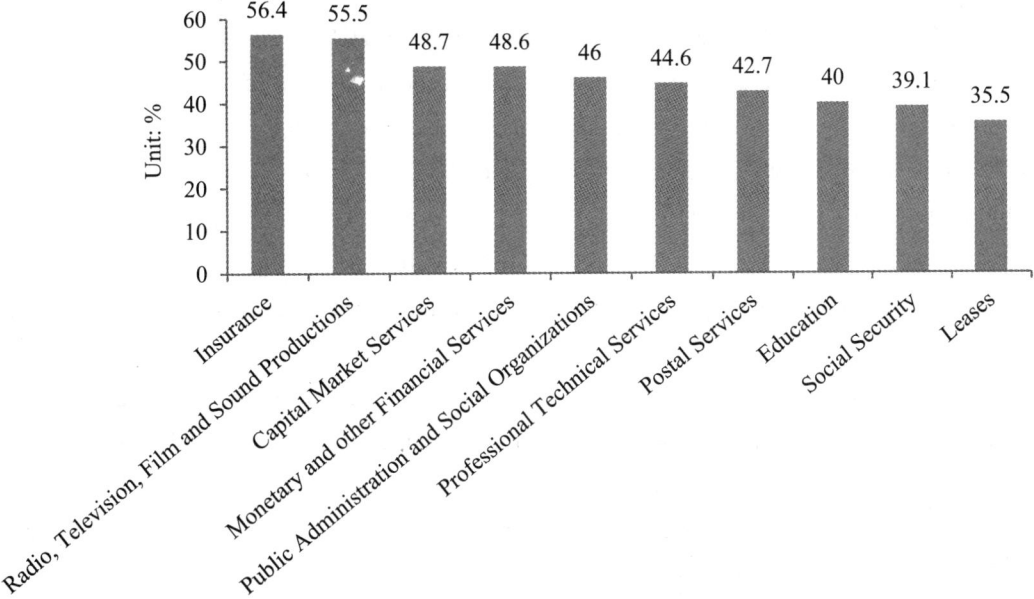

■ Proportions in digital economy of the industry

Figure 2.27   Proportion of each sector of the service industry in digital economy in 2018

Source: China Academy of Information and Communications Technology, "White Paper on China's Digital Economic Development and Employment (2019)".

The proportion of each sector of the agriculture industry in digital economy is ranked from high to low: forestry, fishery, agriculture, and livestock. The forestry products sector has the highest proportion with less than 13%, and the lowest proportion is from the livestock products sector with less than 5%②.

2.4 "AI+"

2.4.1 Intelligent manufacturing

Intelligent manufacturing is the application of artificial intelligence in the manufacturing industry. It can improve productivity and lower production costs, thus pushing for the upgrading

---

① Source: China Academy of Information and Communications Technology, "White Paper on Chinese Digital Economic Development and Employment (2018)".

② Source: China Academy of Information and Communications Technology, "White Paper on China's Digital Economic Development and Employment (2019)".

of the manufacturing industry. Industrial robots are important indicators to reflect intelligent manufacturing. The number of industrial robots used in the industry can, to a very large extent, reflect the degree of intellectualization in the industry. Enterprises in China that are currently producing artificial intelligence robots include Yaskawa (China) Robotics Co., Ltd., Foxconn Technology Group, Harbin Boshi Automation Co., Ltd., and Siasun Robotics and Automation.

From the perspective of flow, according to statistics from the Mechanical Engineering Industry Association (VDMA) in Germany, there were 154,032 new industrial robots in 2018, of which 41,366 units were supplied by China, accounting for 26.84% of the total amount. The compound annual growth rate of newly added industrial robots in China from 2013 to 2018 was 33%, positioning China first in the world. In terms of functions, the following accounted for the top three largest proportions of the newly added industrial robots in China in 2018: 41% were handling robots, 26% were welding robots, and 15% were assembly and dismantling robots. The industries with the highest usage of the newly added industrial robots in China in 2018 were the electrical/electronic industry, which took up 30%, and the automobile industry, which took up 26%.

In terms of stock, according to VDMA statistics, China had 649,400 industrial robots in 2018, up 30% year-on-year. The compound annual growth rate from 2013 to 2018 was 37%, coming in first globally. In terms of functions, the top three largest proportions of China's stock of industrial robots in 2018 belonged to handling robots (39%), welding robots (30%), and assembly and dismantling robots (15%). The industries that had the largest stock of China's industrial robots in 2018 were the automobile and electrical/electronic industry with 31% and 27% respectively.

2.4.2 Autonomous driving

Autonomous driving is the main direction that intelligent driving is developing toward. At present, China's intelligent driving is developing from a partial autonomous driving stage toward a conditional autonomous driving stage. In China, there are organizations such as Baidu that are actively taking part in the project operations of intelligent cars. As of 2018, autonomous driving-related projects in China had reached the testing phase and Baidu's autonomous driving bus "Apollo" had begun mass production. At the same time, the autonomous driving vehicles industry has also begun its layout across the Chinese market. In April 2018, the Ministry of Industry and Information Technology, the Ministry of Public Security, and the Ministry of Transport issued the "Notice on the Management Standards of Road Testing for Connected Automated Vehicles (for Trial Implementation)", which shows the PRC central government's supportive attitude toward the industry. According to statistics from China Automotive Information Net, as of April 2019, 109 autonomous driving pilot road-testing licenses had been issued across 16 cities in China. The two cities that gave out the most licenses were Beijing and Chongqing, giving out 59 and 12 licenses respectively.

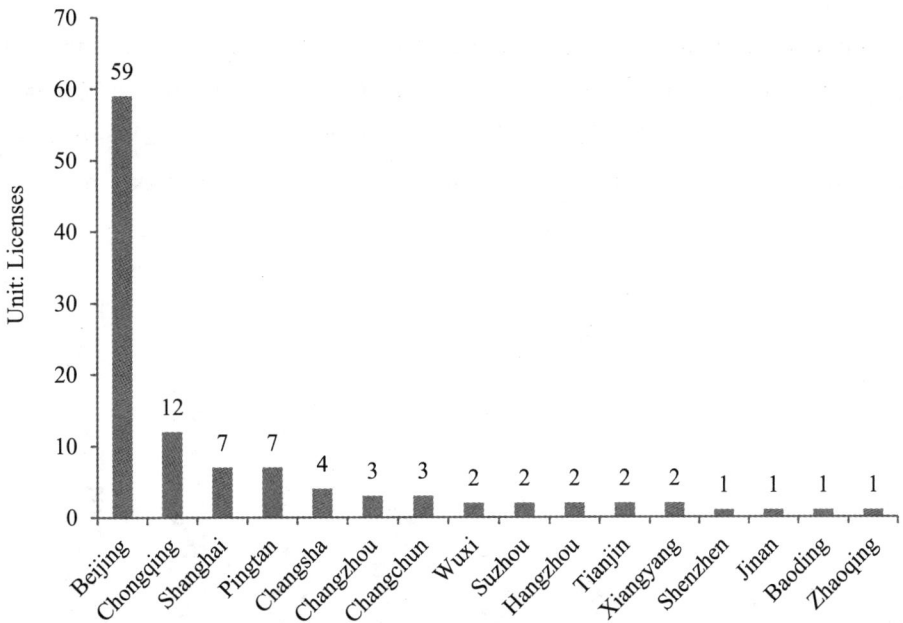

Figure 2.28 Numbers of licenses for autonomous driving pilot road-testing in China

Source: China Automotive Information Net, Qianzhan Industry Research Institute, https://bg.qianzhan.com/report/detail/459/101801-70e85945.html.

2.4.3 Smart homes

In recent years, the development of smart homes has made people's lives more comfortable, safe, convenient, and efficient. According to statistical data from the "Report on the Foresight of China's Smart Home Device Industry Market and Investment Strategy Plan" issued by Qianzhan Industry Research Institute, the scale of China's smart home market has increased year by year. It reached 72 billion yuan in 2014, hitting over 100 billion yuan in 2016, and amounted to 142.8 billion yuan in 2017. By 2018, the scale of the smart home market in China was expected to exceed 170 billion yuan, and it was predicted that the market size would reach 198.5 billion yuan in 2019.

Looking at just enterprises in China, currently, the two enterprises occupying the largest proportion of the smart home market are Alibaba and Xiaomi. Alibaba's Tmall Genie occupied 50% of the market in China and Xiaomi's MiOT Ecosystem contributed 18.1 billion yuan in revenue in the first half of 2019[①].

2.4.4 Online education

Online education is a highlight of all vertical applications of artificial intelligence. It can overcome the limitations of time and space and has many advantages, such as the maximization of resources, the autonomy of learning, interactive learning methods, and complementing

---

① Source: IT Juzi, http://www.199it.com/archives/705222.html.

teaching methods.

China's online education has been booming in recent years. Its user scale and market size have been growing continuously. As of the first half of 2019, the number of China's online education users reached 110.14 million, which was an increase of 15.52% from the fourth quarter of 2018[①]. As of 2017, the scale of China's online education market reached 200.26 billion yuan, a year-on-year increase of 27.93%[②].

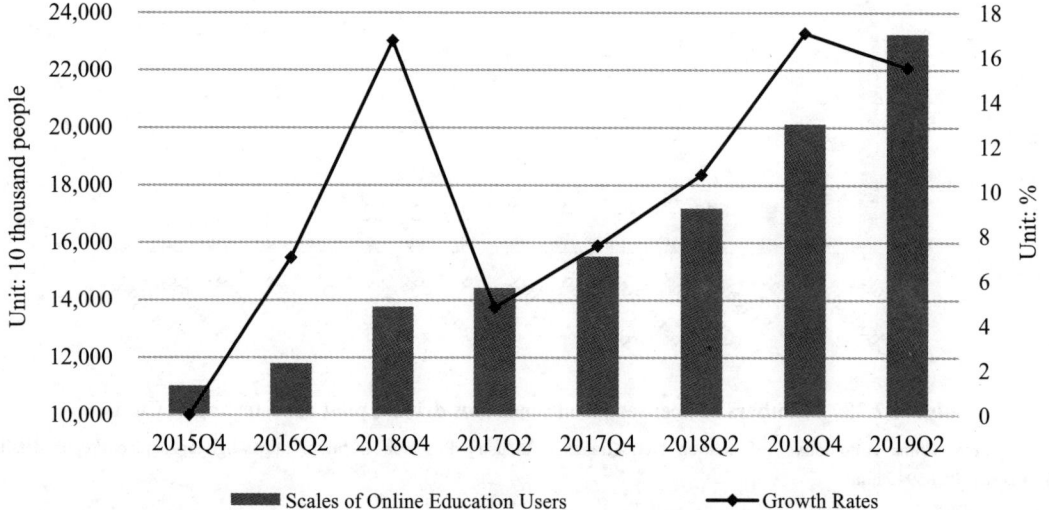

Figure 2.29 Scales of China's online education users

Source: Wind Economic Database.

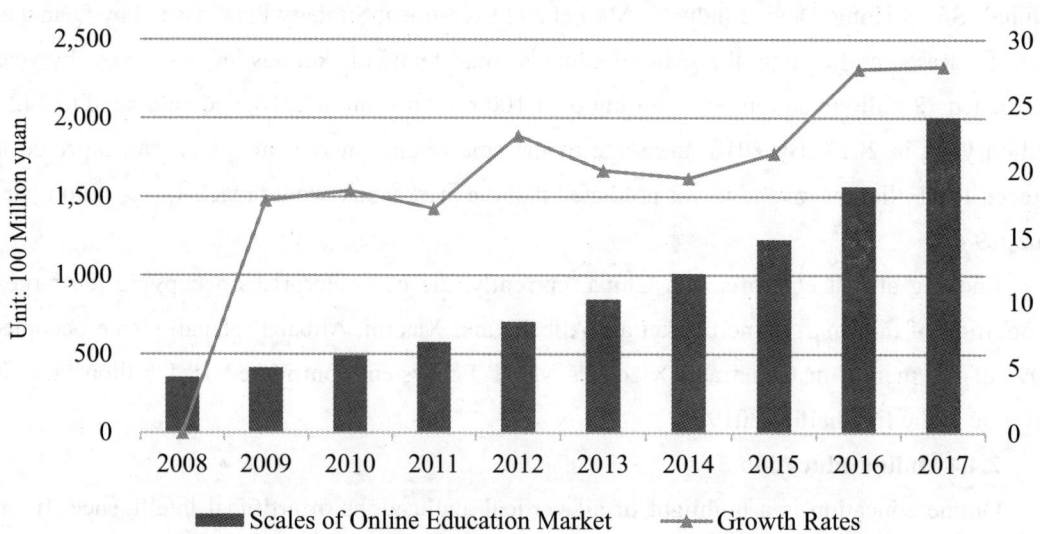

Figure 2.30 Scales of China's online education market (2008-2017)

Source: Wind Economic Database.

---

① Source: Wind Economic Database.
② Source: Wind Economic Database.

According to the breakdown of the market structure, the basic education sector of China's online education industry has shown a gradual growth. According to statistics from China National Information Infrastructure, the proportion of the online education market for primary and secondary schools in 2018 was 17.6%, which was an 8.6% increase from 2012. The proportion of the online education market for higher education showed a gradual decline from 61.8% in 2012 to 53.3% in 2018. In the meantime, the proportion of the online education market for vocational training was relatively stable.

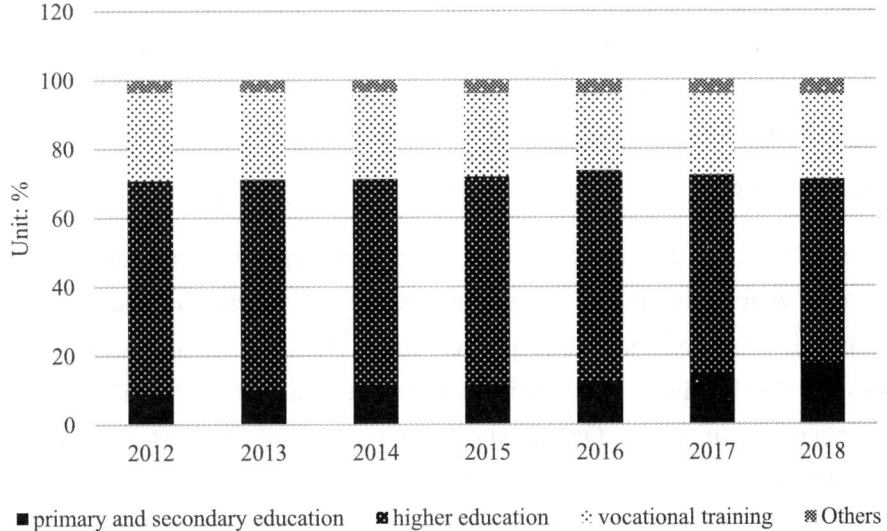

Figure 2.31 China's online education market size structure (2012-2018)
Source: China Industrial Information Network, https://www.chyxx.com/industry/1904/730058.html.

2.4.5 Smart medical care

On the one hand, smart medical care can provide accurate service for patients, thus providing personalized medical services and reducing search costs. On the other hand, it can optimize the medical treatment process and improve medical institutions' operation efficiency. As of July 2019, there were 126 active medical artificial intelligence enterprises in the Chinese market, about the same number as the statistics from 2017 (131). The majority, 57 of them, carried out medical imaging businesses, and 41 enterprises carried out disease risk prediction businesses. As compared to 2017 statistics, there is an increase in the number of enterprises carrying out medical assistance, medical imaging, and drug research and development. Many enterprises have expanded into the auxiliary medical research business. Hence, the number of enterprises in the medical research field has increased. As compared to 2017 statistics, there is a decrease in health management as well as disease risk prediction enterprises.

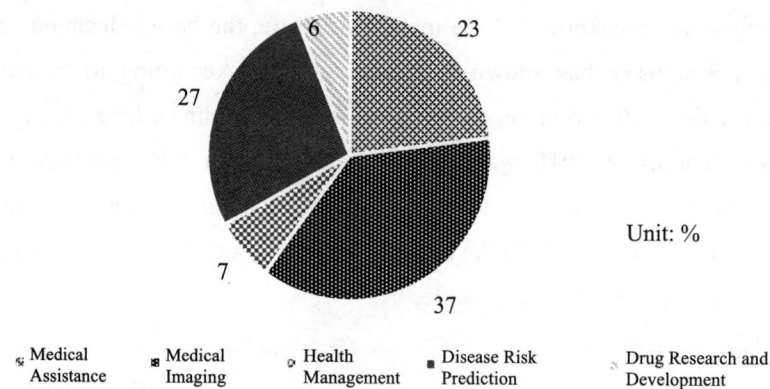

Figure 2.32 Distribution structure of the breakdown of China's smart medical care enterprises in 2019
Source: Wind Economic Database.

2.5 E-commerce

In 2019, China's e-commerce continued its rapid and high-quality development as well as deep integration with industrial businesses. Cross-border e-commerce continued to grow rapidly and maintained its position as the world's largest online retail market. The scale of e-commerce transactions was 34.81 trillion yuan. Among them, online retail sales exceeded 10 trillion yuan, a year-on-year increase of 16.5%. Online retail sales of physical products exceeded 8.5 trillion yuan, accounting for 19.5% of the total retail sales of consumer goods.

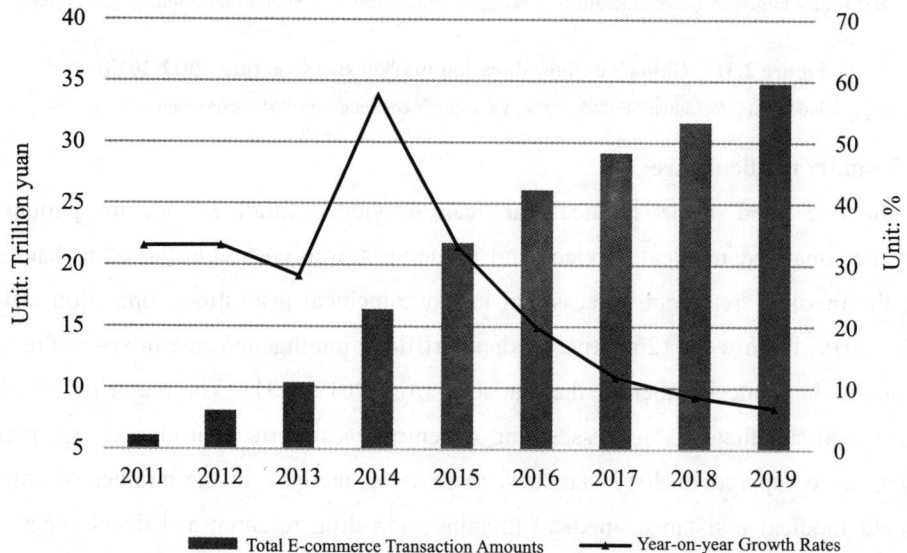

Figure 2.33 An overview of total transactions and growth of e-commerce (2011-2019)
Source: National Bureau of Statistics.

Rural e-commerce has entered a new round of innovation and growth. According to statistics of the Ministry of Commerce, in 2018, the volume of rural online retail sales in China reached 1.37 trillion yuan, a year-on-year increase of 30.4%. This is 6.5% faster than the growth rate of nationwide online retail sales.

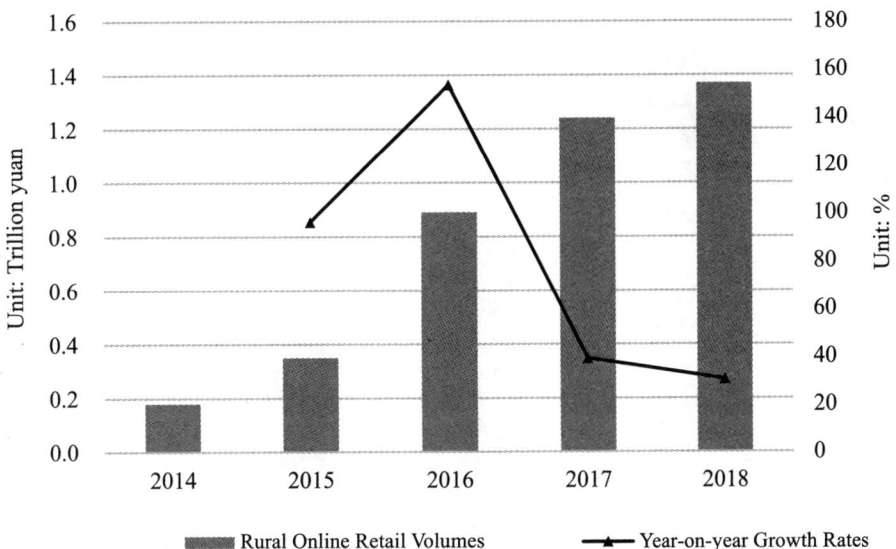

Figure 2.34 An overview of rural online retail volume and growth (2014-2018)

Source: Ministry of Commerce of the People's Republic of China, http://data.mofcom.gov.cn/.

2.6 E-government

China's e-government services continue to uphold a good overall standard. The various government departments have become skillful in organizing their new media platforms and creating uniform platforms, as well as using new technologies. This further improves the standard of governance and effectively enhances people's satisfaction and sense of gain. As of June 2019, the size of China's e-government service users has reached 509 million, accounting for 59.6% of the total number of netizens①.

As of June 2016, there were 61,514 government websites in China, mainly including government portals and departmental websites. Among them, the departments of the State Council, as well as its internal and vertically-managed organizations, contributed a total of 1,001 government websites. Administrative departments at the provincial level and below have a total of 14,142 government websites, which are distributed among 31 provinces (regions and cities) as well as the Xinjiang Production and Construction Corps②. The effective reduction in the number of government websites can simplify administrative procedures and improve the efficiency of the people's work and of the government's operations.

---

① Source: China Internet Network Information Center, "Statistical Reports on Internet Development in China".
② Source: China Internet Network Information Center, "Statistical Reports on Internet Development in China".

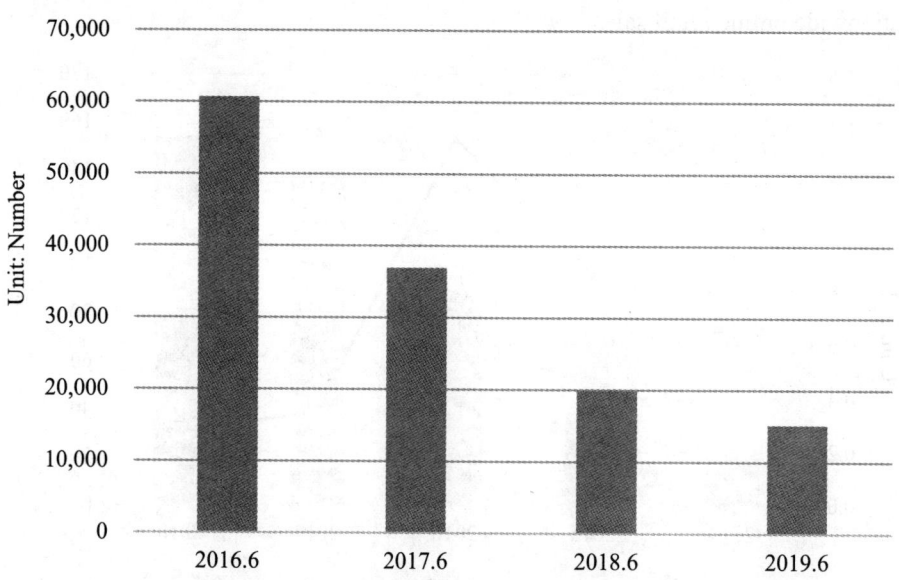

Figure 2.35 Cumulative numbers of Chinese government websites

Source: China Internet Network Information Center, "Statistical Reports on Internet Development in China".

The government has been developing its new media platforms at a good momentum. In this era of the mobile Internet, using new media in governance is an important means to accelerate the transformation of government functions and build a service-oriented government. It is an important path to explore new models of social governance and improve social governance capacity. As of June 2019, China's WeChat City Services have cumulated 620 million users, a year-on-year increase of 24%.

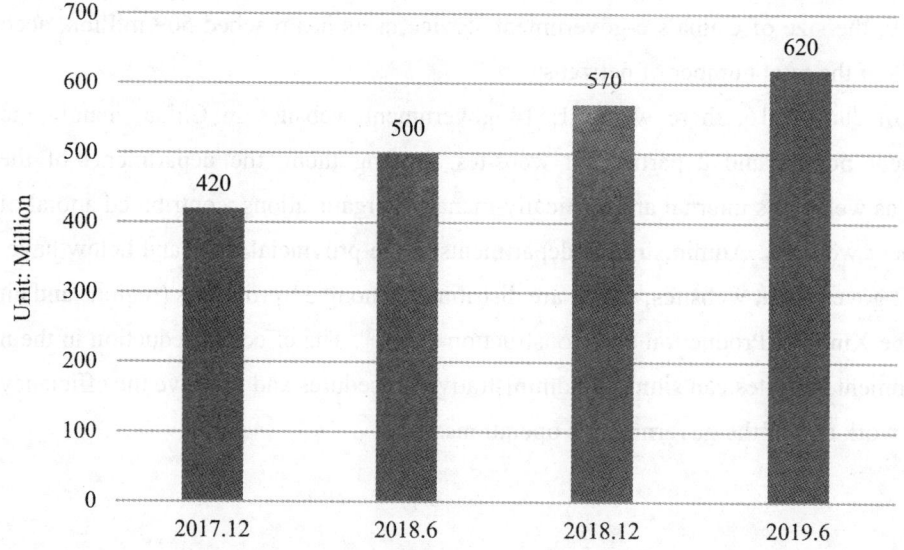

Figure 2.36 Cumulative number of users of China's WeChat City Services

Source: China Internet Network Information Center, "Statistical Reports on Internet Development in China".

Section 3 The Relationship between China's Digital Economic Development and the World

3.1 The status and influence of China's digital economic development in the world

3.1.1 The overall ranking of China's digital economy in the world

Digital technology continues to permeate various fields of economic society, thus becoming a guide in leading economic development. Digital economy has brought about the transformation and upgrading of industries all around the world. In this global informatization era, countries across the world have successively introduced relevant policies to promote the implementation of their digitalization strategies. Digital economies around the world have thus reached varying degrees of development. From the perspective of investments, China's investments in digital technology take the lead across the globe. China's venture capital industry has been paying continuous attention to the digitization field. According to a report by McKinsey, the investments from China's venture capital industry have rapidly increased from 12 billion USD in 2011-2013 to 77 billion USD in 2014-2016. Its proportion in the global venture capital has increased from 6% to 19%. The majority of the venture capital investments flowed to digital industries such as big data, artificial intelligence, financial technology, etc. China's venture capital for some key digital technologies is listed among the top three in the world, including virtual reality, autonomous driving vehicles, 3D printing, robots, drones, and artificial intelligence. This shows that China has placed substantial emphasis on relevant digital technologies. In the future, China's digital economy will grow rapidly. In 2019, China Academy of Information and Communications Technology released "New Prospect of Global Digital Economy", in which they calculated that among the top 30 countries in the size of digital economy across the world in 2018, the digital economy of Germany, the United Kingdom, and the United States accounted for the majority of their respective GDP. The numbers are 60.78%, 60.54%, and 60.07% respectively. This puts them in the top three spots. The digital economy of Korea, Japan, Ireland, and France accounted for more than 40% of their respective GDP, which are 47.15%, 46.07%, 42.30%, and 41.58% respectively, placing them in the fourth to seventh positions. The digital economy of Singapore, China, Finland, Canada, and Mexico also accounted for more than 30% of their respective GDP. The digital economy of Denmark, Sweden, Malaysia, Brazil, and Norway accounted for 20%-30% of their respective GDP. Nine other countries, including India, Belgium, Australia, Italy, and Switzerland, accounted for 16%-20% of their respective GDP. The digital economy of the Netherlands, Thailand, and Indonesia accounted for 10%-14% of their respective GDP. Turkey ranked the lowest, with its digital economy accounting for merely 7.03%

of its GDP.

Table 2.1 Proportion of major countries' digital economy in their respective GDP

Country	Proportion (%)	Country	Proportion (%)	Country	Proportion (%)
Germany	60.78	Canada	31.18	Italy	18.37
the United Kingdom	60.54	Mexico	30.06	Switzerland	18.11
the United States	60.07	Denmark	25.59	Poland	17.84
Korea	47.15	Sweden	23.31	Russia	17.75
Japan	46.07	Malaysia	21.75	South Africa	17.24
Ireland	42.30	Brazil	20.51	Spain	16.85
France	41.58	Norway	20.45	the Netherlands	13.56
Singapore	37.02	India	19.92	Thailand	11.49
China	34.75	Belgium	19.44	Indonesia	11.38
Finland	34.15	Australia	18.58	Turkey	7.03

Source: Derived from the size of each country's digital economy; According to "New Prospect of Global Digital Economies" released by China Academy of Information and Communications Technology in 2019, and the respective GDP of each country provided by the World Bank.

As seen from Table 2.1, the countries with large proportions of digital economy tend to be developed countries. This is because digital economy is an economic entity that requires knowledge-based technological progress. It has a close relationship with the overall economic development standard of the country. Developed countries have advantages such as good information technology infrastructure and scientific talent reserves that allow enterprises and consumers to use information technology at a lower cost. Thus, the overall development standard of their digital economy is generally higher than that of developing countries. In today's digital economy era, developed countries generally maintain a higher standard in the digital economic development process. Taking the United States as an example, it has complete infrastructure amenities and a mature industrial development system. At the same time, it values the basic research in information technology fields, application-based patents, commercial transformation capabilities of technologies, etc. These are the factors that place the United States in the lead for digital economic development. As the world's largest developing country, China's complete manufacturing system and huge consumption market led to the rapid development of its digital economy, making it the only developing country in the world's top 10 digital economy with the largest proportion in GDP.

Looking at the top 30 in the "2018 Global Digital Economic Development Index" released by AliResearch, multiple countries in Europe and Asia are at the top of the digital economy competitiveness rankings. As the only developing country in the top 10, China has beat many developed countries and ranked second place based on its own digitalized competitive advantage and market potential. The report also points out that China's overall digital economic standard is not high on the global scale, but is at a medium level. However, this does not directly reflect

China's current digital economic development. This is because China has chosen a different path in digital economic development as compared to developed countries. Although China's digital economic development has regional imbalances, with a complete information infrastructure, a huge digital consumer group, and a huge market size, China has a broad development prospect in the field of digital economy.

Table 2.2 Top 30 countries or regions in terms of global digital economic competitiveness

Country/region	2018 Ranking	Score	2017 Ranking	Score	Change in Ranking
the United States	1	86.37	1	85.61	0
China	2	81.42	8	78.30	−6
Korea	3	81.32	4	81.45	−1
Singapore	4	80.78	2	82.67	2
Japan	5	79.98	5	80.62	0
the United Kingdom	6	79.43	3	81.60	3
Germany	7	79.00	6	80.53	1
Sweden	8	78.08	9	78.26	−1
France	9	78.08	7	79.67	2
Norway	10	77.57	13	77.13	−3
Switzerland	11	77.05	11	78.00	0
Australia	12	76.61	15	76.12	−3
the Netherlands	13	76.42	10	78.01	3
Austria	14	76.13	14	76.55	0
Ireland	15	75.71	12	77.35	3
Canada	16	75.55	17	75.03	−1
Estonia	17	74.94	23	73.84	−6
Israel	18	74.77	19	74.79	−1
Denmark	19	74.33	16	75.81	3
Finland	20	74.11	20	74.73	0
Hong Kong, China	21	74.01	31	70.12	−10
Taiwan, China	22	73.99	34	69.55	−12
New Zealand	23	73.82	22	74.31	1
Russia	24	73.43	25	73.49	−1
Belgium	25	73.2	21	74.37	4
Iceland	26	73.16	18	74.89	8
United Arab Emirates	27	72.90	28	71.63	−1
Luxembourg	28	72.52	24	73.72	4
Lithuania	29	72.51	29	71.22	0
Czech Republic	30	72.08	26	72.81	4

Sources: AliResearch, "2018 Global Digital Economic Development Index".

3.1.2 Global ranking of the breakdown of China's digital economic industry

At present, digital economy around the world is gradually penetrating all aspects of traditional industries, bringing intense changes to the modes of production and organization. As a whole, the proportion of the service industry in digital economy is relatively high across the world, closely followed by the manufacturing industry. Meanwhile, the digital development of the agriculture industry is relatively slower.

In terms of the proportion of digital economy in the added value of the service industry, in 2018, digital economy of the service industries across the globe has become an important field in leading digital economic development. According to "New Prospect of Global Digital Economies" released by China Academy of Information and Communications Technology in 2019, the United Kingdom had the largest proportion (57.2%) of its service industry's digital economy accounting for the added value in the industry. Germany and the United States followed closely behind with proportions of more than 50%, at 57.1% and 55.1% respectively. Japan and France ranked fourth and fifth. China had 35.9% and ranked sixth. At the same time, it was also the only developing country in the top 10. The majority of the remaining countries accounted for 10%-30%. There were only nine countries, including Indonesia, the Netherlands, New Zealand, and Turkey, that had less than 10%.

Table 2.3 Proportion of service industry's digital economy in the industry's added value for each country

Country	Proportion (%)	Country	Proportion (%)	Country	Proportion (%)
the United Kingdom	57.2	Estonia	18.0	Switzerland	13.8
Germany	57.1	India	17.9	Spain	13.4
the United States	55.1	Hungary	17.5	Lithuania	13.2
Japan	41.0	Russia	17.3	Vietnam	11.6
France	36.7	Croatia	17.0	Slovenia	11.5
China	35.9	Belgium	16.5	Thailand	10.8
Finland	29.8	South Africa	16.4	Indonesia	9.6
Mexico	27.7	Romania	16.4	the Netherlands	9.0
Ireland	27.3	Sweden	16.3	New Zealand	9.0
Korea	25.3	Malaysia	15.9	Cyprus	8.0
Singapore	23.6	Czech Republic	15.7	Portugal	8.0
Canada	22.3	Italy	15.5	Slovakia	7.6
Denmark	21.3	Luxembourg	14.9	Greece	7.1
Norway	19.4	Poland	14.9	Austria	6.3
Brazil	19.1	Bulgaria	14.8	Turkey	4.3
Australia	18.5	Latvia	13.9		

Source: China Academy of Information and Communications Technology, "New Prospect of Global Digital Economies (2019)".

The rapid development of digital economy in all countries is an essential path for the transformation, upgrading of industrial businesses, and the improvement of their quality and efficiency. According to "New Prospect of Global Digital Economies" provided by China Academy of Information and Communications Technology, in 2018, the countries whose industrial digital economy accounted for larger proportions in the industry's added value were still developed countries, of which Korea ranked first with 44.5%. Germany, the United States, Ireland, the United Kingdom, and Japan had more than 30%, accounting for 42.5%, 37.7%, 34.6%, 31.5%, and 30.8% respectively. Singapore, France, Finland, and some other countries had more than 20%. China ranked 11th with 18.3%.

Table 2.4 The proportion of each country's industrial digital economy in the industry's added value

Country	Proportion (%)	Country	Proportion (%)	Country	Proportion (%)
Korea	44.5	Malaysia	12.1	South Africa	8.0
Germany	42.5	Russia	11.6	New Zealand	7.8
the United States	37.7	Estonia	11.6	Czech Republic	7.3
Ireland	34.6	Brazil	10.9	Bulgaria	7.3
the United Kingdom	31.5	India	10.8	Spain	6.8
Japan	30.8	Norway	10.4	Thailand	6.7
Singapore	28.9	Poland	10.2	Latvia	6.6
France	24.8	Romania	9.8	the Netherlands	5.6
Finland	20.9	Italy	9.3	Slovakia	5.4
Denmark	19.3	Luxembourg	9.0	Portugal	4.1
China	18.3	Lithuania	8.9	Indonesia	3.7
Mexico	15.6	Vietnam	8.5	Austria	3.6
Canada	15.3	Switzerland	8.4	Greece	3.2
Croatia	15.1	Slovenia	8.3	Cyprus	2.4
Sweden	12.5	Belgium	8.1	Turkey	2.1
Hungary	12.5	Australia	8.1		

Source: China Academy of Information and Communications Technology, "New Prospect of Global Digital Economies (2019)".

Compared with the digitalization of the service industry and industrial businesses, the digital economic development of agricultural industries across the world is relatively slow, thus becoming a shortcoming for digital economic development. According to "New Prospect of Global Digital Economies" provided by China Academy of Information and Communications Technology, in 2018, there were only two countries whose agricultural digital economy accounted for more than 20% of the industry's added value. They were the United Kingdom and Germany, accounting for 27.1% and 21.9% respectively. For 10 other countries, including Korea, the United States, and Finland, the numbers were between 10%-15%. The remaining countries had less than 10%. Among them, China ranked 15th with 7.3%.

Table 2.5 Proportion of agricultural digital economy in the industry's added value for each country

Country	Proportion (%)	Country	Proportion (%)	Country	Proportion (%)
the United Kingdom	27.1	Croatia	6.5	Switzerland	4.6
Germany	21.9	Belgium	6.5	the Netherlands	4.4
Korea	13.7	Sweden	6.4	Brazil	4.3
the United States	13.7	Romania	6.4	Malaysia	4.0
Finland	13.4	Lithuania	6.4	Thailand	3.7
New Zealand	13.4	Australia	6.1	Mexico	3.5
Japan	12.7	Hungary	6.1	India	3.5
France	12.6	Latvia	5.8	Portugal	3.2
Singapore	11.3	Canada	5.7	Slovakia	2.5
Ireland	10.9	Czech Republic	5.3	Vietnam	2.3
Denmark	10.1	South Africa	5.2	Austria	2.3
Russia	10.0	Luxembourg	5.1	Indonesia	2.0
Estonia	7.6	Poland	5.0	Greece	2.0
Norway	7.6	Spain	4.9	Cyprus	1.4
China	7.3	Bulgaria	4.9	Turkey	1.2
Italy	6.6	Slovenia	4.9		

Source: China Academy of Information and Communications Technology, "New Prospect of Global Digital Economies (2019)".

As stated above, China's overall digital economic development is at the forefront on a global scale, with its digital economy accounting for 34.75% of the GDP, putting it in ninth place. Specifically, the proportion of digital economy of the service industry in the industry's added value is the highest at 35.9%, putting it in sixth place. The industrial digital economy accounts for 18.3% of the industry's added value, putting it in 11th place. Meanwhile, agricultural digitalization development is relatively slower and accounts for less than 10% for the industry's added value, putting it in 15th place.

3.2 Cooperation between China and the world in the field of digital economy

Digital economy continues to become a new engine for global economic development. Digital economic development brings about opportunities not just in China but also across the world. Hence, bridging cooperation between China and the world in terms of digital economic development is more meaningful in today's context.

At the 2018 National Cybersecurity and Informatization Work Conference, General Secretary Xi Jinping pointed out that international cyberspace governance should adhere to multilateral participation and multi-participation. The main roles of the government, international organizations, Internet enterprises, technical communities, non-government institutions, and citizens as individuals should also come into play. Secretary Xi also said there is a need to make use of opportunities such as the construction of the "Belt and Road Initiative" to strengthen cooperation with other Belt and Road countries, especially developing ones, in terms of network infrastructure construction, digital economy, cybersecurity, etc., to build the Digital Silk Road in the 21st century. In recent years, China has been continuously strengthening its cooperation and development with the world's digital economy. On the one hand, it forms digitalized industrial partnerships with countries around the world. On the other hand, China constantly pushes its enterprises to venture overseas and actively devote themselves to the digitalized construction line. The idea of the Digital Silk Road was formed on the basis of benefiting from relevant partnerships with different countries. On November 7, 2018, the 23rd China-Russia PM's Regular Meeting was held. Based on the principle of equality and mutual benefit, cooperation will be strengthened in the field of telecommunications and continue to enhance the competitiveness of the Transit Europe-Asia (TEA) Terrestrial Cable Network, strengthen China-Russia digital economic partnership, and actively push relevant authorities to sign digital development partnership papers, creating new growth areas for cooperation.

In addition, China has also launched relevant digital economic cooperation initiatives. In the 2016 "G20 Digital Economic Development and Cooperation Initiative", the G20 explored ways to use digital opportunities and challenges to promote digital economy for realizing inclusive economic growth and development paths, realizing co-construction in network infrastructure, promoting industrial digitalization of relevant traditional industries, and pushing for the realization of partnership in e-commerce. In the "G20 Digital Economic Development and Cooperation Initiative", the group members agreed to provide favorable conditions for digital economic development, promoting economic growth and ensuring digital inclusiveness on the principles of "innovation, partnership, synergy, flexibility, inclusion, an open and supportive business environment, and the flow of information for promoting economic growth, trust, and security".

On December 3, 2017, the "Belt and Road Digital Economy International Cooperation Initiative" was launched by multiple countries at the Fourth World Internet Conference. The initiative included 13 initiatives such as "expand broadband access and improve quality, promote digital transformation, promote digitization of agricultural production, operation, management, and network transformation of agricultural products distribution, encourage e-commerce cooperation, promote the development of MSMEs, strengthen digital capability training, promote investment in the ICT sector, and promote inter-city cooperation of digital economy". Through expanding and realizing partnerships in digital economy, the initiative can lead to an interconnected Digital Silk Road.

China's partnership with ASEAN's digital economy has become increasingly close. As digital economy gradually becomes a development focus, e-commerce, smart cities, 5G, and other fields are gradually becoming the focus of bilateral cooperation. In May and November 2017, China signed the Memorandum of Understanding (MoU) on E-commerce Cooperation with Vietnam and Cambodia respectively to strengthen cross-border e-commerce cooperation. In

August 2018, China and Malaysia launched the signing process of the bilateral cross-border e-commerce cooperation MoU. China and Thailand have established a ministerial-level dialogue mechanism for digital economy cooperation and held its first meeting in March 2019. The 2019 ASEAN-China Digital Economy Industry Forum was a dialogue mechanism between China and ASEAN countries regarding digital economy. The forum served as platform support for multiple areas such as the realizing of bilateral investment partnerships as well as high-quality resource-docking and development strategies. This is beneficial for China to provide capital and technical experience to ASEAN countries, to provide great support for the digital economy development in ASEAN countries, to encourage ASEAN countries to actively transform their economic development models, and to co-build the Digital Silk Road. On the enterprise level, the top three telecom operators in China have already begun investing partnerships in ASEAN countries to varying degrees. Since 2018, China Mobile has accelerated its overseas layout and focused its business on emerging technology areas such as 5G network, IoT, etc. China Unicom has already established branches in eight ASEAN countries. In November 2018, China Telecom partnered with local groups to form a consortium bid, thus becoming the third telecom operator in the Philippines. In the digitalization of traditional industries, enterprises such as Alibaba (and Ant Financial), Tencent, ByteDance, Didi Chuxing, JD, Meituan, and Xiaomi have started active investing, mergers and acquisitions, technology output, and strategic cooperation in fields such as e-commerce, mobile payment, digital content, mobile travel, and online tourism respectively.

China's digital development is constantly pushing the global digitization process forward. In the future, more countries will have even closer partnerships with China in the digital economy field, and China will also continue to inject new impetus into the global digital economic development.

Section 4　The Policy System of China's Digital Economic Development

4.1 Opportunities and challenges of China's digital economic development

4.1.1 Opportunities

Firstly, in terms of the construction and completeness of new infrastructure, digital economy is built on a new information technology platform, which is different from the supporting infrastructure necessary for economic development in the industrial economy era. The infrastructure of the digital economy era is mainly represented by "cloud-network-terminal". It created a completely new business environment for digital economic development, and changes the existing business management model in the economic society. Therefore, constantly building new infrastructure can provide a solid foundation for digital economic development in

China.

At the same time, the completeness of the new infrastructure represented by "cloud-network-terminal" makes the flow and sharing of data possible, fully realizing the breadth and depth of data mining. This forms a new intelligent ecological environment that provides a basis for the inclusivity of technology, finance, and trade. In the science and technology application scenarios, the technologies represented by cloud computing enable individuals and enterprises to obtain their calculation and network resources at lower costs. This thus reduces the enterprises' operating costs. Through Internet technologies, the financial application scene has built a credit rating model with big data as its basis. This increases the transparency of information and allows more individuals to choose financial services that are suitable for their personal risk preferences. In the context of trade application, economic entities can all partake in global trade, allowing for the trade environment to become more open and inclusive.

Secondly, from the perspective of enterprises, in the digital economy era, social production is gradually transforming from supply-centric to consumer-centric. Digitalized consumers have become the core elements of digital economy. This is because they are also data generators at the same time. By providing intellectualized solution plans and data circulation of consumers' behaviors and demands, businesses can solve consumers' pain points and become a promising market. China has a huge population base, which means a huge consumer potential. Thus, this will create a gigantic data system, and a huge demand for digital consumption, becoming an essential driving force for China's economic growth in the future.

In the digital economy era, with the application of technologies such as the Internet, the Internet of Things, and big data, the factors required by enterprises are not only labor and capital. As a new form of a core element, data is gradually becoming a considerable factor. Therefore, the relationship of production also has changed. With the advancement of the third industrial revolution, information technology has never stopped developing. The degree of internal digitalization in enterprises has been constantly increasing. As an important part of policy-analysis for enterprises, data has helped make the most optimal plans and decisions.

For SMEs, digital economy is a new opportunity. The original company-driven large-scale investment in information systems to complete the digitization of the company is no longer the normality. The emergence of digital platforms has promoted the digitalization of the whole society, providing an affordable yet vast digital infrastructure for the individual, medium, small, and micro enterprises. Additionally, the openness and inclusivity of digital economy also help maximize the potential of these enterprises and solve the development bottlenecks that they might be facing, such as capital financing. By providing these enterprises with the possibility of development, digital platforms have ignited the entire society's production vitality, constantly lowering information costs for the whole society and continuously realizing the possibility of overall large-scale collaboration. During the COVID-19 outbreak, with the guarantee of government policies as a basis, SMEs have relied on financial technology, making full use of the Internet of Things, blockchain, and other information system tools to achieve rapid financing. This serves as a convenient tool to guarantee the steady resumption of work and production for SMEs.

Thirdly, digital economy is a new opportunity at the governmental level. The government can rely on digital technology infrastructure such as big data, the Internet, and cloud computing to realize a new model of digital management. In terms of public service management, the government can constantly encourage digital innovation and entrepreneurship through relevant measures. They can also continuously realize the application and development of digital economy through various roles like an investor, developer, and consumer.

Fourthly, from the perspective of the whole society, the development of digital economy will become an economic development trend. By applying it in various fields such as medical care, environment, security, and education, social welfare and people's standard of living can be improved. With the continuous realization of digital globalization, China is currently using new business models such as investments and mergers and acquisitions, as well as having more technical cooperation, to continually push China to become a strong force in leading global digital economic development. In the future, China's digital technology will continue to have a comparative advantage. China can achieve a vast application of digital economy thanks to its huge population. In addition, China can also make full use of its regional advantage to build economies of scale in regions with better standards of economic development. This will help China keep its leading position in the international arena.

The arrival of the digital economy era will make great changes to our production methods as well as our lifestyle. It will subvert the models that the traditional economic industry is developing in, and form a completely new business model economic paradigm. In the future, the technical scalability of economic development will continue to strengthen, thus bringing new motivators for economic growth and realizing the high-quality development of China's economic growth.

4.1.2 Challenges

Since digital economy development has a unique trait of shareability, it blurs the boundaries between physical reality, virtual world, and individuals. This will result in many complex problems such as legal, security, and ethical issues.

Firstly, from the social management level, although China has relatively well-developed platforms and can obtain huge data resources, the short period of digital economic development places limitations on management in terms of planning and management of data resources. In addition, the openness of the Chinese government's data is still restricted. The restriction in cross-border data traffic also puts China in a relatively disadvantaged position in global cooperation.

Secondly, in terms of data security, digital assets such as core data and key technology patents play a very critical role in the development of enterprises, be it in the industrial field or other industries. However, China lacks the relevant laws and regulations in the digital sharing process. This poses relevant digital security risks and forms an important obstacle to digital technology development in the future. At the same time, there are also a series of problems regarding the protection of digital technology patents, including the lack of foundational technology patents, weak awareness in the protection of commercial confidentialities, lack of a database for professional patents, and the shortage in digital technology standardization tools.

Thirdly, in terms of algorithm, the standard of China's digital economic application is not much different than that at the international level. China also has breakthroughs in artificial intelligence algorithms such as in the fields of speech recognition and targeted advertising. However, China still lags behind some developed countries in terms of the research and development of foundational algorithms. China's basic scientific research level is still comparatively low on a global scale. Hence, China will have to increase investments in basic research and strengthen the research and development in related fields in the future.

Fourthly, there are also some problems with the digital transformation of real economy. Some industries are unable to go through the transformation. In terms of the agriculture industry, the application of digital economy shows relatively scattered characteristics. Since the agriculture industry itself has existing limitations, the degree of digitalization is relatively low. At the same time, there is a lack of accumulation of relevant agricultural data. There is also some time lag in the application of digital technology in agricultural scenarios. The characteristics of agricultural production in China are mainly large output, small scale, low quality, and low added value. Due to various problems such as the low concentration of production and processing, low mechanization level, and lack of standardization of agricultural production, there is still a long way to go for the application of digital economy in the agricultural industry.

China faces the problem of high costs in its application of digital economy due to the lack of a self-driving force in enterprises during the process of their transformation. As compared with relatively developed countries, Chinese enterprises still face a certain degree of cost restriction in introducing digital technologies. On the one hand, China has a shortage of high-quality talents in the corresponding fields of digitalization. On the other hand, compared with digital technology, the labor cost is lower. This leads to enterprises not having enough drive to introduce advanced digital technology, thus resulting in the impact of the labor market and leading to structural unemployment.

All in all, in the process of digital economic development, on the one hand, China should actively seize transformation opportunities and make full use of the advantages of digital development. At the same time, China must always pay attention to the series of problems and challenges brought about by the application of digital technologies so as to push our economy toward a higher-quality development.

4.2 Integration of digital economy and real economy

The digital transformation of traditional industries is one of the important steps for China's economy to turn toward a high-quality development phase. With the continuous development of digital economy, it will have an important impact on China's traditional economy, thus promoting the deep integration of China's digital economy and real economy. With support from the huge local market and active policies, China's real economy will continue to be pushed toward integration with digital economy in the future. In conclusion, such integration mainly starts from some leading fields, which mainly include retail, healthcare, security, and other living and public services. It will then further expand into the production field of agriculture and manufacturing. At present, various industries such as finance, automobile, catering, and logistics have integrated with digital economy, and the relevant fields of application will become increasingly complete.

In the manufacturing sector, "Made in China 2025", officially issued by the State Council on May 19, 2015, is the first 10-year action program implemented by the Chinese government to achieve manufacturing power. In 2015, the State Council issued the "Guiding Opinions on Actively Promoting 'Internet' Action". It pointed out that promoting the integration of the Internet and the manufacturing industry, improving the digitalization, networking, and intellectualization level of the manufacturing industry, and strengthening industrial chain coordination and development are foundations to a new model of collaborative manufacturing using the Internet. In 2016, the Ministry of Industry and Information Technology and Ministry of Finance also issued the "Intelligent Manufacturing Development Plan (2016-2020)". They pointed out that by 2020, the infrastructure and support for intelligent manufacturing development would have increased significantly. The key traditional manufacturing industries would have realized foundational digitalized manufacturing. The application of digital economy in the manufacturing industry would have increased the capacity for data analysis and processing in traditional enterprises in various fields such as innovation, production, and sales. It would have also pushed the industry toward intellectualization and service-based developments. Digital economy would empower traditional manufacturing industries and increase the intellectualization standard of the manufacturing industry. Through new business models and new forms, it would also push the manufacturing industry to undergo a service-based transformation. Enterprises would have changed the existing supply-centric production model to a consumer-centric one, hence transforming the industry's production model from homogenization to customization, focusing on solving consumers' pain points and promoting the rationalization of the manufacturing industry. In addition, digital economy can promote the extended development of manufacturing services to be more service-based. Enterprises' production models transform from simple productions to product-based services. The value added to products increases, hence lifting profits for enterprises and utility for consumers.

In recent years, China has placed great emphasis on the development of digital agriculture and rural areas. Following the guidance of a series of documents released by the departments such as the Ministry of Agriculture and Cyberspace Administration of China, China's digital agricultural development has achieved remarkable results. The documents include: "Action Plan on Promoting the Development of Big Data", "Outline of Development Strategy for Digital Rural Areas", "Three-year Implementation Plan for Modern Agriculture under 'Internet Plus'", "Implementation Opinions on Promoting the Development of Big Data in Agriculture and Rural Areas", "Development Plan for the Informatization of China's Agriculture and Rural Areas under the '13th Five-year Plan'", and "Development Plan for Digital Agriculture and Rural Areas (2019-2025)".

In 2016, the Ministry of Agriculture, National Development and Reform Commission, and eight other departments jointly issued the "Three-year Implementation Plan for Modern Agriculture under 'Internet Plus'". They pointed out that in 2018, the agriculture industry's movement to go online and digitized has made significant progress. In the same year, the Ministry of Agriculture formally issued the "Development Plan for the Informatization of China's Agriculture and Rural Areas under the '13th Five-year Plan'". It pointed out that in 2020, modern agriculture construction under "Internet Plus" would have achieved great results. In 2019, the Ministry of Agriculture and the General Office of the Cyberspace Administration issued the "Digital Agriculture and Rural Areas Plan (2019-2025)". The document pointed out that by 2025, the construction of digital agriculture in rural areas would achieve significant progress and become capable of supporting the implementation of the digital rural areas strategy. In order to realize the deep integration of digital technologies and traditional industries, various stakeholders, such as the government, society, and enterprises, will need to work closely together. On the one hand, all stakeholders need to invest more, strengthen basic research, increase original innovation capacity, strive to a new peak in innovation, and gain new industrial advantages. On the other hand, stakeholders have to explore a multilateral collaborative governance system, explore the development models for a combined digital industry, and improve new infrastructure. In the process of pushing the agricultural industry toward digital transformation, existing agriculture businesses mainly focus on labor and mechanized operation standards. As the application of digital economy increases, streamlined agricultural production continues to advance, thus improving the quality and growth of Chinese agriculture. This has resulted in a streamlined production based on data elements such as soil and weather conditions. Digital technology platforms have increased efficiency in production, processing, and sales, increasing the competitiveness of agriculture products. At the same time, it has also increased the shareability of agriculture information. Digital technology platforms built by the government, enterprises, and other economic entities have effectively reduced the uncertainty factors of agriculture through large-scale collecting, processing, analyzing, and predicting of data. They also alleviated information asymmetry in the agriculture industry and increased production efficiency. However, looking at this from a horizontal contrast, in 2018, digital economy of Chinese agriculture only accounted for 7.3% of the industry's added value. This comes far lower than the industrial businesses' 18.3% and the service industry's 35.9%. In terms of financial investments, in 2018, 25.2% of the counties received less than 100,000 yuan, and only 20.0% received more than 5 million yuan. This shows that the current digital agricultural development in China is still relatively lagging behind with a huge potential to develop further.

The development of digital economy continually deepens the service industry. The impact of this is mainly concentrated in the fields of finance-centric productive services, retail-centric living services, medical care, education, and others. The scale and efficiency of the service industry are greatly lifted, as is the standard of living. In 2015, the State Council pointed out in the "Guiding Opinions on Actively Promoting 'Internet Plus' Action" that deep integration of "Internet Plus" with financial inclusion, services for the people, highly-efficient logistics, e-commerce, convenient transportation, and other fields should be actively promoted, thus enhancing the innovation and productivity of real economy.

In the finance field, financial institutions can analyze the differentiated characteristics of borrowers through digital technologies such as big data and cloud computing. They can thus provide exclusive portfolio investment products for different investors. At the same time, it also improves risk management and control abilities in the financial industry. In addition, it also realizes financial inclusion by tapping into the inclusivity of digital economy. This thus makes it possible for SMEs to enjoy digital economic advantages. In the retail industry, large e-commerce companies can continually meet the differentiated needs of consumers through digital platforms. They can also maximize interests through the vertical breakdown of professional market fields and gathering real-time consumer needs and demands through market data. During the COVID-19 outbreak, a large number of offline activities moved online. This provided excellent opportunities for industries like online medical care and online education.

In the pharmaceutical retail field, the drainage of virus prevention materials and the demand for stay-at-home virus protection supplies have led to a surge in the number of users and orders on O2O platforms. In the spring of 2020, the order volume on Dingdang Medicine Express increased by 700% on a year-on-year basis. The sales volume of prescription drugs for chronic diseases on Meituan's doorstep delivery service increased by 237% year-on-year[1]. In the online medical services field, multiple platforms have started online consultation services, thus reducing the risk of the public contracting COVID-19 while going to visit a doctor.

---

[1] iResearch, "Impact of the COVID-19 Outbreak on New Economy Sectors—An Investment Research Perspective", 2020.

Table 2.6 Promotion measures used by online medical platforms during the COVID-19 outbreak in 2020[①]

Main Online Functions	Product Name	Date
Map of Real-time Outbreaks	Dingxiang Garden	21 January
Videos and Live Broadcasts on COVID-19 Information	Tencent Medpedia	22 January
Online Free Clinic for Hubei Province	Faint Pulse	24 January
	Dingxiang Garden	24 January
	Ali Health	24 January
	Yiyaowang	24 January
Special Pandemic-prevention Free Phone Consultation	Ping An Good Doctor	26 January

Due to the outbreak of COVID-19, in 2020, the Ministry of Education sent out an urgent notice to delay the opening of school in all parts of the country. At the same time, they also advocated for "Suspending Classes without Stopping Learning". As a result, many online education companies provided free courses for secondary and primary students across the country. Online education businesses that relied on the Internet also experienced unprecedented popularity. With Xueersi Online School as an example, the development of online education was more balanced across different cities.

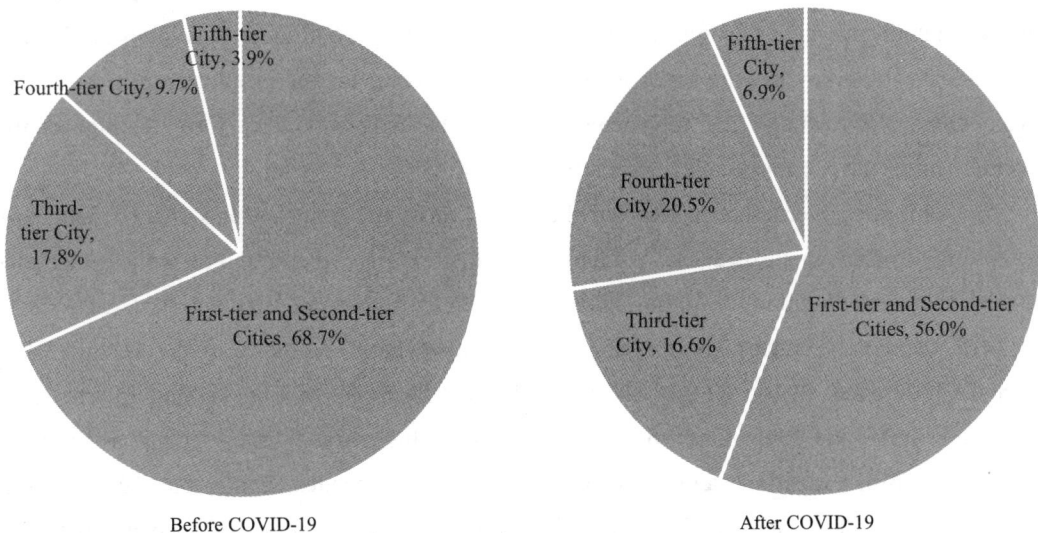

Before COVID-19　　　　　　　　　　After COVID-19

Figure 2.37 Changes in the structure of Xueersi Online School's total standalone devices before and after the COVID-19 outbreak on the city level[②]

---

① iResearch, "Impact of the COVID-19 Outbreak on New Economy Sectors — An Investment Research Perspective", 2020.
② iResearch, "Impact of the COVID-19 Outbreak on New Economy Sectors — An Investment Research Perspective", 2020.

4.3 Incentives of China's digital economic development

In March 2017, digital economy was mentioned in the Government Work Report for the first time. It was explicitly stated that the government would "push forward with the Internet Plus action plan and speed up the development of digital economy. (The government is) confident that all these steps will benefit both businesses and (its) people". In 2019, digital economy was once again mentioned in the Government Work Report. It was stated that "(the government) will strengthen R&D and the application of big data and artificial intelligence technologies, foster clusters of emerging industries like next-generation information technology, high-end equipment, biomedicine, new-energy automobiles, and new materials, and expand digital economy". In 2020, digital economy was included in the Government Work Report for the third time. It was pointed out that "new forms of business such as e-commerce, online shopping, and online services have played an important role during the COVID-19 response, and more policies will be introduced in support of such businesses. (The government) will advance Internet Plus initiatives across the board and create new competitive strengths in digital economy". As seen from the three appearances in Government Work Reports, digital economy is not merely an economic development trend. At the same time, it is also a developing field that the government puts heavy emphasis on. As digital economy continues to develop in China, it will gradually be a key driving force for supply-side reform, for the promotion of productivity development, for realizing the replacement of growth drivers, and in turn the high-quality development of the economy, and for constructing a modern strong China.

The Chinese government has seized the opportunity and launched a series of policies to promote the improvement of digital technology infrastructure construction as well as to realize the continuous development of digital industrialization and industrial digitization. On December 16, 2015, General Secretary Xi Jinping attended the opening ceremony of the Second World Internet Conference. In his speech, he stressed that "China is working on the 'Internet Plus' Initiative to impel the construction of 'digital China'". This marks "digital China" as the target for China's informatization development in the coming decades. Since the 19th National Congress of the CPC, General Secretary Xi Jinping has made a series of speeches regarding advancing digital economy development. He made major strategic deployments based on "implementing China's National Big Data Strategy, constructing a digital economy with data as the key element, and advancing the construction of digital China". In the National Cybersecurity and Informatization Work Conference held on April 20, 2018, General Secretary Xi Jinping stressed that we have to "be sensitive and seize this historical opportunity of informatization development and maximize the leading role of informatization on economic society. In this new era where science and technology develop rapidly, all the more should China catch up with it, promote the integration of digital economy with real economy, and constantly improve its own competitive advantage".

The construction of new infrastructure has laid a solid foundation for China's digital economic development. China's economy has already shifted from a high-speed growth stage to a high-quality development stage. The core of the new digital infrastructure is this new generation of digital technology. The innovation and application of digital infrastructure in fields such as manufacturing and service industries can not only subvert production models of traditional industries, but also promote the formation of new industries as well as the innovation and combined development of all industries. Hence, this effectively promotes structural optimization for the high-quality development of China's economy. This is precisely why the country highly values emerging information technologies like the 5G network and artificial intelligence. In 2018, it was clearly pointed out in the Central Economic Work Conference that there was a need to quicken the pace of the commercial application of 5G network, as well as to strengthen the construction of new forms of digital infrastructure such as artificial intelligence, industrial Internet, and the Internet of Things. In the 2019 Meeting of the Political Bureau of the CPC, it was further emphasized that there was a necessity to grab hold of opportunities for digital economic development and quicken the layout of the new form of digital infrastructure. In the 2020 Meeting of the Standing Committee of the Political Bureau of the CPC, the need to quicken the construction of new forms of infrastructure like the 5G network and data centers was brought up once again. In 2020, the Ministry of Industry and Information Technology released the "Notice of Promoting the Accelerated Development of Industrial Internet" and requested the integrated innovation of the industrial Internet on a broader, wider, and higher standard level, as well as called for the cultivation and expansion of a new growth driver for economic development. This is a higher expectation of the construction of the new forms of digital infrastructure in China. In order to better improve the construction of the new infrastructure, on top of improving the relevant overall planning, the government can carry out rational usage of the new infrastructure and clarify the ownership of the public infrastructure brought about by the cooperation between the government and social capital. In addition, the government should strengthen the legal protection of information network investment to attract more investors to participate in the new infrastructure construction.

In 2015, the State Council issued the "Guiding Opinions on Actively Promoting 'Internet Plus' Action", emphasizing taking full advantage of the importance of data as China's foundational strategic resource. In 2019, the State Council issued the "Guiding Opinions on Promoting the Standard Healthy Development of Platform Economy" and encouraged platform economy to develop new formats. While promoting the rapid development of digital technologies such as artificial intelligence, big data, and cloud computing, the role of platform economy also became more obvious. China has pointed out in the "13th Five-year Plan" abstract that there is a need to utilize big data as our foundational strategic resource to carry out a full-implementation push for big data development as well as quickening the promotion of data resources' open sharing and innovative applications. Since data is the foundational and constituent element of digital economic development, in order to hit the goal of rapid development for our digital economy, China should push for the realization of new progress in data-centric industrial development. China needs to continually push forward the application of digital technologies such as cloud computing, big data, and the Internet in the economy. China also needs to construct a new economic form that has data as its key production element. We need to maximize the development of new forms of economies such as the Internet economy, platform economy, and sharing economy so that they can become an essential driving force to push forward the high-quality development of our economy. Digital economic governance is an important form of national governance in the field of digital economy. With the emergence of new types of economic forms such as big data, artificial intelligence, and digital platforms, the complexity of digital governance has been increased. While maximizing market autonomy, China also needs to maximize the government-led effect and actively push for the realization of promotion for relevant digital industries. At the same time, China needs to strengthen digital infrastructure construction and maximize the goose effect of new types of economic forms such as the Internet economy and platform economy.

Table 2.7 Important policies and plans for China's digital economy development

Date of publication	Document name and document number	Key words
January 1999	Circular of the General Office of the State Council on Forwarding "Notice of Opinions on Accelerating the Development of Mobile Communication Industry" by the State Development Planning Commission of the Ministry of Information Industry (No. 5 [1999] of the General Office of the State Council)	Mobile Communications
July 2001	Circular of the General Office of the State Council on Forwarding the "Opinions on Promoting Space Information Infrastructure Construction and Application in China" by the National Planning Commission and Other Departments (No. 53 [2001] of the General Office of the State Council)	Infrastructure Construction for Space Information
September 2002	Circular of the General Office of the State Council on Forwarding "Notice on the Action Outline for Promoting the Software Industry" by the State Council Information Office (No. 47 [2002] of the General Office of the State Council)	Software Industry
March 2005	Circular of the General Office of the State Council on "Opinions on Accelerating the Development of E-commerce" (No. 2 [2005] of the General Office of the State Council)	E-commerce

Continued

Date of publication	Document name and document number	Key words
March 2014	"2014 Report on the Work of the Government"	Big Data Written in China's Government Work Report for the First Time
January 2015	Circular of the State Council on Printing and Distributing the "Opinions of the State Council on Promoting the Innovative Development of Cloud Computing and Cultivating New Business Forms of the Information Industry" (No. 5 [2015] of the General Office of the State Council)	Cloud Computing
May 2015	Notice of the State Council on Issuing "Made in China 2025" (No. 28 [2015] of the General Office of the State Council)	Made in China
July 2015	Circular of the State Council on "Guiding Opinions on Actively Promoting 'Internet Plus' Action" (No. 40 [2015] of the State Council)	Internet
August 2015	Circular of the State Council on "Action Plan on Promoting the Development of Big Data" (No. 50 [2015] of the State Council)	Big Data
April 2016	Circular of the Ministry of Agriculture on "Implementation Opinions on Promoting the Development of Big Data in Agriculture and Rural Areas" (No. 6 [2015] of the Ministry of Agriculture)	Big Data in Agriculture and Rural Areas
May 2016	"Guiding Opinions of the State Council on Deepening the Integrated Development of the Manufacturing Industry and the Internet" (No. 28 [2016] of the State Council)	Internet, Manufacturing Industry
August 2016	Notice of the Ministry of Agriculture, National Development and Reform Commission, Cyberspace Administration of China, Ministry of Science and Technology, Ministry of Commerce, General Administration of Quality Supervision, Inspection, and Quarantine, and State Food and Drug Administration, and National Forestry and Grassland Administration on Issuing the "Three-year Implementation Plan for Modern Agriculture under 'Internet Plus'" (No. 2 [2016] of the Ministry of Agriculture)	Internet, Modern Agriculture Industry
August 2016	Circular of the Ministry of Agriculture on "Development Plan for the Informatization of China's Agriculture and Rural Areas under the '13th Five-year Plan'" (No. 5 [2016] of the Ministry of Agriculture)	Informationization of Agriculture and Rural Areas
September 2016	"Guiding Opinions of the State Council on Accelerating the Work of 'Internet + Government Services'" (No. 55 [2016] of the State Council)	Internet, Government Affairs

Continued

Date of publication	Document name and document number	Key words
October 2016	36th Collective Study of the Political Bureau of the CPC Central Committee	Building a Big and Strong Digital Economy
November 2016	"Notice of the State Council on Issuing the '13th Five-Year Plan' for the Strategic Development of China's Strategic Emerging Industries" (No. 67 [2016] of the State Council)	Digital Creative Industry
December 2016	"Notice of the State Council on Issuing the '13th Five-Year Plan' for China's Informatization Plan" (No. 73 [2016] of the State Council)	Information Industry
December 2016	"Intelligent Manufacturing Development Plan (2016-2020)" by the Ministry of Industry and Information Technology, and Ministry of Finance (No. 49 [2016] of the Ministry of Industry and Information Technology Joint Plan)	Intelligent Manufacturing
January 2017	"Work Notice of the Ministry of Industry and Information Technology on Issuing the Development Plan for Big Data Industries (2016-2020)" (No. 412 [2016] of the Ministry of Industry and Information Technology Joint Plan)	Big Data
December 2017	General Secretary Xi Jinping's Address at the Second Collective Study of the Political Bureau of the CPC Central Committee	Integrated Development of the Real and Digital Economies
April 2018	National Work Conference on Cyber Security and Informatization	Network Security, Informatization
December 2018	Central Economic Work Conference	Digital Infrastructure Construction
May 2019	Circular of the General Office of the Central Committee of the CPC and the General Office of the State Council on Printing and Distributing the "Outline of Development Strategy for Digital Rural Areas"	Digital Rural Areas
July 2019	"Cloud Computing Services Security Assessment Measures" Promulgated by the Cyberspace Administration of China, National Development and Reform Commission, Ministry of Industry and Information Technology, and Ministry of Finance (No. 2 [2019])	Cloud Computing
August 2019	Circular of the General Office of the State Council on "Guiding Opinions on Promoting the Standard Healthy Development of Platform Economy" (No. 38 [2019] of the General Office of the State Council)	Platform Economy
October 2019	Collective Study by the Political Bureau of the CPC on the Development Status and Trend of Blockchain Technology	Blockchain Technology
January 2020	"Development Plan for Digital Agriculture in Rural Areas (2019-2025)"	Digital Agriculture in Rural Areas

Continued

Date of publication	Document name and document number	Key words
2020	Circular of the Ministry of Industry and Information Technology on "Notice of Promoting the Accelerated Development of Industrial Internet"	Internet
2020	Convened meeting by the Politburo of the CPC Central Committee on studying the prevention and control of COVID-19 and "New Infrastructure Construction", emphasizing pushing for the accelerated development of biomedicine, medical equipment, 5G network, industrial Internet, etc.	5G New Infrastructure Construction, Industrial Internet

Source: Sorted data gathered online.

Table 2.8 Digital economic development policies and plans in certain provinces and cities

Province/City	Time	Name of Policy
Shanxi Province	2019.09.19	"Opinions on Implementing Acceleration on Digital Economic Development in Shanxi Province"
Inner Mongolia Autonomous Region	2019.01.11	"Construction and Development Plan for Digital Inner Mongolia (2018-2025)" (Draft for Comment)
Heilongjiang Province	2019.06.04	"'Digital Longjiang' Development Plan (2019-2025)"
Jilin Province	2018.07.17	"Opinions on the Construction of Digital Jilin to Lead Acceleration of Replacing Old Growth Drivers with New Ones and Promoting High-Quality Development"
Zhejiang Province	2018.09.14	"Five-Year Growth Plan for Digital Economy in Zhejiang Province"
Zhejiang Province	2016.11.15	"13th Five-year Plan for Informatization Development of Zhejiang Province" ("Digital Zhejiang 2.0" Development Plan)
Anhui Province	2019.03.04	"Detailed Rules for Implementation of Several Policies to Support Digital Economic Development"
Anhui Province	2018.10.23	"Notice of the Anhui Provincial People's Government on Issuing Several Policies to Support Digital Economic Development"
Anhui Province	2018.09.12	"Guiding Opinions on Accelerating the Construction of 'Digital Jianghuai'"
Fujian Province	2018.09.21	"Management Measures of Dedicated Funds for Digital Economic Development of Fujian Province"
Fujian Province	2018.04.02	"2018 Digital Fujian Key Work Points"
Fujian Province	2018.02.06	"Opinions on Accelerating the Innovation and Development of the Industrial Digital Economy in the Province"
Fujian Province	2017.08.31	"Notice on Launching the First Batch of Key Laboratories for the Digital Fujian IoT Field"
Fujian Province	2016.05.17	"Digital Fujian Special Plan for Fujian Province's 13th Five-year Plan"
Fujian Province	2015.09.29	"Issuance of Interim Measures Regarding Construction and Operation Management for the Collaboration between the Digital Fujian Public Platform, Government, and Social Capital"

Continued

Province/City	Time	Name of Policy
Jiangxi Province	2019.02.18	"Opinions on Jiangxi Province Implementing the Digital Economic Development Strategy"
Shandong Province	2019.07.09	"Opinions on Shandong Province Supporting Digital Economic Development"
	2019.03.13	"Digital Shandong Action Plan 2019"
	2019.02.27	"Digital Shandong Development Plan (2018-2022)"
Henan Province	2019.09.20	"Henan Province Digital Economic Development Major Project"
	2019.07.02	"Key Points for the Henan Province Digital Economy in 2019"
Guangdong Province	2018.04.10	"Guangdong Province Digital Economic Development Plan (2018-2025)" (Draft for Comment)
Guangxi Zhuang Autonomous Region	2019.07.08	"The Guangxi Zhuang Autonomous Region Digital Economy Industry Development Guidance Catalogue" (for Trial Implementation)
	2018.09.17	"Guangxi Digital Economic Development Plan (2018-2025)"
	2018.09.17	"Three-year Action Plan for the Development of Digital Economy in Guangxi (2018-2020)"
	2018.08.30	"Digital Guangxi-Implementation Plan for 'Guangdianyun' Three-year Engineering Battle in Rural Villages and Households (2018-2020)"
	2018.08.29	"Digital Guangxi-Three-year Action Plan for Information and Communication Infrastructure Campaign (2018-2020)"
	2018.08.29	"Measures to Accelerate Construction of Digital Guangxi"
Sichuan Province	2019.04.02	"Implementation Opinions of the People's Government of Sichuan Province on Accelerating the Digital Economic Development" (Draft for Comment)
	2018.11.16	"Implementing Opinions of the People's Government of Sichuan Province on Accelerating the Deep Integration of Sichuan Province's Digital Economy with Real economy"
Guizhou Province	2018.06.21	"Opinions of the People's Government of Guizhou Province on Promoting the Innovation and Development of Big Data, Cloud Computing, and Artificial Intelligence to Accelerate the Construction of Digital Guizhou"
	2018.02.11	"Notice of the People's Government of Guizhou Province on Issuing the Guizhou Province Implementing 'All Enterprises Unite' to Fight the 'Digital Economy' Battle Plan"
	2017.03.21	"Opinions of the CPC Guizhou Provincial Committee of the People's Government of Guizhou Province on Promoting the Acceleration of Digital Economy Development"
	2017.02.07	"Guizhou Province Digital Economic Development Plan (2017-2020)"
Yunnan Province	2019.02.19	"Notice from the General Office of the People's Government of Yunnan Province on the Establishment of 'Digital Yunan' Group of Leaders"
Tibet Autonomous Region	2019.07.10	"Digital Economic Development Plan of the Tibet Autonomous Region (2019-2025)"
Shaanxi Province	2018.04.17	"Key Points for the Shaanxi Province Digital Economy in 2018"

Continued

Province/City	Time	Name of Policy
Gansu Province	2019.04.01	"Construction Plan for Gansu Province Digital Economy Innovation and Development Pilot Zone"
	2018.06.11	"Special Action Plan for the Development of Data Information Industry Development in Gansu Province"
Qinghai Province	2018.10.16	"Notice from the General Office of the People's Government of Qinghai Province on Establishing the Leaders Group for Coordinating and Promoting Digital Economy in Qinghai Province"
Tianjin	2019	"Action Plan for Promoting Digital Economic Development in Tianjin (2019-2023)"
Shenyang	2019.10.22	"Action Plan for Accelerating Digital Economic Development in Shenyang (2019-2021)"
	2019.05.23	"Several Policies for Supporting Digital Economic Development in Shenyang" (Draft for Comment)
Changchun	2018.07.27	"Opinions on Accelerating the Construction of Digital Changchun and Promoting the Comprehensive Vitalization of Old Industrial Bases"
Hangzhou	2018.10.09	"Hangzhou City's Action Plan for Completely Advancing Digital Industrialization, Industrial Digitization, and City Digitization to Build the City with the Best Digital Economy (2018-2022)"
Ningbo	2019.03.27	"Digital Ningbo Construction Plan (2018-2022)"
	2017.05.13	"The Middle and Long-term Development Plan for Ningbo to Become a Smart City (2016-2025)"
Hefei	2019.10.16	"Guidelines for the Construction of an Innovative Pilot Zone for Digital Economy in Hefei"
Fuzhou	2018.06.05	"Three-year Action Plan for the Construction of 'Digital Fuzhou' (2018-2020)"
Jinan	2019.01.03	"Several Policies and Measures for Promoting Advanced Manufacturing and Digital Economic Development in Jinan"
Qingdao	2019.07.10	"Digital Qingdao Development Plan (2019-2023)"
Nanning	2018.11.23	"Three-year Action Plan for the Development of the Digital Economy in Nanning (2018-2020)"
Chengdu	2019.03.01	"Implementation Plan for Promoting Digital Economic Development in Chengdu"

Source: China Academy of Information and Communications Technology and sorted data gathered online.

Chapter 3 Digital Economy and Industrial Upgrading

This chapter discusses the relationship between China's digital economy and industrial upgrading. The first section discusses the mechanism of the impact of digital economy on industrial upgrading. The second section introduces the general impact of digital economy on industrial upgrading. The third section introduces the impact of digital economy on industrial upgrading, focusing on key industries. The fourth section introduces the impact of digital economy on industrial upgrading from the perspective of enterprises.

Section 1   Impact of Digital Economy on Industrial Upgrading

1.1 Digital economy and restructuring of the internal value chain of enterprises

The development of digital technology restructures the internal value chain for enterprises, optimizing traditional business processes such as R&D, manufacturing, circulation, and sales.

During the process of research and development, the development of cloud platforms helps shorten the duration of R&D, and is especially beneficial to solve R&D-related issues for small and medium-sized enterprises caused by insufficient labor and lack of experience. Cloud application centers are often equipped with online R&D functions, which facilitate product design and simulation analysis. Simulation analysis plays an important role especially in mechanical design, electronic design, circuit simulation, weight estimation, etc. The emergence of collaborative R&D platforms helps enterprises reduce the cost of software resources and reduce the cost of trial and error. In addition, the database of the cloud platform can help analyze various data in the research and development process, visualize the data, and facilitate the real-time storage of research and development results, thus reducing the demand for hardware and ensuring the flexibility of research and development.

In terms of production, the promotion of the Industrial Internet and the Industrial Internet of Things allows more and more enterprises to take part in the construction of smart factories. The development of smart manufacturing gives rise to technological advancements such as remote control and automated assembly lines, which improves production efficiency comprehensively. In particular, when the demographic dividend is gradually disappearing, commissioning industrial robots to perform repetitive, simple, and dangerous tasks not only increases the density of technology, but also expands the boundaries of the curve of the possibility of production.

In terms of circulation, the loose distribution and the lack of timely feedback between supply and demand cause the supply chain to bring difficulties to enterprises. The creation of intelligent warehousing and digital logistics is solving such problems. For example, based on big data, third-party enterprises (represented by Cainiao) can predict business flows and consumer demand, and provide quick feedback for enterprises to stock up and distribute warehouses in a rational way. On the one hand, this approach reduces the occurrence of stockout, thus effectively reducing the risks of missing sales opportunities due to decision-making errors. On the other hand, it also increases the turnover rate and improves operational capabilities.

In terms of sales, big data can tap into customers' needs more precisely. On the one hand, algorithms can be used to push the information of existing products to potential customer groups. On the other hand, low-cost marketing can be achieved with tools such as mini-programs and corporate WeChat accounts to increase customer stickiness. In this process, the in-depth information of the customer group can be further investigated and reported to the production side, so that the production is fully integrated with the customers' needs. By recreating a streamlined management procedure that combines online and offline, the production side and the demand side are connected, and the production side is able to react to the market quickly, thereby introducing customized services that satisfy the diverse and multi-dimensional needs of users. Diversified production introduces economies of scope within enterprises, the production cost is diluted, and the overall competitiveness of enterprises is improved.

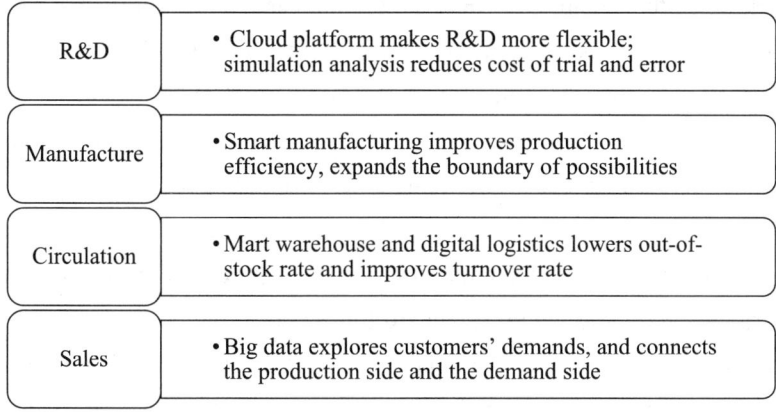

Figure 3.1   Impact of digital economy on the restructuring of the internal value chain of enterprises

1.2 Digital economy and restructuring of the value chain of the industry

The restructuring of the value chain within the industry changes the overall value acquisition mode of the industry. Under the traditional model, the way the manufacturing industry develops itself is through vertical integration. The logic of most enterprises is to reduce costs as much as possible, such as extending to the upstream to reduce production costs and extending to the downstream to reduce transaction costs. However, in digital economy, platform-oriented development becomes the main mode of upgrading. The platform-oriented economic model allows the once single form of business to transit toward complex modes of businesses and promotes a radical change in the business model through the establishment of a multilateral market, thereby forming a complete end-to-end platform. Platform-oriented development reshapes the composition of the value chain in many ways by influencing the forms of industries.

First, establishing a platform in the industry facilitates matching the supply side with the demand side. The presence of resources allows both parties to obtain more information at a lower cost and select more suitable products and resources. In addition, it also broadens the original customer base and focuses on the long-tail effect on the demand side. In the past, due to the constraints of geographical location, cost budget, and other factors, the focus was often on the "head" of the demand curve. However, platform-oriented development allows enterprises to be free from traditional methods such as printing and distributing flyers and buying billboards, which greatly reduces the marginal cost to attract customers.

Second, the development of the platforms improves the price mechanism, and the pricing is more precise. When the demand outweighs the supply, the platform would start automatic premium functions. For instance, there is a premium during rush hours for online car-hailing platforms, and there is an increase in delivery fees during the Spring Festival for takeaway platforms. On the contrary, when the demand is less than the supply, the platform would subsidize to stimulate consumption, such as online car-hailing discounts for ordering on workdays, and "red packets" (bonuses) for ordering afternoon tea/snacks on takeaway platforms. They are all reflections of the self-regulation of the price mechanism. Abundant data effectively regulates prices and alleviates the issues caused by asymmetric information between the supply and demand sides, avoiding the cost of bargaining and saving both sides from being taken advantage of.

Third, platforms can regulate the fair resolution of disputes and reduce maintenance costs. The platform-oriented economy would safeguard transactions, which is especially beneficial for small and micro-businesses to reduce the default rate and bad debt rate and protect the property of the enterprises. Platform-oriented development can improve the business environment within the industry. For example, platforms such as Taobao can guarantee the authenticity of products. Disputes can be resolved based on the records on the platform, which greatly reduces the maintenance cost of individual sellers and protects the interests of consumers.

Through platform-oriented development, the strategic advantages of various industries are no longer limited to the cost. Multilateral markets broaden consumer groups, and the value-added services embedded in the platform also become a new approach to value growth, thus expanding the space for value to grow. Under the influence of digital economy, the innovation of business models within the industry is complete.

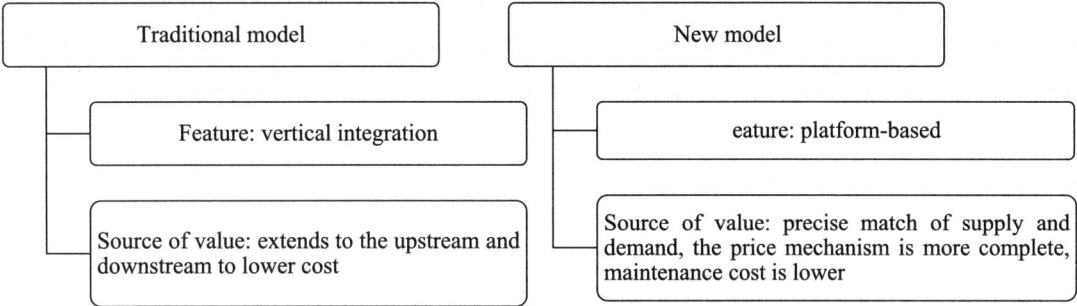

Figure 3.2 Comparison of modes of value acquisition within industries

1.3 Integration between digital economy and industries

Digital economy also promotes the transformation and upgrading of industries by accelerating the crossover and integration of industries. Internet finance, online education, mobile healthcare, online news, etc., are all new business formats or new models formed when traditional industries are merged with digital economy. According to data from the China Internet Network Information Center, as of June 2019, the numbers of users of online news, travel booking, online education, and Internet wealth management reached 686 million, 418 million, 232 million, and 170 million, respectively. The effect of industrial integration is significant.

Thanks to digital economy, many traditional industries have moved from offline to online and entered the field of technology industry. Taking online news as an example, new breakthroughs have been made in both news dissemination and news content. The advancement of Internet technology diversifies the dissemination of news. Multiple platforms such as WeChat corporate accounts and Weibo are integrated with the news industry. For instance, the *People's Daily* has adopted a variety of online platforms for news dissemination. In addition, the introduction of elements such as vlogs and short video clips by the news industry enriches news content. Keeping up with the times allows proper dissemination and attracts a bigger audience.

Another example is the emergence of online education. Digital technology changes the traditional model of education, and effectively alleviates the problem of the lack of teachers in remote areas. According to the data of iResearch Consulting, in the third quarter of 2019, users in Tier 5 cities and below accounted for the highest proportion in online education apps, reaching 21.5%. This means that the development of the Internet and communications technology solved the cost of movable distance. The results of this inter-industry integration achieve the goal of fully sharing educational resources, enabling underdeveloped areas to enjoy high-quality resources and enabling children from rural areas to immerse themselves in the classrooms of famous teachers across the country.

Internet finance is also a result of industrial integration formed under the development of digital technology, and is developing toward financial technology. Initially, financial businesses introduced IT facilities, then Internet financial services such as third-party payment, and now financial services begin to provide technical output in risk control and anti-fraud activities. The integration of the financial industry and the Internet industry drives the financial industry toward higher quality and completes the transformation and upgrading. The application of financial technology also improves the valuation level of enterprises, helps financial institutions safeguard their internal data security, and effectively mitigates payment security risks.

It shows that with the drive of digital technology, two or more industries begin to penetrate the same industrial chain, and even transform from low-end industries into the component of high-end industries. In this way, some traditional industries quickly elevate the relative position in the value chain. Crossover and integration make it possible for traditional industries to switch to higher positions in the value chain.

Online news
- Channels such as WeChat public accounts and Weibo diversify the means of dissemination
- Vlog and short video clips add more elements to the content of news

Online education
- The Internet and communication technology lower the accessibility cost of education resources, making education shared by more people

Internet finance
- The integration of Internet and finance improves the development quality and safety coefficient of financial industry

......

Figure 3.3 Impact of digital technology on the development of crossover and integration of traditional industries

Section 2 Digital Economy and China's Industrial Upgrading: An Overview

2.1 Industrialized development of digital economy

The industrialization of digital economy is the fundamental digital economy. With its continuous technological development and demand, digital economy has developed new business forms in recent years and has gradually formed an industrial chain. In 2018, the cumulative contribution rate of China's information transmission, software, and information services to GDP exceeded 15%. Since the fundamental digital economy started to develop, the industrial technology and industrial models have become stable and mature. This includes four industries: electronic information manufacturing, telecommunications, software and information technology services, and the Internet.

2.1.1 The electronic information manufacturing industry faces challenges but still has room for development

Due to the huge domestic and foreign demand for mobile phones, computers, and color TVs, China's electronic information manufacturing industry has been booming, ahead of the national average level. But in the past two years, due to the impact of trade friction, China's electronic information manufacturing industry has been faced with new challenges. The lack of core technology and R&D capabilities slows down the growth of the electronic information manufacturing industry. Although its added value remains positive, the growth rate drops significantly. In 2018, the monthly growth rate remained above 10%, with the lowest at 10.5%. However, the lowest monthly growth rate in 2019 was only 4.7% (see Figure 3.4).

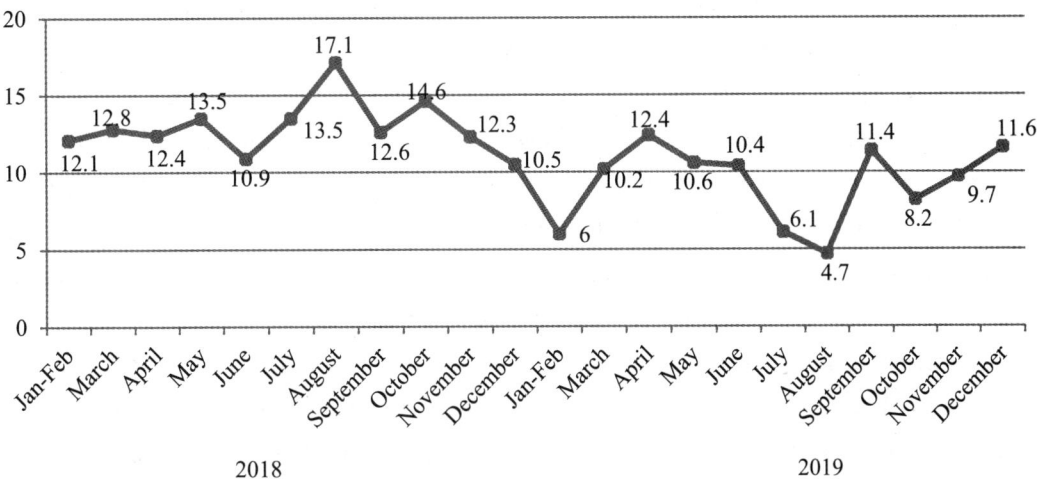

Figure 3.4 2018-2019 growth rate of added value of the electronic information manufacturing industry (%)

Source: Official website of the Ministry of Industry and Information Technology.

From the perspective of changes in revenue and profit growth, since 2018, the revenue of the electronic information manufacturing industry has been declining compared with the previous period. In 2018, the income of the main businesses of the electronic information manufacturers with annual revenue of more than 20 million yuan increased by 9.0% year-on-year, but the total revenue fell by 3.1%. The data for the first three quarters of 2019 is not optimistic either. Compared with 2017, it dropped significantly. The revenue in the past two years shows negative growth (see Figure 3.5).

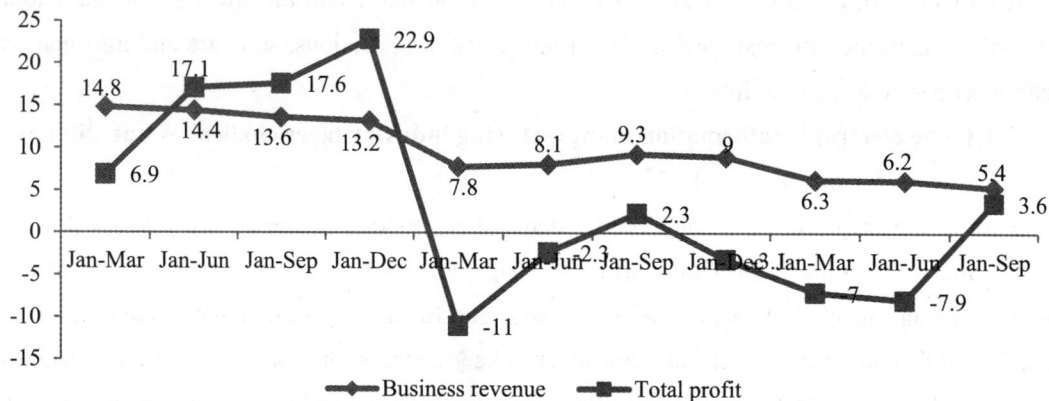

Figure 3.5 Changes in revenue and profit growth of the electronic information manufacturing industry since 2017 (%)

Source: Official website of the Ministry of Industry and Information Technology.

The reasons for the slow growth of China's electronic information manufacturing industry can be attributed to two aspects. First, previously, the industry already reached a certain scale, and it already experienced a period of steady growth. The economic dividends were gradually disappearing. Electronic information products were embracing a transition period, which drove electronic information manufacturing toward higher quality. The electronic information manufacturing industry is a technology-intensive industry. The long R&D cycle and high R&D cost of high-quality products make this industry enter a bottleneck. Second, since 2018, the US has imposed export restrictions on products of the integrated circuit industry, such as chips. Leading enterprises in the electronic information manufacturing industry, such as ZTE, Huawei, and Hikvision, have all been sanctioned to varying degrees. Meanwhile, in September 2019, the US Department of Defense, General Services Administration, and NASA jointly announced the prohibition of US contractors from purchasing equipment and technology from five Chinese companies, including Huawei, ZTE, and Hikvision. This increases the uncertainty in the demand of China's electronic information manufacturing industry, and causes a negative impact on the electronic information manufacturing industry and its upstream and downstream industries to some extent.

However, in recent years, China continues to introduce tax reduction policies for the electronic information manufacturing industry. In May 2019, according to the announcement of the Ministry of Finance and the State Administration of Taxation, qualified integrated circuit design enterprises and software enterprises that are established legally will enter a "preferential period" starting from December 31, 2018. During the first and second years, enterprises are exempted from corporate income tax. From the third to the fifth years, enterprises pay half of the 25% legal corporate income tax, until the end of the preferential period. This measure plays a significant role in increasing the intensity of corporate R&D, encouraging the development of related industries, and improving the business environment. Although the development of the industry has experienced twists and turns, new and stable growth points will emerge with the advent of the 5G era. The improvement of 5G technology will undoubtedly introduce a large amount of demand for related equipment. From the statistics, China's integrated circuit output has been increasing over the past decade. The output in 2018 was 40 times higher than that of 2009 (see Figure 3.6). In 2018, the output of microcomputer equipment, laptops, and monitors in China was 307 million, 173 million, and 166 million, respectively. The development momentum of the industrialization of China's digital economy is steadily improving, and a fixed industry model has been formed.

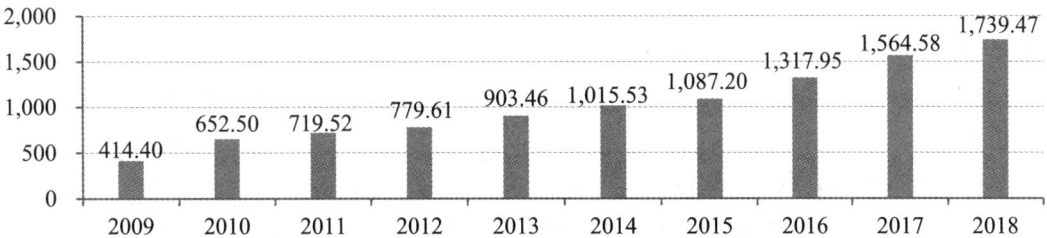

Figure 3.6　2009-2018 changes in integrated circuit production in China (100 million pieces)

Source: National Bureau of Statistics.

Furthermore, China's development in intelligent manufacturing and the Internet of Things optimizes the environment of the fundamental digital economy. The fundamental digital economy and the emerging digital economy complement each other and form a virtuous circle, which will further stimulate the vitality of the electronic information manufacturing industry. The advantages of the electronic information manufacturing industry still remain, and the future development prospects are very bright.

2.1.2 Transformation and upgrading of the telecommunications industry and the continuous optimization of the internal structure

The scale of revenue of the telecommunications industry was comparable in recent years, but the internal structure is undergoing changes. From the perspective of telecommunications services, due to changes in people's lifestyles, instant messaging services such as WeChat are gradually replacing traditional telephone services. As of June 2019, the scale of instant messaging users in China reached 825 million. Mobile phone call service is no longer the main source of income in the telecommunications industry. In recent years, the length of outgoing calls on mobile phones has continued to decrease. In 2019, the revenue of telephone service decreased by 15.5% compared to 2018. On the contrary, the volume and revenue of mobile SMS businesses keep growing. Driven by services such as SMS advertisement push and verification code authentication, the volume of mobile SMS business enters a stage of rapid growth. In 2019, the volume of mobile SMS business increased by 37.5% compared with the previous year. Meanwhile, mobile Internet services become a major component of the revenue of telecom businesses, and the average mobile Internet access traffic per household continues to increase. In 2019, the monthly average mobile Internet access traffic per household reached 7.82GB per household.

From the perspective of the development of telecommunications users, the number of mobile phone users in 2019 exceeded 1.6 billion, and the proportion of 4G users grew steadily. According to data from the Ministry of Industry and Information Technology, by the end of 2019, the number of 4G users was 1.28 billion, accounting for 80.1% of mobile phone users. Secondly, users of fixed Internet broadband access continue to grow rapidly. The gigabit era has arrived. In 2019, the total number of users of fixed Internet broadband access of three major telecommunications companies reached 449 million. The number of fixed Internet broadband access users with an access rate of 100Mbps and above reached 384 million, accounting for 85.4% of the total number of users. The number of users with 1,000Mbps and above reached 870,000.

The popularity of 4G and the development of 5G have brought new vitality to the telecommunications industry in recent years. Driven by the demand for the Internet of Things, the construction of infrastructure of China's telecommunications industry gradually improves, and communication capabilities continue to grow. By the end of June 2019, the number of Internet broadband access ports reached 903 million nationwide, an increase of 22.19% in two years. In the first half of 2019 alone, the length of new optical cable pipelines nationwide reached 1.87 million kilometers, and the total length of optical cable pipelines reached 45.46 million kilometers (see Figure 3.7).

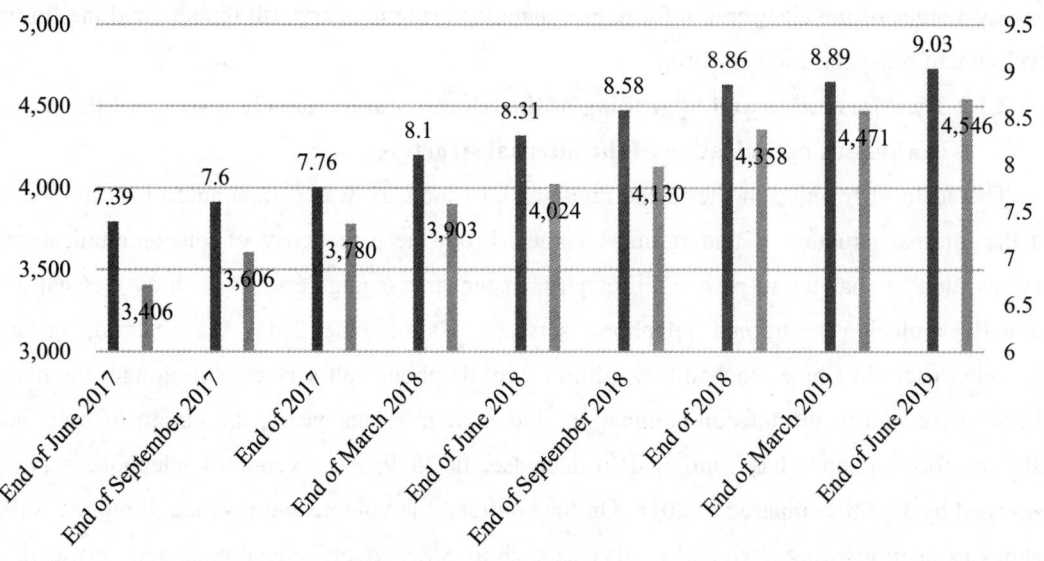

Figure 3.7 Communication capabilities of the telecommunications industry from June 2017 to June 2019

Source: Official website of the Ministry of Industry and Information Technology.

2.1.3 The software and information technology service industry shares a huge market and the revenue continues to grow

In the past two years, China's software industry has developed steadily and progressed, and it is becoming an important force in the development of digital economy. The advent of the intelligent age further increases the demand for the software industry, and business revenue and total profits continue to grow. In 2019, the revenue of China's software businesses reached 7,176.8 billion yuan, a continuous rise for many years, and about 5.28 times higher than that of 10 years ago (see Figure 3.8). Meanwhile, per capita business income was 1.066 million yuan, a year-on-year increase of 8.7%, and the total industry profit reached 936.2 billion yuan, a year-on-year increase of 9.9%. Industry profits attract a continuous increase in the number of employees. By the end of 2019, the average number of employees in the software industry in China reached 6.73 million, an increase of 280,000 over the end of the previous year.

In terms of different fields, the sub-industries of the software industry include software products, information technology services, information security products, and embedded products. In 2019, the revenue of each category of products accounted for 28.0%, 59.3%, 1.8%, and 10.9% respectively. The revenue of software products grew steadily, and the demand for industrial software increased significantly with a revenue of 172 billion yuan, an increase of 14.6%. The revenue of information technology services increased slightly, reaching 4,257.4 billion yuan. Due to the vigorous development of cloud computing, big data, and e-commerce platforms, the corresponding technical services generated significant revenue. Cloud services and big data services achieved revenues of 346 billion yuan, and technical services on e-commerce platforms received revenues of 790.5 billion yuan. Information security is an emerging business form. As residents raise their awareness of privacy and security, the market size of information security products is expanding. In 2019, the revenue of information security products and services received a total revenue of 130.8 billion yuan. Embedded products are an indispensable key factor in China's digitalization and intelligence, with a revenue of 782 billion yuan.

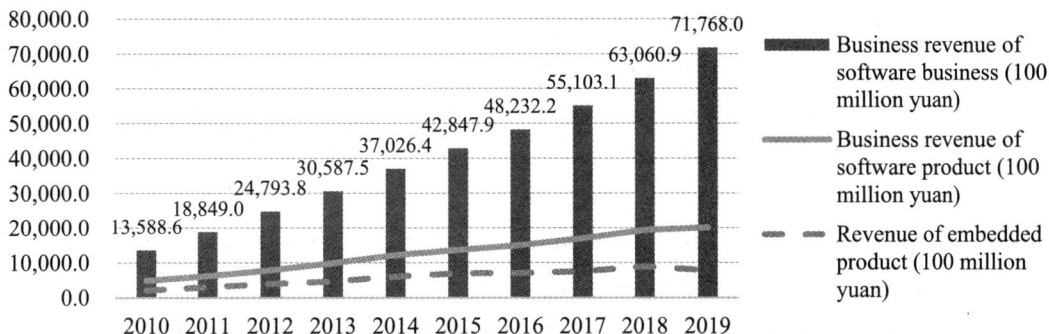

Figure 3.8   2010-2019 development of the software industry

Source: Compiled from public information.

2.1.4 The Internet industry is ascending with booming diversified demand

China's Internet and related service industries are developing steadily with positive momentum. Business revenue, profits, and R&D investment are all growing, and various Internet service businesses are developing rapidly. The Internet industry has many forms of demand, involving many fields such as online music, online video, and online reading. As of June 2019, the numbers of users of online video, online news, and online food delivery in China were 759 million, 686 million, and 421 million, respectively. According to the 2019 Express data, the business revenue of China's Internet enterprises was 1,206.1 billion yuan, a year-on-year increase of 21.4%. The industry achieved a total operating profit of 120.4 billion yuan and invested 53.5 billion yuan in research and development. In terms of different businesses, in 2019, the revenue of information service reached 787.9 billion yuan, that of Internet platform service enterprises was 319.3 billion yuan, and that of Internet data service achieved by Internet enterprises was 11.62 billion yuan (see Figure 3.9).

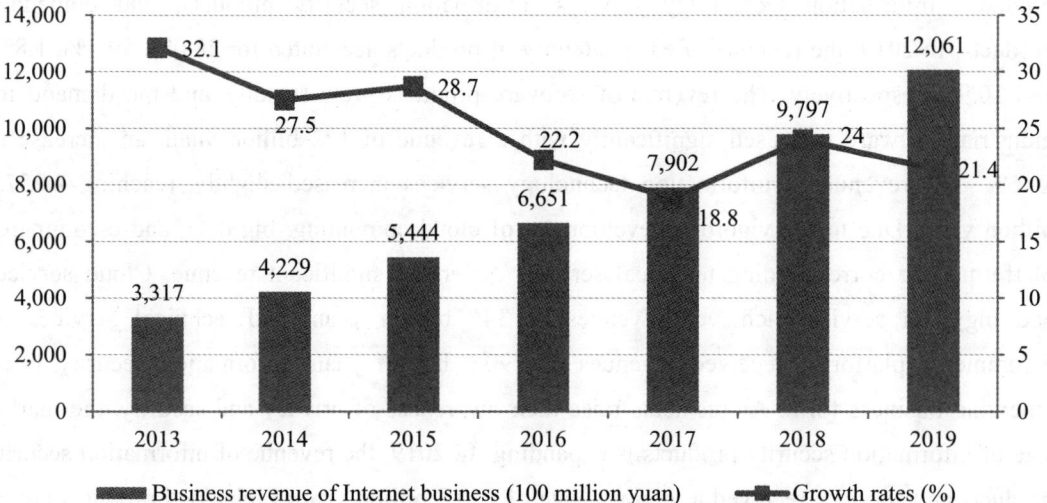

Figure 3.9   2013-2019 development of the Internet industry

Source: Official website of the Ministry of Industry and Information Technology.

The development of the Internet industry profoundly changes the lifestyle of residents, and people's consumption habits are slowly changing. With the transformation of traditional payment methods, the market size of third-party payments is rapidly expanding. According to statistics, the market size of third-party payments in 2018 was 190.5 trillion yuan, while the market size in 2009 was only 0.5440 trillion yuan. This amount increased by 350 times (see Figure 3.10). Meanwhile, according to the data released by the Central Bank, the business volume of electronic payments also increased rapidly in 2018. Banking financial institutions processed a total of 175.192 billion electronic payment transactions, of which 57.013 billion were online payments and 60.531 billion were mobile payments. Year-on-year increases were 17.36% and 61.19% respectively.

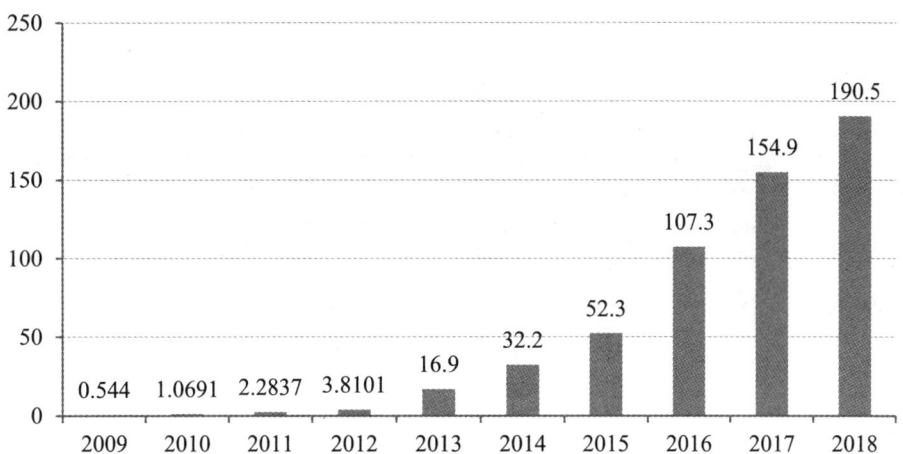

Figure 3.10 Changes in the scale of the third-party payment market from 2009 to 2018 (trillion yuan)
Source: Wind.

By the end of June 2019, the number of Internet users in China reached 855 million, and the Internet penetration rate was 61.2%. As the Internet penetration rate continues to rise, the demographic dividend of the Internet industry is disappearing. Due to the popularization of electronic devices such as smartphones, the traffic and stickiness of PC-side Internet users are constantly declining. According to data from iResearch, in September 2019, the monthly coverage of PC Internet users in China was 499 million, a year-on-year decrease of 2.8%. The loss of PC users has become a trend. In the third quarter of 2019, the total length of visits per capita and the number of visits per capita decreased by 11.8% and 5.7% respectively year-on-year.

2.2 Digitalized development of traditional industries

The digitization of traditional industries refers to the overflow and penetration of digital technologies such as cloud computing, big data, artificial intelligence, and the Internet of Things into traditional industries such as R&D, procurement, production, sales, and services, thereby enabling the innovation, production, and management practices of traditional industries to be constantly improved. According to data from the Institute of Information and Communications Technology, in 2018, the scale of China's industrial digitalization reached 24.9 trillion yuan, accounting for about 80% of the growth of digital economy. It has maintained an upward trend in recent years. Industrial digitalization has become the main driving force of the development of digital economy, as shown in Figure 3.11. With the in-depth integration of digital technology and traditional industries, total factor productivity continues to increase and a series of new models and formats emerge, providing a direction for China to optimize the industrial structure, transform the economic growth model, and seek new momentum for economic development.

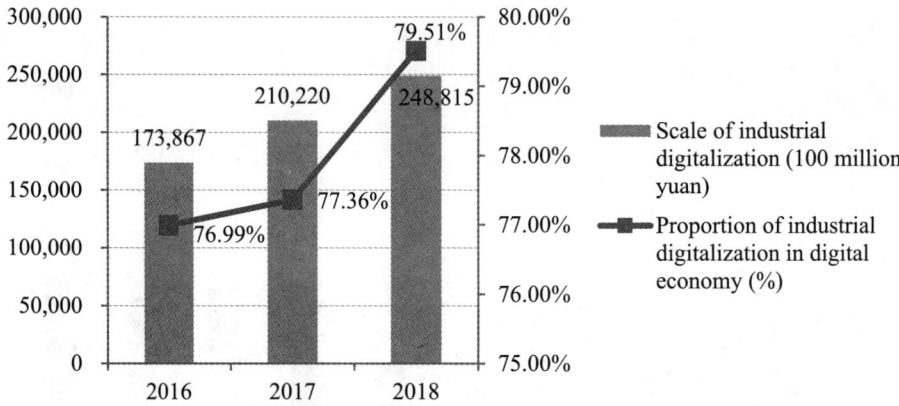

Figure 3.11 Scale of industrial digitalization and its proportion in digital economy
Source: China Academy of Information and Communications Technology.

The combination of traditional industries and digital technology generates a convergent economy. The level of the combination of industrialization and informatization reflects the development level and trend of this convergent economy. The integration of industrialization and informatization index is an indicator to measure the development level of industrialization and informatization integration of enterprises. It mainly evaluates three major aspects: enterprises' basic environment index, industrial application index, and application benefit index. The goal is to accelerate the digitalization, level of networking, and intellectualization for enterprises. The higher the integration index is, the higher level the integration industrialization and informatization of enterprises is, and the higher level the digitalization of China's traditional industries is. Figure 3.12 shows that from 2012 to 2019, the integration index in China continued to increase, reflecting the gradual increase in the digitalization of China's traditional industries.

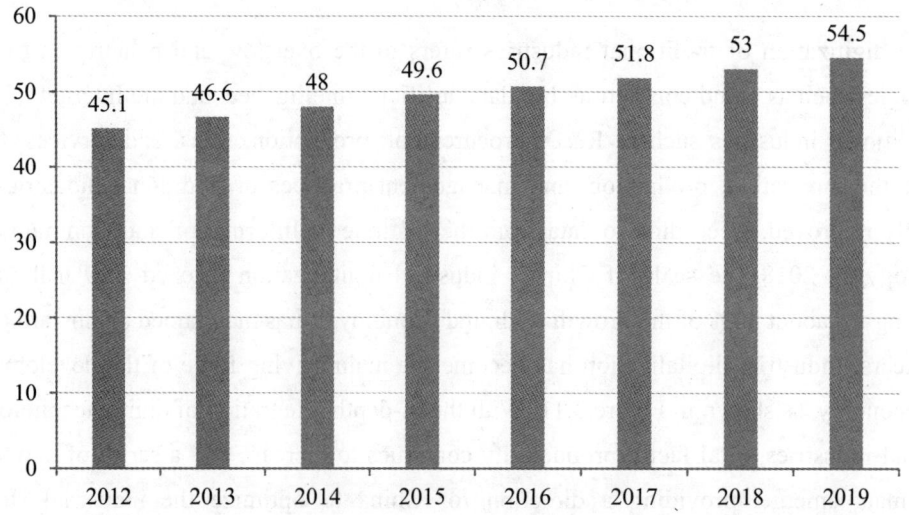

Figure 3.12 Integrationindex of informatization and industrialization
Source: Service platform website of informatization and industrialization.

2.2.1 New infrastructure: the foundation for the digitalization of traditional industries

After the agricultural economy and industrial economy, human society has now entered digital economy era. In the agricultural era, land and labor were the main production factors, whereas in the industrial era, technology and capital are the main production factors. In the digital economy era, data is the most important production factor. The effective application of data determines the digitalization process of all industries. Therefore, new infrastructure, represented by cloud-network-terminal (cloud computing, the Internet/Internet of Things, smart terminal/APP) plays a detrimental role in the digitalization of traditional industries. As shown in Figure 3.13, in addition to cloud-network-terminal, new technologies such as big data, artificial intelligence, blockchains, and biometrics work together and merge with traditional industries and jointly promote the digitalized development of traditional industries. Generally, before the economic potential bursts out, new technologies would go through a period when it popularizes related facilities, so the application of these facilities can reflect the degree of digitalization of industries.

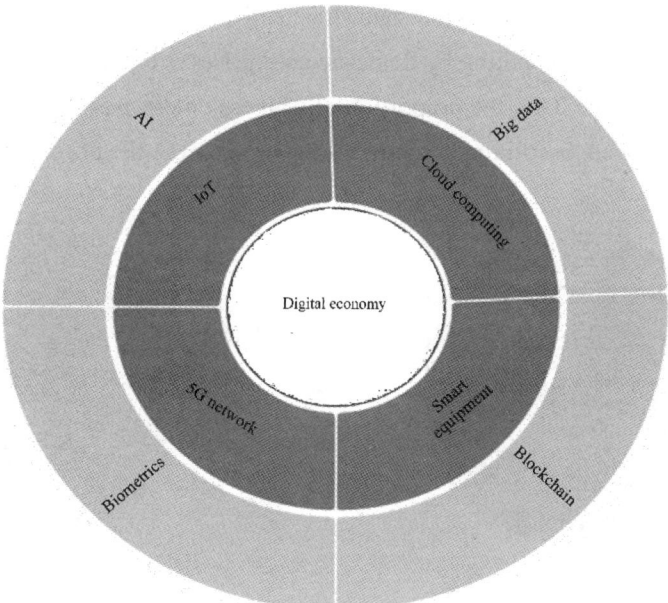

Figure 3.13   Infrastructure and technology system of digital economy
Source: AliResearch.

(1) Cloud computing

The National Institute of Standards and Technology (NIST) defines cloud computing as a pay-as-you-go model. Users can access a configurable computing resource sharing pool through available, convenient, and on-demand network access provided by the model. Cloud computing has three service models and three deployment methods (see Figure 3.14).

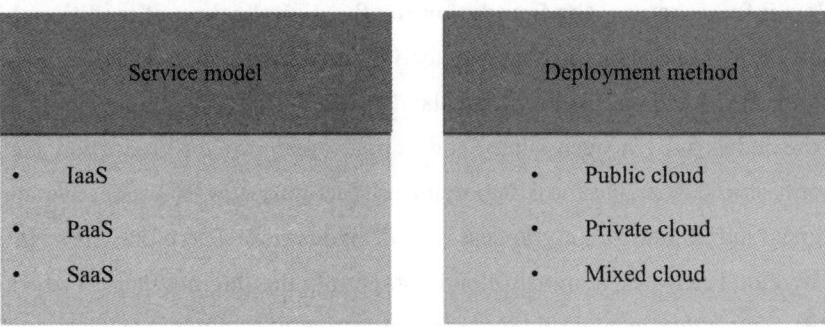

Figure 3.14 Service model and deployment method of cloud computing
Source: Qianzhan Industry Research Institute.

China's cloud computing started in 2007 and has now matured. However, compared with the US, it is still about five years behind. It is in the stage of widespread application. According to Figure 3.15, the proportion of public and private clouds globally in 2018 increased compared with the previous year, and the proportion of using at least one public cloud or private cloud was 96%. Cloud computing has become the mainstream in the construction of IT for enterprises. Although the use of cloud computing by domestic enterprises is extensive, it still lags behind the world. As shown in Figure 3.16, the proportion of Chinese enterprises using cloud computing in 2018 totaled 58.6%. There is still much room for improvement in the utilization rate.

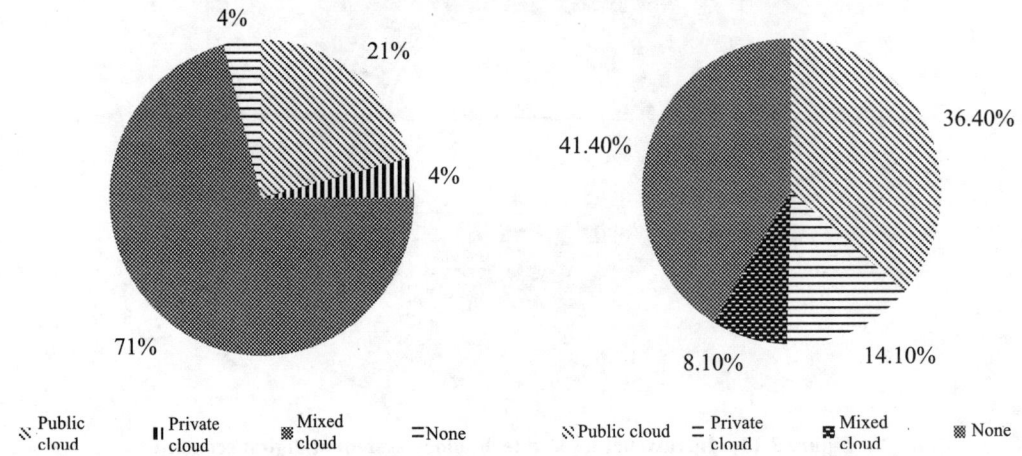

Figure 3.15 Utilization of cloud computing by enterprises worldwide in 2018
Source: RightScale "2018 Cloud Computing Research Report".

Figure 3.16 Utilization of cloud computing by enterprises in China in 2018
Source: China Academy of Information and Communications Technology.

From the perspective of industries, currently, users of cloud computing are mainly from the Internet, transportation, logistics, finance, telecommunications, government, and other fields. In recent years, the amount of data in various industries has increased significantly, with more and more fields starting to tap into the value of data with cloud computing technology. Although the Internet industry is still dominant, the scale of cloud computing in traditional industries such as transportation logistics and finance also constitutes a big presence (see Figure 3.17).

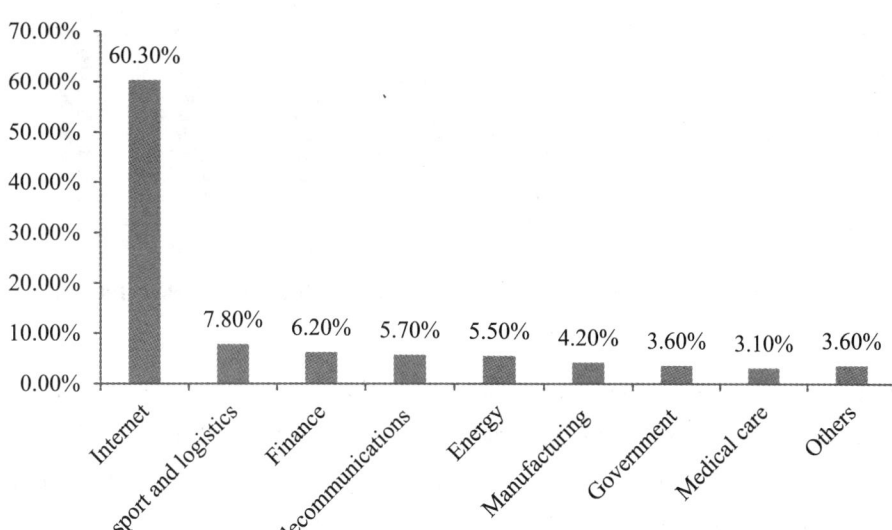

Figure 3.17 Structure of China's cloud computing industry in 2018
Source: Qianzhan Industry Research Institute.

(2) The Internet of Things + 5G

The Internet of Things is a highly integrated and comprehensive application of the new generation of information technology. It is an important foundation for national strategies such as "Cyberpower" and "Made in China 2025", and plays an important role in the upgrading and optimization of industrial structure. The landing of the Internet of Things in industry is the "Industrial Internet of Things", which is the nervous system of intelligent manufacturing. The Industrial Internet of Things is a high-level integration of industrial systems and the Internet, advanced computing, analysis, and sensing technologies. It is also a high-level integration of industrial production and processing and the Internet of Things. It integrates manufacturing, monitoring, enterprise management, supply chain, and the information system such as customer feedback, and intelligently processes data from different channels through the data center, thereby improving production efficiency.

Having been through conceptual speculation, fragmented applications, and closed-loop development, China's Internet of Things has entered a new stage of crossover and integration, integrated innovation, and large-scale development. It is playing an important role in the transformation and upgrading of traditional industries, urbanization, informatization, and agricultural modernization. As shown in Figure 3.18, as for the scale of industry, China's Internet of Things has grown rapidly in recent years, and the market size in 2019 reached 1.77 trillion yuan. The future growth of the Internet of Things market is promising, and the market size is expected to exceed 2 trillion yuan in 2020.

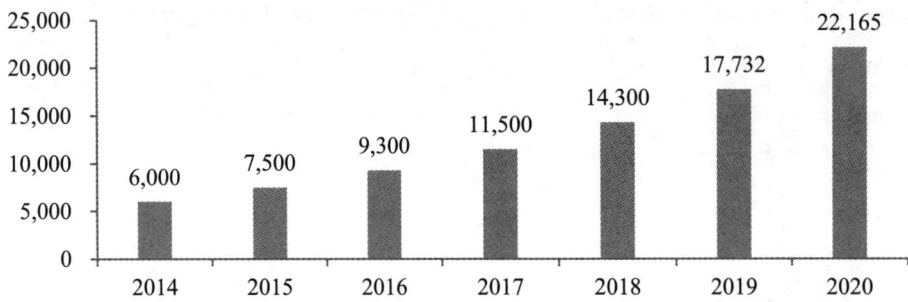

Figure 3.18 2014-2020 summary and forecast of the scale of China's IoT market (100 million yuan)
Source: Chinese Academy of Industry Economy Research.

As more and more enterprises start to use IoT devices and technologies, the data collected in the future will increase exponentially. Traditional technologies will not be able to meet the needs of data transmission and computing. 5G technology will effectively solve this problem. Miao Wei, Minister of the Ministry of Industry and Information Technology, commented that 80% of 5G applications will be communication between things, that is, the Internet of Things will be the main scenario in which 5G technology will be utilized, and the development of 5G plays a critical role on the construction of the Internet of Things. In 2019, China entered the pre-commercial stage, and will soon enter the stage of large-scale commercial use. It is estimated that in 2025, the scale of the 5G market will reach the trillion level, which will benefit the entire industry chain. China's 5G development is in a leading position in the world. Huawei's 5G network patents are far ahead. The number of patents of ZTE and the Datang Group is also among the top 10 in the world. Looking forward, it is expected to accelerate the digital transformation of various industries through 5G.

(3) Smart terminal

Smart terminals, also known as smart hardware, utilize new-generation information technologies such as smart sensor interconnection, biometrics, new displays, and cloud computing, with new designs, new materials, and hardware manufactured by new processes as carriers, and platform-based underlying hardware and software. Smart terminals are the foundation for "things online". In the past 20 years, the terminals were mainly mobile phones, computers, and mobile phone applications. Looking forward, smart terminals will be more diverse based on the mature Internet of Things, including not only smart devices in daily life, but also various equipment on the production side.

2.2.2 Digitalization of traditional industries introduces new models and formats

With the improvement of industrial digitalization and the country's strong support for developing new manufacturing models, the production, organization, and services of traditional industries are shifting toward networked collaborative manufacturing, service-oriented manufacturing, and customization.

Under networked collaborative manufacturing, enterprises overcome the communication barriers between consumers and upstream and downstream partners with the Internet on the consumer and production ends, and encourage multiple parties to join the company's R&D and production activities, making enterprises' activities more efficient and more targeted. From 2013 to 2018, the proportion of enterprises in China that achieved networked collaboration increased from 23.3% to 33.7%, with an average annual growth rate of 8.9% (see Figure 3.19).

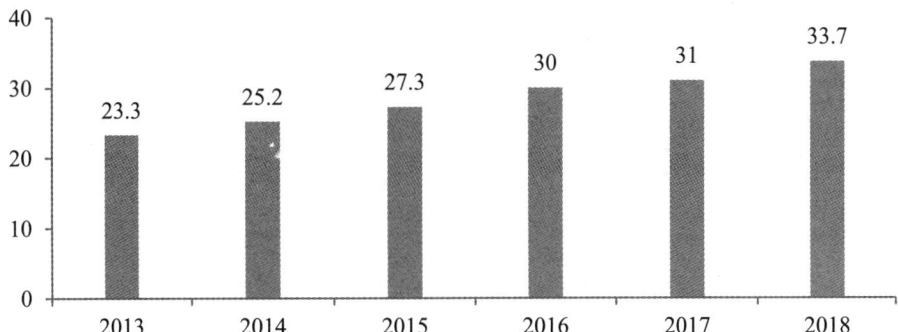

Figure 3.19 Proportion of enterprises achieving networked collaboration (%)
Source: Service platform website of informatization and industrialization.

For a long time, China has been relying too much on the demographic dividend to participate in the international division of labor. As labor costs rise, China is bound to lose its competitive advantage in the international market. Service-oriented manufacturing is to make service an important part of the added value of the manufacturing industry, so that enterprises can move toward the ends of the smiling curve to obtain more value. Figure 3.20 shows that in 2018, the proportion of enterprises providing service-oriented manufacturing in China reached 24.7%, an increase of about two times compared with 2013, which is significant progress.

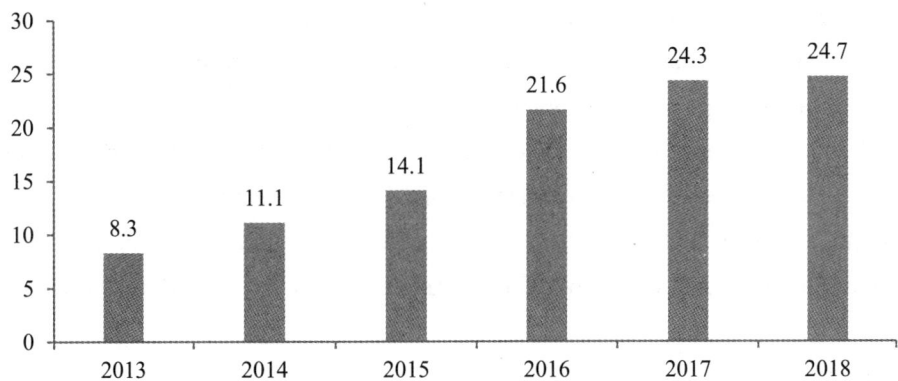

Figure 3.20 Proportion of enterprises providing service-oriented manufacturing (%)
Source: Service platform website of informatization and industrialization.

ICTs such as smart terminals, the Internet, big data, and cloud computing allow enterprises to understand customer needs more easily, accurately, and faster. With these technologies, customization comes very naturally. Enterprises collect customer information through the Internet, conduct targeted R&D, design, and manufacturing, and form positive interactions with customers, dynamically following changes in customer needs and enhancing customer loyalty. Figure 3.21 indicates that the proportion of enterprises carrying out customization in China increases year by year since 2013 with a visible growth rate. The proportion in 2018 was about three times that in 2013.

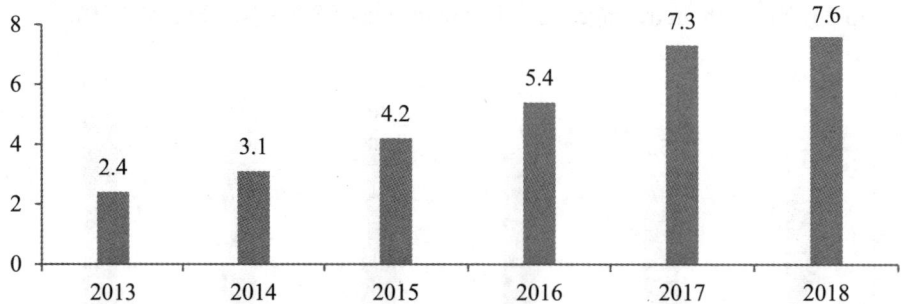

Figure 3.21   Proportion of enterprises carrying out customization (%)

Source: Service platform website of informatization and industrialization.

The above three aspects suggest that with the help of digital technology, China's industrial transformation and upgrading have shown initial results. Looking forward, it is expected that the economic development model and the quality of economic growth will improve with the full awareness of allowing the digital economy to exercise its power.

2.2.3 E-commerce platforms promote the digitalization of traditional industries

In the digital economy era, platforms are the fundamental organization for coordinating and allocating resources. Among them, e-commerce platforms play an important role in business society. Fast and accurate matching between the supply and demand parties through the platform helps save transaction, searching, and contracts costs, and helps reduce information asymmetry between the two parties and improve the quality of the transaction. Meanwhile, with the help of big data, cloud computing, and other technologies, platforms also refine user information and provide user portraits to guide the supplier's R&D, manufacturing, and services to meet the diverse needs of consumers. As a result, enterprises manufacture according to need and their dependence on data increases, thus breaking the traditional production model and regrouping into a new model with a higher level of data utilization. Through aggregation and diffusion, changes at the enterprise level will lead to digital transformation and upgrading of the industry as a whole.

(1) To B

Corporate procurement e-commerce can be divided into a "platform-based" model and a "self-operated" model according to the operating model. Platform-based e-commerce focuses on the role of platforms to integrate information. They are like transaction brokers that match buyers and sellers for transactions without participating in the construction of supply chains. In this model, the platform will provide services such as brand building, marketing, and assistance in product upgrade and development so as to help enterprises increase the number of acquired customers and customer stickiness. Self-operated e-commerce enterprises participate in the supply chain and build their own systems for purchasing, warehousing, and distribution to provide customers with sources of goods. Currently, there are more platform-based models in China's corporate procurement e-commerce market. These platforms use their ability to match resources so as to empower enterprises, thereby promoting the digitalized transformation of the industry. As Figure 3.22 shows, China's B2B e-commerce has been developing in recent years. In 2018, the transaction scale reached 1.95 billion and the online penetration rate reached 15.5%.

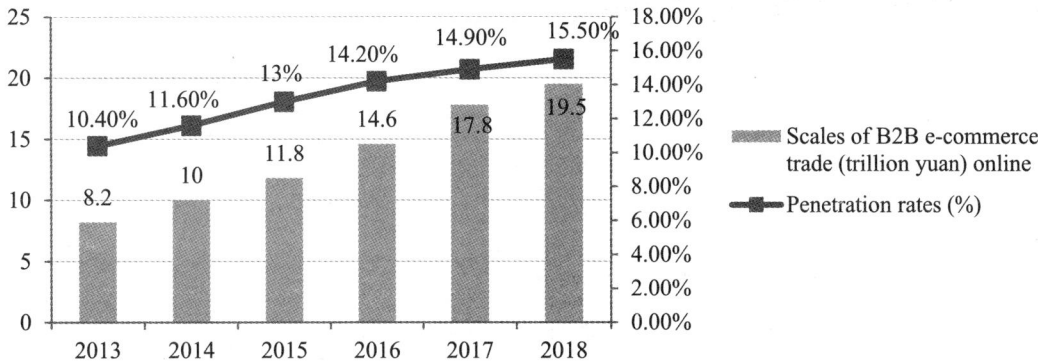

Figure 3.22   2013-2018 scales and online penetration rates of China's B2B e-commerce transaction
Source: iResearch Consulting.

(2) To C

Like enterprise e-commerce, the "to C" e-commerce platform provides vendors with consumption big data, such as order data, traffic data, and customer group data, to provide guidance for manufacturing, help manufacturers predict sales, and realize customization, thus helping manufacturers realize smart manufacturing and promote the development of industrial digitization.

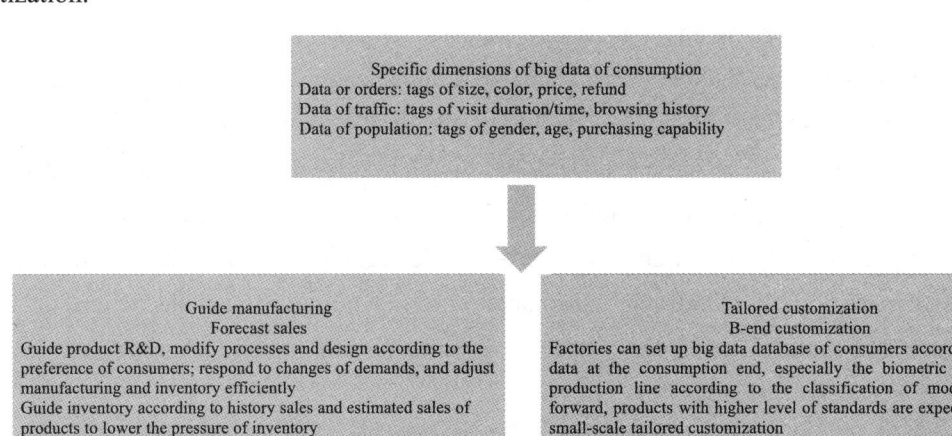

Figure 3.23   Consumption big data helps smart manufacturing
Source: iResearch Consulting.

(3) Development of e-commerce in various industries

As shown in Figure 3.24, the top five industries in e-commerce transactions in 2018 were accommodation and catering, cultural and sports entertainment, wholesale and retail, manufacturing, and leasing and business services (information transmission and software and information technology services belong to digital industrialization, therefore were excluded from consideration). According to the current development of various industries, the level of digitization for these industries is relatively high. It suggests that e-commerce plays a role in the digitization of traditional industries.

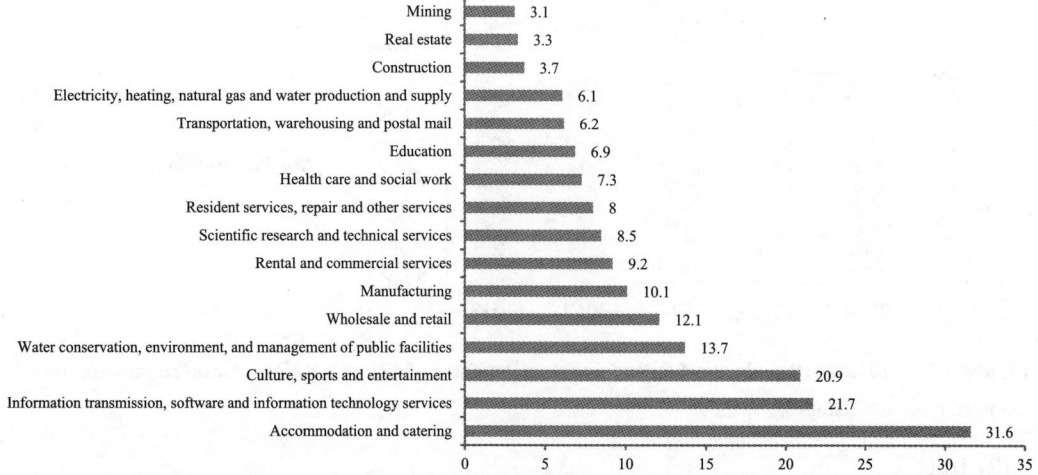

Figure 3.24 Proportions of enterprises with e-commerce transaction activities in various industries in 2018 (%)

Source: National Bureau of Statistics.

2.3 Development of digital economy in the tertiary industry

2.3.1 An overview

According to the "White Paper on China's Digital Economic Development and Employment (2019)", the scale of China's industrial digitalization exceeded 24.9 trillion yuan in 2018, accounting for 27.6% of the GDP. However, the level of development of digital economy among industries varies. The service industry has the highest level of development. In 2018, the proportion of digital economy accounted for 35.9% of the service industry's added value, followed by industry, accounting for 18.3%, while agriculture has the lowest level of digitization, only 7.3%. (Electronic information manufacturing is excluded from industry; information and communication services and software and information technology services are excluded from the service industry.)

Figure 3.25 shows that from 2016 to 2018, the proportions of digital economy in agriculture, industry, and service industries increased year by year. In addition, the average growth rate and absolute level of the digitalization of the three industries present a similar pattern, with the service industry, industry, and agriculture in descending order.

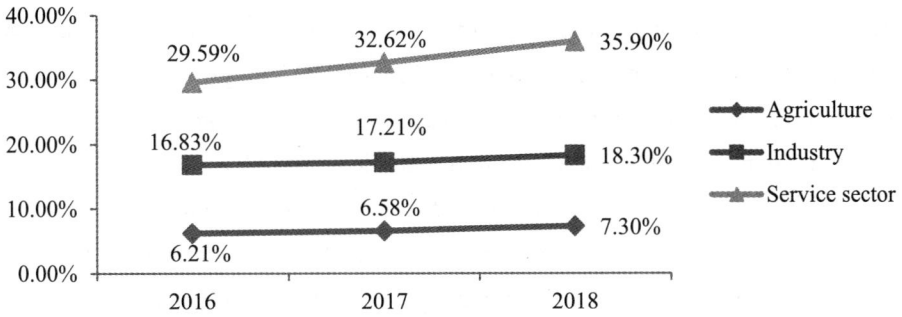

Figure 3.25 2016-2018 changes of the proportions of digital economy in China's tertiary industry
Source: China Academy of Information and Communications Technology.

2.3.2 Industry-specific

(1) The level of agricultural digitalization is less advanced

According to data from China Academy of Information and Communications Technology, the proportion of China's agricultural digital economy in 2018 was only 7.3%, much lower than those of the industrial and service industries. Based on the input-output table, the proportion of the ICT industry as an intermediate input of the three industries can be calculated. This proportion represents the utilization rate of ICT in the three industries and can reflect the level of digitalization of the three industries. Figure 3.26 shows that the utilization rate of ICT in China's agriculture is much lower than those of the secondary and tertiary industries. This is consistent with the conclusion drawn by China Academy of Information and Communications Technology. The digitalized transformation process of China's agriculture indeed lags behind.

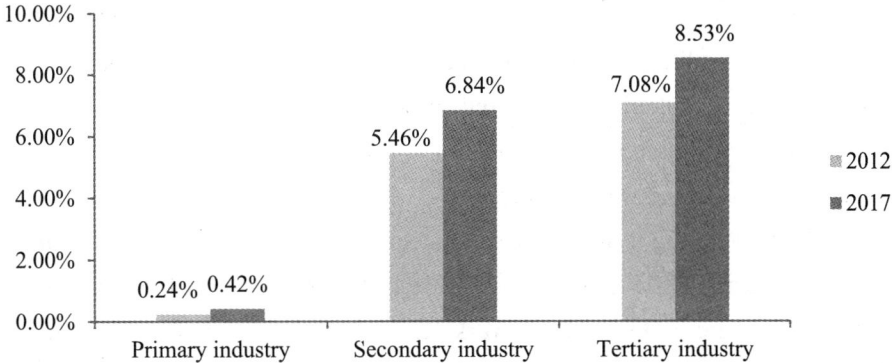

Figure 3.26 Proportions of ICT in the intermediate input of the three industries in 2012 and 2017
Source: National Bureau of Statistics.

The digitalization of agriculture focuses on the application of emerging technologies in agricultural production, such as big data, artificial intelligence, the Internet of Things, remote sensing, GPS, and geographic information system (3S). At present, the development of digitalized agriculture in China is in the early stage, so there are different opinions about the mature model of digitalized agriculture. Tianfeng Securities believes that a mature digitalized agriculture consists of the agricultural Internet of Things, agricultural big data, precision agriculture, and smart agriculture. The agricultural Internet of Things collects agricultural data. Precision agriculture and smart agriculture process the data into agricultural big data. After analysis and extraction, agricultural data can in turn guide other links.

Technical methods induced by the integration of digital technology and traditional agriculture can effectively solve the problems in agricultural production. According to the "Agricultural Information Technology Development Research Report", in agricultural plantation, technologies such as the agricultural Internet of Things, integration of water and fertilizer, and unmanned remote sensing can make the dosage of fertilizers, pesticides, and water more accurate and improve efficiency. In husbandry, the husbandry Internet of Things and artificial intelligence can effectively solve the problems of high feed costs, poor breeding environments, and low labor efficiency. In fishery, i.e. the aquaculture industry, the aquaculture Internet of Things can reduce breeding water pollution and unregulated administration of medication.

In 2011, China issued the "Twelfth Five-Year Plan for the Development of National Agricultural and Rural Informatization", which marks the official launch of the construction of agricultural informatization in China. In the past two years, China has paid more and more attention to the development of agriculture and rural areas, and has introduced related policies, especially the "rural revitalization" strategy proposed in the report of the 19th National Congress, which emphasized the importance of building the agricultural Internet of Things and promoting the development of agricultural science and technology. In the process of implementing these policies, agricultural digitalization-related projects can receive high subsidies and a variety of preferential policies, the implementation of projects accelerates, and the integration of ICT with agriculture will also go further. On the other hand, the continuous progress of emerging technologies and the reduction of costs of utilization will also accelerate the advancement of agricultural digitalization.

(2) Steady progress of industrial digitization

Intelligent manufacturing is an important strategic deployment for China to realize Industry 4.0 and "Made in China 2025", which emphasizes the application of digital technology in industry. The 2019 Chinese Government Work Report stated: "We will ... expand 'Intelligent Plus' initiatives to facilitate transformation and upgrading in manufacturing." Industrial robots, industrial Internet, industrial software, industrial cloud platforms, etc., are important foundations for building intelligent manufacturing. Their development and penetration in the industry reflect the level of industrial digitalization.

1) Industrial robots

Industrial robots refer to multi-joint robotic arms or multi-degree-of-freedom mechanical devices that are able to perform tasks automatically and perform various functions with their own power and control capabilities. Industrial robots are used in traditional production processes such as moving, welding, assembly, and disassembly. The automation of industry is a key task in the initial stage of intelligent manufacturing.

According to the IFR's (International Federation of Robotics) "World Robotics 2019", from 2016 to 2018, the operational inventory (total number of robots used at the time) and installations (the number of new robots at the time) of China's industrial robots topped the world. In other words, China's industrial robot market is the largest and fastest-growing market in the world. As shown in Figure 3.27, in 2018, the operating inventory of China's industrial robots reached 649,447, an increase of about four times compared to 132,784 in 2013, with a compound annual growth rate of 37%.

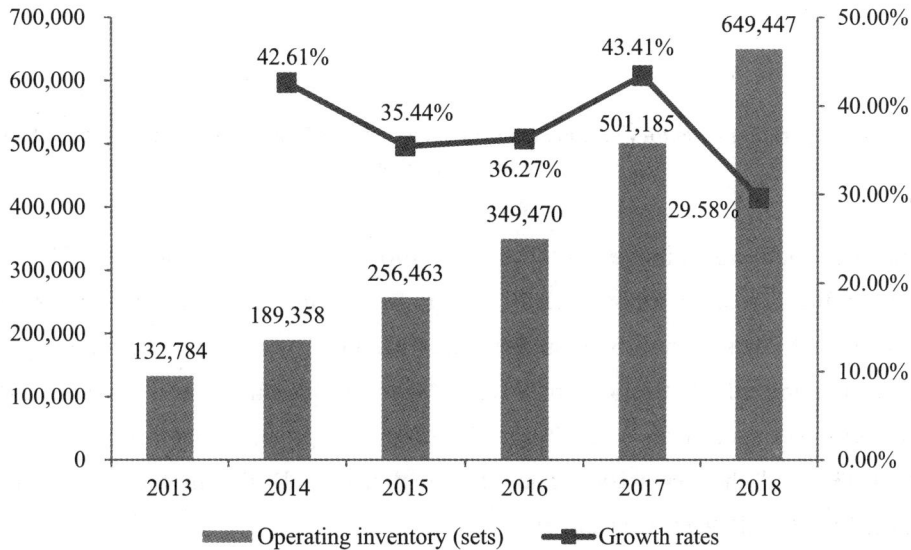

Figure 3.27 2013-2018 China's industrial robot operating inventory

Source: IFR.

On the other hand, as for industry distribution, in 2018, the operating inventory of industrial robots in the manufacturing industry was 524,273, accounting for 82% of the total operating inventory of 649,447, indicating that most industrial robots were deployed in the manufacturing sector. Figure 3.28 shows the deployment of industrial robots in various segments of the manufacturing industry in 2018. The application volume of industrial robots in the automotive industry and the electronics industry exceeds that of other segments, which is due to the characteristics and development status of the industry: on the one hand, there are many streamlined operations in these two industries; on the other hand, China is the world's largest automobile consumer market and production base, as well as a major producer of electronic equipment, batteries, semiconductors, etc., therefore, the demand for industrial robots is relatively high.

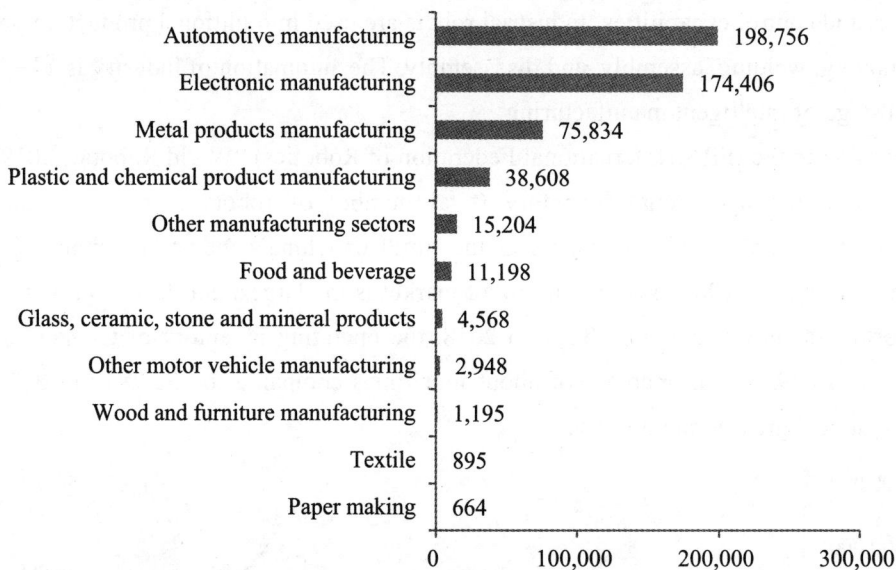

Figure 3.28 Operating inventory of industrial robots in various industries in China's manufacturing industry in 2018

Source: IFR.

Industrial robots are an important tool for enterprises to achieve automation. Thanks to the prosperity of the industrial robot industry, the level of automation of enterprises has kept growing in recent years. Figure 3.29 suggests that according to the data of the integration of industrialization and informatization, in 2018, the level of digitalization of Chinese enterprises had maintained steady growth since 2013. The rate of digitalized control of key processes reached 48.4%, and the penetration rate of digitalized R&D design tools reached 67.4%, increases of 21.6% and 29.9% respectively.

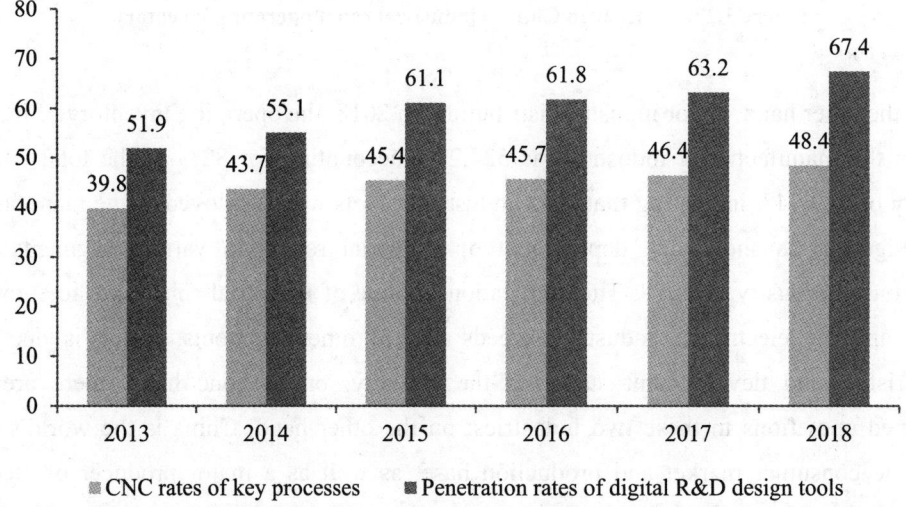

Figure 3.29 2013-2018 enterprise automation level (%)

Source: Service platform website of informatization and industrialization.

2) Industrial Internet

As the consumer-side Internet becomes mature, the construction of the enterprise-side Internet enters a critical stage. The Industrial Internet is the product of the deep integration of ICT and modern industrial technology, as well as the new commanding height of industrial competition in various countries around the world. Predix, an industrial Internet platform product launched by General Electric in 2013, made many enterprises join the competition of the Internet platform, thereby laying the foundation for the later layout of international competition. At the end of 2019, the Ministry of Industry and Information Technology of China issued the "5G + Industrial Internet" 512 project promotion plan, hoping to seize the opportunity in the fourth industrial revolution. According to Figure 3.30, from 2015 to 2020, the scale of China's industrial Internet continued to expand with a significant growth rate, indicating that China's industrial Internet construction was rapidly advancing and expanding its layout.

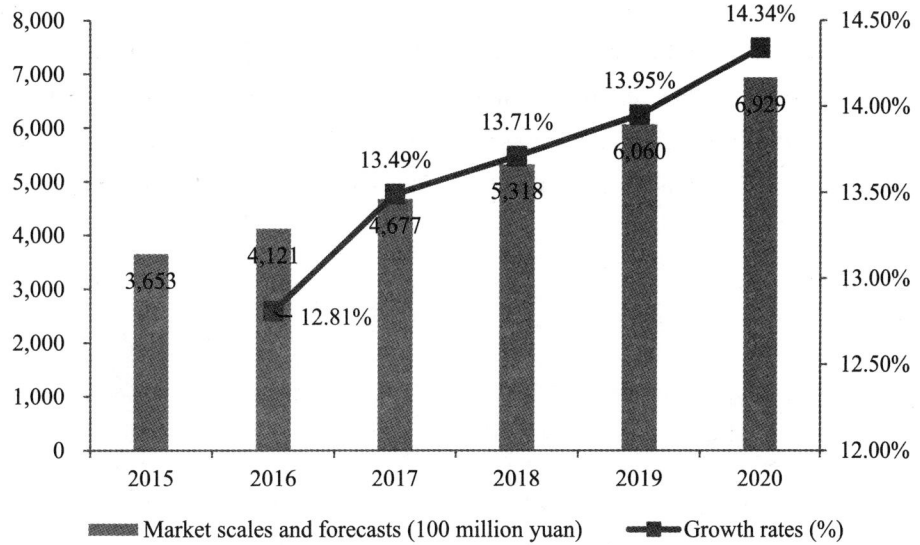

Figure 3.30　2015-2020 industrial Internet market scales and forecasts

Source: Chinese Academy of Industry Economy Research.

3) Industrial software

Industrial software is an important tool for enterprises to realize the digitalization of R&D, design, production, and service. According to Table 3.1, among the three major types of industrial software, the popularity of production control is insufficient, and the performance of product research and development is also insufficient. Only the use of management software is common. However, to realize intelligent manufacturing, the development and popularization of key industrial software have to be improved.

Table 3.1 Penetration rates of major industrial software in 2018 (%)

Types of Software	Names of Software	Popularity
Operation and management	ERP	57.60
	SCM	28.50
	CRM	28.90
Product research and development	PLM	17.30
	PDM	11.00
	CAD/CAE/CAPP	51.00
Production management and control	MES	21.60
	CAM	21.00
	SCADA	17.30

Source: Service platform website of informatization and industrialization.

4) Industrial cloud platform

As shown in Figure 3.31, in terms of industrial cloud platforms, the proportion of industrial enterprises that use cloud platforms in 2018 totaled 43.5%, a limited utilization rate. That can be attributed to two reasons—the supply and demand of cloud platforms: on the supply side, the level of technology is insufficient, and the service quality is below customer expectations; the demand side does not have enough understanding of the cloud platform, and the demand is yet to be stimulated.

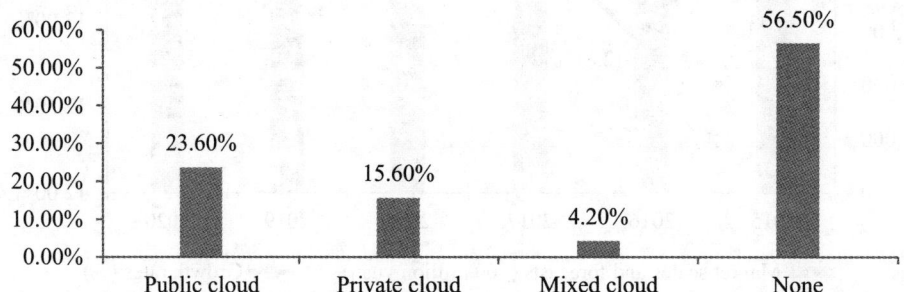

Figure 3.31 Proportions of industrial enterprises using cloud platforms in 2018

Source: Service platform website of informatization and industrialization.

The above aspects show the current situation of China's industrial digitalization: Certain progress has been made in intelligent manufacturing in recent years, but because 5G, big data, and other digital technologies are still developing and yet to be commercialized, the realization of intelligent manufacturing still has a long way to go.

(3) Outstanding performance in the digitalization of the service industry

The digitalization of the service industry is significantly better than that of industry and agriculture, and has maintained a high level of rapid development. The new generation of information technology has different application scenarios in different segments in the tertiary industry. These emerging technologies penetrate the industrial chain of various industries, restructuring the entire chain and constantly innovating and expanding new industry development formats and patterns. Next, a few segments of the tertiary industry are selected to analyze the development of the new generation of information technology in these segments.

1) Transportation

The transportation industry is deeply associated with everyday life. With the development of the economy, people's desire to travel continues to increase, and the load of sea, land, and air transportation increases. Congestion and safety issues have become the primary reasons that affect the travel experience. The solutions to these problems require the improvement of the interaction efficiency between people and vehicles, ships, etc., and a plan at the macro level. The application of 5G, cloud computing, artificial intelligence, and other technologies in the transportation industry gives rise to intelligent transportation, which can significantly improve travel quality through optimization of network transmission, overall planning, and intelligent applications.

Smart transportation is the primary stage of intelligent transportation, which consists of a traffic management system and a traffic information service system. Currently, China's integrated applications of smart transportation are among the best in the world. Cities such as Beijing, Shanghai, Guangzhou, and Shenzhen have built smart transportation management systems with leading international standards. Taking expressway toll collection (ETC) as an example, as of June 2019, 29 provinces, municipalities, and autonomous regions in China opened ETC toll gates and built more than 20,884 ETC lanes. With the dual assistance of policy and technology, the market size of China's smart transportation industry expands year by year. As shown in Figure 3.32, the industry market size reached 48.6 billion yuan in 2018, and this growth trend is expected to continue in the future.

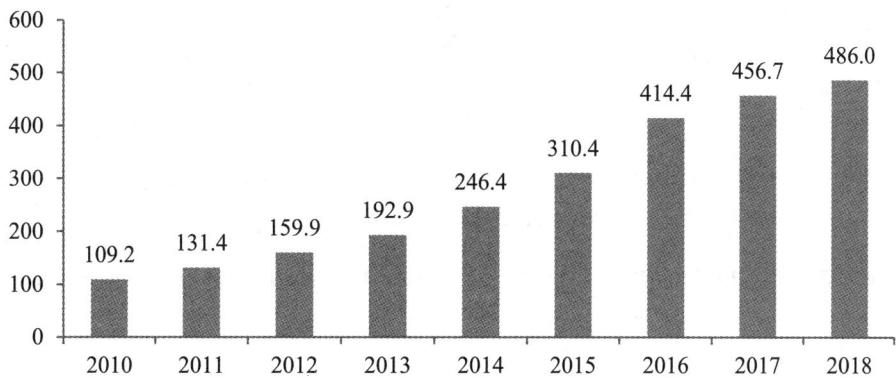

Figure 3.32 Market scales of China's smart transportation industry (100 million yuan)
Source: Qianzhan Industry Research Institute.

The Internet of Vehicles, a topic of current interest, is an important part of future smart transportation. According to Guosen Securities, the development of the Internet of Vehicles can be divided into three stages: it started from the in-vehicle information where vehicles were equipped with basic networking capabilities; currently, it is at the stage of smart networking, where vehicles and roads begin to collaborate through V2X technology; looking forward, the vehicle-road collaboration will be used extensively in smart transportation and advanced autonomous driving. China is in the second stage of the development of the Internet of Vehicles—smart connected cars. Autonomous driving is the issue to overcome for this stage. In China, autonomous driving is still in development and testing. According to the "2019 China Urban Traffic Report", as of the end of 2019, a total of 22 cities in China had issued autonomous driving test policies; many cities issued autonomous driving road trial licenses. Six cities—Guangzhou, Changsha, Shanghai, Wuhan, Cangzhou, and Beijing—started manned tests. There are also many cities that have set up national autonomous driving/connected automated vehicle testing and demonstration areas, such as Changchun in Jilin in the north and Wuhan in the south.

According to the Qianzhan Industry Research Institute, the scale of China's Internet of Vehicles market is expected to reach nearly one trillion yuan in 2025 (see Figure 3.33). Thanks to China's leading position in 5G technology, China's Internet of Vehicles is developing rapidly and will occupy more than half of the global market in the future.

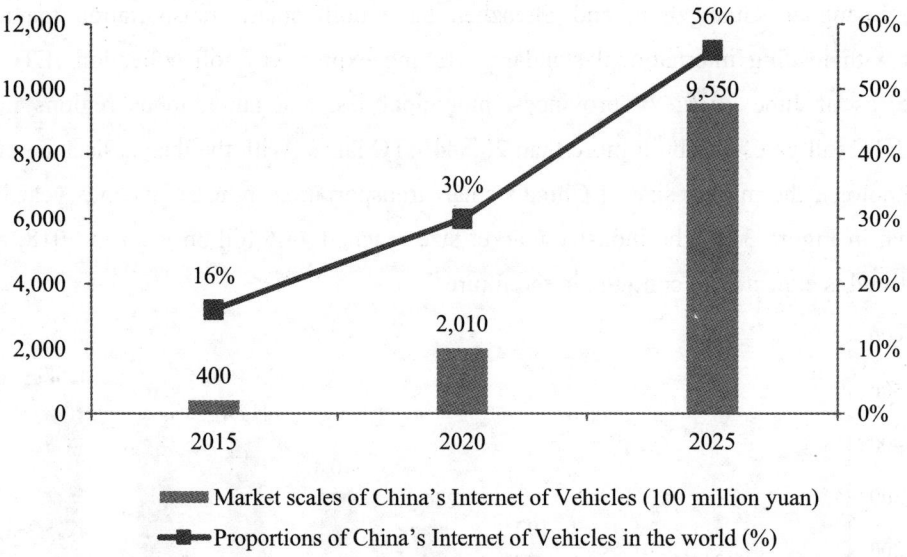

Figure 3.33 2015-2025 market scale of China's Internet of vehicles and its global proportion
Source: Qianzhan Industry Research Institute.

2) Logistics

The huge volume of China's real economy generates a rich demand for logistics, making the logistics industry a supporting industry for China's national economy. Every time technology upgrades, the logistics industry goes through dramatic changes. China's logistics industry went through mechanization and automation and has now entered the stage of intelligence. This is due to the rise of big data, cloud computing, artificial intelligence, and other technologies (see Figure 3.34).

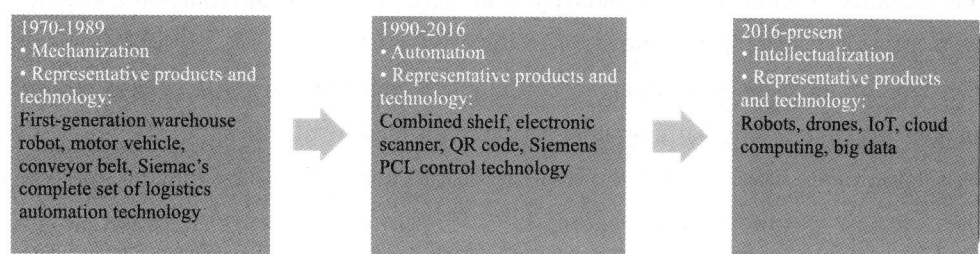

Figure 3.34 Three development stages of China's logistics industry
Source: iiMedia Research.

iiMedia Research believes that with the development of technologies such as the Internet of Things and artificial intelligence, as well as the higher requirements for logistics in new retail, intelligent manufacturing, and other fields, the scale of the smart logistics market will continue to expand, and it is expected to reach the scale of a trillion yuan by 2025. Figure 3.35 also shows that since 2013, the market size of smart logistics has been expanding continuously, and the growth rate stays at approximately 20%.

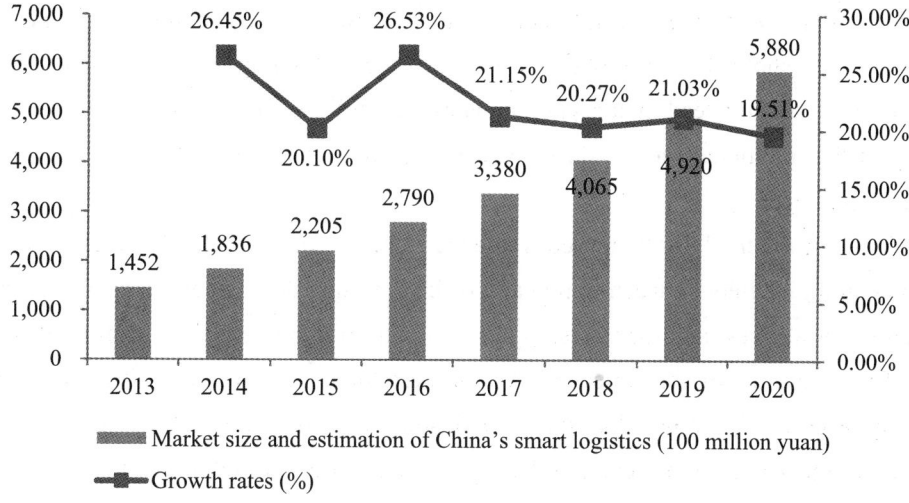

Figure 3.35 Development of China's amart logistics market
Source: Data center of iiMedia Research.

With the maturity of 5G technology, logistics enterprises are expected to upgrade in terminal distribution, warehousing and sorting, etc., to create a more efficient and low-cost intelligent logistics system.

3) The retail industry

Retail is an intermediate link between consumers and producers. It has experienced four revolutions, namely department stores, supermarket chains, supermarkets, and e-commerce. It is currently in the fifth revolution—new retail. "New retail" was first proposed by Jack Ma in 2016. Various understandings of this concept remain in the market. In general, new retail is a consumer-oriented form of the retail industry with the purpose of cost reduction and efficiency improvement, with technological innovation as the driving force.

The rise of the new generation of consumption and the boom of a large number of technologies promote the digital upgrading of the traditional retail industry. The post-'80s and post-'90s generations have become the main force of consumption in China. At present, the post-'80s and post-'90s in China account for 30%. This group has a better education background and a higher level of income, and are ready to embrace novelty. They are highly digitalized. As the level of purchasing capability of this group continues to rise, their consumption demands gradually incline toward quality products. They pursue individualization and differentiation. Their shopping sources are not limited to one channel, but rather omnichannel shopping. Accenture's 2018 research results confirm the above conclusion. There is no clear preference between online and offline shopping. The two have gradually reached a balance and complemented each other. Online shopping is convenient and fast, while offline shopping allows consumers to enjoy a diverse experience of dining, shopping, and entertainment.

On the other hand, new-generation information technologies, such as 5G, artificial intelligence, cloud computing, the Internet of Things, mobile Internet, big data, and VR, are maturing. The threshold for the application of emerging technologies is significantly lowered. Some enterprises take the lead in applying the latest technologies, thus promoting the digitalized upgrading of the traditional retail industry and improving operational efficiency as well as the consumer experience.

As shown in Figure 3.36, taking convenience stores as an example, domestic convenience stores open up the barriers between online and offline through deployment in smart distribution, unmanned stores/shelves, and membership systems, and promote the digitalization of the retail industry. The proportion of convenience stores in these three areas reached 77%, 38%, and 60% respectively. Figure 3.37 shows that since 2016, more and more domestic convenience stores have begun to introduce online retail, and the proportion of online sales revenue increases year by year, and the form of new retail is increasingly visible.

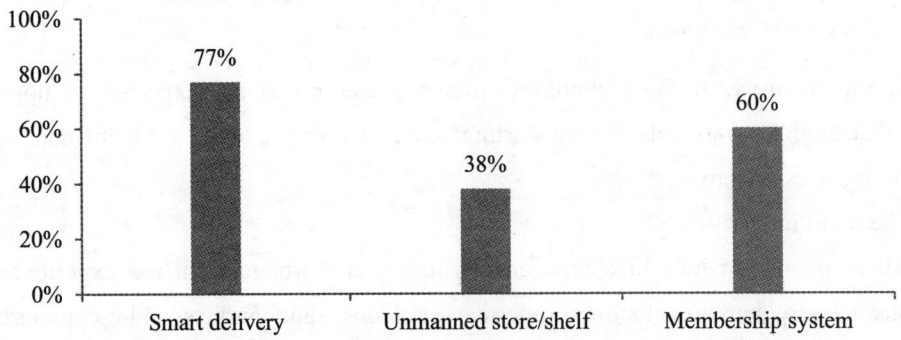

Figure 3.36 Digitization ratio of domestic convenience stores in 2018

Source: KPMG & China Chain Store & Franchise Association, "2019 China Convenience Store Development Report".

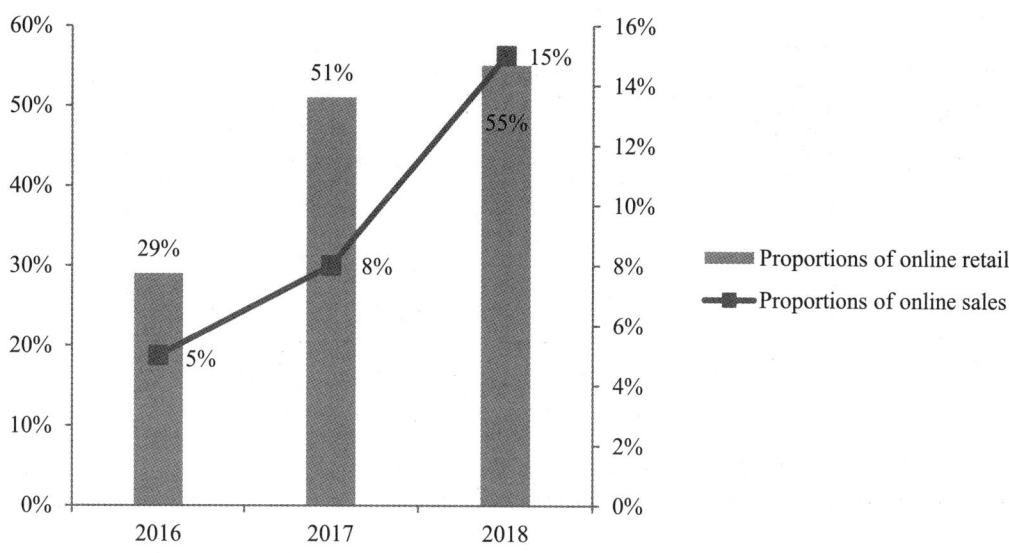

Figure 3.37   2016-2018 introduction of online retail by convenience stores in China and the proportions of online sales
Source: KPMG & China Chain Store & Franchise Association, "2019 China Convenience Store Development Report".

2.4 Development of digital economy in various regions and upgrading of industrial structure

China has a vast territory, and the level of development of each province varies. There are significant differences in industrial environment, factor endowment, and policy orientation. These realities result in significant region-specific characteristics of the development of digital economy. The inconsistency of the integration between digital economy and industries leads to inconsistencies in the pace of upgrading of the industrial structure. The combined effect is significant in eastern coastal provinces and cities. The level of integration between the manufacturing industry and the Internet is higher and the pace is faster, thus taking the lead nationwide. They have become an important force in the first echelon of China's digital economy development.

2.4.1 The fundamental digital economy

From the perspective of the development of the software industry, there is a huge gap in the level of development in different regions. The combined effect of the software industry in the eastern region is significant, and the income is nearly four times the total value of the other three regions. In terms of growth rate, the central and western regions both surpass the eastern region, reaching 22.2% and 18.1% respectively. This means that although the central and western regions are slower, the momentum of development is better. The northeast region is at a disadvantage in terms of business revenue and growth rate, and it lacks an industrial environment.

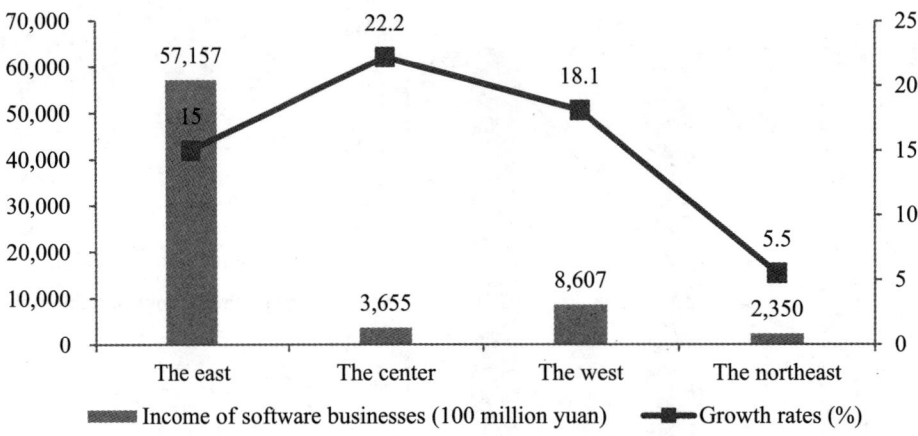

Figure 3.38 2019 growth of the software industry by region

Source: Official website of the Ministry of Industry and Information Technology.

The revenue of the software business in 2017 suggests a huge difference among provinces (see Figure 3.39). Guangdong, Jiangsu, and Beijing led the development of the software industry nationwide, and a relatively stable industrial model and a sound foundation for digital economy had been formed. The annual software business revenue of Guangdong Province in 2017 was 968.12 billion yuan, accounting for 17.6% of the country's total revenue. The development of Shanghai, Zhejiang, and Shandong followed closely, but the gap between the amount of income of these three provinces and the top three provinces was large. The software industry in Sichuan, Fujian, Liaoning, and other provinces started to scale up. On the contrary, the development of the software industry in many provinces such as Qinghai, Ningxia, and Inner Mongolia lagged behind, and vitality was needed for the development of digital economy.

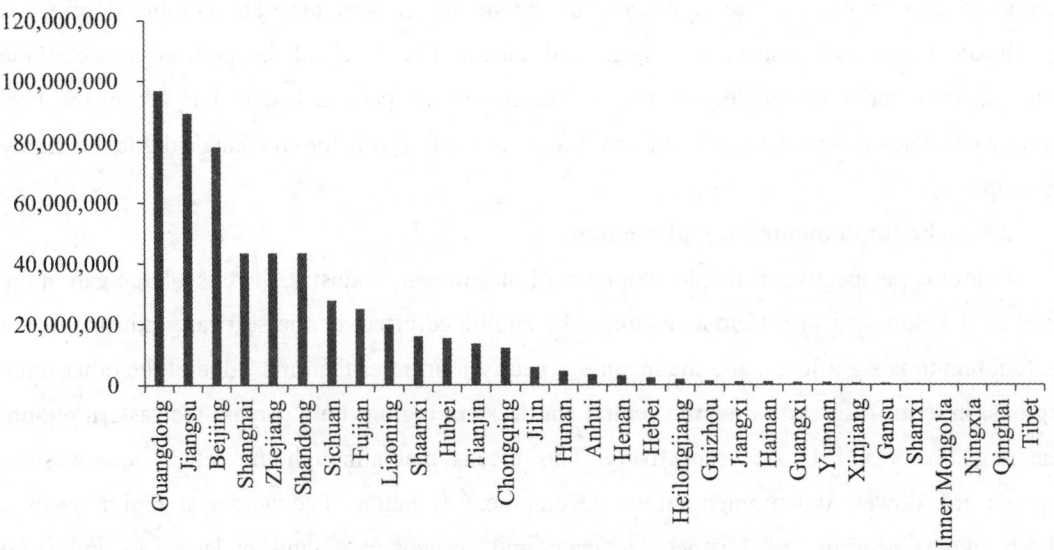

Figure 3.39 Revenue of software business nationwide in 2017 (10 thousand yuan)

Source: Official website of the Ministry of Industry and Information Technology.

From the perspective of the operation of the Internet industry, in 2019, the revenue of Internet businesses in the eastern region accelerated, and the revenue of the Internet industry accounted for 90.9% of the national revenue. The central and western regions grew significantly with potential. The development of Internet services in the northeastern region lagged behind, far below the level of other regions.

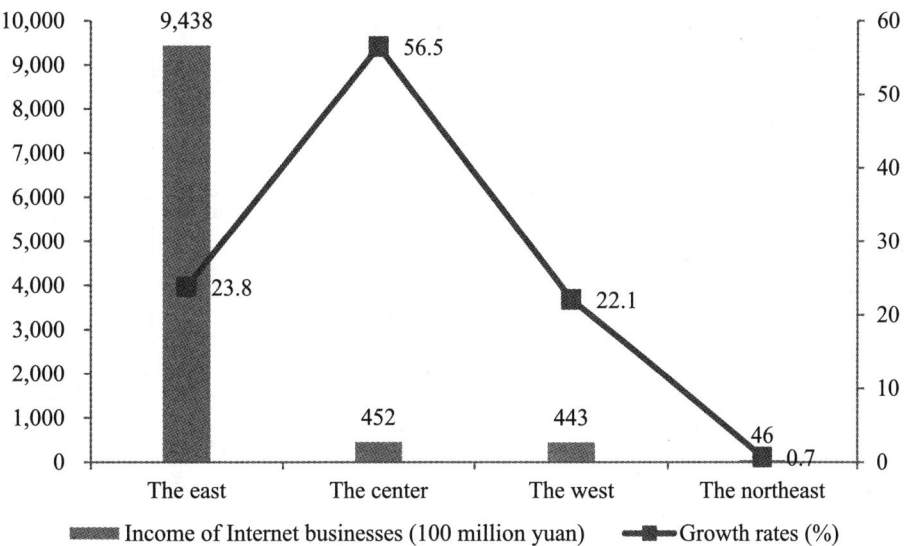

Figure 3.40　Growth of the Internet industry by region in 2019

Source: Official website of the Ministry of Industry and Information Technology.

In 2019, the top five provinces with cumulative Internet revenues were Guangdong, Shanghai, Beijing, Zhejiang, and Jiangsu. The total revenues of the Internet business of these five provinces accounted for 87.1% of the total national revenue. Provinces such as Ningxia, Anhui, Hainan, and Jiangxi increased significantly.

2.4.2 Integration of digitalization and informatization

According to the 2019 statistics data of the service platform website of informatization and industrialization, the national index of integration of industrialization and informatization was 54.5. The indexes of Jiangsu, Shandong, Zhejiang, Shanghai, Beijing, Guangdong, Chongqing, Tianjin, Fujian, and Sichuan were ahead of the national average level (see Figure 3.41). Most of these provinces are in the eastern region, the Bohai Rim region, and the Sichuan-Chongqing region. The leading GDP and sound economic foundation made them the first to start industrial upgrading and integrate manufacturing with the Internet. In comparison, provinces with a slowing pace of informatization are in the western region. The economic foundation of these regions is relatively weak, and the development of the fundamental digital economy is therefore constrained by factors such as industrial structure and factor endowments. In regions with less developed industries, the pace of integration of the two is relatively slow.

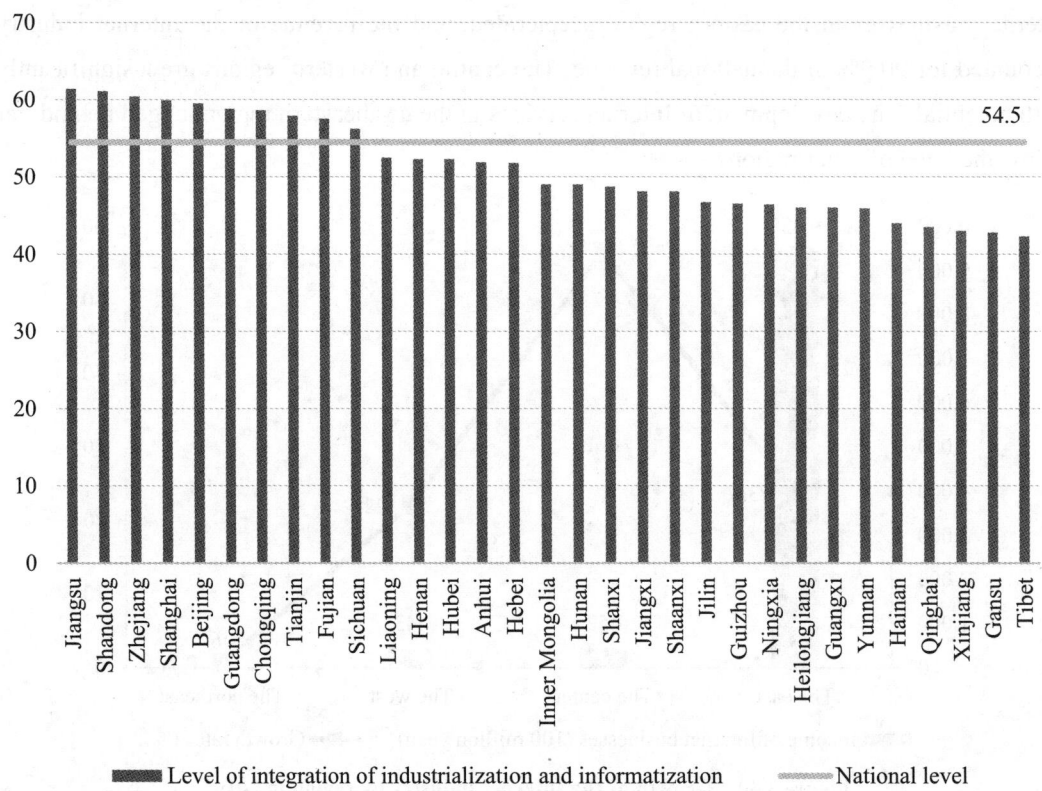

Figure 3.41 Level of integration of industrialization and informatization in various provinces across the country (%)

Source: Service platform website of informatization and industrialization.

The process of industrial informatization is one that optimizes the industrial structure within the province and improves production efficiency. With the development of intelligent technologies, intelligent manufacturing can set enterprises free from traditional industrial models. Enterprises can hand over the simple and repetitive tasks in the production process to smart machines, thus developing toward automation and improving economic benefits. In addition, intelligent manufacturing systems are often equipped with self-learning functions, which means they can constantly optimize performance in practice, and play a role in helping producers make decisions, which will save a lot of labor costs. The "readiness" of intelligent manufacturing is an indicator to measure the status of intelligent manufacturing in an enterprise, and it reflects the process of industrialization and informatization in China. In terms of the readiness of intelligent manufacturing, Zhejiang, Shandong, and Jiangsu took the lead, reaching more than 13%. However, the western and northeastern regions were lower than the national level, and there was a big gap between provinces. The difference in the readiness of intelligent manufacturing between Zhejiang Province and Gansu Province was about 14% (see Figure 3.42).

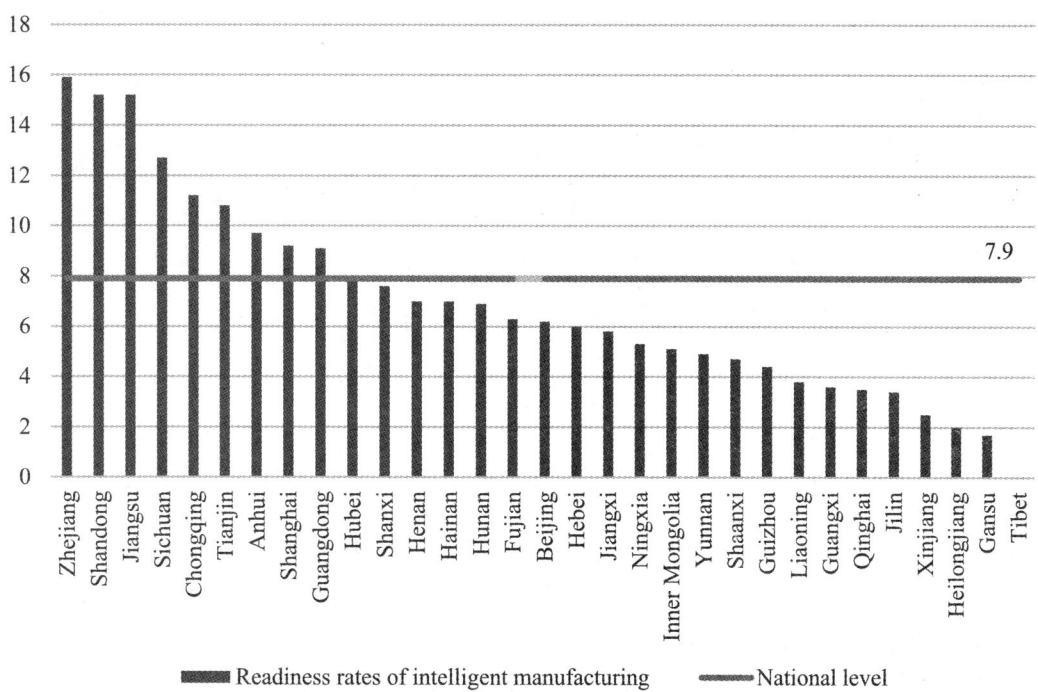

Figure 3.42   Readiness rates of intelligent manufacturing in different provinces across the country (%)
Source: Service platform website of informatization and industrialization.

The industrial cloud platform integrates multiple functions such as data analysis, technical communication, and simulation, and is equipped with multiple excellent performances such as high-speed computing and flexibility, thus optimizing the production process for enterprises. The application of industrial cloud platforms can improve the efficiency of enterprises in many aspects. First, to improve production efficiency. The application of industrial cloud platforms enables producers to see real-time production data, and its data analysis function assists producers in decision-making. Second, to reduce costs. The emergence of cloud platforms allows more enterprises to focus on their advantages and reduce the costs of fixed investment and operation and maintenance personnel. The "on-demand" characteristics also optimize the allocation of resources. Third, the virtual reality and simulation application technology of industrial cloud platforms can solve many problems such as the low efficiency of manufacturing and R&D and the long cycle of product design. The application rate of industrial cloud platforms is an important indicator of the integration of digital economy and manufacturing. Currently, the application rate of industrial cloud platforms in Zhejiang Province is 64.6%, ranking first, far exceeding the national average. Eastern China is above the national average, thanks to its excellent economic foundation and transformation and upgrading concept. In comparison, the application rate of industrial cloud platforms in Qinghai Province is only 20.8%. There is a large gap among provinces, and the scale of development of digital economy is uneven. More policies are needed to promote industrial upgrading in the western region.

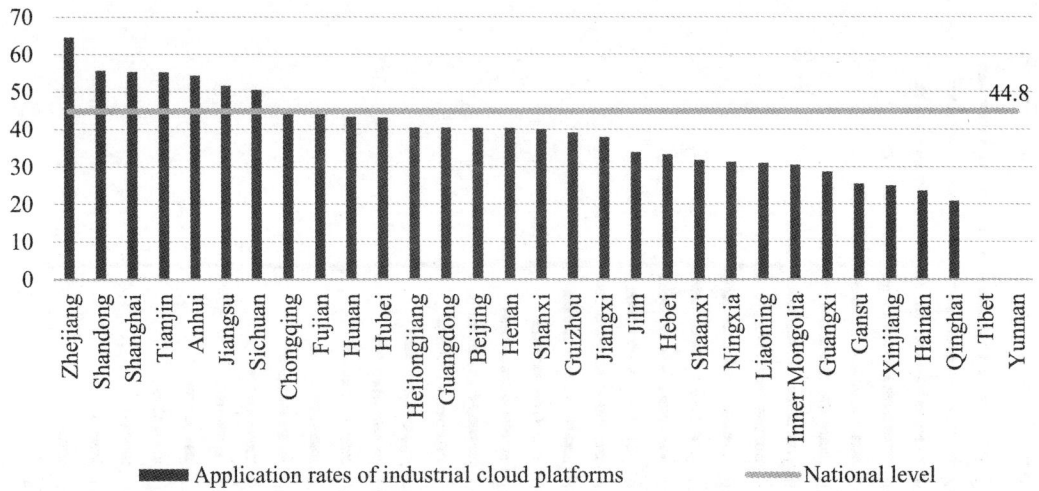

Figure 3.43 Application rates of industrial cloud platforms in different provinces across the country (%)
Source: Service platform website of informatization and industrialization.

2.4.3 Informatization of Enterprises

According to the statistics of iResearch Consulting, the transaction scale of China's enterprise procurement e-commerce market in 2018 exceeded 600 billion yuan. Undoubtedly, the development of e-commerce platforms increases economic benefits for enterprises. On the one hand, the development of e-commerce platforms lowers the cost of obtaining information and helps enterprises find more suitable upstream enterprises and find higher-quality raw materials at a lower cost. In a traditional business model, the expansion of upstream enterprises is restrained by regional characteristics. The development of information technology enables enterprises to obtain supplier information from farther away, so as to identify products that are more suitable for them. In addition, the advantages of logistics and distribution, purchase prices, and the richness of products are all attractive features for enterprises. On the other hand, the rapid development of e-commerce platforms also improves the sales environment and expands sales for enterprises. Enterprises identify customers and expand the scale of demands by setting up product display windows on e-commerce platforms. Meanwhile, enterprises reduce sales costs and facilitate the sound development of production.

In 2017, the proportion of enterprises with e-commerce transaction activities nationwide was 9.5%. The electronic sales of different provinces show that Beijing ranks first with 19% of enterprises, far exceeding the national average. Hainan, Zhejiang, Tibet, Sichuan, Anhui, and other provinces also have excellent performance, leading the national level with 14.8%, 12.7%, 12.4%, 11.7%, and 11.5% respectively. Provinces such as Hainan, Tibet, and Yunnan are in need of the popularization of e-commerce due to geographical factors. The regional restrictions of the traditional business model make the resources of these provinces scarce, and the products circulating on the market are not diverse. The development of e-commerce solves these problems. It allows provinces to send out better or distinctive products of the province and buy the products that they do not produce well. These advantages are the major motivation for local enterprises to engage in e-commerce transactions and promote the increase of the application of e-commerce in these provinces. On the contrary, the proportion of e-commerce transactions in northeast China is the lowest, and the development of e-commerce lags behind, with only 4.7%, 4.3%, and 4.3% (see Figure 3.44).

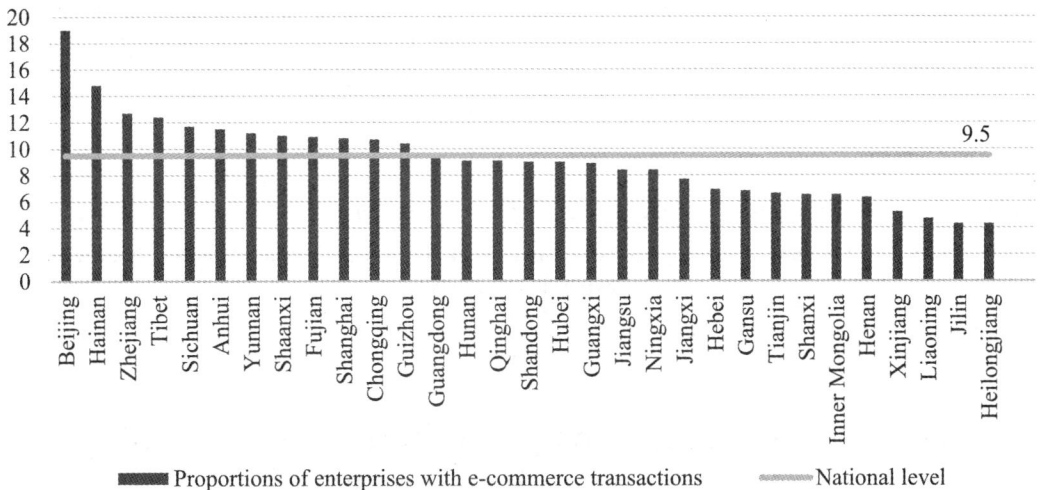

Figure 3.44 Proportions of enterprises in e-commerce transactions in different provinces in 2017 (%)
Source: Chinese Research Data Services.

With the development of Internet technology, the processes of enterprises are simplified. Information-oriented technology has penetrated the daily operation, management, promotion, and other activities of enterprises. In 2017, the proportions of enterprises nationwide that adopted computers, the Internet, information management, and carried out production and business activities through the Internet were 99.7%, 99.5%, 96.7%, and 99.5%, respectively, all close to 100%. Enterprises in different provinces are almost fully covered by the informatization of technology, and there is no significant difference among provinces. In the past five years, the proportion of enterprises using the Internet and the proportion of enterprises carrying out production and business activities through the Internet both increased by 16.5%.

However, by the end of 2017, the proportion of enterprises using the Internet for publicity and promotion was 84%, an indicator needs further improvement. The utilization of the Internet, to a certain extent, helps reduce promotion and publicity costs. For a certain fee, enterprises can deploy relevant promotions on third-party platforms, and these promotions will also be pushed to the mobile phones of targeted users. This approach is more efficient and result-oriented than before. Nationwide, Shandong, Henan, Hubei, Hunan, and Anhui are higher than the national level, the proportions of which are 91.5%, 89.4%, 89.3%, 88%, and 87.9%, respectively. The proportions of Tibet, Liaoning, Tianjin, Shanxi, and Xinjiang are relatively low, about 10%

below the national level (see Figure 3.45).

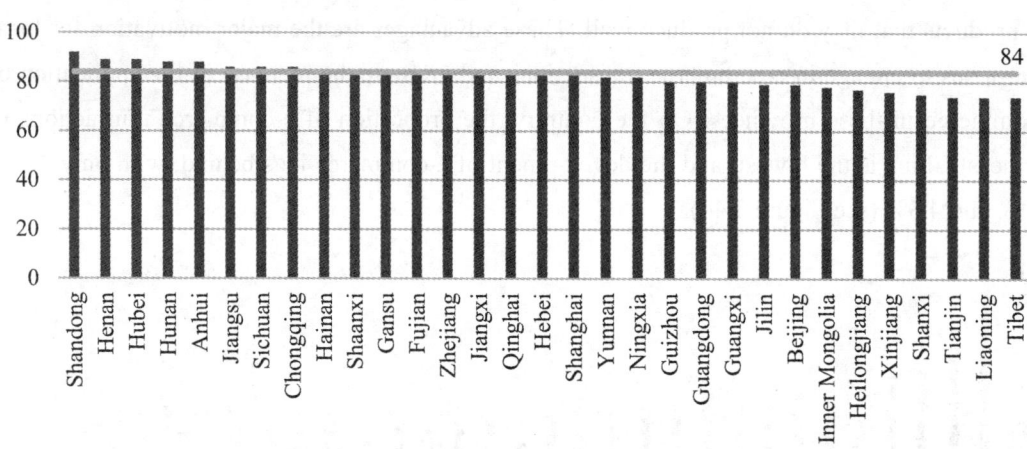

Figure 3.45 Proportions of enterprises using the Internet for publicity and promotion in different provinces in 2017 (%)

Source: Chinese Research Data Services.

Section 3 Digital Economy and Industrial Upgrading: Development of Key Industries

The level and stage of China's digital economy in key industries vary, and the development needs and production characteristics of different industries are also different. Based on the major requirements for digitalization, networking, and intellectualization, various industries start individual explorations based on different aspects of the development of informatization. Major problems and issues discovered during the exploration will be the direction of efforts for the next stage of the industry.

3.1 Digital agriculture: promoting the transformation and upgrading of traditional agriculture

Digital agriculture is a typical application for the transformation and upgrading of traditional industries through digital restructuring in the context of digital economy. As a new form of agricultural development, it uses digital information as a new factor of agricultural production. Digital information technology is used for visual expression, digitalized design, and information management for the objects, environment, and the whole process of the agriculture industry. The expansion of population and continuous consumption of resources have caused an increasingly severe shortage of resources for the world. There are many issues such as low production efficiency, high costs, and scattered scale in traditional agriculture; meanwhile, agricultural production is closely related to resources, and its sustainable development is faced with huge challenges. Subject to factors such as shortage of resources, rising resource prices, and fragmented production, China's agricultural product market is faced with problems such as sharp price fluctuations and lack of security of agricultural products. Digital agriculture can achieve cross-discipline and multi-field organic integration, which is beneficial to increase agricultural income, improve the quality of agricultural products, utilize resources rationally, improve circulation efficiency, and protect the environment. Digital agriculture empowers traditional agriculture and introduces a large number of new businesses. It is a natural choice to support the development of modern agriculture in China.

The fundamental difference between digital agriculture and traditional agriculture lies in the transformation of key decision-making factors. In this process, the key decision-making factor transfers from "people" to "digital". Modern information technologies such as remote sensing, big data, the Internet, and artificial intelligence are widely used, profoundly changing the means of agricultural production (Figure 3.46).

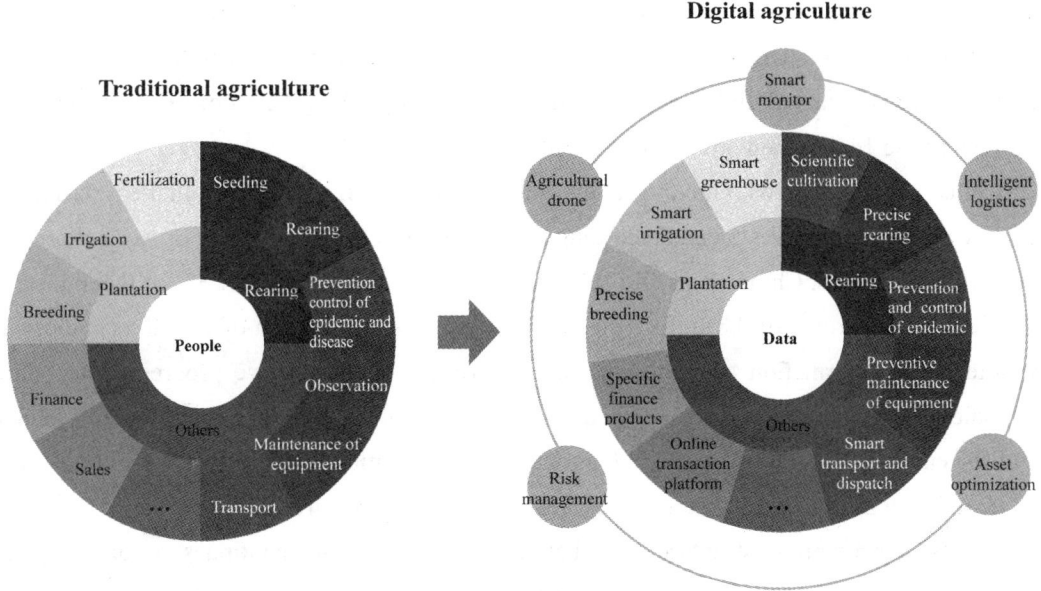

Figure 3.46 Comparison between traditional agriculture and digital agriculture
Source: TF Securities Research Institute.

With technological progress and innovation upgrading, many agricultural developed countries have prioritized digital agriculture as a national strategic focus and priority development direction. Modern information technologies such as remote sensing, big data, the Internet, and artificial intelligence are widely used in the whole process of agricultural development to strive for new advantages in the new round of industrial revolution, resulting in profound changes in the production and lifestyle of human society.

On the one hand, the crossover and in-depth integration of digital technologies are noticeable. For example, when digital technology integrates with plantation, agriculture, fishery, and agricultural product processing industries, digital agriculture will develop rapidly and a large number of cross-discipline agricultural Internet platforms will emerge. The major directions for the application of new technologies such as the Internet of Things and cloud computing to promote the transformation of the momentum of agricultural development are service-oriented production, customization, and cloud-based management and configuration of production resources. Currently, based on cutting-edge technological changes, digital agriculture presents increasing global interconnection, ecosystem cooperation, and technological empowerment. Looking forward, agricultural technology will face fiercer competition than ever before.

On the other hand, digital technology creates a huge market demand and growth potential. Digital technology, represented by the Internet of Things, not only promotes the production and supply of agricultural production materials, but also accelerates the division and cooperation of the global labor market in terms of storage, transportation, processing, and sales of agricultural products. The agricultural industry system, production and management system, agricultural material and machinery system, and agricultural product supply and sales system are going through major changes. Digital technology is transforming traditional agriculture. More farmers will share the dividends of digital economy. It is predicted that the Internet of Things technology alone can create 14.4 trillion dollars for agriculture.

China is the country with the largest investment in digital transformation in the Asia-Pacific region, with over 60% investment. According to data released by the Ministry of Agriculture and Rural Affairs, in 2018, China's agricultural digital economy accounted for 7.3% of the industry's added value, an increase of 0.8% from the previous year. The utilization of digital technology to promote the transformation of traditional agriculture has made positive progress. The online retail sales of agricultural products reached 230.5 billion yuan, a year-on-year increase of 33.8%. As of the end of 2018, a total of 272,000 agricultural information cooperatives were established, providing 95.79 million public welfare services and 314 million convenient services.

As the consumption structure of urban and rural residents continues to upgrade, the demands for high-quality agricultural products and services steadily increase, and the development of the agricultural industry is shifting from increasing yield to improving quality. Following the strategy of "agricultural modernization" and "rural revitalization", with technological innovation and mechanism innovation as the driving forces of transformation, China's agriculture will embark on a journey of agricultural digital development with Chinese characteristics.

3.2 Intelligent manufacturing: promoting manufacturing reform

In recent years, China's labor costs have increased, and the demand for industrial transformation has grown. With the support of policies and technologies, China's intelligent manufacturing industry has entered a stage of practicality. With many segments in the manufacturing industry, China's manufacturing industry is currently in the stage of "electrical automation + digital". Differences remain in industrialization reform in different segments, and there is a vast space for intelligent manufacturing due to the demands derived from different stages.

Intelligent manufacturing organically combines a series of emerging technologies and applications. Its definition includes three aspects: "intellectualization", "digitalization", and "networking" (Figure 3.47). "Intellectualization" refers to improving the level of automation of manufacturing processes through artificial intelligence technology; "digitalization" refers to the conversion of production information into digital format and the use of computers for management and control; "networking" refers to the use of hardware technology to connect producers and machines, machines and machines, and consumers and producers so as to realize the connectivity of data and processes.

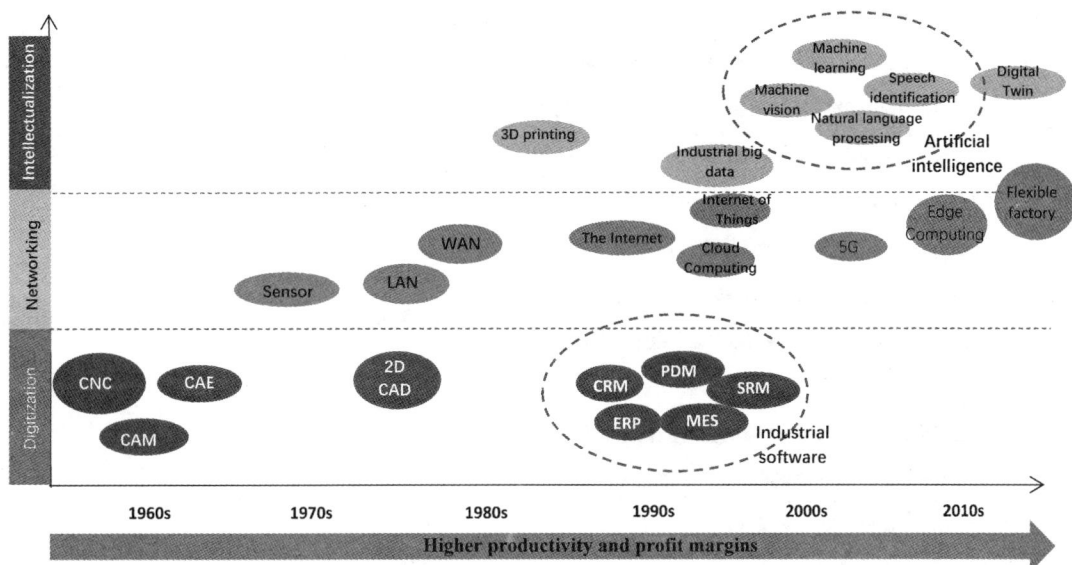

Figure 3.47 Development path of key technologies of intelligent manufacturing
Source: EO Intelligence.

The fundamental elements of intelligent manufacturing are gradually constructed. New transmission technology, high-end CNC machine tools, robots, and other intelligent equipment are put into use, and industrial software is upgraded constantly. The application of big data, the Internet, and artificial intelligence are connected, calculated, and iterated, forming a highly collaborative manufacturing model of self-cognition, self-decision, and self-execution.

China overtook the US in 2010, becoming the country with the highest added value of manufacturing in the world. In 2017, the added value of China's manufacturing industry ranked first in the world, reaching 3.6 trillion USD. The compound annual growth rate remains at 12% over the past 10 years. China will play an important role on the global manufacturing stage in the future.

Although China is a big manufacturing country, it has not become a manufacturing power. As for per capita industrial added value, China only accounts for 1/5 of that of the US and 1/3 of that of Korea. Traditional manufacturing countries of the 20th century, such as the US, Germany, Japan, and the UK, continue to develop advanced manufacturing technologies to enhance their competitiveness. China's manufacturing industry is facing fierce international competition.

3.2.1 Development of China's intelligent manufacturing

As for the global intelligent manufacturing development index, China's intelligent manufacturing belongs to the second echelon in the world, with a generally lower level. Although China is ahead of Brazil, Spain, and other countries, there is a big gap between it and leading countries such as the US, Japan, and Germany (Figure 3.48).

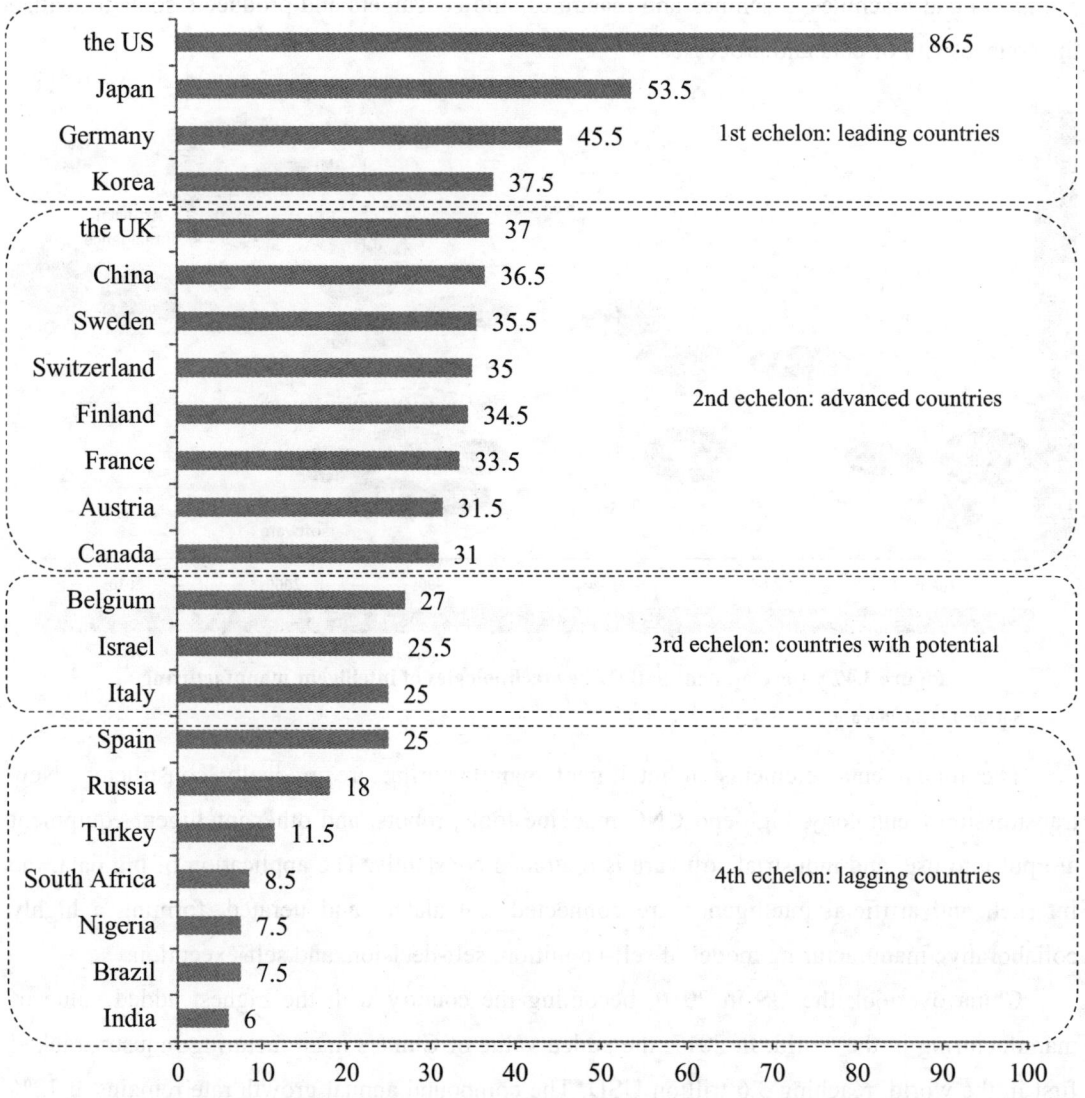

Figure 3.48   Global intelligent manufacturing development index

Source: China Economic Information Service.

Generally speaking, China's intelligent manufacturing industry is at the stage of "electrical automation + digital" (Figure 3.49). Currently, 90% of manufacturing enterprises are equipped with automated production lines, but only 40% are managed digitally, 5% have access to factory data, and 1% use intelligent technology. In 2025, it is expected to enter the stage of "digitalization + networking", and the proportion of digitalized, networked, and intelligent manufacturing enterprises will reach 70%, 30%, and 10%, respectively.

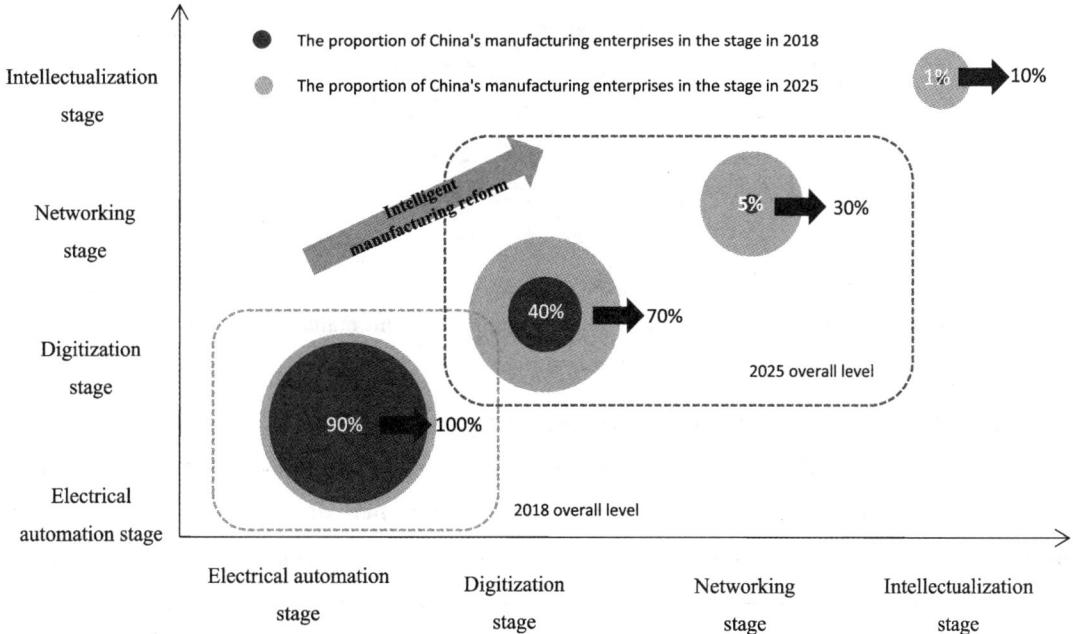

Figure 3.49 General progress of China's intelligent manufacturing

Source: EO Intelligence.

There are many segments in China's manufacturing industry: Based on the classification of the Bureau of Statistics, China's manufacturing industry is now divided into 19 sub-industries (Figure 3.50). Among them, textile and garment, machinery and equipment, and food and beverage enterprises make up the majority; among listed enterprises, the number of enterprises in computer communications equipment, machinery, and pharmaceutical manufacturing is the largest. The concentration and scale of different segments vary significantly. The discrete manufacturing industry accounts for a higher proportion of intelligent manufacturing industry, which is reflected in industries such as electronics, automobiles, and industrial equipment.

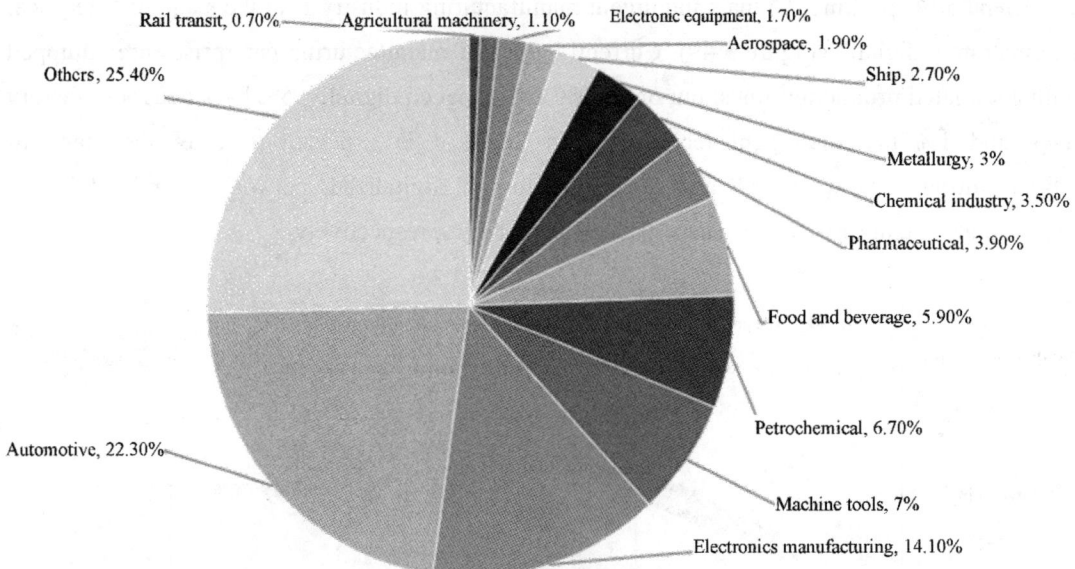

Figure 3.50 Proportions of degments of China's intelligent manufacturing industry
Source: China Intelligent Manufacturing System Integrator Consortium.

3.2.2 Key segments of China's smart manufacturing industry

Leaders of the intelligent manufacturing industry include: computer, communications, and other electronic equipment manufacturing, automobile manufacturing, home appliance manufacturing, home furnishing materials manufacturing, and pharmaceutical manufacturing. These industries are highly automated, with a higher cost and lower return of labor. They also share general characteristics: high demand in terms of market upgrading, complex manufacturing processes, and large downstream markets. Among them, industries with the fastest upgrading and the most extensive market are computers, mobile phones, automobiles, and medical industries. The average depreciation and amortization and average human efficiency of these leading industries continued to increase from 2013 to 2018, and the annual average value was greater than challengers and speculators, indicating that their foundation of intelligent manufacturing is better; their 2013-2018 average labor costs are the highest, and ROP is low. see Figure 3.51 to Figure 3.54.

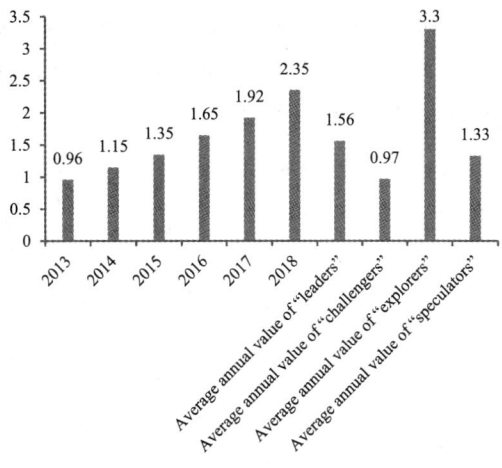

Figure 3.51 2013-2018 average depreciation and amortization of "leaders"

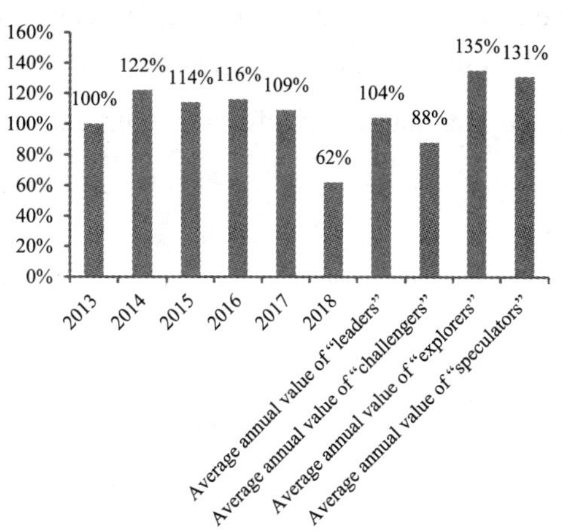

Figure 3.52 Average ROPs of "leaders" from 2013 to 2018

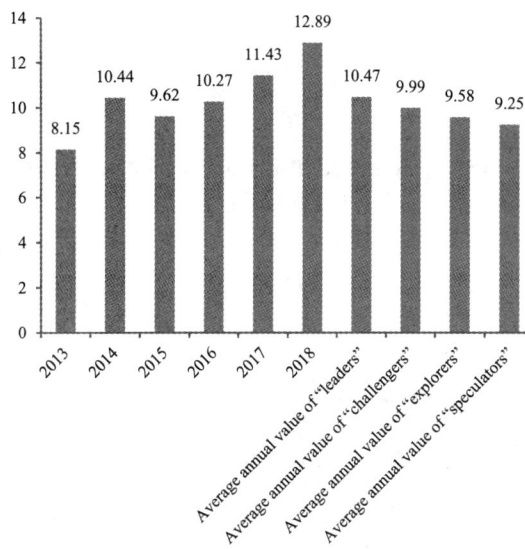

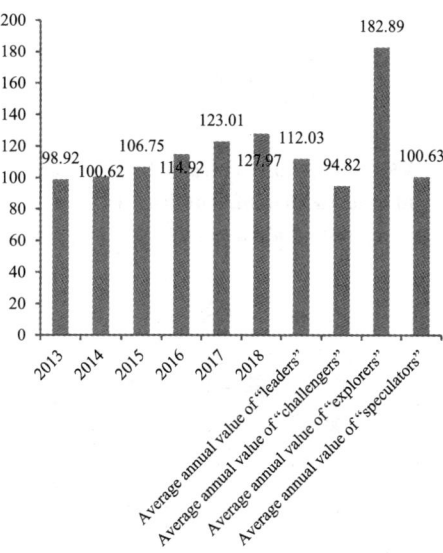

Figure 3.53 Average labor costs of "leaders" from 2013 to 2018

Figure 3.54 2013-2018 average personnel effectiveness of "leaders"

Source: Wind database.

Intelligent manufacturing "challengers" include: the textile and garment industry, machinery and equipment manufacturing, instrumentation manufacturing, electrical equipment manufacturing, and aerospace, railway, and ship manufacturing. Generally speaking, these industries have lower technical thresholds, lower levels of automation, and a rapid decline in returns on labor input. The common characteristics are: products are in the midstream, the market size is not as large as the "leader", customers have lower demand to upgrade products, and labor costs have a greater impact. There is a strong demand for the transformation of intelligent manufacturing. Although from 2013 to 2018 the average depreciation and amortization continued to rise, and labor efficiency "challengers" continued to increase, generally it remained the lowest, indicating that the foundation of intelligent manufacturing is weak; ROP declined faster from 2013 to 2018, indicating that rising labor costs had a significant impact. Manufacturing reform is in urgent need. see Figures 3.55 to 3.58.

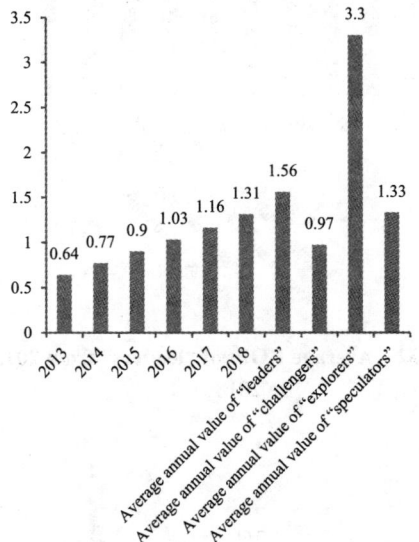

Figure 3.55 2013-2018 average depreciation and amortization of "challengers" (100 million yuan)

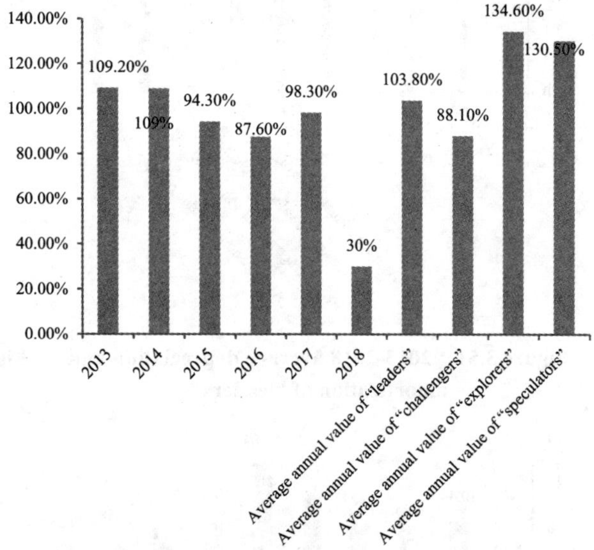

Figure 3.56 Average ROP of "challengers" from 2013 to 2018 (%)

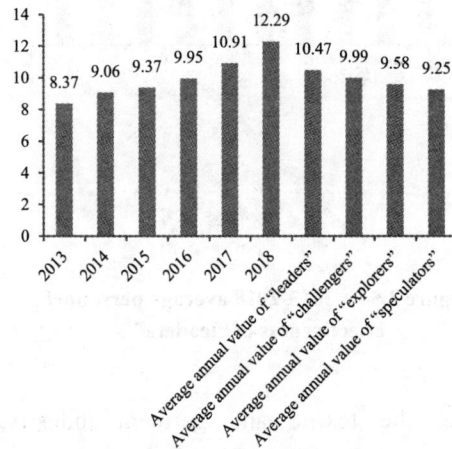

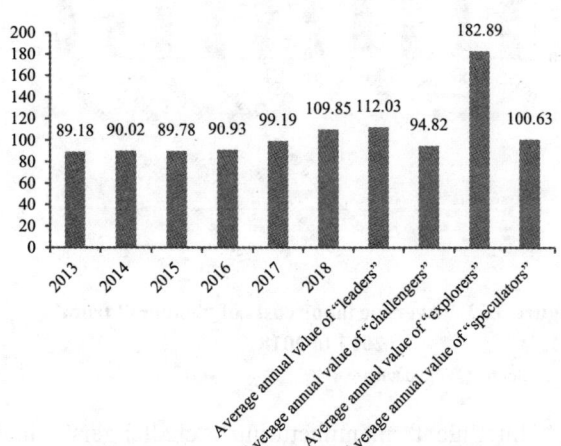

Figure 3.57 Average labor cost of "challengers" from 2013 to 2018 (10 thousand yuan)

Figure 3.58 2013-2018 average personnel effectiveness of "challengers" (100 million yuan)

Source: Wind database.

Intelligent manufacturing "explorers" include: petroleum processing, coking and nuclear fuels, chemical ingredients and products, non-metallic mineral products, non-ferrous metal smelting and processing, and ferrous metal smelting and processing. Generally speaking, the technical threshold of "explorers" is high, the industrial foundation is solid, the labor cost is low, and the returns are high. The general characteristics are: they are mostly in industries based on technological processes with strict production requirements, and are all in the upstream of the industry, but the industry is slow to update and the demand for transformation is weak. The average depreciation and amortization and per capita efficiency of the "explorers" from 2013 to 2018 were higher than those in other quadrants, indicating that the industrial foundation is strong and the level of automation is high; meanwhile, the return of labor is the highest and keeps increasing, indicating that the impact of labor costs is minimal and the demand for intelligent manufacturing comes from lean production. see Figures 3.59 to 3.62.

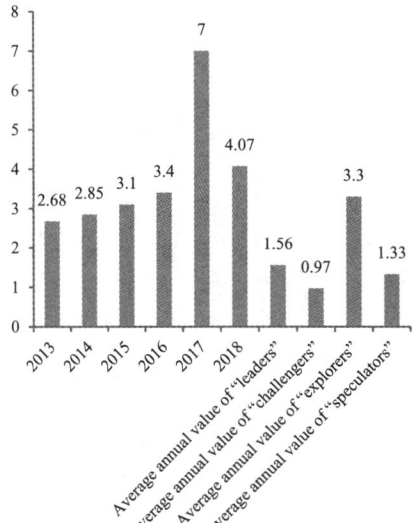

Figure 3.59 2013-2018 average depreciation and amortization of "explorers" (100 million yuan)

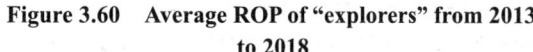

Figure 3.60 Average ROP of "explorers" from 2013 to 2018

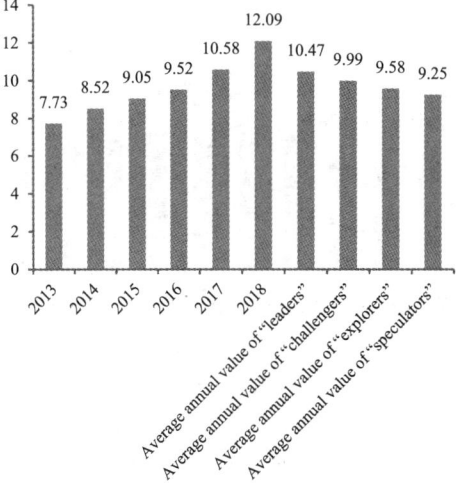

Figure 3.61 2013-2018 average labor costs of "explorers" (10 thousand yuan)

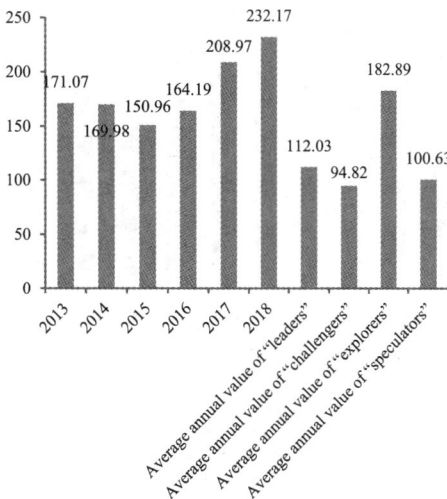

Figure 3.62 Average personnel effectiveness of "explorers" from 2013 to 2018 (100 million yuan)

Source: Wind database.

Intelligent manufacturing "speculators" include: food and beverage manufacturing, cultural, sports, and entertainment products manufacturing, and rubber and plastic products manufacturing. Generally speaking, these industries have lower technical thresholds and larger gaps among enterprises, as well as lower labor costs, but the returns of labor are slowly decreasing. The general characteristics are: low technical threshold, weak industrial foundation, high labor intensity, fragmentation of the industry, slow product upgrading, stable domestic market, and less impact on labor costs compared with "challengers". At present, ROP of "speculators" is relatively high, but overall it is decreasing. Intelligent manufacturing reform is in urgent need. see Figures 3.63 to 3.66.

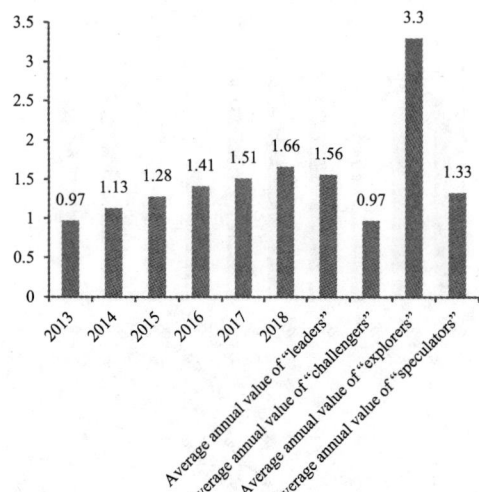

Figure 3.63 2013-2018 average depreciation and amortization of "speculators" (100 million yuan)

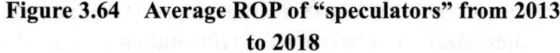

Figure 3.64 Average ROP of "speculators" from 2013 to 2018

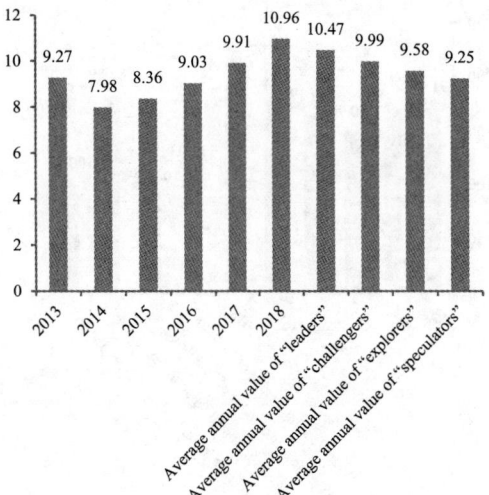

Figure 3.65 2013-2018 average labor costs of "speculators" (10 thousand yuan)

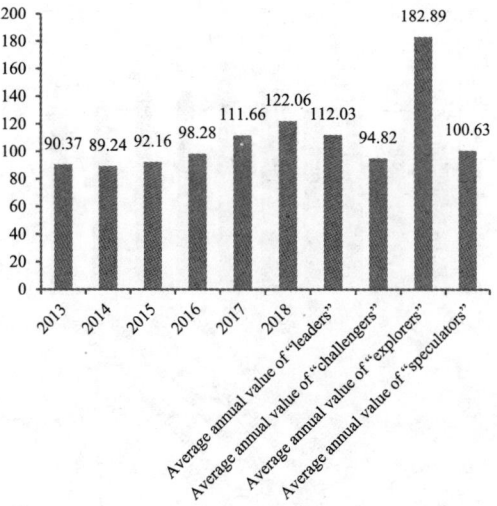

Figure 3.66 average personnel effectiveness of "speculators" from 2013 to 2018 (100 million yuan)

Source: Wind database.

3.3 Logistics: traditional logistics is gradually upgrading toward digital logistics

3.3.1 Digital logistics

The logistics industry is a supporting industry of China's economy. According to the Logistics Industry Big Data Platform, from 2009 to 2016, the proportion of total social logistics costs in the GDP fell from 18.1% to 15.5%. It is a big gap compared with the proportion of logistics costs in developed countries, which accounted for about 10% of the GDP. Improving efficiency and reducing costs become goals that governments, logistics enterprises, and their customers strive to achieve. With the widespread application of information science and technology, digital technology gradually penetrates the logistics industry, promoting the transition from traditional logistics to digital logistics.

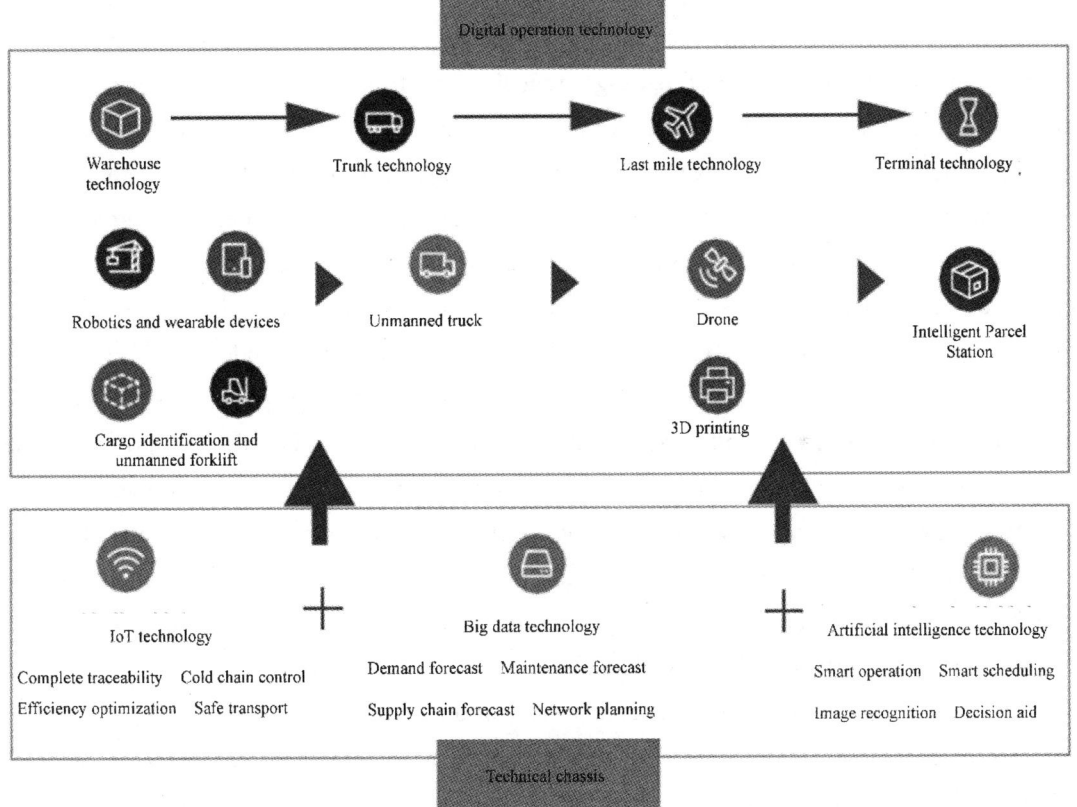

Figure 3.67　A technical overview of digital logistics

Digital logistics refers to the use of digital technologies and means such as intelligent hardware, the Internet of Things, and big data to improve the ability of the analysis, decision-making, and intelligent execution of the logistics system, thus improving the level of intelligence and automation of the entire logistics system. Digital logistics integrates multiple service functions and reflects the needs of modern economic operation characteristics, i.e., emphasizing the fast, efficient, and smooth operation of the flow of information and flow of goods, so as to reduce social costs, improve production efficiency, and integrate social resources.

3.3.2 Upgrading effect of digital technology on the logistics industry

(1) Big data

The driving effect of big data on the logistics industry is reflected in the following four aspects: Firstly, it promotes the accurate matching between the supply and transportation capacity. In O2O platforms, intelligent distribution and intelligent vehicle searches are realized based on big data technology, which improves the utilization rate of transportation resources. For example, Yunmanman and Huochebang effectively reduce the empty-loaded rate of vehicles with the precise matching of vehicles and goods through big data, saving a total of 86 billion yuan in fuel consumption in 2017 alone, reducing carbon emissions by 10 million tons. Secondly, it makes logistics route-scheduling smarter. With big data and artificial intelligence technology, logistics enterprises realize intelligent route planning for vehicles, thus optimizing logistics transportation paths. For example, the intelligent routing service of SF Express can identify the most suitable routing plan for each package, reducing the dispatch rate of customer service by more than 32% and reducing the amount of manual review by more than 60%, thus ranking first in time-efficiency among all express services. Thirdly, it promotes logistics storage and transportation to transform from passive response to active perception. The e-commerce platforms predict the demand according to the consumption trend and big data so that the consumers' orders can be delivered to the door in the shortest time and with the shortest distance. For example, Alibaba Tmall uses big data algorithms to distribute products to areas where consumers are concentrated in advance for storage, thus reducing transportation costs by 40%, and the ratio of same-day and next-day delivery exceeds 80%. Fourthly, it promotes the improvement of coordination of the logistics industry. Internet technology enterprises develop logistics network platform services to promote efficient coordination. For example, Cainiao Network uses big data to predict the congestion of transportation of parcels across the country, which played the role of core coordination hub during the peak of online shopping during the "Double 11" in 2018. It solved the overloading problem during the "logistic peak", i.e., when the business volume of same-day parcel delivery was over one million units for the entire industry.

As of 2018, the scale of China's big data industry reached 438.45 billion yuan. The scale of China's big data service market was 131.73 billion yuan, a year-on-year increase of 36.6%. According to the forecast of the China Center for Information Industry Development, by 2020, the market size of China's big data service market is expected to reach 239.31 billion yuan.

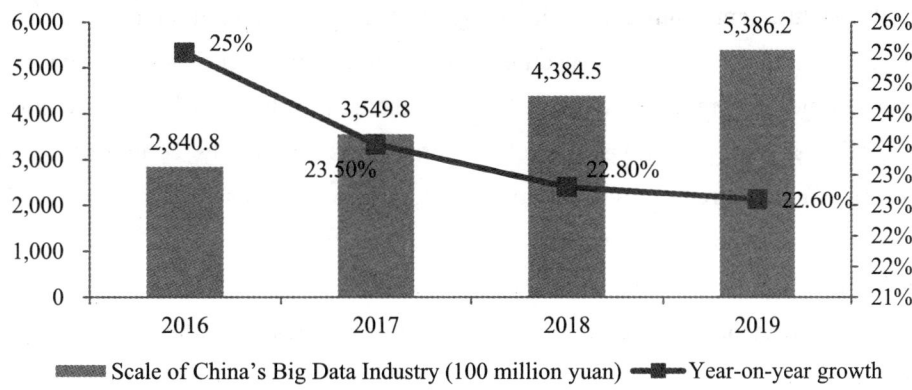

Figure 3.68　Scale and growth of China's big data industry

Source: Qianzhan Industry Research Institute.

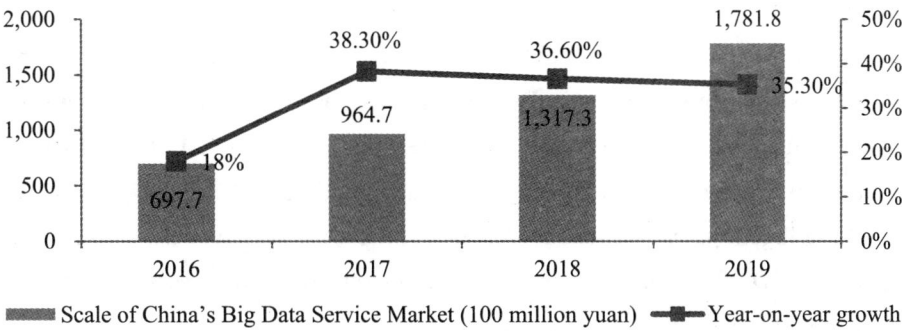

Figure 3.69　Scale and growth of China's big data service market

Source: Qianzhan Industry Research Institute.

(2) The Internet of Things

The Internet of Things and big data analysis rely on each other. The former provides data for the latter to analyze, and the latter commercializes the data of the former. The concept of the Internet of Things is popularized. The Internet of Things is used in three aspects of the logistics industry: warehousing, transportation monitoring, and intelligent terminal of parcels.

Firstly, warehousing. In traditional warehousing, manual scanning and data entry are often required, which results in low efficiency. Meanwhile, warehousing space is unclear, unorganized, and has a lack of process tracking. Applying the Internet of Things technology to traditional warehousing would form an intelligent warehouse management system that improves the efficiency of the entry and exit of goods, expands storage capacity, and reduces labor intensity and labor costs. It also displays and monitors the entry and exit of goods in real time to improve the accuracy of delivery, and completes tasks such as receiving goods into the warehouse, inventory and dispatch, sorting, and exit, as well as data query, backup, statistics, report preparation, and report management of the entire system.

Secondly, transportation monitoring. Real-time monitoring of trucks and goods through the logistics vehicle management system allows real-time location tracking of vehicles and goods, monitors the status, temperature, and humidity of the goods, and monitors the speed, tire temperature, tire pressure, and fuel consumption of vehicles and other driving behaviors such as the number of times the brakes were applied. During the transportation of goods, the information of goods, drivers, and conditions of vehicle driving is efficiently combined to improve transportation efficiency, reduce transportation costs, reduce cargo losses, and clearly understand everything about the transportation process.

Finally, intelligent parcel stations. Based on the Internet of Things, intelligent parcel stations are able to identify, store, monitor, and manage objects. Together with the PC server, they form an intelligent parcel delivery system. The PC server can process the information data collected by the intelligent parcel terminal and update it in the data at the back end in real time. It facilitates users to request parcel delivery information, dispatch parcels, and maintain the parcel terminals.

After the courier delivers the parcel to the designated location and deposits it in the station, the intelligent system would automatically send the user a text message, including the pickup address and verification code. Users can go to the intelligent terminal at any time within 24 hours to pick up the parcel conveniently and quickly. Figure 3.70 shows that the rate of utilization of intelligent parcel stations increases significantly. "Contactless delivery", a concept generated by COVID-19 in 2020, is expected to accelerate educating users, and the penetration of intelligent parcel stations will be significantly increased.

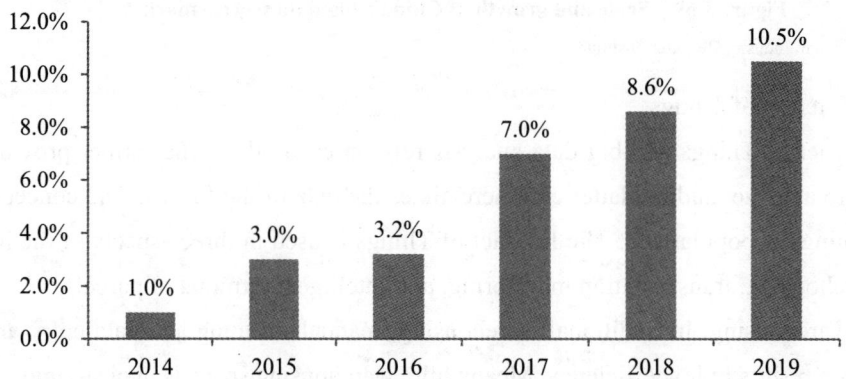

Figure 3.70 Ratio of parcels placed into intelligent parcel stations nationwide (%)
Source: Compiled from public information.

(3) Artificial intelligence

Artificial intelligence technology includes the following five application scenarios: First, management of intelligent operation rules. Through machine learning, the operation rules are equipped with self-teaching and self-adaption capabilities, and make independent decisions after sensing business conditions. For example, artificial intelligence can set production methods, delivery time, transportation cost, abnormal order processing, and other operational rules for orders in scenarios different from regular scenarios during e-commerce peaks (Double 11), thus realizing artificial intelligence processing.

Second, site of the warehouse. Artificial intelligence can fully optimize and learn according to various constraints, such as the geographical locations of customers, suppliers, and manufacturers, economical transportation, availability of labor, cost of construction, taxation systems, etc., and provide the site that is close to the optimal solution.

Third, decision-making assistance. Machine learning and other technologies can identify the status of people, objects, equipment, and vehicles inside and outside the site; learn excellent management experience, dispatch experience, and decision-making from operators; and gradually acquire decision-making assistance and automatic decision-making.

Fourth, image recognition. Utilize computer image recognition, address library, and convolutional neural network to improve the recognition rate and accuracy of handwritten waybill machines, thereby significantly reducing the workload and possibility of erroneous manual input.

Fifth, intelligent dispatching. Through the analysis of basic data such as the quantity and volume of commodities, dispatch various links such as packaging and transportation vehicles intelligently. For instance, by calculating the volume and size of packaging of millions of SKU commodities and by using deep learning algorithm technology, the system intelligently calculates and recommends consumables and packing orders so as to arrange the type of packaging and the placement plan of commodities in a rational way.

3.4 The medical care industry: continuous empowerment of digital technology

3.4.1 Digital medical care

Digital medical care refers to the use of information technology to digitize and informatize the entire medical process. Broadly speaking, it includes not only the informatization of hospital diagnosis and treatment processes, but also the informatization of regional medical collaboration, public health and epidemic prevention, medical supervision, and medical insurance management, involving the comprehensive application of equipment, computer software, (mobile) Internet, and other technologies. Digital medical care is not only a technological application, but should also be regarded as a revolutionary medical method. In the long run, digitalization will have a profound impact on the entire medical process, doctor-patient relationship, and health management methods, just like what we see in the financial and retail industries. It is therefore the direction and management goal of modern medical care.

Initially, digitization in the medical field was reflected primarily in diagnostic equipment, such as bio-signal collecting and processing equipment like electrocardiograms and electroencephalograms, as well as optical, electromagnetic, and acoustic imaging equipment such as CT, color Doppler ultrasound, digital X-ray, and ultrasound. They helped the medical industry better realize the visualization of patient information and strengthen doctors' diagnostic capabilities. Currently, the connotation of medical informatization refers to the application of computer software and hardware in the medical care industry, including traditional software informatization technologies, as well as new generation IT such as cloud computing, big data, artificial intelligence, and the Internet of Things. As Chinese people desire a better life and have higher requirements for a better quality of lifestyle, China's total expenditure of medical care increases year by year, and the market scale of information technology-based medical services, such as mobile medicine, is also rapidly expanding. see Figures 3.71 and 3.72.

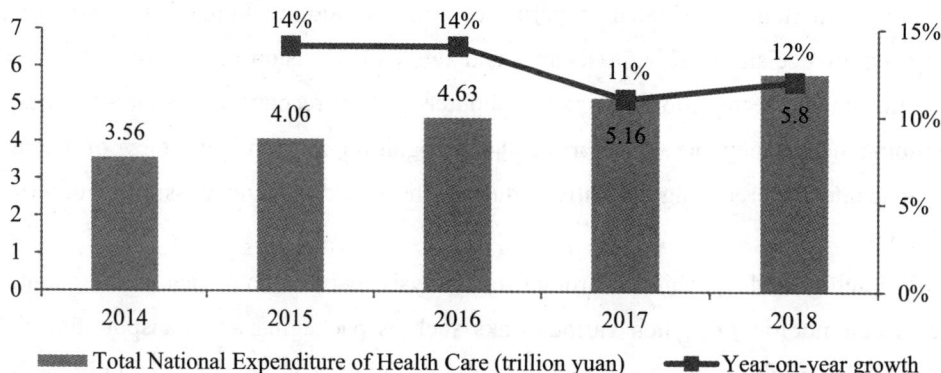

Figure 3.71   Changes in total national expenditure of health care from 2014 to 2018

Source: National Health Commission.

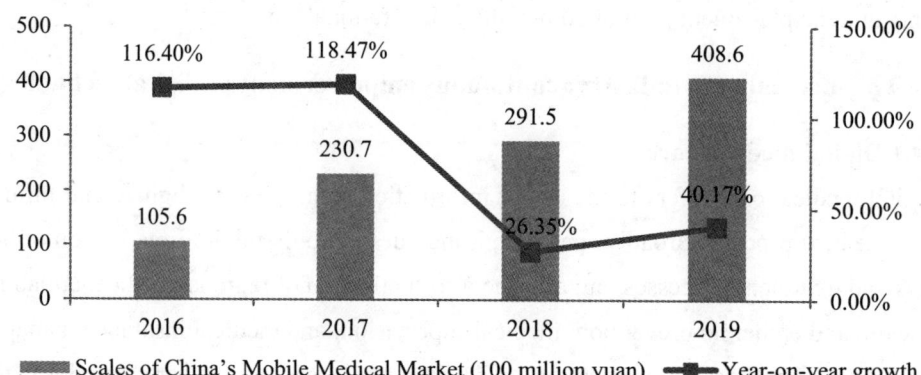

Figure 3.72   2016-2019 China's mobile medical market scale and changes

Source: Analysys.

3.4.2 The role of digital technology in upgrading medical services

Just like in the fields of logistics and finance, new-generation information technologies such as cloud computing, big data, artificial intelligence, the Internet of Things, and blockchain are also penetrating the medical industry. Formally, this penetration includes not only the integration of new technologies with existing IT systems, helping them deepen and upgrade functions, but also new forms of applications driven by new technological features that did not exist in the past. At present, digital technology is affecting the medical care industry in the following aspects:

(1) Cloud computing

As a revolution in IT infrastructure, cloud computing not only brings changes to the hardware infrastructure of medical institutions at the IaaS level, but also has a more important impact on the medical information system at the software architecture level. Currently, most medical information systems are C/S (Client/Server) architecture based on traditional single or vertical architecture software design, while cloud systems are based on SOA or B/S (Browser/Server) architecture constructed by microservice technology.

Compared with traditional IT systems, cloud systems are loosely coupled through componentization or microservices, which are technically more scalable with low operation and maintenance costs, facilitate the deployment and application of innovative technologies, and are easier to support complex large-scale or heterogeneous systems. This is especially important for implementing inter-agency regional medical care and the integrated application of large medical care groups. Secondly, for the hospital, the use of cloud architecture makes it easier for departments to open up data exchange channels, thus maintaining data consistency, and easier to deploy delivery than traditional software. see table 3.2.

Table 3.2 Main differences between traditional medical IT systems and cloud architecture systems

Dimensions of comparison	Cloud systems	Traditional systems
Realization of technology	SOA architecture/microservice architecture	Monolithic architecture/vertical architecture
Software architecture	B/S architecture	C/S architecture
possibility of extension	componentization, loose coupling, easy to expand	tightly coupled, difficult to expand
integrated application within groups	support	doesn't support
operation and maintenance management	once built, used by multiple parties	difficult to maintain, high cost

Source: CSDN.

(2) Big data

Big data technology uses massive or even full data for analysis. It has a large volume of data, excellent real-time performance, and diverse types. Despite the low density of data value, it integrates massive structured or unstructured data sources and diversified data analysis technologies that can tap into information that cannot be obtained through traditional methods. The development of medical care activities relies heavily on information and data. After years of accumulation, the medical care industry has accumulated a considerable amount of data (diagnosis and treatment data, health data, R&D data, operational data, etc.). Although the quality of data needs to be improved, it constitutes the basis for big data analysis in many aspects.

Now, big data technology is rapidly penetrating the medical care industry, which is reflected in the following aspects: ① Analysis based on the clinical data of a large number of patients helps doctors make a more accurate diagnosis in the diagnosis and treatment activities; ② Wearable equipment can monitor patients' vital signs remotely and can realize the management of chronic diseases or health conditions more efficiently and at a low cost; ③ With the help of big data, public health departments can monitor multi-dimensional data such as medical and public opinions, which helps carry out epidemic prevention and control in a forward-looking approach; ④With big data technology, medical insurance departments analyze medical behavior patterns and the spread of doctor-patient relations to make up for the shortcomings that are easy to be exploited under fixed rules. Medicare expense control and medical quality improvement shift from "empirical decision-making" to "data decision-making"; ⑤ Insurance enterprises use big data technology to manage commercial insurance claims in order to reduce reimbursement fraud and excessive medical risks; ⑥ Pharmaceutical enterprises use big data technology to assist pharmaceutical research and development activities, which can reduce the cost of trial and error of research and development.

(3) Artificial intelligence

Currently, artificial intelligence (AI) remains a relatively vague concept. Generally speaking, it is a discipline that studies and develops theories, methods, technologies, and application systems used to simulate, extend, and expand human intelligence. At the technical level, mainstream AI technologies include machine learning, language recognition, image recognition, natural language processing, knowledge graphs, etc. Some of the above have begun to be applied in the medical care field, but due to the complexity of medical activities, it all still remains at a generally primitive level.

Currently, AI technology is based on algorithms, computing power, and data, therefore it is closely integrated with cloud computing and big data technology. In particular, AI and big data technology are so deeply integrated into many application scenarios that it is difficult to distinguish one from the other. In medical care, typical applications of AI are as follows: ① AI-based medical image recognition has started trials in imaging departments or regional imaging centers, and is currently targeted at relatively simple scenarios such as tuberculosis recognition, fundus screening, bone age testing, etc.; ② Voice interaction technology is being applied in systems or equipment such as voice electronic medical records, intelligent diagnosis guides, etc.; ③ knowledge graphs, machine learning, natural semantic processing, and other technologies are combined with big data and applied in medically assisted decision-making, epidemic prediction, and medical research, pharmaceutical development, and other fields; ④ AI technology is also applied in the management and performance evaluation of hospitals or medical insurance.

(4) The Internet of Things

Different from mobile Internet, which connects people to people, the Internet of Things establishes an extensive network among things, and between people and things. Medical behaviors include diagnosis, treatment, monitoring, medication and equipment management, and other activities, involving the interaction between doctors, nurses, patients, medication, equipment, and other objects. The Internet of Things technology significantly improves efficiency in information collection and interaction control.

As the Internet of Things matures, the medical Internet of Things starts to show signs of accelerated development. Domestically, leading hospitals are deploying more Internet of Things applications in their medical systems. Specifically, medical IoT applications are primarily reflected in the following aspects: ① Real-time collection of data of patients' physical signs to help medical staff make a more comprehensive and accurate diagnosis or timely prevention, and improve the level of intellectualization; ② More convenient access to patient's identity, location, and other information so as to reduce the probability of accidents, such as the incorrect administration of medication, and to find the patient in time in case of emergency and ensure the safety of patients; ③ Collecting medical equipment operation data to operate and maintain it more efficiently; ④ Tracking and management of medication, consumables, blood, etc., to ensure the information matches patients accurately and improve the level of asset management.

(5) Blockchains

In its essence, blockchains are distributed ledgers, which means they are difficult to falsify, are decentralized, and are traceable. These satisfy the requirements for data protection. The zero-knowledge proof technology helps protect privacy. Based on this feature, the potential application scenarios of blockchains in the medical care industry are related to the protection and sharing of patient data, such as data authorization and management in diagnosis and treatment, scientific research, medical insurance reimbursement, and commercial insurance claims; secondly, data management of wearable devices related to medical care can also be combined with blockchain technology; besides, the supply chain and internal circulation management of medical devices and pharmaceutical consumables can also apply blockchain technology due to its difficulty to be falsified. Currently, blockchain technology is yet to mature, and its application in medical care is extremely limited. The level of technology and its ecosystem need to be improved to determine the possibility of future promotion.

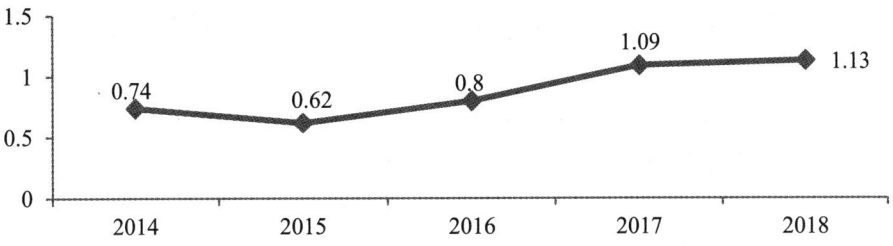

Figure 3.73 Changes in the proportion of the annual budget of informatization investment of Chinese hospitals (%)

Source: CHIMA.

3.5 E-commerce: new retail becomes the future "tailwind"

3.5.1 Development and current status of e-commerce

As a product of the Internet era, e-commerce is centered on information technology and makes all links of transaction networked and informatized; thanks to the popularization of network infrastructure and the upgrading of digitalized information technology, the form of e-commerce constantly updates and iterates. New forms of business, such as live e-commerce and social e-commerce, emerge.

In recent years, the scale of online retail has continued to grow, and its share in total social retail has continued to increase. As offline experience and online consumption divert flows mutually, the integration of the two channels further expands the scale of online retail. According to the data of the China e-Business Research Center, the transaction volume of China's online shopping market in 2017 was 7.2 trillion yuan, a year-on-year increase of 39.2%, accounting for 19.6% of retail sales of consumer goods. On the whole, the growth of the online retail market has gradually slowed down, but the market scale has remained large, and its proportion in the total retail sales of consumer goods will continue to increase.

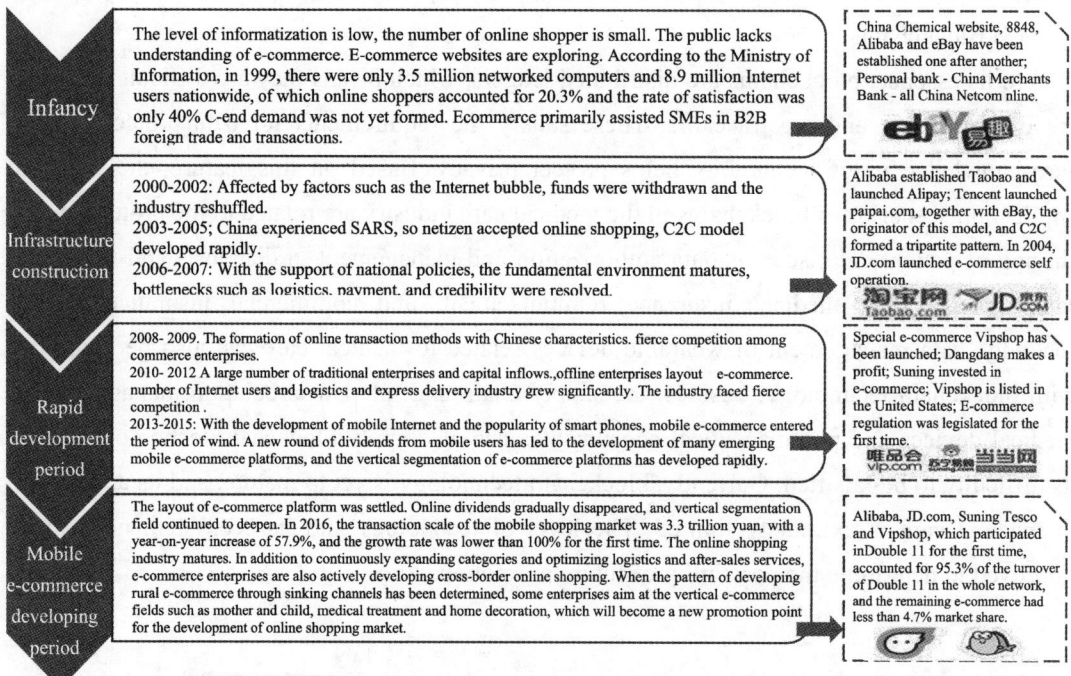

Figure 3.74 Development of China's e-commerce

Source: Compiled from public information.

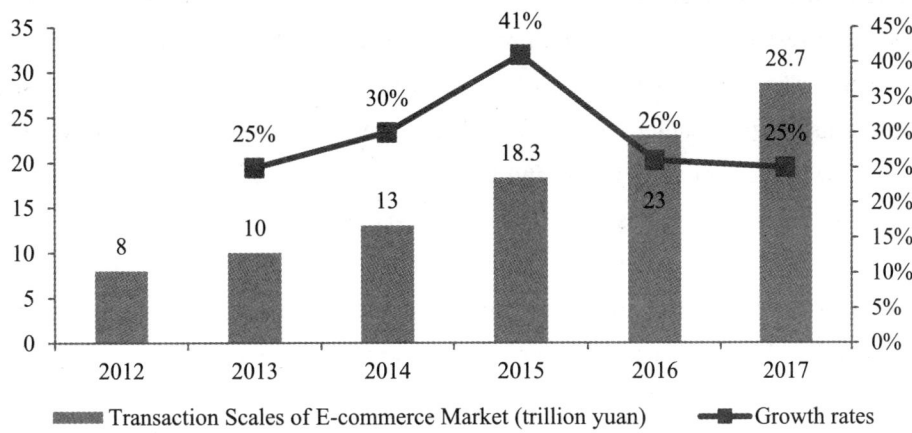

Figure 3.75　Transaction scale of China's e-commerce market
Source: China e-Business Research Center.

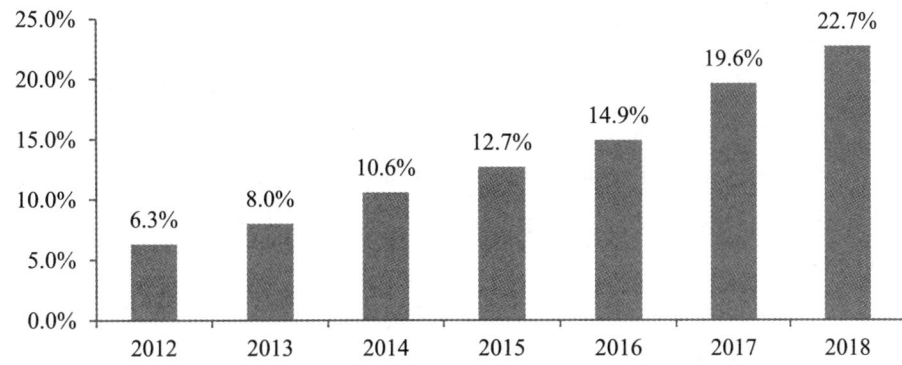

Figure 3.76　Proportions of social retail sales in China's online shopping market (%)
Source: China e-Business Research Center.

3.5.2 Digital economy upgrades the e-commerce industry

Digital economy and e-commerce interact and promote each other: On the one hand, e-commerce provides platforms and opportunities for the digitization of traditional industries; on the other hand, digital economy provides technical support for the generation and development of e-commerce. Its driving mechanism is reflected in the following aspects:

Firstly, it breaks the geographical restrictions and achieves full network coverage of sales. Traditionally, offline businesses are subject to geographical restrictions. The business environment of physical stores is complex. The operation environment for individual stores and for chain stores varies significantly. However, with the popularization of the infrastructure of digital economy, the scale of online shopping malls is increasingly large, and they are free from geographical restrictions and category restrictions. Its characteristics decide that in each subdivision track and category, e-commerce focuses on marketing across the entire network and unlimited expansion of users. Within 3-5 years, the combination of online hot-selling strategy and the scale effect of e-commerce would achieve the brand influence that offline brands can only achieve in more than a decade.

Secondly, it reshapes the circulation process and shortens the distance between businesses and consumers. The traditional relationship between production and sales was: supplier> manufacturer>distributor>retailer>customer. There are limitations such as disorganized distributions, low transaction efficiency, and high cost. E-commerce compresses multiple levels of agencies. Platform-based stores or self-operated e-commerce stores face a large number of consumers directly and undertake large-volume needs of commodities. Therefore, platform-based stores or self-operated e-commerce stores can conduct centralized large-scale procurement and scale warehousing and logistics, thus reducing supply chain costs and logistics costs and forming a scale advantage.

Thirdly, it depicts consumer profiles accurately and then achieves accurate recommendations of products and advertisements. E-commerce platforms use big data to count consumption data in various dimensions, including population-specific data (age, gender, purchasing capability, etc.), traffic data (browsing history, browsing duration, etc.), and order data (color, price, refund status, etc.) to depict consumers' portraits accurately and build models; then artificial intelligence algorithms are used to recommend products for consumers and place information traffic-based advertisements accurately according to requirements and product characteristics of the brand, thus avoiding damaging the user experience and improving the efficiency of sales.

Fourthly, it accumulates a large amount of data to form a bilateral "moat". The real advantage of e-commerce platforms lies in the massive data they accumulate. Through data accumulation and calculation, platforms can provide all stores with accurate information about the purchase, sales, and storage of goods, thereby effectively improving product turnover and reducing storage and distribution costs. When the platform accumulates a certain amount of data, enterprises will start a self-sustaining growth process, superimposing the first-mover advantage in obtaining data and feeding back shops at the B-end and users at the C-end. The behaviors of shops and consumers will influence each other. Data advantage becomes the "moat" of the head platform.

3.5.3 Future development trend of e-commerce: integrating online and offline, initiating a new era of retail

2017 is called the "first year of new retail". In recent years, the growth rate of mobile Internet users in China has slowed down, and the demographic dividends are disappearing. The cost of online customer acquisition rises, and the space of e-commerce shrinks. Offline channels still account for more than 74% of national FMCG sales, and profitable accesses of e-commerce platforms are transferring offline. Alibaba first proposed the concept of "new retail" in October 2016. Retail giants such as JD, Yonghui, Bailian, Gome, and IKEA began to deploy it.

Table 3.3 **Understanding of new retail by major e-commerce platforms**

Enterprises	Understanding of new retail
Alibaba	New retail is a concept and technology based on the Internet. It fully reforms and upgrades the existing social retail through the integration of online, offline, and logistics, and improves the efficiency of the production, circulation, and service process of goods.
Xiaomi	The nature of new retail is to improve efficiency and release consumer demand through product upgrades.
Haier E-commerce	New retail is the integration of enterprises and user experience, providing consumers with the best experience, realizing customized solutions, and overturning the existing manufacturing system.
Suning	Under new retail, the Internet of Things will be combined with AI to perceive consumers, predict consumption trends, and guide manufacturers to provide diversified and customized services.
JD	Under the fourth retail revolution, the infrastructure will be intelligent and coordinated to upgrade cost efficiency and experience.

Source: Compiled from public information.

Although the understanding of new retail by major e-commerce platforms varies, the understanding of the nature of the emergence of new retail coincides: new retail is the result of increasingly mature technologies such as the mobile Internet, the Internet of Things, and big data. Looking forward, new retail will realize a retail model of "all scenarios, all customer groups, all data, all channels, all time periods, all experiences, all categories, and all links", which is reflected as the following:

All-channel operation and marketing: Connecting online and offline to form an all-channel business model is a consensus reached by the retail industry. Amazon's acquisition of Whole Foods Supermarket and Ali's investment in commercial supermarkets are typical all-channel-oriented thinking. Be it from the technical side or from the consumer demand side, all-channel has become a "standard configuration" for new retail. In terms of offline physical stores, with the help of sensor integration, face recognition, and voice recognition, applications such as smart shopping guides, consumer behavior data collecting, and commodity status tracking can be realized.

Data drives manufacturing: In the era of new retail, all commodities, users, and consumer behavior will be digitized, and user identification and service accesses will also be digitized. Meanwhile, as big data applications cover sales analysis, inventory analysis, consumer behavior analysis, precision marketing, etc., the efficiency of retail business operations will be improved, such as using the flow of consumers and clicks to study consumption habits and achieve precision marketing.

Scenario-based experience penetrates products and services: Enterprise products will be designed to function based on scenarios to improve the user experience. Enterprises will use big data to analyze and predict consumption scenarios to improve the customer experience. Through consumer big data analysis, enterprises can understand customer needs, predict scenarios, and optimize products and services.

Communities become the main entrance of traffic: As rents rise and profits drop, it has become inevitable that physical stores in China are getting smaller and smaller. Convenience stores, boutique supermarkets, community-based shopping malls, and other community businesses will become an important direction for retail enterprises that look for transformation and upgrading. The role of the communities as the main entrance of traffic will become increasingly important.

Section 4   Representative Digital Enterprises in China

4.1 Fanmi technology: reaching out the source of planting, tracking the entire industry chain of quality control

In March 2014, Beijing Fanmi IoT Technology Co., Ltd. was established. Fanmi Technology reaches out to the source of planting with the help of Internet technology and launches the core product "Fan Mi Li" IoT operating system. With quality control as the core, it connects the front ends with the back ends and creates a platform that connects the entire industry chain. Agriculture, as a traditional industry, has significant pain points: farmers who are at the production end are faced with information asymmetry and low management levels; consumers who are at the consumption end find it difficult to trace the process of planting agricultural products, and food safety issues frequently occur. Fanmi Technology believes that quality control must start from the source to solve the problem. Through real-time monitoring and guidance of planting procedures of agricultural products, the quality of agricultural products is improved, and consumers are better aware of the process of how agricultural products grow. The investment cost at the early stage is relatively high when quality control sensors are deployed. Currently, Fanmi limits the cost to 1,000 yuan/mu and plans the duration of each sensor/mu for five years. This means the equipment cost is about 200 yuan/mu/year at the early stage.

As shown in Figure 3.77, after completing the quality control sensor and platform construction, Fanmi's Internet of Things plays an important role: the installation of collecting and monitoring sensors in customers' plantations to monitor the growth information of agricultural products in real time; the information collected by sensors is passed to the quality control center of the platform; the platform updates the data to the product archives, and gives on-site feedback based on the monitoring results; product identification codes are generated to facilitate consumers to scan and trace; eventually, the customer experience at the terminal is sent back to the platform to provide real-time information for the evaluation of product quality.

Chapter 3 Digital Economy and Industrial Upgrading • 169 •

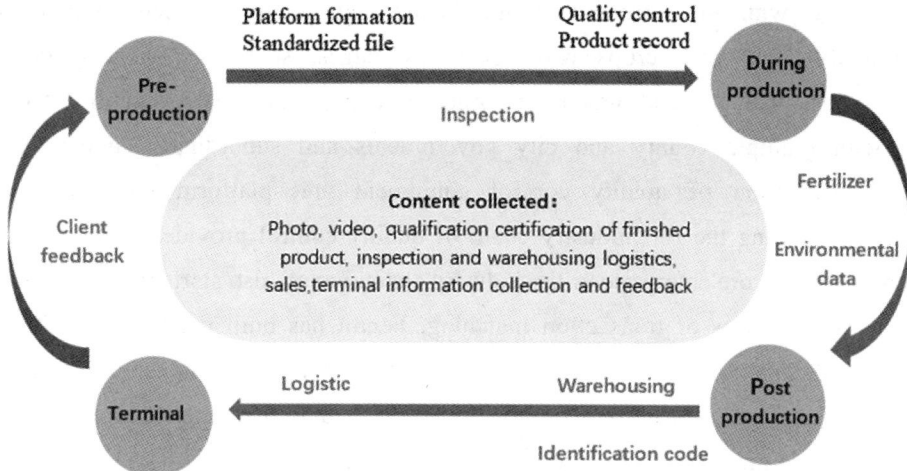

Figure 3.77 Fanmi quality control sensor platform and deployment

Source: TF Securities Research Institute.

Finally, when consumers purchase agricultural products, they can see the identification codes displayed on them. By scanning the identification code, consumers would understand essential information such as growth, transportation process, and quality of agricultural products through text, pictures, videos, and other methods. As consumers upgrade consumption and are increasingly concerned about food safety issues, products tested by Fanmi are expected to be recognized by the market and consumers.

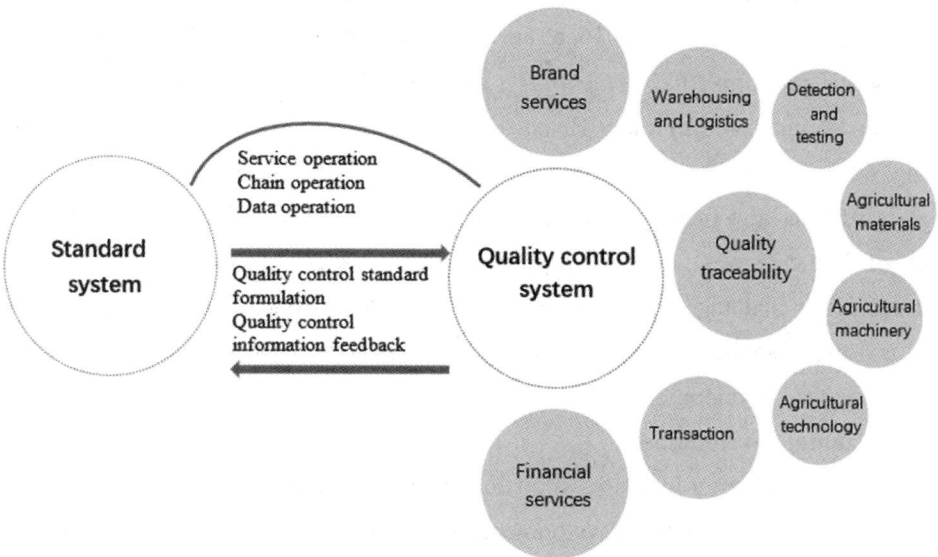

Figure 3.78 Fanmi quality control system

Source: TF Securities Research Institute.

Fanmi focuses on regional, individual products to build brands and deploy with a variety of services for future development. As a young brand, Fanmi focuses its resources in Weifang,

Shandong Province, with an awareness of introducing high-quality products. It deploys its platforms around a few cash crops with local advantages, such as radish, ginger, and watermelon, to establish a brand image. In order to expand the scale, Fanmi establishes cooperation with multiple county and city governments and subordinate cooperatives to complete the installation of quality control equipment and platform deployment. The characteristics of tracking the full industry chain of quality control provide Fanmi with great potential to become the core enterprise of the industry chain. Fanmi also starts to deploy in every link. For example, in terms of transaction matching, Fanmi has built cooperation with TOC platforms (such as JD) as well as TOB wholesale markets, chain restaurants, and boutique fruit and vegetable markets; in the financial sector, it has established an industrial fund with the local government to provide financial services to platform partners.

4.2 RootCloud: a pioneer of the industrial Internet platform

On June 25, 2019, internationally-renowned research organization Gartner announced the results of the 2019 IIoT (Industrial Internet Platform) Magic Quadrant. It is reported that there were more than 40 platforms in the world that met the selection criteria of the Magic Quadrant. 16 platforms were selected. With its industrial Internet platform ROOTCLOUD, RootCloud became the first Chinese enterprise to enter the list since Gartner launched the Magic Quadrant in 2018.

RootCloud was previously known as Root Cloud Platform, which was introduced as an IoT platform within the Sany Group. In 2016, after resource integration, "Root Cloud" was upgraded to an open public platform "ROOTCLOUD", and RootCloud became an industrial Internet platform enterprise incubated by Sany Heavy Industry. In 2017, RootCloud developed rapidly, empowering 42 industries and connecting more than 400,000 high-value devices. At the beginning of 2018, its first financing amounted to several hundred million yuan. In June 2019, its B-round of financing was 500 million yuan. As the advancement of the industrial Internet platform faces many challenges, it is worth investigating how RootCloud has stood out in just three years and better applied digital technology to industrial scenarios. This is reflected in the horizontal and vertical development of the industrial Internet platform of RootCloud.

4.2.1 Horizontal development

Incubated by Sany Heavy Industry, RootCloud is embedded with powerful industrial genes. From the perspective of horizontal development, thanks to industrial "know-how", RootCloud developed a path of "equipment -> factory -> industry chain -> general platform". During the first two years after it was founded, RootCloud positioned its most experienced aftermarket services as its core business, i.e., providing equipment networking, real-time monitoring, remote operation and maintenance, predictive maintenance, and other services around industrial equipment assets. Currently, it not only provides equipment aftermarket services, but also focuses on the other three industrial application scenarios with rigid demands: asset management of the production line, energy consumption management, and industry chain financial services. In terms of industrial segmentation, RootCloud has extended from its best engineering machinery and equipment to other areas of high-value and key equipment, including air compressors, stamping, casting equipment, etc., and has covered 61 segments. It has also helped leading enterprises build 14 industrial cloud platforms including the casting industry chain, injection and molding industry chain, and textile industry chain.

Based on the experience of Sany Heavy Industry in the aftermarket service of construction machinery, RootCloud gradua!ly expands to the aftermarket service of high-value and key equipment in other industries, and then expands to the production optimization services of the factories where these equipment are applied, thereby forming an industrial Internet platform solution at the level of industry chain; meanwhile, it expands to multiple industries horizontally and eventually forms a cross-industry, cross-discipline, universal industrial Internet platform.

4.2.2 Vertical deployment

Vertically, the industrial Internet platform of RootCloud is divided into three parts: IoT, data, and application. This vertical structure is presented with the example of "big data cloud platform of the new energy lithium battery drying equipment".

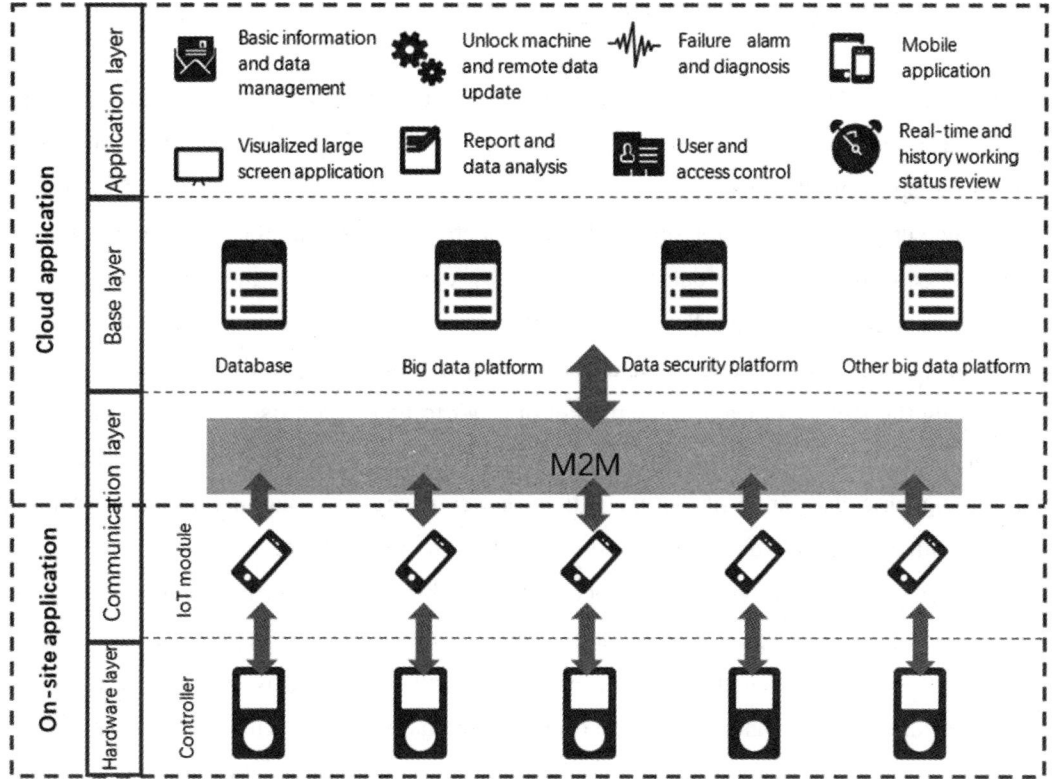

Figure 3.79 Big data cloud platform of the new energy lithium battery drying equipment
Source: Official website of RootCloud.

On this structure, IoT is at the bottom. Taking the practical status of China's industry into consideration, RootCloud focuses on API and multi-protocol compatibility that can integrate various ICS systems, enabling its powerful IoT access capabilities. Now, RootCloud supports more than 400 types of industrial protocols such as Modbus, Profinet, OPCDA/OPC UA, etc., which can be connected to a series of PLC, CNC, sensors, and other special equipment of OEM manufacturers; the ROUTCLOUD platform covers 95% of the mainstream industrial control systems and is compatible with 100% of the general international hardware interfaces with quick access to the equipment. Specifically, the ROUTCLOUD platform has access to more than 560,000 pieces of industrial equipment and has connected more than 450 billion assets.

Data is in the middle. As more and more devices are connected and served by RootCloud, it pays more and more attention to the value of data. The data collected by various production line equipment can solve many internal problems related to production for factories, such as predicting the damage from cutting devices according to the data of the machines, etc. Currently, RootCloud supports PB-level industrial big data processing and analysis capabilities, millisecond-level data distribution, over 8,000 data indicators, and a data processing speed of 1.5+ million pieces per second. Based on mainstream data mining, machine learning, and artificial intelligence technologies, RootCloud conducts big data mining and analysis and establishes failure diagnosis, failure anticipation, health assessment, quality control, and other data models.

Application is at the top, which satisfies the data application requirements of various manufacturing enterprises. This is combined with the horizontal development of services based on industrial application scenarios.

Taking service providers for lithium battery electric vehicle manufacturers as an example, RootCloud can collect battery data in real time by empowering the monitoring of the UNe electric drive lithium battery. It allows electric vehicle manufacturers to implement full life-cycle management of new energy batteries, and dynamically monitor the operating data of the batteries from leaving the factory to leaving the market in order to help enterprises understand the health status of the equipment. It also allows manufacturers to improve and optimize the battery life cycle through big data analysis. Users will be better aware of remaining battery power and remaining mileage so as to avoid electricity exhaustion in the middle of a trip.

In order to allow data visualization technology to bring lean improvements to enterprises, RootCloud proposes the idea of sinking data analysis and visualization capabilities into business processes: if customers can use a huge amount of data collected by the industrial Internet platform efficiently, they can empower the digitalized transformation of more industries.

Thus, a product positioned at the data layer and serves the application is introduced—big data workshop. Adopting a graphical and interactive approach, the big data workshop is a data service platform that provides user management, data management, task scheduling, and task monitoring functions. Data analysis and visualization are derived from Data Analytics, a data visualization analysis product provided by DataHunter, which is a specialized data visualization analysis and business intelligence service provider in China. It allows data experts and employees with no engineering background to have easy access and collect massive amounts of data and obtain data analysis results more easily and in a more straightforward way. Presenting the data results in the form of a report allows the data to speak for itself. For example, users can view the status of the equipment in real time, predict equipment failures in real time, and evaluate the health value of the equipment so as to quickly maintain equipment with insufficient health values with the equipment health status model.

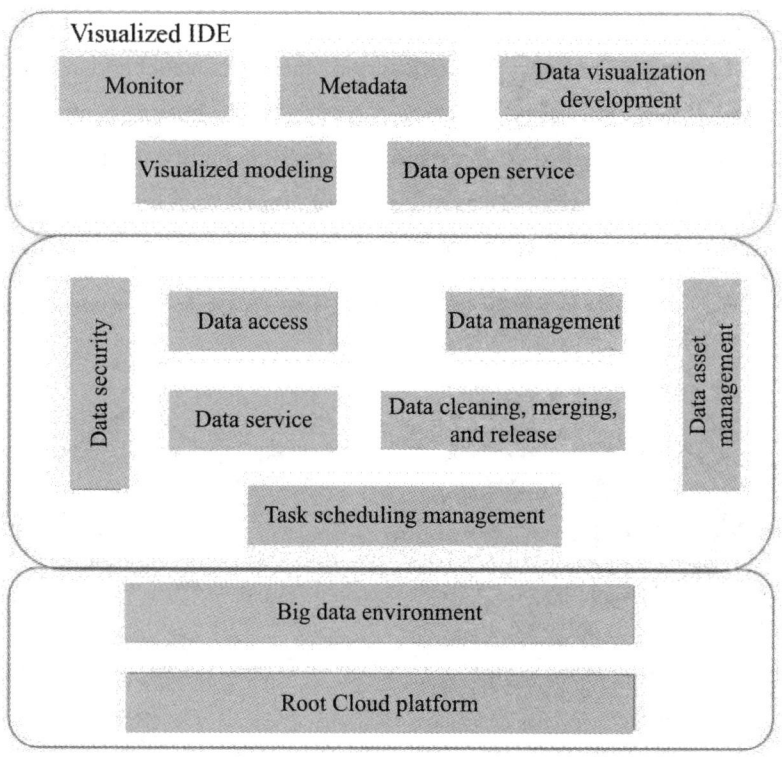

Figure 3.80 Structure of big data workshop

Source: Compiled from public information.

The strategic model of RootCloud has been generally recognized by the market, with customers all over the world and numerous practical cases. Based on the accumulation in the manufacturing industry, RootCloud has built a complete industrial Internet platform system covering the connection layer, platform layer, application layer, and other structures so that digital technology can be better applied to real industrial scenarios. It also forms a standard package that allows enterprises to quickly build application models with specific attributes based on the ROUTCLOUD's bottom platform to empower domestic and international enterprises.

Following the nationwide transformation and upgrading of the manufacturing industry and the construction of intelligent manufacturing parks, RootCloud expanded its national deployment. It has been in Guangzhou and settled in Beijing, Shanghai, Changsha, Suzhou, and Xi'an. It not only focuses on clustering in the areas of China's advanced manufacturing industry, but also radiates into the Beijing-Tianjin-Hebei region, the Yangtze River Delta, and Central China, and drives the nationwide industrial Internet application and helps the Chinese manufacturing industry overtake.

4.3 SF Express: a benchmark in the logistics industry

SF Express was established in 1993. Since its establishment, SF Express has adopted a centralized and differentiated strategy to position itself in the mid-to-high-end market and has occupied an absolute advantage. In terms of business strategy, the forward-looking direct sales model helps SF Express secure service quality and market control, and establishes a sound reputation and brand premium, all of which help secure higher business unit prices. Its higher prices correspond with high-quality services and delivery punctuality. SF Express focuses on the delivery of mid-to-high-end parcels, especially small items, and has built a reputation and formed a positive brand image among C-end users.

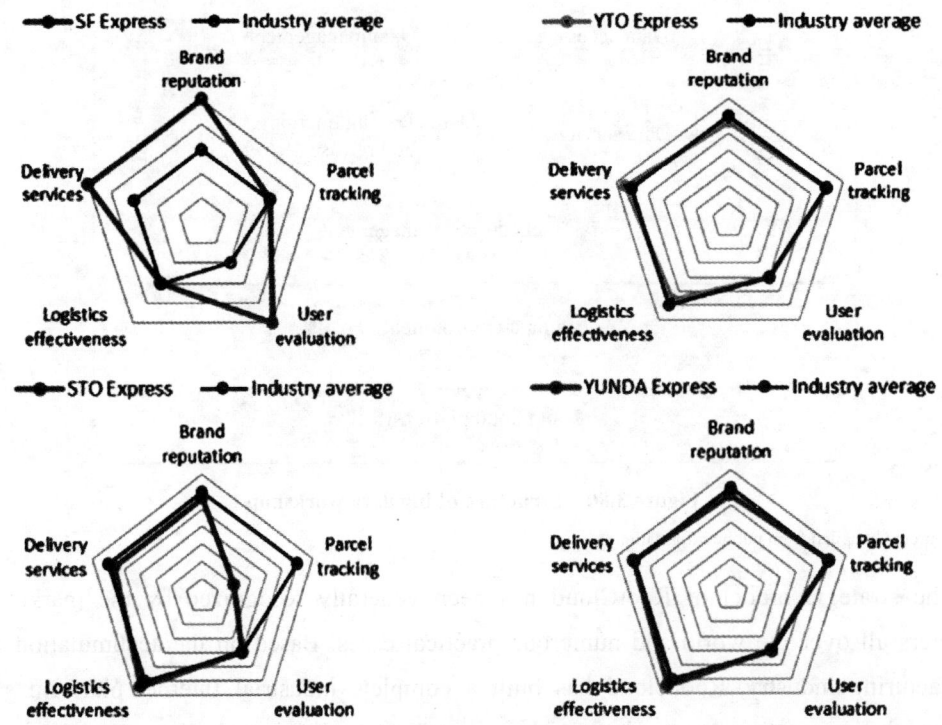

Figure 3.81 Comparison of Taobao parcel index among SF Express, YTO, STO, and Yunda
Source: Taobao.com.

In the context of digital economy, based on its judgment on the development of domestic urbanization and international trade, SF Express focuses on data as its core and uses technologies such as "warehousing, automation, AGV, and artificial intelligence" to realize the interconnection of data, thereby reducing the cost of the logistics supply chain. Therefore, SF Express is dedicated to increasing its efforts on research and development. From 2015 to 2018, its annual compound growth rate of R&D investment was 60.55%. In 2018, it invested 2.723 billion yuan in technology, accounting for 3% of its revenue, a 1.36% increase from 2017.

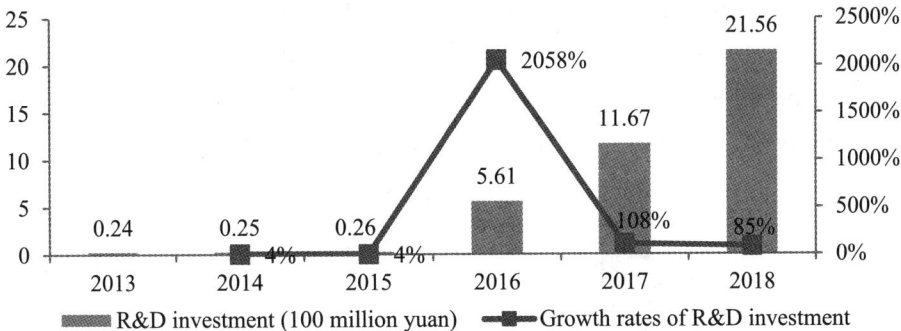

Figure 3.82 SF Express's R&D investment and growth rates from 2013 to 2018

Source: Enterprise announcements.

The significance of R&D to SF Express is reflected in the following: (1) Cost reduction and efficiency improvement: The courier industry is a typical labor-intensive industry. As China's demographic dividend gradually disappears, it is inevitable that technology will replace labor. (2) Business volume increase: The courier delivery industry has a significant scale effect. Cost reduction and efficiency improvement would further increase the scale. In addition, the market of commercial parcels requires enterprises to respond fast and place information in advance. The process of R&D and innovation is also one that constantly consolidates the base. (3) The accumulation and transformation of big data: In this essence, the disagreement between SF Express and Cainiao in June 2017 was a fight for data at the delivery end of future logistics e-commerce. For enterprises, accurate and efficient business forecasts based on data will be one of the core foundations for traditional decision-making to transform toward smart decision-making.

As the investment in science and technology continues to grow, the central direction of development for SF Express includes the following aspects.

4.3.1 IoT robots

Before 2009, SF Express was committed to introducing high-tech from the outside. SF Express equipped every delivery vehicle with GPS to record all the details of courier delivery. After 2009, SF Express changed its views on courier delivery, transit, and other details, started to look at the details with a holistic thinking, started to set up cloud computing and big data centers, and built a logistics system through its own network and data centers, laying the foundation for the future.

From 2009 to 2015, SF Express continued to prepare technical resources such as the

Internet of Things, distributed data networks, etc., to prepare for future data access. After 2016, the technical foundation of cloud computing matured. SF Express began to focus more on artificial intelligence and big data, and combined them with the Internet of Things. For instance, there are RFID tags that can intelligently identify parcels, and smart sensors that can identify the temperature and humidity of parcels. Based on these, SF Express establishes a multi-level network that can transmit this information to data centers from across the country.

Once these foundations are built, they can be applied to many scenarios. For example, in the medical care sector, SF Express has its own smart parcels that can control the temperature of the transportation process. It is able to show if the parcel is handled with violence during the process, and the speed with which the parcel is dropped can be recorded.

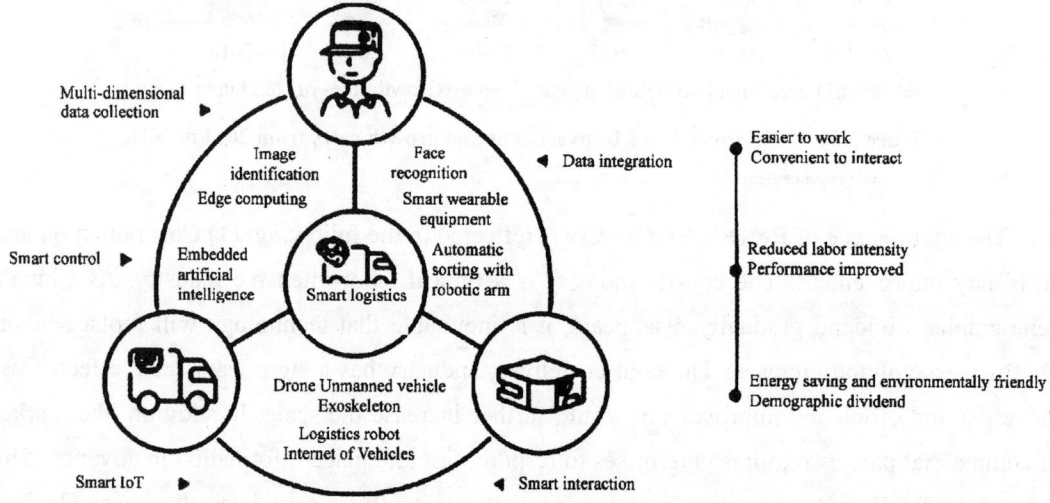

Figure 3.83   The logistics system supported by the Internet of Things
Source: Official website of SF Express.

In order to achieve full process control, SF Express hired experts from abroad to control operation and mobile robots on-site so that these robots can be applied to all links of sorting and transportation.

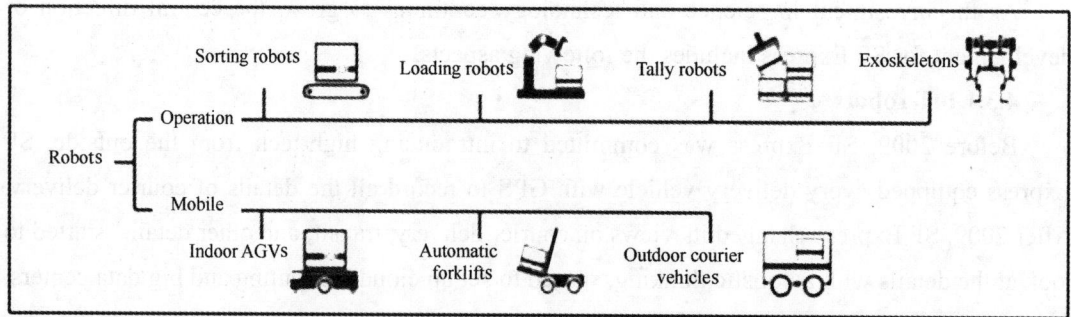

Figure 3.84   IoT robots of SF Express
Source: Official website of SF Express.

4.3.2 Artificial intelligence

SF's artificial intelligence has three major directions. The first is natural speech recognition, such as using smart customer service for after-sales problems. The second is computer vision. For example, OCR technology replaces the manual input of orders, saving a lot of repetitive work and making the address recognition and correction of 10 million pictures a day into an automated process. The third is the decision-making update. SF Express combines GIS, multimedia compression, and database technology to effectively establish a visualized warehouse management and order management system. In the intelligent warehouse management system, the monitoring equipment based on image/video recognition and analysis technology collects video, image, and other data information and assembles them at the main control center, so that decision-makers at all levels can obtain information of the abnormalities of the front-end warehouse, to realize timely decision-making, command scheduling, and investigating. In the intelligent order management system, image/video recognition and analysis technology can effectively realize order tracking management and reduce the damage and loss of goods during transportation, thereby helping to formulate production plans and scheduling and ensure that goods reach their destinations in time and safely.

4.3.3 Smart logistics map

SF Express started to build its own map in 2016, and its main target is a 4D map based on logistics. In order to draw such a map, SF Express first renamed the address according to the coordinates; meanwhile, it performs high-precision positioning with the movement data of 800,000 couriers across the country and adds real-time data that does not exist on the map, such as height, floor height, and load, to achieve a comprehensive positioning state.

4.4 Pinduoduo: another approach to developing e-commerce with social attributes

E-commerce with social attributes has flourished in recent years, and Pinduoduo is an example. The platform focuses on consumer-to-business (C2B). It attracts the capital market with unique business thinking, i.e., allowing users to share their experience and group purchases of low-priced products. Pinduoduo was officially launched in September 2015; in 2016, it received 110 million dollars from top investment institutions such as Tencent and Gaorong Capital; in 2018, it received 3 billion dollars from investment institutions such as Tencent and Sequoia. Pinduoduo has turned the table in just four years with 400 million active users and secured its place in the domestic competition of e-business.

4.4.1 Pinduoduo's e-commerce model with social attributes

The rapid development of Pinduoduo is closely related to "social e-commerce", a new type of e-commerce. Social e-commerce uses Weibo, social media, and network media to assist in the purchase and sale of goods through social interaction and other means. Pinduoduo takes advantage of the characteristics of social e-commerce platforms to open and occupy the market through social media. Traditional e-commerce platforms, such as JD, are striving to build a complete logistics system across the country by rapid logistics and after-sales service, and have established their position in e-commerce. Pinduoduo has to change its model of e-commerce if it wants to stand out from the competition, with mature e-commerce enterprises such as Taobao and JD. Pinduoduo uses social media such as WeChat to promote its platform and products, rather than waiting for customers to search and purchase on the shopping platform after they realize they want to buy certain products. It promotes itself through consumers.

With the support of Tencent, Pinduoduo developed a WeChat mini program to share its platform on WeChat's "Moments" feature without any barriers. It attracted tens of millions of active fans within six months. The WeChat mini program becomes the access of the Pinduoduo platform. Users who have purchase experience can enter the platform through the WeChat mini program to purchase again. The mini program improves user experience, guarantees the return of users, and improves the brand's popularity.

In traditional online shopping platforms, there is no difference in price between an individual purchase and a group purchase. Pinduoduo's group purchase model stimulates consumers' desire to purchase. For each product, there is an "individual price" and a "group price" with a significant price difference, which encourages consumers to choose the group-buying model. In order to enjoy relatively low prices, users will share and interact with their family, friends, and colleagues, and buy products in groups. In this way, Pinduoduo can attract potential users, and stimulate users' interest in participating in the next group purchase.

4.4.2 Pinduoduo's consumer positioning

Pinduoduo focuses on ordinary user groups and takes the "high cost-effective" path that targets an extensive population. It targets price-sensitive consumers with limited purchasing power and relatively lower expectations for prices.

Aiming at users in third- and fourth-tier cities and towns, a large consumer group that has not been covered by other e-commerce giants, and analyzing the needs of these people for dislocation competition, Pinduoduo has stood out within a short time.

4.4.3 Pinduoduo's profit model

The positioning of Pinduoduo is to use low-priced products to attract consumers and create group purchasing. Taking advantage of WeChat's huge social traffic dividends, users use WeChat for bargains. The huge traffic has also attracted a large number of shops that focus on high-margin products, thus achieving a win-win situation with shops. After obtaining orders of the products users put down on Pinduoduo, shops arrange factories to manufacture as per the actual number of products and sell the products directly to users after production, thereby compressing the supply chain and sales links. It reduces production costs because warehouse rent and many intermediate links are skipped, thus lowering prices and improving customer satisfaction, achieving "small profits but quick turnover".

In the face of the fierce competition of the e-commerce industry, Pinduoduo needs to form a stable and high-end talent team to maintain its current position and continue to make profits. As of 2018, the proportion of Pinduoduo engineers exceeded half of the company's total staff. To prevent the loss of talents, Pinduoduo issues employee equity to encourage talents to stay.

4.4.4 Current status and direction of Pinduoduo

In 2019, the number of active users of Pinduoduo was 440 million, which made Pinduoduo stand out with its resources of a "low-consumption market". Because the products on Pinduoduo are cheaper than other platforms, there are businesses that produce products below the standards in order to further reduce costs. In the beginning, Pinduoduo introduced a "zero-deposit" and "zero-threshold" policy to attract shops to join. Some unqualified, even illegal shops were included and a large number of fake and shoddy products appeared on the platform. If Pinduoduo's products are labeled fake and inferior, it will reduce consumers' trust in the long run. In order to achieve long-term and healthy development, attract high-quality shops, and fully protect the rights and interests of consumers, Pinduoduo launched the "New Brand Plan" in 2018 to support high-quality production capacity. This prevents the loss of users and attracts new users.

Pinduoduo quickly established its own brand by "e-commerce + social networking". Admittedly, it needs to continuously improve its brand image if it wants to gain a foothold in the e-commerce market. Regardless of its future prospects, Pinduoduo will become a remarkable model in China's technology and business field.

Chapter 4　Digital Economy and Trade

China is a major global trading country, and its trade in goods and services occupies an important global position in terms of volume. Trade is also an important engine fueling China's economic growth. With the advent of the digital economy era, China is also actively developing its digital trade, reflected in its use of digital technology to carry out production and sales activities, its use of digital elements to input production, and its output of digital products and services. In the report "Digital Revolution: How Can China Attract Digital Trade Opportunities at Home and Abroad" released by the Center for China and Globalization (CCG) in 2019, the economic value of China's digital trade was evaluated through data analysis. The report pointed out that through the application of digital technology, digital trade currently supports an economic value of up to 3.2 trillion yuan in China's domestic economy. If various trade barriers affecting digital trade at home and abroad are excluded, this value is expected to increase 11-fold by 2030, reaching 37 trillion yuan.① This shows the impact of digital trade in economic and trade development. So, in the context of China's growing digital economy, what changes is it undergoing in its trade? Where will digital economy lead China's trade? What problems and challenges will China face in its trade development in the digital economy era? This chapter will provide research and analysis to deepen our understanding of digital economy's impact on China.

Section 1　The Advent of the Digital Trade Era

1.1 Global trade enters a new phase

The rise of information and communications technology has inaugurated a wave of "digital revolution" around the world, profoundly affecting all aspects of social life. The new generation of information technologies, such as artificial intelligence, big data, cloud computing, and services, are advancing with each passing day, driving the rapid growth of digital economy and injecting new impetus into international trade. First, digital technology enables trade to overcome the limitations of time and space, reducing its dependence on geographical trade

---

① Data source: Center for China and Globalization (March 2019). Digital Revolution: How Can China Attract Digital Trade Opportunities at Home and Abroad. Retrieved from https://www.useit.com.cn/thread-22789-1-1.html.

proximity and on traditional business networks. Virtualized negotiation methods and digital logistics operations reduce trade costs. Secondly, digital technologies such as electronic methods and the Internet make the trade process easier and more convenient, enabling trade parties to negotiate directly, greatly reducing intermediary links and improving trade efficiency. Moreover, digital economy expands trade objects, not only in e-commerce platforms of traditional physical goods, but also in digital knowledge and information such as digital products and services. At the same time, digital trade can effectively break channel monopolies, lower trade barriers for vulnerable groups like small and medium-sized enterprises to enter the international market, and promote trade inclusion.

With the advent of the digital economy era, trade as an important link in the active economy and society has entered a new phase of digital development, with worldwide changes in economic trends and product structure. As demarcated by Javier López González and Marie-Agnes Jouanjean (2017),[1] the development of world trade can generally be divided into three stages. The first is the traditional trade stage, which usually requires a fixed or permanent venue of business establishment, completing transactions through paper documents and certifications. It is often restricted by time and space, and characterized by final product trade. However, in international trade, the decrease in transportation costs has led to a separation between production and consumption across borders, so consumers can benefit from a wide range of new and more competitive products from various countries. The second stage can be called the global value-chain trade (GVC trade) stage. This stage is characterized by trade in intermediate goods. As the world economy develops, transportation costs and coordination costs continue to decrease, allowing companies to use comparative advantages in location to allocate production across national boundaries. The third stage is the current stage of trade. It is the trading of products and services under digital technology. The application of digital technology has reduced the cost of information and trade. The process of trade negotiation, contract signing, and payment of funds can all be completed digitally. Trade efficiency is improved, and the trade method is paperless. Virtualization and digital technology in the trade field have transformed the overall format of trade and reinvigorated it. At the same time, current trade policies involve more issues, like the free flow of information, data privacy protection, intellectual property rights, and other policymaking issues under the present digital economy. Therefore, in the context of the digital economy era, a new stage of global trade has arrived, allowing traditional trade to develop afresh, giving rise to new forms of trade. Hence, we will call this new era the digital trade era.

---

[1] López González, J. and M. Jouanjean (2017). Digital Trade: Developing a Framework for Analysis. *OECD Trade Policy Papers*, No. 205, OECD Publishing, Paris. Retrieved from http://dx.doi.org/10.1787/524c8c83-en.

1.2 The concept and definitions of digital trade

1.2.1 The extension of the concept of trade in the digital economy era

With the rapid development of the global digital economy, more than half of the global service trade has been digitized, and more than 12% of cross-border physical trade is realized through digital platforms.① The global industrial structure, organizational production methods, and product content have undergone profound changes. A new form of trade with vast digital trade potential has come into being. As a new form of trade, it is the product and result of the growing digital economy at a certain stage. The birth of digital trade has subverted former trade operation forms, extending the original concept of trade in the digital economy era.

Trade is a general term for transaction behavior. Trade in the digital economy era has not changed in essence and is still a transaction behavior. Yet under the influence of digital economy, its objects, modes, and other aspects have been newly extended and expanded. However, compared with the original trade concept, common understanding of this new form of trade in the digital economy era is still largely at the descriptive stage, with no universally recognized and accepted definitions. The "Manual on Statistics of International Trade in Services", jointly written by the United Nations, the World Trade Organization (WTO), and six other international organizations, defines digital trade as transactions made through online orders. The transactions are divided into tangible and intangible commodities. The intangible commodity part is called digital service trade.② In the paper "Work Programme on Electronic Commerce" adopted by the World Trade Organization in 1998, e-commerce is used to represent digital trade, which defines it as the production, distribution, marketing, sale, or delivery of goods and services using electronic means.③ In July 2013, the United States International Trade Commission (USITC) first proposed the concept of digital trade in "Digital Trade in the U.S. and Global Economies, Part 1", defining it as commercial activities that realize products and services transactions through Internet transmission.④ In August 2014, USITC included physical goods into digital trade in their paper "Digital Trade in the U.S. and Global Economies, Part 2", emphasizing that digital trade is a trade realized through digital technology, expanding on its original definition.⑤ In 2017, in the report "Market Opportunities and Key Foreign Trade Restrictions" issued by

---

① Data source: Ministry of Commerce, P.R.C. (2018). China Digital Trade and Software Export Report 2017. Retrieved from http://cipa.mofcom.gov.cn/article/f/201806/20180602760921.shtml.

② UN, IMF, UNCTAD, WTO, OECD, EU (2002). *Manual on Statistics of International Trade in Services*. Retrieved from https://unstats.un.org/unsd/publication/Seriesm/Seriesm_86e.pdf.

③ WTO (September 1998). Work Programme on Electronic Commerce. Retrieved from https://www.wto.org/english/tratop_e/ecom_e/wkprog_e.htm.

④ U.S. International Trade Commission (July 2013). Digital Trade in the U.S. and Global Economies, Part 1. Investigation No. 332-531. USITC Publication 4415. Retrieved from https://www.usitc.gov/publications/332/pub4415.pdf.

⑤ U.S. International Trade Commission (August 2014). Digital Trade in the U.S. and Global Economies, Part 2. Investigation No. 332-540. USITC Publication 4485. Retrieved from https://www.usitc.gov/publications/332/pub4485.pdf.

USITC, the definition of digital trade was further expanded. Here, digital trade includes not only the sale of personal consumer goods on the Internet and online services, but also the provision of data flow, intelligent manufacturing services, and other platforms and applications in the global value chain under four categories: digital content, social media, search engines, and other digital products and services.① Chinese research institutions have offered three main definitions of digital trade: One, that digital trade is a business mode based on digital electronic information, relying on wired or wireless digital networks and using digital exchange technologies; Two, that digital trade is the cross-border payment of tangible products and intangible services using digital technologies and digital formats as its basic tools, mainly including three aspects: digital services, digital-supported trade, and digital-driven trade; Three, that digital trade is trade enabling companies in different industries to conduct product and service transactions on the Internet using related equipment. Among the definitions of digital trade, the most representative can be found in the "Bluebook on the Development of Digital Trade between the World and China 2018", which defines digital trade as trade conducted through modern information networks using communications technologies effectively to achieve efficient exchange of products and services, digital knowledge, and information. This in turn promotes the transformation of consumer Internet into industrial Internet, hence realizing a new type of trade activity in which the manufacturing industry is intellectualized.②

Based on the above definitions of digital trade by representative global organizations, we can understand digital trade as trade relying on information networks, digital technology, and digital production factors for production, integrating online and offline consumers, producers, suppliers, and intermediaries on digital information platforms to conduct transactions, and ultimately realizing a form of trade in which products and services are produced by digital technology, digital knowledge, and information. It is a form of transaction that can realize cross-border goods and services. From this concept, the concept of trade in the digital economy era can be extended to the following areas: The first is the input and use of new production factors, such as digital production technology and digital knowledge in the front-end production of trade activities; The second is that it entails trade activities, products, and services produced by digital technology, digital knowledge, and information as its main trade objects, in addition to traditional goods and services; The third is that it involves the digital operation of transaction processes in trade activities, using modern information networks as the carrier, fully utilizing communications technologies to realize the transaction process.

---

① U.S. International Trade Commission (August 2017). Global Digital Trade 1: Market Opportunities and Key Foreign Trade Restrictions. Investigation No. 332-561. USITC Publication 4. Retrieved from https://www.usitc.gov/publications/332/pub4716_0.pdf.

② Zhejiang University Regional Opening and Development Research Center (September 2018). Bluebook on the Development of Digital Trade between the World and China 2018. Retrieved from http://www.zjskw.gov.cn/u/cms/www/201809/29142313hdlq.pdf.

1.2.2 The expansion of trade specifications in the digital economy era

The rapid development of digital economy and the rapid application of digital technologies, such as artificial intelligence, big data, and the Internet of Things, have promoted the gradual digitalization of production and sales in the trade process. In the digital economy era, trade is based on the Internet, with digital exchange technology as a means, and Internet transmission as a medium. This has not only changed the production modes and delivery of many goods and services, but also directly shortened space-time proximity, reducing transaction costs and improving efficiency and benefits. As a result, the trade system is optimized, the trade process is simplified, and trade opportunities are increased. In addition, most of the trade objects are intellectual property-intensive products and services, characterized by high knowledge, high technology, high interaction, and high innovation. Therefore, while providing products and services to customers, trading entities must continue to innovate, absorb new knowledge, and learn new technology to create a knowledge-applicable model suitable for new technology and production development. Furthermore, with the continuous emergence of new technologies such as cloud computing and big data, the forms of trade will continue to increase, not only expanding the range of trade products and services, but also providing customers with a broader choice of goods and services. It is possible to adapt to the special and individual needs of customers, stimulating their wants, and providing customers with real-time, interactive, and low-cost personalized products and services.

Based on the current development of global digital trade, as well as analysis and definitions from representative digital trade perspectives, we believe that digital trade is mainly identified through three aspects: The first is digital purchase—that is, the cross-border, digital-order transactions that reflect international goods and services trade in e-commerce. The second is digital platforms. One of the distinctive features of international trade digitization is the emergence of intermediary platforms such as Amazon, Uber, eBay, and Alibaba. Although not all digital trade transactions involve this type of intermediary platforms, its impact on domestic and foreign economic and competitive landscape is clear. The third is digital production and delivery. Digital trade captures digitalized service and data streams in the form of downloadable products, such as software, e-books, and data and database services. Therefore, compared with physical goods mainly transacted in traditional trading stages, the statistical specifications of digital trade in the digital economy era mainly cover four areas. The first is digital products, such as office software, electronic games, digital products like online videos (derived from the developing digital technology), and digital equipment products such as computers and mobile phones that integrate digital technology. The second involves digital services like online courses and 3D printer services that rely on digital technology. These new services also include ICT services, digital financial services, and other services that use digital technology to achieve digital transformation. The third area involves physical goods that are traded through digital information and communications technology—that is, trade goods on electronic platforms. It can be understood as the trade of goods driven by digital economy. The fourth area is digital knowledge and information, such as electronic databases, supplier and customer information flows, and other specific products composed of digital elements. Therefore, in the digital economy era, the scope of trade has significantly expanded, mainly involving new trade objects and the application of digital technology in traditional goods trade.

In summary, compared with traditional trade stages, trade activities in the digital economy era have shown new characteristics and differences. The first is virtualization: digital knowledge and information are used in the production of products and services to achieve element virtualization. Transactions are conducted on a virtualized Internet platform, virtualized electronic payment is used to realize transaction virtualization, and circulation virtualization is realized in the transmission of digital products and services. The second is platformization. A platform-based operation has become the main business mode for Internet companies. Platforms have become economic organizations that coordinate and allocate resources and converge data streams. The third is inclusiveness. The application of digital technology has greatly reduced barriers to trade. Small and medium-sized enterprises and individuals who were in a disadvantageous position in traditional trade can now attract global consumers by applying digital technology. The fourth is service globalization. Jiang Xiaojuan's (2017) research pointed out that the development of digital technology has overturned traditional theories about the low efficiency, high cost, and non-tradable judgments of service industries, leading to a significant increase in the production efficiency and globalization level of such industries, while promoting economies of scale and scope of production.[①] Jiang Xiaojuan and Luo Libin (2019) further called attention to the products and services of various countries provided to the global market through a global cyberspace built by digital technology. Service suppliers, consumers, and related production factors have become the internal driving force of globalization in service industries, thus accelerating the globalization of service production, the globalization of consumption, and the globalization of investment.[②]

[①] Xiaojuan Jiang (2017). Resource reorganization and the growth of the service industry in an interconnected society. *Economic Research Journal*, 52(03): 4-17. Retrieved from http://kns.cnki.net/KXReader/Detail?TIMESTAMP=637263915544436250&DBCODE=CJFQ&TABLEName=CJFDLAST2017&FileName=JJYJ201703002&RESULT=1&SIGN=Z0l8Mtu02t%2beLIDisyqUuQ7YrFc%3d.

[②] Xiaojuan Jiang, Libin Luo (2019). Service globalization in the network era: new engine, acceleration and great power competitiveness. *Social Sciences in China* (02): 68-91+205-206. Retrieved from http://kns.cnki.net/KXReader/Detail?TIMESTAMP=637263916018655000&DBCODE=CJFQ&TABLEName=CJFDLAST2019&FileName=ZSHK201902006&RESULT=1&SIGN=MoRMf3%2bKIlArZ%2bApIkg2TEwUk14%3d.

1.3 The impact and significance of digital trade

1.3.1 The study of the impact of the digital economy and its channels on trade

With the development of digital economy, its relationship with trade has attracted widespread attention from government departments and academic circles around the world. Whether research reports of related institutions or of academic journals, a significant amount of research has been conducted on digital economy and trade. However, in general, current research on digital economy and trade generally has three characteristics. The first, the actual impact of digital economy on trade is only touched on generally, merely analyzing how digital economy integrates with trade from the perspective of trade volume and value chain. Yet in fact, the scope of trade is relatively wide and includes not only different types of trade, but also different trading entities. The second, the analysis of how digital technology is being integrated into trade, and is relatively superficial. There is a lack of in-depth analysis based on trade theory. The third, a lack of focus. Most of the research is from a global perspective, lacking a country-specific analysis, without exploring its internal impact on a certain country. This chapter introduces digital economy factors into the analysis framework. It analyzes the impact of digital economy on intermediate links of trade activities from a theoretical perspective, and studies production costs, market access, and the degree of controllable trade risks brought about by production intellectualization, production standardization, and production and circulation integration in digital economy. Through the research in this chapter, we can see how the application of digital technology in trade will reduce trade costs, intermediate links, and trade barriers, and ultimately improve trade efficiency. We will intuitively grasp the ways digital technology develops vigorously, and understand how manufacturing and service industries can adjust their industrial structure in the digital economy era, thereby enhancing their competitiveness and increasing their profitability.

1.3.2 Providing ideas for China's participation in formulating a new trade regulation system

Studying the relationship between digital economy and trade is a vital requirement for China's participation in formulating relevant rules. At present, only the United States has clearly separated digital trade from digital economy, yet a mature and complete regulatory system has not been formulated globally. As a major global trading country, with rapid development in its digital economy, it is vitally important for China to participate in the formulation of relevant trade rules and policies. Through the research in this chapter, we will fully grasp the direction China will take while developing domestic and international trade in the digital economy era. We will systematically analyze and summarize the mutual influence of digital economy and trade, as well as clarify the internal mechanism behind digital economy's impact on trade. This will help China formulate and implement high-level trade policies in the digital economy era, and for it to have a say in the formulation of trade regulations. It will provide the much-needed framework and references for China to participate in the formulation of international trade rules.

1.3.3 Locating the important breakthrough point for realizing trade transformation and upgrading in the digital economy era

Over the years, the development of digital technology has continuously injected new impetus into China's economic growth. Through their reliance on the Internet, companies have used digital technologies like big data and electronic means to upgrade and transform their production, circulation, and sales processes, and build new digital business formats, thus enhancing their production capacity and improving the quality of their goods and services. In 2018, China's digital economy reached 31.3 trillion yuan, accounting for 34.8% of the GDP; digital industrialization reached 6.4 trillion yuan, accounting for 7.1% of the GDP.[①] Based on this, and in the context of China's economic upgrade and transformation, digital economy can promote trade as a new channel for Chinese products to open up overseas markets. This can play a fundamental role in China's trade transformation and further promote trade to become an important engine in fueling its high-quality economic growth. However, developing digital economy does not change the fundamental nature of trade; instead, it promotes the transformation and upgrading of trade activities in object, mode, system, and function. Digital economy brings a new delivery model into world trade, and therefore will give rise to new trade policies. The advent of the digital trade era will intensify international division of labor, change trade methods, and reshape the trading system. Using research, we can more fully grasp the impact of digital economy on China's trade, and provide a strong basis for it to promote China's international trade growth, improve its trade structure, promote regional economic development, and help later companies enter the international market. This can help China find an important breakthrough point in its digital trade transformation and upgrading, offer advice for new problems and new phenomena that it may encounter as digital trade develops, thus accelerating China's goal in becoming a great trading nation.

1.3.4 Providing an analysis framework for the digital economy, so as to direct the development of new trade formats

With the rapid development of digital economy, the digitization trend of global service trade and cross-border physical trade has been slowly intensified. The wide application of new digital technologies such as cloud computing, big data, and artificial intelligence has an important impact on global economic growth. Internet globalization and cross-border data flows have encouraged the strong growth of digital trade on an international scale, and digital trade has become increasingly important in international trade. From 2012 to 2016, the global digital trade

---

① Data source: China Academy of Information and Communications Technology (2019). White Paper on China's Digital Economic Development and Employment (2019). Retrieved from http://www.caict.ac.cn/kxyj/qwfb/bps/201912/t20191230_272898.htm.

value increased from USD 19.3 trillion to USD 27.7 trillion.① In 2017, China's software and information technology service industry had a software business revenue of 5.5 trillion yuan, and its software export value was USD 37.556 billion, an increase of 9.72% from the previous year, equivalent to 2.6 times that of 2011.② China's digital trade is at the global forefront in terms of development. Digital trade conforms to the country's national economic strategy by adapting to a growing and open world economy. It is very important to provide in-depth analysis of trade changes brought about by digital economy, as China ushers in a new digital era. We will summarize the opportunities and challenges that digital economy will bring to China's international trade development.

Section 2 The Impact of Digital Economy on Trade

2.1 Digital economy and changes in trade products

In recent years, the development of China's international trade has gradually shifted from traditional trade to digital trade, with cross-border e-commerce as its mainstay. The percentage of cross-border e-commerce transactions in total import and export trade increased from 5% in 2010 to 20% in 2015 (as shown in Figure 4.1). The development of China's international trade promoted by digital trade has also shifted China's trade subjects from traditional goods to digital products and services. Digital products refer to content products that are transmitted and delivered over the Internet. These products are created by traditional or core copyright industries, are digitally encoded and electronically transmitted via the Internet, and are independent of physical carriers. They are classified as follows: movies and pictures; sound and music; software; video, computer, and entertainment games. Digital services include transmission services of signals, texts, images, and other information; broadcast services of audiovisual content; and services implemented by electronic networks.③

---

① Data source: United States International Trade Commission (2017). Global Digital Trade 1: Market Opportunities and Key Foreign Trade Restrictions. Retrieved from https://www.usitc.gov/publications/332/pub4415.pdf.

② Data source: Department of Electronic Commerce and Informatization, Ministry of Commerce, P.R.C. (2017). China's E-commerce Report 2017. Retrieved from http://dzsws.mofcom.gov.cn/article/ztxx/ndbg/201805/20180502750562.shtml.

③ In 1998, the WTO defined "digital products" in its "Work Programme on Electronic Commerce" as content products that are transmitted and delivered over the Internet. These products are created by traditional or core copyright industries, are digitally encoded and electronically transmitted via the Internet, and are independent of physical carriers. They are classified as follows: movies and pictures; sound and music; software; video, computer, and entertainment games. In June 2014, the European Commission released the "What is a digital service?" report, and its definition of digital services includes: signals, texts, images, and other information transmission services; audio-visual content broadcast services; services implemented by electronic networks.

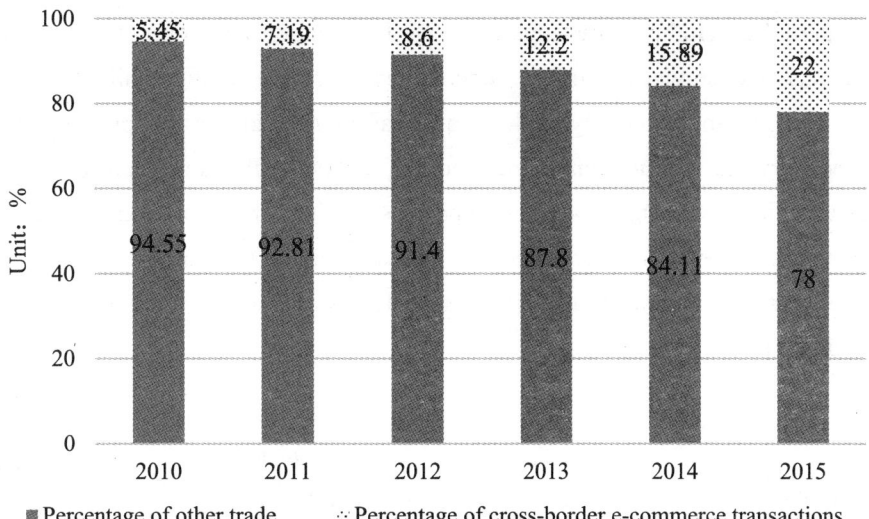

Figure 4.1　Changes in the percentage of cross-border e-commerce transactions in China (%)
Source: National Bureau of Statistics, "China's E-commerce Market data Inspection Report 2015".

As China's digital products and services trade grows vigorously as a part of its international trade, it has gradually emerged that the development speed of its information services cannot match the development speed of its digital trade. The developing digital economy has played an important role in promoting the production of new trade subjects based on digital products and services, as well as trade circulation. Traditional physical goods trade has developed from intra-industry trade to intra-product trade. The production of a good is no longer dependent on a single enterprise and is transferred to collaborative upstream and downstream enterprises in the same production chain. This kind of trade in the form of value chain has higher requirements for information symmetry between enterprises. Digital economy uses modern information networks as an important carrier, and the effective use of information and communications technologies has promoted information flow between upstream and downstream enterprises. On the one hand, this rapid information transmission reduces information asymmetry between enterprises; on the other hand, it unifies the requirements of intermediate suppliers and demanders, reduces transaction costs, and ultimately encourages the production and development of value-chain trade. Compared with traditional physical trade targets, the production of digital products and services reaps more economies of scale and scope, relying on a networked platform based on electronic communication infrastructure. Therefore, its production is reliant on digital economy, with production and circulation completed using digital technologies.[①] The World Bank (2016) has pointed out that digital technology promotes the production of digital products and services

---

① Digital technology includes the Internet, mobile phones, and all other tools that collect, store, analyze, and share information digitally. Its specific manifestations are in cloud computing, big data, mobile Internet, social media, etc.

in three main aspects: information searches, automated production, and platform provision[①] (as shown in Figure 4.2). Highly knowledge-intensive information is an important raw material for digital products and services. Digital technologies represented by mobile Internet and the Internet of Things can effectively collect information needed for the production of digital products and services. Cloud computing and big data are the key representatives. Digital technology coordinates the entire production process of digital products and services through an automated model, achieving further economies of scale. Digital technology represented by social media builds a user-communication platform to help manufacturers provide customized digital products and services.

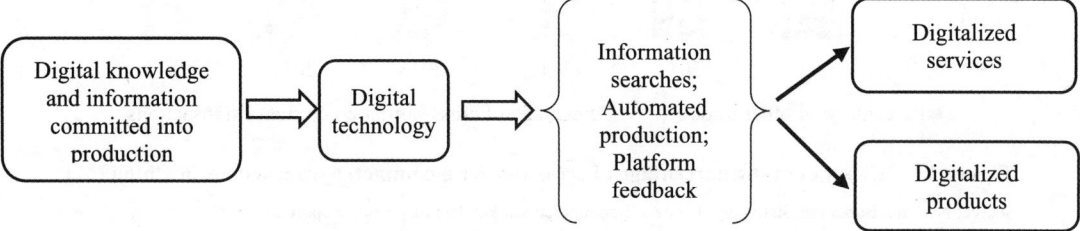

Figure 4.2   The impact of the digital economy on digitalized products and services production

Digital economy promotes the production of digital products and services by providing electronic communication infrastructure and digital technology support. Besides the production phase, digital economy also plays an important role in the transaction and circulation of digital products and services. Digital economy is based on digital technologies and promotes the entry of digital products and services into the international and domestic markets in three important aspects: transaction, transportation, and payment (as shown in Figure 4.3). First, the paperless and virtualized characteristics of digital product and service transactions mean that they do not rely on physical trading venues. At the same time, the network platform provided by digital technology provides a trading platform for digital products and services. Since traditional trade usually involves wholesalers, retailers, and other trade intermediaries earning intermediary fees, such intermediary fees are particularly prominent when conducting international trade. The digital product trading platform provided by digital technology enables buyers and sellers to trade directly. By reducing transaction costs and saving transaction time, it optimizes trade efficiency and encourages the efficient entry of digital products and services into international and domestic markets. In addition, digital trading platforms can improve information symmetry between buyers and sellers, and help reduce the fixed costs of digital products and services entering these markets. Second, transportation cost, as an important part of trade cost, is a key link for such products. Digital products and services are mainly based on digital knowledge and

---

[①] World Bank (2016). World Development Report 2016: Digital Dividends. Retrieved from https://openknowledge.world bank.org.

information. Therefore, developing digital technology represented by electronic communications technology can accelerate trade circulation of digital products and services in these markets, effectively reducing trade costs. Third, the global e-commerce payment and security certification system established by digital technologies, represented by smart terminals, cloud computing, big data, and mobile Internet, provide effective support for the payment of digital products and services. They allow for secure payments for both parties, provide effective protection, reduce the risk of default, and ultimately reduce the transaction cost of trade.

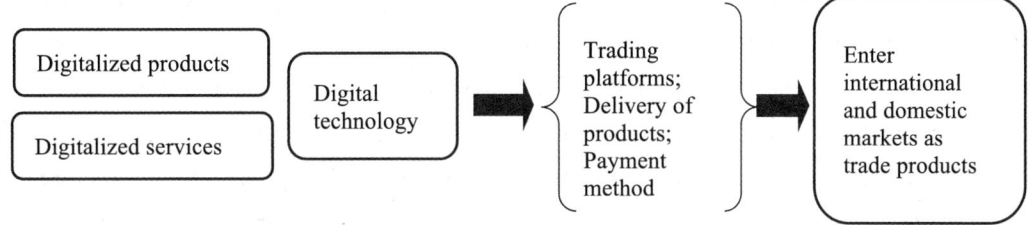

Figure 4.3 The impact of digital economy on trade products

2.2 Digital economy and the number of trading companies

Since China joined the WTO, international trade has developed rapidly, an important manifestation being the rise in the number of companies participating in import and export trade. Figure 4.4 shows that, from 2000 to 2014, China's export and import trading companies had clearly grown. Andrew B. Bernard, Jonathan Eaton, J. Bradford Jenson, and Samuel Kortum (2003) pointed out the core factors affecting Chinese manufacturers' entry into international and domestic markets: production costs, trade risks, and entry barriers.[①] The research of Marc Melitz (2003) shows that total factor productivity of manufacturing enterprises determines production cost. When production cost is low enough so that the benefits of export products exceed their fixed cost, manufacturers will choose to enter the international market.[②]

Under the current background of economic de-globalization, uncertainties in national policies represent trade risks and are an important factor affecting the exports of Chinese manufacturers. Fluctuations in export product demand caused by trade risks make sales profitability of export enterprises more volatile. When fixed production costs cannot be covered, Chinese manufacturers will withdraw from the international market. As global trade turns to value-chain trade, Chinese manufacturers are facing the urgent task of integrating into the global production chain. Product exports, being indispensable intermediate products for downstream enterprises, represent an important linkage in such integration, but they are dependent on how

---

① Bernard A. B., Eaton J., & Jensen J. B. (2003). Plants and productivity in international trade. *American Economic Review*, 93(4): 1268-1290. DOI: 10.1257/000282803769206296.

② Melitz M. J. (2003). The impact of trade on intra-industry reallocations and aggregate industry productivity. *Econometrica*, 71(6): 1695-1725. DOI: 10.1111/1468-0262.00467.

intermediate exports conform to the intermediate requirements of downstream enterprises. When intermediate products exported by Chinese manufacturers cannot meet the production needs of downstream enterprises, they will face entry barriers. Compared with the manufacturing industry, service industry companies have a higher need for information communication between trade parties, and stricter requirements in their use of cutting-edge technologies. Therefore, the core driving forces for Chinese service companies entering the international market mainly involve three aspects: communication costs, production technology, and market thresholds. The service industry must face customers directly when providing service products, and the demands of different groups of people are different. In order to provide better-customized services, both trade parties need to maintain a high level of information communication. Therefore, the cost of communication is an important factor in Chinese service companies entering the international market. In the final stage of industrial upgrading, the service industry has a higher requirement for production technology, as companies strive to shorten their technological gap with the world's elite. Improving production technology is another driving factor for Chinese service companies entering the international market. The non-tradable nature of the service industry also raises the threshold for service companies competing internationally.

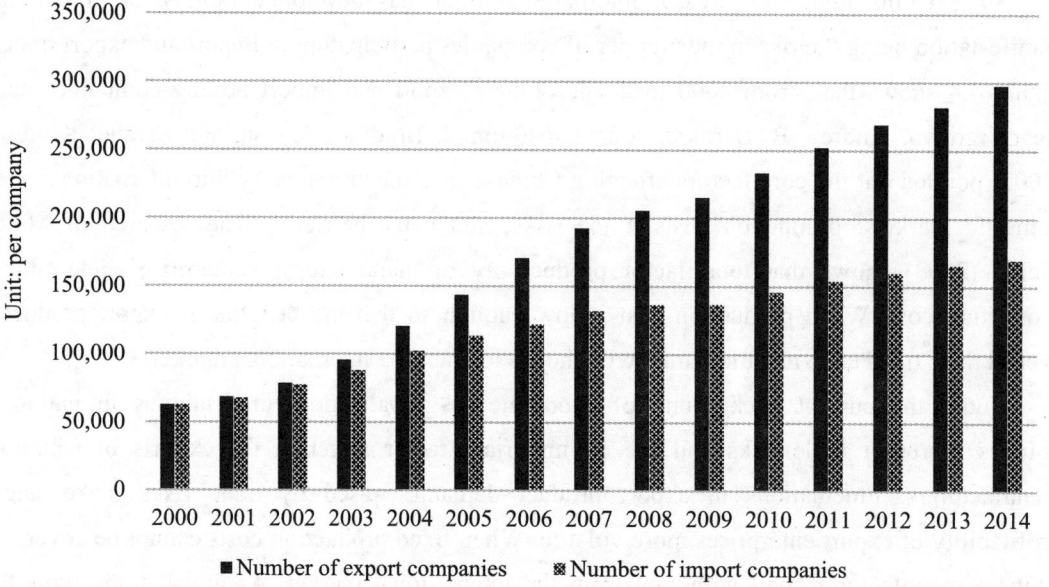

Figure 4.4 Changes in the number of Chinese trading companies

Source: Computed by the author, based on the Chinese customs database.

The development of digital economy has expanded trade objects from physical goods to digital products and services, and is effectively supporting the production and trade of digital products and services. Digital economy also plays an important role in traditional trade. This can best be seen in the fact that digital economy has increased the number of traditional manufacturing and service companies. Figure 4.5 shows digital economy's impact on Chinese trading companies entering the international market. For Chinese manufacturing companies, production costs, trade risks, and entry barriers are important factors determining their entry into the world market. The development of digital economy has an impact on manufacturers in three aspects. First, digital technology represented by artificial intelligence effectively replaces labor through intellectualized production, and the economies of scale brought about by intellectualized production have improved production efficiency and reduced production costs for manufacturing enterprises. Their cost advantage in production is attracting more Chinese manufacturers into the international market. Second, digital technologies represented by big data and cloud computing can estimate the potential export market demand by integrating production and distribution, so that production and trade flows are as consistent as possible. This effectively reduces trade risks and attracts more Chinese manufacturers into the international market. Third, digital technology improves the standardization of production by integrating the production process and digital expression of product properties, effectively reducing mismatches between upstream and downstream enterprises. Hence, it reduces entry barriers for Chinese enterprises joining the global value chain, enabling more of them to enter the international market.

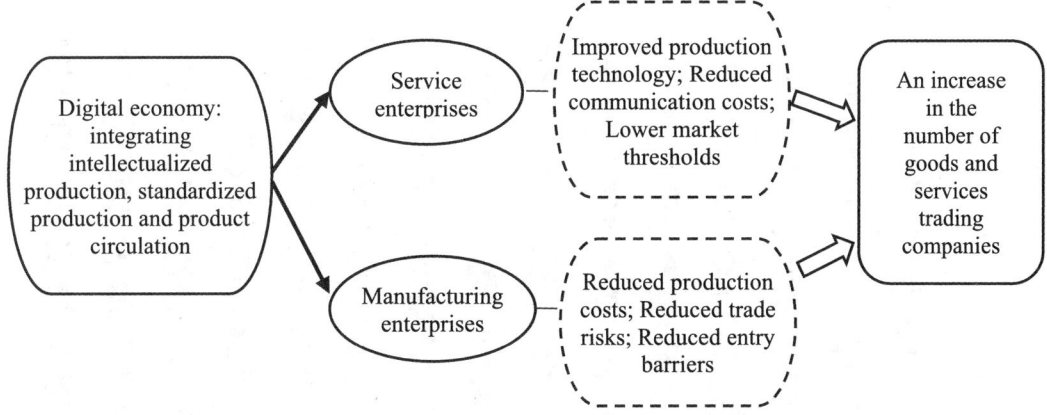

Figure 4.5 The impact of digital economy on trading companies

For Chinese service companies, production technology, communication costs, and market thresholds are important factors determining their entry into the international market. The developing digital economy has an impact on service companies in three aspects. First, digital technology represented by artificial intelligence has improved the production technology of service products through intellectualized production, strengthening the customization of service products. Improved customized services have become an important advantage of Chinese service companies in the international market. Second, digital technology represented by electronic communication through production standardization makes information between both trade parties more symmetrical, with faster and smoother information flow, thus reducing the information communication cost between the two parties. Thanks to this, more Chinese service enterprises are willing to enter the international market. Third, digital technology represented by the mobile Internet reduces the non-tradability of service products. The threshold for Chinese service companies entering the international market has dropped, enabling more entrants.

2.3 Digital economy and international trade network expansion

Another important feature of China's international trade development is the continuous expansion of the international trade network of Chinese import and export companies. From 2000 to 2014, the export destinations of Chinese import and export enterprises grew gradually (as shown in Figure 4.6). The main factors driving such expansion are the fixed costs required to expand into the new international market, and variable costs required to pay for product sales. New companies entering the international market need to pay a fixed cost to understand international product demand. They also need to locate sales channels and establish overseas sales platforms. After paying the fixed costs, new companies also need to consider the cost of transporting the products to their export destinations, as well as any possible trade risks that may hinder product sales.

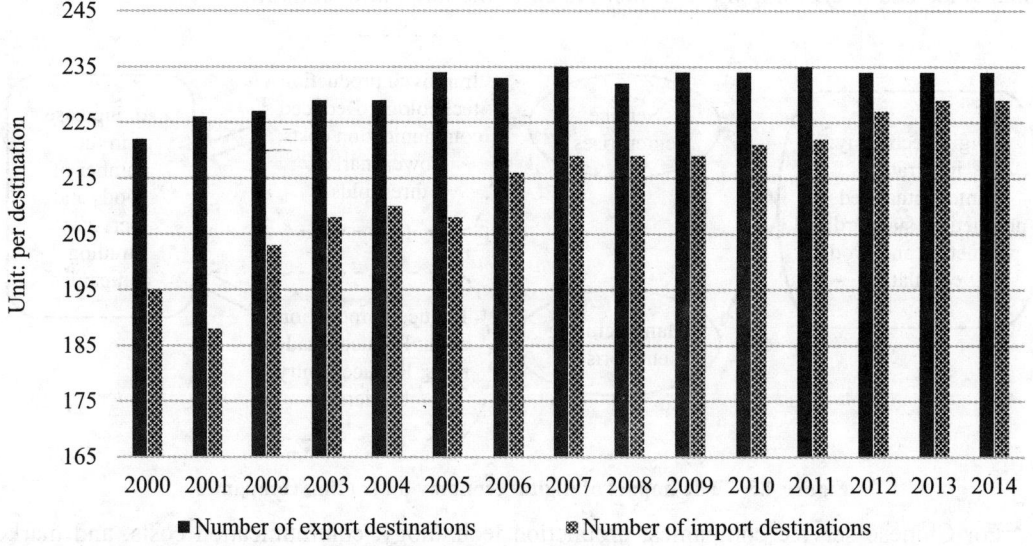

Figure 4.6   Changes in the numbers of trade market destinations for Chinese enterprises
Source: Computed by the author, based on the Chinese customs database.

As digital economy increases the number of Chinese trading companies, it also broadens the international trade network for such existing companies, seen in the diversification of international trade markets for exports and imports. Digital economy has broadened the international trade network of companies through the use of modern information networks as the main infrastructure carrier, represented by information and communications technologies (as shown in Figure 4.7). The construction of modern information networks provides material guarantees for effective communication between companies and trading partners in the new international market. Information and communications technologies, represented by the Internet, mobile Internet, and social media, have achieved cross-border exchanges between trading parties. This reduces the search cost of existing companies looking for product demand in potential international markets. It provides efficient communication with trade intermediaries and reduces the cost of channel construction for product sales. These two factors are increasing the diversification of existing companies in international markets. The fixed cost required by market entrants has been greatly reduced, which in turn opens up international markets for companies. While reducing fixed market entry costs, the establishment of modern information networks and the use of information and communications technologies have also reduced the variable costs of product sales. The increased efficiency of information communication between companies and trading partners improves the efficiency of contract negotiations and the transaction process, especially when digital products and services are the trade objects. At the same time, it accelerates the circulation of trade products and reduces trade costs significantly, improving information communication efficiency between trading parties. This also enables companies to grasp the demand situation of their target market, allowing them to make timely adjustments to their production strategy to adapt to their destination market demand, thereby reducing economic losses and supply-and-demand mismatches caused by trade risks. These two factors have greatly reduced the variable costs of companies expanding into international markets, increasing their diversification. Import trade is a mirror image of export trade, and the two are symmetrical. The above analysis is also applicable to enterprises diversifying in international import markets. The construction of modern information networks and the use of digital information and communications technologies have improved communication efficiency between trading companies and potential trading partners. This reduces the search cost for companies looking for suitable intermediate products. It also reduces the cost of companies looking for suitable intermediate goods purchase channels, greatly reducing the fixed cost of imported intermediate goods. It improves communication efficiency between trading parties, and enhances the efficiency of the import transaction process when exporting intermediate goods. At the same time, the timely grasp of the production situation will help overseas suppliers adjust their production strategies and avoid economic losses caused by insufficient intermediate product supply, further reducing the variable cost of imports. The decline in fixed and variable costs of imports will finally lead to the diversification of trading companies entering international markets.

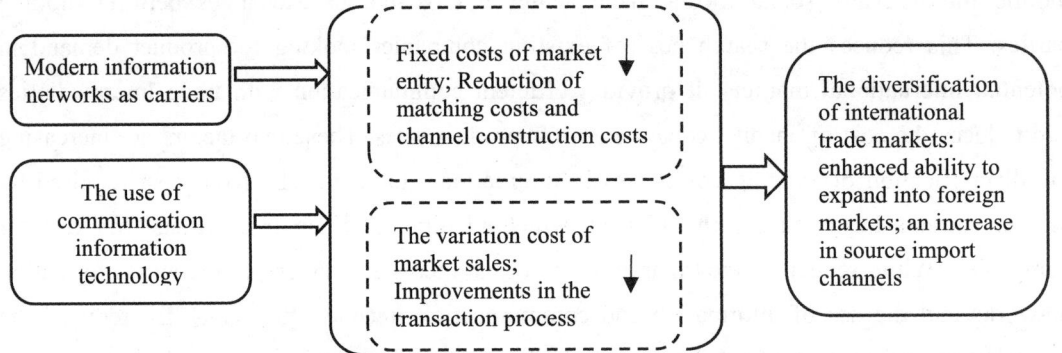

Figure 4.7 The impact of digital economy on international trade networks

2.4 Digital economy and the transformation and upgrading of the processing trade modes

Processing trade refers to business trade activities in which all or part of the raw materials—parts, components, packaging materials, etc.—are imported by the enterprise engaging in such trade activities, with the finished products re-exported after processing or assembly. Its specific forms include the processing of local or import materials. All products of processing trade are sold abroad and are not sold in the country; goods imported under processing trade are tariff-free. The emergence of processing trade cannot be separated from the international division of labor. In the middle of the 20th century, the vertical division of production and the convenience of international trade allowed developed countries with advanced production technology to transfer part of their production to developing countries, leveraging on their labor cost advantage to complete the intermediate processing or assembly. Developing countries also began undertaking such processing of intermediate products to kickstart their economic development. Hence, a special trade called processing trade was born.

Since the late 1970s—that is, since the start of its reform-and-opening-up era—China has focused on developing processing trade. The Chinese government not only introduced a series of preferential policies like tax reduction and exemption, and tariff reduction and exemption, but also constructed export processing zones to attract foreign investment, developing the country through processing trade. Barry Naughton (2006) pointed out that, unlike other East Asian economies, China is not subject to specific regional restrictions when developing its processing trade; processing trade can be carried out nationwide.[①] Therefore, China's processing trade has experienced a phase of rapid growth and has become its main import and export mode. Figures 4.8 and 4.9 show the changes in processing trade from 2000 to 2017. One can see that during this period, both processing trade exports and imports rose gradually, and the total amount was huge. As can be seen from Figures 4.8 and 4.9, processing trade exports accounted for more than 50%

---

① Naughton, B. (2006). China's emergence and prospects as a trading nation. Brookings Papers on Economic Activity 2, 273-313. Retrieved from https://www.brookings.edu/wp-content/uploads/1996/... a_naughton_lardy.pdf.

of China's total exports before the 2008 financial crisis. Processing trade imports accounted for more than 30% of China's total imports. Although affected by the financial crisis, with the proportion of China's processing trade in import and export trade decreasing, it still plays a pivotal role in China's trade.

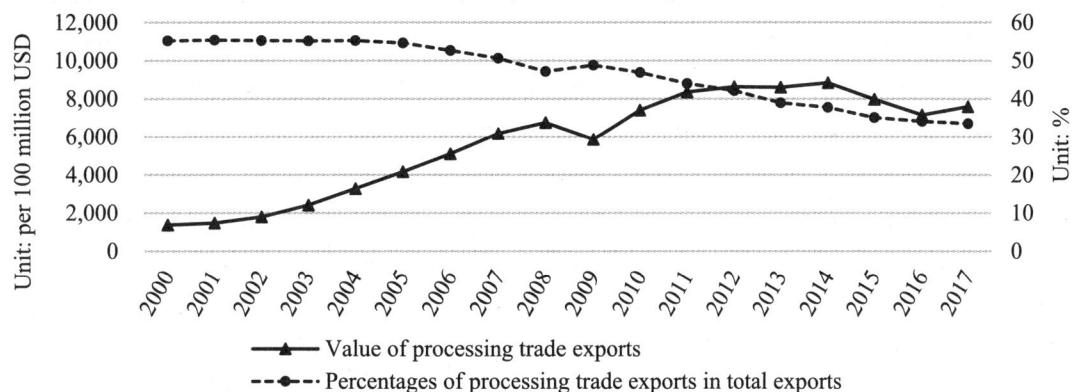

Figure 4.8   China's processing trade exports from 2000 to 2018

Source: Department of foreign trade and economic statistics, National Bureau of Statistics of China (2018). 2018 China Trade and External Economic Statistical Yearbook. Retrieved from http://navi.cnki.net/KNavi/YearbookDetail?pcode=CYFD&pykm=YSCTJ&bh=.

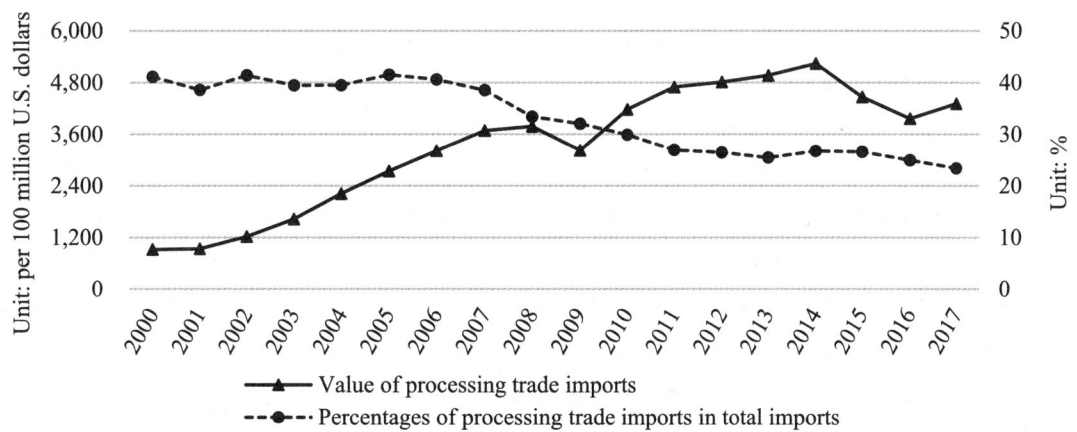

Figure 4.9   China's processing trade imports from 2000 to 2017

Source: Department of foreign trade and economic statistics, National Bureau of Statistics of China (2018). 2018 China Trade and External Economic Statistical Yearbook. Retrieved from http://navi.cnki.net/KNavi/YearbookDetail?pcode=CYFD&pykm=YSCTJ&bh=.

One can see that processing trade has experienced decades of growth in China and occupies an important position in China's import and export trade. What cannot be ignored is that China's processing trade methods have unique characteristics, manifested in the following aspects: in addition to foreign direct-investment enterprises, processing trade firms in China are mainly small and medium-sized enterprises. Both their management and production technology are lacking, and their ability to operate independently and conduct external marketing is also weak. Under the processing trade model, the added value of exports is very low, and its effect on the economy is limited. According to calculations made by Robert Koopman, Zhi Wang, and Shang-Jin Wei (2008),[①] only 18.1% of China's processing trade exports are manufactured in China, with the remaining 81.9% coming from imported intermediate products. Thus, the added value of exports under China's processing trade is very low, mainly relying on its cheap labor force to inject new value, and not obtaining added export value through high-technology production. China's processing trade also has the characteristics of being anonymous and brandless. Most of the product manufacturers engaging in processing trade have not formed their own market brands, and their brand awareness is weak, especially in processing orders. Chinese enterprises are mainly engaged in OEM production. Under the import materials processing mode, most Chinese enterprises have not formed products with market-brand advantages. Thus, in the highly competitive international market environment, sales of China's processing trade products are polarized: First, developed countries have high-production technology in high-end products, while Chinese processing trade companies lack the corresponding technological innovation incentives and support, mainly relying on foreign orders to survive. Second, low-end products do not have independent brands and technical fundamentals, and hence lack international market competitiveness, mainly relying on foreign market demand to survive. All these have led to China's processing trade model relying heavily on labor-cost advantage, with low added-value of exports, poor independent management capabilities, and weak ability to withstand external risks.

Given such characteristics of China's processing trade mode, one cannot ignore the development and application of digital economy in transforming and upgrading processing trade. One may say that the key to transforming China's processing trade is for enterprises to change their production organization model, break the Western monopoly on production technology, and develop their own production technology and market brand. They should enhance their international competitiveness and achieve full independence in export production, operation, and sales. Digital economy can boost the transformation and upgrading of processing trade through internal and external channels (as shown in Figure 4.10). From the perspective of external influences, the developing digital economy technology has enabled Chinese processing trade companies to access international network platforms. The opening of such external network platforms has largely reduced information asymmetry. For Chinese processing trade enterprises, especially small and medium-sized ones, the use of external network platforms with unobstructed international market information allows them to quickly understand the trends and changes of international markets, while implementing the transformation and upgrading of processing trade. It helps them adjust their own production and operation in a timely fashion, reducing the adverse impact of international market risks on their companies. At the same time,

---

[①] Koopman, R., Wang, Z., & Wei, S.-J. (2008). How much of Chinese exports is really made in China? Assessing domestic value-added when processing trade is pervasive. NBER Working Paper 14109. Retrieved from https://www.nber.org/papers/w14109.

it improves the companies' ability to withstand risks and reduces potential risks that may arise from such transformation. Also, market product supply information brought by these network platforms encourages enterprises to acquire more advanced production knowledge, learn market sales knowledge, and enhance their learning ability by mastering processing trade transformation. While external network platforms promote the fluency of market information, they also provide an important channel for Chinese exports. The wide application of digital trading platforms and payment methods can help enterprises carry out import and export trade in a more standardized manner, allowing them to establish and protect their own brands in the international market and gain breadth and depth in their marketing promotion. This will reduce the time and monetary costs of the channel construction that is required for transforming processing trade into general trade.

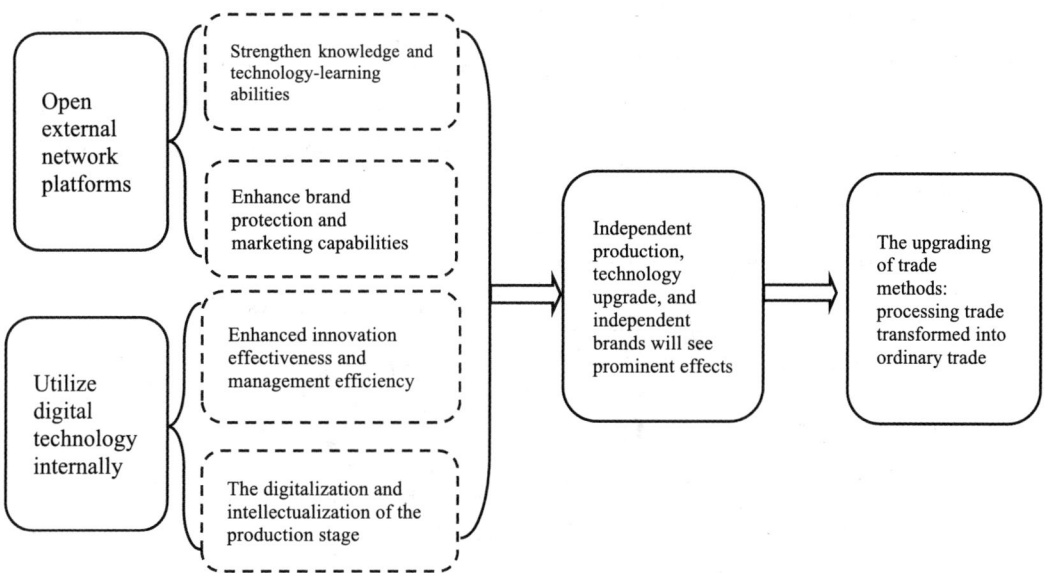

Figure 4.10   The impact of digital economy on the transformation and upgrading of processing trade

In terms of internal channels, the use of digital technology in internal production management is also an important factor in processing trade transformation. Specifically, the use of management information systems can reduce management complexity faced by enterprises during their processing trade transformation and promote management efficiency. At the same time, improving internal management and operation efficiency will also promote the efficiency of enterprises in absorbing advanced technology, innovation, and transformation. In terms of actual production, the digital age and the use of digital technology in the production process, like automation and intellectualized machinery and equipment, will greatly enhance production efficiency and boost the enterprises' transition from processing trade to general trade. From the above analysis, one can see that the developing digital economy plays a role both internally and externally, helping the transformation and upgrading of processing trade. It can comprehensively reduce risks and costs faced by the industrial upgrade, and increase the capabilities and technologies required for its transformation. Technological upgrading of independent production and the management of independent brands will show prominent effects, accelerating China's transition from processing trade to general trade.

2.5 Digital economy and participation in global value chains

Every product, from its initial production to its sale to the consumer, undergoes several intermediate stages. This series of intermediate activities includes product innovation research and development, high-tech parts production, simple parts production, assembly manufacturing, and marketing and after-sales services. As each intermediate activity is completed, value will be added to the product, so this chain generates value and is called a value chain. Broadly speaking, the added value generated by R&D and design, high-tech parts production, simple parts production, and marketing and after-sales services is relatively high on the right side of the curve, while added value generated during assembly manufacturing is low, on the middle part of the value chain. Hence, the value chain presents a positive U-shaped curve, as seen in Figure 4.11, called a smiling curve.

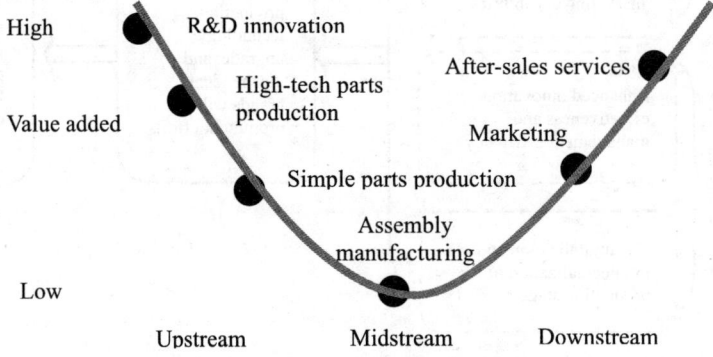

Figure 4.11 A "smiling curve" graph

In a traditional production-and-management model, almost all production activities in this chain are completed by a single enterprise. However, with the refinement of the division of labor, the upstream, midstream, and downstream links in the chain can be completely differentiated and outsourced. Especially in the case of global trade and international division of labor, the production chain of a specific product can be differentiated, produced, and completed in different countries, thus forming a global value chain. Global value chains have become an important feature of globalization today. As a global trading country, China occupies an important position in global value chains. Figure 4.12 shows the top 15 economies with the highest participation in global value chains in 2010. One can see that most of the countries with high participation in global value chains are developed countries, while China's participation in global value chains has reached 59%. In fact, China occupies large sections of intermediate stages in the global value chain, mainly helped by its large-scale, low-cost labor advantage, and preferential import-and-export trade policies. Although China has a high degree of participation in global value chains, it is mainly concentrated in the manufacturing sector, and its participation in service industries is very low. In terms of manufacturing participation, China's part of the value chain lies in midstream manufacturing, including but not limited to the procurement of product parts, supply-chain management, production, and assembly. Most Chinese companies act as original equipment manufacturers, their main job being to assemble product parts—that is, using labor to complete assembly—with China's added value mainly deriving from labor. This is also inseparable from the fact that China's participation in global value chains is closely connected with the manufacturing powers of Europe and the United States.

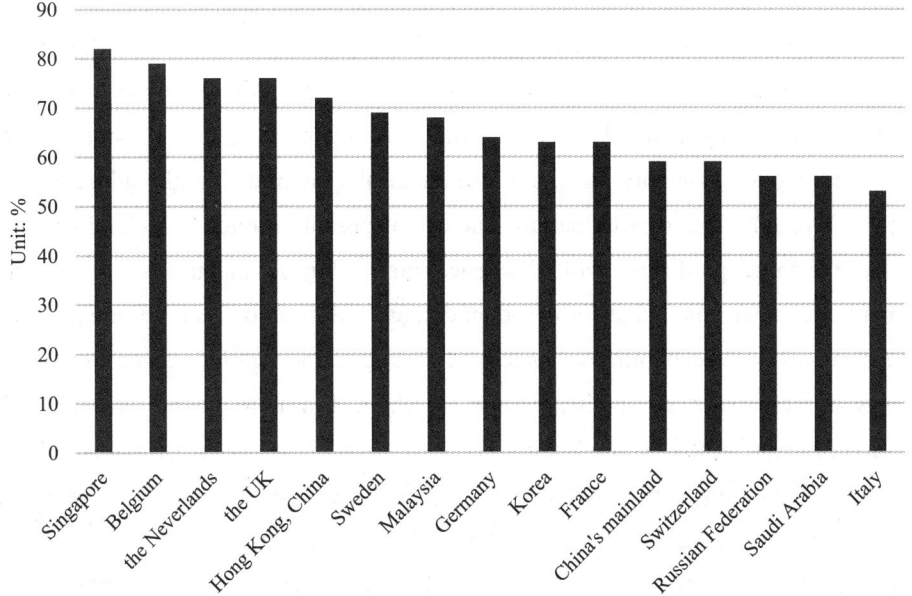

Figure 4.12 The top 15 economies with the highest participation in global value chains in 2010

Source: UNCTAD (2013). "World Investment Report 2013." Retrieved from https://unctad.org/en/PublicationsLibrary/wir2013_en.pdf.

With the development of digital economy, the trading system of global value chains is also undergoing profound changes. For the traditional manufacturing value chain, the application of digital technology has further refined the division of labor. For example, the use of the Internet and digital technology in the transportation process has reduced trade barriers and trade costs, gradually subdividing the formerly indivisible production chain, allowing for more global participation. Thanks to the use and promotion of digital information technology, the former information communication barriers are broken, especially in the intangible R&D design, marketing, and service links. New service parts are joining the organizational structure of the value chain. For example, the use of online sales platforms and electronic payment has replaced the original market retail model and become a new part of the global value chain. Furthermore, digitalization also promotes the creation of a new global value chain—the service products value chain. As digital economy develops, digital products have also become a new form of global value chain. For example, in the digital gaming industry, the value chain includes game content creation, game content digital processing, game distribution, and sales. This new global value chain has gradually become one of the main forms of value chains.

As a major country participating in global value chains, China is in an era when profound changes are being effected by digitalization. Digital economy has also prompted changes in the way China participates in global value chains. For the traditional manufacturing sector, companies use digitalized and intellectualized production technologies that increase production efficiency, enabling them to undertake more parts of the value chain and increase their participation. At the same time, thanks to the use of advanced digital production technology, companies can make products with higher technological content. With this ability, the international competitiveness of companies in global value chains will increase, and companies are participating more in global value chains. Chinese companies can now not only participate in low-end processing and assembly links, but also undertake the mid-to-high-end parts, expanding the depth and breadth of their participation. The use of digital production technology and digital information exchange platforms will also encourage Chinese manufacturers to understand external market competition and absorb product demand information more efficiently, improving their innovation level and capabilities, hence contributing to their global value. This will result in their increased international competitiveness in the chain. From the perspective of the changing external environment, global value chains are now driven by digital economy. The original manufacturing global value chain has changed, with the emergence of a new service industry global value chain, allowing Chinese companies to further participate in the chain and providing them with important opportunities. Chinese companies can rely on digital information technologies such as the Internet to deepen their timely and effective connections with the world. At the same time, they can make use of reduced transaction costs brought about by digitalization to attract more Chinese SMEs into the global value chains. With improvements in production efficiency, production technology, and innovation capabilities, Chinese enterprises will gradually move toward the high-end parts of global value chains, such as R&D, design, and marketing services. China can further exploit the developing digital economy and human capital to serve these global value chains, especially in the service production parts. On the whole, the developing digital economy will change China's participation in global value chains, specifically reflected in its enhanced international competitiveness, as it moves toward the high-end parts and increases its participation.

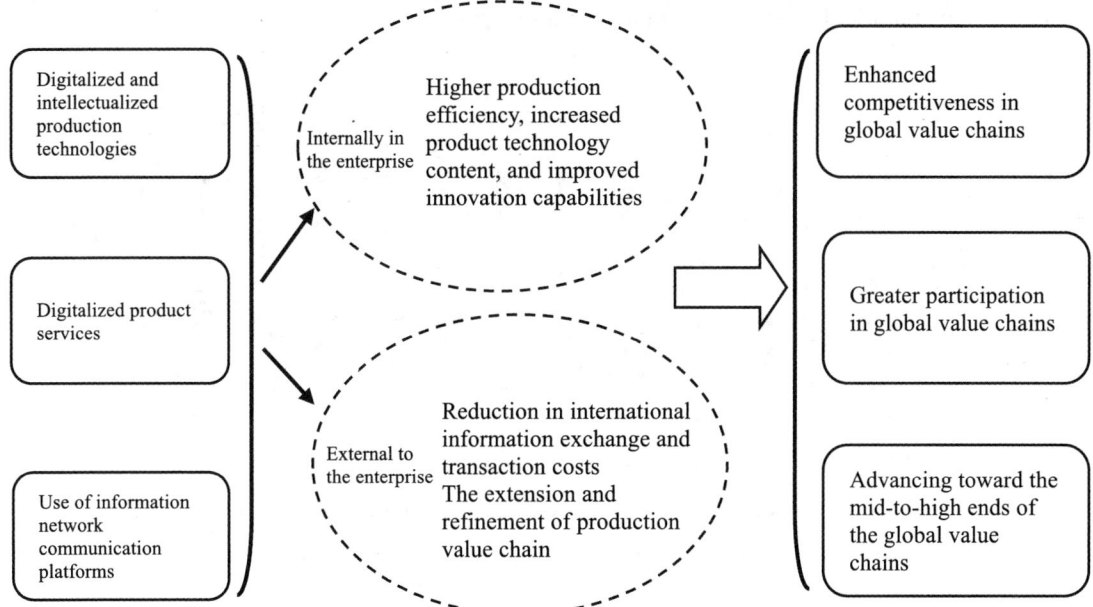

Figure 4.13 The impact of digital economy on participation in global value chains

2.6 Digital economy and the international status of trade

As the world's third-largest trading nation, China's status and influence in global trade cannot be underestimated. Since the beginning of its reform and opening-up era in the late 1970s, China has been actively developing foreign trade and implementing an "export-oriented" policy. Especially after its entry into the World Trade Organization, China's foreign trade development has entered a period of accelerated growth. Its international trade is increasing annually on the overall scale. Figure 4.14 shows the percentage of China's export of goods as a part of the global export of goods, as well as its export of services as a part of the global export of services from 2005 to 2017. From the figure, we can see that from 2005 to 2017, China's goods export share showed a clear upward trend. Especially after 2014, China's goods export has accounted for more than 10% of the world's total. In comparison, its service export share is relatively low. Although it has increased slightly, it is maintaining a level between 3% and 5%. Therefore, concerning the current state of China's trade, we can say that although China occupies a key position in world trade in terms of goods traded, it does not show an absolute advantage in service trade.

Under the new global trade situation, China is utilizing digital development to bring about economic development, and at the same time promoting its share and status in international trade. First, as China's digital economy develops, Chinese companies are able to transform and upgrade their original production technology digitally, boosting the manufacturing production efficiency and technology level of their manufacturing industry. In this way, the international competitiveness of their export goods is enhanced. China's developing digital economy will help it maintain its important global trade status in export goods.

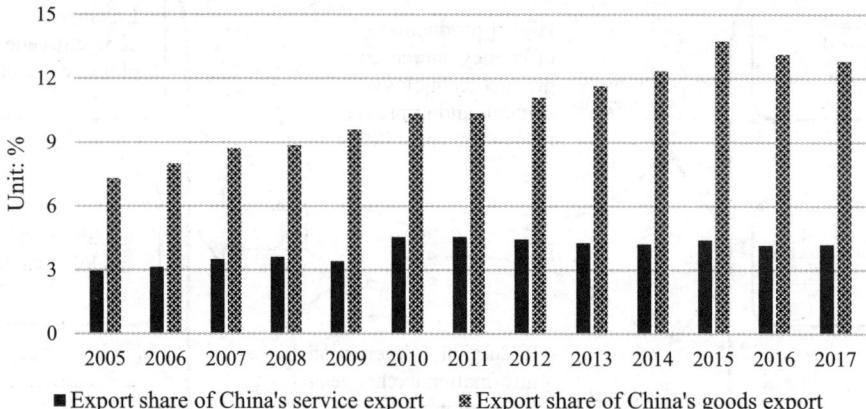

Figure 4.14 Changes in China's world share in goods and service export, 2005-2017

Source: WTO Database. Retrieved from https://www.wto.org/english/res_e/statis_e/merch_trade_stat_e.htm.

At the same time, with its original manufacturing industry as the foundation, China can realize its transition to a high-end manufacturing industry driven by digital economy. China will be able to export high-tech products and related ICT products, and re-establish itself in the process of digital upgrading. New comparative advantages will enhance its position in global trade. Also, China's developing digital economy has popularized and facilitated online transactions in traditional export industries, reduced communication barriers for Chinese companies engaging in foreign trade, and helped reduce fixed and variable costs as China trades with the world. It has expanded the scale of China's export products in the international market, further increasing its total volume in foreign trade. Lastly, service products produced using digital knowledge and digital technology have become new tradable goods. Driven by digital economy, China is developing a digital service industry, adding new channels and new products to its foreign trade. This also contributes to China's rising international trade share and status.

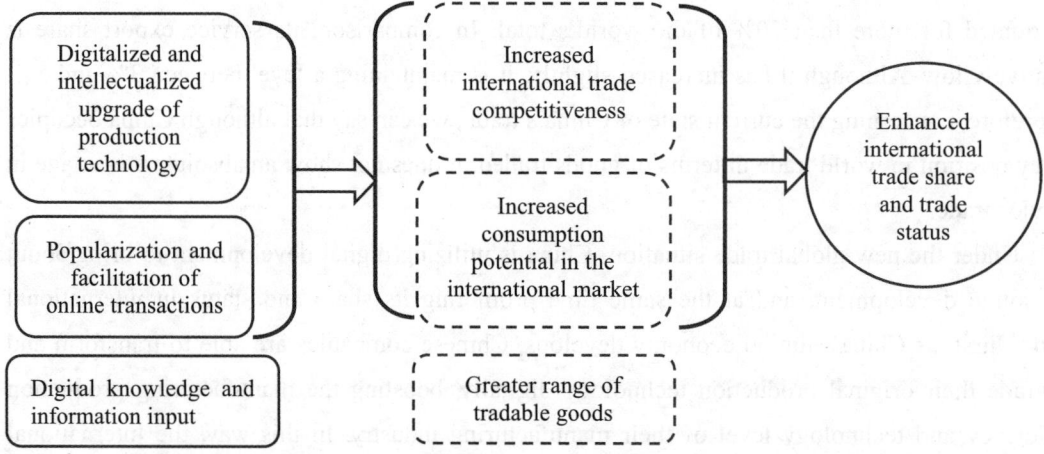

Figure 4.15 The impact of digital economy on raising international trade status

Section 3 Typical Enterprise Case Studies of China's Digital Trade

3.1 Tmall Global: building a digital trade value chain

3.1.1 The development process of Tmall Global

With the rapid development of Internet technology, online shopping has become one of the most important shopping channels in consumers' lives. In order to satisfy their needs for material diversity, various cross-border e-commerce platforms have emerged. As e-commerce develops rapidly in digital economy, the growth prospects of such platforms are quite impressive. We can see from the monitoring data of the China E-commerce Research Center that, as of the end of June 2018, the number of regular cross-border online shoppers in China had reached 75 million. From Figure 4.16, it is easy to see its rapid growth from 2013 to 2016. After that, e-commerce has been growing more gradually.

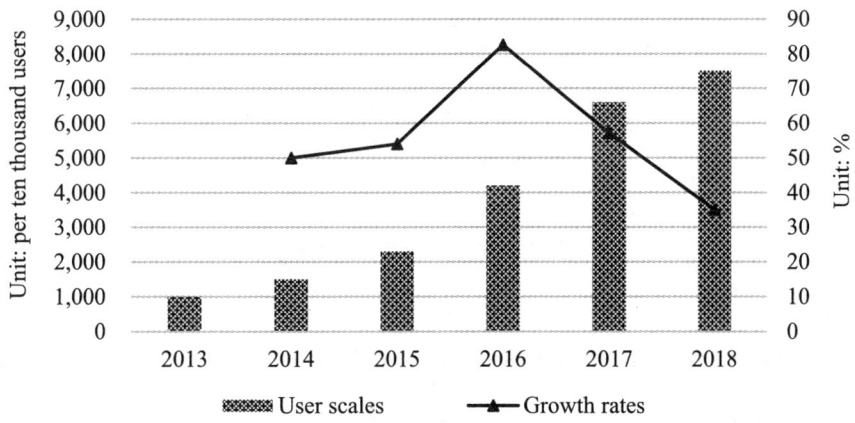

Figure 4.16 The scales of Chinese cross-border online shoppers from 2013 to mid-2018

Note: The data in 2018 in this graph is as of June 2018.
Source: WWW.100EC.CN. Retrieved from http://www.100ec.cn/.

It was in this context that Tmall Global was formally launched on February 19, 2014. Tmall Global is a cross-border e-commerce platform under Alibaba. Through its reliance on Alibaba, Tmall Global has inherent advantages in product supply. Soon after its launch, Tmall Global collaborated with the China (Hangzhou) Cross-border E-commerce Pilot Area, Zhengzhou Xinzheng Comprehensive Protective Tariff Zone, and Ningbo Free Trade Zone. On June 24, 2015, the Alibaba Group's Juhuasuan platform and Tmall Global jointly launched the "global village" models, with 11 national pavilions from the United States, the United Kingdom, France, Spain, Switzerland, Australia, New Zealand, Singapore, Thailand, Malaysia, and Turkey all unveiled on Tmall Global. By relying on Alibaba's strong resource support, Tmall Global is growing vigorously and has achieved remarkable results. Relevant data show that in the fourth quarter of 2018, China's cross-border import retail e-commerce market was ¥114.56 billion, with Tmall Global accounting for 31.7%,[①] far more than any other cross-border e-commerce platform. Tmall Global ranked first in market share for five consecutive times.

At present, there are two main platforms on Tmall Global. One is the direct shopping platform. After consumers place their orders on the Tmall Global platform, the platform directly contacts the overseas merchant, and the merchant directly exports the goods to the destination. It takes about 20 days for the delivery to reach customers. The second model is the global flash-shopping platform, which purchases overseas products in batches in advance and stores them in domestic bonded warehouses. When a consumer places an order, the product will be delivered directly from the bonded warehouse. It takes about seven days for logistics companies to deliver a product to the customer. This method reduces the time spent in international logistics and improves the speed and ease in which consumers can purchase cross-border goods.

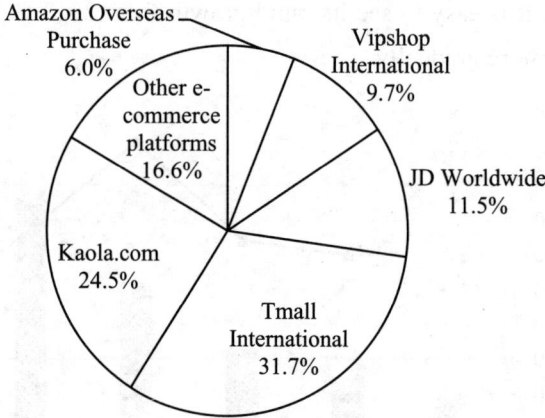

Figure 4.17   China's cross-border import e-commerce market competition pattern in the fourth quarter of 2018

Source: Analysys (March 6, 2019). Retrieved from https://www.analysys.cn/article/analysis/detail/20019146.

3.1.2 A study of Tmall Global's production value chain in the digital economy era

By relying on the digital economy background, China's e-commerce has developed rapidly. Different from the traditional sales model, online platform e-commerce connects various economic entities in the production value chain, drawing them closer. It helps realize the sharing of resources and information. As a result, the effectiveness of the value chain becomes increasingly prominent.

First, in terms of product flow, Tmall Global relies on platforms such as the Internet and logistics systems to complete transactions and distribute its products to customers. It can directly contact upstream suppliers and downstream consumers, reducing traditional retail costs at

---

① Source: Enfodesk (January 2019). "Quarterly Monitoring Report of China's Cross-Border Import Retail E-Commerce Market, Fourth Quarter of 2018." Retrieved from https://www.analysys.cn/article/analysis/detail/20019146.

different stages of distribution. On the one hand, it reduces cost for enterprises; on the other, the relatively low commodity prices also bring welfare to consumers, and optimize benefits to suppliers, Tmall Global, and consumers simultaneously. Tmall Global relies on big data and cloud computing to better capture consumer preference data, realizing a two-way flow of information and reducing information costs. For consumers, it enables them to obtain more product information and more convenient after-sales services. It also allows suppliers to understand market demand and recent consumption trends using the e-commerce platform database.

Second, the rapid development of digital economy has also broadened Tmall Global's advertising marketing and consumption model. Besides using common marketing methods like search engine promotion and precision marketing, the continuously developing social-media streaming and self-media have resulted in social-media streaming marketing and "entertainment" marketing becoming the mainstream. Tmall Global uses variety shows, online dissemination, and offline activities to successfully build demand, increasing traffic and popularity and enabling downstream consumers to purchase more freely. Tmall Global also uses the international version of Alipay (Escrow) for cross-border transactions, with Alibaba International Station and the domestic Alipay jointly providing third-party guarantee services to International Alipay. Payment is processed in this way: after consumers complete their purchase of goods and pay through Alipay, their payment will be temporarily stored in Alipay. After the merchant processes the order and sends the delivery, and when the consumer finally receives the purchased good, payment will be transferred to the merchant's account. One can see that Tmall International protects the interests of both merchants and consumers through transitional third-party supervision, standardizing capital flow for both parties, thus ensuring safe capital flow in the value chain.

Finally, in terms of logistics distribution, Tmall Global's logistics distribution is handled by Cainiao Logistics. Compared with other traditional logistics companies, Cainiao Logistics is not so much a logistics company, but more of an "artificial intelligent system of express logistics". Its main duty is to coordinate between various logistics companies. Cainiao's processing involves the capture, modeling, and calculation of cross-border, warehousing, and distribution information and terminal big data. It incorporates logistics companies into the logistics network, thereby accelerating the entire logistics system, enhancing the whole value chain while acting as a "lubricant".

3.2 Huawei: innovative trade modes in digital economy

3.2.1 An overview of Huawei's mobile phone export situation

As a key representative of a high-tech product, a mobile phone is a very complex product, involving many parts and components. Mobile phone manufacturing cannot be completed unless every part is present. Therefore, the mobile phone industry is bound to involve international trade. At present, China's mobile phone industry has made considerable progress, with Huawei mobile phones being the chief exemplar. Huawei is a mobile phone company that has emerged in China over the past 10 years. Thanks to its continuous technological innovation and mastery of high-level information and communications technologies, Huawei's well-made mobile phones have occupied an important market position in the global mobile-phone market. Huawei achieves mobile-phone sales mainly through exports. Numerous countries and regions are the export destinations of Huawei mobile phones. Huawei mobile phones can be said to exemplify China's digital product exports. Therefore, by analyzing Huawei's mobile-phone export model, we can further study digital economy's impact on China's trade methods.

Huawei is able to maintain rapid growth, leveraging on the opportunities brought about by China's digital transformation. True digital transformation is not about a company opening an online store or shopping mall and digitalizing only the sales section. Instead, it involves the re-engineering of production processes and the creation of new businesses and products. It is an integrated process. Huawei's consumer business mainly involves mobile phones, driven by AI to create a hardware-and-service ecological platform for core-end cloud collaboration. At the same time, Huawei continues to innovate in core technology fields, such as 5G, artificial intelligence, and AR/VR, creating an integrated and intellectualized experience for consumers while leading industry reform. By investing in consumer business and persistently pursuing patented technology, Huawei's global exports have increased significantly (see Table 4.1 for details).

Table 4.1 Huawei's global sales data analysis (unit: per million yuan)

Region	2018	2017	Changes in percentage
China	372,162	312,532	19.1%
Europe, the Middle East, and Africa	204,536	164,603	24.3%
Asia Pacific	81,918	71,199	15.1%
The Americas	47,885	39,470	21.3%
Others	14,701	15,817	−7.1%
Total	721,202	603,621	19.5%

Source: Huawei Investment & Holding (2019). Huawei Annual Report 2018. Retrieved from https://www-file.huawei.com/-/media/corporate/pdf/annual-report/annual_report2018_cn_v2.pdf?la=zh.

One can see from Table 4.1 that the domestic Chinese market is still an important sales market for Huawei. Countries in Europe, the Middle East, Africa, and the Asia-Pacific region are Huawei's main export markets. The Americas only account for a small proportion of Huawei's global market. In addition to the significant increase in exports, digital economy has also caused a fundamental change in the way Huawei exports its mobile phones. Due to the global hardware support of mobile phones, with centralized cooperation between multiple enterprises, Huawei mobile phones mainly used a combination of general trade and imported material processing in the past. They imported foreign mobile phone hardware, put them together in local hardware factories, and then used these domestic factories to assemble mobile phones before exporting them. One can see from Table 4.2 that some core hardware in Huawei mobile phones still has to be processed with imported materials in order to ensure quality control. The hardware products are imported from other companies for domestic assembly. These products are exported once assembly is completed.

Table 4.2 A few component suppliers of Huawei mobile phones

CPU	Main camera	Screen	Casing	Battery	Fingerprint recognition
Qualcomm	Sony	JDI	Jabil	SDI	Fingerprint Cards

Source: Huawei Investment & Holding (2017). Huawei Annual Report 2016. Retrieved from http://www-file.huawei.com/-/media/CORPORATE/PDF/annual-report/AnnualReport2016_cn.pdf?la=zh.

3.2.2 Changes in trade modes in Huawei's mobile phone exports

With the continuous growth of digital economy and the continuous transformation and upgrading of global industrial structures, Huawei is transforming from a combination of imported processing and general trade to a general trade model. There are three main reasons behind this change.

The first is innovation-driven, that is, big data, artificial intelligence, and high-end talents play a significant role in boosting Huawei's mobile phone production. At present, Huawei has developed many breakthrough innovations in the fields of mobile phone performance, photography, artificial intelligence, communications, and design. Its product competitiveness and user experience have been greatly enhanced. The Kirin 980 chip developed independently by Huawei has reached the 7-nanometer standard, breaking the US monopoly on high-end mobile-phone chips. Its revolutionary graphics processing acceleration technology, GPU Turbo, has broken through the processing bottleneck when using the EMUI operating system, GPU, and CPU. Its flexible "Leica triple camera" system utilizes artificial intelligence to offer a professional photographic experience when using their slim and stylish phones. The graphene-plus-liquid cooling system brings outstanding rapid cooling performance. The 40W wired super-fast charging, 15W wireless fast charging, and wireless reverse charging have provided users with three new fast and safe charging systems.[①] Huawei has applied the above innovations to its high-end mobile phone products. Huawei is paying more and more attention to the domestic manufacturing environment, gradually reducing the cost and scale of input processing. In doing so, it lowers the cost of mobile phone production, expands the scale of its ordinary trade, and reduces the costs of its mobile phone business.

The second reason is its reliance on Internet technology to improve trade efficiency. The continuous emergence of new technologies such as Huawei's mobile terminal, artificial

---

① Source: Huawei Investment & Holding (2019). Huawei Annual Report 2018. Retrieved from https://www-file.huawei.com/-/media/corporate/pdf/annual-report/annual_report2018_cn_v2.pdf?la=zh.

intelligence, and big data has enabled more tangible products to eliminate physical limitations, transforming themselves into digital products and services, for direct dissemination on the Internet. At the same time, the development of a global e-commerce payment system, a security certification system, and other technologies has greatly benefited the electronic level of production, delivery, and payment, while encouraging the formation of a mobile phone digital product-and-service market. Driven by the transformation and upgrading of the industrial structure and the rapid growth of information technology, the individualized and specialized needs of consumers for information products and services have been further stimulated and expanded. They have become the mainstream of Internet consumption. As the global industrial structure transforms and upgrades itself, driving the industry, newly developed technologies will act as a guarantee, and new demand will act its traction, boosting scientific progress in digital trade. Digital trade uses digital exchange technology on the Internet as a means and Internet transmission as a medium to directly shorten time and distance. It reduces transaction costs, simplifies trade processes, and increases trade opportunities while expanding Huawei's mobile-phone export share.

The third involves uncertainties facing the trading environment. After the financial crisis, every country is aiming to stimulate its economic growth through digital economy. The trade friction between China and the United States and their technological competition will continue. Presently, the US Department of Commerce has added Huawei and 70 affiliates to the "entity list" for export control. US companies must obtain approval from the US government before they can trade with Huawei. Deglobalization and protectionism have turned into prominent risks in global trade. Trade restrictions have increased, and global trade tensions have intensified. Despite these factors, Huawei has already developed many core technologies domestically, such as radio frequency, power amplifier chips, FPGA chips, etc.[①] These breakthroughs in key technologies have enabled Huawei to overcome its mobile-phone export disadvantages and enhance its export strength.

Thanks to the continuously developing digital economy, Huawei (including its Honor sub-brand) had shipped 206 million smartphones in 2018, an increase of 35% from the previous year.[②] Its growth rate is relatively rapid, greatly surpassing that of its top two competitors, Apple and Samsung. Despite the rapid growth of its mobile-phone exports, some of Huawei's core mobile phone hardware still needs to be processed with imported materials, to ensure quality control. However, in recent years, Huawei has turned gradually from a combination of imported processing and general trade to general trade. Huawei has developed the HiSilicon

---

① Source: Huawei Investment & Holding (2019). Huawei Annual Report 2018. Retrieved from https://www-file.huawei.com/-/media/corporate/pdf/annual-report/annual_report2018_cn_v2.pdf?la=zh.

② Source: Huawei Investment & Holding (2019). Huawei Annual Report 2018. Retrieved from https://www-file.huawei.com/-/media/corporate/pdf/annual-report/annual_report2018_cn_v2.pdf?la=zh.

processor and Kirin processor independently, using them in its high-end mobile phone products. Huawei is gradually reducing the cost and scale of input processing, expanding its scale of general trade while lowering the cost of production of its mobile phones. At the same time, it aims to expand its export share, overcome its export disadvantages, and improve its export strength.

Section 4 Trade Development in the Digital Economy Era

4.1 The development status of digital trade

4.1.1 Digital product trade

(1) Information and communications technology (ICT) products trade

In the United Nations Commission on Trade and Development (UNCTAD) database, the trade of ICT products is divided into four types: computers and peripheral equipment; communication equipment; consumer electronic equipment; electronic components. ICT products include both finished and intermediate products, and trade is mainly carried out between Asia, Europe, and the United States. Statistics show that 49% of global ICT product imports in 2015 were made by developing Asian countries with many large manufacturing enterprises and manufacturing equipment in participation.① We can interpret the statistics of global information technology-related ICT product trade exports as a percentage of the total merchandise trade. Although the share of ICT products has fluctuated since 2005, it is still increasing on the whole. Especially since 2011, the proportion of ICT products is rising gradually, accounting for 12.12% of the world's total exports in 2018 (see Figure 4.18).

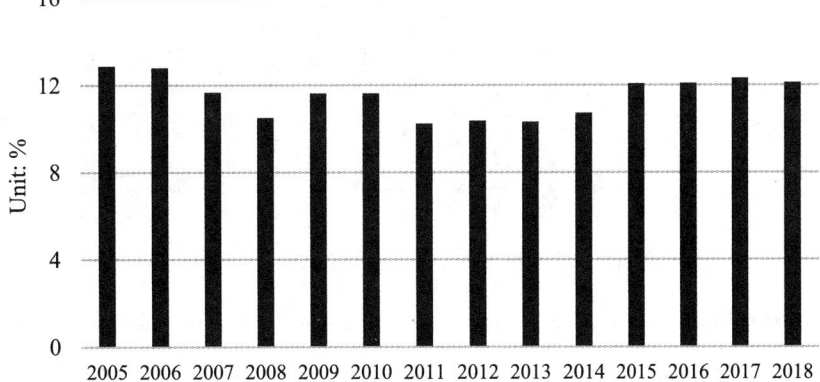

Figure 4.18 Global ICT product exports as a percentage of total merchandise exports, 2005 to 2018

Source: UNCTAD STAT. Retrieved from https://unctadstat.unctad.org/wds/ReportFolders/reportFolders.aspx.

---

① Source: UNCTAD (October 2017). Information Economy Report 2017: Digitalization, Trade and Development. Retrieved from https://unctad.org/en/pages/PublicationWebflyer.aspx?publicationid=1872.

As far as China is concerned, the import and export of China's ICT products and its proportion in the total merchandise trade are shown in Figure 4.19 and Figure 4.20. First, in terms of ICT products trade volume, other than a decline in certain years (2009 and 2016), China's ICT product imports and exports had both been growing from 2005 to 2018, with its export value being significantly higher than its import value. China reached a peak in its exports and imports in 2018. Exports were valued at USD 681.1 billion and imports at USD 484.1 billion in 2018.

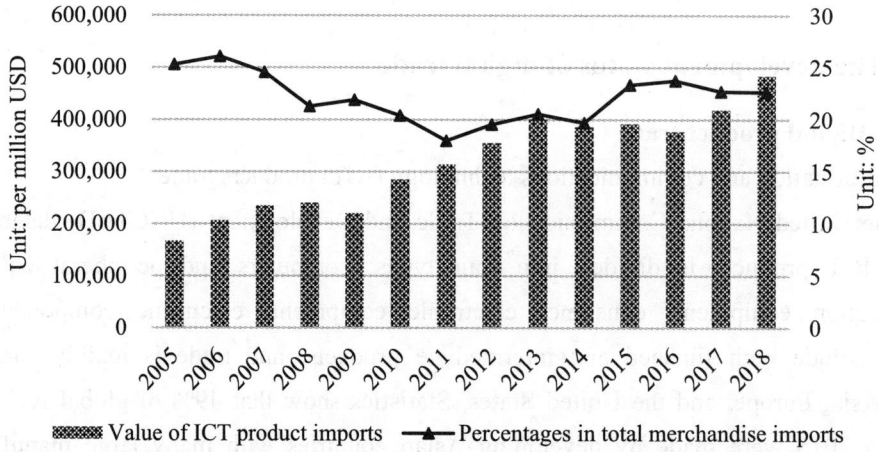

Figure 4.19 China's ICT product import scales and percentages in total merchandise imports, 2005-2018

Source: UNCTAD STAT. Retrieved from https://unctadstat.unctad.org/wds/ReportFolders/reportFolders.aspx.

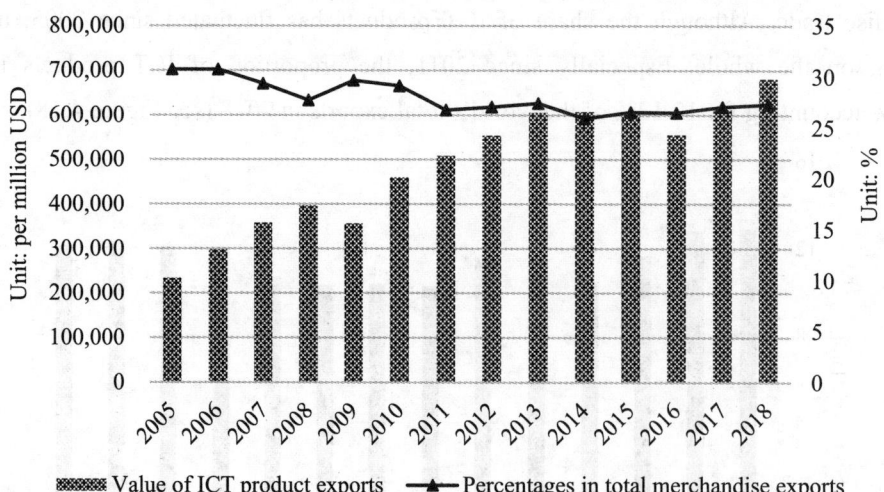

Figure 4.20 China's ICT product export scales and percentages in total merchandise exports, 2005-2018

Looking at China's percentage of imports and exports within the total merchandise trade, one can see the same trend in its import and export. The percentage of its export within the total ICT products is significantly higher than that of its import. In the 14 years from 2005 to 2018, the percentage of ICT product exports was at its highest in 2006, reaching 30.72%. Although it has declined since then, the proportion had been still always higher than 25%. Its ICT import percentage had been still growing. It reached a peak of 26.07% in 2006, and then hit a trough of 18% in 2011. Since then, it had been showing a rising trend. Imports accounted for 22.67% of the total in 2018. However, one can see that although the share of imports and exports reached their peak in 2006, the value of imports and exports was very small in 2006, only two-fifths of 2018's value. This shows that China's ICT products had increased significantly in the past decade, while its total volume of merchandise trade was also increasing.

(2) Cross-border e-commerce

In 2016, the Universal Postal Union, the United Nations Conference on Trade and Development (UNCTAD), Asia-Pacific Economic Cooperation (APEC), and World Trade Organization (WTO) launched a cooperative project to measure cross-border e-commerce transactions, now widely regarded as an important component of digital trade.[1] In China, the early days of its digital economy focused on information construction and the development of e-commerce.

According to the United Nations 2019 Digital Economy Report, global e-commerce activities are dominated by large economies. In 2017, the value of global e-commerce transactions reached USD 29.367 trillion, with the value of e-commerce transactions in the United States, Japan, China, and Germany accounting for 56.5% of the global e-commerce total. In the field of B2C e-commerce, China leads the world thanks to its convenient electronic payment system, accounting for about 26% of the world's transactions in 2017. Yet in 2017, China's B2B was only valued at USD 869 billion, accounting for 49% of its e-commerce. China has the lowest proportion of B2B commerce among the top 10 countries,[2] indicating that its developing B2B e-commerce still lags far behind those of developed countries, especially the United States. The future application of new information technology, such as AI, blockchain, and the Internet of Things, will usher in an innovative peak in China's e-commerce.

The reason for the rapid growth of cross-border e-commerce is that it is replacing the traditional trade market. There is huge room for the future development in digital technology application. In 2015, the world's top five economies imported 1.4% of global total imports using B2C. China ranked first in B2C and cross-border e-commerce, and its total cross-border e-commerce ranked second.[3]

---

[1] OECD (March 2017), "Working Party on International Trade in Goods and Trade in Services Statistics, Measuring Digital Trade: Towards a Conceptual Framework." Retrieved from http://www.oecd.org/officialdocuments/publicdisplaydocument pdf/?cote=STD/TBS/WPTGS(2012)15&docLanguage=En.

[2] Source: UNCTAD (2019). "Digital Economy Report 2019: Value Creation and Capture: Implications for Developing Countries." Retrieved from https://unctad.org/en/PublicationsLibrary/der2019_en.pdf.

[3] Source: UNCTAD (October 2017). "Information Economy Report 2017: Digitalization, Trade and Development." Retrieved from https://unctad.org/en/pages/PublicationWebflyer.aspx?publicationid=1872.

Table 4.3 Cross-border B2C e-commerce in the top five countries in 2015, in terms of import value

Country	Total value of cross-border B2C e-commerce (billion USD)	Percentage of cross-border B2C import market (%)	Percentage of B2C market (%)	Total value of B2C (billion USD)	Number of cross-border merchants (million)
the US	40	1.7	7	612	34
China	39	2.3	6	617	70
Germany	9	0.8	10	93	12
Japan	2	0.3	2	114	9
the UK	12	1.9	7	200	14
Global total	189	11	70	2904	380

Source: UNCTAD (2017). "Information Economy Report 2017: Digitalization, Trade and Development.".

The penetration rate of China's cross-border e-commerce has been increasing over the years. According to the 2019 Global E-commerce Data Report, the transaction value of China's cross-border e-commerce industry reached 9.1 trillion yuan in 2018, an increase of 11.6% from the previous year, and a 9.83-fold increase from 840 billion yuan in 2009. The export e-commerce transaction value reached 7.1 trillion yuan, with import e-commerce transaction value reaching 1.9 trillion yuan, an increase of 26.7% from the previous year.[①]

Since 2018, China's cross-border e-commerce industry has ushered in favorable policies. The e-commerce law and a series of new cross-border e-commerce policies have been introduced. The Chinese government has further increased personal cross-border e-commerce consumption limits and added cross-border e-commerce comprehensive pilot zones. It has gradually perfected e-commerce platforms online and offline, launching an "online and offline" omni-channel model, slowly improving upstream and downstream supply chains, all of which will be standardized to promote cross-border e-commerce growth. The industry's e-commerce import retail market has grown rapidly since 2013. Although the growth rate had slowed down in the past three years, it was as high as 161.34 billion yuan in 2018. The consumer base of imported cross-border e-commerce has also increased, with a rise in transaction volume and growth, reaching 101 million customers in 2018. Among the world's top 10 e-commerce companies, Alibaba ranks first globally, with a market share of 26.6%. Amazon ranks second, with a market share of 13%.[②] One can see that rapidly developing cross-border online transactions are expected to spearhead China's foreign trade development.

With the explosive growth of cross-border e-commerce in China, countries in the "Belt and Road Initiative" have also made important contributions, beyond developed markets such as Europe and the United States. The "'Belt and Road' Cross-Border E-Commerce Consumption

---

① Source: www.100EC.CN (November 2019). "Global E-Commerce Data Report 2019." Retrieved from http://www.100ec.cn/zt/2019sjbg_world/.

② Ministry of Commerce. P.R.C. (2018). E-Commerce in China 2018.

Report 2019" pointed out that China's products have been successfully sold to more than 100 countries through cross-border e-commerce, including Russia, Israel, Vietnam, and Korea, all having signed cooperation treaties for the construction of the "Belt and Road Initiative". As a result, China's online commerce relationship has expanded to many countries in Asia, Africa, and Europe within the "Belt and Road Initiative".①

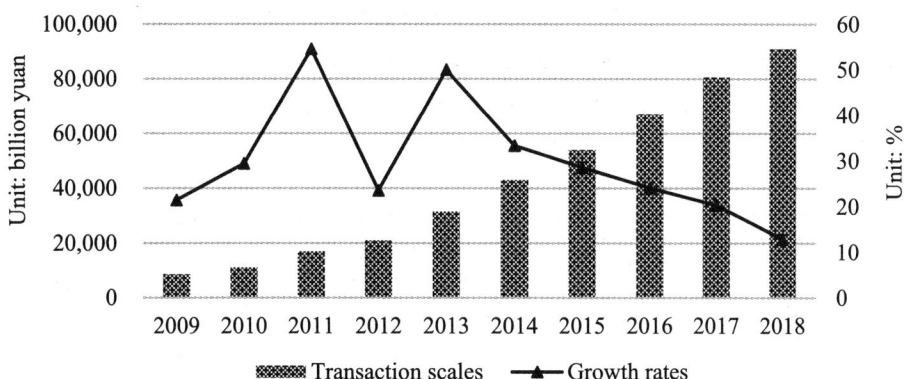

Figure 4.21   China's cross-border e-commerce transaction scales and growth rates, 2009-2018

Source: www.100EC.CN(November 2019). Global E-Commerce Data Report 2019. Retrieved from http://www.100ec.cn/zt/2019sjbg_world/.

4.1.2 Digital service trade

(1) Software

Software export is an important component of digital service export and an important indicator in measuring the competitiveness of a country's digital service export. In 2018, China's software exports generally maintained a medium- to high-speed growth, achieving a software export value of USD 41.227 billion, an increase of 9.8% from the previous year.

Table 4.4   China's software export scales (100 million USD) and growth rates, 2010-2018

Year	Negotiation amount	Percentage growth (%)	Execution amount	Percentage growth (%)
2010	126.20	24.42	97.30	34.01
2011	190.68	51.09	143.39	47.37
2012	234.20	22.82	194.16	35.40
2013	320.71	36.94	253.56	30.59
2014	377.15	17.55	30.57	18.51
2015	425.78	12.89	333.93	11.10
2016	464.89	9.19	342.3	2.51
2017	571.82	23.00	375.56	9.72
2018	560.89	−1.90	412.27	9.80

Source: Ministry of Commerce of the People's Republic of China (October 8, 2019). China Trade in Digital Services Report 2018. Retrieved from http://coi.mofcom.gov.cn/article/y/gnxw/201910/20191002901732.shtml.

---

① JD Big Data Research Institute (April 2019). "Belt and Road" Cross-Border E-Commerce Consumption Report 2019. Retrieved from https://research.jd.com/.

In terms of software export modes (as shown in Table 4.5), information technology outsourcing is the main mode of software export. In 2018, completed information technology outsourcing was USD 40.131 billion, accounting for 97.43% of the total, with a growth rate of 10.2%.[①] One can see that its scale continues to grow and its structure is constantly optimized. The export structure of information technology outsourcing is mainly based on software R&D outsourcing. In 2018, the execution amounts of software R&D outsourcing, information technology and service outsourcing, and operation and maintenance outsourcing were USD 25.59 billion, USD 8.817 billion, and USD 5.335 billion respectively, accounting for 64%, 22%, and 13% of the total.

Table 4.5　Statistics of China's software exports in 2018 by export mode

Types of contract	Negotiation amount (100 million USD)	Percentage growth (%)	Execution amount (%)	Percentage growth (%)
Information technology outsourcing	544.99	−1.6	1.31	10.2
Software development outsourcing	305.68	−22.4	255.90	5.1
Information technology services outsourcing	122.66	46.2	88.17	28.2
Operation and maintenance services	112.06	48.9	52.35	1.6
Cloud-based services outsourcing	4.57	N/A	4.53	N/A
Software products	15.90	−12.7	10.96	−3.5
System software	2.73	−24.2	2.08	−12.4
Application software	11.67	−19.7	8.25	−7.4
Supporting software	1.51	1,493.3	0.63	804.9
Total	560.89	−1.9	412.27	9.8

Source: Ministry of Commerce of the People's Republic of China (October 8, 2019). China Trade in Digital Services Report 2018. Retrieved from http://coi.mofcom.gov.cn/article/y/gnxw/201910/20191002901732.shtml.

(2) Satellite navigation and location services

According to statistics in the "China Satellite Navigation and Location Service Industry Development White Paper (2020)"[②] released by China Satellite Navigation and Positioning Association, the output value of China's satellite navigation and location service industry reached 301.6 billion yuan in 2019, an increase of 14.4% compared with 2018. The output value of core industries directly related to the development and application of satellite navigation

---

① Source: Ministry of Commerce of the People's Republic of China (October 8, 2019). China Trade in Digital Services Report 2018. Retrieved from http://coi.mofcom.gov.cn/article/y/gnxw/201910/20191002901732.shtml.

② GNSS and LBS Association of China (May 19, 2020). White Paper on China's Satellite Navigation and Location Service Industry Development (2020). Retrieved from https://tech.sina.com.cn/roll/2020-05-19/doc-iircuyvi3918768.shtml.

technology was 116.6 billion yuan (including chips, devices, algorithms, software, navigation data, terminal equipment, infrastructure, etc.), accounting for 33.8% of the total output value. One of the highlights of this industry is the BeiDou satellite positioning and navigation system, independently developed and operated by China, which began global services in 2018. According to data released by GNSS and LBS Association of China, BeiDou contributes 80% of the core output value of the satellite navigation, positioning, and location services industry, and the associated output value derived from satellite navigation is 194.7 billion yuan. At present, the satellite navigation and positioning products of Chinese companies have been sold in more than 100 countries worldwide. "BeiDou" has also been used in more than 30 countries and regions within the "Belt and Road Initiative". China's satellite navigation and location service industry has entered the world development stage.

(3) Digital content products and services

The export scale of content services such as video on demand, electronic games, digital music, and electronic publications is expanding rapidly. The "2018 China Gaming Industry Report" details that China's rapidly developing online gaming has greatly increased its independent research and development capabilities. Overseas gaming markets have become an important source of income for Chinese gaming companies. From 2009 to 2018, the actual sales revenue in overseas markets for independently developed Chinese online games increased rapidly, from USD 110 million to USD 9.59 billion, an 87-fold increase in 10 years,[①] as shown in Figure 4.22.

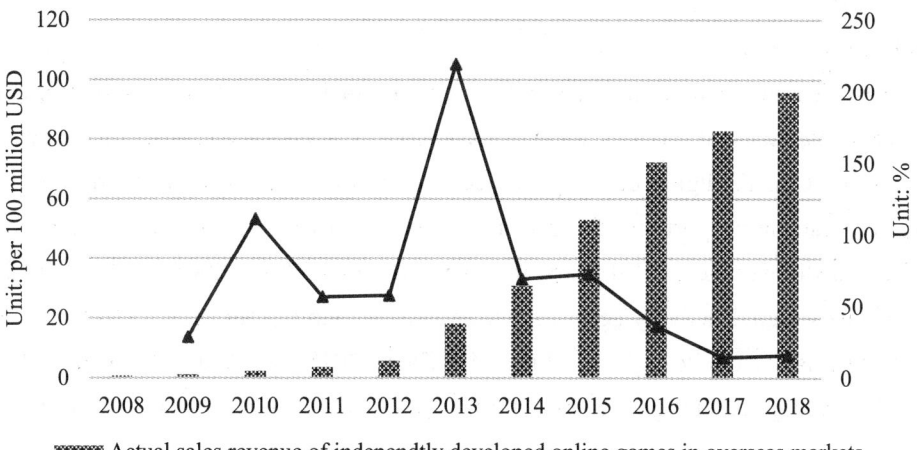

Figure 4.22 China's independently-developed online gaming overseas market sales revenue, 2008-2018

Source: Ministry of Commerce of the People's Republic of China (October 8, 2019). China Trade in Digital Services Report 2018. Retrieved from http://coi.mofcom.gov.cn/article/y/gnxw/201910/20191002901732.shtml.

---

① GPC, IDC (December 2018). *2018 China Gaming Industry Report* (Abstract). Beijing: China Book Press. Retrieved from https://www.useit.com.cn/thread-22501-1-1.html.

The digital publishing industry is relatively weak. The "2018 Statistical Analysis Report on Cultural Development" reports that China's publication exports in 2018 were USD 3.56 billion, including USD 1.79 billion for traditional publications such as books, newspapers, and periodicals, and digital publishing such as audiovisual products and electronic publications. Exports were USD 50 million, accounting for only 1.4% of publication exports.[①]

(4) Social media and search engines

Chinese social media is rapidly expanding overseas, constructing a global social-media network platform. This trend is manifested in two areas. First, the number of users and the scale of app downloads are expanding rapidly. According to data released in "Global Digital 2019 Reports," global social media users reached 3.48 billion in 2019.[②] Among the top eight platforms with active users, Chinese social media occupies three spots: WeChat (1.083 billion users), QQ (803 million users), and Qzone (531 million users). Second, the development of China's social media shows brand diversification, and short video, live broadcast, and communication are showing good growth. According to the 2018 Global App download rankings released by the Internet Information Center, Apptopia, TikTok is second only to WhatsApp and FB Messenger, ranking third in the social app category.[③]

As search engines expand in overseas markets, Chinese local search engine companies like Baidu are actively promoting internationalization. As the world's largest Chinese-language search engine, Baidu has successively launched search engines in Japanese,[④] Arabic (Egypt), Portuguese (Brazil), and Thai (Thailand) since 2008, steadily advancing its internationalized search business.

(5) ICT services

ICT service trade includes service trade categories such as information services, computer software services, financial services, and business services. Figure 4.23 shows the percentages of the world's and China's digital delivery service trade in total service trade from 2005 to 2018. One can see that the proportion of the world's digital delivery services has generally shown continuous growth over the past 14 years, increasing from 44.37% in 2005 to 50.15% in 2018. In contrast, China's digital delivery services started late, accounting for only 22.01% in 2005, but its growth rate is relatively high, reaching 49.26% in 2018, less than 1% behind the world average. The average annual growth rate during these years was 8.8%. This shows that digital

---

① Ministry of Culture and Tourism, P.R.C (November 2018). *2018 Statistical Analysis Report on Cultural Development*. Beijing: China Statistics Press.

② The data statistics are from January 2018 to January 2019. Data is collected from the world's top social platforms used in 230 countries and regions. Source: We Are Social (January 2019). Global Digital 2019 Reports. Retrieved from https://www.useit.com.cn/thread-22153-1-1.html.

③ Source: 199IT Apptopia (December 2018). 2018 Worldwide Download Leaders. Retrieved from https://www.sohu.com/a/283157696_100196087.

④ Baidu ceased its Japanese search-engine operation in March 2017.

technology-related products in global service trade are always an important component of world trade. Digital-related service trade is becoming a new trade growth point, and China's digital service trade is also growing rapidly.

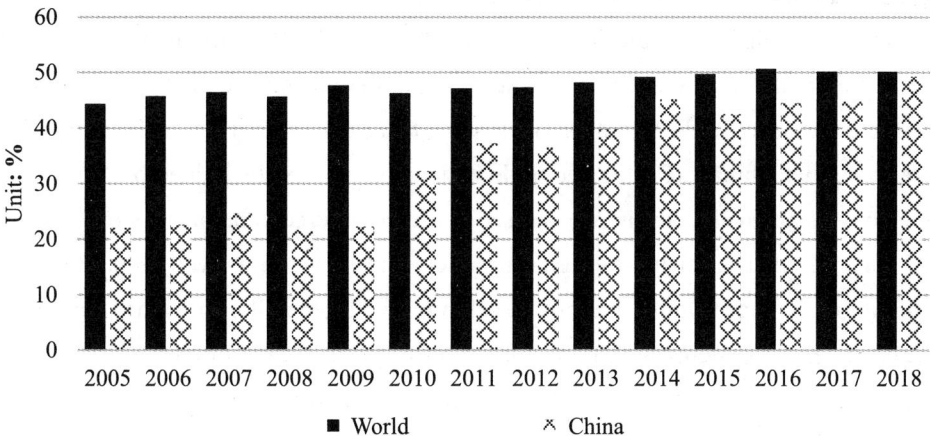

Figure 4.23 The percentages of the world's and China's digital delivery service trade in total service trade, 2005-2018

Source: UNCTADSTAT. Retrieved from https://unctadstat.unctad.org/wds/TableViewer/tableView.aspx?ReportId=158358.

Table 4.6 The export value of ICT service trade in major economies in the world (100 million USD) and their proportions

Economy	2014	2015	2016	2017	2018	Percentage of market in 2018
India	542.93	548.50	534.69	539.61	579.27	28.24%
China	201.73	257.84	265.31	277.67	470.58	17.64%
Germany	280.31	284.43	328.17	356.63	386.04	11.66%
the United States	275.30	292.94	313.62	338.20	342.87	4.14%
the UK	227.26	212.88	214.94	213.31	230.71	6.13%
France	180.57	163.05	164.04	174.93	197.80	6.79%
Belgium	115.05	103.13	103.59	118.56	131.41	10.65%
European Union	2,411.90	2,352.50	2,414.90	2,661.70	3,068.70	12.06%
Global total	4,407.70	4,426.00	4,585.60	4,953.90	5,682.50	100%

Source: UNCTADSTAT. Retrieved from https://unctadstat.unctad.org/wds/TableViewer/tableView.aspx.

As shown in Table 4.6, in terms of global ICT service trade exports, India and China ranked first and second respectively, with USD 57.927 billion and USD 47.058 billion in 2018. The sum of the two countries' exports accounted for 18.47% of the world's total. The total exports of the 28 EU countries in 2018 were valued at USD 306.87 billion, accounting for 54% of the world's total exports in ICT services. US exports were worth USD 34.287 billion, accounting for 6%.[1] This also reflects, to a certain extent, the positions of the world's major economies in the global Internet. However, many developing countries are currently only using electronic

---

[1] Source: UNCTADSTAT. Retrieved from https://unctadstat.unctad.org/wds/TableViewer/tableView.aspx.

communications when participating in ICT. For example, in countries like Colombia, Honduras, Thailand, Turkey, and Zambia, electronic communications accounted for more than 85% of their total ICT service exports.[①]

China's ICT service trade export value has maintained rapid growth since 2008. In 2008, its export value was USD 7.822 billion, increasing to USD 47.058 billion in 2018, a five-fold increase. It now ranks second in the world. Looking at the percentage of ICT product exports in total service trade, it was 5.38% in 2008, increasing to 17.64% in 2018, as shown in Figure 4.24. All these show that China's ICT service trade is developing rapidly, guided by digital economy. From the above statistical analysis, we can see that e-commerce is booming worldwide, and the potential for trade that is related to digital products and services, as well as digital knowledge and information, is huge. Digital trade is developing well generally. In China, digital economy has integrated very thoroughly with trade. One can foresee that digital trade will become the new engine fueling China's trade growth and will play an important role in driving its sustained economic growth.

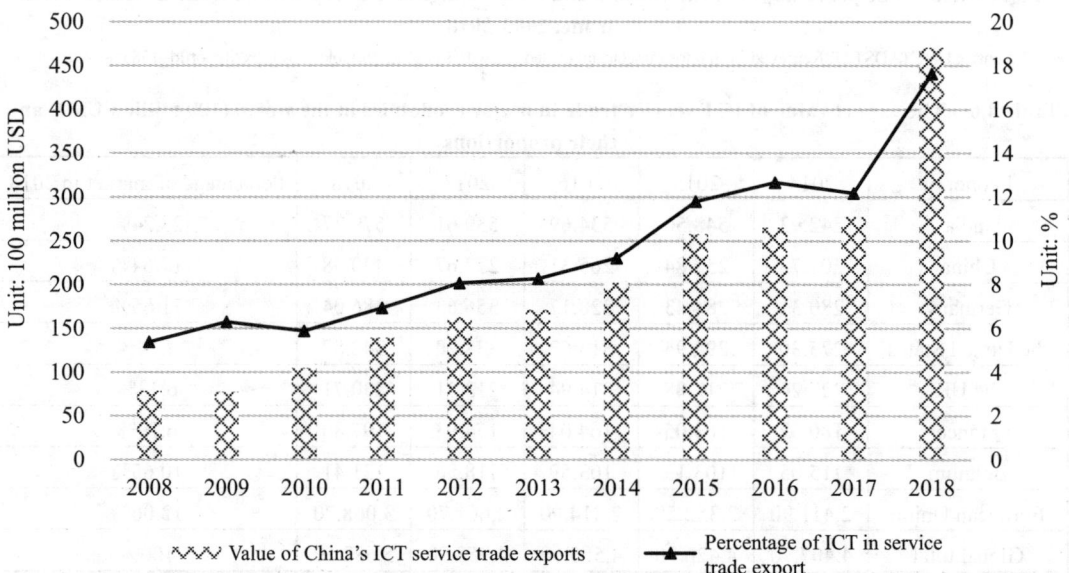

Figure 4.24 China's ICT service trade export value and its percentage of service trade export, 2008-2018

From these trends and facts, we can thoroughly examine the actual impact of digital economy on trade, clarify the relationship between digital economy and trade, and reveal the mechanism of digital economy on trade. We can also analyze the trade activities and entities that will be affected by digital economy. The answers to these questions will help deepen our understanding of digital economy and trade, and provide an important reference and basis for

---

① Source: UNCTAD (October 2017). Information Economy Report 2017: Digitalization, Trade and Development. Retrieved from https://unctad.org/en/pages/PublicationWebflyer.aspx?publicationid=1872.

China's developing digital economy and trade.

4.2 Problems and challenges facing China's digital trade development

The growth of digital economy has pushed global trade into a new stage, bringing about new developments and opportunities. In the digital economy environment, the emergence of a new trade mode integrating digital technology has greatly facilitated trade in all parts of the world. Digital economy accelerates information flow among trade entities and promotes the categorization and efficient use of information, effectively reducing trade cost and information friction between countries. This has not only promoted international and domestic trade, but also changed the traditional trade model, bringing about improvements to consumer welfare. At the same time, driven by digital technology, the emergence of new trade objects has also injected new elements into trade. One can say that the new digital trade era is a process of global trade renewal and the start of a new cycle of trade development. As a major global trading country, China faces changes in domestic and foreign trade environments in its digital trade developmental stage. China's trade development also faces many problems and challenges, specifically manifested in the following areas.

4.2.1 An urgent need for the digital-trade development environment to be optimized

The characteristics of digital trade are mainly manifested in the digitization of the trade process and the digitization of trade products. These have promoted traditional trade efficiency and new trade forms, profoundly changing the structure and order of international trade, especially accelerating global trade activities. China has established itself as a global trading country, with more than 40 years of trade development. It has a huge volume of exports and imports. By relying on labor cost advantage, it has established processing trade as its main mode of trade, and its main trade products are also concentrated in labor-intensive processing and manufacturing. On the whole, the trade environment China has nurtured is a trade environment compatible with China's processing and manufacturing-based trade characteristics. However, with the rise of the digital trade era, it is clear that China's traditional development environment still needs to be optimized. Taking into consideration its growth trend and the characteristics of its digital trade, China's digital-trade development environment still faces many problems.

Fundamentally, the development of digital trade must be supported by digital technology. Specifically, advanced digital technology will gradually replace the original production technology, becoming the technical standard for trade products in various countries. The upgrading of trade products is also inseparable from the update of digital technology. The production of tradeable digital products and digital service trade all rely on digital technology. Moreover, the digitization of the trade transaction process is entirely dependent on information network technology. Thus, the main problem facing the growing digital trade environment lies in the development of digital technology. First, the development of digital technology relies on its acquisition and management of data, but China has relatively weak data collection and management abilities. At present, its data collection system is still in its infancy. It has not established a national data platform to uniformly record detailed trade behaviors between trade entities at the national level, such as the trade entities engaging in trade, the products they are trading in, etc. There are serious data gaps in the statistics of smaller trade volumes. Hence, there is an urgent need for comprehensive, unified, and detailed data collection in the booming data economy. Second, with regard to digital trade regulations, China still lacks protection for data acquisition and transmission, and has not yet formulated strong and detailed provisions or laws to regulate data acquisition and transmission at the national level. When data is being transferred, especially in cross-border data or information transfer, the transfer of data across borders needs more coordination and regulations due to the big differences in content and methods of data control between various countries. The imperfections and discrepancies of data policies increase the cost of data transmission across countries, weaken the convenience of cross-border information transmission, and will have an adverse impact on China's developing global digital trade. Next, in terms of digital talents and policies, China is still deficient in management and creative talents with a comprehensive grasp of digital trade technology. Its supporting policies are not perfect, resulting in insufficient impetus for digital trade growth. Furthermore, China's digital trade has insufficient supporting industries and regulatory policies. The development of digital trade is inseparable from logistics industry support, especially when the trade cycle is greatly reduced under digitization. The high efficiency of the logistics and transportation industry is important in maintaining the normal growth and impetus of digital trade. Although China's logistics industry is growing at a high speed, a transportation mode suitable for the rapid operation of digital trade has not yet been established, resulting in developmental challenges. Moreover, in addition to the above-mentioned intangible digital products and services that require regulatory measures in cross-border trade, the trade of other trade objects like tangible digital products and cross-border e-commerce trade products also needs relevant adaptive regulations. Especially for emerging digital cross-border e-commerce, new measures are needed in terms of entry and exit procedures, inspection and quarantine, and warehousing and logistics. Although China's Customs has issued new customs declaration laws in response to these changes in digital trade, it still lacks regulatory measures to promote digital trade that can regulate any risks that may arise.

4.2.2 Unbalanced development of digital trade

Although China's internal regions have shown vigorous growth after a long period of trade development, it is still showing uneven regional development in the new era of digital trade. First, in terms of policy support, the Chinese government approved the construction of cross-border e-commerce comprehensive pilot zones in 2015. The first zone was in Hangzhou, approved in March 2015. The second batch of such pilot zones was approved in January 2016 and includes those in Ningbo, Tianjin, Shanghai, Chongqing, Hefei, Guangzhou, Shenzhen, Chengdu, Dalian, Qingdao, and Zhengzhou. The third batch was approved in July 2018 and includes those in Yiwu, Zhuhai, Dongguan, Shenyang, Weihai, Nanjing, Wuxi, Beijing, Hohhot, Changchun, Harbin, Nanchang, Wuhan, Tangshan, Changsha, Nanning, Haikou, Guiyang, Kunming, Xi'an, Lanzhou, and Xiamen. Within these national-level cross-border e-commerce comprehensive test areas, development seems unbalanced. The cross-border e-commerce comprehensive test areas in the provinces of Guangdong and Zhejiang deal in cross-border e-commerce. The scale of their imports and exports far exceeds those of other provinces. Moreover, compared with other test areas of China, the scale and speed of their cross-border e-commerce development are much higher. The study by Shuzhong Ma, Jiwen Guo, and Hongsheng Zhang (2019) also pointed out the imbalance between China's digital trade development regions: development is strong in the eastern and southern regions, and weak in the western and northern regions. The southeast coastal region shows stronger development momentum, while the central and western regions clearly lag behind.[1] The information network construction and transportation logistics in the central and western regions are still very backward, lacking support from high-end service industries like finance, software development, and market management. This has caused difficulties in developing digital trade in rural and economically-underdeveloped areas.

Such unbalanced regional development is clearly not conducive to China's comparative advantages in the digital economy era, with a need to fully utilize regional characteristics to achieve comprehensive trade development. It is also not conducive to developing China's new trade competitiveness in the digital trade era. More importantly, this imbalance in regional development is closely related to imbalances in China's digital-trade industry structure. The unbalanced industry structure is another important manifestation of China's unbalanced digital trade development. The main digital trade operations are concentrated in the eastern and southern regions, excessively concentrated in certain industries. For example, cross-border e-commerce has become the main form of China's developing digital trade. China's cross-border e-commerce mainly relies on small developing e-commerce enterprises focusing on labor-intensive products, while trade in digital content products, such as software, video, and digital publishing, lags behind in both scale and quality. On the whole, the unbalanced development of China's digital trade between regions and in industrial structure, as well as its lack of competitiveness in digital trade, are important factors hindering its digital trade growth.

4.2.3 Poor digital trade innovation ability

Digital trade is a new kind of trade arising in the digital economy era. China's digital trade development can only adapt to the global environment through continuous innovation, thereby

---

[1] Ma, S., Guo, J., & Zhang, H. (2019). Policy analysis and development evaluation of digital trade: an international comparison. *China & World Economy*, 27(3). DOI: 10.1111/cwe.12280.

sustaining its high-quality growth. The innovation of digital trade is mainly reflected in two aspects: one is the innovation of trade-related digital technology; the other is the innovation of the digital trade mode. Digital technologies that promote digital development include digital production technologies like automation and intelligence (used in digital product production), information network technologies that realize digital trade transactions, artificial intelligence technologies, and management systems for digital trade production and transactions, like cloud computing and big data technology. Since China's trade development is dominated by processing trade, it mainly exports labor-intensive products, and undertakes processing and assembly. Its main business entities are small enterprises. Many production technologies and equipment must be imported from overseas, and its enterprises lack the ability to innovate. Their abilities to use and innovate digital production technologies with high technical requirements are even weaker. Secondly, although China currently has achieved much in developing digital trade network platforms, it is still slightly inadequate in its innovative ability to replace key technologies under the changing digital technology environment. Its integration of high-end digital technologies such as artificial intelligence—used to upgrade its digital trade—still lags behind. Finally, in terms of management technology, digital trade will generate a large volume of data streams. This data and information are the key to digital trade decision-making and the core of digital-trade production and transaction supervision. At present, few Chinese companies are actually using cloud computing and big data technologies to deal with data flow. The integration of digital-trade needs and their ability to use cloud computing and big data technology innovatively are also clearly lacking. In terms of digital-trade model innovation, China's participation in digital trade often extends from the original trade mode. It only utilizes digital technologies in a few trade links. In China generally, few trade business entities know how to flexibly apply existing digital technologies to produce a new digital trade mode. This has led to the emergence of a homogeneous developing digital trade that lacks differentiated competitive advantages.

4.3 The prospects of China's developing digital trade

First of all, on the enterprise level, digital trade continues to grow with increasing participation of enterprises. Digital trade makes full use of the advantages of the Internet and digital technology, effectively reducing the cost of various trade links. Firstly, the collection of digital trade information can help trade participants fully understand transaction information, greatly reducing information and transaction costs of cooperation and communication between trade parties. Secondly, the process of digital trade negotiation, contract signing, fund payment, and customs declaration can be done digitally. This paperless and virtualized operation model greatly saves negotiation costs, contract costs, payment costs, and customs clearance costs. Thirdly, digital trade uses digital logistics operations, which are highly efficient and precise, reducing logistics costs in international trade. At the same time, the emergence of digital trade has increased the range of products that companies can trade (new digital products and related services). As a result, the continuous increase of corporate trade participation is manifested in the participation of more service and goods production companies, as well as more small- and medium-sized enterprises.

Secondly, on the industrial level, the development of digital trade shows that the value chain system is still expanding. On the one hand, thanks to the effective use of digital trade technology and the continuous increase in the tradability of products and services, production activities can be outsourced to more countries, thus extending the value chain's spatial layout. On the other hand, thanks to the effective use of digital trade technology and the increasing tradability of products and services, linkages within production have become more meticulous and detailed. Production has become more finely segregated, extending the value chain from the production link.

On the national level, the development of digital trade has promoted the reconstruction of the global trade order. This reconstruction of the global trade order is reflected in two aspects: (1) The development of digital trade has continuously increased the proportion of digital products and services trade in global trade, elevating the status of countries exporting such products; (2) The developing digital trade has caused changes in comparative advantages, enabling developing countries to rise in status through such comparative advantage.

Chapter 5 Digital Economy and International Investment

The rapid development of information technology and the ever-increasing market demand for digital products and services have led to an investment boom in digital economy. Investment hotspots continue to emerge in cloud computing, cloud storage, virtual reality, artificial intelligence, blockchain, online medical services, and ridesharing. It is not difficult to understand that despite the decline of global economic growth in recent years, the hindrances to globalization, and an overall decline in international investment, the international investment in digital economy is still growing steadily. As the world's second-largest digital economy country, China occupies a pivotal position as both an investment destination and a capital exporter.

Section 1 The Development of Global Digital Economy Investment

1.1 Analysis of total investment volume

The core driving force in the development of digital economy, especially during its rapid growth over the past decade or so, is digital economy investment[①]. According to statistics provided by PitchBook Data, after the bursting of the Internet bubble in 2002, there were only 1,254 investment transactions in the global digital economy that year, amounting to USD 28 billion. By the end of 2019, this figure had increased by more than 17 times, reaching 21,488. Investments increased by more than 20 times, reaching USD 569.8 billion. The rapid development of digital technology has led to an investment boom in digital economy. From 2002 to 2019, investments in the global digital economy increased from 17.9% (in transaction volume)

---

① According to digital economy's need to "produce value with digital factors," this chapter defines 26 industries in the PitchBook database as digital industries. This corresponds roughly to the "digital industrialization" departments as defined by China Academy of Information and Communications Technology, excluding the broader "industrial digitization" sectors. The same transaction may involve multiple industries. We treat all transactions involving digital economy industries as digital economy investments, while the rest are treated as non-digital economy investments. At the same time, this report covers three types of equity transactions: mergers and acquisitions (M&A), private equity investments (PE), and venture capital (VC).

and 8.29% (in monetary transaction amount) to 52.66% and 28.59% respectively (see Figure 5.1 for details).

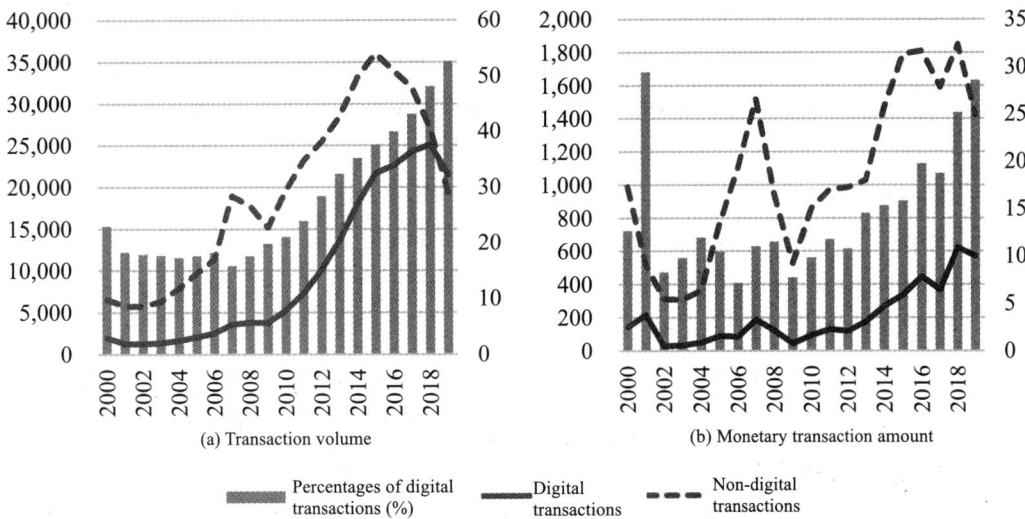

Figure 5.1 Changes in total investment volume in the global digital economy

Note: the unit of transaction number: transaction; the unit of transaction amount: billion USD.
Source: compiled from the PitchBook database.

Figure 5.1(a) shows the specific changes in investment transaction volume in the global digital economy and non-digital economy from 2000 to 2019. This figure shows that before the 2008 financial crisis, overall digital economy transactions were increasing in total volume, but the percentage that digital economy constituted in total transaction volume did not increase; it even declined slightly. This indicates that the global digital economy investment during this period was growing slowly, lagging far behind that of the non-digital economy. During the financial crisis of 2008 to 2010, investment in the global non-digital economy was hit hard, and its transaction volume also decreased significantly, while investment in digital economy remained stable, showing only a decline in growth. From 2008 to 2018, investment in the global digital economy maintained an upward momentum. Although its transaction volume was still less than that of the non-digital economy, it is worth noting that transactions continued to rise rapidly, from 21.13% in 2010 to 52.66% in 2019. Its growth rate exceeded 149% in these 10 years. Looking back at the non-digital economy over the same period, we find that although its total growth rate increased significantly from 2010 to 2015, it declined substantially thereafter, returning to the same rate in 2010. Throughout 2000-2019, global investment in the non-digital economy was still the prevailing trend, but digital economy is in the ascendant and rapidly growing into a new trend in global investment.

Figure 5.1(b) shows the changes in the monetary transaction amount in the global digital economy and non-digital economy from 2000 to 2019.① They are quite different from the changes in transaction volume. Before the financial crisis, the monetary transaction amount in the global digital economy was fluctuating greatly, but showed slow growth after 2002. During the financial crisis of 2008 to 2010, both digital and non-digital economies were showing a significant decline in the monetary transaction amount. It was not until 2010 that it just barely returned to the level of 2008. After the financial crisis, although the absolute increase in the monetary transaction amount of non-digital economy was greater than that of digital economy, but their growth of transaction volume was the same during this period. The growth rate of digital economy transactions also gradually increased during this period, rising from 9.81% in 2010 to 28.59% in 2019, an increase of 191%.

Taking into account the growth rate of transaction volume in digital economy from 2010 to 2019, it is not difficult to conclude that investment in digital economy has grown rapidly in the last decade. Digital economy becomes increasingly important with the passage of time. At the same time, the single monetary transaction amount in digital economy is decreasing gradually. In other words, compared with non-digital economy, digital economy has a higher proportion of small-scale transactions.

1.2 Analysis of subdivided investment types

We have offered analyses on the transaction volume of these three types of transactions: M&A, PE, and VC. Let us now take a closer look at the investment situations of these different types of transactions. Of the three types of transactions, M&A has the most procedures, the longest transaction cycles, and the largest monetary transaction amount, so their total transaction volume is relatively low. VC investors make short-term profits through frequent advances and retreats in investment outlets. So they take more risks, their transaction cycles are short and their single transaction amount is the smallest, so their transaction volume is larger. PE investors mainly make profits by buying Pre-IPO companies or companies with strong profitability to double their value, or reap profits through their performance growth. Their monetary transaction amount is also higher and their transaction volume lower.

Figures 5.2(a) to 5.2(c) show the changes in transaction volumes of M&A, PE, and VC transactions in digital and non-digital economies. We find that in the field of digital economy, the transaction volume of these three types is growing. Between them, the growth of VC transactions

---

① The monetary transaction amounts come from the completed transactions in the PitchBook database. Since some of them involve transactions between non-listed companies or person to person, the monetary transaction amounts are not disclosed. It is inevitable that the transaction amount of some transactions may not be computed. However, such uncomputed monetary transaction amounts account for less than 30% of the total, an acceptable percentage in all databases.

is particularly rapid, especially after 2010. Its VC transactions even exceeded that of non-digital economic investment in 2014. Digital economy has become the main driving force for the growth of global VC transactions. This is not difficult to understand. Technologies are updated frequently, leading to shorter technology life cycles, as well as compatibility requirements after technologies are incorporated into the system. Most investments in digital economy choose enterprises with market potential that are not yet mature. They may even help support startups, although their high returns are accompanied by high risks. Correspondingly, investors are required to improve their capability to take risks, and investors are more inclined to adopt VC transactions as their ways of investment. At the same time, it can be seen that, similar to the trend in global transaction volume, the proportions of these three types of transactions have continued to grow after the financial crisis.

At the same time, we also show the changes in the monetary transaction amount in these three types of transactions in Figures 5.2(d) to 5.2(f).① Figure 5.1(b) shows that the global investment market began to pick up in 2010, and has since entered a long period of vigorous growth. Transaction volume hit a new high from 2010 to 2019. Therefore, we will mainly analyze the changes in the monetary transaction amount from 2010 to 2019 for these three types of transactions. One can see that in the field of digital economy, there were big changes in transaction volume for these three types. M&A and PE showed slow growth in the monetary transaction amount during this period, while VC growth rate rose sharply since 2010, showing an almost geometric growth after 2012. In recent years, digital startups in the world (especially in China and the United States with their huge digital economies) have grown rapidly, attracting a large influx of VC capital, forming a situation that is driven by the twin engines of "capital" and "innovation". Compared with non-digital economy, the differences between these three types of transactions in digital economy are more prominent. Inferring from their monetary transaction amounts, the main investment destination of M&A and PE is still non-digital economy; while for VC, digital economy has grown so rapidly that the monetary investment amount of VC has already vastly exceeded that of non-digital economy, becoming the new darling of VC transactions.

---

① We must note that for M&A and PE, monetary transaction amounts fluctuate greatly in non-digital economy. This is because there are a few transactions involving large sums of money in certain years, which boosted the scale of such transactions. VC transactions, on the other hand, are smaller in scale and higher in volume. Even if there are a few transactions involving large sums, it cannot upset the overall scale of transactions in that year.

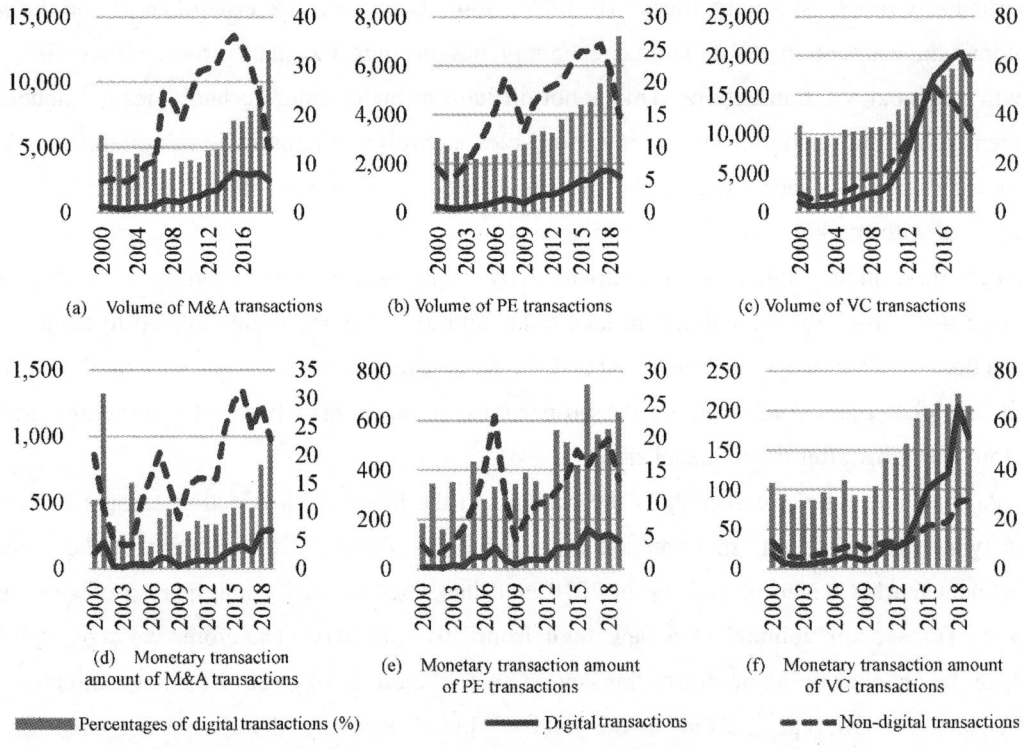

Figure 5.2 Global digital economy investment (by transaction type)

Note: the unit of transaction number: transaction; the unit of transaction amount: billion USD.
Source: compiled from the PitchBook database.

To sum up, as of 2019, although global equity investment was still dominated by non-digital economic industries, the rapid rise of digital economy had become difficult to stop. It has become a new destination and trend in global investment and plays an increasingly important role in the global investment environment. Recently, VC transactions in the digital economy sectors have surpassed those in the non-digital economy sectors in both volume and monetary amount. This fully demonstrates that, for VC investment, an "incubator" for startups, its enthusiasm for technological innovative economies, such as digital economy, continues undiminished, which in turn fuels the rapid growth of digital economy and other technological economies.

1.3 Major investment industries

To understand the key investment industries of the global digital economy and to better compare such dynamic changes in these key investment industries, we list the top 10 global digital economy sectors receiving the largest global investment volume (see Figure 5.3). First, we discover that in 2018, the total transaction volume in global digital economy investment far exceeded that of 2010. Second, Software as a Service (SaaS) and Financial Technology (FinTech) are still among the top three, while Big Data, the Internet of Things, Artificial

Intelligence, and Machine Learning have risen in ranking, especially AI and Machine Learning, which ranked second in transaction volume in 2018. It is not difficult to see that in recent years, the focus of foreign investment in the global digital economy has shifted from relatively mature leading industries, such as E-commerce and Advertising Technology (AdTech), to more technology-intensive sectors, such as Artificial Intelligence and Machine Learning, Big Data, the Internet of Things, and Cryptocurrency/Blockchains.

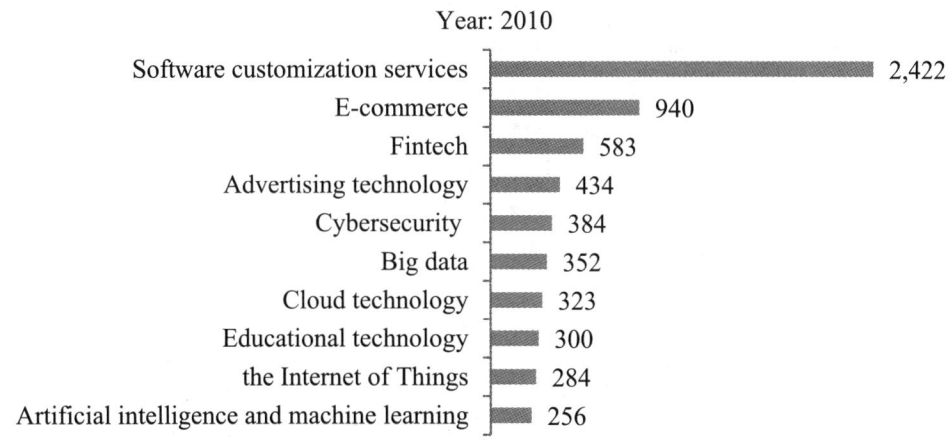

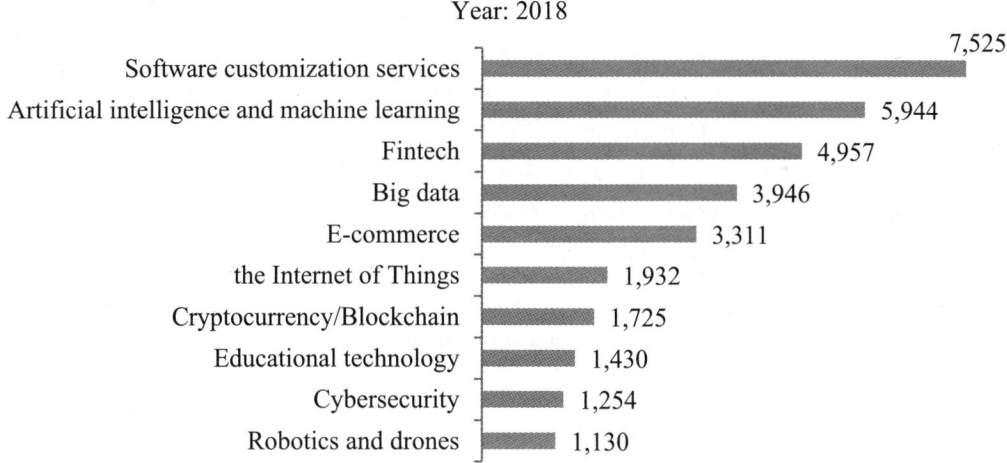

Figure 5.3 The top 10 sectors attracting the most global digital economy investments (ranked by transaction volume)

Source: compiled from the PitchBook database.

Sorted by monetary transaction amount, the top 10 sectors remain largely unchanged (see Figure 5.4). Software as a Service (SaaS), Financial Technology, E-commerce, Big Data, Artificial Intelligence, and Machine Learning are still among the top 10 sectors. Yet at the same time, we notice that CloudTech did not rank within the top 10 in transaction volume in 2018, but ranked sixth in monetary transaction amount that same year, reaching USD 62.68 billion. It indicates that the cloud technology sector has experienced a large surge in monetary transaction amount per single transaction, and its concentration of investment capital is higher. The same trend can be seen in sectors like Supply Chain Tech and Autonomous Cars.

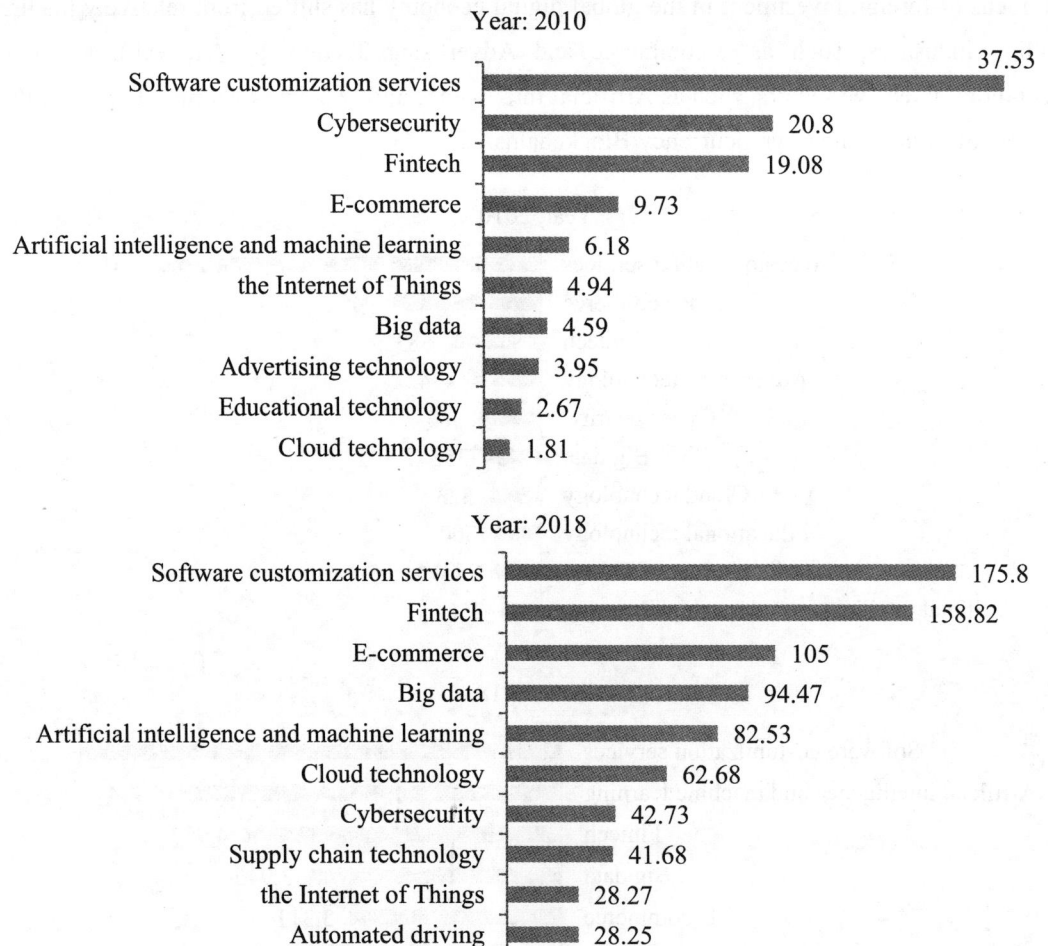

Figure 5.4 The top 10 sectors attracting the most digital economy investments (ranked by monetary transaction amount, billion USD)

Source: compiled from PitchBook database.

1.4 Major investment destinations

Table 5.1 summarizes the top 10 investment destinations of global digital economy investments. The United States is the most important investment country for all types of investments, be it in transaction volume or monetary transaction amount, and its volume or amount far exceeds that of other countries in percentage. This is not surprising. The United States has always been the most active country globally as a capital market. At the same time, the United States is the world's strongest digital economy in terms of technological research, with the most active startups and VC. That is why it has attracted more digital economy capital than any other country. Other than developed countries in the West, China's digital economy capital market is also very active, with its various investment amounts ranking in the top three globally. The United Nations Conference on Trade and Development (UNCTAD) pointed out in their "Digital Economy Report, 2019" that the United States and China are the two giants in the global digital economy. The sum of capitalization value in these two countries' digital economies accounts for 90% of the total value of the global digital economy market. The global digital economy is mainly concentrated in China and the United States, in terms of markets, technology, unicorns, and investment opportunities.

Table 5.1 Distribution of investment destinations in the global digital economy (2008-2019)

VC			PE			M&A		
Country	Volume	Percentage	Country	Volume	Percentage	Country	Volume	Percentage
The top 10 investment destinations in the global digital economy (sorted by number of transactions, unit: per transaction)									
the United States	82,316	46.98%	the United States	6,264	49.30%	the United States	11,666	46.26%
the United Kingdom	14,067	8.03%	the United Kingdom	1,325	10.43%	the United Kingdom	2,273	9.01%
China	12,898	7.36%	France	691	5.44%	Canada	1,194	4.74%
Canada	6,780	3.87%	Canada	653	5.14%	Germany	1,168	4.63%
France	6,221	3.55%	Germany	493	3.88%	France	1,041	4.13%
India	6,195	3.54%	the Netherlands	317	2.49%	China	853	3.38%
Germany	5,348	3.05%	Sweden	317	2.49%	India	708	2.81%
Israel	3,116	1.78%	Australia	284	2.23%	Australia	619	2.45%
Australia	2,523	1.44%	China	242	1.90%	Sweden	487	1.93%
Sweden	2,475	1.41%	India	190	1.50%	the Netherlands	465	1.84%
The top 10 investment destinations in the global digital economy (sorted by transaction amount, unit: billions of USD)									
the United States	1,446.97	55.87%	the United States	622.41	64.36%	the United States	897.01	61.08%
China	380.94	14.71%	China	76.53	7.91%	the United Kingdom	155.16	10.57%
the United Kingdom	198.81	7.68%	the United Kingdom	72.82	7.53%	China	85.03	5.79%
India	88.06	3.40%	France	22.50	2.33%	India	43.83	2.98%
Canada	41.76	1.61%	Canada	18.10	1.87%	Israel	28.02	1.91%
Israel	39.88	1.54%	Germany	17.75	1.84%	Canada	24.59	1.67%
Germany	39.88	1.54%	Denmark	11.68	1.21%	Germany	21.40	1.46%
France	36.34	1.40%	Korea	9.82	1.02%	France	19.92	1.36%
Australia	24.29	0.94%	Italy	8.87	0.92%	Finland	17.83	1.21%
Sweden	24.10	0.93%	Australia	8.22	0.85%	Australia	16.45	1.12%

Source: compiled from the PitchBook database. If the invested firm has subsidiary companies (like branches) in multiple countries, the volume or monetary transaction amount will be calculated multiple times in the corresponding countries.

1.5 Main investment source countries

Since China and the United States are the two digital economy giants, then what are the percentages of investors' transactions from these two countries within the overall global digital economy investment? To study this, we further compiled the percentages of these two countries in the global digital economy investment source countries (see Figure 5.5). Generally speaking, the United States is the absolute giant in digital economy investments. Although China is also a major source of global investments, it still lags far behind the United States. The volume of investment transactions and the monetary transaction amounts between these two countries are different as well. In terms of transaction volume, that completed by US investors accounts for most of the global digital economy transactions, while the transaction volume completed by Chinese investors is relatively small. On the other hand, in terms of the monetary transaction amount, the percentage of monetary transaction amount originating from US investors has decreased significantly, while the percentage of the monetary transaction amount originating from Chinese investors has increased significantly. This indicates that within all types of investments, the average single monetary transaction amount completed by Chinese investors is larger than that by American investors. Especially for VC investments, the percentage of monetary transaction amount completed by foreign investment institutions is much higher than the percentage of transaction volume. This indicates that the average investment of Chinese capital in digital economy is larger in scale than that of American capital, and much higher than the rest of the world. In fact, this also explains to a certain extent why foreign investors, such as those from the United States, are more flexible in their use of capital, diversifying their investments. In today's fast-changing business environment, this investment model that does not rely on intermittent "Big Bang" transactions can often reduce the debt-to-EBITDA ratio, thereby achieving higher rates of return and further promoting capital flow.

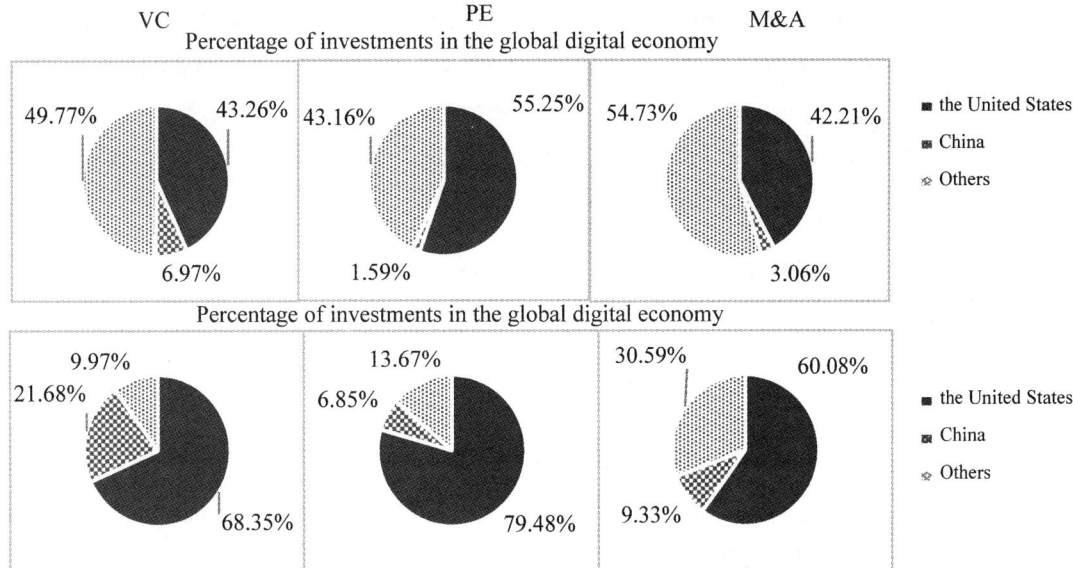

Figure 5.5 Proportions of global digital economy investments from source countries
(China and the United States)

Note: The data in this figure is based on the location of the investment institution's headquarters. In view of the facts that there are many foreign investment institutions in China (absorbing local capital) and that some Chinese investment institutions and foreign investors set up independent investment companies in the United States' Silicon Valley, data in this figure tends to overestimate the percentage of American investments and underestimate the percentage of Chinese investments.

Source: compiled from the PitchBook database.

Section 2 International Investment in China's Digital Economy

As a representative of emerging economies, China has made great strides in its digital technology investment and application. China's reliance on a huge digital consumer base and a wide range of digital applications has helped it promote the testing and development of digital business models. According to the "Global Innovation 1000" report released in 2018 by PricewaterhouseCoopers, there are 175 Chinese companies among the 1,000 listed companies with the highest R&D expenditures in the world. At the same time, McKinsey Global Institute believes that China has the world's most active digital investment and entrepreneurial ecosystem, and China's digital achievements far exceed the expectations of most followers: in 2016, China's retail e-commerce transactions accounted for 42.4% of the world's total, ranking first in the world, while accounting for less than 1% 10 years ago. The mobile payment transaction volume as related to personal consumption was as high as USD 790 billion, which was 11 times that of the United States.① Clearly, China has become an important force in shaping the global digital landscape, and its digital globalization is ascending. In order to improve their digital technology

---

① McKinsey Global Institute (2017). China's digital economy: a leading global force.

and achieve better digital transformation, Chinese companies have been extensively investing in foreign digital companies. As China's digital economy develops rapidly, driven dually by policy support and consumer demand, it has also attracted capital from astute foreign investors. This directly drives the investment in the digital economy field China has participated in, whether as an investor or a country attracting investment.

2.1 Foreign investment in China's digital economy①

2.1.1 Historical changes in overall scale

Figure 5.6 plots the changes in total foreign investments in China's digital economy from 2000 to 2019. It can be seen that the percentage of digital economy transactions by foreign investors investing in China is very high. In the last five years, this proportion has reached 68.96% (the percentage of transaction volume in 2019) and 67.43% (the percentage of transaction amount in 2016). This also demonstrates China's vast investment potential as a digital economic power. In recent years, more than 60% of foreign investments in China are digital economy investments, and nearly half of the investment funds have flowed into the country's digital economy industries. At the same time, by looking at the historical investment scale, one can see that transaction volume and monetary transaction amount of foreign investments in China have risen sharply since 2014. In particular, digital economy investments have grown even more rapidly, exceeding the transaction volume of non-digital economy investments in China.

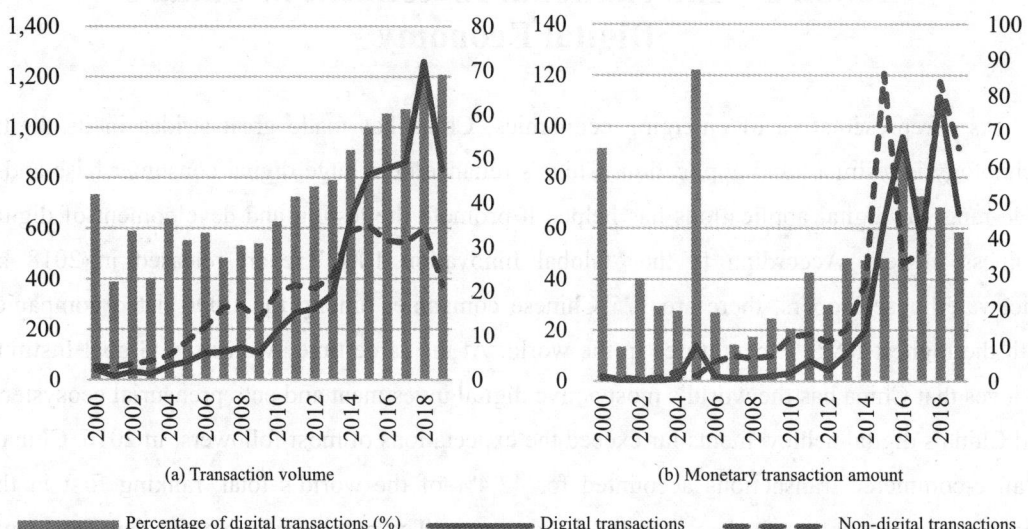

Figure 5.6 Changes in total foreign investments in China's digital economy

Note: the unit of transaction number: transaction; the unit of transaction amount: billion USD.
Source: compiled from the PitchBook database.

---

① The foreign investments in China in this section do not include Sino-foreign joint investment transactions, so the true scale of foreign direct investments may be somewhat underestimated.

2.1.2 Analysis of subdivided investment types

To further analyze the differential performances of foreign investments in China's digital economy for different investment types, we will also analyze three types of foreign investments in China's digital economy, namely, mergers and acquisitions (M&A), private equity investments (PE), and venture capital (VC). Looking at transaction volumes in Figure 5.7, foreign M&A in China has shown a significant decrease in non-digital economy investments in recent years, while digital economy investments continue to increase, causing a rise in the percentage of digital economy investments. Seen from the perspective of the monetary transaction amount, since a single M&A transaction is large and certain transactions do not disclose the transaction amount, the total monetary transaction amount between the years fluctuates greatly. However, one can still roughly conclude that the monetary transaction amount for foreign mergers and acquisitions in China is on the rise.

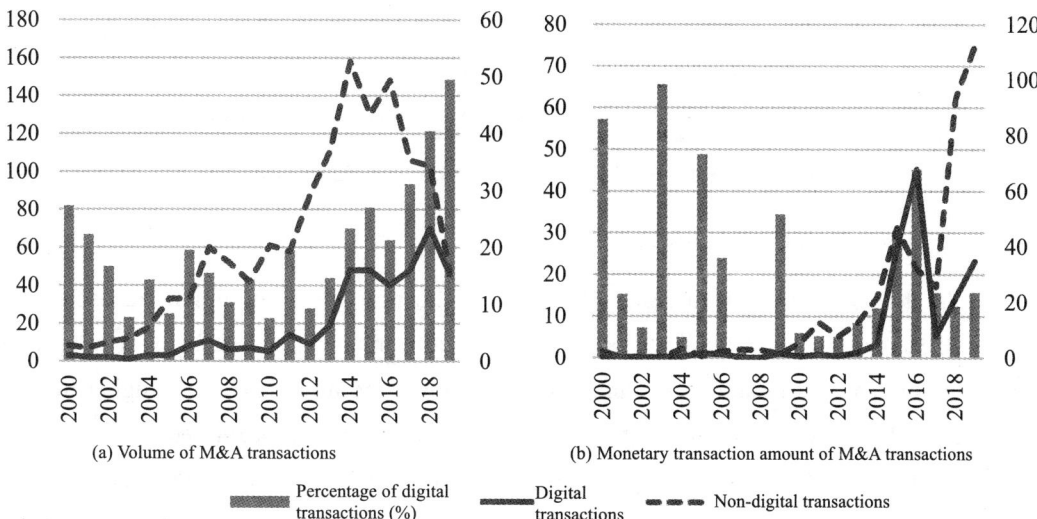

(a) Volume of M&A transactions　　　　(b) Monetary transaction amount of M&A transactions

Percentage of digital transactions (%)　　Digital transactions　　− − − Non-digital transactions

Figure 5.7　Foreign M&A investments in China's digital economy

Note: the unit of transaction number: transaction; the unit of transaction amount: billion USD.
Source: compiled from the PitchBook database.

Similar to the M&A investment situation, the transaction volume for foreign PE investments in non-digital economy sectors within China has decreased significantly over the years, while the transaction volume in digital economy sectors has remained largely unchanged, further boosting the percentage of PE investments in digital economy (see Figure 5.8). However, unlike M&A investments, the monetary amount of China's foreign PE investments has fallen sharply recently, and the influx of PE capital flowing into the country's non-digital economic sectors has dropped significantly. This may be caused by weaknesses in the global PE investment market in recent years. The global PE market has been struggling over the past few years, and long-term primary and secondary market valuations have caused a decline in the underlying valuation, severely affecting investor confidence. By September 2019, the shares of the two major American online car-hailing giants, Lyft and Uber, had fallen in value by one-third since they went public the year before. Furthermore, WeWork suddenly withdrew its listing application due to its plunge in valuation in the third quarter of that year, dealing PE investors withdrawing from expectations a heavy blow[①].

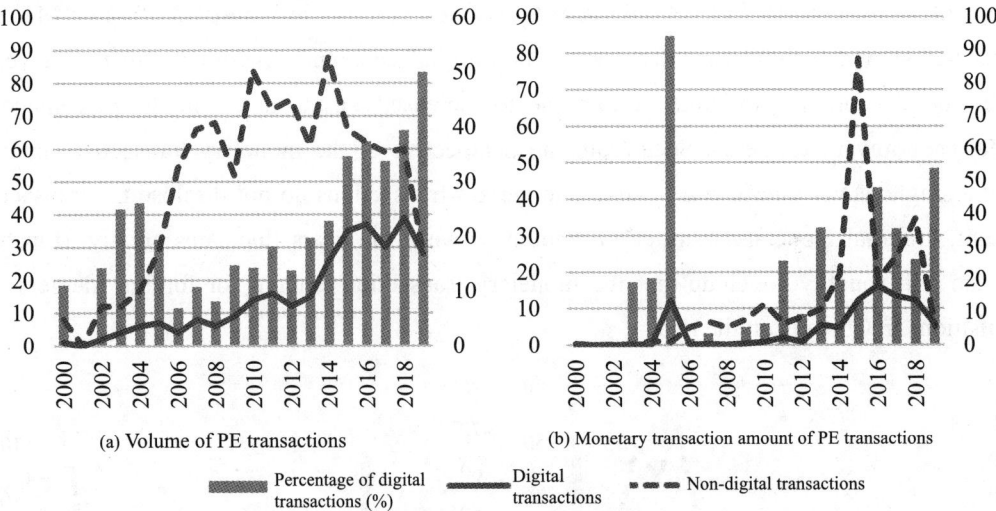

Figure 5.8 Foreign PE investments in China's digital economy

Note: the unit of transaction number: transaction; the unit of transaction amount: billion USD.
Source: compiled from the PitchBook database.

Similar to the global VC investment situation, the proportion of digital transactions in foreign VC investments in China has risen since the 2008 financial crisis for both transaction volume and monetary transaction amount, even exceeding 70% after 2016. It is higher than the percentage of VC investments in the global digital economy over the same period (see Figure 5.9). In other words, China's digital economy VC market is more active and higher than the global average. A reasonable explanation is that digital economy, as a technology-based economy, holds more attraction for VC investors preferring to invest in startups with good growth potential. Secondly, although China's VC market started late compared with those in Europe and the United States, Chinese enterprises have greatly increased their investments in digital technology research and development over the years, and governments at all levels have issued successive policies to support digital technology-based startups, providing these companies with a good growth environment and huge development space. Therefore, the large influx of overseas VC capital flowing into China's digital economy is also due to such investment trends. According to a report by McKinsey Global Institute, China's VC market has grown rapidly since 2010. Its total investments increased rapidly from USD 12 billion in 2011-2013 to USD 77 billion in 2014-2016. Correspondingly, the percentage share of global VC

---

① Condra, P. (2020). The Ripple Effects of COVID-19 on Emerging Technologies: How the crisis is affecting the startup ecosystem. Emerging Tech Research, PitchBook.

transactions has increased from 6% to 19%, gradually evolving into a major contributor to global VC investment growth. At the same time, China is now the world's leading digital technology investment and application country, nurturing one-third of the world's "unicorn" companies[①], and digital companies represented by such "unicorns" are seen as emerging forces in digital economy, widely favored by global VC investors.

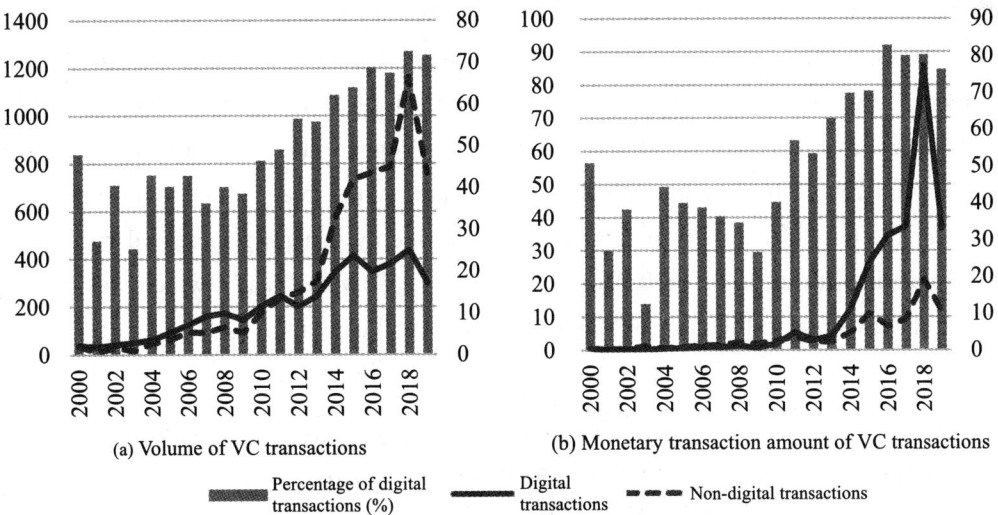

Figure 5.9 Foreign VC investments in China's digital economy

Note: the unit of transaction number: transaction; the unit of transaction amount: billion USD.
Source: compiled from the PitchBook database.

2.1.3 Main investment industries

The above analysis is mainly based on the differential performances of foreign investments in China's digital economy in terms of the different transaction types. Does technological innovation, as the core driving force behind digital economy, also affect the preference for certain industries and products? To understand this, we combined the above-mentioned analysis and listed the top 10 industries attracting foreign investments in China's digital economy from 2010 to 2018, by monetary transaction amount, in Figure 5.10. To ensure the analysis' completeness, we also listed the top 10 investment industries according to transaction volume in Figure 5.11. However, due to the large differences in the average single transaction amount between different industries, it is hard to compare the transaction volume between different industries. The monetary transaction amount of each industry also reflects the overall financing situation and preference for capital investment, so we will mainly analyze the monetary transaction amounts according to rankings.

By comparing Figures 5.10 and 5.11, we discover that the top 10 industries attracting foreign investments in China's digital economy are relatively similar in transaction volume and

---

① McKinsey Global Institute (August 2017). China's digital economy: a leading global force. "Unicorns" refer to non-listed startups with a market value of more than USD 1 billion.

monetary transaction amount. In 2010, they included Software as a Service (SaaS), Cybersecurity, Financial Technology (FinTech), the Internet of Things, E-commerce, and Advertising Technology (AdTech). In 2018, they included these seven industries: Software as a Service (SaaS), Financial Technology (FinTech), E-commerce, Artificial Intelligence and Machine Learning, Big Data, Ridesharing, and Supply Chain Technology (Supply Chain Tech). Of course, with the passage of time, the changes in industry structure are still very significant. China is the well-deserved leader of the global e-commerce industry. In 2010 and 2018, China's e-commerce was the world leader, attracting USD 1.19 billion and USD 34.66 billion respectively. The No.3 sector in 2010, Cybersecurity, dropped out of the list in 2018 and was replaced by FinTech, which ranked 8th in 2010. In addition, the total foreign investment volume in 2018 for the top 10 industries in China's digital economy generally increased more than 30 times compared with those in 2010. Even Software as a Service (SaaS), which was declining, jumped from USD 600 million to USD 26.8 billion during this period.

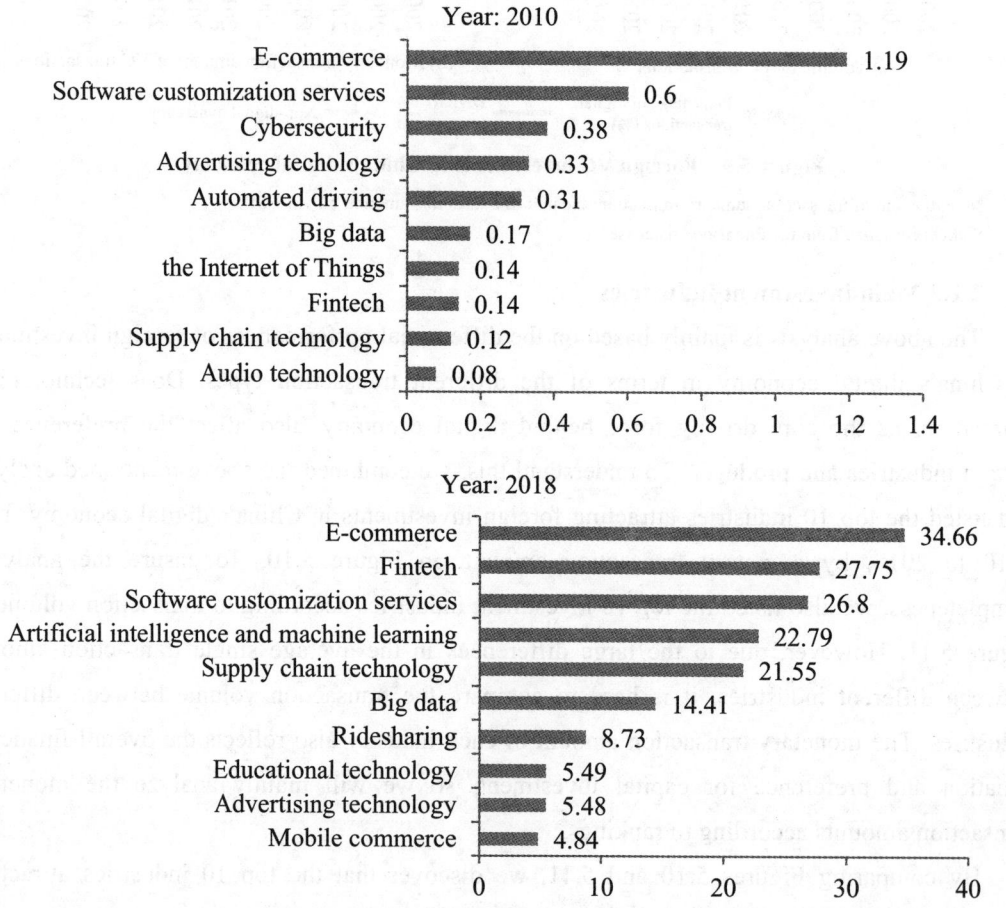

Figure 5.10 **The top 10 industries attracting foreign investments in China's digital economy (ranked by monetary transaction amount, billion USD)**

Source: compiled from the PitchBook database.

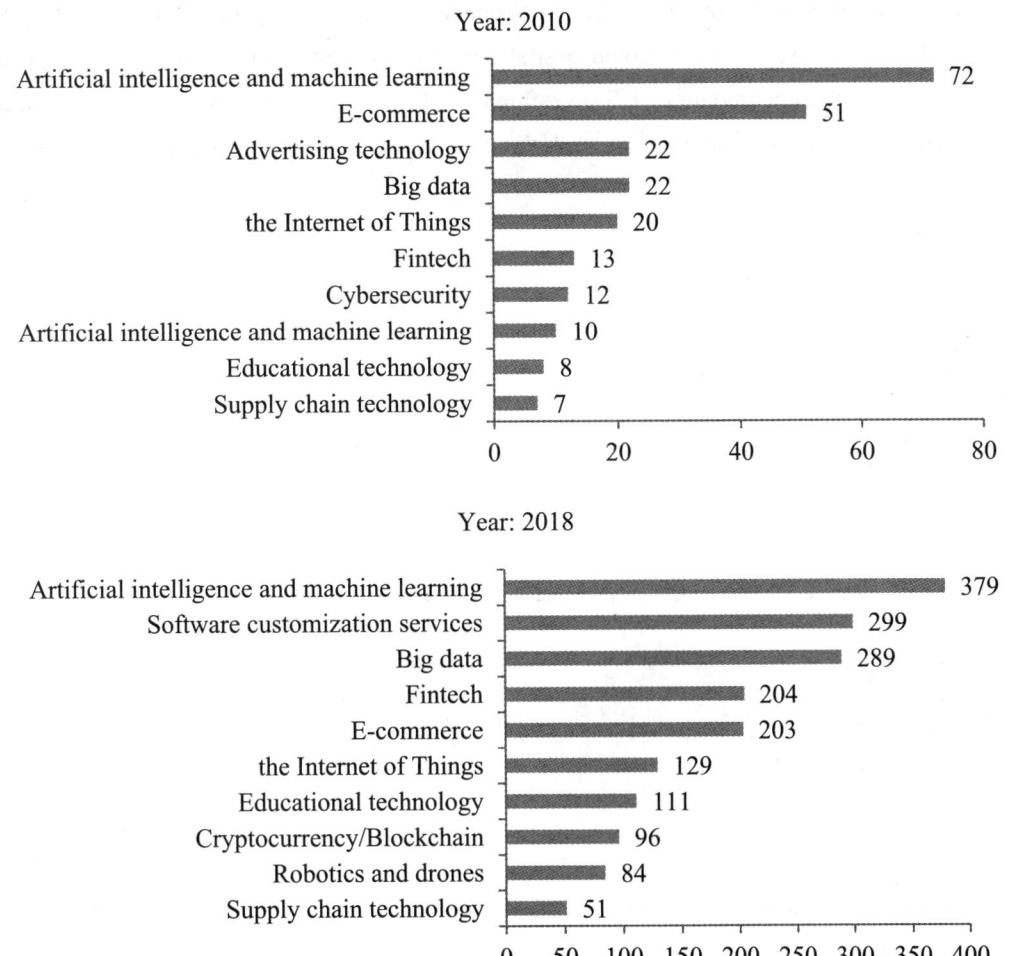

Figure 5.11 The top 10 industries attracting foreign investments in China's digital economy (ranked by transaction volume)

Source: compiled from the PitchBook database.

2.1.4 Main investment source countries

Similarly, the main foreign countries investing in China's digital economy are also worth analyzing. In this section, we mainly examine the digital investments from the United States, the global digital economy hegemon, in China. Figure 5.12 shows the proportion of US investments to all foreign investments in China's digital economy from 2008 to 2019. It can be seen that in terms of transaction volume, US investments in China's digital economy have an absolute advantage in all three types of transactions. This is not surprising at all. As mentioned earlier, the United States and China are the world's two largest digital economy giants, and the comparative advantages of these two countries complement each other: the United States has strong R&D capabilities, and its B2B advantages are obvious. China has huge market potential, and there are many application scenarios for B2C, and the development of B2B is lagging but has potential (with its strong manufacturing base). So both countries have a strong potential for cross-border investments. However, it is similar to the situation of digital economy investment transactions completed by US investors in the global digital economy, as seen in the previous section, the average single transaction amount of US investments in China is relatively small, reflected in the high proportion of transaction volume and the low percentage of the monetary transaction amount.

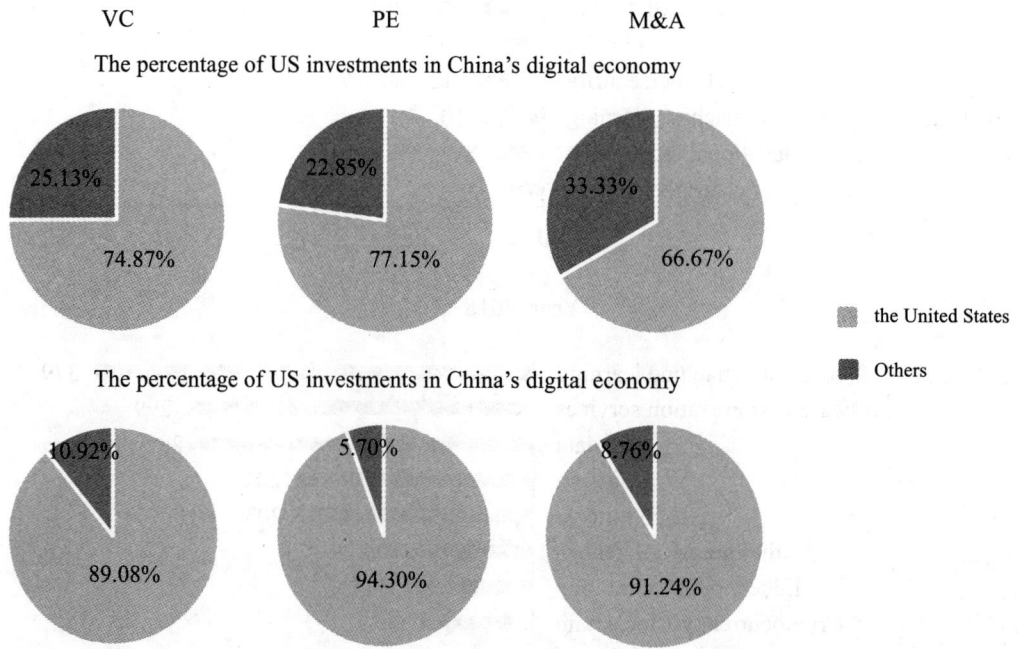

Figure 5.12 The percentage of US investments in China's digital economy (2008-2019)
Source: compiled from the PitchBook database.

It is worth noting that with the rapid development of China's economy, competition between the two countries will become increasingly prominent, and the antagonism between China and the United States will inevitably cast a dark shadow on the future of China's digital economy and foreign investments. Furthermore, as practical requirements such as national security, privacy rights, and intellectual property protection in the digital field become stronger, developed countries have in recent years substantially strengthened their protection of high-tech and core assets (including data) in their digital economies, strengthening checks on overseas mergers and acquisitions, as well as introducing policies to encourage returning investments from high-tech companies. This will hinder the overseas expansion of digital multinational companies, but at the same time, will also help further regulate the market rules of digital economy. The most typical example is the General Data Protection Regulation (GDPR), which took effect in the European Union in May 2018, detailing comprehensive regulations for data collection, storage, transfer, and use. While setting a model for global digital policies, it will also have a significant impact on digital international investments. Cross-border investments in digital economy may face more policy restrictions, and international coordination needs to be strengthened urgently.

2.2 China's foreign investment in digital economy

2.2.1 Historical changes in overall scale

Figure 5.13 plots the changes in China's external digital economy investments from 2000 to 2019[①]. It can be seen that transaction volume and monetary transaction amount of China's digital economy investments in foreign countries are significantly greater than those received from foreign investors. Between them, the percentage of digital transactions has steadily increased since the 2008 financial crisis, exceeding 50% (that is, the number of digital economy transactions exceeded the number of non-digital economy transactions) for the first time in 2017, reaching 60% in 2019. This growing foreign digital investment momentum mainly stems from China's thirst for foreign advanced digital technology and R&D resources (mainly through outbound mergers and acquisitions), as well as investment opportunities for excellent digital startups from Western developed countries, especially the US (mainly through VC and PE). The growth momentum of the Chinese digital economy is very strong, and Chinese investors will inevitably enter the overseas digital market in the course of this process.

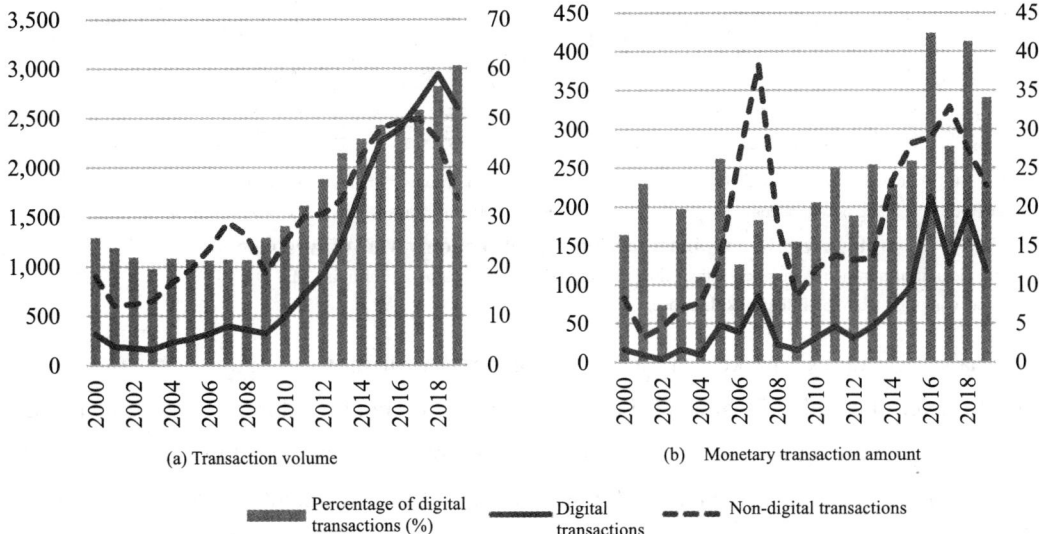

Figure 5.13 Changes in China's foreign digital economy investment, in transaction volume

Note: the unit of transaction number: transaction; the unit of transaction amount: billion USD.
Source: compiled from the PitchBook database.

2.2.2 Analysis of subdivided investment types

Similarly, in order to have a clearer understanding of the different performances of such transaction types, we have plotted a graph of China's foreign digital economy investment changes by transaction type from 2000 to 2019. In Figure 5.14, in terms of transaction volume,

---

① Investors here include Chinese companies, as well as branches and subsidiaries of foreign companies in China.

China's outbound M&A investments in overseas non-digital economy fields decreased significantly, while its digital economy investments continued to increase, resulting in a continuous rise in the percentage of digital economy investments. This conforms with the performances of foreign mergers and acquisitions in China. But in absolute terms, the volume and monetary amount of China's outbound mergers and acquisitions were greater than those of foreign M&A during the same period. In general, under the "digital disruption" associated with the digital age, outbound M&A often play a more important role in digital economy investments: they help domestic companies realize their strategic transformation in the "winner-takes-all" digital age, and find new suitable development directions, thereby augmenting their own survivability and competitiveness. This also explains why digital economy investments have remained popular in recent years, while global investments have been declining.

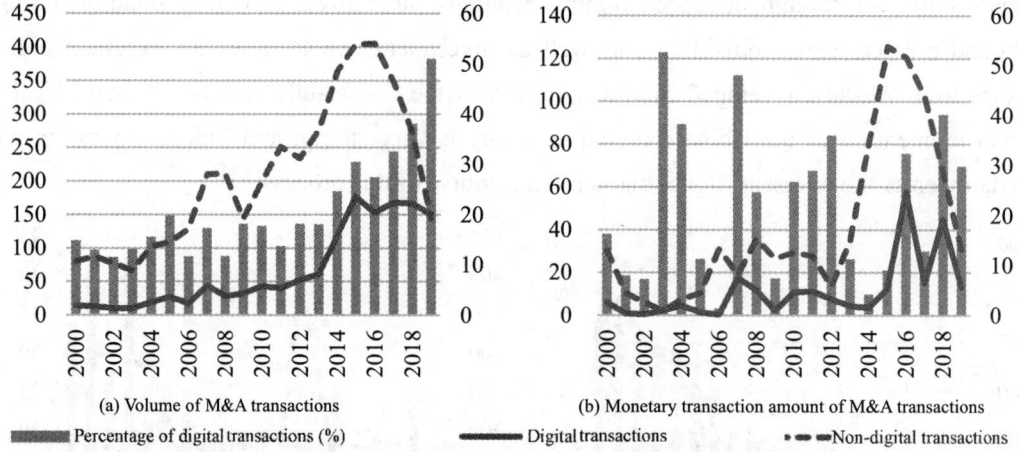

Figure 5.14 China's foreign digital economy M&A investments

Note: the unit of transaction number: transaction; the unit of transaction amount: billion USD.
Source: compiled from the PitchBook database.

China's PE and VC markets started late compared with those of Europe and the United States. However, the scale of China's PE and VC markets has continued to grow over the past 20 years, gradually evolving into an important investment hotspot in the world market. Figure 5.15 plots the changes in China's external digital economy PE investments from 2000 to 2019. Although the share of investments in digital economy has increased steadily after the financial crisis, it did not reach 29.3% in all PE transactions until 2019, indicating that non-digital economy is still a major part of China's participation in the global PE market. However, similar to the situation of outbound mergers and acquisitions, regardless of whether they are outbound or inbound investments, the volume of PEs invested in non-digital economic sectors has decreased significantly in recent years, pushing up the proportion of digital investments further, but always lower than the percentage of foreign digital investments in China. At the same time, one also observes that the monetary amount of China's foreign PE investments rose sharply before the global financial crisis in 2008, and then declined sharply during the financial crisis. It has been increasing slowly since then, but has not yet reached the level of 2007. In general, Chinese PE investors investing abroad and foreign PE investors investing in the Chinese market are not only differentiated in investment fields, but also in transaction scales. China's foreign PE investors are more inclined to conduct large-scale transactions.

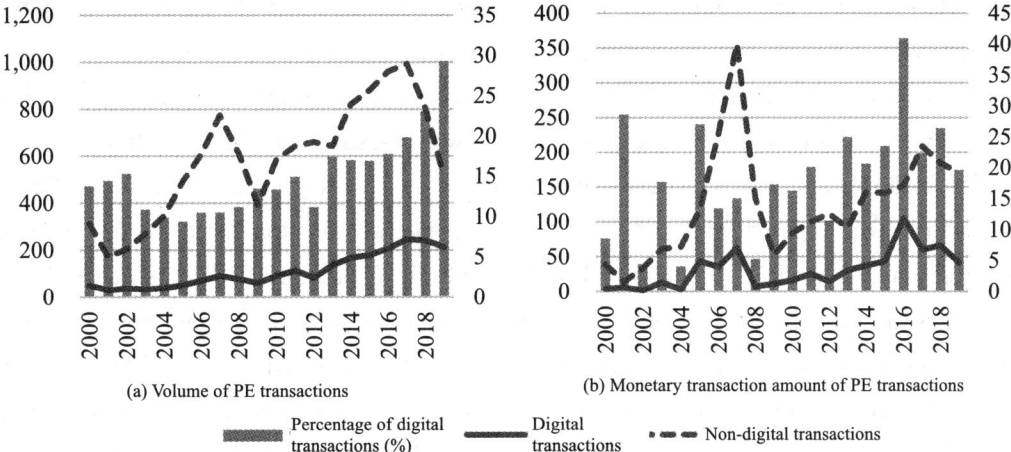

Figure 5.15　China's external digital economy PE investments

Note: the unit of transaction number: transaction; the unit of transaction amount: billion USD.
Source: compiled from the PitchBook database.

Similar to the situation of global VC investments and foreign VC investments in China, China's VC investments in foreign digital economy sectors have exceeded those in non-digital economy sectors in recent years, both in transaction volume and monetary transaction amount (see Figure 5.16). In contrast, however, China's foreign digital economy VC investments have surpassed its non-digital economy VC investments earlier, and the upward momentum is stronger. This indicates that China's astute investors are investing in overseas digital startups earlier, and their investments grow faster.

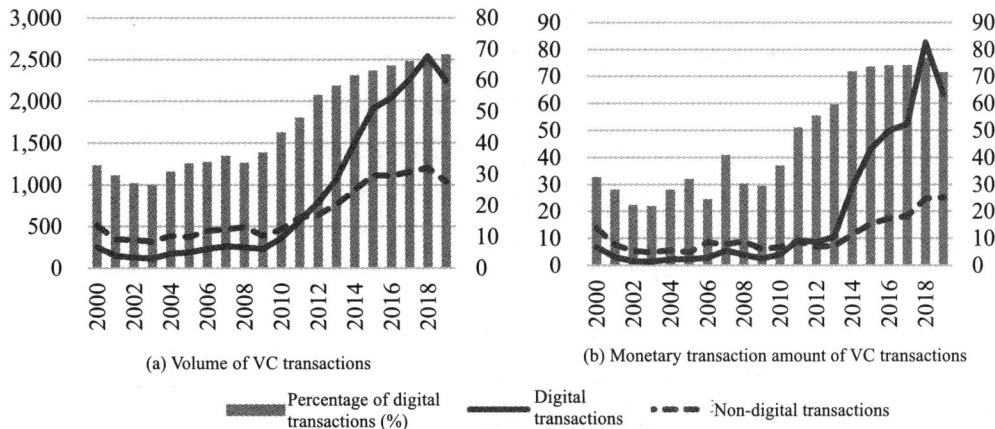

Figure 5.16　China's external digital economy VC investments

Note: the unit of transaction number: transaction; the unit of transaction amount: billion USD.
Source: compiled from the PitchBook database.

2.2.3 Main investment industries

We list in Figures 5.17 and 5.18 the top 10 industries of China's external digital economy investments in 2010 and 2018, sorted by the monetary transaction amount and transaction volume. It is not difficult to see that China's investments in foreign digital economies far exceed the monetary amount and volume of foreign investments in China's own digital economy. Compared with 2010, the top 10 industries of China's foreign digital economy investments in 2018 underwent major changes. Software as a Service (SaaS) and Financial Technology (FinTech) were still in the top three, and these two industries are basic technical service industries in the digital economy field, always favored by investors. The Artificial Intelligence and Machine Learning industry had grown further, entering the top three in the monetary transaction amount, while Cybersecurity had dropped out of the top 10. This is driven by the dual engines of "national policy support" and "high-tech development", led by the three mature Internet giants BAT (Baidu, Alibaba, and Tencent) and the new Internet giants TMD (Toutiao, Meituan, and Didi). This is the result of many enterprises investing in foreign technology companies in order to foster technological innovation and seize investment opportunities. At the same time, investors have keen instincts. Guided by technological trends in recent years, the rapidly developing Supply Chain Technology, Ridesharing, and Autonomous Cars were among 2018's top 10 sectors in China's foreign investment in digital economy. At the same time, taking into account their transaction volume, we draw a similar conclusion as from the previous ranking analysis. We discover that sectors such as Cybersecurity and Artificial Intelligence and Machine Learning in 2010, as well as Autonomous Cars and Ridesharing in 2018, had larger average single transaction amounts. It can be concluded that in the field of digital economy, there are significant differences in the single transaction amounts between different industries, as they evolve gradually with technological innovation over time.

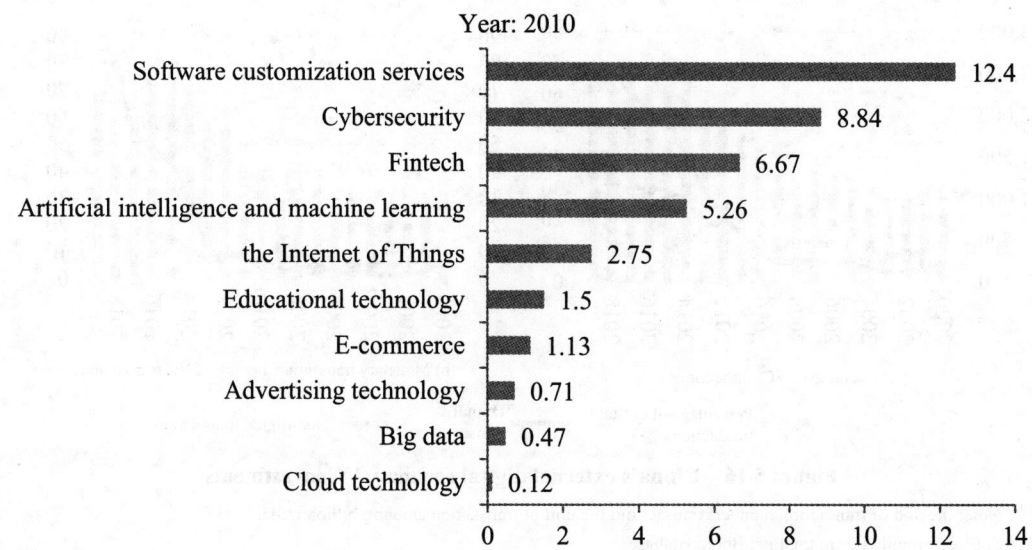

Chapter 5 Digital Economy and International Investment

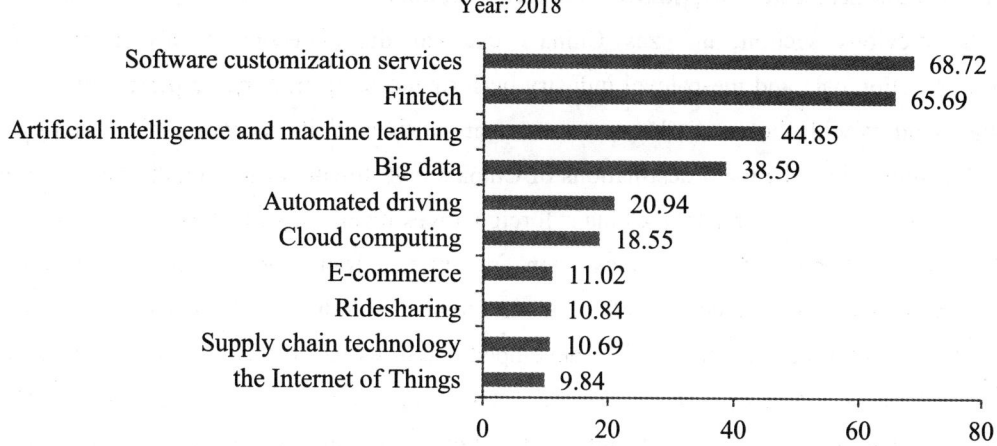

Figure 5.17 The top 10 industries of China's foreign digital economy investments (ranked by monetary transaction amount, billion USD)

Source: compiled from the PitchBook database.

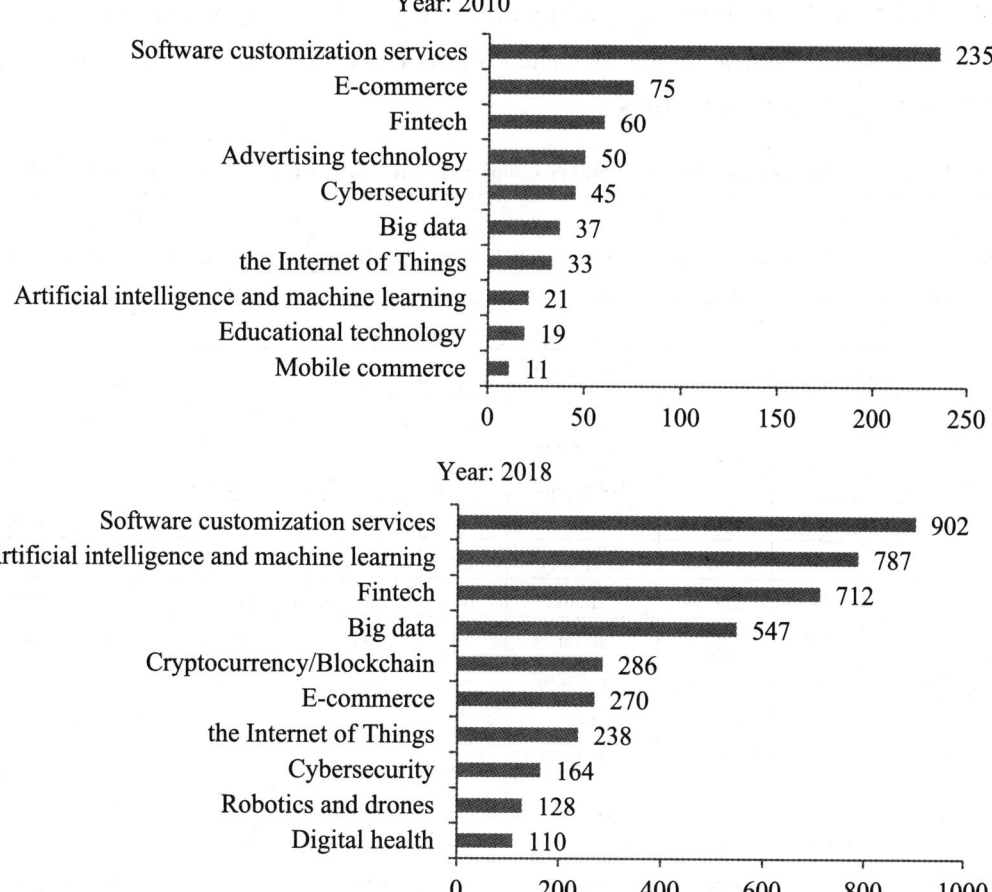

Figure 5.18 The top 10 industries of China's external digital economy investments (ranked by transaction volume)

Source: compiled from the PitchBook database.

2.2.4 Main investment destination countries/regions

The previous section analyzes China's external digital economy investments from micro-transaction data and meso-level industry performances. From a macro perspective, which are the countries with the most Chinese investments in their digital economies? To study this, Table 5.2 summarizes the main destinations of China's investments in foreign digital economies from 2008 to 2019. We find that China's foreign investments in digital economies are very concentrated, with both monetary transaction amount and transaction volume in the top 10 investment destinations exceeding 80% of the total (excluding VC monetary transaction amount). In general, besides investing in developed countries like the United States, the United Kingdom, Canada, Germany, France, Australia, the Netherlands, as well as regions like Hong Kong, China has also invested significantly in the digital economies of developing countries like Israel and India. This can be seen in Israel, which has strong fundamental scientific research capabilities in certain digital fields such as information security, and in India, which has advanced technology in digital fields such as financial technology, based on implementation of the "Digital India" plan and establishment of the world's largest biometric system, Aadhaar. At the same time, as important nodes of the "Belt and Road Initiative", they have become new "targets" of China's digital foreign investments.

Table 5.2 Distribution of China's digital economy outbound investment destinations (2008-2019)

VC			PE			M&A		
Country/region	Volume	Percentage	Country/region	Volume	Percentage	Country/region	Volume	Percentage
Distribution of China's digital economy outbound investment destinations (sorted by number of transactions, unit: per transaction)									
the United States	8,765	56.20%	the United States	890	48.42%	the United States	556	46.92%
the United Kingdom	822	5.27%	the United Kingdom	183	9.96%	the United Kingdom	101	8.52%
India	768	4.92%	France	117	6.37%	Canada	51	4.30%
Israel	419	2.69%	Germany	69	3.75%	Germany	47	3.97%
Canada	397	2.55%	Canada	61	3.32%	Israel	45	3.80%
Singapore	375	2.40%	India	56	3.05%	France	41	3.46%
Germany	364	2.33%	Australia	41	2.23%	India	35	2.95%
France	357	2.29%	the Netherlands	37	2.01%	Australia	28	2.36%
Japan	271	1.74%	Sweden	33	1.80%	Hong Kong, China	26	2.19%
Hong Kong, China	193	1.24%	Brazil	28	1.52%	the Netherlands	26	2.19%
Others	2,866	18.38%	Others	323	17.57%	Others	229	19.32%

Continued

VC			PE			M&A		
Country/region	Volume	Percentage	Country/region	Volume	Percentage	Country/region	Volume	Percentage
Distribution of China's digital economy outbound investment destinations (sorted by monetary transaction amount, unit: billion USD)								
the United States	197.0	53.74%	the United States	303.9	65.45%	the United States	77.2	39.63%
India	28.5	7.76%	the United Kingdom	43.0	9.27%	the United Kingdom	46.9	24.05%
Singapore	12.6	3.44%	France	13.4	2.88%	Israel	20.5	10.50%
the United Kingdom	11.2	3.07%	Germany	11.6	2.50%	Finland	10.4	5.34%
Indonesia	7.2	1.98%	Denmark	9.6	2.06%	Luxembourg	8.6	4.41%
France	5.6	1.54%	Korea	8.1	1.74%	France	4.0	2.07%
Germany	5.2	1.41%	Hong Kong, China	7.6	1.64%	Germany	3.5	1.79%
Israel	4.3	1.19%	India	5.5	1.18%	Australia	3.1	1.59%
Sweden	3.6	0.99%	Italy	5.5	1.18%	Canada	3.1	1.59%
Canada	3.4	0.91%	the Netherlands	5.1	1.10%	Hong Kong, China	1.7	0.86%
Others	87.9	23.96%	Others	51.1	11.00%	Others	15.9	8.17%

Source: compiled from the PitchBook database. If the invested firm has subsidiary companies (like branches) in multiple countries, the volume or monetary transaction amount will be calculated multiple times in the corresponding countries.

Section 3 Typical Enterprise Case Studies of China's Digital Investment

3.1 Baidu

3.1.1 Investment structure and philosophy

Baidu's investment history is relatively short, mainly operated by Baidu Ventures, Baidu Capital, and Baidu Investment and M&A Department.

Baidu Ventures: It concentrates on the latest trends in technological innovation, mainly focusing on the fields of artificial intelligence (AI) and virtual reality (AR), investing in early-stage projects.

Baidu Capital: It focuses on Baidu's strategic synergy, mainly investing in mid-to-late-stage projects on the Internet and in the mobile Internet field, with a broad range of investment areas.

Baidu Investment and M&A Department: It concentrates on strengthening the competitiveness of Baidu's core businesses, focusing on projects that are complementary and closely integrated with Baidu's existing businesses.

3.1.2 Investment scale and types

According to statistics from PitchBook, Baidu has completed 220 investments of various types since 2013, with an announced investment amount of USD 41.326 billion. Due to the highly active technological innovations in the digital field, the short life-cycle of digital technology, and the obvious "winner-takes-all" phenomenon in market applications, venture capital (VC) and private equity (PE) account for a very high proportion of investments in digital enterprises. Their main goal is to occupy a favorable position for investment before the potential value of the new technology market is clear, and to prepare for subsequent investments or mergers and acquisitions. Like other investments in digital enterprises, Baidu's investments are mostly of the VC or PE types, with fewer mergers and acquisitions. Take 2018 as an example: more than half of their investments are of the venture capital type before the Series A round, with investments before the Series B round accounting for 84% of the total investments (see Figure 5.19).

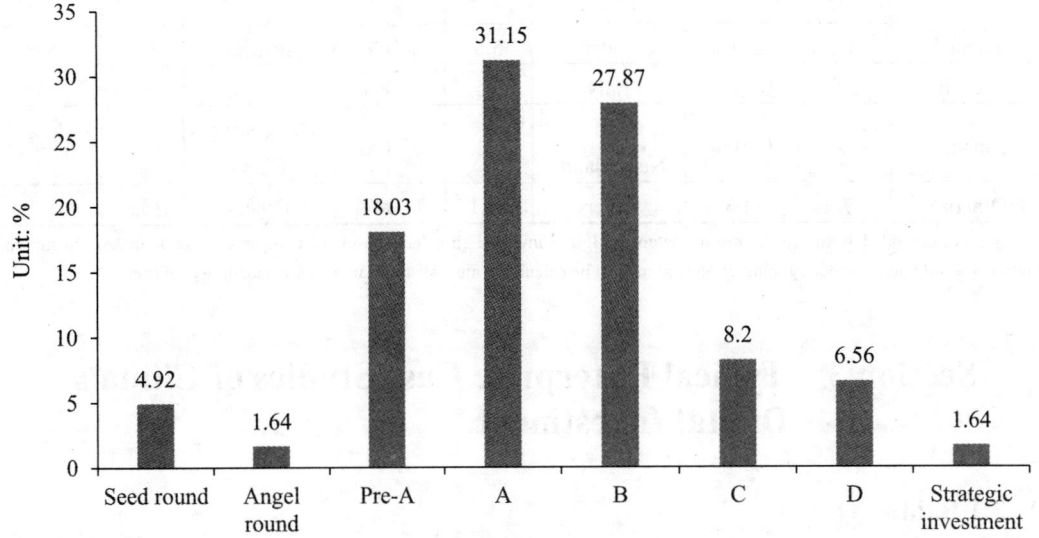

Figure 5.19　Distribution of Baidu's investment rounds (2018)

Source: IT Juzi.

3.1.3 Investment areas

Baidu formulated a development strategy of "consolidating the mobile foundation and decisively winning the battle in the AI era", with its investments mainly focusing on artificial intelligence and intelligent driving. In 2017 for instance, it invested in AI companies like SmarterEye, SoundAI, Knowbox, and YI Tunnel, as well as in automobile transportation companies like Bitauto and WM Motor. The three companies wholly acquired by Baidu's Investment and M&A Department in 2017 are also in the AI field. Raven Tech undertakes the important task of R&D and also manufactures hardware equipment. Its Raven H smart speakers was unveiled at the Baidu World Congress and CES, attracting attention at home and abroad.

Both KITT.AI and xPerception have advanced global technologies and talents. One complements Baidu's voice interaction technology without wake-up words, while the other strengthens Baidu's machine-vision capabilities to accelerate Baidu's AI strategy. In 2017, the Investment and M&A Department financed Shouqi Limousine & Chauffeur and SmarterEye to help promote and implement Baidu's Apollo technology in the field of smart transportation. According to the "Deep Analysis Report on Artificial Intelligence Technology Patents" released by the China Patent Protection Association at the end of 2018, Baidu ranked first in China with 2,368 AI patent applications—twice that of Tencent and more than three times that of Alibaba, topping the AI patent chart.

By consolidating its advantages in business AI technology, Baidu's investments extend to broader fields, such as corporate services, medical and healthcare, education, finance, and advertising. It strives to combine its strengths in artificial intelligence with these businesses in order to create a complete AI business ecology.

3.1.4 Internationalization strategy

Baidu does not have a long history in investment, but it is highly internationalized. According to statistics from PitchBook, Baidu has invested in 58 countries and regions outside of China, with most of its investments in the United States, accounting for 21.8% of Baidu's total investment projects (83% of its total foreign investment projects). However, in terms of the monetary transaction amount, although its investment scale in the United States is large, it only ranks second in Baidu's foreign investments. Hong Kong (China) ranks first. The main reason for that is due to Baidu's relatively large strategic investment in China Unicom, Hongkong reaching US 11.7 billion. As inferred from the announced transaction amount, Baidu has close to 40% in international investments[①].

Table 5.3 The countries/regions invested in by Baidu

Country/region	Number of investment projects	Percentage	Amount (million USD)	Percentage
China's Mainland	162	73.64%	25,081.76	60.69%
Hong Kong, China	3	1.36%	12,548.7	30.37%
the United States	48	21.82%	3,636.23	8.80%
Israel	3	1.36%	38	0.09%
Finland	1	0.45%	10	0.02%
Singapore	1	0.45%	10	0.02%
Switzerland	1	0.45%	1.5	0.00%
Brazil	1	0.45%	Unknown	-

Source: compiled from the PitchBook database. Statistics are as of November 2019.

---

① In the PitchBook database, nearly 30% of transactions lack information in monetary transaction amount. Relatively speaking, there is a higher percentage of missing transaction amounts in Chinese investments. Therefore, calculations based on existing investment amount will overestimate the internationalization ratio of corporate investment to a certain extent.

For investments in Europe, the United States, and other countries, Baidu's main goal is to acquire related advanced technologies such as AI and connected driving, as Baidu has invested in Velodyne, the originator of global lidar, and Visual Threat, an American provider of the Internet of Vehicles (IoV) security solutions. In addition, strategic investments in leading industrial companies around its core businesses, such as Uber, is also one of Baidu's key strategies for foreign investment.

3.2 Tencent

3.2.1 Investment structure and philosophy

There is no clear distinction between Tencent's financial investments and strategic investments, and they do not have a clear goal to achieve. Tencent's investments and businesses remain relatively independent, with independent concepts and values. The mission of the investment department is to explore future possibilities for Tencent, not just to serve Tencent's current strategies or businesses.

Tencent adopts a circle-type investment method, its core being "society + content". The closer one moves to the circle's center, the stronger the control. In the outer fields, Tencent adopts a minority equity investment in order to build an ecosystem and export its basic capabilities to partners, thereby gaining opportunities to enter new fields. This method is complementary to Tencent's connection strategy.

Tencent focuses its core capabilities on Internet traffic and capital, and believes that it is impossible for a company to participate in all Internet products, and has since proposed an open strategy. By treating investment as one of its core strategies and establishing ecological partnerships, it "only seeks symbiosis, not ownership". In 2011, Tencent announced the establishment of a Tencent Industry Win-Win Fund, investing ¥5 billion into projects. Its main mission is to invest in high-quality companies in the industrial chains and better serve users on Tencent's open platform.

3.2.2 Investment scale and types

Among the Chinese digital companies, Tencent is the most active in investment. According to PitchBook statistics, Tencent has made a total of 437 investments since 2013, with a reported investment amount of USD 192.533 billion. According to the database, the number of Tencent's investment projects has risen sharply since 2014 and has maintained an upward trend. The decline in investment data in 2019 is due to the fact that there are no statistics available about situation of the end of that year, and also due to the domestic economic downturn in that year (see Figure 5.20).

Chapter 5 Digital Economy and International Investment • 253 •

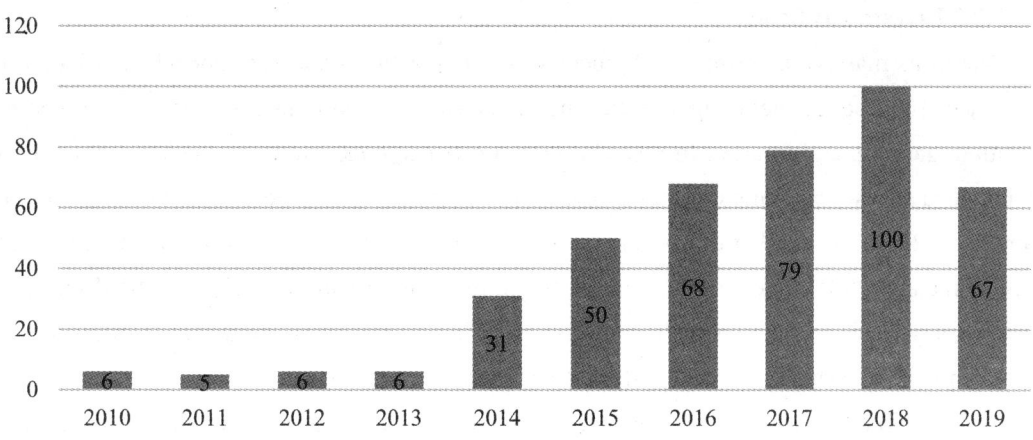

Figure 5.20 The numbers of Tencent's investment projects over the years (2010-2019)
Source: compiled from the PitchBook database.

In terms of investment types, Tencent tends to invest in companies or technologies that are not fully mature. Take its investments in the field of artificial intelligence as an example: its investment projects before the Series A round account for more than half of its total number of projects, and the investment projects before the Series C round account for nearly 80% (see Figure 5.21).

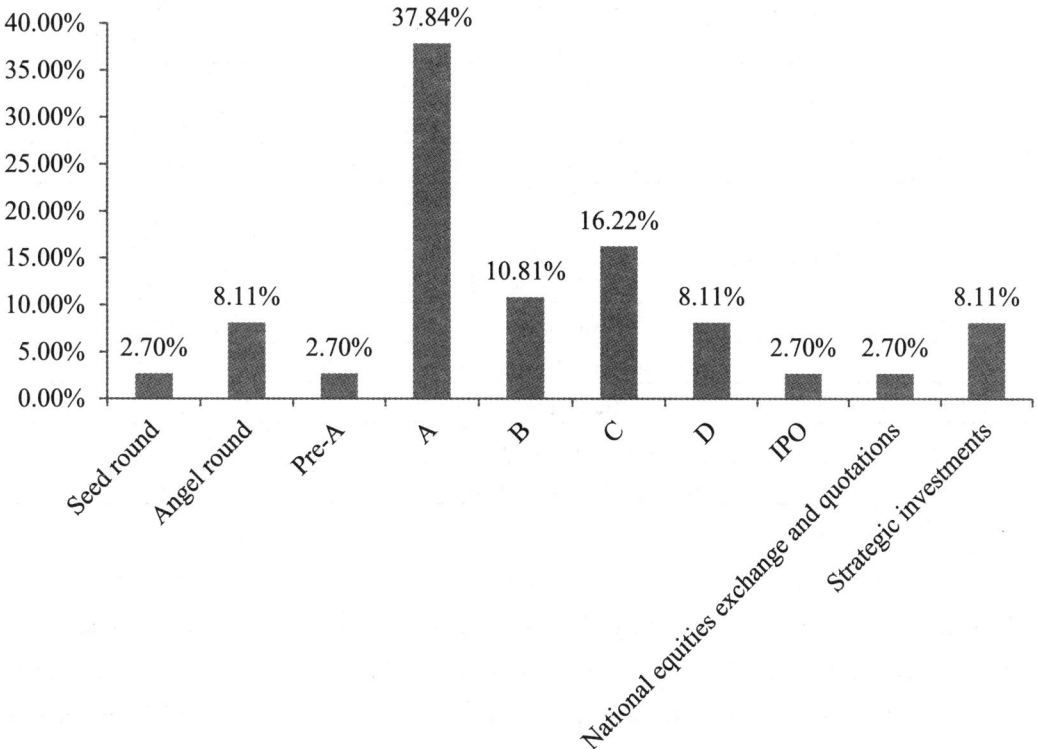

Figure 5.21 Tencent's investment rounds in the AI field
Source: IT Juzi.

3.2.3 Investment fields

Due to its massive investments, Tencent's investment fields are also more diversified, with more than 10 sectors, including culture and entertainment, corporate services, e-commerce, education, gaming, and finance. In recent years, in order to concentrate on the key fields, it has strengthened investments in culture and entertainment, corporate services, and e-commerce. For example, in 2018, the number of investment projects in these three industries accounted for 60% of the company's total investments. Among them, the culture and entertainment field has been Tencent's key field over the years. Tencent invested in 56 projects in 2018. The subdivisions of investments include short video, animation, live broadcast, and audio.

In 2018, Tencent's newly established Cloud and Smart Industry Group (CSIG) attracted much attention from the outside world, inaugurating their transformation from 2C to 2B, thereby promoting the digital upgrade of the industry. From the perspective of investment portfolio, the number of Tencent's investments in corporate services has ranked top two in the past two years.

Table 5.4 Distribution of Tencent's investments in key fields

Ranking	Industry	Percentage
1	Culture and Entertainment	34.00%
2	Corporate Services	14.00%
3	E-commerce	9.00%
4	Education	7.00%
5	Gaming	7.00%
6	Finance	6.00%
7	Transportation	6.00%
8	Sports	3.00%
9	Logistics	3.00%
10	Life Services	3.00%
11	Software Tools	2.00%
12	Medical and Healthcare	2.00%
13	Hardware	2.00%
14	Real Estate Services	1.40%
15	Advertising and Marketing	1.00%

Source: IT Juzi.

Social e-commerce is a popular field in the e-commerce industry in recent years. Based on the WeChat ecosystem, Tencent is actively investing in startups in the field of e-commerce, posing a challenge to Alibaba. For example, Tencent has invested in the social e-commerce platform "Pinduoduo", the lifestyle-sharing community e-commerce platform "Xiaohongshu", the mobile retail-service provider "Youzan", the fresh food e-commerce platform "Missfresh", etc. At the same time, in the field of education in 2018, it invested in "Baby English" and "BaiCiZhan" based on the WeChat ecosystem.

3.2.4 Internationalization strategy

Judging from the volume and monetary amount of its overseas investments, Tencent has the strongest overseas investment capability among the three BAT giants, with the highest monetary amount and the widest scope. Through investments or mergers and acquisitions, Tencent has appeared on six continents: Europe, Asia, North America, South America, Africa, and Oceania. According to the PitchBook database, based on projects for which the monetary transaction amount has been announced, 58.87% of Tencent's investments are in China's mainland, with the remaining 41.13% invested overseas[①].

Table 5.5 The top 10 countries/regions invested in by Tencent

Country/region	Number of investment projects	Percentage	Investment amount (millions USD)	Percentage
China's Mainland	271	62.01%	113,335.9	58.87%
the United States	74	16.93%	32,138.88	16.69%
Finland	2	0.46%	15,424.63	8.01%
Hong Kong, China	10	2.29%	12,977.63	6.74%
India	20	4.58%	8,779.67	4.56%
France	2	0.46%	2,450	1.27%
Korea	9	2.06%	1,460.59	0.76%
Germany	3	0.69%	719.51	0.37%
Brazil	2	0.46%	580	0.30%
the United Kingdom	9	2.06%	497.16	0.26%

Source: compiled from the PitchBook database. Statistics are as of November 2019.

Among them, American companies are Tencent's first choice for overseas investments, with 74 investment projects accounting for 44.6% of its overseas investments, amounting to USD 32.14 billion—more than 40% of its overseas investment amount. The investment fields of Tencent in the United States are hardware, software tools, and medical and healthcare. This is not difficult to understand, because the technology level in the United States still leads the world globally, and investments in these companies can also help Tencent's own technological development. Tencent's investments in Finland are few, but the monetary investment amount is huge, with two projects reaching USD 15.42 billion—second only to the investment scale in the United States. Tencent's investment portfolio in India is relatively diversified, with many different fields, most of which are leading companies in the region in their related industries, including the acquired Ola, Flipkart, and the well-known Indian fantasy-sports gaming-platform Dream 11. Korea is a key area for Tencent's overseas investments, mainly due to a large number of Korean gaming companies, including Bluehole Studios (which developed the popular game

---

① In the PitchBook database, nearly 30% of the transactions lack information of transaction amounts. There is a slightly higher percentage of missing transaction amounts in domestic investments. Therefore, calculations based on existing investment amounts will overestimate the proportion of international corporate investments.

"PUBG"), and its established gaming company, Kakao Games.

Moreover, in recent years, Tencent has also been actively expanding its global portfolio in the field of financial technology. For example, Tencent has invested in financial OTC (Over The Counter) compliance solution provider "QTrade", consumer core-competence finance provider "WeShare", supply-chain financial business service-provider "Linklogis", global cross-border payment platform "Airwallex", cross-border financial technology company "iPayLinks", Philippines digital-payment solution-provider "VoyagerInnovations", African online-payment provider "Paystack", German digital bank "N26", and Brazilian fintech startup "NUBANK" and so on.

As investors rush to invest in global artificial intelligence, Tencent is also one of the busiest corporations. Tencent's AI investments span the entire world, from China to the United States and Canada. There are eight investments in the United States and one in Canada, accounting for about a quarter of Tencent's AI investments, among which are well-known companies like Tesla and SoundHound. In addition, Tencent has also invested in agricultural technology startup Phytech in Israel. This company invented an agricultural IoT technology to help users install sensors around their crops, so as to record data related to their growing environment, which also involves artificial intelligence to a certain extent.

3.3 JD

3.3.1 Investment structure

JD.com has five main investment entities, namely, JD's parent company and its subsidiaries: JD Digital, JD Logistics, Qianshu Capital, and JD Cloud. The following are the introduction of JD Investrment Repartment, JD Digital, and Qianshu Capital.

(1) JD Investment Department

The JD Investment Department is mainly responsible for investments and mergers of the JD Group, and its headquarters is located in Beijing. JD Investment focuses on investments based on its own businesses, including e-commerce retail, finance, logistics, and technology, covering all stages of a company's growth, maturity, and pre-IPO. The juridical person of Beijing JD Shihang Zhuoneng Zhongchuang Investment Funds Management Center (limited partnership) is Shanghai Jinshundong Investment Management Co., Ltd., and Liu Qiangdong is the legal representative and executive director of Jinshundong.

(2) JD Digital

JD Digital Technology was preceded by JD Finance. The JD Finance Group, which started independent operation in October 2013, is positioned as a technology company serving financial institutions. 11 business sectors have been established: corporate finance, consumer finance, wealth management, payment, crowdfunding and crowd innovation, insurance, securities, rural finance, financial technology, overseas business, and urban computing. In addition to serving financial institutions, JD Finance is also preparing itself technically to serve non-financial enterprises and cities by providing a wider range of technological services to the whole society.

In terms of data acquisition capabilities, JD Finance relies on JD Group's more than 240 million active users, with hundreds of thousands of suppliers, partners, and transaction data. At the same time, it enriches its data resources through investment and cooperation. In terms of data technology capabilities, it uses big data as the basis for technology applications, such as learning, artificial intelligence, image recognition, graph network, and blockchain. In terms of data model product capabilities, it develops risk quantification models, marketing models, and user insight models. Using cutting-edge big data application technology, the JD Finance Group has established a complete set of financial infrastructure, such as a risk control system, payment system, investment research system, investment advisory system, DaaS (data as a service) platform, and SaaS (software as a service) platform.

On September 17, 2018, the official WeChat account of "JD Finance" was renamed "JD Digital".

On November 20, 2018, JD Finance was rebranded as JD Digital Technology. JD Digital Technology has become the parent brand of the entire corporation, with JD Finance a sub-brand of JD Digital Technology. In addition, JD Digital Technology also includes sub-brands like JD iCity, JD Farm, JD Mo Media, and JD Shaodongjia.

JD Digital Technology connects financial and physical industries with digital science and technology to help improve their Internet, digitalization, and intellectualization levels.

(3) Qianshu Capital

Qianshu Capital, established on August 10, 2017, is an early-stage fund of JD Digital, focusing on consumption upgrades in the Chinese market. Qianshu Capital's investment targets are angel investments or Series-A-round startups. Its core concept is to use data as the investment decision-making engine, with crowd-innovation ecology and financial technology functioning as post-investment supports in order to hold small percentages of shares through investment. With minimal interference in the invested companies, it won't strategically and operationally restrict them, aiming for mutual growth with them.

As an early-stage investment fund focusing on consumers under JD Finance, Qianshu Capital has invested in subdivisions such as living technology, personal healthcare, fashion accessories, and entertainment content, including well-known startups like 8H, Muzhen Radios, Runmi, and a-life. In the future, Qianchu Capital will focus on investment in new consumption areas to promote the consumption upgrade of consumers from material needs to spiritual needs.

Qianshu Capital relies on JD Finance's crowd-innovation service system. It integrates high-quality resources in the system and provides invested companies with customized post-investment support, like training, services, channels, and financial services. Specifically, it relies on JD University's School of Innovation to build a community of well-trained enterprise founders, providing a platform for mass innovation entrepreneurs to communicate with such successful entrepreneurs for four consecutive terms, with more than 170 entrepreneurs participating in. It uses big-data product systems, online SaaS platforms, industrial parks, and other services to provide standardized operation support for startups. Through JD.com and JD's crowdfunding, it optimizes corporate consumption channels, directly reaching billions of customers. Through JD Finance's supply chain finance and rural finance, it can provide mass entrepreneurship enterprises with full life-cycle funding and resources.

3.3.2 Investment scale and types

Using PitchBook's statistics, we calculated that JD.com made a total of 91 investments from 2013 to 2019, with a total announced transaction amount of USD 43.659 billion. JD's total investment amount is slightly more than Baidu's, but its number of investment projects is less than half of Baidu's, indicating that its average investment per project is relatively large. Looking at the situation over the years, there is an overall rising trend, but the number of investments was at its peak in 2015 and 2018, with investment activities being the most active during this period. Compared with Baidu and Tencent, JD's investment is less stable in pace.

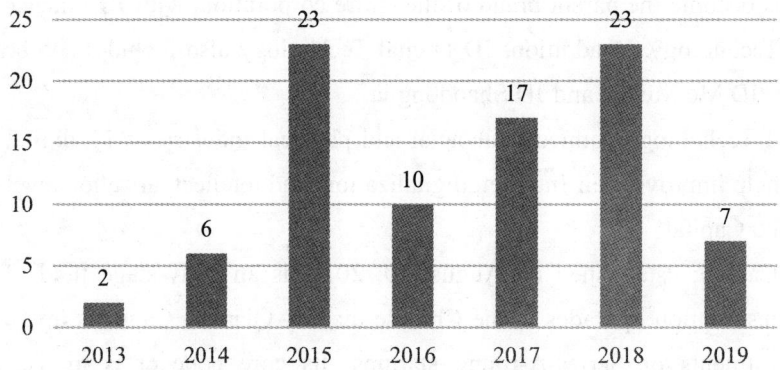

Figure 5.22   The numbers of JD investment projects over the years

Source: compiled from the PitchBook database.

Seen from the perspective of investment rounds, although JD's investment projects are relatively small, nearly two-thirds of them are projects before the Series A round. Most of its investments are angel investments or from the Series A round, indicating that JD's investment style is more radical. The fact that angel investment round projects account for the most proves that JD prefers investing in the early stage of projects, such as team formation and daily operations, making investments of lower amounts. Secondly, JD prefers A round investments. One can see that JD prefers making decisions to invest in projects to accelerate their development after collecting sufficient data.

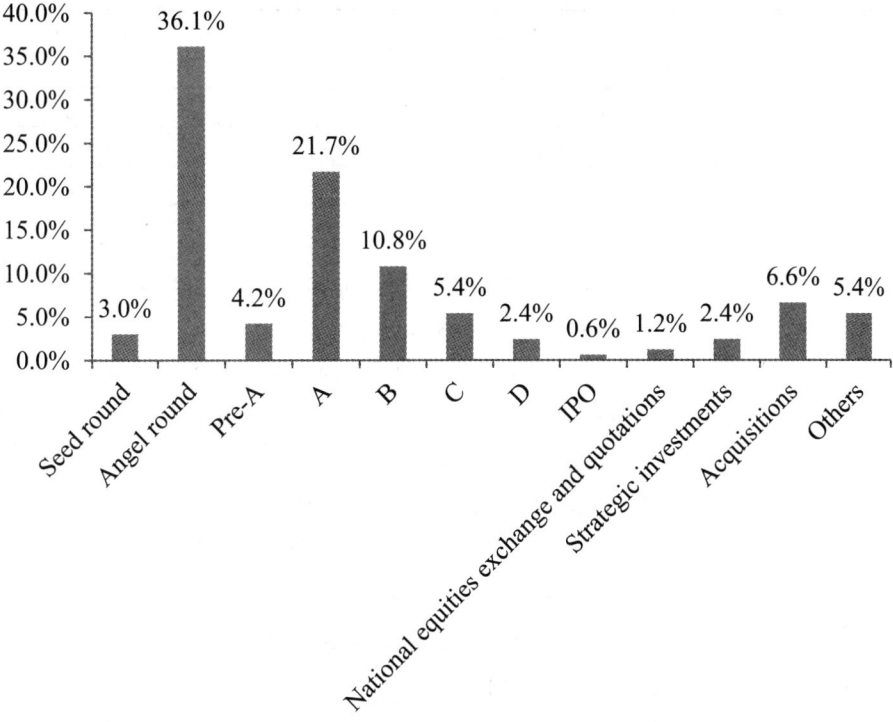

Figure 5.23 Distribution of JD investment rounds

Source: compiled from the PitchBook database.

3.3.3 Industry distribution

JD's overall investment portfolio is extensive, mainly concentrated on the fields of corporate services, e-commerce, hardware, life service, finance, and transportation (see Table 5.6). One can see that JD's investment strategy is mainly to serve JD's corporate development, focusing on its corporate ecological development and platform construction, while taking into account capital operation.

Table 5.6 Distribution of JD's main investment areas

Ranking	Industry	Percentage
1	Corporate services	15.4%
2	E-commerce	14.3%
3	Hardware	13.1%
4	Life service	12.7%
5	Transportation	7.7%
6	Finance	7.1%
7	Travel	4.6%
8	Entertainment media	4.6%
9	Logistics	3.9%
10	Medical and Healthcare	3.5%
11	New industries	2.7%

Continued

Ranking	Industry	Percentage
12	Education	2.5%
13	Others	4.9%
14	Social media	1.5%
15	Software tools	1.5%

Source: IT Juzi.

JD's investment targets include companies like Vipshop that are similar to traditional industries but whose business scopes are complementary to JD, making up for its shortcomings. At the same time, it uses JD Digital Technology's investments to transform itself from an e-commerce company into a technology development giant, covering all major areas of digital economy. JD Digital Technology, formerly known as JD Finance, was founded within the JD Group and started operating independently in October 2013. Based on cutting-edge technologies such as big data, artificial intelligence, the Internet of Things, and blockchain, JD Digital Technology has established core digital risk-management capabilities, user-operation capabilities, industry-interpreting capabilities, and B2B2C business-service capabilities. At present, JD Digital Technology has basically completed its portfolio layout, in the fields of digital finance, smart city, smart agriculture, digital marketing, and digital campus. Its subbrands include JD Finance, JD iCity, JD Farm, JD Mo Media, and JD Shaodongjia. It has integrated the personal, enterprise, and governmental sides based on its customer base.

3.3.4 Internationalization strategy

Relatively speaking, JD has relatively low internationalization, and its pace of internationalization is relatively slow. According to PitchBook's statistics, nearly 70% of JD's investment projects are in China's mainland. Overseas investments are mainly located in Southeast Asia, with a few others in Europe and the United States. In terms of the investment amount, the majority of its overseas investments are mainly in Hong Kong (accounting for 27.5% of JD's total investments), with fewer in other regions.

However, JD Digital Technology has established an AI laboratory in the United States' Silicon Valley, and is also expanding its business portfolio in countries and regions such as Thailand, Indonesia, and Hong Kong, China. Taking its own businesses into consideration, the main purpose of JD's overseas investments is to expand its overseas businesses, taking advantage of its strengths in core businesses like e-commerce and logistics. It is less likely to invest in new technologies in Europe and the United States.

Table 5.7 The countries/regions invested in by JD

Country/Region	Number of investment projects	Percentage	Investment amount (million USD)	Percentage
China's Mainland	71	78.02%	27,141.15	62.17%
Hong Kong, China	2	2.20%	12,006	27.50%
Indonesia	4	4.40%	2,850	6.53%
the United States	3	3.30%	951	2.18%
Thailand	3	3.30%	526.83	1.21%
Vietnam	3	3.30%	161	0.37%
Taiwan, China	1	1.1%	Unknown	
Singapore	1	1.1%	Unknown	
Germany	1	1.1%	Unknown	

Source: compiled from the PitchBook database. Statistics are as of November 2019.

Chapter 6   Digital Economy and Finance

Digital finance is the product of the mutual integration and evolution of finance with science and technology. After more than 10 years of rapid development, the global digital financial ecosystem has already taken form. At present, digital finance permeates almost all financial businesses across the world, such as credit, loan, remittance, deposit, and investment businesses. Thus, it has become an indispensable part of the financial system and represents the future direction of the financial industry's development.

The application of digital technology has brought about both opportunities and challenges to the development of China's financial industry. Digital finance reduces credit reporting costs, improves the accuracy of fraud prevention, promotes the personalized development of financial products, enhances the operation and management standards of financial institutions, and enhances the innovation of financial models. All of these lead to the creation of technologies such as digital currencies and blockchains, which in turn has significantly increased the efficiency of financial activities and promoted the inclusiveness of financial activities. At the same time, the flow of digital currency outside the banking system has challenged the effectiveness of traditional monetary policies. The rapid and broad transmission of risks in digital finance has challenged the traditional financial regulatory model. Risk prevention and control has thus become a very important segment of the development process of digital finance.

This topic will be further elaborated on according to what was covered above, and corresponding policy recommendations for all aspects will be listed.

Section 1   An Overview of Digital Finance

1.1 The concept and content of digital finance

In reality, digital finance refers to traditional financial institutions and Internet companies using digital technology to achieve financing, payment, investment, and other new financial business models. This concept is basically similar to "Internet finance" (traditional financial institutions and Internet enterprises using Internet technology and ICT to achieve funds accommodation, payment, investment, and infomediary services) as well as "financial technology" (financial innovation through technological means, forming business models, technology applications, business processes, and innovative products that have a significant impact on financial markets, institutions, and financial services). Generally, Internet finance is more often regarded as an Internet company engaging in financial businesses, while financial technology has more prominent technical characteristics. In contrast, the concept of digital finance is more neutral and it covers a broader scope.

The development of the digital financial system has its own unique path, characteristics, and regularity. Research on digital finance helps to further stimulate the vitality of the global financial ecosystem and enhances the upgrading of business formats in the financial industry. The development of financial technology has seven trend drivers: artificial intelligence (AI), big data processing, core system replacement, distributed ledger technology, e-payment, inclusive finance, and financial technology governance.

1.2 Development history of digital finance

Financial technology has been sprouting since the middle of the 19th century. It has gone through three stages of development (as shown in Figure 6.1). From the original complement and assistance to the traditional financial industry, to becoming its competitor and in the trend of replacing it, the impact of the digital finance wave is unstoppable.

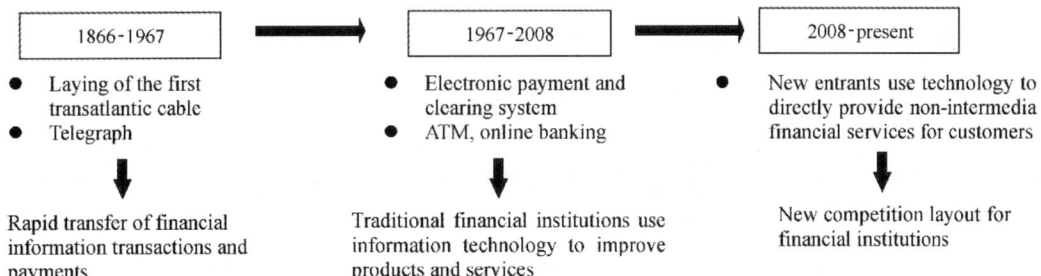

Figure 6.1 Development history of global financial technology

Source: Consumer International (2017, July), Banking on the Future: An Exploration of Finance and the Consumer Interest, Consumer International: Coming Together for Change.

From 2014 to 2017, global investments in financial technology have increased steadily from USD 19.9 billion to USD 39.4 billion. According to data released by CBInsights, the total amount of investments and financing put into financial technology across the globe reached USD 39.57 billion in 2018. China's digital finance started later with the birth of the Alipay system at the beginning of the 21st century. However, the industry generally takes the opening of Yuebao in 2013 as the start of digital finance development in China. Today, China's digital finance has developed into a leading global banner. The rapid development of businesses such as Alipay's Ant Financial, Jingdong Finance, as well as some third-party payment platforms, online loans, digital insurance and currencies, etc., have made China a global leader (as shown in Figure

6.2)[1]. According to the "2018 Global Financial Centres Index", Asia and the Americas are currently leading in financial technology while Europe's development is slightly lacking in comparison. The index also showed that the "Belt and Road Initiative" economy is actively catching up.

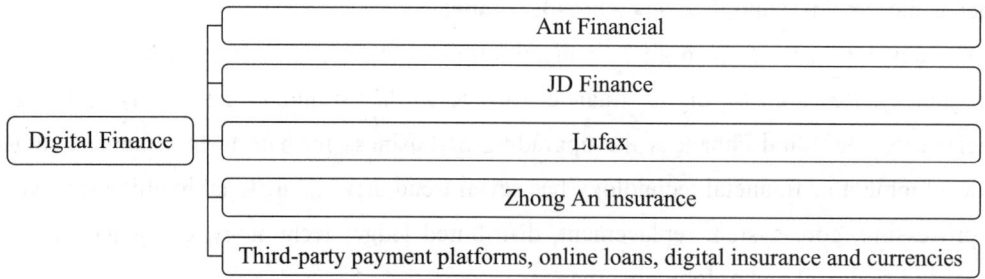

Figure 6.2　Composition of digital finance in China

Source: Sorted according to relevant information.

1.3 Digital finance models

1.3.1 Digital financial models abroad[2]

Currently, digital financial models overseas mainly include credit reporting and loan services.

Credit Karma and ZestFinance are relatively successful digital finance institutions offering credit reporting services. Credit Karma mainly provides five free credit reporting products including concise credit reports, credit rating, credit analysis, and credit monitoring, as well as the recommendation of credit products. Among these, the first four products mainly aim to satisfy customers' rigid credit reporting requirements while the fifth product satisfies customers' potential credit requirements. In order to provide customers with high value-added financial services, Credit Karma has built its own mobile application as well as a platform called Insight. The former mainly enables customers to check their credit status in real time while the latter enables customers to understand the overview of their financial situation and how each financial activity can affect their credibility. In this credit-inquiry process using big data, Credit Karma mainly works with many partners to realize this data expansion and upgrading of technology. On the one hand, Credit Karma actively cooperates with traditional credit industry giants like TransUnion and Equifax. At the same time, they absorb investments from Internet giant Google. On the other hand, Credit Karma enhances cooperation with traditional banks to build a platform for credit card recommendation, searching, and management. At present, the data used by Credit Karma mainly comes from traditional credit bureaus as well as platform users. The credit reports and credit ratings that Credit Karma offers come directly from TransUnion and Equifax. At the

---

[1] Jinying Luo (2019). On the development of digital finance in China. *Science and technology economic guide*, 27: 207-208.

[2] Fei He (2019). Research on digital finance models at home and abroad. *Rural Finance Research*, 6: 23-29.

beginning of its establishment, ZestFinance mainly offered money-lending services from the platform ZestCash. Later on, they focused on offering personal credit analysis. Regarding the notion of credit inquiry through big data, ZestFinance firmly believes that "all data is credit data" and "missing data is information", and it strives to offer services to crowds that the three credit bureau giants in the United States could not cover. This crowd generally does not have a history of poor credit (FICO scores lower than 500, about 15% of Americans). In terms of the notion of big data rating, unlike how traditional rating models use "strongly relevant" data, ZestFinance places more emphasis on "weakly relevant" data to reflect a user's repayment capacity and willingness.

Typical loan service institutions mainly include Kreditech, Affirm, Upstart, and Visual DNA. They work on a basic principle that is to reduce credit risk through big data analysis. For example, Kreditech collects about 20,000 dynamic data points for specific borrowers and uses algorithms to match and analyze the borrower's behavior. In this process, Kreditech pays particular attention to analyzing the social and consumer data of the applicant. For example, they would ask to visit the applicant's Facebook or Twitter homepage to analyze the applicant's social circle, social dynamic, and even private messages; they would ask to visit the applicant's eBay or Amazon homepages to understand the applicant's e-commerce consumption habits, mobile phone usage, personal location information, and other important data; they would also understand how they use their browsers, how they fill in questionnaires, and other seemingly "irrelevant" behaviors. Through the combination of big data technology and social data, it is indeed possible to lower credit default rate.

1.3.2 Domestic digital finance models[①]

The existing digital financial models in China are roughly divided into four categories: banking, e-commerce, social, and operators.

In the banking sector, take ICBC, one of the "four major banks" as an example. At the beginning of 2015, ICBC issued the "e-ICBC" strategy, which advocated its "three platforms, three product lines" plan. The "three platforms" refer to "e-Buy", "e-Connect", and "e-Banking". "e-Buy" is ICBC's e-commerce platform. "e-Connect" is an instant message platform to aid communication between users, enterprises, and internal staff. "e-Banking" is a "direct banking" that ICBC has come up with by combining existing mobile and online banking services. The "three product lines" refer to financing, payment, and investment financial management. At the end of the same year, ICBC also launched version 2.0 of its "e-ICBC" strategy, which builds an overall framework comprised of online e-commerce, financial management, and social networking. In early 2017, ICBC launched the personal credit consumer loan product "e-Loan". This product comprehensively applied the large database that banks have contributed to over the

---

① Jinying Luo (2019). On the development of digital finance in China. *Technology and Economic Guide*, 27: 207-208.

years, and it offers all-round credit services to customers by using big data technology.

The usage of digital finance by e-commerce giant Alibaba can be considered a classic case study. In 2004, Alipay was established and perfectly solved financial credibility problems. It even promoted the rapid development of online platforms headed by Taobao and Tmall. In 2014, Ant Financial was launched, and it had a huge number of subsidiary products that are represented by Sesame Credit, Ant Credit Pay, Ant Cash Now, and Ant Insurance. These products served customers from different income groups. At the beginning of 2019, Alipay had more than one billion users worldwide, marking a new era for online payment.

Speaking of social platform giants, we have to talk about Tencent. Since the new millennium, QQ and WeChat have been launched in succession, thus spreading Tencent users across the country. Tencent's digital financial development came relatively late, but in view of its huge user base, its digital financial services have been developing rapidly in recent years. In the early stage, Tencent only had Tenpay Payment. Afterward, Tencent built on this and launched both QQ Wallet and WeChat Pay. This provides a very convenient payment experience for the huge user base. This easily became the foundation for the deep integration between social platforms and payment. Also, there were no concerns about its security due to the rapid development of information technology. When the development of social payment platforms was relatively mature, Licaitong was pushed into the market to satisfy the multiple needs of users, such as securities, funds, insurance, and many others.

Telecom operators were relatively early in expanding digital financial services. They mainly cooperated with banks, loan companies, and financial service agencies on the principle of mutual benefit. They ventured into cross-border cooperation and strove toward a win-win goal, thus building an "innovative Internet-based financial ecological environment and service model" system. Compared with banks and e-commerce data, operators have high real-time data and strong scalability. With just a mobile number, one could assess an overview of information from various platforms. For example, in March 2011, China Telecom, one of the three big operators in China, established Tianyi E-Commerce Co., Ltd., and created a third-party payment company Bestpay. The application scope of Bestpay involves shopping, living, finance, and many other fields, of which the financial sector is the focus of China Telecom's development strategy. Built on the foundation of Bestpay, Tiancheng Finance has already become important in China Telecom's branching out in digital finance. Tiancheng Finance mainly carries out six core businesses: payment, credit reporting, consumer finance, wealth management, supply chain finance, and information technology.

Section 2   Effect of Digital Finance

2.1 Influence of digital finance on traditional financial business formats and market operating mechanism

2.1.1 Support from digital finance to traditional financial business formats and market operating mechanism

Finance is a high data-intensive industry. As a result, financial institutions have always been the most active users of information technology. Modern information technologies such as cloud computing, big data, artificial intelligence, the Internet of Things, and blockchains are gradually being applied in all aspects of the financial ecosystem. The impact of digital finance on traditional financial industries is mainly reflected in how financial technologies have transformed the traditional payment channels. They have mastered their control over payment entrances, blocked off direct contact between traditional banks and consumers, and thus caused traditional banks to retreat from the rear end of payment channels. This has allowed financial technology enterprises to gain control over the transaction habits and data of a massive group of consumers while also settling a large amount of small, idle funds. Given the advantages of data and funds, financial technology enterprises can use algorithms to provide users with low-cost, easy-to-operate, personalized, and rationalized financial services such as online loans, wealth management, and insurance. This formed a closed loop in the financial ecology centered around remittance, loans, and deposits.

Digital technologies such as big data, cloud computing, artificial intelligence, and blockchain have a far-stretching influence on traditional financial institutions in terms of operational efficiency, risk control, business models, and so on. Big data has characteristics such as large volume, high speed, diversity, etc. Big data uses customer profiles to depict the spending power and risk appetite of banks' individual customers. It also depicts the upstream and downstream activities of enterprise clients, such as their productivity, distribution, operation, finance, sales, and relevant industries. This helps to broaden banks' understanding of customers. With customer profiles, banks can effectively carry out precision marketing and achieve greater probability in referral traffic. At the same time, with the vast ocean of information in hand, banks can use big data mining methods to conduct loan risk analysis and quantify the credit line of enterprises. Cloud computing can realize mass data storage in the cloud, making the application of big data in the financial market more efficient and convenient. Artificial intelligence can use robots, image recognition and other technologies to sift out the information needed for operations easily such as customer identification and credit analysis. This also allows banks to provide intelligent services, quickly resolving user problems, greatly improve the user experience, and significantly improve customer stickiness. The openness of blockchain can connect both parties of a transaction, making the process opened to them and minimizing risks of information mismatch in traditional financial businesses. At the same time, the trustlessness and decentralization of blockchains results in the immutability of data, increases transaction security, lowers transaction-related costs, and is equipped with the potential to subvert traditional financial businesses in banks such as payment, clearing, financing, securities, and loans. As various digital technologies become more popularized, brokerage enterprises have gradually internalized their outsourced financial technology businesses. Currently, 60% of banks and 29% of payment organizations have developed a financial technology plan (as shown in Figure 6.3).

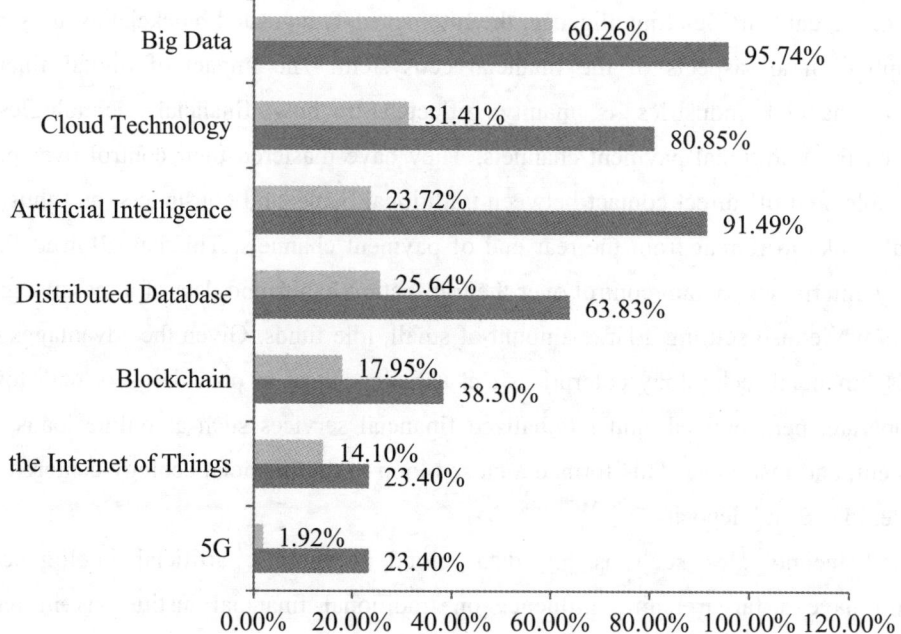

Figure 6.3 Comparison of financial technology fields covered by banks and financial institutions

Source: Payment and Clearing Association of China (March 2020). "Investigation Report on the Development of Financial Technology Businesses in Commercial Banks and Non-bank Payment Institutions".

In general, the support provided by financial technology toward the development of traditional financial business formats and market operation mechanism can be divided into several aspects shown in Table 6.1. Each of their proportions in respective services is shown in Figure 6.4.

Table 6.1 Financial technology support

Industry Support				Market Support Services
Deposit, loan, and financing services	Payment, clearing, and settlement services		Investment management services	Portal and data aggregator
				Ecosystem (infrastructure, open source, APIs)
Crowdfunding	Retail	Wholesale	High-frequency trading	Data application (big data analysis, machine learning, predictive modeling)
Loan market	Mobile wallet	Value delivery network	Copy transaction	Distributed ledger technology (blockchain, smart contract)
				Security (customer identification and verification)
Mobile bank	Peer-to-peer transmission	Wholesale foreign exchange	Electronic transaction	Cloud computing
				the Internet of Things/Mobile technology
Credit rating	Digital currency	Digital trading platform	Robo advisors	Artificial intelligence (robot, financial automation, algorithm)

Source: Bank for International Settlements (2018, February). Sound Practices: Implications of Fintech Developments for Banks and Bank Supervisors. Basel Committee on Banking Supervision.

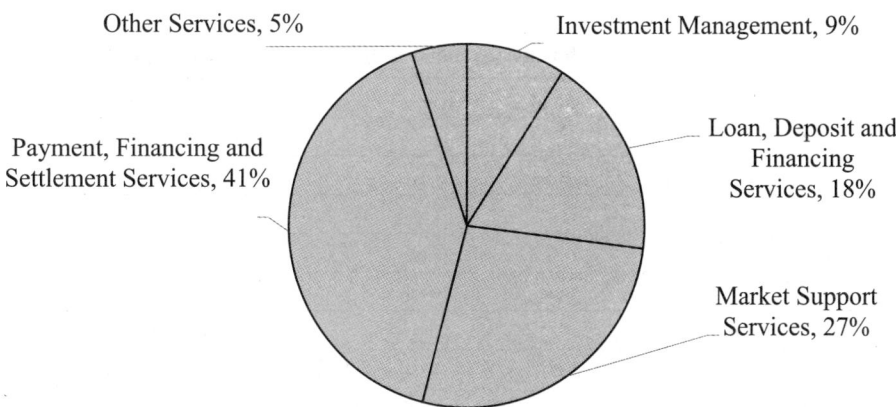

Figure 6.4 Percentages of services provided in financial technology activities

Source: Bank for International Settlements (2018, February). Sound Practices: Implications of Fintech Developments for Banks and Bank Supervisors. Basel Committee on Banking Supervision.

As seen in Figure 6.4, the proportion of deposits, loans, and financing services related to traditional financial businesses accounts for 18% while the proportion of payment and clearing services was as high as 41%. With such a broad spectrum of applicability, digital finance is indeed exciting. However, it comes as a complement to, a strong suppressor of, and even a replacement for traditional finance, which easily results in worries. Hence, the impact on financial stability and the risks that come after have also become problems that need close attention. Next, a few classic examples will be used to elaborate on the above points.

(1) P2P lending

The growth in P2P lending mainly happened after the financial crisis in 2007-2009. Compared with bank loans, the size of P2P loans is still very small, but it is expanding rapidly. In 2015, the amount of P2P lending across the world was only USD 26.16 billion, but Morgan Stanley predicted that by 2020, the amount would increase to USD 150 billion and even USD 490 billion. Even so, compared to the USD 13.116 trillion that American commercial banks had loaned as of December 2018, this number still pales in comparison.

European and American P2P lending started earlier, thus resulting in the formation of a batch of well-known P2P lending platforms: LendingClub Corporation, Prosper Marketplace, Upstart, Funding Circle, Borrowers First, SoFi, etc. After recent years of development, China has evolved to become the largest P2P lending market in the world with over 4,000 platforms[①].

P2P lending platforms engage in many overlapping business activities with traditional banks (refer to Table 6.2), which makes it extremely easy for P2P lending to take over the bank industry's market share. However, in the short term, it will not replace bank loans. Table 6.2 shows that P2P lending has many advantages and disadvantages as compared to banks. For example, while P2P lending allows for lower operating costs and regulatory burdens, it also faces the risk of overlending.

Table 6.2 Comparison of businesses between banks and P2P lending platforms

Banks	P2P Lending Platforms
A. Services provided	A. Services provided
• Improve risk-sharing and consumer insurance systems	• No
• Filter	• Yes
• Regulatory	• No
• Liquidity creation	• No
B. Capital structure	B. Capital structure
• High leverage of the banks' equity capital	• Since lending platforms do not invest in equity capital, the investor will be the equity holder of the loan
C. Incentive problems	C. Incentive problems
• Insufficient filtering	• Yes
• Insufficient regulation	• No
• Excessive risks due to high leverage and safety net	• No
• Insufficient liquidity creation	• No
• Distorted incentive mechanism due to insufficient safety net and insufficient capital, resulting in overlending and excessive growth	• Profit-maximization incentives resulting in overlending and excessive growth
• Insufficient capital due to safety nets	• No

---

① Anjan V. Thakor. (2019). FINTECH AND BANKING. Retrieved from http://dx.doi.org/10.2139/ssrn.3332550.

Continued

Banks	P2P Lending Platforms
D. Management	D. Management
• Deposit insurance and capital regulation	• No
• High regulatory costs and limitations	• Low regulatory burden
• High operating costs	• Low operating costs
E. Target functions	E. Target functions
• Maximizing the value of bank assets	• Maximizing ownership claims over P2P platforms, including initiation and other costs, with the addition of the borrower's repayment

Source: Anjan V. Thaksor (2019). FINTECH AND BANKING. Retrieved from http://dx.doi.org/10.2139/ssrn.3332550.

A large number of empirical studies and factual evidence suggest that the development of the platform increases competition, reduces banks' interest revenue on loans, increases the interest rate of bank deposits, lowers the growth rate of bank system loans and deposits, and brings about more risks[①]. All of these show that while P2P lending platforms can complement the loopholes in traditional banking businesses, P2P lending also plays an obvious role as a replacement.

The technical advantages of P2P platforms may allow them to become complementary to banks in terms of the size of their loans. Given the lower fixed costs of loan issuance on P2P platforms and that they are more willing to give out riskier loans than banks, they can serve marginal and below-margin bank borrowers. They can focus on providing loans that are smaller than what banks can loan, thus serving as a complement to this sector of the market. The operating costs of banks are higher than those of P2P lending institutions, so they must have a collection of branched networks and ATMs and bear the costs for more stringent regulations on their loans. Welltrado (2018) estimates that the operating costs of the Lending Club account for 2.7% of outstanding loans, while the ratio in banks would be close to 7%[②]. However, although the operation costs of P2P lending institutions are lower, the loans they provide might not be cheap.

P2P platforms are also a substitute for banks because they serve the same borrower group. P2P lending institutions are competing with bank loans. P2P lending institutions often have a competitive advantage when banks face certain temporary shocks that limit their credit supply. This effect will be even stronger when the bank's financial position was already not performing well without the shock.[③]

---

① Zhongfei Chen, Kexin Li & Ling-Yun He (2019). Has Internet Finance Decreased the Profitability of Commercial Banks?: Evidence from China. *Emerging Markets Finance and Trade*, (6): 1-18. DOI: 10.1080/540496X.2019.1624159.

② Welltrado (2018, March). Global Blockchain-Backed Loans Marketplace ICO. White Paper.

③ Tang, H. (2019). Peer-to-Peer Lenders Versus Banks: Substitutes or Complements?. *Review of Financial Studies*, 5(32): 1900-1938. de Roure, Calebe, Loriana Pelizzon and Anjan V. Thakor. (2019). P2P Lenders Versus Banks: Cream Skimming or Bottom Fishing?. SAFE Working Paper, 206(1): 1-62. DOI: 10.2139 / ssrn.3174632.

However, besides talking about benefits and costs, banks do have some fixed advantages. Thakor and Merton (2019) proposed a theory regarding bank and non-bank loans. In this theory, banks have more advantages than non-bank loan institutions (including P2P lending platforms). Although banks face more incentive problems, and also more complex ones than P2P platforms, in terms of developing investors' trust, banks enjoy more advantages and can also provide more intermediary services.① Goetz's (2018) research shows that the stiffened competition in the banking industry causes banks' profitability and capital quality to increase, thus improving stability in banks. Competition forces banks to increase efficiency and perhaps lower their tendency to overlend and remain "evergreen".② Hence, the emergence of digital finance in the form of P2P lending platforms, for example, is not just a challenge to the traditional banking industry, but also a transformation opportunity.

(2) Smart Contracts

The essence of smart contracts is that they can enable non-trusted delegates to collaborate without a neutral central authority. That is to say, smart contracts replace trusted intermediaries, like the bank, to link two parties together. As a result, its core is to create a credible machine solution. Smart contracts have huge potential to improve efficiency and reduce costs for contracts and checking. This is because smart contracts eliminate the need for reconciliation between both parties and speed up the transaction settlement.

In low-income countries, the impact of smart contracts has begun to surface. For example, Nigeria, Kenya, Uganda, Tanzania, Senegal, and the Democratic Republic of the Congo have developed the BitPesa remittance service blockchains. They are used by BitPesa as open-source digital account books, which will constantly update all transaction records to make this platform transparent and secure. For example, when transacting via BitPesa, the platform can directly accept local currency and then send bitcoin to digital brokers, who would then deposit the bitcoin as a local currency in the receiving country.

Smart contracts appear to pose an imminent threat to banks and other financial intermediaries. As a trusted third party in a contract, if their roles get played down, their profitability will decrease significantly. Banks can adjust to become providers of smart contracts and to use the increased contracting opportunities offered by smart contracts to modify existing contracts and create new contracts.

2.1.2 "Open bank" and "monetary policy" in digital finance

On the whole, the development of digital finance has indeed caused an impact on traditional finance business formats. However, traditional financial institutions have not remained unchanged. While riding along on this wave, they have accomplished self-innovation, increased

---

① Thakor, Richard and Robert C. Merton (2019). Trust in Lending. Paper presented at the AFA Meeting, Atlanta, (1): 1-58. DOI:10.2139 / ssrn.3201689.

② Goetz, Martin R. (2018). Competition and Bank Stability. *Journal of Financial Intermediation* 35, Part A, (6): 57-69.

efficiency, and gradually transformed into a completely new collaboration and service method. Since 2018, state-owned big banks, joint-stock banks, and private banks have gradually rolled out "open-bank" strategies. Promptly after, commercial banks opened up API (Application Programming Interface) terminals to connect online platform service providers of all sorts. Through working with service providers, banks have delved into various specific consumer scenario services. The open bank is an innovative business model and concept. Within the boundaries permitted by regulators, commercial banks receive authorization from customers to use technologies such as API to share their information and services with other financial institutions in the banking industry, financial technology companies, vertical industry companies, etc. This allows for "plug and play" between bank services and products, and they co-work together to build an open bank-induced ecosystem.

Table 6.3 Main business models of open banks

Development models	Main characteristics	Cases
Standard Open Type	Banks open basic financial services to various types of enterprises in a standardized form.	Shanghai Pudong Development Bank launched the first API Bank non-boundary open bank in the industry. Customers can utilize the bank API through various channels including enterprise portal websites, enterprise resource management systems, WeChat mini-programs, and partner applications.
Customized Cooperation Type	Banks create customized solutions for business scenarios specified by partners.	The Bank of China works with property managers in communities to develop an application. With the application, users can directly use the application to pay bills, property managers can publicize community consultation, track bill payments, etc., and banks can expand resources.
Innovative Business Type	New forms of digital banks will induce new forms of Internet finance businesses, build inclusive financial services, and serve long-term and micro customer groups.	Ping An Bank's subsidiary, OneConnect, launched the Gamma O platform. The platform connects to a large number of technology service providers, one-stop accesses, and financial institutions represented by banks to share technologies, scenarios, customers, and establish a financial technology ecosystem.

Source: Boston Consulting Group (2019). Wefore "Internet Finance Monthly Journal".

It has been proven that this type of transformation is very effective. The proportion of retail in financial profits has been continuously increasing, there are now more non-interest income sources, and a large number of user resources have been absorbed, becoming the cornerstone of successful banking transformation. The advancing of open banks is parallel to the digitalization process of commercial banks and is paving the best path for commercial banks to fully embrace financial technology.

However, in the processes of enhancing financial services and promoting the transformation and upgrading of the financial industry, digital finance has brought about challenges for the effectiveness of monetary policies. Traditional Chinese monetary policies are focused on currency supply, bank loans, and total social financing. Digital technology has promoted the development of credit services provided by non-financial payment institutions, allowing large amounts of funds to run outside of the banking system. This increasingly blurs the boundaries between different levels of currency supplies, making it more difficult for the Central Bank to measure and regulate different levels of currency supplies. This potentially undermines the effectiveness of quantitative monetary policies. On the other hand, digital finance broadens the channels for individuals and enterprises to participate in the financial market, which increases the sensitivity of enterprises and individuals to interest rate increases, which aids in allowing price-based monetary policies to become important.

2.2 Digital finance boosting inclusive finance: current status, mechanism, and successful business models

2.2.1 Current development status, mechanism, and successful business models of international inclusive finance

Digital finance effectively solved the problems that the agriculture industry, small and micro enterprises, innovative enterprises, and supply chain enterprises are facing, such as financing difficulties and high prices. This helps to increase financial inclusion and supports and empowers servicing real economy, preventing and controlling financial risks and deepening the supply-side structural reform in finance. Among all of these, the biggest advantage is to support the development of inclusive finance. Digital technology has provided a solution to overcome the natural problem faced in financial inclusivity. Digital finance, driven by the rapid development of e-commerce and communication technologies, can reduce the dependence of traditional finance on physical bank branches. With stronger geographical penetration and low-cost advantages,[①] digital finance has created conditions for providing financial services for the masses of less-developed regions. In particular, digital currency plays a vital role in aspects such as increasing the coverage of financial services and reducing service costs.[②] This has helped to optimize the allocation of financial assets, improve the financing situation of small and medium-sized enterprises, and realize profitability uplifting while promoting financial stability.[③]

In 2005, the concept of inclusive finance was proposed to provide appropriate, effective,

---

① Jizun Li (2015). Thinking about Internet finance. *Management World*, (7): 1-7,16.

② Jinpu Jiao, Tingting Huang, Tiandu Wang, Shaohua Zhang, Tian Wang (2015). China's inclusive financial development process and empirical research. *Shanghai Finance*, (4): 12-22.

③ Ying Wang, Lei Lu (2012). The GSP financial system and financial stability. *Journal of Financial Development Research*, (1): 4-10.

and affordable financial services for all segments and groups of society. The main target groups are SMEs, farmers, low-income groups in urban areas, etc. The World Bank estimates that more than 38% of adults in the world, which is roughly two billion people, have no bank accounts, and cannot access formal bank services.① Finance inclusivity bridges the gap between using and accessing funds physically, digitally, and psychologically for those without bank accounts and those with insufficient funds.② In today's digital world, physical cash is rapidly becoming the remains of traditional social customs and the legacy left behind by the financial system. These customs and the financial system put those without bank savings in an unfavorable position. By combining digital finance tools (e.g. mobile remittances that use blockchain technology) and psychological tools (e.g. financial education), people without bank accounts can receive financial services and break their poverty cycle.③

The number of adults across the world who have no bank accounts has fallen significantly every year. What is more exciting is that big-scale inclusive finance is reaching the poorest and most remote areas of the developing world, including China, India, and sub-Saharan Africa. In some cases, emerging markets have surpassed developed countries in digital financial innovation, forming a number of successful business-model cases, such as M-Pesa in Kenya, EKO in India, and bKash in Bangladesh.④

(1) M-Pesa

In March 2007, the leading mobile-phone provider in Kenya, Safari.com, and a London-based British telecommunications group, Vodafone, jointly developed the M-Pesa mobile-phone-based financial transaction platform. Over the past 10 years, the M-Pesa platform has completely changed Kenya's inclusive financial services, providing users with more than 75% of financial services. These measures now include commercial banks' virtual savings accounts, as well as the smooth integration of commercial banks and microcredit institutions (as shown in Figure 6.5). M-Pesa currently has 20.5 million active clients, accounting for more than 70% of the adult population in Kenya. It has more than 150,000 active agents and handles more than two billion transactions every month.

---

① Demirguc-Kunt, A., Klapper, L., Singer, D., Van Oudheusden, P. (2015, April). The Global Findex Database 2014: Measuring Financial Inclusion Around the World. World Bank Policy Research Paper 7255, World Bank Group, 4-5.

② Mas, I. (2012). Payments in developing countries: breaking physical and psychological barriers. *Transaction World Magazine*, December.

③ Pande, R., Cole, S., Sivasankaran, A., Bastian, G., Durlacher, K. (2012). Does Poor People's Access to Formal Banking Services Raise Their Incomes? EPPI-Centre, Social Science Research Unit, Institute of Education, University of London.

④ Howard Thomas, Yuwa Hedrick-Wong (2019). How Digital Finance and Fintech Can Improve Financial Inclusion. *Inclusive Growth*, (4): 27-41.

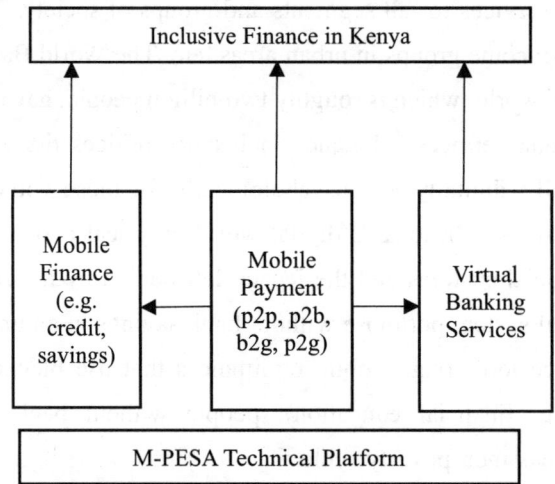

Figure 6.5 M-Pesa's platform and financial service chart

Source: Ndung'u, N. S. (2016, October). The M-Pesa technological revolution for financial services in Kenya: A platform for financial inclusion. Paper presented at Mastercard Conference, Singapore.

There are two reasons for the rapid growth of M-Pesa. Firstly, Kenya has a law requiring all citizens over the age of 18 to carry identity cards. This identification has improved the security, quality, and measurability of currency transactions and transfers. Secondly, in 2006, the Kenyan government changed the management regulations of financial services, allowing M-Pesa to operate a legal financial-service company in Kenya. Because of this, M-Pesa has undergone four stages of development: ① Acting as a mobile phone technology platform for users to transfer between one another, before allowing for payment and settlement. This happened after legislation allowed M-Pesa products to be used in the market with electronic multiple units (EMUs). The Kenyan government revisited the communication law, acknowledging EMUs and non-bank organizations as financial service providers. ② Combining virtual savings accounts, such as M-Shwari, to provide virtual banking services, realizing free transfers from M-Pesa to savings accounts. ③ Using data analysis methods serving as a foundation to create consumer credit ratings using existing customer transaction and savings data, allowing financial institutions to evaluate and set the price for the loans and credit that an individual receives. ④ As the platform becomes more complex, some cross-border payment systems and international remittances functions were allowed to be added.

After years of steady development, for small-value accounts that do not have adequate technologies to manage abnormal flows, the M-Pesa technology platform is providing account management, including that for micro-accounts. This allows several Kenyan banks to use this platform to reach more Kenyans and create more deposits for the banking system. For example, by carefully observing the growth of micro-accounts, we can see that there were only 4.12 million accounts in 2007, which doubled by 2009, reaching eight million accounts. Now, financial inclusion has already reached 80% of the population. In 2009, Safari.com included payment services in M-Pesa to enable consumers to pay for utilities, loans, and insurance. In addition, the Kenyan government has also launched an e-citizenship plan with M-Pesa to enable citizens to apply for and pay for government services with mobile currency.

(2) EKO

EKO India[①] began in 2007 in India (a huge banking market) in a similar way as M-Pesa did. Now, it has become a modern mobile-wallet payment system. In 2016-2017, its annual transaction amounted to USD 10.7 billion, with 10 million clients and 20,000 agencies. EKO provides basic bank accounts, payments, deposits, and withdrawal services. The uniqueness of its business model is that it uses its own technology platform, Simplibank, to ensure ordinary mobile phones can be used to conduct safe capital transfers. Its business correspondent (BC) system is designed to overcome the dependence of the banking departments on the banks' branches (cost is usually high in rural areas). The BC of EKO is mainly local retailers (thousands of retailers). They are very familiar with their customers, can keep track of customers' deposits and payments, and provide them with convenience, which effectively complements bank branches and mobile network operators.

(3) bKash

bKash is a mobile financial service (MFS) provider initiated in Bangladesh in July 2011. It is responsible for providing basic services such as CICO remittance, call time top-ups, and bill payments through agents in small shops. According to the Institute of International Finance (2016), there are more than 110 million people in Bangladesh who are 15 years old and above. The per capita GDP is more than USD 1,000. Although the proportion of mobile phone usage is 80%, the penetration of smartphones is only around 15% (in 2015). In the population of those 15 years old and above, nearly 30% have an account in a financial institution while only 6% have a mobile banking account. In this context, the development of bKash from 2011 to 2017 was inevitably crucial. By 2017, the company's shares in the mobile-banking market have already grown by 50%. There were 53.7 million mobile-banking accounts in the market with transactions amounting close to USD 120 million. Among these mobile accounts, there were nearly 28 million active accounts, which accounts for about 25% of the population of those 15 years old and above. They are mainly using the accounts for withdrawals and savings. Apparently, financial inclusion has increased significantly.

From the various successful digital inclusive financial models such as M-Pesa, we can summarize these key elements for providing digital infrastructure standards, and digital financial inclusion should be extended to all citizens (as shown in Figure 6.6):

- Achieving digital connectivity through mobile phones or digital interface systems.
- The CICO network helps poverty-stricken customers convert cash into digital currency

---

[①] CGAP (2017). EKO India. Presentation by Matteo Chiampo at Mastercard Symposium, Singapore.

and vice versa.

• A payment platform that can connect the other party of the transaction (other payment providers, institutions, etc.).

• Rules that make cross-platform payments clearer.

• Universal customer data standards and analysis.

• Payment platforms are cheap and can be used for multiple purposes other than transfers.

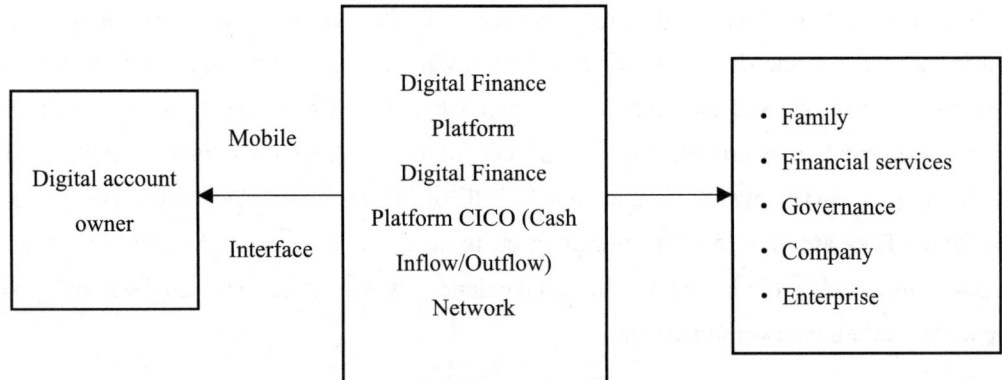

Figure 6.6   Mechanism for digital finance platform inclusivity

Source: Radcliffe, D., & Voorhies, R. (2012). A digital pathway to financial inclusion. SSRN Paper No. 2186926, Gates Foundation, U.S. (working paper).

2.2.2 Current development status, mechanism, and successful business models of inclusive finance in China

When compared with the world's progress, the beginning of China's digital inclusive finance was not too late and has even developed rapidly. Since 2006, China has been vigorously promoting the development of inclusive finance by rolling out measures such as establishing micro-credit companies, establishing the "Inclusive Finance Business Unit" in financial institutions, and running pilot programs of loans with a mortgage of the "two rights". From 2013 to 2018, the average number of bank accounts and credit cards owned by each Chinese national increased from 4.1 to 7.2 for the former and from 3.1 to 5.5 for the latter. By the end of 2018, the outstanding loan of the RMB inclusive finance sector had reached 13.39 trillion yuan, a 13.8% year-on-year increase. The growth rate increased by 5.3% as compared to the end of the previous year. There was an increase of 1.62 trillion yuan in the year, which was 695.8 billion yuan more than the previous year. The balance of inclusive small and microloans was 9.36 trillion yuan, a 21.79% year-on-year increase. It was 9.2% higher than the growth rates of all other loans. Inclusive small and microloans supported 17.2323 million small and micro business entities, which was an increase of 4.5507 million entities from the beginning of the year. The lending rates from small and micro businesses decreased. The lending rate of newly-opened inclusive small and micro businesses in the fourth quarter of 2018 was 7.02% on average, which was 0.8%

lower than that of the first quarter. However, financial inclusion faces high costs and pricing risks, which often leads to a lack of business sustainability.

Inclusive credit places great emphasis on eliminating financial exclusion and realizing social equality. Traditional bank loans exclude those who have real financial needs but do not have a house, car, and social security, thus forming financial exclusion in the traditional sense. The application of digital technology uncovers the "realizable value" of soft data such as social, online consumption, and payment, which effectively lowers transaction costs and the bar for credit services. However, as "Internet Plus" continues to mine deeper into online user data, new financial exclusions are also generated. Those whose production and business operations are mainly carried offline, as well as those small and micro businesses, farmers, and low-income groups in rural areas who might not have enough capacity in utilizing the Internet or experiences in operating mobile smart devices, have reasonable and real needs for funding. If they had funds with reasonable risk prices to help them "generate blood", they could be fully capable of uplifting their livelihood and business standards while repaying the principal and interest. However, because they do not access the Internet as often and lack online behavioral traces, they fall into the vacuum zone of the "Internet Plus" era.

In order to solve the problems and contradictions in the development of inclusive credit, the convergence model emerges. The so-called convergence model dismantles the segments in inclusive credit and forms independent business "joints" such as gaining customers, data, risk control, capital, and credit enhancement. It then relies on financial technology to build a uniform platform that connects various organizations that specialize in these different joints to form an inclusive credit business model in an organic ecosystem. In this convergence model, under the premise of meeting their own business qualification requirements and cooperating between organizations, many business participants will fully maximize their differentiated advantages in business attributes, service networks, data accumulation, science and technology research and development, financing channels, etc., so as to eliminate business shortcomings in a collaborative manner and generate economies of scale. This helps to provide diversified, affordable, and convenient credit solutions for an inclusive financial crowd.[1]

As compared with the traditional inclusive finance business model, the innovation of the inclusive finance business model brought about by digital finance is more suited for the needs of the target group, which is mainly reflected in these areas: In terms of expanding the coverage and enhancing the availability of financial services, digital finance can lean on the traffic flow brought about by the Internet's mobile data terminals and the block-to-block network in blockchain to extend the radius of inclusive financial services, expand the services coverage, break the geographical restriction, extend financial services to remote areas and low-income

---

[1] NIFD (2019). Research report on convergence model of inclusive finance.

groups, and improve the availability of financial services. In terms of reducing transaction costs and balancing commercial profits and social benefits, digital finance can make use of big data and cloud computing technology to analyze and process data gathered from various aspects such as online socializing, consumption, work, and life. This allows digital finance to effectively produce a credit rating for customers. By relying on blockchain technology, digital finance can also form a traceable and accountable credit system that can alleviate information asymmetry and cut information and customer acquisition costs. In terms of simplifying business processes and increasing productivity of financial services, digital finance can sort through massive amounts of data and effectively screen user information. This helps make risks more explicit and simplifies the reviewing process significantly. By using blockchain technology, digital finance can automatically record and store all information, thus effectively shortening the financial back-end business process.[1]

As shown in Table 6.4, there is no lack of successful digital inclusive finance business models in China. For example, in 2007, Ali cooperated with state-owned banks to open up micro-credit application services to Taobao merchants. In 2011, Alipay received the first domestic "Payment Business Permit" issued by the Central Bank. At the same time, Ali began to carry out micro-credit businesses independently. In June 2013, Ali launched the online currency fund "Yuebao", which blew up the market. In 2014, building on top of Alipay businesses, Ant Financial Services Group (Ant Financial in short) was officially established. Currently, Ant Financial is already offering various financial services such as payment, small loans, credit, financial management, etc. Among all these digital finance products under Ant Financial, Sesame Credit, Ant Credit Pay, and Ant Cash Now are more well known. "Sesame Credit points" is a rating product that Sesame Credit released to the public. Currently, it is already being applied in various scenarios such as clothing, food, housing, and transportation. Among these, the most direct application of Sesame Credit points is to branch out consumer finance businesses. Ant Credit Pay and Ant Cash Now are online consumer finance products that Ant Financial has designed for the general public. According to personal Sesame Credit points, Ant Credit Pay can provide users between 500 to 50,000 yuan in personal loans for use on the Taobao shopping platform. Different from Ant Credit Pay, Ant Cash Now can provide users with personal loans in cash, and usage is no longer limited to specified online platforms and can also be used in any offline retail store. According to statistics, the main user group of these two services is people born in the 1980s and 1990s. They are especially welcomed by lower-income groups.

---

[1] Mingxian Li, Qilan Li (2020). Research on the business model innovation of inclusive finance driven by fintech. *Rural Finance Research*, (4): 10-15.

Table 6.4 Innovation of inclusive finance models in digital finance

Innovative Business Models in Inclusive Finance	Representative Enterprises
Online Crowdfunding	Jingdong Dongjia, Taobao Crowdfund, etc.
Internet Insurance	ZhongAn Insurance, Ant Insurance, etc.
Third-party Payment	Alipay, WeChat Pay, etc.
P2P Online Loans	Ppdai, Renrendai, etc.
Robo Advisor	Machinegene Investment, Ant Fortune, etc.
Online Banks	WeBank, MYbank, etc.

Source: Mingxian Li, Qilan Li (2020). Research on the business model innovation of inclusive finance driven by fintech. *Rural Finance Research*, (4): 10-15.

Digital technology combines with inclusive finance to build "scenarios" such as Taobao or WeChat on Internet platforms to connect millions of mobile end-terminals, integrate finance deeply into day-to-day scenarios, and provide ubiquitous financial services. At the same time, they rely on cloud computing, big data, and other financial technologies to analyze the data gathered from social media and online shopping platforms to understand users, identify risks, and conduct credit ratings. Without the need to be face to face with customers, these technologies lower acquisition and risk costs and greatly improve the feasibility of inclusive finance development. Although most residents do not have credit records, they can accumulate credit on WeChat and Alipay when paying bills, such as water, electricity, gas, etc., shopping, or paying for meals. These can all serve as credit reports, which are already being used for review purposes on digital financial platforms (such as Ant Cash Now and WeChat Loan).

The Institute of Digital Finance at Peking University and the Ant Financial Services Group have used data from Ant Financial's transaction records to arrive at China's digital financial inclusion index of multiple administrative levels between 2011 to 2018. The results show that digital finance is an important model for the realization of low-cost, wide-coverage, and sustainable inclusive finance in China. It has provided the possibility for economically-lagging areas to catch up[①] and has greatly accelerated the development process of inclusive finance in China.

Section 3 Digital Financial Innovation

3.1 Digital currencies

3.1.1 Development of non-legal digital currencies

Ever since blockchain technology developed digital currencies like Bitcoin and Ethereum, capital investors, financial institutions, and governments from all over the world started to pay

---

① Feng Guo, Jingyi Wang, Fang Wang, Tao Kong, Xun Zhang, Zhiyun Cheng (2019). Measuring the development of digital inclusive finance in China: Index compilation and spatial characteristics. *China Economic Quarterly*, accepted.

great attention to this development and invested heavily in research. Blockchain technology is the main technology of digital currency research, and as compared to traditional currencies, digital currencies built on this technology have advantages such as lowering issuance and transaction costs, increasing payment efficiency, and improving transaction security.

Cryptocurrency is becoming increasingly popular as an emerging digital currency, but it is unlikely to replace the legal digital currency. Take Bitcoin as an example, it is a transaction medium, but it can only be used on a limited number of commodities, so it takes up a smaller proportion out of all payments. Also, although Bitcoin was initially created as a peer-to-peer payment system, many Bitcoin transactions between consumers and enterprises involve a middle man who converts the Bitcoin into real currency[1]. This takes up both time and money. Another disadvantage of Bitcoin is that its value fluctuates significantly and it is not a stable value source.

Ripple will be used to discuss the unique nature of non-legal digital currencies. Ripple was launched in 2012 by a private company of the same name as a substitute for Bitcoin to address all existing and imagined currencies, including the exchange between these currencies and broader financial transactions. Ripple follows a "no one trusts anyone" principle. Each Ripple user can specify a commission amount and establish trusted relationships with their chosen account. As a whole, these links form a trusted network between accounts. When two accounts want a settlement, there must be a "trusted path" existing between them. Ripple regularly records information such as account statuses, account balances, etc., with timestamps in a "ledger". In transaction validations, only the latest released ledger and the next ledger undergoing validation are used to effectively speed up the validation process.[2] In addition, all Ripper users can realize the free exchange between currency A and currency B.

3.1.2 Countries' attitudes toward non-legal digital currencies

Governments and financial institutions have different attitudes toward non-legal digital currencies. On one side are the countries supporting digital currencies, including Singapore, Canada, the United Kingdom, Australia, and Switzerland, and these countries have introduced corresponding incentive polices. Those on the other side are more cautious, represented by the United States, Russia, France, China, Korea, and other countries. The measures that each country came up with are shown in Table 6.5.

---

[1] Foley, S., Karlsen, J. R., & Putniņs, T. J. (2019). Sex, Drugs, and Bitcoin: How Much Illegal Activity Is Financed Through Cryptocurrencies?. *Review of Financial Studies*, 32(5): 1798-1853.

[2] Gérard Dréan (2018). Bitcoin and Other Cyber-currency. DOI:10.1002/9781119102687.ch6.

Table 6.5 Attitudes of the world's major countries toward non-legal digital currencies

Attitude	Country	Specific Measure
Supportive	Japan	Japan has the most relaxed policies. Not only does it recognizes that digital currency payments are legitimate, but it also exempts digital currency transaction taxes.
	Singapore	Singapore treats digital currency as a special commodity and does not interfere with the merchants' acceptance of digital currency.
	Canada	Canada has realized the legalization of its first domestic ICO project.
	the United Kingdom	the UK regulates the use of regulatory sandboxes in digital currencies and gives them more relaxed development space.
	Australia	Australia approved regulations on Bitcoin transactions in 2017 and canceled double taxation.
Cautious	the United States	States in the US subject non-legal digital currencies and related derivatives to licensed strict regulations.
	Russia	Since 2014, Russia has banned domestic digital currency transactions and has closed numerous digital currency platforms. However, its attitude has been improving in recent years.
	France	France set up a special task force to enact laws and regulations on cryptocurrency and also strengthened the regulation on relevant derivatives.
	China	The relevant regulatory authorities in China have issued relevant documents prohibiting the implementation of non-legal digital currency relevant businesses and also closed existing digital currency trading platforms in China.

Source: Collation of relevant information.

In regards to both legal and non-legal digital currencies, from the perspective of historical laws and risk regulation, it can be seen that legal digital currency is the trend of future development. It is mainly based on the following two considerations: The first one is determined by the decentralization, anonymity, and high volatility of non-legal digital currencies. These characteristics will impact the stability of financial markets, forcing countries to issue legal digital currencies. Secondly, the legal digital currency issued by the central bank is supported by the state credit and has strong stability. Moreover, the supply and circulation of currencies are easy to be managed as a whole, which is beneficial for effective state-implemented macro-control and monetary policies.

3.1.3 Overseas research on legal digital currencies

In regards to legal digital currencies, all countries have paid close attention to and actively followed up on the research. Numerous central banks have indicated that they would issue legal digital currency in the future, and some countries have even attempted to do so.

Countries whose central bank has already issued digital currency include Ecuador, Venezuela, and Uruguay in South America, Tunisia and Senegal in Africa, and the Marshall

Islands in Oceania. Studies found that these countries either have low international status or are facing a severe economic crisis, so issuing legal digital currencies was an attempt to seek a way out. However, none of these were carried out nationwide, and results deviated from expectations. Taking Venezuela as an example, this is the first legal digital currency endorsed by government assets. On February 21, 2018, the Venezuelan government issued the official digital currency "Petro", which uses the country's rich petroleum as an anchor currency. This makes Venezuela the second country to release a central bank digital currency after Ecuador. However, since Venezuela faces a series of problems such as intense fluctuations in its economy, serious inflation, and domestic political crisis, ever since the issuance of "Petro", many people have viewed it as a capital scam controlled by the government. In addition, the United States has imposed economic sanctions on Venezuela, making the future prospects of "Petro" very worrisome.

The central banks of countries such as the United Kingdom, Canada, Russia, Sweden, Thailand, Lithuania, and the Bahamas plan to launch their own digital currencies. On the contrary, as economic giants, the United States and Japan do not have plans to do so.

The central bank of the United Kingdom was much faster in its research on legal digital currency. In 2015, the Bank of England proposed the legalization of digital currencies. It worked with the University of London to study and issue the digital currency "RSCoin", aiming to create a scalable digital currency controlled by the central bank. At present, RSCoin is still in the prototype design stage.

In March 2016, Canada launched a pilot project for the legal digital currency "Jasper", which was based on blockchain technology. The project involved the Canadian payment system, the Bank of Canada, the main banks in Canada, and the R3 alliance. The project uses distributed ledger technology to mimic the wholesale payment system, which is implemented in three stages. The first stage is to use the Ethereum platform to build prototypes and concepts to validate the system. It is also used to investigate the usage status of digital receipts issued by the central bank. The second stage uses the R3 open-source ledger platform Corda to build the prototype for further exploration. The third phase (current stage) attempts to settle multiple assets on the same account book.[①]

The Monetary Authority of Singapore (MAS) also launched the Ubin project quite early and began to study the central bank digital currency system. The project, like the Canadian Jasper project, invited the R3 alliance to participate. It also mirrored many characteristics of the Jasper project. At present, the Ubin project has already evaluated the feasibility and possible impact of a distributed ledger. Problems have been discovered and elements that need to be strengthened have been identified.

[①] Yang Gao (2018). Dynamics of digital money development and regulatory policy options. *Credit*, 37 (02): 89-92.

3.1.4 China's research on legal digital currencies

The People's Bank of China has always held a positive attitude toward digital currencies and blockchain technology. It organized institutions in the financial industry to participate in the design and construction of the legal digital currency system.

The payment services and products provided by commercial institutions have commercial profitability and cannot benefit everyone like public services and products. Therefore, in regards to digital currencies, the vast majority of the population can only obtain fair and inclusive currency services through a state monopoly. From the historical and economic perspectives of currency development, the legal digital currency may be the digital currency that has the least social cost, is the most trustworthy, and is also the most competitive. Therefore, China's research on legal digital currencies will help occupy an advantageous position in future international financial system reforms.

In 2014, the People's Bank of China established the legal digital currency research institute. This group mainly studies the feasibility of issuing legal digital currencies and has also carried out research such as digital currency issuance and business operation framework, the key technologies of digital currencies, and the issuance and circulation environment. The group has achieved phased results.

In January 2016, the People's Bank of China held a seminar on digital currencies and clearly listed the issuance of legal digital currencies as its strategic goal. The seminar asked for the research team to accelerate their research on the key technologies and multi-scenario applications of legal digital currencies. In November of the same year, the central bank also established the Institute of Digital Money to conduct intensive research in the field of digital currencies. It was clearly stated that the "central bank-commercial bank" two-tier delivery system will be adopted to realize the issuance and circulation of digital currencies. There is a "two treasuries, three centers" foundational system framework, and blockchain technology is used to construct the prototype system for a digital receipt trading platform.

In 2017, the People's Bank of China successfully tested the blockchain-based digital receipt trading platform. In December of the same year, the Institute of Digital Money was officially established.

On June 15, 2018, the Institute of Digital Money of the People's Bank of China invested in the establishment of the "Shenzhen Financial Technology Co., Ltd." This company's operations cover the related services of financial technology, such as technology development, consulting, and transfer, as well as the construction, operation, and maintenance of financial, technology, related systems. On August 28 of the same year, the Nanjing Fintech Research Innovation Centre was officially unveiled. The center is a joint-collaboration between the Nanjing Provincial People's Government, Nanjing University, the Bank of Jiangsu, the Nanjing Branch of the People's Bank of China, and the Institute of Digital Money of the People's Bank of China.

The China International Big Data Industry Expo was held in Guiyang in May 2019. The PBITFP trade financing blockchain platform developed by the Institute of Digital Money of the People's Bank of China was unveiled. On September 5, 2019, it was reported that the "closed-loop test" of the People's Bank of China's digital currency has begun. The test would mimic some payment plans, and some commercial and non-governmental institutions will be involved.

RMB 3.0 is the digitalization of the central bank of China's currency, which is known as "DC/EP" for short. "DC" is an acronym for "Digital Currency", "EP" is an acronym for "Electronic Payment", and their main function is to act as an electronic payment method. What makes it different from RMB 2.0 is that it defines the different nature between legal digital currencies and mobile payments such as Alipay, WeChat, PayPal, etc. At present, the M1 and M2 of the commercial bank account system have realized electronification and digitalization, and there is no need for reform in the short run. Therefore, according to information released by the central bank of China, the proposed digital currency soon to be released will aim to replace M0 instead of M1 and M2, and realize the digitalization of paper money.

At present, the Chinese central bank uses a "double-layer operation" structure for its distribution channel. The central bank will follow the 100% reserve banking system to convert the central bank's digital currencies for commercial banks. Then, commercial banks or commercial institutions will convert these digital currencies to the public. This structure can allow the central bank and commercial banks to complement each other's advantages and disadvantages, stimulate full competition among commercial banks along the central bank's preset path, promote the formation and development of a new financial ecology, and prevent potential risks for the central bank in terms of talents, resources, and operations.

Compared with the world's major developed countries, the central bank of China's digital currency technology system has many advantages. First of all, China has many original related technologies. As of September 2019, the central bank's four institutions have applied for 84 patents. Also, the research on foundational science conducted by Chinese universities and research institutions has advanced rapidly. The research has the potential to learn from international digital currency technological achievements. At present, the core technology of the central bank's digital currency lies in the "Digital Currency Wallet/Chip Card" feature.

3.2 Blockchain technology

3.2.1 Development of overseas blockchain technology

In 2008, Satoshi Nakamoto published the article "Bitcoin: A peer-to-peer electronic cash system". In the article, he first elaborated on blockchain technology. Afterward, with the gradual popularity and stable development of Bitcoin, its foundational technology, blockchain technology, has attracted attention from people from all sectors. According to a research report by McKinsey, blockchain technology is the core technology that has the most potential to spark the fifth wave of revolution, after steam engines, electricity, information, and Internet technology.[①]

A blockchain is a chain structure connecting data blocks in chronological order, in which each block records a transaction or status at a certain point in time. Blockchains consists of Public Blockchains, Consortium Blockchains, and Private Blockchains. Among these, Public Blockchains were developed the earliest, and its range of applications is the widest. In Public Blockchains, all nodes are free to enter or leave. As a decentralized distributed computing technology, blockchain technology has advantages that centralized technologies do not have, such as common maintenance, non-temperable data, traceability, high credibility, etc., which generally include distributed storage, consensus mechanisms, encryption algorithms, and peer-to-peer transmission. The transaction process of blockchains is shown in Figure 6.7.

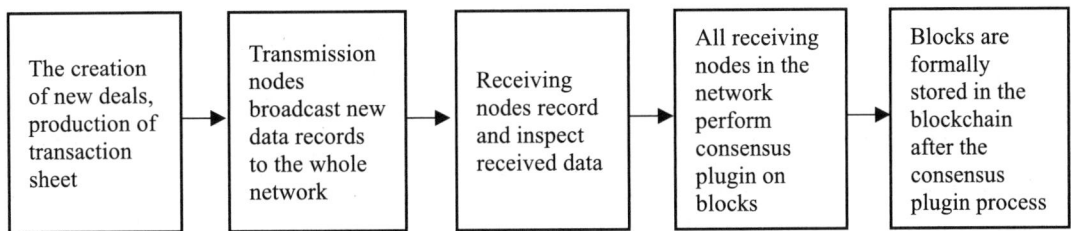

Figure 6.7　Transaction process of blockchains

Source: Yuandi Wang, Li Li, Die Hu (2014). Review of blockchain research. *Journal of China University of Mining and Technology (social science edition)*, 20(03): 74-86.

As an innovative and forward-looking technology, blockchains are regarded as the cornerstone of digital economy. Currently, they are widely used in many fields such as finance, intelligent manufacturing, digital asset transactions, etc. In recent years, its development in the financial sector has been particularly rapid, and it is even the core of many encrypted digital currencies, such as Bitcoin and Ethereum. Currently, banks in countries all over the world have participated actively in the realization of blockchains (refer to Table 6.6).

Table 6.6　Part of the blockchain projects around the world

Country or Organization	Institution	Investment Project or Start-up	Application Areas	Start Time
Australia and Germany	Commonwealth Bank of Australia, German Fidor Bank	Ripple	Transfer payment	2013

---

① Aodi Liu, Xuehui Du, Na Wang, Shaozhuo Li (2014). Blockchain technology and its progress in the field of information security. *Journal of software*, 29(07): 2092-2115.

Continued

Country or Organization	Institution	Investment Project or Start-up	Application Areas	Start Time
Spain	Banco Bilbao Vizcaya Argentaria (BBVA)	Coinbase	Digital Currency, Payment Settlement	2015.07
the United States	Citibank	Internal Laboratory	Digital Currency, Payment Settlement	2015.07
Switzerland	Union Bank of Switzerland	Internal Laboratory	Payment Settlement	2015.10
Korea	Shinhan Bank	Streami	Settlement Clearing	2015.12
the United States, the Netherlands, etc.	Wells Fargo, ABN AMRO Bank, etc.	Hyperledger	Digital Currency, Payment, Settlement, etc.	2016.03
the United States	Bank of America	Internal Research Institutions	Trade Finance	2016.03
Transnational Organizations	R3 Alliance (R3CEV)	Corda	Payment Settlement, Financial Transactions, etc.	2016.04
the United Kingdom	Barclays Bank	Circle	Digital Currency, Payment Settlement	2016.04

Source: Wei Luo (2018). Innovation and application of blockchain technology in the field of finance. *Technological economy and management research*, 08: 90-95.

3.2.2 Blockchain technology development in China

In 2015, Cao Lei published "Blockchains: Another Possibility of Finance". This formed the beginning of China's academic research on blockchains. In August of the same year, China's Wanxiang Holding funded and established Wanxiang Blockchain Labs. This was the first Chinese research institution committed to promoting the practical application of blockchain technology.

In April 2016, the ChinaLedger Alliance was established. At that time, it was the most influential blockchain alliance. On July 31 of the same year, Ant Financial announced that it would try to apply blockchains in charity scenarios. In October of the same year, the Ministry of Industry and Information Technology released the "China Blockchain Technology and Application Development White Paper". It highlighted the importance of the blockchain system in the development of areas such as education and employment. In December of the same year, blockchain technology was included in the "13th Five-year Plan for National Informatization Planning" issued by the State Council.

In 2017, the Ministry of Industry and Information Technology established the Trusted Blockchain Open Lab and accelerated the development process of blockchain technology in China.

On February 26, 2018, the *People's Daily* published a whole-page report titled "Three Questions on Blockchains", further reflecting China's proactive stance. In May of the same year, the Ministry of Industry and Information Technology officially issued the "2018 China Blockchain Industry White Paper", which was the first official blockchain industry white paper issued by officials.

On October 25, 2019, in the 18th Collective Study of the Political Bureau of the CPC Central Committee, General Secretary Xi Jinping emphasized the need to put blockchain technology as an important breakthrough in the self-innovation of key technologies.

China still faces many challenges in the process of developing blockchain technology. The first challenge is overcoming the problem of scalability. In the blockchain system, scalability, non-centralization, and security can only be implemented for at most two of them. Therefore, any framework strategy of a blockchain system will contain the pros and cons of the three. The second challenge is to overcome interoperability issues. To realize the "credibility" of blockchains, the size of the blockchain network must be large enough. However, at present, many organizations and institutions are attempting to apply blockchains in a small-scale scope, leading to the diversification of blockchain technologies and platforms. This thus causes the problem of connecting these heterogeneous blockchains. The third challenge is the problem of regulations. Under the premise of maintaining the "self-governance" of blockchains, we need to incorporate blockchains into the regulatory system as soon as possible so as to achieve widespread application.

Although there are still many problems regarding blockchains to be solved, it does not affect its development and application in many fields such as financial technology, digital currency, etc. It will remain a popular research topic in the future.

3.2.3 Application of blockchain technology in supply chain finance

Supply chain finance involves multiple fields such as supply chain, finance, and logistics. The financing model can be broadly divided into inventory financing, purchase order financing, and accounts receivable financing. From the birth of supply chain finance until now, there are still numerous pain points. Factors such as asymmetric information, a lack of trust transmission mechanism, cumbersome processes, and high risk-control costs, etc., all restrict its development. Ever since the blockchain technology was applied in this field in 2015, these problems have been gradually solved. Blockchain technology presented each asset and node of the logistics supply chain in a digital form on the cloud platform. This guarantees that information is clear, transparent, real, and credible. Its unique privacy and security protection mechanism eliminates all obstacles in information sharing in every aspect of the supply chain. At the same time, blockchain technology has built a new credit system in the supply chain, thus reducing transaction costs, and solving credit risks in supply chain financing. The specific improvements made toward traditional supply chain financing are shown in Table 6.7.

Table 6.7　Specific solutions for supply chain finance based on blockchains

Types	Supply Chain Finance Problems	Blockchain Solutions
Inventory Financing	Incorrect, unclear, or forged storage documents may cause banks to provide financing risks for incorrect amounts of funds or non-existent goods.	Blockchain-driven activity registry can provide chances to connect to a large number of users on the Internet. This, in turn, maintains the status of warehouses and the completeness of receipt data, thereby avoiding counterfeiting.
	The same commodity is financed by a number of banks without them knowing.	Shared databases in blockchains can avoid dual overhead problems.
	Tracking ownership of financing goods	Using blockchains and smart contracts to transfer property rights can increase transparency and reduce financing risks.
Purchase Order Financing	Involving third parties such as auditors, or contacting third-party logistics companies to improve transparency, thereby increasing financing costs	The blockchain layer creates transparency, thus realizing the direct financing process and reducing the associated risks and costs.
	Tracking the actual flow of goods	The combination of blockchains and the Internet of Things makes it possible to track the actual supply chain. This allows for risk adjustment at each step of the transport process to complete the order.
Accounts Receivable Financing	High costs to prevent repeat consumption and falsification of invoices	Blockchains create unique and unchangeable documents, which can be effectively exchanged on the Internet and be used as a secure collateral.

Source: E. Hofmann et al. (2018). Supply Chain Finance and Blockchain Technology. DOI 10.1007/978-3-319-62371-9_6.

Yizhanwang's "logistics financial chain" is a commercial case of exploring the blockchain + supply chain model. The logistics financial chain offers open, transparent, and mutually-beneficial financial agreements to bring in participants from industries, such as funders, logistics platforms, and transport suppliers. They form an economically mutually-beneficial ecosystem that solves restriction problems that SMEs' logistics suppliers face in their funding channels. In terms of technology, Yizhanwang's logistics financial chain researched and developed its own blockchain technology, Vector.Link. It speeds up and optimizes high availability of system high-frequency data and prolongs the syncing of stored data, taking care of performance, data privacy, and security. In terms of innovation, the logistics financial chain proposed the concept of "transport value" for the first time. After anchoring the accounts receivable that have been confirmed, the platform will provide a guarantee. The enterprises' credibility in the supply chain will affect the parameters of transport capacity, ensuring that the credibility is positively correlated to profits. Building on the "transport value" mechanism, small, medium, and micro suppliers' short-term and dispersed accounts receivable can turn into effective data value evidence. In view of this, these suppliers can quickly receive funding from financial institutions. At the same time, they can enjoy various highly effective and flexible financial services in terms of transport loans, transport consumption, gas loans, loans to buy cars, etc., thus enhancing liquidity.

3.3 Regulatory sandbox

3.3.1 Regulatory sandboxing practices in foreign countries

The FinTech Regulatory Sandbox mechanism refers to the creation of a safe space that enables financial technology enterprises to test innovative financial products, services, business models, and marketing methods within their scope of control. These enterprises do not need to be subjected to immediate regulatory control when they encounter problems.

The concept of the regulatory sandbox was first introduced in November 2015 when the Financial Conduct Authority (FCA) proposed the "Sandbox Regulatory" to Her Majesty's Treasury in the United Kingdom. The operation model of the regulatory sandbox is shown in Figure 6.8.

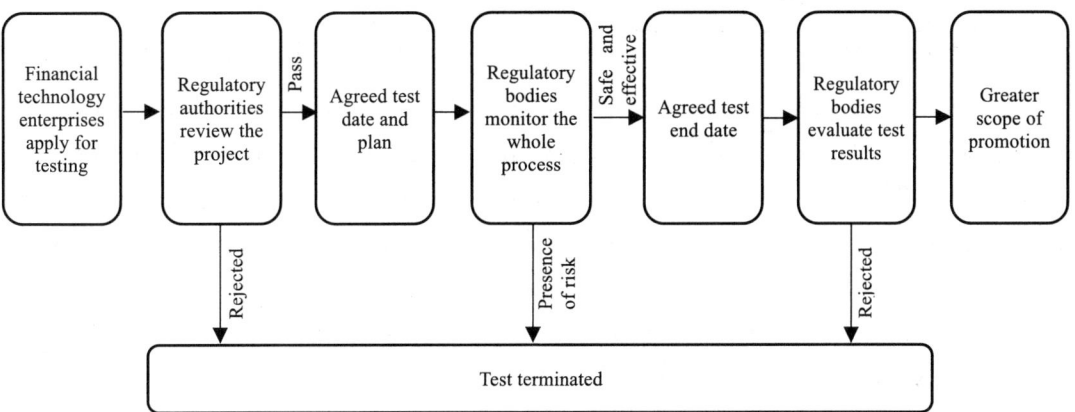

Figure 6.8 Regulatory sandbox test flowchart

Source: Yaoyao Lu, Huawei Zhao (2018). The impact of "regulatory sandbox" mechanism on China's financial innovation regulation. *Finance and accounting monthly*, 19: 160-164.

Ever since the United Kingdom proposed the regulatory sandbox in 2015, it has received wide attention on the international scale. It was even crowned as the best option to effectively balance innovation and risk regulation. Other countries and regions such as Australia, Singapore, Thailand, Indonesia, Malaysia, and Canada have started to copy it and release their own regulatory sandbox projects. The countries and regions that have implemented regulatory sandbox as of now are shown in Table 6.8. Through the implementation of this measure, these countries and regions have created a good financial development environment for their own country or region, thus enhancing the coordinated development of financial innovation and stability.

Table 6.8 Countries or regions carrying out regulatory sandboxing

Country or Region	Implementing Institution	Start Time
the United Kingdom	United Kingdom Financial Conduct Authority	June 2016
Australia	Australian Securities and Investment Commission	June 2016
Abu Dhabi	Abu Dhabi Global Market	June 2016
Malaysia	Central Bank of Malaysia	October 2016
Mauritius	Mauritius Board of Investment	November 2016
Singapore	Monetary Authority of Singapore	November 2016
Indonesia	Indonesia Financial Services Authority	December 2016
Thailand	Bank of Thailand	December 2016
Thailand	Office of the Insurance Commission of Thailand	June 2017
the Netherlands	Netherlands Authority for the Financial Markets	January 2017
the Netherlands	De Nederlandsche Bank NV	January 2017
Canada	Canadian Securities Administrators	February 2017
Bahrain	Central Bank of Bahrain	June 2017
Arizona, the United States	Attorney General's Office, Arizona	March 2018

Source: Fan Liu (2019). Sandbox regulation: Introducing logic and local construction. *Southwest finance*, 03: 53-63.

The United Kingdom is the first country in the world to implement regulatory sandboxing, and it is also the country with the most projects running currently. On May 9, 2016, the FCA officially launched the regulatory sandbox. By the beginning of 2019, 276 enterprises had already submitted applications to the FCA, of which 89 have been accepted and have been or are conducting relevant tests. The average acceptance rate is 30%.[①] The main participants in the test include big financial institutions such as HSBC and Nimbla, as well as financial technology startups such as Nextday Property Limited and Swave. The test covers investment management, payment and clearing, market foundation implementation, financing, insurance, and other fields. The technologies involved include artificial intelligence and blockchain technology. The FCA adopts a regular centralized testing method with strict screening standards. After a project successfully passes through 3-6 months of testing, it will be put into the financial market to be promoted. Meanwhile, the FCA will also work on regulation gaps found in the test process in a timely manner and constantly improve the breadth and depth of supervision.

In June 2016, the Monetary Authority of Singapore (MAS) proposed a regulatory sandbox mechanism. In November of the same year, it issued the Sandbox Guidance on Fintech Regulation and established its own regulatory sandbox. In the paper, the MAS listed a detailed description of the applicable targets, access conditions, and operation procedures, and exit and transition strategies for its regulatory sandbox. Unlike what the UK did, Singapore adopted a case-by-case approval method for the regulatory sandbox project. There was no limit on test duration, and the management method is more flexible. It also allows the product to be tested for

---

[①] Klingler D. (2019). RegTech and the Sandbox—Play, Innovate, and Protect!. DOI: 10.1002/9781119362197.ch21.

six months on a client base with a maximum of 50 people. However, it is currently mainly involved in the insurance sector, and its coverage is relatively narrow. PolicyPal Pte Ltd. was the first regulatory sandbox project in Singapore, and it began testing in March 2017. The project is a model that verifies a user's identity via mobile phone facial recognition. It uses artificial intelligence technology to calculate clients' premiums, thus providing convenient and efficient services for consumers.

In June 2016, the Australian Securities and Investment Commission (ASIC) issued the "Further Measures to Facilitate Innovation in Financial Services (Draft for Comment)". The paper proposed policies for regulatory sandboxes, and the first local project testing started in May 2017. The ASIC allows newly-established enterprises without a financial services license to conduct no longer than 12 months of testing, but the scope is limited to the field of financial technology. Compared with the UK and Singapore, Australia's regulatory sandbox is more stringent. The ASIC has strict restrictions regarding the regulatory sandbox testing projects, such as the number of clients, the balance of product funds, and the size. It also requires participants in testing projects to provide a sufficient compensation plan through methods such as insurance. Therefore, other countries view the Australian regulatory sandbox as a "minimal touch" regulatory environment.

Many countries and regions in Europe and Asia have also come out with, or are in the midst of developing, their own regulatory sandbox projects. In November 2016, the European Banking Federation recommended launching a Europe-wide Financial Technology sandbox to allow enterprises to test cross-border financial innovation services. In the same year, the Swiss Federal Council also proposed implementing regulatory sandboxes to create a financial innovation environment without the need for approval and authorization, allowing SMEs to provide financial services without receiving permission. In addition, Malaysia, Thailand, the Netherlands, and Canada have also implemented regulatory sandboxes in a timely manner.

3.3.2 Practice of regulatory sandboxing in China

In September 2016, the HKMA proposed a regulatory sandbox plan targeted for the banking industry, mainly involving a fast payment, virtual bank, application programming interface, voice and vein identification of clients, and other businesses. It will adopt a case-by-case approval method for test projects that fall within the scope of businesses. The HKMA allows banks entering the sandbox to conduct pilot tests on limited customers, and they do not need to fully comply with the usual regulatory requirements during the period of testing. This encourages banks to undergo financial innovation.

Hong Kong's success also indirectly implies the feasibility and necessity for regulatory sandboxing in China's mainland. On the one hand, regulatory sandboxing guides the lawful development of financial innovation, which will alleviate the contradiction between financial stability and innovation, thus promoting the friendly interaction between regulators and regulated subjects. Therefore, it is necessary to introduce regulatory sandboxes in China. On the other hand, the regulatory sandbox model is compatible with China's financial market, regulatory system, financial reform path, and many other factors, which makes it feasible to introduce the model. Currently, cities such as Beijing, Shanghai, Guiyang, and Ganzhou have already started carrying out testing of regulatory sandboxes.

Drawing on the experiences from countries and regions around the world, this paper puts forward some constructive suggestions on the local structure of China's regulatory sandboxes.

Firstly, the "delegated legislation" model should be established. In order to promote regulatory sandboxing in China, the first problem to be solved is the relevant legislative issues. It can only undergo the right operation with the right guidance from laws and regulations. As China's financial regulatory legislation falls under the CPC's exclusive legislative power, in order to make regulatory sandboxing more convenient and faster, it can imitate the practice of the free-trade area and set up a "legal zone" in a specific pilot area. The State Council may adjust the laws according to time and place and suspend some law-mandated administrative approvals on blockchain financial activities. In addition, the legislature in the region shall be granted the right to delegate legislative power and make appropriate adjustments at any time. Furthermore, the relevant legal system shall be localized in terms of four areas: implemented entity, applicable targets, main content, and representation (see Table 6.9).

Table 6.9 Local structure of the legal system for regulatory sandboxing

Main Aspects	Specific Content
Implementing Entity	Regulation of sandboxes in China shall be carried out by the newly established Financial Technology Regulatory Body, which is subordinate to the Financial Stability and Development Committee. However, the People's Bank of China will be responsible for specific operations. It is not recommended to separate the regulatory work between the Banking and Insurance Regulatory Commission and the China Securities Regulatory Commission. It is also not recommended to hand it over to local financial regulatory authorities.
Applicable Target	1. Innovative entities should be limited to financial technology institutions, excluding individuals; technology enterprises, Internet enterprises, or professional financial technology companies with profound technical background must be included in the scope of trial; the scale of the enterprise need not be limited.
	2. Innovative formats: Financial technological formats that allow the legal regulation of sandboxes must meet two conditions—"financial activities developing in China, and development, design, and application should have a substantive association with China" and "substantive, forward-looking, and responsible innovation".

Continued

Main Aspects	Specific Content
Main Content	1. Implement the "No Enforcement Measure Document", and reduce regulatory exclusion in financial technology innovation.
	2. Regulatory authorities may provide separate compliance guidelines on a case-by-case basis and may provide guidelines alongside "One Bank, Two Commissions" (the People's Bank of China, the Banking and Insurance Regulatory Commission, and the China Securities Regulatory Commission).
	3. "Restrictive authorization" and "exemption and modification of rules" are the main features of sandbox regulation.
	4. Protect financial consumers in a static "mandatory standard" and a dynamic "protection and compensation scheme" mechanism.
Representation	The State Council shall formulate administrative regulations on the specific matters related to regulatory sandboxing, specifically including factors such as the implementation entity, applicable targets, qualification for application, regulatory process, system design, exit procedure, consumer protection measures, and legal liabilities. In addition, it shall clearly define the collaborative supervision obligations for One Bank, Two Commissions and other organizations of the State Council.

Source: Sorted according to relevant summarized literature.

Secondly, there is a need to reasonably determine the entry threshold for regulatory sandboxing. When building a regulatory sandbox platform in China, it is necessary to ensure that the tested enterprises are qualified and have good credit conditions. Specifically, it should copy Australia's practice. For enterprises with better credit and possessing financial business qualifications, they can extend further into the approved business scope and are permitted to enter the sandbox. At the same time, in regards to the registration and approval processes for the financial innovation business, the enterprises will be given the right to engage in financial businesses. Regulatory authorities will be undergoing strict regulations. Due to the high administrative management characteristic of the financial market in China, the case-by-case approval method is currently not feasible.

Thirdly, the sandbox exit mechanism should be developed in detail. Due to the limited resources of sandboxes, in order to achieve a reasonable allocation of resources, there is a need to develop a clear and feasible sandbox exit plan. This includes criteria for relevant components such as test duration and feasibility. For enterprises with maxed-out test periods or with non-innovative or non-feasible products, they should exit the sandbox in a timely manner. The responsibility to set specific criteria shall be handed to the regulatory authorities. The regulatory authorities must act in accordance with the law in the process of implementation to ensure that all enterprises are treated fairly.

In the process of promoting the localization of regulatory sandboxes in China, we must pay attention to the many challenges that come with it. Regulatory sandboxing is not the perfect financial regulation system. It also has potential risks. Firstly, test failures will lead to serious consequences. The test requires high-cost support. When faced with a failure, the test enterprise is unable to compensate for the relevant losses of the tested subject. Moreover, the long test cycle will cause the financial product to miss the best time to enter the market, thus affecting the credibility of the regulator. Secondly, the authenticity of the test results is to be discussed. The regulatory sandbox has eased regulatory constraints so that the test environment cannot simulate the real financial market environment, so it is possible to underestimate the financial risks it faces during the product promotion.

Section 4   Risks of Digital Finance and Risk Prevention and Control

4.1 Risks faced in digital finance

4.1.1 The authenticity of big data is difficult to guarantee

The authenticity of big data is difficult to guarantee, thus reducing the effectiveness of test results. The source of big data is very broad, including online searches, electronic platform transaction data, public platform interaction, etc., which makes it more comprehensive, timely, and transparent compared with traditional statistical data. However, in many situations, it is impossible to determine data authenticity. If there appears to be data falsification, the results from the risk control model will deviate from the real situation, and there will be serious mistakes in risk management decision-making. For example, some financing entities will commit fraud in order to meet loan conditions or obtain higher loan amounts. There might even be imitations of other entities, which will bring difficulties for financial supervision.

4.1.2 Challenges from digital currencies

(1) Digital currencies based on blockchain technology will face the risk of decentralization

Most digital currencies use shared blockchains. Under the influence of different consensus plugins, different digital currencies show different degrees of decentralization in aspects such as currency distribution and transfer, currency information recording, currency system maintenance, etc.[1] The varying degrees of decentralization undoubtedly increase the difficulty of financial regulation. In the traditional financial format, the risk is mainly spread within the financial system and seeps into real economy. However, in the decentralized system, financial risks are often spread throughout the whole network at a more rapid speed and affect a continuously increasing range, increasing the destructivity of risks.

---

[1] Da Ke (2019). Reflection and reconstruction of the regulatory approach of digital currency—from "the law of money" to "the currency as law". *Business research*, 07: 133-142.

(2) Risks due to the high anonymity of digital currencies

The encryption algorithm in blockchains gives digital currencies their anonymity. Anonymity prevents regulators from being able to track the specific situation of digital transactions. This allows illegal and criminal activities, such as evasion of tax and capital control, asset transfer, and ICO and asset scams, to become more rampant. This will further damage the investor's relevant profits. In addition, when digital currency exchanges are hacked and a large number of digital currencies are stolen, the irreversibility and anonymity of the transaction activities prevent owners from recovering their own assets through any means including by law. This results in heavy losses, and regulators face even greater regulatory pressure.

4.1.3 Greater difficulty in seeking regulatory paths to balance financial innovation and financial stability

In order to avoid external regulatory constraints, financial institutions adopt various innovative financial instruments, trading methods, financial products, etc., to obtain extra profits. However, this comes with an increase in systemic risks, leading to an increase in the risk of a financial crisis.

The role of government regulators lies in preventing the risks that may arise in excessive financial innovation. They also have to promote the stable operation of financial markets. In the face of financial innovation, regulators will constantly adjust the regulation control. However, when financial regulation is too strict, it will lead to the decline of corporate profits. In cases like this, both parties are in a mutually enhancing and mutually restraining relationship. This will result in a continuous, dynamic game process of "innovation - regulation - innovation again - regulation again". Then, it is possible for innovation and regulation to achieve a balance in the continuous game dynamics and a win-win situation. However, there is currently a clear imbalance between financial innovation and financial stability, and the latter is the optimal choice made by regulators when formulating policies. Policymakers not only have to consider realizing the stability and control of financial markets and meeting the requirements of the central bank's requirement for "financial deleveraging", but also have to pay attention to ensuring the sustainability of financial innovation. In addition, they need to prevent disruptions to normal market operations. Such multiple contradictions are one of the difficult challenges faced by regulators.

4.1.4 Traditional neutral financial regulators are weak in digital financial regulation

Traditional financial regulation mainly revolves around commercial banks, policy banks, securities companies, insurance companies, and other financial institutions. They have detailed regulatory requirements for them in terms of capital funds, interest-rate caps, auditing, and financial information disclosure. For financing guarantee companies, small-loan companies, limited partnership private equity investment funds, and other non-financial institutions, they are not subject to regulation from financial regulators (One Bank, Two Commissions). Only some local governments and industry associations may be in charge of regulation, but it is also possible to not even have self-regulation. In the rapidly developing environment for digital finance, the centralized traditional financial regulation shows obvious disadvantages. Chaos in the financial sector will surface, such as loopholes in regulatory perimeters resulting in regulatory failures and financial risks spreading uncontrollably. All of these will adversely affect the stability of financial markets.

4.1.5 Impact of the mixed operation model on the separated regulatory system

At present, the financial regulatory system in China still falls under separate regulations. On the one hand, the scope of financial regulation is narrow. It overemphasizes the management and legal compliance of market access conditions in financial institutions, and it does not pay enough attention to risk control in enterprises' operations and the handling of problematic financial institutions. On the other hand, the regulatory authorities are all independent, which causes data to be scattered. When the sharing system was implemented, this greatly hindered the availability and completeness of regulatory information.

Digital financial service platforms provide comprehensive financial services. It is very common for the same platform to carry out different businesses such as peer-to-peer lending, investment, insurance, and so on. The trend of a mixed-business model in digital financial institutions and products makes innovated financial instruments and products more complex. In this case, it will result in regulatory gaps and overlaps. Regulatory institutions will fall into dispute and adversely affect regulatory efficiency. As a result, the current separated regulatory model is no longer suitable for digital financial development. Different financial regulatory institutions should strengthen cooperation with each other. In addition, due to the transnationality of digital technology and the globalization of financial services, regulatory coordination is no longer only restricted to a country. An all-round regulatory system is also needed to strengthen international communication.

4.1.6 Digital finance improving the difficulty of regulating anti-money laundering

Digital finance provides financial services to low-income groups through digital forms, allowing those excluded from traditional financial institutions to obtain financial support. This is beneficial for financial inclusivity and promotes the inclusive growth of the economy. However, digital financial institutions have yet to perfect risk control and management in financial decision-making in terms of loans, investment, insurance, etc. They do not have complete control over information related to enterprise operations and personal credit. There is a need for a uniform platform to share comprehensive financial regulatory information across the country and a need for another one for risk detection and warning. In terms of transaction evaluation and process, there is still a lack of substantial testing, thus creating a risk of information asymmetry. Hence, the risks in anti-money laundering and tackling terrorist financing will be increased.

Moreover, the high anonymity of digital currencies also makes anti-money laundering even more challenging. The slow development of big data risk control and the rapid development of digital currencies have put great regulatory pressure on regulatory authorities to deal with anti-money laundering.

4.2 Risk prevention and control in digital finance

4.2.1 Big data risk control

(1) Research progress of big data risk control in foreign countries

Risk assessment based on big data analysis can support financial decision-making such as loans, investments, and insurance. This makes up for the shortcomings of traditional financial institutions that rely solely on financial data and mortgage assets for risk control. Digital finance uses big data technology for screening, analyzing, and value mining enterprise operations information and personal credit information. It uses frontier technology to establish risk model systems, provide a basis for credit risk assessment, and enhance banks and other credit service institutions' capabilities in risk identification and business credit evaluation for SMEs and individual entities.

The United States has more than 170 years of history in credit reporting. Thus, it has a better performance in risk control compared to other countries. In America, big data risk control is mainly used in the credit rating system in the financial industry. The FICO Credit Score (refer to Table 6.10) is a personal credit risk assessment method developed by Fair Isaac Corporation. It mainly considers factors such as the customer's repayment history, liabilities, duration of credit history, credit product portfolio, newly opened accounts, etc. Usually, the assessment does not consider factors such as race, skin color, occupation, position, address, request for credit report inquiry, etc. ZestFinance uses emerging big data risk control technologies to build a risk control model for multiple loan services. In addition, it also includes non-credit elements in the risk control system and expande its service audience to include customers who have FICO scores of less than 500 and have been rejected by other financial institutions, thus significantly reducing loan default rates. Additionally, Upstart provides credit assessment targeting the young population (especially college students who have just graduated) through supplementary information such as their alma mater, their GPA scores, and the companies they work for.

Table 6.10 FICO score content

Main Constituent Elements	Scope of Assessment
Payment History (35%)	Includes specific reports on all kinds of repayment records for various credit accounts, public records, check deposit records, and overdue payments.
Amounts Owed (30%)	Mainly analyzes how many credit accounts are sufficient, reflecting customers' repayment capacity.

Continued

Main Constituent Elements	Scope of Assessment
Length of Credit History (15%)	Includes the age of the oldest account, the age of the newest account, and the average age of all accounts.
New Credit (10%)	Includes the number of newly opened credit accounts, current number of credit applications, duration of creditor's inquiry on customer's credit, and recent credit status.
Credit Mix (10%)	Includes the type of credit account being held and the number of credit accounts for each type.

Source: Sorted according to information found on the website.

India's Aadhaar (a universal biometrics digital identity database) is a unique 12-digit identifier given to all citizens by the government. It has now involved more than 1.1 billion people in India, with 99.7% coverage. The Aadhaar digital system mainly collects from users a photo, identity card information, 10 fingerprint data, and two iris scans. It then shares the information with banks for risk identification and assessment. In 2018, the government reached an agreement with a large number of financial institutions to allow them to enter the identity database in the form of KYC (know your customer).

For a special group of people like refugees, especially those without actual identification documents such as ID cards or passports, it is difficult to prove their identity and obtain international assistance in other countries. The Finnish Immigration Office and MONI Company have developed a system to provide refugees with prepaid MasterCard that are linked to users' digital identities and the blockchains recording their financial transactions. This helps build data on the refugees' credit history and serves as a reliable credit data source for financial institutions when making financial decisions such as providing loans and insurance.

(2) Big data risk control in Chinese commercial banks

Commercial banks mainly focus on credit inquiry data when it comes to traditional risk control for personal businesses. This hinders business development for the group without credit reports. With the development of information technology and the popularization of mobile interconnectivity, behavioral data such as customers' consumption, travel, and communication can be obtained through mobile terminals such as Taobao, Jingdong, and Meituan. These terminals serve as rich databases for big data risk control. The intellectualization of commercial banks includes the above-mentioned non-credit behaviors data into the system. By relying on new algorithms such as big data and machine learning, it can mine into the relevance between customers' non-credit behaviors data and potential risks. This broadens the radius for commercial banks' risk control and enriches the customers' risk profile as well as the dimension for risk identification. In addition, smart risk control can also capture the information dimension that banks were unable or had difficulty to actualize. For example, by using social media, device data, and neural network technology, smart risk control can identify fraudulent applications and transactions. At the same time, the data it uses has a new characteristic of being high-frequency. This helps commercial banks quickly capture changes in a customer's risk characteristics and make timely financial adjustments.

In the individual retail business, commercial banks use AI technology, big data, facial recognition, cloud computing, etc., to construct 360-degree profiles of customers. Yang Jun (2018) proposes carefully examining individual customers' credit from three dimensions (as shown in Table 6.11). For enterprise financing businesses, big data and other related technologies can be used to establish a smart early warning monitoring system for enterprise customers. The system can obtain real-time data about the enterprise, such as its financial condition, litigations, public opinion, and announcements, as well as information such as the industry the enterprise is in. This actualizes the monitoring of the whole industry chain and uses AI decision making for risk warning. With the continuous accumulation of bank system data, it can also conduct a correlation analysis of various risk warning signals and default probabilities. This helps identify various indicators related to corporate default, continuously optimize the bank credit evaluation model, and improve the accuracy of decision-making and loan recovery rates.

Table 6.11 Individual retail business credit reporting system in commercial banks

Evaluation Dimension	Specific Indicator	Detailed Scope
Front-end Credit Capacity	Repayment Capacity	Emphasizes analyzing individual credit information, bank statements, consumption, asset strength, etc.
	Willingness to Repay	Mainly includes information verification, blacklist comparison, fraud screening, multi-head borrowing, etc.
Rear-end Investment Capacity	Objective Financial Capabilities	Analyzes personal basic information, asset information, investment behavior, consumption behavior, and other aspects.
	Risk Appetite	Focuses on individual investment planning, investment experience, cognitive level, risk sensitivity, etc.
Side Anti-money Laundering Investigation	—	Enhances customer identification and transaction monitoring.

Source: Jun Yang (2018). The value and development of risk control in the new era. *China finance*, 02: 87-88.

(3) Big data risk control on China online loan platforms

P2P is short for "Online-Peer-to-Peer Lending", which is the actualization of lending between individual entities or between an entity and an enterprise via the Internet. P2P online loans have developed relatively rapidly in China in recent years. However, investors are generally weaker in reviewing financiers' repayment situations according to their history, credit reports, and assets condition. Besides, each platform has varying capacities in credit reporting. On top of that, there is a lack of industry self-discipline. From 2015 to 2019, there were increasing cases of problematic platforms (refer to Figure 6.9 for more details).

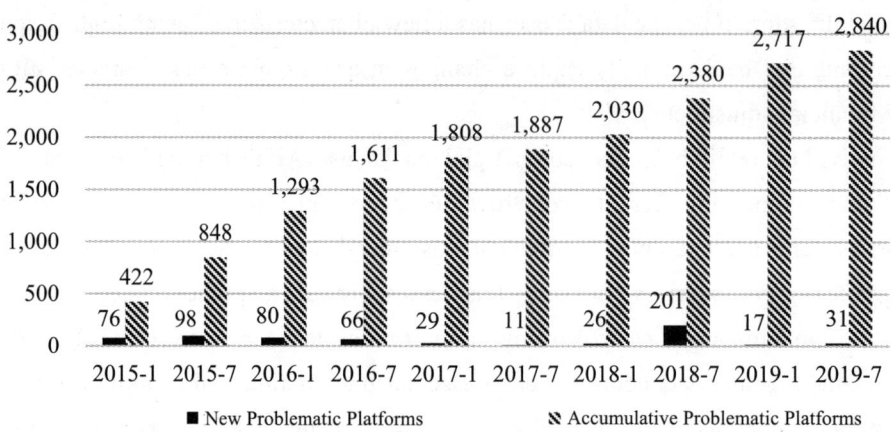

Figure 6.9 Number of problematic platforms

Source: WDZJ.

Currently, some online loan platforms have started cooperation with third-party credit bureaus such as Sesame Credit, Tencent Credit Services, and AnRong Credit. Some online loan platforms even tried self-building credit reporting systems. The current main task of China's credit bureaus is to screen and analyze customer data for online loan platforms (refer to Table 6.12). On January 4, 2018, the People's Bank of China issued a notice on its official website stating that it would officially accept applications for personal credit reporting businesses from Baihang (in preparation) and formally mark the beginning of the credit data integration era. "Credlink" is a credit reporting alliance and is recognized as the official individual credit bureau. It is led by the National Internet Finance Association of China (NIFA), which occupies 36% of its shares. Each of the eight other individual pilot credit bureaus such as Sesame Credit, Tencent Credit Services, and Qianhai Zhengxin holds 8%. Before the establishment of "Credlink", the above institutions monopolized the credit reporting market and formed an oligopoly market. This resulted in the inaccuracy and low coverage of credit data. The forming of "Credlink" integrates the data from all institutions and has helped to create a more realistic and complete customer profile, thus enhancing the development of big data risk control.

Table 6.12 An overview of certain big data credit bureaus

Credit Bureaus	Evaluation Dimensions	Data Source	List of Partner Platforms
Sesame Credit	Identity traits, contractual capacity, credit history, interpersonal relationship, behavior preference	Alibaba e-commerce data, Ant Financial Internet financial data, data from public security network and other partners	Xinwang Baoku, WangShang Credit, Laifenqi, etc.
Tencent Credit Services	Contract fulfillment, security, wealth, consumption, social activities	User social communication data (only with user authorization), consumption and credit on WeChat Mini Programs, and other data	China Rapid Finance

Credit Bureaus	Evaluation Dimensions	Data Source	List of Partner Platforms
AnRong Credit	Dimensions such as multi lending, expiry, blacklist, attribute association, fraud, justice, etc.	Integrate credit data from public security, judicature, business, education background UnionPay, e-commerce, etc.	www.jysp2p.com, www.yrd100.com, www.bxjr.com
Qianhai Zhengxin	Social credit, contract fulfillment capacity, spending power	Enterprise and individual customers of Ping An Group, as well as records of Ping An Bank and Ping An Insurance	www.bxjr.com, otouzi.com, lufax.com

Source: Assorted data from information gathered online.

4.2.2 Regulatory technology

(1) Regulatory technology development in foreign countries

Regulatory technology refers to applying new technologies to the existing regulatory process to achieve more effective risk identification, risk evaluation, regulatory requirements, data analysis, and other activities. This helps minimize corresponding cost expenditure. Countries around the world have already begun to actively use regulatory technology products.

The FCA was the first to propose regulatory technology as the product of the organic integration of technology and financial regulation. Regulatory technology is based on data collection, complex data analyses, and even greater data storage capacity. Compared with traditional regulation, regulatory technology has four advantages: the agility to rapidly decouple and combine big data, generate a solution in a timely manner, combine the different requirements into one uniform compliance standard, and intellectualize information mining and analysis. Currently, it is already being applied in various fields such as regulatory data management, real-time monitoring of financial transactions, scenario simulation and prediction, implementation of KYC principles, and machine interpretation of regulatory rules.

Currently, the application of regulatory technology in trade-reporting systems and anti-money-laundering monitoring systems in exchanges has become relatively mature. Regulators can detect abnormal transactions in a timely manner through real-time monitoring of the transaction reporting system. It can then decide whether to take action to control them. In addition, regulators can use the anti-money-laundering system to monitor the flow and quantity of currencies in real time to ensure the orderly operation of the currency market. In 2009, the United States Securities and Exchange Commission (SEC) established the Economic and Risk Analysis Department to study how to use data to improve regulation. Afterward, the SEC also used the Market Information Data Analytics System to monitor high-frequency transactions in real time.

The United States Financial Industry Regulatory Authority (FINRA) uses the SONAR (Securities Observation, News Analysis, and Regulation) system to detect potential insider trading and misleading trading behaviors. This system can handle 10,000 messages every day, assess the price model of 25,000 securities, generate 10-60 pieces of warning information, and effectively improve the efficiency and quality of regulation.

In 2014, the British government announced in its 2015 budget that the Financial Conduct Authority (FCA) and Prudential Regulation Authority (PRA) will jointly promote the development of regulatory technology. In April 2016, the FCA issued the 2017-2018 Business Plan and clearly proposed the development plan for regulatory technology in the next two years. It sent out a wide invitation to regulatory technology-related entities to participate in the TechSprint conference. As of now, the British NatWest Bank has conducted quantum calculation testing in order to improve efficiency in solving problems. The hardware used in the test is Fujitsu's Digital Annealer, and the quantum software is provided by 1QBit. The calculation model runs at 300 times the speed of a traditional computer. This test helps investment managers decide on the correct components in an asset portfolio. In addition, Standard Chartered Bank's subsidiary SC Ventures participated in the Series A round of financing held by regulatory technology start-up Silent Eight. The company mainly uses artificial intelligence technologies to monitor the financing of anti-money laundering and counter-terrorism. Standard Chartered Bank uses the company's technology to screen potential customers and avoid high-risk enterprises and customers.

On March 16, 2016, the Financial Stability Board (FSB) held its 16th meeting in Japan. Regulatory technology was formally incorporated into the meeting agenda. Afterward, subsidiary committees in industries such as banking, securities, and insurance all accelerated their research in the field of regulatory technology.

The Austrian Oesterreichische Nationalbank (OeNB) has developed a data software platform in which banks can submit the industry's single contracts, loans, deposits, and other data. This collection method based on data input changes information-reporting methods that were based on static templates in the past. This increases regulatory efficiency significantly. In the past, the supervision of regulatory agencies is mainly reflected in the regular examination of the reports submitted by financial institutions. In such a situation, there is the possibility of human alteration of data in financial institutions. This platform effectively curbs this behavior, allowing regulators to be more timely, accurate, and objective in making their assessment of financial institutions' risk status.

At present, the research on the application of regulatory technology has gradually increased in popularity in various countries and regions around the world. By 2019, the financial regulatory authorities of several major economies such as Australia, Canada, Ireland, and Singapore have designated institutions to oversee the policy research, planning, coordination, etc., of regulatory technology works. The focus is on the risk guidance of regulatory arbitrage, aimed at promoting the incubation and development of financial technology industries. In addition, on a global scale, some regulators have also developed compliance systems to monitor the compliance of staff behavior in real time. They use this indicator as a reference factor for regulatory authorities to approve licenses and businesses.

(2) Regulatory technology development in China

In May 2017, the People's Bank of China set up a financial technology committee. It emphasized strengthening the application of regulatory technology and enriching financial regulatory means through the active use of big data, artificial intelligence, cloud computing, and other technologies. In 2018, the China Securities Regulatory Commission officially implemented the Regtech General Establishment Plan, marking the Commission's completion of the top-level design for regulatory technology construction work, and it has entered the full implementation stage. At present, Internet finance giants and network banks have applied a large number of regulatory technologies in customer credit evaluation models and the KYC field. These phenomena indicate that China's regulatory technology is developing at a rapid momentum and has a promising future.

At present, the technical departments of banks and payment institutions are still taking the lead in financial technology development. Of these, 14.89% of banks and 10.26% of payment institutions have set up dedicated financial technology departments. The main way for banks to develop financial technology businesses is through external cooperation and internal incubation in work units. Meanwhile, payment institutions are mainly going for external incubation. In addition, financial technology investments are relatively higher in banks than in payment institutions. Banks are also relatively doing better in financial technology standard system construction, but there are still gaps.

From the perspective of the application of technological development, there are more institutions involved in big data, and their development speed is the fastest. There are relatively more institutions involved in cloud computing, artificial intelligence, and distributed databases, and their development speed is relatively slower. There are fewer institutions involved in blockchain, the Internet of Things, and 5G, and their development speed is the slowest. From the perspective of institution type, in general, banks are involved in more areas than payment institutions. Their use of financial technology has enhanced many areas, of which the most is in improving risk-monitoring models to monitor suspicious transactions.

However, according to Deloitte's research report, it was found that most of the enterprises in the field of regulatory technology are distributed in Europe and America. China still faces many problems in applying regulatory technology and needs to be constantly improved. In the future, solutions for regulatory technologies need standardization, which will help spread out development costs. However, it is clear that the standardization of regulatory technology is difficult to realize in the short term. First, regulatory data has not been standardized. This will affect the accuracy and comparability of relevant indicators. Second, standardization has high requirements for technical safety, and studying it takes a long time. Third, standardization plans cannot be chosen through administrative means and need to be determined through the market-based competitive survival mechanism. However, this process is lengthy.

Chapter 7 Digital Economy and the Labor Market

In recent years, with the vigorous development of digital economy with digital knowledge and information as the key factor of production, new technologies, new formats, and new models have emerged one after another, becoming a new engine that drives economic growth. Countries around the world place the development of digital economy as an important strategy to promote economic development, further promote the integration of the innovative achievements of digital economy into different fields of real economy, and deploy competition and cooperation around the new round of technology and industrial commanding heights. The strategy of developing digital economy has been elevated to national competitiveness and has been promoted by the national strategic deployment. Currently, the world is at a critical point for a new round of technological revolution and industrial transformation. Digital technologies such as the Internet of Things, big data, cloud computing, and artificial intelligence are constantly changing. Digital economy, with data resources as an important factor of production and total factor digital transformation as the major driving force, is booming. Employment in digital economy is accelerating, with new models and new business formats constantly emerging. As digital economy has an expansion effect on employment in new business formats, it also has a substitution effect on employment in traditional industries. Meanwhile, the development of digital economy empowers workers with more choices and freedom, and generates many new flexible employment forms, forming an innovation effect in employment. The combination of multiple effects forms a huge impact on the scale and structure of the supply and demand of the traditional labor market.

This chapter analyzes the multiple impacts and impact mechanisms of the development of digital economy on the labor market. We will also analyze the impact of digital economy on the supply and demand of the Chinese and international labor markets, and analyze the relationship between digital economy and employment. Based on the research conclusions, we will propose policy recommendations from the perspectives of the government, enterprises, and individuals to stay tuned to the impact of the development of digital economy on the labor market.

Section 1 Typical Characteristics of the Labor Market in the Digital Economy Era

1.1 Employment characteristics of digital economy

1.1.1 Scale of employment

Digital economy is a new form of economy following the agricultural economy and the industrial economy. On the one hand, the Internet, E-commerce, software, communications, and IT services create a large number of new jobs in digital economy. On the other hand, traditional employment fields are also seeking digital transformation, which will generate new employment opportunities. The top two countries for digital economic development are the US and China. Their total digital economy in 2017 was 11.5 trillion dollars and 4.02 trillion dollars respectively. The scale of employment in digital economy in the two countries is also increasing. According to data released by the US Bureau of Economic Analysis (BEA), digital economy supported 5.1 million jobs in the US in 2017, accounting for 3.3% of the total 152.1 million jobs, and the average annual salary of employees employed in digital economy was 132,223 dollars, significantly higher than the average annual salary of 68,506 dollars for the overall employment. Figure 7.1 shows the employment status in China's digital economy from 2007 to 2017. It suggests that in terms of both absolute and relative employment, employment in digital economy grew rapidly. By 2017, employment in digital economy accounted for 22.1% of the overall employment. According to the "White Paper on China's Digital Economic Development and Employment (2018)", the number of employees in digital economy in China in 2018 was 191 million, and digital economy employment accounted for 24.6% of the total employment, continuing its growth after 2017.

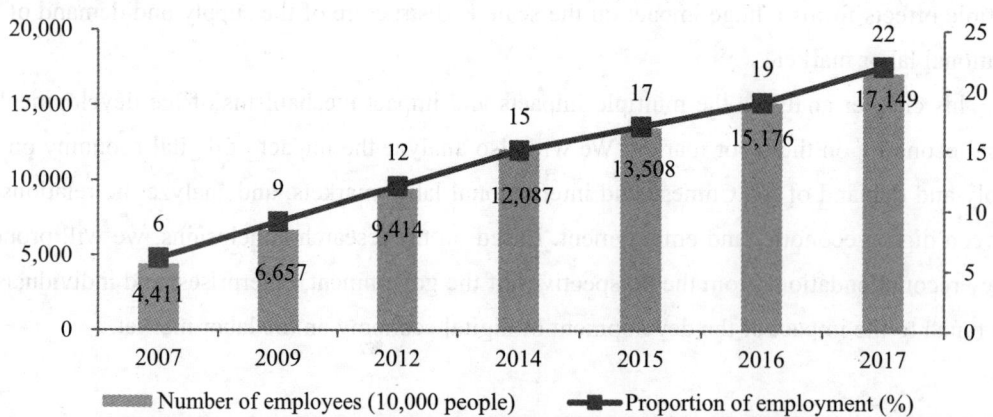

Figure 7.1 2007-2017 overview of China's digital economy employment

Source: China Academy of Information and Communications Technology, "White Paper on China's Digital Economic Development and Employment 2018".

1.1.2 Employment structure

In terms of the industrial structure of employment, the tertiary industry is the main force to absorb employment. In 2017, the digital transformation of China's tertiary industry absorbed about 120.16 million workers, accounting for 34.3% of the total employment in the tertiary industry, significantly higher than the primary industry (7.8%) and the secondary industry (22.4%); the proportion of employment in the digital transformation of the primary, secondary, and tertiary industries all increased, of which the tertiary industry increased by about 4% year-on-year, higher than the primary and secondary industries.[①]

Changes in the industrial structure of employment are associated with industrial attributes. For the primary industry, with the popularization of new-generation artificial intelligence technologies such as robots, agriculture will be large-scale, intensive, and intelligent, and the productivity will increase accordingly, releasing more agricultural labor. The digital transformation of the secondary industry has great potential for attracting labor. The manufacturing industry has low transaction costs, high proportion of fixed assets, high technology intensity, etc. Therefore, digital transformation is not easy. Currently, there are few workers with related digital knowledge and skills, which increases the difficulty of transformation. In contrast, the tertiary industry, with high transaction costs, low proportion of fixed assets, and low technology intensity, is able to carry out digital transformation easier. Meanwhile, the combination of big data, artificial intelligence, and other technologies with the consumer service industry promotes the development of high-end consumer service industries such as elderly care, sports and health, and education and training. The significant rise in the demand for service drives the increase in the demand for employment. From the perspective of employment, within the services, industry, and agriculture, the development of digital economy varies.

Table 7.1 Proportion of digital economy in typical sectors of each industry in 2017

Service industry	Proportion of digital economy	Industry	Proportion of digital economy	Agriculture	Proportion of digital economy
Insurance	49.30%	Transmission, distribution, and control equipment	24.20%	Forest products	11.30%
Radio, TV, and film production and recording	48.50%	Metal processing machinery	21.30%	Fishery industry	8.80%
Capital market services	42.90%	Ships and related devices	19.30%	Agricultural products	6.80%

---

① Source: China Academy of Information and Communications Technology

Continued

Service industry	Proportion of digital economy	Industry	Proportion of digital economy	Agriculture	Proportion of digital economy
Monetary finance and other financial services	42.90%	Batteries	16.30%	Livestock products	4.10%
Specialized technical services	42.40%	Railway transportation and urban rail transport equipment	15.70%		
Public management and social organization	40.50%	Material handling equipment	13.40%		
Postal	37.70%	Whole automobile	10.70%		
Education	35.30%	Special equipment for chemical, wood, and non-metal processing	10.60%		
Social security	34.40%	Steel, iron, and castings	8.90%		
Leases	33.20%	Coking products	8.80%		

Source: China Academy of Information and Communications Technology, "White Paper on China's Digital Economic Development and Employment (2018)".

Table 7.1 shows that compared with the consumer service industries represented by the accommodation and catering industries, the proportion of digital economy in producer service industries, represented by finance, technology, and other industries, is higher. The reason may be that most of the producer service industries are capital- and technology-intensive industries. The input of ICT-related capital and technology is relatively high, thus having a significant facilitating effect on the output of industries. Consumer service industries are mostly labor-intensive industries. Although the capital and technology investment related to ICT is relatively small, it may play a greater role in driving employment. Compared with the light industry sector that provides consumption materials such as wood and castings, the digital transformation of the heavy industry sector that provides production materials, such as shipping and railway industries, is faster. The proportion of digital economy in all sectors in agriculture is relatively low. The potential for digital development of agriculture is significant.

In terms of the regional structure of employment, on the one hand, with rapid technological innovation and the decline of production costs, digital economy will promote the regional transfer of industries, and the regional structure of labor will be adjusted accordingly. From a global perspective, developed countries are usually equipped with foundations and innovative capabilities for developing digital economy, which is in sharp contrast to low- and middle-income countries where the penetration rate of the Internet remains low. Among the world's 7.4 billion people, 4.2 billion have no access to the Internet, and the majority of these people are in developing and emerging countries (in India, China, and Nigeria, the proportions are 80%, 55%, and 61% of their population, respectively). In addition, the previous advantages of low- and middle-income countries are mainly their low labor costs. This advantage may be weakened by the widespread application of artificial intelligence and other technologies. Therefore, in the context of digital economy, advantageous industries will be transferred from low- and middle-income countries to developed countries, and from underdeveloped regions to developed regions, becoming the driving force for the flow of labor across countries and regions. On the other hand, developing countries used to be a global human-resource pool with multi-level labor resources, but the existence of immigration barriers has hindered the flow of labor to developed countries and regions. The extensive application of intelligent interconnection technology and the rapid development of platform economics enable workers in low- and middle-income countries to enter the labor market of developed countries and regions without immigration, providing efficient and convenient conditions for labor to flow to developed countries and regions.

In terms of the skill structure, on the one hand, knowledge and information are key factors of production in the digital economy era. For the employed, digital skills have become fundamental abilities, just like listening, speaking, reading, and writing. In 2011, the European Commission defined the "digital skills", which "involves the confident and critical use of Information Society Technology (IST) for work, leisure, learning, and communication. It is underpinned by basic skills in ICT: the use of computers to retrieve, access, store, produce, present, and exchange information, and to communicate and participate in collaborative networks via the Internet." The pressing problem in the current labor market is a mismatch between supply and demand. The rapid development of digital economy requires highly digitally-skilled talents, and the shortage of such talents leads to the shortage of top digital talents and talents who combine digital technology and industry experience. Training of digital talents with primary skills also lags behind the growing demand. "The Digital Transformation of Chinese Economy: Talents and Employment" divides digital talents into six categories: digital strategic management, in-depth analysis, product R&D, advanced manufacturing, digital operations, and digital marketing. The shortage of digital talents in product R&D is 87.5%, which has an overwhelming advantage. Digital operations account for about 7%, while advanced manufacturing and digital marketing account for less than 1%. Currently, big data, business intelligence, and other fields are developing rapidly, but still with a huge shortage of talents.

On the other hand, the labor force can be divided into three levels: high-skilled, medium-skilled, and low-skilled. The skill structure of employment will change with the development of digital economy. There will be two types of technological progress in digital economy: deskilling-biased progress and skill-biased technical progress. Deskilling-biased progress will increase the demand for low-skilled labor, while skill-biased technical progress will increase the demand for high-skilled labor. These two types of technological progress will polarize jobs. The employment rate of high-skilled and low-skilled jobs will increase, while the employment rate of medium-skilled jobs will decline, and gradually be separated and rejected by the labor market. The World Bank also pointed out in the "World Development Report 2016: Digital Dividends" that one of the future trends in the global labor market is that the skill structure of employment will be polarized.

1.1.3 Forms of employment

Internet information technology and Internet platforms break the boundaries of traditional organizations and lower the threshold for individuals to enter the economy. Individuals are able to engage in economic activities without entering traditional enterprises. Flexible employment forms such as self-employment, freelance employment, and part-time employment are emerging. The 2016 McKinsey Global Institute's "Independent Work: Choice, Necessity, and the Gig Economy" pointed out that there were 162 million people in Europe and the US engaging in independent work, accounting for 20%-30% of the total working-age population. In "Future Employment 2018" released by the World Economic Forum in 2018, it is predicted that the content, location, and form of future work will undergo tremendous changes. If the value can be achieved with the help of platforms on the basis of "on-demand gathering and dispersion", enterprises would choose temporary workers, freelancers, or specialized contractors. Stable full-time job opportunities will become fewer and fewer.

Compared with traditional employment, flexible employees have greater power in decision-making, and have greater flexibility in the location, hours, and content of their work; and the labor relationship is no longer a long-term and stable one, but rather a part-time, market transaction or cooperation relationship. The short-term relationships also mean that flexible employees have to take greater risks.

Compared with traditional flexible employment, flexible employment in the context of digital economy relies on technologies and platforms to break the limitations where individuals have to work locally in fringe fields. Flexible employment gradually becomes an independent choice of workers rather than a forced choice. Meanwhile, the scope of flexible employment has expanded from traditional trade and circulation areas to diversified areas such as express delivery and sharing economy; the proportion of highly educated workers in flexible employment has increased significantly, especially in the field of knowledge payment, while most of the traditional flexible employees are low-educated and low-skilled.

1.2 Scale and measurement of employment in digital economy

While digital economy brings many benefits, it also generates adverse effects. One of the issues that receive much attention is its replacement of existing jobs. The substitution effect will make current employees lose their jobs. For example, the widespread application of intelligent robots may make those who do labor-intensive and highly-repetitive work lose their jobs; the advantages of the low fixed costs of E-commerce will have an impact on physical stores. The closure of physical stores also means that the corresponding staff will face unemployment. Some authorities make predictions related to the substitution of employment. The "2016 Global Human Capital Report" released by the World Economic Forum pointed out that seven million jobs worldwide will disappear in 2020, and 65% of elementary school pupils will eventually engage in a new career that doesn't exist yet. The World Bank predicts in the "World Development Report 2016: Digital Dividends" that in the future, 55%-77% of jobs in China and 43%-69% of jobs in India will be replaced due to low skills, while the replacement ratio of jobs in OECD countries will be 57%. In the "World Development Report 2019: Changes in the Nature of Work", the World Bank estimates that 47% of careers are at risk of being replaced by automation in the US. This data vividly describes the huge impact of digital economy on the job market, but there are problems: many institutions propose data disclosures and predictions, and the measurement methods of each institution vary. Comparability among data is minimal. In terms of measurement in the digital economy field, one of the major problems is that there is no universally accepted definition of digital economy. When it comes to measuring and predicting the scale of employment in digital economy, institutions adopt differentiated measurement methods due to different understandings of digital economy.

According to a report released by the OECD, on average, ICT-related occupations in OECD countries accounted for approximately 3.5% of all employment in 2013. Countries with the highest and lowest proportions were Finland and Turkey, at 6% and 1% respectively. The difference among countries is mainly due to the different proportions of professionals and engineers in the labor force. In terms of sectors of the ICT industry, the employment rate of ICT manufacturing, publishing, and telecommunications services has been declining in all OECD countries since 2000, while the employment rate of IT and other information technology services has been increasing.

According to the data released, the scale of employment in digital economy that the OECD focuses on is the proportion of ICT-related occupations to the total employment. Therefore, a clearer definition of ICT-related occupations is required. ICT-related occupations involve the development, maintenance, and operation of ICT systems, as well as occupations in which ICT is the main part. According to the latest version of the "International Standard Classification of Occupations" (ISCO-08), this definition specifically includes minor groups 133 (information and communications technology service managers), 215 (electrotechnology engineers), and 742 (electronics and telecommunications installers and repairers). Additionally, there are sub-major groups 25 (information and communications technology professionals) and 35 (information and communications technicians). The employment data by occupation comes from the labor force survey, and the employment data of the US comes from the census.

In "Year 2035: 400 Million Job Opportunities in the Digital Age" released by BCG (Boston Consulting Group), it is estimated that China's overall digital economy in 2015 was close to 1.4 trillion dollars, with a digital economy penetration rate of 13% and a total employment capacity of 113 million people. The report also predicts that in the next 20 years, digital economy will continue to develop vigorously. By 2035, China's overall digital economy will approach 16 trillion dollars, with a digital economy penetration rate of 48% and a total employment capacity of 415 million people.

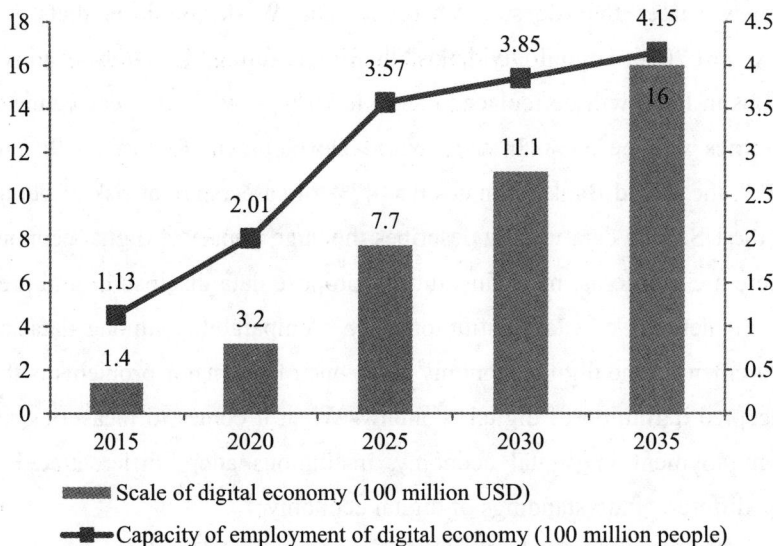

Figure 7.2 China's digital economy and employment from 2015 to 2035
Source: BCG, "Year 2035: 400 Million Job Opportunities in the Digital Age".

BCG adopts the e-GDP method, which was first proposed at the G20 summit in 2011 and is continuously revised in accordance with the development of digital economy. To put it simply, the overall scale of digital economy is quantified into monetary value through corresponding indicators, and all activities related to the creation, production, service provision, and application of digital equipment are evaluated using the expenditure approach. Similar to the expenditure approach of GDP, e-GDP includes consumption expenditure, individual ICT investment expenditure, government ICT expenditure, and the net value of ICT equipment exports, and other forms of digital economy are considered based on actual conditions, such as C2C, represented by Taobao.

Specifically, the content of consumption expenditure refers to all the consumption of individuals to obtain access to the Internet and purchase goods and services through the Internet, such as broadband Internet access fees and purchases of hardware, software and smartphones; personal ICT investment expenditure includes two parts: the capital expenditure of all telecommunications enterprises, and the total private investment in Internet-related ICT; government ICT expenditure also includes two parts: the government's public expenditure for ICT infrastructure construction, and software and service fees needed by the infrastructure construction; the net export value of ICT equipment refers to the difference between the export value and the import value of all ICT-related goods, equipment, and services. After the scale of digital economy is measured using the e-GDP indicator, BCG uses two assumptions for the premise of its prediction: first, the output rate of the labor force in all sectors of e-GDP is the same; second, the average annual growth rate of labor output rate after 2015 is 6%. Based on the above two assumptions to calculate the employment scale driven by digital economy, the formula is:

Total employment capacity in digital economy = scale of digital economy / output rate of labor force.

According to data released by China Academy of Information and Communications Technology, in 2018, the number of jobs in China's digital economy reached 191 million, accounting for 24.6% of the total number of jobs. Taking into account the fact that the total number of employees dropped by 0.07% year-on-year, the number of jobs in digital economy increased by 11.5% year-on-year, a double-digit rapid growth. The number of jobs in digital industrialization reached 12.2 million, a year-on-year increase of 9.4%, and the number of jobs in industry digitalization reached 178 million, a year-on-year increase of 11.6%.

The measurement of the scale of digital economy includes two parts: digital industrialization and industrial digitization. Differences in specific measurement methods remain. The calculation of the scale of digital industrialization is relatively simple, which is to add up all added values of various sectors under the information and communications industry according to the national economic statistics system. This includes the manufacturing, leasing, and sales of electronic information equipment, electronic information transmission services, computer services, and the software industry, as well as emerging industries under the rapid development of digital technology, such as cloud computing, the Internet of Things, big data, Internet finance, etc. The scale of digital industrialization focuses on the increase in output and efficiency brought about by the integration of ICT products and services and traditional industries. The calculation is relatively complicated. The main idea is to separate the contributions of digital technologies in different traditional industries and add these contributions up. It adopts the KLEMS framework. Specifically, it divides the national economy into 139 industries, calculates ICT capital stock, non-ICT capital stock, labor, and intermediate input for each province, and calculates growing accounts and ICT capital stock by industry using mathematical models and corresponding assumptions. Similarly, employment driven by digital economy is divided into two parts: employment driven by digital industrialization, and employment driven by industrial digitalization. The number of job opportunities driven by digital industrialization is calculated by the number of employees in the information and communications industry. The data comes from the "China Labor Statistical Yearbook" and "China Population and Employment Statistics Yearbook". Employment driven by industrial digitalization refers to people engaged in digital transformation in traditional industries. There are no immediate statistics. It needs to be calculated approximately based on industry output, labor productivity of the industry, and the number of employees. The specific formula is:

Employment driven by industrial digitalization = scale of industrial digitalization / average labor productivity of the whole industry.

Based on the above measurement methods, combined with the current development background in which digital economy is extensively integrated with various industries, the employment scale of the broadly-defined digital economy has more advantages than other definitions in terms of the scope, which is conducive to describing the level of integration of digital economy and real economy and better reflecting the impact of digital economy on encouraging new business formats. First, the broad definition is more comprehensive and logical. The core and narrow definitions cannot reflect the penetration effect of digital economy on traditional industries. Ignoring the integration and development of digital economy and the primary, secondary, and tertiary industries will result in low calculation results, which may be contrary to the actual situation in which digital economy develops rapidly. Second, the core and narrow definitions have controversial views about the "core" and "digital sectors", while the broad definition takes direct and indirect impacts of digital economy in the first place, which helps to maintain the intertemporal comparability and sustainability of the measurement. Third, due to the wide scope of the broad definition, the measurement is more complicated. However, the foundation for researching the direct and indirect effects of new technologies on the economy already exists, and its measurement method will be improved and more standardized under the broad definition.

Section 2　The Impact of Digital Economy on the Labor Market

2.1 The impact of digital economy on the scale of labor supply and demand

The impact of digital economy on the scale of labor demand is similar to that of previous technological progress. Scholars divide the impact into "substitution effect" and "creation effect" when they discuss the impact of technological progress on employment. The same approach can be applied when exploring the impact of digital economy on the scale of labor. The difference is that digital economy, based on previous technological advances, acts on the scale of the labor force through compensation effects, bringing more diversified effects.

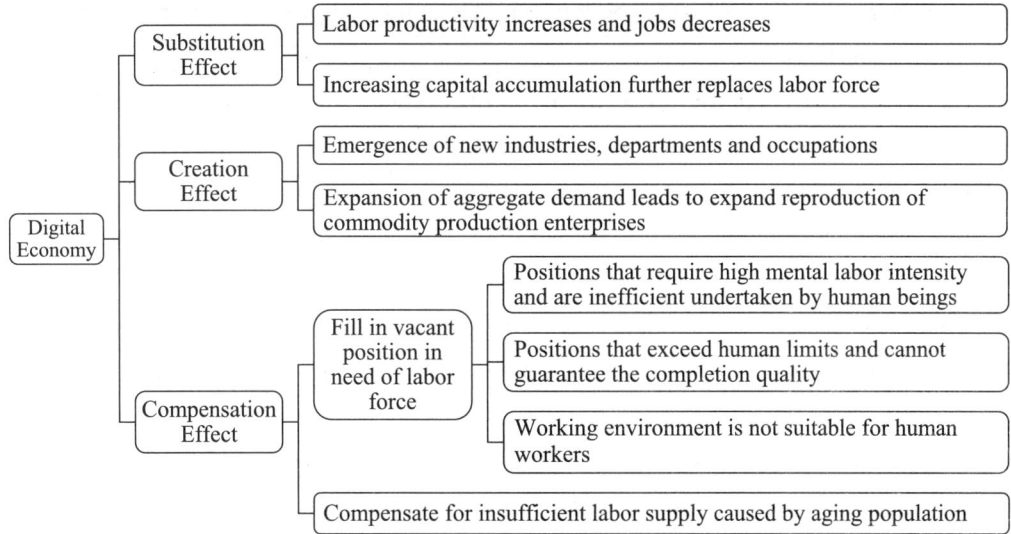

Figure 7.3 The impact of digital economy on the scale of labor supply and demand

2.1.1 Substitution effect of digital economy on the scale of labor supply and demand

Academia defines the development of the new generation of science and technology, represented by artificial intelligence, the Internet of Things, and big data, as the fourth industrial revolution. In history, every industrial revolution brought about major economic changes and the upgrading of industrial sectors and jobs. As an important part of digital economy, artificial intelligence has a more visible substitution effect than previous technological revolutions.①

The substitution effect of digital economy on labor demand is derived from two aspects: labor productivity and capital productivity. On the one hand, the application of big data, cloud computing, artificial intelligence, and the Internet of Things in the industry can increase labor productivity. When the scale of production is constant, jobs will be reduced and labor demand will shrink; on the other hand, the increase of productivity brought about by digital economy means more labor is obtained, thus increasing the accumulation of capital in an industry, and providing an economic foundation for the introduction of a new round of technology. Such a cycle will bring about a further reduction in the scale of labor demand.②

Regarding the development trend of job substitution, the traditional view of technological unemployment still has a strong voice. Some supporters of technological unemployment believe

---

① Cao Jing, Zhou Yalin. Research progress on the impact of artificial intelligence on the economy. *Economic Perspectives*, 2018(01): 103-115.

② Qiu Yue, Du Hui. Research on the influencing factors and mechanisms of artificial intelligence on employment. *Journal of China Institute of Industrial Relations*, 2019, 33(03): 5-14.

that artificial intelligence will replace most jobs in the foreseeable future and will have a negative impact on employment expectations and income distribution.[1] There are also scholars who hold different views: that the risk of work being automated does not mean actual work loss. A more compromised view is that in the long run, technological progress will benefit everyone, but not in the short term.[2]

2.1.2 Creation effect of digital economy on the scale of labor supply and demand

Although digital economy will have a substitution effect on labor demand and lead to some workers losing their jobs, its effects are not all negative. In particular, in the long run, the application of digital economy technology will have a creation effect on labor demand. On the one hand, the development, promotion, and application of new technologies such as big data, cloud computing, and the Internet of Things will have an immediate and positive effect on job opportunities. Digital economy will promote the emergence of new industries, new sectors, and new occupations, which will create massive labor demand. The integration of digital economy and traditional industries will cause some jobs to be replaced by smart machines, but it will also create new jobs and expand the demand for labor during the transformation and upgrading of traditional industries. For example, with the development of artificial intelligence, the demand for intelligent robots will increase. R&D, design, marketing, and other sectors with intelligent robots as the center will emerge and attract many professionals, thereby expanding the scale of employment. On the other hand, as a part of technological progress, digital economy will lead to a rapid increase in labor productivity and accelerate economic growth. Economic growth will lead to a general rise in labor wages, which in turn will increase overall social consumption, i.e., expanding aggregate demand. The expansion of aggregate demand will make enterprises expand the reproduction of goods, thereby expanding the scale of employment.[3] In addition, as digital economy continues to make new breakthroughs, the efficiency of management will improve, enabling industries to increase the scope of management, which will also bring about the expansion of labor demand.[4]

Acemoglu proposes that although automation reduces jobs, it also generates new job opportunities by creating new tasks. Newly created jobs include two parts: one is the increase in labor demand due to the increasing business volume because of the application of artificial intelligence; the other is new types of jobs generated by artificial intelligence.[5] Ji Wenwen and

---

[1] Trajtenberg M. (2018). AI as the Next GPT: A Political-Economy Perspective. Nber Working Paper. No. 24245.

[2] Cortes G.M., Jaimovich N., Nekarda C.J., Siu H.E. (2014). The Micro and Macro of Disappearing Routine Jobs: A Flows Approach. Nber Working Paper No. 20307.

[3] Yin Zhenyu, Wu Chuanqi. The employment effect of artificial intelligence and its inspirations for China. *Reform and Strategy*, 2019, 35(02): 90-97.

[4] Qiu Yue, Du Hui. Research on the influencing factors and mechanisms of artificial intelligence on employment. *Journal of China Institute of Industrial Relations*, 2019, 33(03): 5-14.

[5] Acemoglu D., Restrepo P. (2017). Robots and Jobs: Evidence from US Labor Markets. Nber Working Paper No. 23285.

Lai Desheng point out that the efficient allocation of information would overcome the limitations of time and space, allowing more people to participate and generating new jobs.[①] Zhang Chenggang believes that new employment forms with digital economy as the foundation can not only create more jobs, but also increase employment opportunities for disadvantaged groups.[②] Wang Jun and Yang Wei also point out that the impact of new technological progress, such as artificial intelligence, on total employment is expansive and will help improve the quality of work.[③]

2.1.3 Compensation effect of digital economy on the scale of labor supply and demand

Unlike traditional technological progress, digital economy has a compensation effect on the scale of labor supply and demand. On the one hand, artificial intelligence can fill in many vacant positions so as to complete the entire economic chain, thereby making up for the supply of labor. The vacant positions include the following categories: First, positions with such a high intensity of mental work that if humans took these positions the efficiency would be very low, such as scanning and recognition of surveillance images; second, positions beyond the limits of human senses and response, humans thus cannot guarantee the quality of completion, such as inspection and testing of precision instruments; third, positions where the working environment is not suitable for human, such as on a spacecraft for deep space exploration.[④] If these positions are intelligent and automated during the process of digitalization, the demand for labor will be reduced, and the shortage of labor supply will be alleviated.

On the other hand, digital economy can compensate for the lack of labor supply caused by the aging of population. Currently, while the global population growth rate slows down, the aging degree increases rapidly. Labor shortage is about to become a common problem for global economic and social development. With the intensification of the aging problem, the scale of labor supply will be further reduced in the future. The improvement of school education and vocational education will change the skill structure of the labor force. Workers are inclined to choose jobs with higher skill requirements and higher wages, which will result in an insufficient supply of low-skilled jobs. However, in the context of digital economy, the radius of the traditional labor market expands greatly, which means it is more tolerant to workers. The emergence of new forms of employment enables the labor force to obtain more flexible and fair employment opportunities, and increases the employment participation rate. With the help of

---

① Ji Wenwen, Lai Desheng. Influence Mechanisms and Practical Analysis of Employment in the Network Platform to Industrial Relations. *Journal of China University of Labor Relations*, 2016, 30(04): 6-16.

② Zhang Chenggang. A Growing Trend of Employment? Analysis of Concept and Impact of New Forms of Employment. *Human Resources Development of China*, 2016(19): 86-91.

③ Wang Jun, Yang Wei. Historical analysis and the advance of the impact of artificial intelligence and other technologies on employment. *Review of Economic Research*, 2017(27): 11-25.

④ Deng Zhou, Huang Yana. A Study of Influence of Artificial Intelligence Development on Employment. *Study & Exploration*, 2019 (07): 99-106, 175.

induced innovation, the labor force will be replaced, so as to make up for the lack of labor supply and compensate for the structural imbalances of the labor market caused by aging.①

2.2 The impact of digital economy on the structure of labor supply and demand

In the context of digital economy, the structure of the labor market will undergo profound changes. From the perspective of enterprises, with the transformation and upgrading of industrial sectors, labor will be redistributed among the three industries. The rapid development of emerging technologies also increases the requirements for labor skills. From the perspective of the labor force, with the innovation of employment patterns, the threshold of the labor market is lowered. Many non-labor workers enter the labor market, which will greatly increase the labor participation rate.

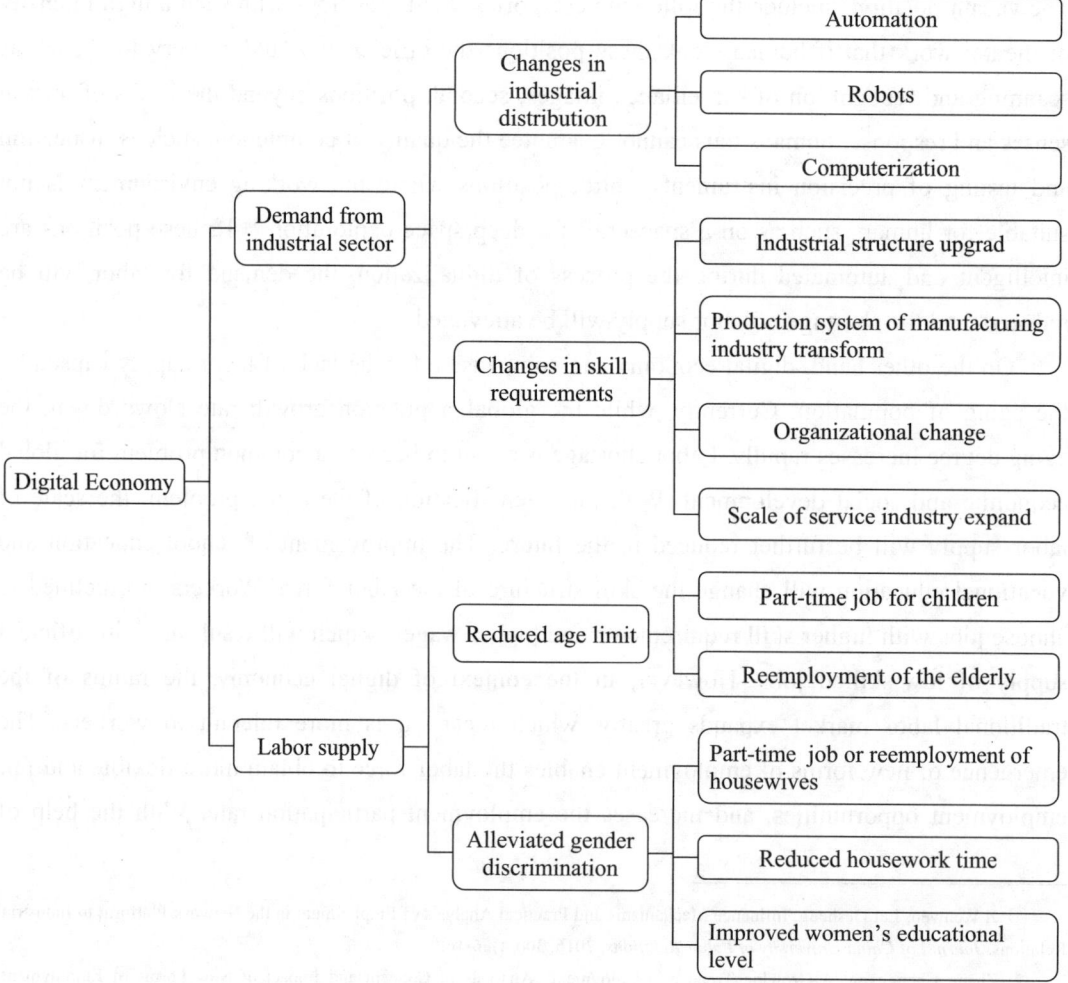

Figure 7.4 Impact mechanism of digital economy on the structure of labor supply and demand

---

① Yang Junkai, Zhao Hui. An analysis of labor supply in the era of artificial intelligence. *People's Tribune*, 2019(21): 46-47.

2.2.1 The impact of digital economy on the industrial structure of labor force

With the widespread application of technologies such as big data, cloud computing, artificial intelligence, and the Internet of Things, the rapid development of the high-tech service industry and the transformation and upgrading of the industrial structure bring about changes in the distribution of labor industries. According to Autor et al., workers in the manufacturing sector will be gradually transferred to the service industry due to the substitution effect of artificial intelligence.① Research by the US Bureau of Labor Statistics also shows that by 2024, almost all new job opportunities will be in the service industry, especially in health care and social assistance services.②

In the primary industry, artificial intelligence will transform habits and methods of product and work, and strengthen the connection with the market. Ampatzidis et al. point out that the current automation and robots can realize human-machine cooperation throughout the agricultural production process from crop selection, sowing, disaster prevention, etc., up to crop harvesting.③ Lele et al. believe that the speed and scope of the transformation of smart and digital technologies are beneficial to an inclusive agricultural and rural development, truly connecting farmers to the market in each production link and increasing farmers' income through the provision of higher levels of education, health care, finance, and market services.④

In the secondary industry, the development of digital economy has a significant impact on the labor demand of the manufacturing industry. This is not only because the manufacturing industry is easily affected by industrial robots and automation, but also because the manufacturing industry absorbs a large amount of ordinary labor force. Compared with the agriculture and service industries, the distribution of labor force is more concentrated. Acemoglu et al. find that the large-scale application of industrial robots has a significant negative correlation with employment and wages, and propose that the substitution effect of industrial robots on the labor market is greater than its creation effect at the emergence stage.⑤

As for the tertiary industry, in addition to accepting workers from the manufacturing industry, Frey finds that many workers in the service industry are at risk of being replaced by computerization.⑥ Workers in telemarketing, insurance, transportation services, photography, data maintenance, and other occupations are considered to be most likely to be replaced by

---

① Autor D.H., Dorn D. (2013). The Growth of Low-Skill Service Jobs and the Polarization of the US Labor Market. *American Economic Review*, 103(5): 1553-1597.

② Trajtenberg M. (2018). AI as the Next GPT: A Political-Economy Perspective. Nber Working Paper. No. 24245.

③ Ampatzidis Y., Bellis L.D., Luvisi A. (2017). iPathology: Robotic Applications and Management of Plants and Plant Diseases. Sustainability, 9(6): 1-14.

④ Lele U., Goswami S. (2017). The Fourth Industrial Revolution, Agricultural and Rural Innovation, and Implications for Public Policy and Investments: A Case of India. *Agricultural Economics*, 48(S1): 87-100.

⑤ Acemoglu D., Restrepo P. (2017). Robots and Jobs: Evidence from US Labor Markets. Nber Working Paper No. 23285.

⑥ Frey C.B., Osborne M.A. (2017). The Future of Employment: How Susceptible are Jobs to Computerization. *Technological Forecasting and Social Change*, 114: 254-280.

computerization. But the creation effect of artificial intelligence also promotes the labor demand in some occupations. The fastest-growing ones are kindergartens (and elementary schools) teachers, accountants and financial personnel, nurses, health consultants, rehabilitation specialists, and social information workers.①

Domestic scholars also study the impact of digital economy on China's industrial structure. Xia Yan et al. find that the impact of digital economy on the employment of the secondary industry has been increasing year by year, calculating data based on the input-occupancy-output model. It is found that the manufacturing employment brought by digital economy is primarily in the ICT industry (accounting for 35.9%). Employment in the tertiary industry is mainly in wholesale and retail and commercial services. Meanwhile, digital economy affects the employment scale of technology-intensive manufacturing and production services. The close relationship between production services and manufacturing explains that digital economy can play a greater role in the dual functions of absorbing jobs in the manufacturing and service industries.②

2.2.2 The impact of digital economy on the labor skill structure

With the rapid development of emerging technologies, the upgrading of the industrial structure increases the demand for high-quality, high-skilled labor. Meanwhile, with the expansion of the service industry, the demand for low-skilled labor also increases. Autor believes that the impact of the rapid development of artificial intelligence on jobs presents primarily in the decrease in the number of medium-income and medium-skilled jobs.③ Goos et al. also believe that both high-income mental work (cognitive work) and low-income labor positions increase. The polarization of the labor market appears, and it affects employment choices.④

With the development of emerging technologies, the structure of enterprises also goes through changes, which has an indirect influence on the demand for labor skills. More comprehensive databases and more convenient access to information allow workers to operate on the whole process rather than on a single step. The utilization of automated machines and programmed processes also require workers to have stronger analysis and problem-solving capabilities. The improvements of the organizational structure bring more communication tasks to managers. Enterprises need workers to have interpersonal skills that computers do not have. Adapting to new tools, organizational structures, and production methods requires workers to

---

① Yang Weiguo, Qiu Zitong, Wu Qingjun. A review of the employment effects of artificial intelligence applications. *Chinese Journal of Population Science*, 2018(05): 109-119, 128.

② Xia Yan, Wang Huijuan, Zhang Feng, Guo Jianfeng. Impact of the Digital Economy on China's Economic and Non-agricultural Employment: Based on the Input-Occupancy-Output Model. *Bulletin of Chinese Academy of Sciences*, 2018, 33(7): 707-716.

③ Autor D.H. (2013). The "Task Approach" to Labor Markets: An Overview. *Journal for Labor Market Research*, 46(3): 185-199.

④ Goos M., Manning A. (2007). Lousy and Lovely Jobs: The Rising Polarization of Work in Britain. *The Review of Economics and Statistics*, 89(1): 118-133.

have stronger cognitive ability, flexibility, and self-management capabilities compared with previous fixed production operations, which also requires a higher level of labor skills.① Caroli and Reenen believe that high-skilled workers are better at dealing with increasing uncertainties and responsibilities.② Zammuto et al. believe that high-skilled workers are better at communication to reduce information redundancy.③

Meanwhile, artificial intelligence is affecting the production mode and production system of the manufacturing industry, and changing the skill requirements of workers in these production systems.④ When Yin et al. analyze the changes brought about by previous industrial revolutions, it is found that compared with the assembly line, the Toyota Production System (TPS), and modular manufacturing created by the second industrial revolution, the flexible manufacturing system (FMS), and the Seru production system based on computerization and industrial robots as the software and hardware foundation can satisfy the needs of mass customization under the conditions of Industry 4.0.⑤ This will not only change the pattern of future development of the manufacturing industry, but also pose higher requirements on the skills of future workers.

2.2.3 Impact of digital economy on the age structure of the labor force

With the development of digital economy and the emergence of new forms of employment, the flexibility of working hours, locations, and entry and exit of job positions will lower the age restriction on the labor force, allowing more people to enter the labor market, thereby increasing labor participation rate and alleviating the labor shortage caused by aging.

On the one hand, curious young people and children are more likely to accept new things. Based on the Internet platform, they use their spare time to enter the labor market and develop flexible employment such as live-streamers. While investigating the impact of online job hunting on wages, Shahiri and Osman propose that online job hunters may be young and highly educated workers.⑥ Xia Yan et al. find that under digital economy, employees tend to be younger, calculated with the input-occupancy-output model. Non-agricultural employees between 16 and 34 years old are the main driving force of digital economy, in particular, the group between 25 and 29 years old. The proportion of non-agricultural employees over 34 years old in the overall

---

① Ning Guangjie, Lin Ziliang. Application of information technology, organizational reform of enterprises and changes in demand for labor skills. *Economic Research Journal*, 2014, 49(08): 79-92.

② Caroli E., J. V. Reenen (2001). Skill-biased Organizational Change? Evidence from a Panel of British and French Establishments. *Quarterly Journal of Economics*, 116(4): 1449-1492.

③ Zammuto R., E. O'Conner (1992). Gaining Advanced Manufacturing Technologies Benefits: The Roles of Organization Design and Culture. *Academy of Management Review*, 17(4): 701-728.

④ Yang Weiguo, Qiu Zitong, Wu Qingjun. A review of the employment effects of artificial intelligence applications. *Chinese Journal of Population Science*, 2018(05): 109-119, 128.

⑤ Yin Y., Stecke K.E., Li D. (2017). The Evolution of Production Systems from Industry 2.0 Through Industry 4.0. *International Journal of Production Research*, 56: 848-861.

⑥ Shahiri H., Osman Z. (2015). Internet Job Search and Labor Market Outcome. *International Economic Journal*, 29(1): 161-173.

employed population under digital economy gradually increases, especially those aged 40-49.[①] This suggests that the acceptance of digital economy by the middle-aged population is increasing, and the multi-dimensional generation and integration of digital economy are deepening.

On the other hand, digital economy has a positive role in promoting the reemployment of the elderly. The reemployment of the elderly is an important measure to promote active aging, and it is also a presentation of allowing the elderly to have opportunities for their own pursuits.[②] In China, many elderly people are able to engage in social production after retirement. The elderly with rich work experience and in sound physical condition deserve to be respected and valued by the society and even return to work. However, the data of the "China Labor Statistical Yearbook" shows that in 2015, the proportion of reemployed elderly over 60 in China's urban areas was 9.18%, and the proportion in 2005 was 9.7%. However, in the same period, the proportion in Japan was as high as 60%. This shows that the reemployment ratio of retirees in China is not high, which increases the burden of pension.[③] However, with the development of digital economy, the labor market relaxes the restriction on age. Retirees, especially younger retirees with energy, can rely on the Internet platform to be reemployed in a diversified approach to better realize their personal value, thus lowering the burden of pension for the entire society.

2.2.4 Impact of digital economy on the gender structure of the labor force

The impact of digital economy on the labor market varies according to different genders. On the one hand, due to traditional concepts and women's advantages in housework, a lot of housework is undertaken by women and it takes a lot of time. Therefore, some women are excluded from the labor market. Additionally, the impact of marriage and childbirth on the labor supply is more apparent for women, making more women full-time mothers. In the context of digital economy, online activities such as online shopping, online food ordering, and online payment can reduce the time for housework, providing women with energy for work, and increasing women's labor participation rate. On the other hand, due to gender discrimination in the labor market in China, women are underemployed and the labor participation rate is low. The development of digital economy lowers the threshold for entrepreneurship, and various forms of flexible employment emerge. These emerging forms of employment often have no special requirements for gender. In certain industries, such as live-streaming, females are preferred. Therefore, in the context of digital economy, gender discrimination faced by female workers can

---

① Xia Yan, Wang Huijuan, Zhang Feng, Guo Jianfeng. Impact of the Digital Economy on China's Economic and Non-agricultural Employment: Based on the Input-Occupancy-Output Model. *Bulletin of Chinese Academy of Sciences*, 2018, 33(7): 707-716.

② Xu Jie. Status and influencing factors of the reemployment of younger elderly in urban areas. Nanchang: Jiangxi University of Finance and Economics, 2018.

③ Peng Qiushi, Zhang Chang, Zeng Qingsen. Current status of reemployment of younger retired elderly in urban areas—taking elderly transportation coordinators in Beijing as an example. *Economic Outlook the Bohai Sea*, 2019(06): 12-14.

be avoided or reduced, thereby increasing the female labor participation rate.[①] Using regional Internet access capabilities as an instrumental variable, Dettling solves an endogenous issue of reciprocal causation. Research finds that women who use the Internet at home are more likely to participate in the labor market. Telecommuting, online job hunting, and saving time in housework are the main factors.[②] Goldin proposes that the generalized utilization of standardized production service processes and computer systems allows colleagues to take over the work without disruption while the productivity does not drop significantly even when a worker stops working.[③] This allows women to flexibly arrange their working hours so as to stay in the labor market despite the pressure of looking after children.

Another important way for digital economy to affect female employment is education. Technological advancement would increase the enrollment rate and education level for women, and the improvement of their education level is the main factor affecting their participation in the labor market.[④] With the help of Becker's family production model, Lewis explains that the advancement of family production technology will lead to an increase in human capital investment in girls, and ultimately lead to an increase in the female labor participation rate.[⑤] Ning Guangjie and Ma Junlong use the CFPS 2014 survey data to analyze the impact of the Internet on women's labor supply, and find that the Internet would increase the labor participation rate of women with primary and junior high school degrees, reduce the possibility of them working in agriculture, and increase the possibility of them becoming self-employed and wage earners. Meanwhile, the use of the Internet significantly reduces the time women spend on housework and improves their human capital level through online learning and business activities. This is an important factor in increasing the female labor participation rate.[⑥]

In addition, while the advancement of automation technology leads to changes in the supply and demand structure of job assignments, it will also lead to changes in the employment structure of different genders. Black and Spitz-Oener study the impact of technological progress on female employment and gender-specific wage gaps under the RBTC analysis paradigm, and conclude that women have an advantage over men in non-programmed work.[⑦] Therefore, the relative changes in job assignments caused by technological progress explain the shrinking wage gap between genders.

---

① Ning Guangjie, Ma Junlong. The influence of the Internet on female labor supply. *Social Science Front*, 2018(02): 75-83.
② Dettling L. J. (2012). Opting Back In: Home Internet Use and Female Labor Supply.
③ Goldin C. (2014). A Grand Gender Convergence: Its Last Chapter. *American Economic Review*, 104(4): 1091-1119.
④ Zhang Pengfei. New progress in artificial intelligence and employment research. *Economist*, 2018(08): 27-33.
⑤ Lewis J. (2013). The Short-run and Long-run Effects of Household Technological Change [EB/OL]. http://www.Hec.ca/iea/Sem-iNaires/131105_Joshua_Lewis.pdf.
⑥ Ning Guangjie, Ma Junlong. The influence of the Internet on female labor supply. *Social Science Front*, 2018(02): 75-83.
⑦ Black S. E., Spitz-Oener A. (2010). Explaining Women's Success: Technological Change and the Skill Content of Women's Work. *Review of Economics and Statistics*, 92(1): 187-194.

2.3 Innovation in the form of employment under digital economy

The concept of "new forms of employment" was first proposed in the communiqué of the 5th Plenary Session of the 18th Central Committee, but there was no clear definition. From the perspective of production relations, Zhang Chenggang believes that the new forms of employment are a de-employer employment pattern that emerges with the advancement of Internet technology and the upgrading of mass consumption, as well as a flexible form of employment that deviates from the traditional, formal employment and upgrades with the help of information technology.① Zhu Songling believes that the new form of employment is a form of employment that is generated by the extension of traditional industries under the conditions of the Internet, and it has not been transformed into an independent form of employment.② Zhu Wanfen believes that the new form of employment is a new flexible employment model derived from the combination of Internet technology and traditional industries.③ All these definitions emphasize that the new form of employment relies on Internet technology and is different from traditional forms of employment. Its "newness" is mainly presented in the new field, new technical means, new methods, and new concepts of employment.④ In the context of digital economy, with the upgrading of mass consumption, the widespread application of Internet technology, and the institutional reform represented by "general entrepreneurship and innovation", new forms of employment in various formats and types emerge on the Chinese market. In summary, there are mainly the following categories:

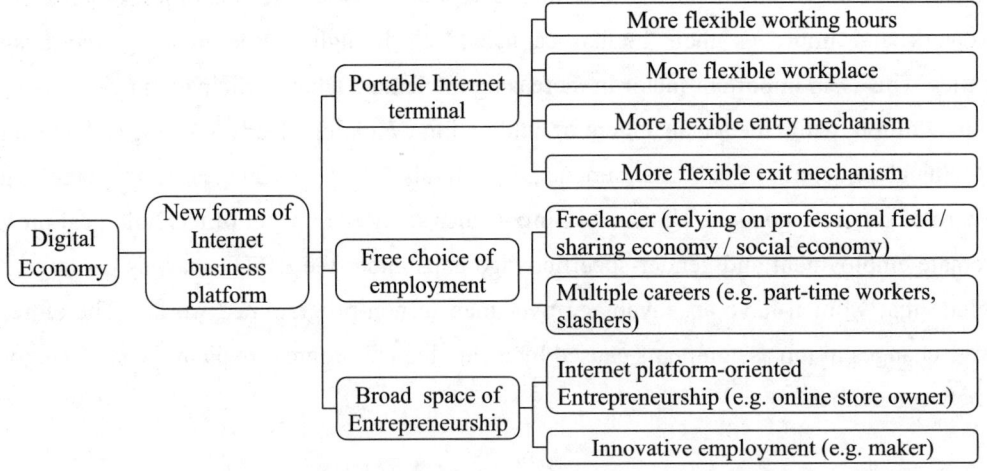

Figure 7.5   Impact mechanism of digital economy on formats of employment

---

① Zhang Chenggang. A Growing Trend of Employment? Analysis of Concept and Impact of New Forms of Employment. *Human Resources Development of China*, 2016(19): 86-91.

② Zhu Songling. New Employment Form: Concept, Pattern, and Prospect. *Chinese Youth Social Sciences*, 2018, 37(03): 8-14.

③ Zhu Wanfen. A Summary of Research on Flexible Employment Personnel under the New Employment Pattern. *Labour Union Studies (Journal of Shanghai Trade Union Management Vocational College)*, 2019(04): 30-38.

④ Ji Wenwen. Digital Economy and Future Work. *Journal of China University of Labor Relations*, 2017, 31(06): 37-47.

2.3.1 Flexible employment under digital economy

The employment scenarios represented by the new Internet business platforms make employment more flexible. The flexibility is presented in the following aspects: First, working hours are more flexible. Under the new Internet business platform, workers can provide services using their fragmented time, choose the time to log in to the platform or APP, and decide the length of service time independently. Second, the working location is more flexible. Under the new Internet business platform, workers do not work at fixed places. They can start working as long as there is an Internet terminal. This makes the choice of location more flexible. Third, job entry is more flexible. Under the new Internet business platform, most enterprises do not restrict workers from providing services on other platforms, and usually do not check whether they have labor relations with other platforms or enterprises. As long as they meet the basic conditions of related skills and services, they can sign a service agreement with a platform. This reduces the threshold significantly. Fourth, the exit mechanism is more flexible. Under the new Internet business platform, workers are less dependent on business organizations, and the flow is free. There is no need for prior notice or consent to leave the new Internet business platform. Generally, workers just no longer log in to the APP or uninstall the APP.[1][2]

2.3.2 Self-employment under digital economy

In the context of digital economy, a large number of freelancers and "slashies" appear in the labor market, and the freedom of workers is improved significantly. According to different sources of job opportunities, freelancers can be divided into three types: The first type is freelancers who rely on a certain specialized field and market segment. Such employees have a higher level of intelligence and technological skills, and richer resources in the industry. Working conditions and income levels are relatively high. The second type is freelancers relying on the sharing economy platforms, which can be further divided into service crowdsourcing and on-demand service. They are free from organizations such as factories, enterprises, and offices, and are connected to the market through virtual platforms. By integrating and providing idle resources, the efficiency of supply and demand is improved, and individual market value is realized. The third type is freelancers relying on the community economy, i.e., an employment model that utilizes the trust and sharing of community members for income in exchange and sharing circles with common interests or occupations. "Slashies" refers to employees with multiple occupations. According to the number of occupations and whether there is a distinction between primary and secondary occupations, they can be divided into two types: The first type is part-time workers who have a second job by using online supply and demand matching

---

[1] Zhang Xianmin, Yan Bo. Investigation and analysis of employment forms of new Internet business platform enterprises. *China Labor*, 2017(08): 14-19.

[2] Chen Mingxin. The path and mechanism of information technology's impact on the form of employment. *Special Zone Economy*, 2019(09): 128-130.

platforms or information channels in addition to their primary job. The second type is those who choose a diverse lifestyle with multiple occupations and identities, which is a proper "slashy". There is no clear distinction between their multiple occupations, and they often switch their roles between multiple job opportunities and employment status, and even between being employed and being entrepreneurs.①

As the proportion of freelancers and slashies rises, the demand for high-skilled labor increases. High-skilled talents with certain knowledge and skills carry knowledge and skills with them. They can get a freer working environment, perform their talents more freely, and realize the pursuit of self-worth. However, there is still a huge demand for some low-skilled jobs. There is a polarization in the demand for skills in the job market. Low-skilled or unskilled groups enjoy considerable freedom in the new Internet business platforms. They can choose whether to undertake job assignments. Due to the flexibility of job entry and exit, workers' dependence on the platform is weakened, making the flow of people freer.②

2.3.3 Innovation and entrepreneurship under digital economy

Digital economy provides a broad space and efficient approach for innovation and entrepreneurship, and even blurs the boundaries between employment and entrepreneurship. It generates an entrepreneurial form of employment that includes self-seeking projects, self-financing, self-management, and self-assumpting risks. This new form of employment includes two types: Internet-platform-oriented entrepreneurship and innovative employment. Online shop owners are representatives of Internet platform entrepreneurship. Thanks to the lowering thresholds of technology, capital, and logistics, starting a business on Internet platforms becomes the first choice for young entrepreneurs, as well as the first choice for employment. Innovative employment refers to opportunistic entrepreneurship, pursuing creativity and innovation. Their businesses are emerging, incubating, and not ready for business registration. The representatives for this type is "Maker".③ The activities of innovative employment are innovative and leading. The locations are primarily in entrepreneurial incubation spaces and platforms. Some enterprises also have entrepreneurial employment models based on their own platforms, such as Haier's HCH and Tencent's "Makerspace". In face of a market with hundreds of millions of consumers, there are unlimited possibilities for innovation and entrepreneurship in China. Among the groups of innovators and entrepreneurs, there are many college students, young people from rural areas, and even less-advantaged groups such as the disabled. This also makes a contribution to improving China's labor participation rate. Driven by China's "general

---

① Zhang Chenggang. A Growing Trend of Employment? Analysis of Concept and Impact of New Forms of Employment. *Human Resources Development of China*, 2016(19): 86-91.

② Chen Mingxin. The path and mechanism of information technology's impact on the form of employment. *Special Zone Economy*, 2019(09): 128-130.

③ Zhang Chenggang. A Growing Trend of Employment? Analysis of Concept and Impact of New Forms of Employment. *Human Resources Development of China*, 2016(19): 86-91.

entrepreneurship and innovation" strategy, the vision of future innovation and entrepreneurship is promising.

Section 3   Development and Changes of China's Labor Market in the Context of Digital Economy

3.1 China's employment status in the context of digital economy

The rapid development of digital economy not only creates a large number of employment opportunities, but also triggers profound changes in China's employment structure, and generates a new form of flexible employment. The following discusses the employment status in China in the context of digital economy from four perspectives: scale of employment, structure of employment, employment methods, and industry and regional differences of employment.

3.1.1 Expanding scale of employment

The "China 'Internet +' Digital Economy Index (2018)" released by Tencent Research Institute pointed out that China's digital economy generated roughly 3.2 million new jobs in 2017, accounting for 22% of the new employees in 2017. According to the "White Paper on China's Digital Economic Development and Employment (2019)", issued by China Academy of Information and Communications Technology, the overall scale of China's "digital economy" in 2018 reached 31.3 trillion yuan, a nominal increase of 20.9% calculated in comparable terms, accounting for 34.8% of the GDP. Moreover, the ability of digital economy to absorb employment increased significantly. In 2018, China's digital economy created 191 million jobs, accounting for 24.6% of the total employees, a year-on-year increase of 11.5%, significantly higher than the growth rate of the national total employment scale in the same period. Currently, digital economy is developing rapidly. According to a report of BCG in 2019,[1] it is estimated that by 2035, the scale of China's digital economy will reach 100 trillion yuan, accommodating 415 million people.

Accordingly, as employment expands, China's digital economy develops rapidly. In the third quarter of 2017, information transmission, computer services, and software industries, representatives of China's digital economy, accounted for 3.6% of the GDP, rising from 2.1% in 2011. In 2017, the digitization rate of production equipment in China was 44.8%, the CNC rate of key processes was 46.4%, and the networking rate of digital equipment was 39%. The penetration rates of ERP, PLM, and MES reached 55.9%, 16.4%, and 20.7%, respectively.[2] According to related studies, the net impact of digital economy on employment is positive. On

---

[1] The Boston Consulting Group (2019). "Year 2035: 400 Million Job Opportunities in the Digital Age".

[2] China Academy of Information and Communications Technology (2019). "White Paper on China's Digital Economic Development and Employment".

the condition that the GDP growth rate remains constant, every 1% increase in digital economy will drive the employment rate by 0.01%, but there is a one-year lag. Given that the average growth rate of digital economy is 10%, its contribution to employment growth is 0.1%.[①] In the past few years, the overall employment growth has remained at 0.2-0.3%. Therefore, digital economy contributed about one-third to half of the overall employment growth.

In terms of the scale of employment, digital economy releases the huge potential of the employment market. This is presented in two aspects: First, the conversion of new and old kinetic energy creates huge space for employment. Research shows that for every 100 employed workers in digital economy, 72 workers upgrade the original jobs, and 28 workers start new jobs. Second, flexible employment brought about by digital economy is growing rapidly, and its proportion in employment is increasing rapidly.[②] Digital economy fully plays the roles of "stabilizer" and "multiplier" for employment.

3.1.2 Changes in the structure of employment

The rapid development of digital industry adjusts the original structure of employment. Many repetitive and low-value jobs in traditional industries have disappeared. The World Bank's "World Development Report 2016: Digital Dividends" states that in the future, 55% to 77% of jobs in China are likely to be replaced due to low skills. Similarly, according to the "World Development Report 2019: Changes in the Nature of Work" issued by the World Bank, it is estimated that 47% of US occupations are at risk of automation, and the possibility that jobs with an hourly salary of fewer than 20 dollars will be replaced by robots is 83%; the possibility of jobs with an hourly salary of 20-40 dollars being replaced is 31%; the possibility of jobs with an hourly salary of over 40 dollars being replaced is 4%. The BBC reported the data system, created by Cambridge University researchers Michael Osborne and Carl Frey, which analyzed the "possibility of being eliminated" of 365 occupations around the world. The occupations with possibilities higher than 90% include accountants, insurance salespersons, bank employees, etc. The 30 occupations with the highest possibility of being eliminated are shown in Figure 7.6.

According to the report[③] released by AliResearch, the positive impact of artificial intelligence on employment outweighs the negative impact. However, at the current stage of development in China, the substitution of employment by three major smart tools are yet to be identified. In a limited number of businesses where technology replaces labor, most of the replaced personnel have the opportunity of an internal transfer. So it is rare to see a reduction in staff due to smart tools. Currently, the software and information technology service industry and

---

① Yi Yan (2019). China's Digital Economy: Opportunities and Risks. *China Money*, 212(6): 64-68.
② Institute of Population and Labor Economics, Chinese Academy of Social Sciences (2019). *Green Paper on Population and Labor: China Population and Labor Issues Report No.19*. Beijing: Social Science Academic Press.
③ AliResearch (2019). "Research Report on the Application of Artificial Intelligence in the E-commerce Industry and Its Impact on Employment".

the Internet industry are growing rapidly, with revenues increasing by 14.2% and 20.3% year-on-year, respectively. The vitality of demand for information consumption, investment in digital economy, and digital trade continues to be released, promoting the development of digital industrialization and employment.

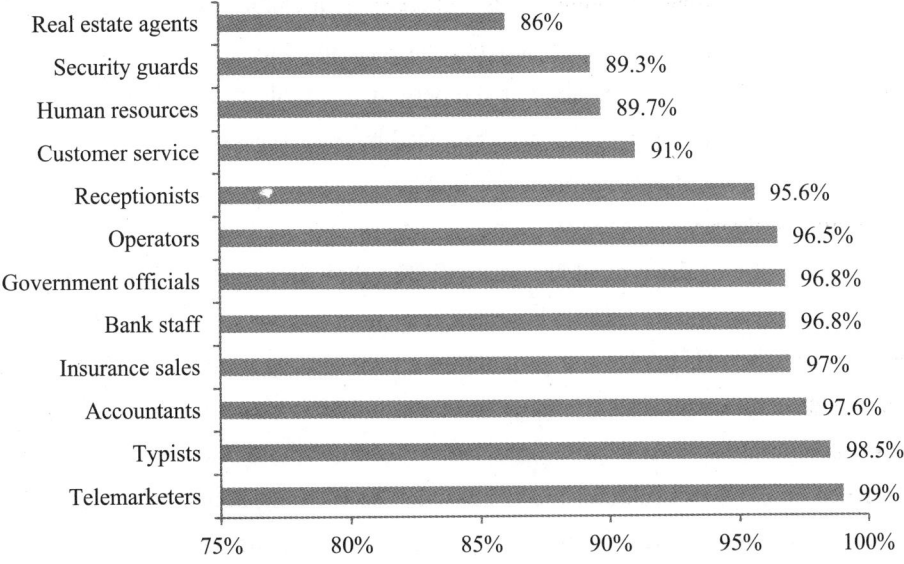

Figure 7.6 Occupations with the highest possibility of being replaced by "artificial intelligence"

Source: BBC analyzed the possibility of 365 occupations being replaced by robots (2017, November 16). Retrieved from https://www.sohu.com/a/204771235_717687.

In terms of the employment structure, with the in-depth development of digital economy, the employment rate of the tertiary industry will continue to rise. Thanks to the extensive and in-depth application of digital information technology, the primary industry will further improve the scale, intensification, and intelligence level, and labor productivity of the agricultural industry. With the popularization of new-generation artificial intelligence technologies such as robots, more agricultural labor will be released by agricultural automation. For example, big data analysis, drip irrigation technology, and spraying of pesticides by drones will help with efficient fertilization and irrigation, thereby saving a lot of agricultural labor. In the secondary industry, the employment scale of traditional manufacturing will continue to decrease. Patterns in the development of digital economy in the secondary industry are: the digital transformation of capital-intensive industries is significantly faster than that of labor-intensive industries, and the digital transformation of heavy industries is faster than of light industries. Meanwhile, the penetration of digital economy into various industries continues to deepen. The development of digital economy in China varies. The average proportion of digital economy in services is 32.6%, in industry 17.2%, and in agriculture 6.5%.[①] The proportion of the tertiary industry is

---

① China Academy of Information and Communications Technology (2019). "White Paper on China's Digital Economic Development and Employment".

higher than that of the secondary industry, and the proportion of the secondary industry is higher than that of the primary industry.

In recent years, the output of industrial robots in China has increased. In the first half of 2018, the cumulative output of nationwide industrial robots was 73,849.1 units, a year-on-year increase of 23.9%.① The use of smart devices and equipment enables manufacturers to deal with the challenges of loss of workers, short delivery periods, and safety issues. In the long run, the employment opportunities brought about by emerging technologies will be greater than the traditional jobs that have disappeared or been replaced by machines.

3.1.3 Diversification of employment methods

In the digital economy era, the boundaries of enterprises are blurred, and platform-oriented enterprises become one of the typical characteristics of digital economy. Digital technology and Internet platforms break the traditional boundaries of organizations, providing individuals with resources such as markets, R&D, and production and lowering the barriers for individuals to enter the economy. Individuals can engage in economic activities without entering traditional enterprises. Accordingly, forms of employment become more flexible and diverse. The traditional fixed employment relationship is broken. The working hours, locations, content, and term of employment are more flexible. The supply and demand relationship in the human resources market is more flexible, and employment and entrepreneurship are more independent and flexible. Digital economy creates a large number of new employment methods.

Digital economy generates a new model of flexible employment. According to the report,② the rapid development of the platform economy, sharing economy, "crowd-sourcing", "crowd-innovation", and other new models and formats of digital economy generates new flexible employment models such as self-employment, freelancing, and part-time employment in addition to the traditional labor-contract-based employment format. Taking Alibaba, a platform economy, as an example, if we take "income opportunities" as a calculation indicator for "employment opportunity", in 2018, Alibaba created 40.82 million job opportunities, including 15.58 million transactional employment opportunities, and approximately 25.24 million driving employment opportunities.

In addition to flexible employment methods, the impact of digital economy also includes empowering employment methods. "Empowerment" refers to the use of platform big data, cloud computing, and artificial intelligence to provide workers with basic tools such as smart devices, transaction payments, and information services, so as to help workers complete their work more efficiently and intelligently. This also means further changes in the way of working and employment approach.

---

① Data from the big data database of the Chinese Academy of Industry Economy Research.

② Institute of Population and Labor Economics, Chinese Academy of Social Sciences (2019). *Green Paper on Population and Labor: China Population and Labor Issues Report No.19*. Beijing: Social Science Academic Press.

3.1.4 Industrial and regional differences of employment

Digital economy develops differently in different industries in China. The digital transformation of the tertiary industry creates the most jobs, accounting for 65% of the employment in digital economy, while the digital transformation of the secondary industry has the greatest potential for absorbing workers, accounting for 23.7% of the total employment in the secondary industry. Specifically, the industrial, services, and agriculture digital economies account for 18.3%, 35.9%, and 7.3% of the industry's added value, respectively.[①]

From the perspective of the transformation and mobility of the labor force, the digital transformation of the labor force in the tertiary industry is the least difficult, and that in the secondary industry is the most difficult. According to preliminary calculations,[②] there were about 19.28 million jobs related to the digital transformation of the primary industry in 2018, accounting for 9.6% of the total employment in the primary industry, an increase of about 2%. The number of digital transformation jobs in the secondary industry was 52.21 million, accounting for 23.7% of the total employment in the secondary industry, an increase of approximately 1.4%. The number of digital transformation jobs of the tertiary industry was 134.26 million, accounting for 37.2% of the total employment in the tertiary industry, an increase of 4%. Industry attributes make the difficulty of digital transformation vary. The tertiary industry, with high transaction costs, low proportion of fixed assets, and low technology intensity, is less difficult to digitally transform. It is easier for industry practitioners to switch to the roles of practitioners with digital skills. The secondary industry, with low transaction costs, high fixed assets, and high technology intensity, is more difficult to digitally transform. Talents in basic industrial processes are lacking in knowledge and experience related to digitalization and intelligence, and the transformation is difficult.

The development of digital economy in Chinese key regions also varies. In terms of total amount, the Yangtze River Delta has the largest amount, with 8.63 trillion yuan; in terms of proportion, the Pearl River Delta has the highest proportion, 44.3%; in terms of growth rate, the Yangtze River Delta has the fastest growth rate, reaching 18.3%.[③] The employment absorption capacity of different provinces varies significantly. Eastern provinces have the highest employment absorption capacity. In 2018, in terms of the proportion of digital economy employment in the total employment, the top seven provinces and cities were Shanghai, Beijing, Tianjin, Jiangsu, Zhejiang, Shandong, and Guangdong, with the proportions all higher than 30%. The employment absorption capacity of digital economy in central and western regions is

---

① China Academy of Information and Communications Technology (2019). "White Paper on China's Digital Economic Development and Employment".

② Data from the big data database of the Chinese Academy of Industry Economy Research.

③ China Academy of Information and Communications Technology (2019). "White Paper on China's Digital Economic Development and Employment".

relatively low.

Meanwhile, the varied level of digitization in each region affects the flow of the labor population. From the perspective of the floating population (CLDS[①] 2017), the net inflows of Beijing, Tianjin, Shanxi, Shanghai, Zhejiang, and Guangdong significantly increase; the net outflows of Hebei, Anhui, Jiangxi, Henan, Guangxi, Sichuan, and Guizhou significantly increase. Currently, regions with a large net inflow attract the floating population through labor-intensive industries and a better economic foundation. Based on a better economic foundation, the development of digital economy in these regions takes the lead, bringing more employment opportunities. However, it remains unclear if it will bring about a larger population flow in the future, or attract different flows of working population based on regional comparative advantages. According to the 2019 China "New Economy Index" report, the catch-up effect of digital economy among provinces increases significantly, indicating that digital economy is playing an increasingly important role in narrowing the gap among provinces.

In the long run, with the expansion of digital economy, industrial production will gradually shift from later-developing regions to developed regions with higher levels of scientific R&D and lower production costs. As the industrial system is being restructured, the regional structure of labor also changes. Digital economy can promote the development of related industries, driving the growth of GDP in these regions, promoting employment growth in all directions, and reducing the overall unemployment rate in the region. In areas with a high level of digital economy development, the unemployment rate will be significantly lower than in other areas.

3.2 Case analysis of China's employment innovation in the context of digital economy

Digital economy, dominated by the Internet industry, provides strong technical support for entrepreneurship and employment. In particular, new business formats and new models continue to emerge, generating a large number of new jobs that are adapted to the new needs of society, becoming the new main force for employment in China. As the most active field in China's economic development, digital-economy-related technologies and business models innovate very fast. On the one hand, digital technology can reduce transaction costs in business models, including but not limited to labor costs, physical costs, and information processing costs. On the other hand, digital technology can improve the effectiveness of risk control. The basis of risk screening is information, and big data technology profoundly changes the efficiency of data collection and processing. Artificial intelligence further improves the ability to process big data. Cloud computing improves the efficiency of big data and artificial intelligence, and reduces the cost of data processing significantly.

---

① China Labor-force Dynamics Survey.

Entrepreneurship activities, in the context of the Internet and digital technology, show new features such as openness, borderlessness, and strong interaction. Taking big data technology as an example, emerging startups can provide more professional solutions to the industry by selling data and services. This new type of startups is becoming an important business model in digital economy. ICT services, generated by digital technologies such as cloud computing, support the entrepreneurship of SMEs effectively and provide SMEs with opportunities to enter the global market and increase cooperation and innovation. The following table compares the characteristics of traditional entrepreneurial employment and digital entrepreneurial employment in detail.[①]

Table 7.2　Comparison of employment characteristics between traditional entrepreneurship and digital entrepreneurship

Element	Traditional entrepreneurship and employment	Digital entrepreneurship and employment
Subjects of entrepreneurship	Enterprises and other organizations, entrepreneurial individuals	Users, entrepreneurial teams, investors, and technicians
Entrepreneurial organizations	Bureaucratic organizations in traditional enterprises or individual-centered network organizations	Virtual teams, online crowdfunding, social media interaction and platformization, ecological entrepreneurship ecosystem
Entrepreneurial opportunities	Individual prior opportunities, new technologies, new knowledge, and new market opportunities	The market created by digital technology and products and service reconstruction, innovations created by user participation, and new application opportunities in new scenarios
Entrepreneurial process	There are clear divisions of time periods and predefined entrepreneurial opportunities.	Fragmented, interactive, dynamic, and borderless iterate innovation and entrepreneurship
Entrepreneurial output	Fixed products and services	Self-sustaining, dynamically evolving products and services
Theoretical basis	Traditional management theory of innovation and entrepreneurship, resource-based theory and uncertainty theory, etc.	Digital innovation theory, opportunity creation theory, technology entrepreneurship theory, platform theory, self-growth theory, digital infrastructure theory, etc.

In the mature stage, digital economy has two major characteristics. First, traditional industries are networked. Based on online retailing, almost all aspects of lifestyle services are shifting online. Users can use "Didi" for car-hailing and "Eleme" and "Meituan" for takeout. Even laundry and housekeeping can be solved with the Internet. Second, Internet-based model innovation continues to emerge. Ridesharing, represented by Mobike, makes a breakthrough compared with the original shared bicycles, which are based on bike stations. It injects vitality

---

[①] Wang Chongming, Wu Ting. Research on Entrepreneurship in the Internet Context. *Journal of Zhejiang University (Humanities and Social Sciences Edition)*, 2016, 46(01): 131-141.

into China's digital economy by taking model innovation as the core.[①]

As of December 1, 2018, among the top five unicorn enterprises in the world, China's three digital enterprises, Didi Chuxing, Xiaomi, and Meituan, were on the list. This indicates that a number of technology giants in China are growing and may lead the future global development of related fields. The following are three cases, "Meituan Model", "5G Mobile Communication Technology", and "Didi Sharing Platform Economy", to illustrate the employment (horizontal expansion) brought by the expansion of the Internet industry under digital economy, employment (vertical expansion) brought by deepening original business under digital economy, and the creation of a new model and new platform (three-dimensional construction) to discuss the approach and form of employment under digital economy.

3.2.1 Meituan model: new models promote employment

According to the "Lifestyle Service Platform Employment Ecosystem and Meituan Dianping Employment Opportunity Report", as China's leading life service e-commerce platform, in 2018, Meituan generated 19.6 million employment opportunities, of which there were 2.7 million online labor transaction (rider) opportunities, 12.77 million online service product transaction opportunities, 4.074 million business-related employment opportunities, and 58,600 corporate employment opportunities. It shows that the Meituan platform has a strong ability to drive employment and becomes an important carrier for workers to obtain income opportunities. According to Meituan's business content and the characteristics of a certain industry, employment opportunities can be divided into four categories: online labor transaction (rider), online service product transaction, business-related, and direct employment of Internet enterprises. Based on the above four forms, the platform creates a large number of new employment forms, such as takeaway riders, professional operators, trainers from cosmetology schools, commenters, "tasting officials", etc., forming a rich ecology of employment.

According to the "2018 Takeaway Riders Group Research Report", issued by the Meituan Research Institute, 31% of the riders of Meituan are workers from industries with overcapacity reduced, which solves the employment problem caused by industrial transformation and upgrading. With the help of marketing, finance, distribution, supply chain, operation, and IT services, Meituan provides 5.8 million shops with solutions to expand channels of customers and improve the efficiency and quality, as well as the management and profitability, of shops. Therefore, real economy and digital economy are developed in an integrated way. On the other hand, driven by innovation, Meituan participates in the development of industry standards and platform governance, serves the development of talents in the life service industry, promotes employment, and helps the standardization and healthy development of the industry. Figure 7.7 shows the new employment ecological model based on "Meituan".

---

① Hu Wen. Review and Prospects of China's Digital Economy Development. *Civil-Military Integration on Cyberspace*, 2018 (06): 18-22.

Meituan has formed a rather mature and complete system. The "Meituan model" refers to the platform product matrix that Meituan has formed: On the consumers' end, users can obtain information about lifestyle and entertainment through applications such as Meituan, Dianping, and Meituan Takeaway; on the shops' end, users can open shops, thereby joining the Meituan platform, or realize mobile management and digital operation of their restaurants through "Meituan butler". Meanwhile, Meituan provides financial services such as small loans, insurance services, and smart payments to help shops develop. As of March 2019, Meituan had 58,600 employees nationwide, of which 60% are post-90s, with an average age of 27 years old. Compared with the employment data at the end of 2017, the number of Meituan employees increased from 42,200 to 58,600, an increase of 39%.

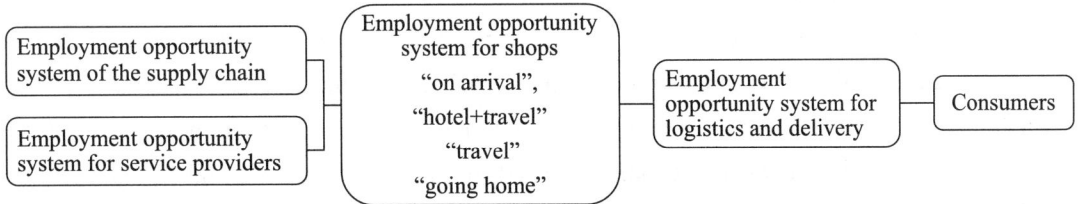

Figure 7.7 Digital economy employment ecosystem of the "Meituan" model

Source: Meituan Research Institute.

With the development of the Internet economy, the Internet and traditional industries are integrated more profoundly. Important changes occur in the form of Internet-based employment. Different from the traditional employment model, where jobs are created by increasing investment and employment, life service platforms, represented by Meituan, take advantage of the platforms to match supply and demand, thus driving employment. They are able to generate huge employment opportunities in a short time by reducing transaction costs and creating new business models. In the foreseeable future, a group of consumer service industries, represented by Meituan, will drive employment to a greater extent. In the new employment ecosystem, the digitization of the consumer service industry not only provides space for entrepreneurship and new occupations, but also improves the overall productivity of the entire industry and improves human efficiency for the entire industry. The data integration between the consumer market and the labor market will reduce the instability of the labor market and play a vital role in stabilizing the labor market.

In summary, the employment mechanism driven by the "Meituan Model" platform is reflected in four aspects: driving employment opportunities, creating new jobs, improving employment quality, and enhancing employability. In terms of driving employment opportunities, it has generated tens of millions of job opportunities; in terms of creating jobs, it has created a large number of new positions and new forms of employment, enriching the ecology for employment; the platform facilitates the digital upgrade of the supply side, expands the scale of business operations, and improves the quality of employment; the platform promotes the standardization of internal management and work processes of enterprises, and helps standardize employees' skills and improve the general level of skills.

3.2.2 5G mobile communication technology: new technologies expand employment

The five core technologies that are currently considered to be able to influence the future are artificial intelligence, the Internet of Things, advanced robotics, additive manufacturing, and augmented reality and virtual reality technologies.[①] Each of these technologies is transformative and disruptive. Together, they will completely overturn traditional business models, communication methods, and even the global economic structure. But these technologies all rely on another technology that has not been widely discussed: 5G technology.

According to the "White Paper on 5G Economic and Social Impact", released by China Academy of Information and Communications Technology, it is predicted that by 2030, 5G is expected to drive China's direct economic output of 6.3 trillion yuan, economic value added of 2.9 trillion yuan, and 8 million job opportunities. In terms of indirect contributions, 5G will drive total output of 10.6 trillion yuan, economic value added of 3.6 trillion yuan, and 11.5 million job opportunities. The White Paper proposes that as a general-purpose technology, 5G will open up a new era for the development of mobile communications, accelerate economic and social digital transformation, and elevate the development of China's digital economy to a new level. At present, China's 5G mid-band system equipment, terminal chips, and smartphones are all in the top echelon of the global industry. 5G will have an impact on almost all industries, especially the automotive, medical, and Internet of Things industries. Regarding the number of patent applications for the new generation of communication standard "5G", China accounts for 34%, leading the world.

At present, there are 559 5G-related enterprises in China, the number of related jobs increases 8-fold, and the demand is far greater than the supply. From the perspective of the distribution of talent demand in four major segments of 5G, 5G applications account for the largest proportion (72.81%), followed by terminals and operators (12.49%), original devices and materials (9.82%), and finally transmission networks (4.88%).[②] These all show great employment prospects. Once officially commercialized, 5G will bring the communications industry into a new round of development, and also drive multiple trillion-scale emerging industries, indicating a larger job market. With the official commercialization of 5G, network-related problems will be solved, and industries such as artificial intelligence and intelligent manufacturing will rise. In addition, the upstream and downstream of the industrial chain, such as chips, electronic components, software, and smart hardware, will also enter an upgrade period, and the opportunities for venture capital are limitless.

---

① Kearney Global Business Policy Council. 2017.
② China Academy of Information and Communications Technology (2019). "White Paper on 5G Economic and Social Impact."

According to calculations by China Academy of Information and Communications Technology, it is estimated that between 2020 and 2025, China's 5G commercialization will directly drive 10.6 trillion yuan in total economic output, directly create an economic value added of 3.3 trillion yuan, indirectly drive a total economic output of about 24.8 trillion yuan, and indirectly drive a total economic value added of about 8.4 trillion yuan. In terms of the contribution to employment, 5G is expected to directly create more than three million jobs by 2025. Different from the Meituan model, the population that benefits from 5G mobile communications technology will be the middle-to-upper-level knowledge population. The human capital structure and output of this population are higher. The economic development and vitality brought by such employment are bigger. Taking Huawei as an example, as a communications company, Huawei has significant advantages in communications technology, leading 4G and 5G technology, camera technology, and battery life cycle fast charging. In addition, Huawei AI has chip advantages. In fact, the employment of high-level technicians driven by Huawei in the past two years exceeds 100,000, which is very impressive from the perspective of the human capital contribution rate.

According to the "2019 Report on Talent Development of the Internet Industry",[1] it is estimated that by 2035, China's 5G will create 9.5 million job opportunities, ranking first in the world. 2018 is known as the "first year of 5G", while 2019 is known as the "first year of 5G development". 5G has become a tailwind of the high-tech field, and the momentum of talent growth is rapid. According to Liepin's big data, the demand for talents in 5G in 2018 increased by 57.62% compared with 2017, and the market is optimistic. Looking forward, more and more cities will need 5G talents, and high-skilled talents will have a bright future for employment.

3.2.3 Didi model: platform economy changes employment

As a new business model under the new round of global technological revolution and industrial transformation, the sharing economy generates a large number of new job opportunities. According to statistics from the "2018 China Sharing Economy Development Report", the size of China's Internet sharing platform economy market in 2018 exceeded 7 trillion yuan. It was estimated that by 2020, the market scale of China's Internet sharing platform economy would reach 9 trillion yuan. The role of the sharing economy in promoting structural optimization, rapid growth, and transformation of consumption patterns in the service industry is becoming increasingly prominent.

The role of the platforms in the platform economy includes three aspects: First, information infrastructure of a modern country, which provides strong support for economic and social development; second, online poverty alleviation provides new methods and new ways to promote targeted poverty alleviation; third, there are three of the four great inventions—"'Scan

---

[1] Liepin (2019). "2019 China AI & Big Data Talent Employment Trend Report".

QR Codes', Bike-sharing, and Online shopping" (the other is high-speed trains)—to provide consumers with accessible, affordable, and excellent network services.

Specifically, the impact of the platform-based sharing economy on the new labor force and its employment model includes four aspects: First, the platform labor market is new. It is an expansion of the fixed workplace labor market, is a product of the new economic form, and makes up for the lack of job creation in the labor market. Second, the number, type, and structure of jobs created on the platform labor market are determined by the scope, cost, and adequacy of information sharing. Employment takes flexibility as the goal, and virtualized contracts, time flexibility, multiple employment relationships, and fragmented career paths as features. Third, employment in the labor market takes stability as the goal, and positions are realized by assignments, and it's characterized by contract legalization, time immobilization, exclusive employment relationships, and career standardization. Fourth, the determination mechanism of wages in the platform labor market is different from the traditional one. Wages for fixed positions are based on job characteristics and personal characteristics, while platform employment wages are based on the access to shared information and feedback from users.[①] The digitalization of the platform-based economy reshapes the market structure through three channels: first, disintermediation—supply and demand sides are connected by the digital platform; second, digitization reduces the threshold of many industries, making smaller traditional enterprises increase; third, the oligopoly of the platform industry has the advantages of scale economy, but lack of competition may cause price distortion.

Didi Chuxing, a model of the shared platform economy, has been operating in more than 400 cities across the country. There are 17.509 million drivers working on the platform, 2.384 million of which were transferred from industries with overcapacity, and 875,000 are retired or demobilized soldiers. Through the digital upgrade and transformation of the entire industry, the Didi platform generates a large number of new employment forms, including online car-hailing drivers, service managers, autonomous driving, road test safety administrators, and autonomous driving tests. These new employment forms enrich the ecology of the entire travel industry and are a new growth point for platform-based enterprises. The "2017 Didi Chuxing Employment Research Report" points out that from June 2016 to June 2017, a total of 21.08 million people earned income on the Didi platform. From June 2017 to June 2018, a total of 30.66 million people earned income on the Didi platform, a significant increase. The research team of the School of Labor and Human Resources of Renmin University released the "Didi Platform Employment System and Employment Quantity Estimation Report". The report shows that in 2018, the Didi travel platform generated 18.26 million employment opportunities in China, including 11.943 million direct employment opportunities, such as online car-hailing and

---

[①] Liu Yi, Xia Jiechang. Research of Theories and Policies of Sharing Economy. *Economic Perspectives*, 2016(04): 116-125.

designated driver services. It also indirectly drove 6.317 million employment opportunities in automobile production, sales, refueling, and maintenance. The latter is the employment opportunities and positions that were indirectly driven by the Didi platform to the upstream and downstream of the travel industry.

According to data from the National Information Center, in 2018, the number of people providing services to the sharing platform economy in China was 75 million, accounting for 9.7% of the national employment of 775.86 million, an increase of about five million over the previous year and a year-on-year increase of 7.1%. The number of employees on the platform was 5.98 million, a year-on-year increase of 7.5%. The shared platform economy has become a new driving force for social and economic development. As policies are gradually regulated and public awareness continues to improve, the industry will continue to maintain rapid and orderly development. According to the forecast of the National Information Center, in the next three years, China's sharing economy will maintain an average annual growth rate of more than 30%, and its potential in stabilizing employment and promoting consumption will be further released. Looking forward, the sharing economy model will bring more jobs, change the traditional employment model, and create more employment methods.

3.3 International comparative analysis

In 2018, the aggregate of the global digital economy exceeded 30.2 trillion dollars, accounting for 40% of GDP. The US has the largest digital economy in the world, followed by China, Germany, Japan, and the UK. The growth rate of digital economy in more than 80% of countries is significantly higher than the GDP growth rate over the same period. Digital economy has become the main driving force behind the global economic recovery. The 2019 Digital Economy Report shows that the leading position of the US and China in the development of digital economy is reflected in many aspects. For example, the two countries account for 75% of blockchain-related patents, 50% of global IoT spending, more than 75% of the cloud computing market, and 90% of the market value of the world's 70 largest digital platform enterprises. The current global competition of urban digital economy is that the US plays a dominant role, developed European countries have strong competitiveness in urban innovation and talents, and cities in emerging Asian economies have strong economic and infrastructure competitiveness and are keeping up.

As an advanced productive force, the empowerment and multiplication effects of digital economy are significant. In terms of labor employment, the population engaged in digital economy in developed countries accounts for a relatively high proportion of the total labor force. According to data from the Bureau of Economic Analysis of the US Department of Commerce, in 2016, there were 5.9 million jobs in the US digital economy, accounting for 3.9% of the 150 million jobs in the US, close to that of the financial and insurance industries and wholesale trade, transportation, and warehousing industries. The average annual salary of employees in digital economy was 114,275 dollars, much higher than the average salary of the overall employed population of 66,498 dollars. In 2017, the average annual salary of employees in digital economy in the US was 132,000 dollars, 1.93 times higher than the average salary in the US. European countries have the strongest overall digital economy, and the gap between digital industrialization and industrial digitalization among countries is relatively small, and the average proportion of digital economy in GDP is 44.7%. Asian countries generally attach great importance to digital industrialization. Digital technology and industrial development have become a key part of driving digital economy. Digital industrialization accounts for an average of 21.7%.[①]

Although China's overall level of digitalization still lags behind that of developed economies, it is becoming a global leader in some important emerging industries, especially in financial technology. China is also a leading global investor in some key digital technologies. Currently, China's venture capital in key digital technologies, such as virtual reality, autonomous driving, 3D printing, robotics, drones, and artificial intelligence, ranks among the top three in the world.

The increase in the concentration of industries in China and the US is driven by technological progress. The development of digital economy in the US is capital-friendly, whereas the development of China's digital economy is labor-oriented. In the US, more and more people worry that machines will replace humans and that ordinary workers will suffer from technological progress. Although there are similar concerns, what we see is the employment opportunities created by food delivery, express delivery, and part-time workers, and the income generated by these jobs often exceeds that of traditional manufacturing. Relevant research conducted by the Chinese Academy of Social Sciences shows that the use of the Internet is particularly helpful in increasing the income and employment of low- and middle-income groups. The difference in the development of digital economy between China and the US originates from population density and labor costs. This means that technological progress is labor-substituting in the US and labor-complementary in China.

Digital economy in the US started developing early, and the scale of digital economy is world-leading. In 2017, the US GDP was 19.3 trillion dollars, and the scale of digital economy was approximately 11.50 trillion dollars, about 60% of the GDP; among which, the scale of industrial digitalization reached 10.11 trillion dollars, accounting for 88% of digital economy.[②] In order to promote the development of digital economy, the US federal government focuses on

---

① Guo Lin. Comparison of Digital Economy Industries between China and the US. *Modern Economic Information*, 2019(07): 407.

② Guo Lin. Comparison of Digital Economy Industries between China and the US. *Modern Economic Information*, 2019(07): 407.

cutting-edge technologies in digital economy and formulates strategies such as the "Federal Big Data Research and Development Strategic Plan". Looking at the comparison of the digital economy development between China and the US, the US does better in digital security and other elements, while China has outstanding performance in the elements of digital international trade. China and the US remain at the same level in terms of digital resource sharing, utilization of digital resources, and digital economic development. However, in terms of digital infrastructure and digital market environment, China is at a disadvantage and has a large gap from the US.

In terms of the development of digital economy, China needs to improve labor productivity. According to a 2017 World Bank report, although China's manufacturing output value ranked the first in the world, the level of overall labor productivity was only 15,500 dollars GDP per worker, seven times lower than the US' 107,200 dollars. In terms of segments, the labor productivity of the information and communications industry is only 1/12 of that of the US, while the labor productivity of manufacturing, financial, and real estate and commerce is 1/10, 1/9, and 1/6 of that of the US, respectively. Only the labor productivity of the wholesale and retail industry is at a high level in the world, but it is still only 1/4 of that of the US. While China's labor productivity ranks low in the world, the effective utilization and vigorous development of digital economy will promote the improvement of labor productivity significantly.

China's digital economy is entering a new stage of rapid development. As for the speed of development, China's digital economy grew by 18.9% in 2016, 12.8% higher than the US (6.1%), 1.9% higher than Japan (17.0%), and 7.4% higher than the UK (11.5%); as for industrial scale, China's digital economy totaled 22.6 trillion in 2016, accounting for 30.3% of the GDP, an increase of 2.8% from 2015, a rapid growth, but still significantly lower than that of other major countries in the world, which was 28%, 16.1%, and 28.3% lower than the US (58.3%), Japan (46.4%), and the UK (58.6%), respectively.[1] The above analysis shows that countries have taken the deepening of the integration of information technology and traditional industries as the focus of their digital economy strategy. The demand for talents with professional digital skills is increasing rapidly. How to attract and train talents needed for the new stage is an important foundation for China to establish a competitive advantage in the development of the global digital economy, and it is also a prerequisite for digital economy to continue to create jobs for China to promote the further development of the labor market.

---

[1] China Info100 (2018). "2017 China Digital Economy Development Report".

Section 4 The Impact of the Development of Digital Economy on the Labor Market

4.1 Problems in the labor market during the development of digital economy

4.1.1 Rapid changes of employment among and within industries

In the book *The Economic Possibilities for Our Children and Grandchildren*, Keynes mentioned: "In a hundred years, the technical standards of the country will be four to eight times higher than the present." "Technological progress can produce sufficient goods, solve economic problems, and also cause unemployment." Just like what he says, the rapid development of digital economy will act on different industrial sectors and drive the transformation and upgrading of the industrial structure of different sectors, and differentiate the labor market.

In the agricultural sector, as the level of digitalization in the agricultural sector continues to deepen, information technologies represented by the Internet of Things and virtual agriculture is being widely used in various links such as agricultural production, processing, and sales, achieving real-time data acquisition and the network of information communication, which improves the competitiveness of agricultural products and achieves large-scale production in the agricultural sector. The digital transformation and upgrading of the agricultural sector not only reduce the demand for labor, but also move toward the technology-oriented requirement. What is in need is a new type of farmers who are familiar with the digital agricultural management system. The immediate impact is the release of a large amount of low-skilled labor. If they cannot be transferred to industrial and service sectors, it will lead to an increase in the number of unemployed in the agricultural sector. On the other hand, due to the technology-oriented demand for labor, most of the rural workers do not have relevant skills and cannot obtain the skills in a short period of time. Therefore, they cannot meet the job demand in the process of agricultural digitalization, which will cause a labor shortage. In addition, the released labor force in rural areas contains the young and middle-aged, while the surplus labor force contains mainly the elderly and women. Therefore, with the development of digital economy, the structural contradiction between supply and demand in the labor market in the agricultural sector will be more severe.

In the industrial sector, unlike workers who only needed to operate equipment simply during the industrial revolution, in digital economy era, with the development of digitization and intellectualization, the traditional manufacturing industry is facing the challenge of transformation and upgrading. Cyber-physical systems will create many smart factories, and smart manufacturing will become the main development trend. In addition, the structure of China's population continues aging, making the cost advantages of the original labor-intensive industries disappear, and the competitive advantages continue to weaken, thus promoting the widespread application of industrial robots and other intelligent economies. As a "virtual labor force", intelligent economies, such as industrial robots, will overturn the original production model, reduce the labor cost of enterprises, and improve production efficiency. It is presented in the labor market as the following: on the one hand, repetitive and easily standardized tasks will continue to be replaced by digital technology, thus reducing the demand for such labor and increasing unemployment in the labor market; on the other hand, the demand for highly skilled labor with skilled application of digital software and programs will continue to increase. The development of digital economy creates relevant technical jobs. However, with the rapid use of industrial robots and other intelligent economies, the overall scale of employment in China will decrease in a short period of time. Generally speaking, the supply and demand structure of the labor market in the industrial sector will reshuffle, thereby driving China's human capital to develop to an advanced level.

In the service sector, although application of information technology started relatively late, the positions gradually begin to be intelligent and digital, and are in a rapid application stage. With the widespread application of digital technology, the employment trend will continue to increase for workers who have access to information tools such as the Internet and network platforms. It should be noted that in the short term, the labor market in the service industry will also replace some repetitive and routine jobs, thereby reducing the total labor demand; but in the long run, the service industry will have more demand for employment.

Generally speaking, although digital economy shows different development processes and trends in different industrial sectors, there is a common phenomenon. The level of digital skills of workers is generally insufficient and cannot satisfy the labor demand required by digital technology. There is a structural imbalance. As a result, the income of workers with different skills will further vary, forcing workers that cannot satisfy digital skills to continue to disconnect from the labor market; meanwhile, the differences in digital technology between different industrial sectors lead to the varied level of employment and level of income in different industrial sectors.

4.1.2 The digital divide between urban and rural areas and labor mobility between regions

From a regional perspective, the scale of digital economy in all regions of China is showing a steady growth trend, but the area with the most digital talents is still the eastern coastal area, and the gap between the western region and the southeastern coastal area is expanding. With the rapid growth of digital economy in the eastern coastal area, digital economy agglomeration is gradually forming, which continuously promotes technological innovation, industrial coordination, urban integration, and institutional innovation, thereby further promoting the region's combined effect and division of labor, collaboration effect, and scale effect. Looking forward, the eastern coastal area will become the main area for the development of digital economy, and it will lead to the cross-regional flow and gathering of labor, especially high-skilled labor.

As the development of digital technology relies on local infrastructure and talent reserves, there is a significant gap between urban and rural areas, and the urban-rural digital divide has gradually formed. The so-called urban-rural digital divide refers to the gap in information resource allocation caused by the gap between urban residents and rural residents in owning and using technology. The urban information infrastructure is relatively complete, and information technology can be widely used in cities. The opportunity for rural residents to use information resources is significantly lower than that of urban residents. This means that the digital skills of rural residents are at a low level. On the one hand, it hinders the popularization and application of digitalization in the agricultural sector; on the other hand, even if the agricultural sector realizes digitalization, there is a lack of skilled labor that is compatible with it, resulting in aggravation of the contradiction between the supply and demand of the labor market. In addition, the industrial sectors in cities continue to transform and upgrade industries, and the requirements for the quality of labor are constantly increasing. Therefore, surplus labor in rural areas will find it difficult to find suitable jobs in cities, which will aggravate the structural imbalance in the labor market, further increasing the income gap between urban and rural areas and deepening the digital divide between urban and rural areas.

4.1.3 Imbalance between the supply and demand of digital technology talents

According to data from the National Bureau of Statistics, there were approximately 3.95 million people engaging in technical services related to information transmission, computer services, and software industries in 2017. Among them, the proportion of digital talents with intermediate and high specialized skills is not high. There were even fewer digital talents with cutting-edge technologies such as artificial intelligence, machine learning, virtual reality, and intelligent manufacturing. However, in the digital economy era, digital talents and data are important driving forces for rapid development. With the rapid development of digital economy and the continuous deepening of the digital transformation of industries, the demand for digital talents will continue to increase.

However, the current situation facing China's labor market is that the proportion of digital talents in China's labor market is relatively low, and the level of digitization of the labor force is generally not high. There is a shortage of digital talents in the labor market, which is reflected in the skill structure; specifically, the contradiction between the supply and demand of digital high-skilled talents. The rapid development of digital economy requires a large number of high-skilled digital talents. However, because of the lack of corresponding labor supply due to China's existing education system and other reasons, a shortage of talents exists across the country.

4.1.4 Substitution and creation of job opportunities

According to the report of the McKinsey Global Institute, after analyzing more than 2,000 job assignments covered by more than 800 occupations around the world, it is concluded that about 50% of the world's job assignments can be automated by improving existing technology. It is also predicted that 51% of the job assignments are likely to be automated in China. Taking into consideration China's huge population base, approximately 397 million workers will face the risk of being replaced in the digital economy era.

Generally speaking, the development of digital economy has a skill-focused impact on the labor market. Limited by current algorithms and computing power, and with the goal of improving productivity, the impact on the labor market is the replacement of workers with simple and repetitive job assignments. Therefore, with the development of digital economy, the demand for low- and medium-skilled workers will continue to decrease, and the employment of low- and medium-skilled labor will face greater risks. In addition, from a gender perspective, the proportion of female employment in computer-related fields is much lower than that of males, and jobs in information technology fields are less likely to be replaced in the future. Therefore, compared with men, women face greater employment risks in the future. Looking forward, the impact of the labor market will first affect low- and medium-skilled workers and female workers.

On the other hand, digital technology, as technological progress, creates some new forms of employment while replacing some traditional jobs and reduces the level of risk for workers. Technological progress will also expand the scale of the economy and increase the demand for labor, especially for highly skilled labor and digitally skilled labor. The jobs created by digital economy will focus on the use of digital technology to complete complex tasks, including R&D and application of digital technologies, as well as the monitoring, authorization, and maintenance of digital technology systems, etc. Most of these jobs are creative and are deeply integrated with digital technology.

4.1.5 Polarization of employment

In the digital economy era, the polarization of employment is also worth our attention. The World Bank report pointed out that in digital economy, one of the changes in the global labor market is job polarization, which means that the employment ratio of high-skilled and low-skilled jobs increases, whereas the employment ratio of medium-skilled jobs decreases, and medium-skilled jobs will be separated and gradually leave the labor market. In the digital economy era, with rising labor costs, medium-skilled workers will be replaced first. According to the cost-benefit analysis, replacing medium-skilled workers will generate higher benefits and will make up for the cost of digital technology input. It is also technically feasible, so medium-skilled workers will be replaced first. Therefore, in the digital economy era, the polarization of the labor market will become more apparent.

Meanwhile, the polarization of the labor market will cause a widening gap in income because the medium-income workers will shift toward high-income jobs and low-income jobs. In the digital economy era, there are technical thresholds for high-income jobs, so only a small number of workers could get high-income jobs in a short period of time through retraining. More workers are turning to low-income job positions and engaging in low-skilled jobs, thus widening the income gap between workers. Additionally, in the short term, most medium-skilled workers turn to jobs that are easily standardized, which causes the squeezing effect of the labor market, and a large number of low-skilled laborers will lose their jobs, thus the unemployment problem in the labor market will intensify.

4.2 Opportunities brought by the development of digital economy to the future labor market

In the report "Year 2035: 400 Million Job Opportunities in the Digital Age", the Boston Consulting Group predicts that China's overall digital economy will be close to 16 trillion dollars in 2035, with a digital economy penetration rate of 48%, and the total employment capacity will reach 415 million. From the above data, in the future, the impact of digital economy on China's labor market will become more significant, and the development of digital economy will bring a series of opportunities and challenges to China's future labor market.

4.2.1 Development of digital economy promotes the conversion of new and old kinetic energy of economic development and the improvement of labor productivity

Currently, the development and application of digital economy are transitioning from the demand side to the supply side. The application of digital technology focuses on consumption, social interaction, travel, communication, payment, etc., thus accumulating a large amount of user data and providing sufficient data sources for further research and development of digital technology. It further promotes the widespread application of technologies such as the Internet, the Internet of Things, and big data in the economic society, thereby driving the employment growth of such technical enterprises, creating many new jobs, increasing employment demand, and driving the employment of the labor market. As digital economy gradually develops toward the supply side, the integration of digital technology and traditional economic industries will be realized, driving the optimization and upgrading of the industrial structure, so that traditional industries such as manufacturing and the medical and health industries have huge development space and potential. Looking forward, traditional industries combined with digital technology will become the core force driving employment in the labor market.

Looking forward, the development of digital economy will further empower the labor market and make the labor market more efficient and productive. The application of digital economy will also promote the transformation and upgrading of the traditional economy, and combine with the traditional economy to produce new industries, new formats, and new models, thereby improving the production efficiency of enterprises, expanding the scale of production of enterprises, and increasing the level of employment in the labor market. On the other hand, the extensive application and development of digital technology will also create more high-skilled and creative jobs and bring about skill-oriented technological advancement, thereby increasing the proportion of skilled workers, which is conducive to increasing labor productivity. This will further promote the structural adjustment of the labor market, improve the efficiency of the allocation of the labor market, and realize the transition from a demographic dividend to a talent dividend.

4.2.2 The development of digital economy is free from the constraints of time and space of the labor market

In the digital economy era, the traditional employment relationship in the labor market will undergo profound changes. Economic subjects can get free from the constraints of time and space, and further improve the efficiency of labor allocation and labor productivity. In terms of employment choices, employment opportunities for workers will increase. The boundaries of entrepreneurship and employment are not limited to physical boundaries, but can be extended to digital platforms, forming platform-based entrepreneurship and employment channels. As Internet technology continues to mature, digital platforms continue to be built and improved. In addition to broadening entrepreneurship and employment, it also reduces the information asymmetry between traditional labor market resource allocation and supply and demand. A more efficient allocation of labor resources lowers the search costs and information costs of labor suppliers and providers, making the transaction more convenient, regulated, and transparent, and it can even help employ some unemployed workers due to industrial restructuring.

In terms of forms of employment, the forms become more diversified, the job responsibilities are clearer, and their level of skills also improves. In addition, employment is flexible and the locations are no longer restricted. Employers are separated from enterprises. The in-house office work gradually becomes decentralized, including home office, online office, etc. This has greatly increased the number of jobs and enriched the forms of employment in the labor market. In addition, the employment concept of the younger generation becomes more profitable. Through flexible forms of employment, they choose to achieve promotion and increase in work income through skill learning, training, and job-hopping.

In terms of time planning, the traditional working hours and working model are eight hours of work and fixed commuting hours. However, in the digital economy era, workers and enterprises focus on the maximization of benefits, so they focus on efficiency rather than duration. Looking forward, the duration of working hours will be shortened, and working hours will become more flexible. Individuals have more flexible working hours, so as to maximize the benefits of various economic entities and promote rapid economic development.

In terms of the distribution of workers, digital economy breaks free of the restrictions of time and space, reduces the gender employment gap, and increases employment opportunities for women. Women can achieve employment through flexible choices of workplaces, thereby increasing the female labor participation rate. Meanwhile, it also reduces the regional employment gap, so that workers in relatively remote areas can obtain employment opportunities through the platform, thereby increasing the overall labor participation rate in the labor market and increasing household disposable income.

In terms of business management, the development of digital economy changes the management approach of the original enterprises. The platformization of enterprises introduces profound changes in the original relationship and forms among workers. Enterprises are free from the originally closed employment status. The ways of recruiting talents are also diversified. The application of digital technology simplifies the recruitment process and improves recruitment efficiency. Through digital platforms such as the Internet, the distance between enterprises and talents is shortened. Meanwhile, enterprises begin to use platforms to transform into platform-based enterprises, allowing them to engage in some tasks of working relationships and partnerships, including labor dispatch, talent leasing, human resources, organizational cooperation, etc., so as to maximize the profits of multiple parties.

4.2.3 Digital economy and aging population

With the continuous development of social productivity and the improvement of medical and health conditions, more and more countries are turning into aging societies. As the elderly population increases, the number of those in the labor force of the suitable age will gradually decrease, and labor costs will gradually rise. Therefore, production and economic development will be affected by a shortage of young labor. The development of digital economy provides realistic and feasible solutions to alleviate the labor shortage caused by the aging of the population. The aging of the population, in turn, promotes the development of digital economy. On the one hand, as the growth of the national labor force is restricted, it is necessary to rely on the advancement of digital technology to replace those who leave the labor force or support elderly workers to continue to do manual work so as to maintain the growth of the economy. On the other hand, as the proportion of the elderly population rises, digital technology may be able to solve the supply and demand issue for elderly care services caused by the growth of the elderly population and the lack of elderly care resources, such as care workers and elderly care institutions. This will generate a huge elderly care consumption and service market, including medical robots, smart medical care, and smart pension, which will further promote the development of digital economy.

In the digital economy era, enterprises can only accelerate the application of digital technology through transformation and upgrading, then replace low-skilled workers, thereby reducing the cost of labor factors, to meet the challenges of an aging society. Meanwhile, despite the age structure of China's population continuing aging, its huge population base, abundant data resources, and broad consumer market potential, including a huge elderly consumer market, provide a broad scope and market demand for the further development of digital technology and digital economy. Chinese enterprises should take this opportunity to accelerate the development of the digital industry, and promote the application of digital technologies such as smart medical care, smart cities, and smart education, so as to better meet the challenges of an aging society.

4.3 Challenges brought by the development of digital economy to the future labor market

4.3.1 The challenge of unemployment

The rapid development of digital economy will have a dramatic impact on the allocation of workers in the labor market. As the application of digital technology is skill-oriented, it may lead to technological unemployment in the labor market. The majority of technological unemployment is the labor force with lower education background who are unable to adapt to the needs of modern digital technology, and repetitive and regular jobs are replaced. If the workers in these replaced jobs cannot master digital skills to adapt to the demands of emerging industries, it may cause an imbalance between the supply and demand in the labor market and cause unemployment. Unattended, unemployment will have an impact on economic and social stability, and affect the further development of digital technology and digital economy.

On the one hand, technological unemployed workers can obtain jobs needed by digital technology applications through vocational education and training, thus successfully transforming into high-skilled workers. However, most of the high-skilled jobs require specialized human resources, and are often the result of long-term professional learning, so only workers who receive professional skills training early can adapt to these positions, which means that workers stick to such specialized skill-based jobs, and it is difficult for technological unemployed workers to obtain such jobs. On the other hand, technological unemployed workers can choose to lower their occupational requirements and choose to engage in low-skilled positions, but this will reduce the working conditions and income of the workers, and make it difficult for the workers to return to their original level. Therefore, it lowers the possibility of workers choosing downgraded jobs, resulting in increased unemployment. Therefore, it remains a huge challenge to alleviate the unemployment problem in the development of digital economy, so that technological unemployed workers can switch and adapt to new jobs.

4.3.2 Challenges of new labor relationships

With the development of digital economy, a variety of new forms of employment emerges, and labor relationships are also changing, which may cause a series of labor relationship problems caused by lagging laws and regulations. There are three aspects: First, it is difficult to confirm the legal status of workers. New forms of employment are difficult to be defined by labor-related laws. Second, in the new form of employment, it is difficult to determine the relationship between employees and organizers. As a result, under the current legal framework, it is difficult to apply traditional social protection mechanisms, such as minimum wages and maximum working hours. Third, in the new form of employment, income is calculated based on commissions or a piece-based price system, which is more flexible and fragmented than the original monthly or annual contract payment system. Therefore, the existing labor-related laws and regulations are lagging behind the development of new labor relations. Looking forward, how to improve and maintain new labor relations as digital technology advances, how to provide continuous labor resources for the development of digital economy, and how to create harmonious labor relations become new topics worth attention.

4.3.3 The challenge of inequality

Changes in technology will have an impact on the labor market. The rapid development of digital technology will further aggravate fluctuations of workers, and the inequality in the labor market may expand. On the one hand, with the development of digital economy, the number of workers and jobs affected by the substitution effect may continue to increase. Inevitably, some workers will be impacted by the development of digital economy. Therefore, the benefits of different worker groups vary as digital economy develops. In the future, the income gap among worker groups of different occupations, education levels, and genders may continue to expand.

On the other hand, the unbalanced development of digital economy between urban and rural areas and regions may also cause a digital divide. China's digital economy is located in the eastern coastal area. The development of digital technology talents and capital promotes technological innovation, industrial coordination, urban integration, and institutional innovation in the eastern coastal area, further accelerating the development of digital economy in that area. The huge gap in infrastructure and digital talents between urban and rural areas will exacerbate the structural imbalance in the labor market and form a segmented labor market under digital economy. Therefore, we should avoid the digital divide as we develop digital economy and be aware of the inequality in the labor market. This remains a challenge in the process of promoting digital economy.

Chapter 8　Digital Economy and Global Governance

As cutting-edge technologies such as big data, cloud computing, the Internet of Things, artificial intelligence, and quantum science continue to achieve revolutionary breakthroughs, the resulting digital economy has become the source and core driving force of global economic growth and globalization. As it spearheads new developments in economic globalization, digital economy also brings new challenges. The failure of governments to efficiently regulate and cooperate will inevitably threaten global economic growth. Therefore, while digital economy continues to rise in status as the world economy develops, it is imperative to perfect the global governance system and the construction of specific institutions.

Digital economic governance generally refers to the governance of all digital-related economic activities. Global governance of digital economy should not only include supervision by governments of various countries, but also introduce digital economic entities such as platforms, third parties, enterprises, and consumers to jointly explore how to create a sustainable and healthy ecological system and enhance the role of digital economy in the economic conversion process. In 2018, the United Nations issued a programmatic report on promoting the development of the global digital economy, emphasizing the need for global governance of digital economy, and urging all member states to work together to resolve the adverse effects of digital technology on society, ethics, and the economy, maximizing the role of digital economy in enhancing social welfare.

By reflecting on the background and significance of global governance systems in digital economy, this chapter will systematically sort out the development strategies and specific policies of the world's major economies for digital economy, as well as the current development status of the more influential digital economic global coordination systems. This chapter will also analyze the more controversial issues in constructing a digital economy global governance system, exploring the historical opportunities and potential risks in its gradual reform and improvement.

Section 1 The Significance of a Global Governance System for Digital Economy

Since the 1990s, new business models represented by e-commerce that uses the Internet as a platform have emerged continuously, and concepts like "new economy" and "Internet economy" have slowly been introduced. Since the early 21st century, as technologies like cloud computing, big data, the Internet of Things, and artificial intelligence develop, modern information and network technologies have become more and more extensive, resulting in a more intensive influence on human society and economic activities. This phenomenon is defined as digital economy. Specifically, digital economy refers to economic activities that use digital knowledge and information as their key production factors, modern information networks as the main carrier, and effective use of information and communications technologies as the driving force for efficiency improvement and economic structure optimization.

Under these conditions, clouds, networks, and terminals have become the new generation of infrastructure, large-scale data has become an important means of production, and computing power has become a key representative of productivity. They promote the intelligent transformation of production tools, as well as changes in the division of labor and organization through network connections. They also play a role in innovating growth models, increasing labor productivity, and cultivating new markets and new industrial growth points. In these ways, they help achieve inclusive and sustainable growth. Digital economy has become an increasingly important engine for world economic growth.

Table 8.1 E-commerce sales in the top 10 countries in the world, 2017

Ranking	Country	E-commerce sales value (billion USD)	Percentage of e-commerce sales to GDP (%)	B2B (billion USD)	Percentage of B2B in e-commerce sales (%)	B2C (billion USD)	Average annual expenditure of a single online buyer (USD)
1	the United States	8,883	46	8,129	90	753	3,851
2	Japan	2,975	61	2,828	95	147	3,248
3	China	1,931	16	869	49	1,062	2,574
4	Germany	1,503	41	1,414	92	88	1,668
5	Korea	1,290	84	1,220	95	69	2,983
6	the United Kingdom	755	29	548	74	206	4,658
7	France	734	28	642	87	92	2,577
8	Canada	512	31	452	90	60	3,130

Continued

Ranking	Country	E-commerce sales value (billion USD)	Percentage of e-commerce sales to GDP (%)	B2B (billion USD)	Percentage of B2B in e-commerce sales (%)	B2C (billion USD)	Average annual expenditure of a single online buyer (USD)
9	India	400	15	369	91	31	1,130
10	Italy	333	17	310	93	23	1,493
Total of top 10 countries		19,315	36	16,782	87	2,533	2,904
Global total		29,367		25,516		3,851	

Source: UNCTAD, "Digital Economy Report, 2019.".

The vigorous growth of digital economy has also promoted a revolutionary change in the global economic and trade model—the large-scale cross-border trade and movement of digital products and services, which has further expanded global trade and investment growth. The deep integration of digital economy and traditional economy has promoted the new development of traditional industries, and continuously created new, unprecedented industries and related economic and trade exchanges. Digital economy makes it easier for more social classes, especially the disadvantaged, to participate in business activities, offering a solid foundation for global economic transformation in a more inclusive direction.

Table 8.2 Cross-border B2C sales in the world's top 10 countries, 2017

Ranking	Country	Cross-border B2C sales value (billion USD)	Percentage of trade exports (%)	Percentage of B2C sales (%)
1	the United States	102	6.6	13.5
2	China	79	3.5	7.5
3	the United Kingdom	31	7.0	15.0
4	Japan	18	2.6	12.2
5	Germany	15	1.0	17.1
6	France	10	1.8	10.6
7	Canada	8	1.8	12.7
8	Italy	4	0.7	16.2
9	Korea	3	0.5	3.8
10	the Netherlands	1	0.2	5.0
Total of top 10 countries		270	3.0	10.7
Global total		412	2.3	10.7

Source: UNCTAD, "Digital Economy Report, 2019".

However, digital economy has also brought about huge challenges to regulatory and governance cooperation at the global level. The growth opportunities created by the application of digital technology coexist with its serious abuse and unexpected consequences, and the dividends of digital technology coexist with its faults. First, the digital economy has brought new challenges to the global trade and investment ecosystem, changing comprehensively the traditional economic growth model, causing a reconstruction in the global supply chain and value chain. Secondly, the "digital divide", such as the access and quality of basic facilities, the penetration rate of digital technology, and digital literacy, has not yet been resolved, which may exacerbate global inequality at all levels. Thirdly, the "barrel principle" in information security has become increasingly prominent, and the global economy must face increasing security threats due to digitalization. According to estimates made by relevant parties, digital security crises such as cybercrime and hacker attacks have cost the global economy more than USD 400 billion annually. Finally, as a new economic form, the digital economy has produced many new types of property rights and economic transaction models that are beyond the scope of existing laws and regulations. A global institutional coordination mechanism is currently absent.

As technological changes accelerate, the construction of corresponding collaborative and governance systems has failed to keep up with the changes. We still lack a global governance coordination system. In 2015, the United Nations recognized 680 cooperation mechanisms related to the digital economy, and the number has now risen to over 1,000. Among these numerous, complicated, and competing mechanisms, a primary systematic and interest-coordination model has not been confirmed.

The essential feature of the digital age is interconnectivity, and clearly differentiated competitive and cooperation mechanisms are destroying this interconnectivity, even resulting in a struggle for dominance, a decline in mutual trust, and an obstruction to the original cooperation process. It was not until the G20 (The Group of Twenty) Hangzhou Summit, held in 2016, that the "G20 Digital Economy Development and Cooperation Initiative" was first proposed, marking the start of policy coordination and cooperation among the world's major digital economies. In 2018, the Secretary-General of the United Nations delivered a speech on global digital economic governance for the first time, which was taken as the start in constructing a global digital economic governance system.

In recent years, there has been a global consensus on the importance of the digital economy. Many international multilateral cooperation platforms like the G20 and the Asia-Pacific Economic Cooperation (APEC) have listed the digital economy as an indispensable priority, actively discussing opportunities and challenges brought about by the new digital economy, and exploring ways to improve its global governance. Committed to cooperation, mutual trust, and mutual benefit, they promote the establishment of a new digital economy global governance system that is conducive to the welfare of all mankind.

Section 2 The Evolution and Development of a Global Governance System for Digital Economy

2.1 WTO negotiations and coordination on global digital trade

As the key representative of the traditional trade governance system, WTO is committed to building a multilateral digital trade regulatory system to meet the challenges of global economic governance in the developing digital economy.

At present, the WTO has not formulated any special rules on digital economic governance. Its relevant regulations are scattered in other agreements and their annexes. These include the "General Agreement on Trade in Services" (GATS) (Articles 1, 2, 3, 6, 14, and Annex on Telecommunications, section 5), which delineates regulations in principle for "access to and use of public telecommunications networks and services", "movement of information across borders", "digital service market access", and "data localization measures". The "Information Technology Agreement" (ITA) has also made some progress in formulating "information technology product tariff reduction". The principles in the "Agreement on Trade-Related Aspects of Intellectual Property Rights" (TRIPS) are also applicable to digital trade. Under the framework of the "Declaration on Global E-commerce", WTO members have also reached a consensus to not impose a "customs duty on electronic transmissions".

However, the aforementioned digital trade rules do not regulate the latest development of digital trade, and are limited by the slow progress of the "Doha Round" negotiations. These regulations also make it difficult to substantially regulate the future development of the global digital economy. In addition, the commitments made by WTO members in the GATS are all listed under a "positive list", which does not cover most digital trade forms that have just emerged. Regulations on the protection and enforcement of intellectual property rights in TRIPS can be partially applied in the field of digital trade, but more specific rulings are needed as guidance. Although the "Declaration on Global E-commerce" of 1998 states that they will not "[impose] customs duties on electronic transmissions", this political commitment does not really have any international legal effect.

Although the WTO has achieved unsatisfactory results in global digital economic governance and trade rules, it is still one of the most important platforms for constructing a future, multilateral governance system for digital economy. In fact, many economies have already made efforts under the WTO framework. For example, since July 2016, China, the United States, the European Union, Russia, and other WTO member states have submitted more than 30 proposals on multilateral digital trade governance. The 11th WTO Ministerial Conference, held in December 2017, unanimously agreed to make e-commerce a core issue. 71

WTO member states jointly issued the "Joint Statement on E-commerce" (referred hereafter as "Joint Statement"), aiming to explore e-commerce issues together under the WTO framework.

Thanks to the efforts of China, the United States, the European Union, Russia, and other economies, the WTO has made a lot of progress in promoting a digital trade governance system in recent years.

Firstly, WTO members agreed to extend the validity period of tariff exemption for electronic product transmission. Although the WTO members failed to unanimously agree to elevate this declaration to international law, its main members all expressed support and reached a general consensus to extend its validity period. In addition, the conclusion of the relevant WTO research report clearly states: "It is recommended that electronic product transmission be made permanently tax-free. This will be conducive to improving enterprises' participation in international trade, further promoting the development of global digital trade."

Secondly, WTO members generally recognize that the WTO framework has unique advantages in digital trade governance. Most WTO members believe that global digital trade based on the Internet and cross-border data flow has natural multilateral attributes, and it is appropriate to gradually establish and improve a unified governance system under a multilateral framework. As an alternative to the multilateral governance system, the negotiations required for a bilateral governance system to achieve the same rule coverage is more time-consuming and labor-intensive, and its more complex trade rules and implementation standards will inevitably lead to the "spaghetti bowl" effect. A free, open, and internally coordinated multilateral digital trade regulation system is difficult to achieve, but it has the conditions to become the most ideal global digital trade framework. In other words, only a mature WTO multilateral system will have the unique advantage of delivering a digital trade multilateral governance system.

Thirdly, some members have already put forward feasible proposals on the regulation and governance of digital trade. In the near future, certain WTO members will work toward "ITA agreement expansion", "upgrading TRIPS", "building a new cross-border data flow coordination mechanism", and "reasonably defining and interpreting the scope of application for GATS rules and commitments", thereby constructing and reforming the multilateral digital trade governance system.

For possible progress the WTO can make in digital economic governance, see Table 8.3

Table 8.3 The progress and potential cooperation between WTO members in digital trade governance

Field	Specific details
(1)	Reaching a consensus on the perpetuation and legalization of "customs-free digital transmissions".
(2)	ITA's tariff reduction law should cover more new information and communications products. The membership coverage of the new round of ITA negotiations should be expanded.
(3)	TRIPS should further emphasize "the protection of source code" and introduce a clause on the "responsibilities of Internet intermediaries".

Continued

Field	Specific details
(4)	The cross-border privacy regulation system under the Asia-Pacific Economic Cooperation (APEC) framework should be promoted among WTO members, so as to achieve a balance between free cross-border data flow and privacy protection.
(5)	Formulate special rules to reduce or completely eliminate unnecessary localized data storage for member.
(6)	The provision of digital services should be regarded as "Mode 1", and will automatically trigger the "Mode 1" commitment of GATS members in that service sector.

Source: compiled by the author.

2.2 G20 coordination and cooperation for the development of digital economy

The G20 is made up of 20 members: China, Argentina, Australia, Brazil, Canada, France, Germany, India, Indonesia, Italy, Japan, Korea, Mexico, Russia, Saudi Arabia, South Africa, Turkey, the United Kingdom, the United States, and the European Union. The total GDP of its member states accounts for 85% of the world's total, and its total population accounts for two-thirds of the world's total. The G20 has become an important part of the global economic governance system.

The G20's contribution to global digital economic governance began with the "G20 Digital Economy Development and Cooperation Initiative" adopted during the 2016 G20 Hangzhou Summit. In 2016, as the chair country of that year, China listed "digital economy" as an important issue for the first time in the "Blueprint on Innovative Growth". During this meeting, the "G20 Digital Economy Development and Cooperation Initiative" was unanimously adopted, indicating that "digital economy" has officially become a vital and inevitable component for economic cooperation among G20 members.

The "G20 Digital Economy Development and Cooperation Initiative" elaborates the concept, significance, and guiding principles of digital economy, and proposes seven aspects: innovation, partnership, synergy, flexibility, inclusion, open and enabling business environment, and flow of information for economic growth, trust, and security. These general principles clarify the key issues of digital economy development and cooperation, such as broadband access, ICT investment, entrepreneurial and digital transformation, e-commerce cooperation, digital inclusion, and the development of micro, small and medium-sized enterprises. At the same time, the initiative encourages all members to strengthen policy formulation and supervision in six areas: intellectual property protection, respect for independent development paths, digital economic policy formulation, development and implementation of international standards, trust enhancement, and radio spectrum management. It promotes exchanges to create an open and secure global governance system to face the future, encouraging its members to carry out multi-level cooperation and continuously deepen exchanges and coordination in the areas of policy formulation, legislative experience, and best practices in training and research. On this basis, the G20 will continue to strengthen its active interaction with other international organizations and groups, jointly promoting the rapid and healthy development of digital economy.①

Since the 2016 Hangzhou Summit, all G20 meetings have listed digital economy as a key topic of focus and discussion. The G20 Summits held in 2017 and 2018 both issued G20 Digital Economy Ministerial Declarations, further enhancing the achievements of the Hangzhou Summit on this issue.

On June 28 and 29, 2019, the 14th G20 Summit held in Osaka, Japan put "Global Digital Governance" as the primary discussion topic of the meeting. Witnessed by leaders of China, the United States, Japan, and other countries, representatives of various countries signed the "Osaka Digital Economy Declaration", officially launching the "Osaka Orbit". This declaration emphasizes that discussions on e-commerce issues should be aimed at establishing international trade rules, and it calls on all countries to make substantial progress in negotiations during the 12th WTO Ministerial Conference to be held in 2020, so as to promote the development of their digital economies.

As the host country, Japan put forward the concept of "trust-based digital flow" and advocated for the establishment of a "data circulation circle", allowing the free flow of data across borders, while promoting global data development based on personal privacy, ethics, intellectual property rights, network security, and reliable regulations that encourage free and global circulation of data. The European Union paid more attention to data localization and privacy protection, while the United States was more concerned about whether it could obtain non-discriminatory market access and realize free data flow.② India did not participate in the meeting, while Indonesia and South Africa refused to sign and endorse the declaration. This shows that there is still a long way to go in establishing a global digital economic governance system that can reconcile the differences of all parties.

The governance innovation section of the declaration pointed out that global governance in the digital age must be innovative. The potential of emerging technologies can only be fully realized through the benefits of innovative support and policy formulation. The G20 will strive for innovation-friendly policies to tap into the potential of digital technologies and remove barriers to innovation. Countries have adopted measures such as regulatory sandboxes to make policies more flexible, comprehensive, and agile. The removal of policies, regulations, or regulatory barriers can promote and accelerate the economic growth and inclusive development of developing countries, as well as micro, small, and medium-sized enterprises (MSMEs).

Global governance in the digital age needs to be innovation-friendly, meanwhile it must not

---

① Feng Kong. G20 Hangzhou Summit adopted the 'G20 Digital Economy Development and Cooperation Initiative' to inject new impetus into the innovation and development of world economy. *China Daily*, September 28, 2016.

② Dong Yan & Zhang Lin. Building Rules for the Global Digital Economy. *Guangming Daily*, July 15, 2019.

lose legal certainty. Interoperable standards, frameworks, and regulatory cooperation can help in this regard. With all stakeholders playing different roles, the formulation of coordinated international and national policies will help cope with a wide range of social challenges and incorporate continuously upgraded new technologies into future policy discussions.

2.3 APEC's cooperation policies and results encouraging the development of digital economy in the Asia-Pacific region

APEC is composed of Australia, Brunei Darussalam, Canada, Chile, People's Republic of China, Hong Kong China, Indonesia, Japan, Republic of Korea, Mexico, Malaysia, New Zealand, Papua New Guinea, Peru, the Philippines, Russia, Singapore, Chinese Taipei, Thailand, Vietnam, and the United States—an economic cooperation organization of 21 member economies. APEC is also the highest-level economic, trade, and investment cooperation platform in the Asia-Pacific region. The organization's focus on digital economy began at the end of the 20th century, and after years of exploration, has entered the specific implementation stage of digital economic cooperation.

The important strategies, blueprints, initiatives, and action agendas of the APEC digital economy cooperation are shown in Table 8.4.

Table 8.4 The progress of the APEC digital economy cooperation

Stage and year		Specific details on cooperation
Initial stage	1998-2000	The release of the "APEC Blueprint for Action on Electronic Commerce"
Full exploration stage	2000-2010	Adopted the "Action Agenda for New Economy" and the "e-APEC Strategy".
Specific implementation stage	2010 to present	Formulated the "APEC Leaders' Growth Strategy" in 2010; Adopted the "APEC Initiative of Cooperation to Promote Internet Economy" in 2014; Adopted the "APEC Framework on Human Resources Development in the Digital Age", "APEC Cross-Border E-commerce Facilitation Framework", and "APEC Internet and Digital Economy Roadmap" in 2017; Formulated the "APEC Action Agenda for the Digital Economy" in 2018.

Source: compiled by the author.

2.3.1 Initial stage (1998-2000)

In 1998, APEC released the first action plan for digital economic cooperation—the "APEC Blueprint for Action on Electronic Commerce", which marked the preliminary cooperative consensus of APEC member economies in the field of e-commerce. Digital economic cooperation has since become one of APEC's important cooperation topics. The "Blueprint" stipulates the main principles for developing e-commerce, based on information and communications technology, in the three areas: enterprises, governments, and markets. It proposes the "Brunei Goals"—realizing paperless trade for developed APEC members before

2005, and for developing APEC members before 2010. Limited by the Internet, especially with mobile Internet technology at the developmental stage and with restrictions on its application, APEC's digital economic cooperation at this stage is focused on promoting the emerging global e-commerce.

2.3.2 Full exploration stage (2000-2010)

In the new millennium, the "Action Agenda for New Economy" and the "e-APEC Strategy" have been adopted successively, marking APEC's entry into the full exploration stage of digital economic cooperation. The "Action Agenda for New Economy" and the "e-APEC Strategy" have formulated specific action plans in priority areas such as Internet infrastructure construction, mechanism innovation, and human resources. In terms of digital infrastructure construction, it planned to increase the number of Internet access points in the Asia-Pacific region by 2005 to three times that of 2000. By 2010, urban and rural residents of various economies can use the Internet to obtain information and services through personal or community channels. In terms of mechanism innovation, a plan was formulated to promote digital economic cooperation using a "pathfinder approach"; that is, to encourage qualified and willing APEC members to practice first, before expanding to other member economies once the earlier group has accumulated enough experience, or when the conditions are ripe. In addition to these two landmark achievements, APEC also issued a series of agendas and action plans related to digital economic cooperation at this stage, expanding the scope of cooperation and reforming cooperation mechanisms.

2.3.3 Specific implementation stage (2010 to present)

In 2010, the formulation of the "APEC Leaders' Growth Strategy" marked a new framework construction stage in terms of digital economic cooperation. In the "APEC Leaders' Growth Strategy", APEC included growth strategy as a formal topic for the first time, proposing to achieve balanced, inclusive, sustainable, innovative, and safe growth in the Asia-Pacific region. Digital prosperity characterized by close cooperation is an important part of the innovative growth goal. Its proposal is based on the rapidly developing Internet and digital economy. This means that cooperation between digital economies in APEC has significantly improved. As the global digital economy rapidly develops, it has gradually become an important pillar in APEC's growth strategy.

Since then, APEC has successively adopted initiatives like the "APEC Initiative of Cooperation to Promote Internet Economy" (2014), the "APEC Framework on Human Resources Development in the Digital Era" (2017), the "APEC Cross-Border E-commerce Facilitation Framework" (2017), and the "APEC Internet and Digital Economy Roadmap" (2017), clarifying the priorities and specific areas for digital economic cooperation. Priorities related to digital economic cooperation include data and privacy protection, e-commerce and digital trade, legal frameworks related to digital economy, entrepreneurship and innovation, human resource development, Internet finance, and the development of micro, small and medium-sized enterprises. In 2017, the "APEC Internet and Digital Economy Roadmap", formulated by the APEC Da Nang Conference, identified 11 key areas, which include digital infrastructure, e-commerce, information security, inclusiveness, and data flow, that will guide future APEC Internet and digital economic cooperation. In 2018, pushed by host economy Papua New Guinea, APEC formulated the "APEC Action Agenda for the Digital Economy". As the only annex to the APEC chairman's statement that year, the agenda showed APEC's deep concern about digital economic cooperation issues. In addition, as understanding and cooperation deepen, APEC has formulated a complete framework and clear mechanism for digital economic cooperation in the Asia-Pacific region.

Table 8.5 Digital economy development index and global ranking of APEC member economies in 2017

Member economy	Development index	Ranking	Member economy	Development index	Ranking
the United States	0.837	1	Chile	0.413	45
Singapore	0.609	9	Thailand	0.411	46
Hong Kong, China	0.484	22	Russia	0.446	38
Canada	0.590	12	Mexico	0.466	29
Republic of Korea	0.621	4	Vietnam	0.367	67
Australia	0.584	15	Peru	0.387	59
New Zealand	0.586	24	Indonesia	0.391	54
Japan	0.615	7	Brunei Darussalam	0.304	89
People's Republic of China	0.718	2	the Philippines	0.376	63
Malaysia	0.459	32	Papua New Guinea	-	-

Source: "2018 Global Digital Economy Development Index", jointly developed by Alibaba Research Institute and KPMG, December 2018.

2.4 The content and impact of the CPTPP agreement on the developing digital economy

Although the United States withdrew from the "Trans-Pacific Partnership" (TPP) after the Trump administration took office, the remaining 11 countries quickly signed the new "Comprehensive and Progressive Trans-Pacific Partnership" (CPTPP). The latter is still a regional trade agreement, with one of the highest levels of global liberalization. The newly-signed CPTPP agreement removes 22 clauses of the original TPP agreement, but still retains more than two-thirds of it. For example, the "e-commerce" chapter (on extensive protection of data created by digital trade), the "government procurement" chapter (opening government procurement contracts equally to all foreign bidders), and the "state-owned enterprises" chapter (mainly restricting member state governments from subsidizing state-owned enterprises and intervening in the market) are not found in any other regional economic cooperation agreements.

The regulations on digital economic cooperation in the CPTPP agreement are also among the most comprehensive and widely applicable regional regulations in current global digital economic governance. The CPTPP inherits the principle of lowering barriers to data flow through new trade rule adjustments as advocated by the United States, thereby promoting the liberalization of digital trade, and may have a significant impact on the formulation of future international trade rules. Its regulations mainly include (1) insisting that the Internet should remain free and open, (2) banning tariffs on digital products, and (3) ensuring that trading partners will not take further protective measures, like not putting contracting parties' digital products at a competitive disadvantage, and not erecting discriminatory and protectionist barriers against cross-border information flow. Governments are prohibited from forcing domestic companies to adopt localization strategies in computing services, and are also prohibited from forcing companies to transfer technology, production processes, or proprietary information to individuals. The e-commerce chapter has 15 clauses that regulate e-commerce policies, including clauses to reduce digital trade barriers, clauses to protect the rights and interests of online consumers, clauses to facilitate digital trade, and clauses to promote international coordination and cooperation.

See Table 8.6 for digital trade clauses in important global economic and trade agreements.

Table 8.6 The status of digital trade clauses covered by important global economic and trade agreements

Digital Trade Clauses	USMCA	CPTPP	KUFTA	EUJEPA	EUSFTA
Removal of tariffs on digital products and/or electronic transmission	Yes	Yes	Yes	Yes	Yes
Principle of non-discrimination of digital goods	Yes	Yes	Yes	No	No
Electronic authentication and electronic signature	Yes	Yes	Yes	Yes	Partially
Paperless transactions	Yes	Yes	Yes	No	Partially
Domestic electronic trading box	Yes	Yes	Yes	Partially	No
Protection of online consumers	Yes	Yes	Yes	Yes	No
Protection of personal data	Yes	Yes	No	No	No
Measures to combat unsolicited commercial electronic communications	Yes	Yes	No	Yes	No
Cybersecurity	Yes	Yes	No	No	No
Cross-border transfer of information	Yes	Yes	Partially	Yes	Yes
Prohibiting data localization requirements	Yes	Yes	No	No	No
Responsibilities of intermediary service providers	Yes	No	No	No	Partially
Non-disclosure of software source code and related algorithms	Yes	Partially	No	Partially	No
Open government data	Yes	Yes	No	No	No
Cooperation	Yes	Yes	Yes	Yes	Yes

Note: USMCA stands for the "United States-Mexico-Canada Agreement", KUFTA stands for the "Korea-United States Free Trade Agreement", EUJEPA stands for the "Japan-EU Economic Partnership Agreement", and EUSFTA stands for the "EU-Singapore Free Trade Agreement".

Source: "Digital Rules in Trade Agreements. Asian Trade Center, 2019-7-24." http://asiantradecentre.org/talkingtrade/. comparing-digital-rules-in-trade-agreements. Retrieved on May 28, 2020.

2.5 Policy coordination among the United States, Japan, and Europe on developing digital economy

2.5.1 Joint Statement of the United States, Japan, and Europe

On January 14, 2020, Japanese Minister of Economy, Trade and Industry Hiroshi Kajiyama, US Trade Representative Lighthizer, and EU Trade Commissioner Hogan met in Washington DC, US, and issued a joint statement. This was the seventh joint statement issued by the United States, Japan, and Europe on international economic governance. It reflects the difficulties that economies like the United States, Japan, and Europe face in dealing with the new global political and economic situation when encountering obstacles in multilateral trading mechanisms such as the WTO, and it reflects their urgent hope in reshaping international rules. In their previous tripartite joint statements, the content related to digital trade and e-commerce included the "Joint Statement on Electronic Commerce", issued in Buenos Aires in 2017, and the "Joint Statement on Electronic Commerce", issued in Davos in 2019. These statements pointed out the need to deepen WTO members' consensus on the major economic benefits of future digital trade agreements, striving to achieve high-standard agreements with as many members participating as possible and to improve the business environment by promoting data security.[①]

2.5.2 The "Data Circulation Circle" of the United States, Japan, and Europe

On January 9, 2019, Japan, the United States, and the European Union conducted a meeting of trade ministers in Washington and issued a joint statement, affirming the guidelines in building a cooperative "data circulation circle" that allows for the free flow of personal and corporate data across borders.

The issue of cross-border data flow has always been a serious and extremely sensitive issue for all countries, and their strategic considerations are not entirely consistent. Concerning this issue, the US and Japan reached a preliminary agreement as early as the Trans-Pacific Partnership Agreement. The European Commission passed an "adequacy decision" with Japan on January 23, 2019, allowing personal data to flow freely between the two economies on the basis of strong protection. However, the US and the EU still have differences on the issue of cross-border data flow. In May 2018, the EU issued the "General Data Protection Regulation", strengthening the protection of personal information, in principle prohibiting the transfer of personal data outside the EU, opposing the stance of the US on the free flow of global data across borders.

The "data circulation circle" jointly promoted by the US, Japan, and Europe will help resolve differences between them on the issue of data circulation and also promote regional and global economic integration.

---

① Liu Ming. Analysis of the Joint Statement of the US, Europe, and Japan Trade Ministers since 2017. *National Governance*, June 2019.

Section 3 Key Issues in Global Governance of Digital Economy

3.1 The battle for dominance between competing global digital economic governance systems

3.1.1 The European Union

The digital economic governance system that the EU hopes to establish is based on the General Data Protection Regulation (GDPR). The EU is committed to promoting its single market by improving data governance and strengthening its absolute control over data, thereby gaining dominance over the other global governance systems. The birth and development of the GDPR is gradually showing its extensive influence and coverage. Important features of the regulation include: First, the GDPR stipulates that EU personal data control has a "long-arm jurisdiction" function; that is, it has control functions for all countries storing EU personal data. Second, the EU data security enforcement mechanism has strengthened the "Budapest Convention", leading to the implementation of high penalties. Third, the GDPR allows for full and flexible control during the implementation process, optimizing the international dialogue mechanism, and gaining greater dominance among global digital economic governance systems.

In addition, the EU has formulated a "Digital Single Market" (DSM) strategy. A "Digital Single Market" refers to a market that meets the three following conditions: goods, people, services, and capital are guaranteed free circulation; residents, individuals, and businesses can connect seamlessly; all online activities are conducted under fair competition conditions. The DSM is an important long-term goal of the EU to unify markets and promote trade and economic growth. It is made up of three main components:

(1) Provide individuals and enterprises with better digital products and services, such as measures to promote the development of cross-border e-commerce; protect consumer rights; provide faster and more affordable package delivery services; break geographical boundaries and change the current situation of different prices for the same commodity in different member states; reform copyright protection laws; promote the provision of cross-border television services.

(2) Create a favorable environment conducive to the prosperity and development of digital networks and services, including a comprehensive reform of the EU's rules and regulations in the telecommunications sector; review the audiovisual media organization framework to meet the needs of the times; comprehensively analyze and evaluate search engines, social media, application stores, etc., and the roles they play on online platforms; enhance security management of digital services, especially personal data.

(3) Maximize the growth potential of digital economy, such as proposing a "European Free

Data Flow Plan" to promote the free flow of data resources across the EU; establish unified standards and interoperability in e-health, transport planning, and other fields that are vital to the development of the DSM; build an inclusive digital society so that citizens can seize employment and other opportunities brought about by the developing Internet.

The EU has introduced a series of important policies around the "Digital Single Market" concept. In terms of platform management, the EU believes that actions such as data collection on online platforms have a profound impact on the online ecological system, playing a key role. Here, the so-called online platforms include search engines, social media, e-commerce and app stores, and price comparison websites. The main concern of the EU is that once these large-scale network platforms use their market power to develop and grow in different economic fields, it may be difficult to apply the EU Competition Law on them. To combat this, the EU is considering a series of management policies, such as trading practices, access clauses, and contract terms (that will improve transparency and prohibit unfair transactions). It will also restrict discriminatory practices of vertically integrated companies, and amend the EU Competition Law to better apply it on online platforms. It will establish a roundtable on EU online platforms to promote their development.

Concerning e-commerce business, the European Commission will amend the rules related to consumer online shopping and value-added tax. First, the EU will further optimize rules regarding the purchase of digital content on the Internet, such as the issuance of after-sales relief for online defective content. Second, the EU will introduce a series of statutory contract rights involving warranty periods and breach of contract relief. Third, the EU will also review the "Consumer Protection Cooperation Regulations" (2011). The promulgation of this will strengthen the power of law enforcement agencies and enhance coordination in monitoring and early warning. In 2015, the EU initially established a pan-European dispute resolution platform. It must be mentioned that the EU also adjusted value-added tax in 2016, easing pressure on member governments. This means that the EU may include digital products in value-added tax in the future. Finally, the EU also introduced measures on parcel delivery in 2016. These measures involve price transparency, fast delivery, and merchandise tracking.

Concerning geo-blocking,[①] some EU member states oppose this restriction, believing that certain geo-blocking measures will hinder intra-European trade. In fact, these restrictions are being applied to the isolated market of each member state, leading to price differentiation and other effects unconductive to competition. In response to this problem, the EU is working to revise the "Electronic Commerce Regulations", which is committed to establishing a unified internal market framework, and Article 20 of the services directive, concerning non-discriminatory provisions for content recipients. These changes will reduce the legitimate

---

① Geo-blocking refers to the practice of restricting users' access to network resources based on their geographic location. The users' geographic location is calculated using positioning technology to determine whether they are allowed access.

reasons for online sellers to deny consumers' access to online services. In addition, the EU is also reviewing the "Satellite and Cable Directive", established in 1993, to assess whether it helps consumers' cross-border access to satellite broadcasting services within Europe. This is expected to expand the application scope of certain broadcasters' network services.

3.1.2 The United States

After his inauguration, President Trump announced that the United States would be withdrawing from the TPP agreement and that NAFTA negotiations would resume. These two actions have had a great impact on the United States' global leadership in the field of digital trade. The Obama administration signed the TPP agreement, intending to use this to promote US leadership in global digital economic governance, and strengthen trade regulations to conform to American interests globally. After the US formally announced its withdrawal from the TPP in 2017, it did not propose an alternative strategy, which undoubtedly marked the waning of its leadership in global digital economic governance. Although some digital trade regulations in the original TPP agreement were adopted in the resumed NAFTA negotiations, with an attempt to multilateralize the "American template", there is no doubt that the US is weakening in its leadership status in digital trade governance.

At the international level, although the United States and Europe have similar positions on basic concepts of global digital economic governance, they have not reached a substantive consensus. For example, the US particularly emphasized the effect of the "Privacy Shield Agreement", but after the invalidation of the Safe Harbor Privacy Principles, the EU is still extremely dissatisfied with the agreement. The fundamental differences in their understanding of human rights and the market have also led to uncertainties for the future development of global digital economic governance.

3.1.3 China

China's main contribution to the construction of an international digital economic governance system is reflected in digital trade chapters of its latest signed bilateral free-trade agreements. For example, in the China-Korea Free Trade Agreement, China-Australia Free Trade Agreement, and other binding trade agreements, e-commerce clauses are adopted, with separate chapters on e-commerce. This "separate chapter" model is also used in telecommunications and financial fields involving digital trade. At present, China is actively promoting e-commerce negotiations in more than 10 free-trade agreements. So far, China has completed negotiations on e-commerce issues in the China-Georgia and China-Chile Free Trade Agreements, as well as the EAEU-China Trade and Economic Cooperation Agreement.

Secondly, China is also actively offering suggestions in discussions on international digital economic governance, helping to formulate international digital trade rules. In November 2016, China submitted "China's Proposal on E-commerce Issues" to the General Council of the WTO, offering opinions and suggestions on e-commerce-related issues. The proposal uses the concept of cross-border e-commerce, which mainly includes business-to-user (B2C) and business-to-business (B2B) cross-border e-commerce transactions. Its content includes creating a trade policy environment that facilitates cross-border e-commerce, improving transparency of the e-commerce policy framework, and upgrading infrastructure and technical conditions for developing cross-border e-commerce. In December 2017, China pushed the 11th Ministerial Conference of the WTO to reach ministerial decisions in its e-commerce work plan. China has also actively participated in consultations on e-commerce under the WTO, the Shanghai Cooperation Organization, the Lancang-Mekong Cooperation, and other multilateral and regional trade arrangements, and has facilitated the founding of the BRICS E-commerce Working Group, resulting in the "BRICS E-commerce Cooperation Initiative". The G20 Trade Ministers' Meeting held in Shanghai in July 2016 also approved the "G20 Strategy for Global Trade Growth", which listed "the promotion of e-commerce development" as one of the pillars of the cooperation. It promised to deepen e-commerce cooperation and strengthen public-private dialogues, as well as promote the study and discussion of trade-related policies, standards, and methods, so as to adapt to new trends in global economic and trade development. At present, China is taking advantage of the "Belt and Road Initiative" to perfect an integrated regulatory system in seven areas of digital trade: the classification of digital products, cross-border digital transmission, trade barriers and tariffs, personal data privacy protection, Internet usage rules, new financial services, and intellectual property rights.

3.2 Free flow of trust-based data

3.2.1 Background of the problem of cross-border data flow

Cross-border data flow in digital trade is generated under digital globalization and economic globalization. This concept was defined by the OECD in "Guidelines on the Protection of Privacy and Transborder Flows of Personal Data" in the 1980s: cross-border personal data flow is the flow of personal data across national borders. The UNCTC defined cross-border data flow in 1982 as the processing, storage, and retrieval of machine-readable data processed by computers across national borders.

In recent years, the volume of transactions generated by countries through digital trade has been increasing from year to year. According to the MGI's "Digital globalization: The new era of global flows" report, the contribution of data flow to global economic growth and investment has exceeded that of traditional cross-border trade since 2008. Data globalization has become an important force in shaping global economic development. In order to protect their economic interests, countries have erected barriers to inhibit free cross-border data flow during transactions. However, due to differences in political background, supervisory strength, economic development status, and digitization level, there are also varying degrees of restrictions on cross-border data flow. Seen from this context, the study of disputes arising from cross-border data barriers and the need for governments to reach a consensus are of great significance to the future growth of international digital trade.

3.2.2 The positions of major global economies on cross-border data flow

At present, the major global economies have different levels of supervision over cross-border data restrictions. There is the open data flow supervisory system of the United States, the European Union system that meets certain conditions of free data flow, and the relatively strict supervisory system of China.

(1) The United States

The US economy is relatively advanced in digital development and is highly dependent on free data flow. Hence, it has adopted a relaxed stance on the issue of data flow restriction, preferring to restrict government power, using the market as the main means of protecting personal data, and relying on the power of commercial organizations to protect personal information. The US believes that any hastily enforced legislation will hamper the development of e-commerce, so it has not issued a protection law regulating cross-border data flow. At the same time, the US has further promoted cross-border data flow by signing bilateral and multilateral agreements. APEC's "Cross-Border Privacy Rules" (CBPR), of which the US is a participant, is considered to be one of the more operational.

Although the US has adopted a relaxed stance on cross-border data restrictions, it does impose restrictions on certain data flow. For example, the US stipulates in its "Export Administration Regulations" that certain products produced using American technology or software, foreign products that are not produced in the US but contain a certain proportion of American technology, or products made by factories outside the US but with key components manufactured using American technology may face export restrictions. China's ZTE Corporation was once affected by this control and was unable to import certain products from the US.

On June 4, 2019, the US Center for Strategic and International Studies (CSIS) website published a report entitled "Data Governance Principles for the Global Digital Economy". The report pointed out that discussions on data governance are not conducted in a vacuum. Laws, practices, frameworks, standards, and agreements related to data processing have existed for decades, and data governance has been explicitly or implicitly included in existing governance mechanisms involving privacy, digital trade, e-commerce, and human rights. However, almost no one could predict that emerging technologies would have extended the boundaries of data tracking to our natural environment, enabling us to obtain detailed insights using vast amounts of data generated by digital economy. The report set out to fill four major gaps in the existing global data governance structure: First, a large number of international, regional, national, and local laws and regulations that affect data flow need to be consistent, interoperable, and coordinated. Second, existing rules, frameworks, and debates around data flow governance tend to focus entirely on personal data and privacy, rarely considering the broader impact of data on competition, mobility, and trade. Third, the existing data flow governance frameworks and global debates mostly focus on controlling data access rather than data use. Fourth, existing differences in positions usually are based fundamentally on the rights and freedom of data subjects, at the expense of other stakeholders and social groups.

(2) The European Union

Unlike the US position of restricting data flow based on self-discipline, the EU recognizes the right to data as a basic human right of its citizens and has stricter restrictions on free data flow. Since the early development of digital economy, EU member states have introduced legislation restricting data flow. For example, Sweden introduced the Data Act in 1973, and the United Kingdom introduced the Data Protection Act in 1984. With the gradual expansion of EU integration, the EU has gradually adopted the "Digital Single Market" as its main development goal. Therefore, data flow within the EU has become a necessity for digital transactions between countries. In June 2015, the EU proposed the "Digital Single Market Strategy". Its main purpose is to eliminate regulatory barriers among member states, unify the markets of its 28 members into a single market, and promote the development of the EU's digital economy.

In 2016, the EU passed the "General Data Protection Regulation" to implement the conditional free flow of data across borders, that is, "lenient internally and strict externally" regulations. When data is exchanged within the EU, it can flow freely and completely if both parties reach an assessment level in the exchange of information. However, when data is transmitted to countries, regions, and industries outside the EU, one must determine the protection adequacy of the other party. The "Regulation" also proposes that the legal model of "long-arm jurisdiction" be used to govern all companies collecting information from EU citizens.

(3) China

China's management system for cross-border data flow was established late and is still being improved. The "Cybersecurity Law of the People's Republic of China" was officially passed in November 2016 and came into effect in June 2017. This was the first time that China had clearly implemented regulatory measures on cross-border data flow in legislation. In April 2017, the draft of "Measures for Security Assessment of Outbound Provision of Personal Information and Important Data" was released. This legislation supplements the Cybersecurity Law through specific content by delineating evaluation methods for outbound data and improving the existing regulatory system.

From the current management framework, one can see that China's attitude toward cross-border data flow is exactly the opposite of that adopted by the US. China implements strict security reviews, filtering and monitoring data content flowing in and out of the country. This regulation is conducive to national and personal data security and has a positive impact on facilitating the efficiency of domestic law. However, excessively strict data export restrictions may also result in trade barriers, reducing the efficiency of international digital product trade.

3.2.3 Disagreements and cooperation among major global economies in cross-border data flow

(1) Disagreements and cooperation between the United States and Europe

As two key components of the world economy, the United States and Europe also play a leading role in the development of the global digital economy. However, there is an irreconcilable difference between the two on the issue of cross-border data flow. There are two main contradictions: The first is in personal information protection. The protection of personal information in the US depends on its citizens' self-discipline. The US has not issued a clear law on the protection of personal privacy, while the EU is based on "human rights" and attaches great importance to such privacy. The second is data flow. The US believes that the Internet should not have national boundaries and that all countries can use it freely. Therefore, in the TPP agreement that the US participated in, the US proposed the free flow of cross-border data on a global scale. The EU emphasizes that every country has sovereignty of data and this should not break each individual country's autonomy.

Applied practically, these two propositions each have their pros and cons. Since the US and Europe are closely connected economically, failure to find a balance between such differences will adversely affect their long-term cooperation. The "Safe Harbor Agreement" was signed under this context. The agreement stipulated that US companies must accept the supervision of the EU or the US government, and the US must provide a list of companies that agree to abide by this rule. This was the first time that the US and Europe reached a consensus on this issue. However, the agreement was invalidated due to the "Prism Gate" incident and its aftermath. In response to its serious consequences, the US and Europe are actively seeking new ways of cooperation to amend the original Safe Harbor Agreement. In February 2016, the "Privacy Shield Agreement" was officially released. This new agreement added provisions as to how private and individual data can be used, greatly enhancing personal information protection.

Although the release of the "Privacy Shield Agreement" marked the gradual restoration of trust between the US and Europe on the issue of data flow, there may be still conflicts in the future. The fear that the US may try expanding its dominance of the Internet and on data flow control along with its commitment to freer access of overseas data are still the crux of the conflicts between the two sides.

(2) Disagreements and cooperation between China and the United States

Both China and the United States are big digital trading nations, and digital trade occupies an important position in the economies of both countries. During President Obama's administration, the US gradually formed a regulatory system by largely promoting the free flow of data across borders. After President Trump took office, he further strengthened this policy. However, there are big differences and contradictions in the positions of China and the US on cross-border data flow, which hinders the development of digital trade between them to a certain extent.

The free flow of cross-border data is the basis for US companies' survival worldwide, but China clearly stipulates in Article 37 of its "Cybersecurity Law" that companies can only collect personal information and important data in China by cooperating with its national cybersecurity and informatization department. The relevant department of the State Council can only transmit data overseas after conducting a security assessment. In addition, because China's information protection technology is not perfect, in order to avoid information leakage, China must implement more restrictive measures, such as the use of the Great Firewall and restrictions on VPNs. The US believes that these restrictions are not conducive to digital trade between China and the US, as they indirectly block US-funded companies from entering the Chinese market.

Faced with this disagreement, it is vitally important for China and the US to seek common ground while reserving differences and build a win-win framework based on respect for their mutual positions on free data flow.

3.3 Personal privacy protection in the development of digital economy

3.3.1 Background of the personal privacy protection problem

The concept of privacy was first put forward by American scholars Warren and Brandeis in the article "The Right to Privacy", published in the *Harvard Law Review* and defined as the right to be let alone. With the development of the theory of privacy rights, countries continue to improve privacy protection systems. The United Nations issued the Universal Declaration of Human Rights in 1984, establishing the right to privacy as one of the basic human rights. However, because it is difficult to maintain the same definition in different fields, it is difficult to define the connotation of privacy.

As human society enters the information age, personal information has become an important factor of production supported by big data technology. As Internet technology develops, the ability of enterprises to obtain and process user information without user knowledge has rapidly increased. This not only leads to more serious privacy issues, but also poses a serious threat to personal life and social stability. Countries worldwide are aware of the importance of personal information protection and have promulgated successive laws and regulations. For example, the United States promulgated the "Fair Credit Reporting Act" in 1970. It was the world's first law to protect personal information. The "Convention for the Protection of Individuals with Regard to Automatic Processing of Personal Data", signed by members of the European Commission in 1981, was the world's first convention for the protection of personal data.

The establishment and protection of one's privacy rights is a common demand of the public and is conducive to the development of the e-commerce industry. This also requires the protection of personal data in cross-border trade in order to adapt to the new pattern of digital international trade.

3.3.2 Personal privacy protection policies of major economies in the world

(1) The United States

The United States was the first country to protect privacy. Since the introduction of the privacy theory, the US has established a relatively complete privacy protection mechanism. In 1974, the "Privacy Act" was promulgated and implemented by the US, regulating the collection and use of personal information by the federal government and balancing the contradiction between public interest and personal privacy to prevent public institutions from misusing its citizens' information and violating their personal privacy rights. With the development of electronic communication technology, the US promulgated the "Electronic Communications Privacy Act" in 1986 to protect citizens' communication and e-mail content, prohibiting the storage and access of personal communication information without permission. At the same time, the US pursues a privacy protection policy combining industrial self-discipline and law. In 1998, the US Department of Commerce issued the "Elements of Effective Self-Regulation for Protection of Privacy", which regulates US website practitioners and requires them to take self-regulatory measures to protect personal data and privacy on the Internet.

As the US information technology industry develops, three forms of self-discipline have been gradually formed: "Recommended Industry Guidelines", "Enterprise Privacy Certification", and "Technology Protection Mode". The "Recommended Industry Guidelines" is led by the "Online Privacy Alliance" and is committed to creating an environment of mutual trust for businesses. The "Enterprise Privacy Certification" is led by TRUSTe, Webtrust, and other organizations, authorizing privacy certification for cross-industry alliances. The "Technical Protection Mode" was led by the "Platform for Privacy Preferences Project", allowing websites to disclose personal data; it was ultimately up to the user to choose whether the data could be published.

(2) The European Union

The EU's privacy protection system also started early. In 1995, the European Parliament and the Council of the European Union passed the "Directive 95/46/EC on the protection of individuals with regard to the processing of personal data and on the free movement of such data", which came into effect three years later. The directive required EU countries to adopt uniform standards to protect personal data. The member states of the EU have successively formulated their own personal data protection laws to meet the unified requirements of the Directive. In 2002, the Council of the European Union and the European Parliament jointly promulgated the "Privacy and Electronic Communications Directive", which replaced the previous "Directive 95/46/EC on the protection of individuals with regard to the processing of personal data and on the free movement of such data". It is the latest legislation regulating privacy protection of e-commerce consumers in the EU. The EU's privacy protection system has been perfected after the "General Data Protection Regulation" came into effect. For the first time, personal privacy was included in data protection, and its "long-arm jurisdiction" feature is applicable to all companies worldwide that collect information from EU member states with undifferentiated jurisdiction. This groundbreaking regulation is widely used as a reference by other countries.

The EU's privacy protection is bound jointly by the domestic laws of its member states and the EU's unified directives. The traditional rights that do not involve personal data flow are bound by domestic laws, while the cross-border flow of private data is protected under the "Electronic Communications Privacy Act".

(3) China

In the digital age, China's legislation on personal privacy protection still needs to be improved. First, due to the late establishment of legislation for privacy rights in China, the right to privacy is not protected as a separate right, but is differentiated separately under different fields. The dependence of privacy rights on such differentiation makes it difficult to separate this from other rights, resulting in overlaps and causing difficulties in the actual act of protection.

Moreover, most of China's existing provisions on privacy remain at the traditional level, that is, they merely ensure that citizens' homes and their personal dignity are not violated. As digital information technology develops, there are certain deficiencies in legislation in digital communications. Existing laws are incapable of dealing with issues like the collection and use of personal information by emerging technology industries, resulting in loopholes in the system. Offenders who expose the personal information of citizens are still beyond the reach of the law.

3.4 Server localization in the development of digital economy

3.4.1 Background of the problem of server localization

Server localization requires data collected and generated in the host country to be stored in a server within the host country to protect national and personal data from being stolen. However, this requirement has had an impact on the free flow of cross-border data. How to balance the benefits of free data flow and data localization has become an important and contentious issue among countries.

Before US withdrawal, the TPP was the first free-trade agreement to restrict server localization. The TPP stipulates in Article 13 of its e-commerce chapter: "No Party shall require a covered person to use or locate computing facilities in that Party's territory as a condition for conducting business in that territory". The computing facilities here include servers and storage devices for processing or storing information for commercial use.

Aside from the United States as the main promoter of these agreements, other global economic agreements prohibiting the host country's server localization have also been recognized by other economies. Even after the US withdrew from the TPP, the CPTPP agreed upon by the remaining 11 economies still retains the relevant provisions. Moreover, the "Trade in Services Agreement" (WikiLeaks Disclosure Edition, round 10, December 2014) also made relevant provisions on server localization: A contracting party shall not, on the provision of local services and investment, force service providers to:

• Use computing facilities in the territory of the contracting party;

• Use computer processing or storage services provided in the territory of the contracting party;

• Use other methods to store or process data in the territory of the contracting party.

The increase in transaction costs brought about by server localization is the chief reason for countries prohibiting server localization. The Leviathan Security Group found that in the quantification of mandatory localization cost, "for many countries that are considering or have considered forced data localization laws, local companies would be required to pay 30%-60% more for their computing needs than if they could go outside the country's borders. This is devastating. Businesses rely on data and computation for every aspect of their business; most businesses cannot afford to increase a base cost of doing business 30%-60%, and when the business grows, so too will their computing costs."[1]

Bauer and his team used the Global Trade Analysis Project (GTAP) to quantify losses caused by data localization in seven economies: Brazil, China, the European Union, India, Indonesia, Korea, and Vietnam.[2] The study pointed out that the production and export of the required services depend on safe and efficient data access. Data localization may affect any enterprise that uses the Internet to produce, deliver, and collect work fees or pay wages and taxes, and may threaten economic recovery. The proposed or promulgated localization requirements of these economies have some adverse effect on their GDP: Brazil (−0.2%), China (−1.1%), the European Union (−0.4%), India (−0.1%), Indonesia (−0.5%), Korea (−0.4%), and Vietnam (−1.7%). If these economies implement localization requirements in all sectors, the GDP loss will be even more severe: Brazil (−0.8%), the European Union (−1.1%), India (−0.8%), Indonesia (−0.7%), and Korea (−1.1%). The simulation results are shown in Table 8.7.

---

[1] Leviathan Security Group. Quantifying the Cost of Forced Localization, 2015. https://www.leviathansecurity.com/s/Quantifying-the-Cost-of-Forced-Localization.pdf.

[2] Bauer, M., Lee-Makiyama H., van der Marel, E., Verschelde B. The Costs of Data Localisation: A Friendly Fire on Economic Recovery. European Center for International Political Economy, ECIPE Occasional Papers No.3/2014.

Table 8.7 Simulation results of the impact of server localization on the GDP of certain economies

Economy	Scenario 1 (%)	Scenario 2 (%)
Brazil	−0.2	−0.8
China	−1.1	−1.1
the European Union	−0.4	−1.1
India	−0.1	−0.8
Indonesia	−0.5	−0.7
Korea	−0.4	−1.1
Vietnam	−1.7	−1.7

Note: Scenario 1 takes into account the actual proposed regulations in each country/region, including the data localization requirements of each country/region; Scenario 2 assumes that data localization requirements are implemented in all industries based on actual proposed regulations.

Source: Bauer, M., Lee-Makiyama H., van der Marel, E., Verschelde B. "The Costs of Data Localisation: A Friendly Fire on Economic Recovery." European Center for International Political Economy, ECIPE Occasional Papers No.3/2014.

Even though global economies have some consensus on the possible losses caused by server localization, the dangers of free data flow on the security of sovereign nations still prompt many economies to propose regulations with "localized data storage" or "restriction on cross-border data". Among the seven economies studied by Bauer et al, five have made clear requirements for data localization.[①] In fact, even the CPTPP agreement provides flexibility for contracting parties to take restrictive measures. Provisions prohibiting the localization of computing facilities need not prevent contracting parties from adopting or maintaining certain computing facilities localization in order to achieve legitimate public policy goals.

3.4.2 Strategic positions of major global countries/regions on server localization

(1) The United States

Cloud servers used by most multinational companies in the United States are located in the US, and the world's major information technology companies are from the United States, with data stored locally (such as Amazon, Alphabeta, Apple). In order to reduce the operating costs of these companies and enhance their international competitiveness, the US government has incentives promoting the free flow of global cross-border data and calls on other countries to prohibit the implementation of server localization. The US is also the primary promoter of "server localization" in international economic and trade rules, having successfully incorporated its demands into agreement clauses of the original TPP negotiations. After President Trump took office, although the US withdrew from the TPP, it does not mean that the US has changed its stance on free cross-border data flow. In 2018, the US, Mexico, and Canada negotiated on cross-border data flow and data storage localization issues, resulting in the USMCA, which clearly states the requirements for non-mandatory data storage localization. In addition, the US Congress promulgated the "Clarifying Lawful Use of Overseas Data Act" in 2018, giving US

---

① Bauer, M., Lee-Makiyama H., van der Marel, E., Verschelde B. The Costs of Data Localisation: A Friendly Fire on Economic Recovery. European Center for International Political Economy, ECIPE Occasional Papers No.3/2014.

law enforcement agencies the right to obtain overseas data.

The US government pointed out that server localization is essentially a trade barrier, which may cause unfair competition between regions and increase business operating costs. Even so, the US itself has implemented server localization in some areas. In 2010, the US government issued the "Federal Cloud Computing Strategy", giving the federal government control over data and the power to formulate relevant policies to determine where data should be stored.① In 2015, the US Department of Defense required all cloud computing service providers to store data within the country. In 2016, the US Internal Revenue Service issued regulations requiring tax information systems to be located in the US. In addition, the US has also imposed cross-border flow restrictions in its foreign security review and contract mechanism on data held by foreign capital entering the infrastructure market.②

(2) The European Union

The EU has relatively comprehensive protection policies for personal privacy, emphasizing the supremacy of "human rights", so the need for data localization is emphasized in multilateral negotiations. One of the foundations for the EU adopting this position is the principle of non-neutrality of technology; that is, technology has social value in addition to intrinsic value. This makes personal information more susceptible to infringement through cross-border transmission. The Swedish "Data Act" passed as early as 1973 restricts the cross-border flow of personal data. In 1995, the EU passed the "Data Protection Directive". This directive allows for the protection of personal data within the EU, especially when personal data flow from member states to non-member states. Upon this basis, the EU then passed the "General Data Protection Regulation (GDPR)" in 2016, which took effect in 2018. On the one hand, the GDPR continues the principles of the Data Protection Directive. While prohibiting member states from using data protection as an excuse to restrict the free data flow within the EU, it also restricts the outflow of data from the EU. The EU has also expanded the jurisdiction of the GDPR, stipulating that no matter where the company is located, the regulation is applicable to any company using data owned by citizens of EU member states or providing goods or services to EU citizens. In addition, the EU has also imposed heavier penalties. For example, companies that process data without customer consent or violate the privacy principle will be punishable by the EU with a penalty of up to 4% of its annual global turnover, or 20 million euros (whichever is higher). It is worth noting that these regulations apply to both decision-makers and "machines". This means that related cloud services also fall under its jurisdiction.③ Although the law does not provide

---

① Federal Cloud Computing Strategy. https://cloud.cio.gov/strategy/. Retrieved on May 22, 2020.

② Huang Daoli, Hu Wenhua & Da Alai. Big Data Governance and Compliance Response from the Perspective of Security. *Confidential Science and Technology*, 2018(10):14-18.

③ Blackmer, W. S. GDPR. Getting Ready for the New EU General Data Protection Regulation. Information Law Group. InfoLawGroup LLP. 5 May 2016 [22 June 2016].

clear legal requirements for server localization, it objectively increases the operating costs of companies whose servers are not in the EU and can therefore be regarded as a soft requirement for service company localization.

In addition to personal data, some EU member states have increased the requirements for server localization in specific areas after the leakage of the US Prism program. Both Germany and France have invested in their own specialized networks in domestic data storage, independent of American technology, thereby realizing server localization.

However, this position of the EU is a clear "double standard". The European Commission has also pointed out that Russia's support for data localization has created trade barriers and is not conducive to EU companies trading in Russia. At the same time, the EU has also criticized China's data localization policies.

(3) Australia

Australia's basic position is similar to the EU's; that is, the requirements for server localization are mainly based on the protection of personal data. In 2012, Australia enacted the "Personally Controlled Electronic Health Records Act". Section 77 prohibits the transmission of health data outside of Australia. If foreign companies wish to collect, store, and process health-related information in Australia, they must establish a data center in Australia or establish a cooperative relationship with a local data center to process their data.

(4) Russia

Russia's "Law on Information, Information Technologies, and Information Protection" promulgated in 2006 and the "Russian Federal Law on Personal Data" signed by its president in 2014 stipulate that the personal data of Russian citizens should be stored in the territory, and information owners and operators are also required to establish a data center in Russia. In addition, the "Bloggers Law", which took effect in 2014, stipulates that individuals or corporate or legal entities engaged in information distribution or exchange must store data on login, distribution, transmission, and processing in Russia for more than six months.

(5) India

India has adopted stricter requirements for server localization. The "Information Technology (Reasonable Security Practices and Procedures and Sensitive Personal Data or Information) Rules" promulgated as early as 2011 stipulates that sensitive personal data must not be transferred outside of the country without explicit consent. In 2014, an action plan published by the National Security Council of India stipulates that all email service providers must establish servers in India, all data generated in India should be stored in India, and the data of all telecommunications and Internet companies are required to be stored and processed by the "National Internet Exchange of India" to ensure that they remain in India. In 2018, India released the latest draft of the "Personal Data Protection Bill, 2019" (the "Indian Act") in accordance with the EU's General Data Protection Regulation, differentiating personal data into three levels:

① Personal data. Personal data refers primarily to data that can directly or indirectly identify the natural person, or related data after taking into account any characteristics of the natural person, or after combining these characteristics;

② Sensitive personal data. Sensitive personal data includes financial data, health data, official identifiers, religion/politics/belief affiliations, sex life, biometric and genetic data, transgender identities, bisexual identities, castes and tribes, and other data categories specified by the DPA;

③ Critical personal data. Critical personal data refers to personal data specified by the central government as critical personal data. The government specifies which data belongs to critical personal data.

For general personal data, the "Indian Act" does not require local storage; for sensitive personal data, it can be transferred across borders under certain conditions, but should continue to be stored in India; for critical personal data, it can only be stored in India for processing.

(6) China

China's position on data storage localization focuses on protecting network security. Its "Cybersecurity Law" stipulates that important data collected and generated by information infrastructure operators must be stored locally, or only transmitted overseas after passing a security assessment. This policy allows for the swiftest response to cyber attacks by foreign criminals, thereby ensuring national information security.

3.5 Intellectual property protection in the development of digital economy

3.5.1 Background of digital intellectual property protection issues

In recent years, as Internet technology develops and with the emergence of new advanced technologies, the Internet has been undergoing disruptive changes. According to a report issued in 2018 by China's National Copyright Administration, China's online copyright industry accounted for 7.35% of its GDP, becoming an important pillar of its economic structural upgrade. However, the problem of piracy and copyright infringement has also risen, and new requirements have been put forward to protect intellectual property rights.

In addition, as the scale of cross-border e-commerce continues to expand, with its characteristics of intangibility and anonymity, it has caused new problems in the supervision of intellectual property. Loopholes in cross-border trade are exploited by criminals, and infringements are on the rise. In the "Special 301 Report" released by the United States in 2018, it is clear that there are serious intellectual property infringement problems in the Chinese e-commerce market. As Sino-US trade friction intensifies, the issue of intellectual property rights protection needs to be resolved urgently.

However, due to the regional requirements of intellectual property rights, domestic intellectual property rights are not protected in other countries. This has obstructed the expansion of international trade. In 1967, 51 countries signed the "Convention Establishing the World Intellectual Property Organization" at the Stockholm Conference, establishing the World Intellectual Property Organization (WIPO) as a specialized agency of the United Nations. At the end of the 20th century, the WTO established the TRIPS Agreement, stating the minimum standards for protecting intellectual property rights for both parties. The agreement marked the maturity of the intellectual property protection system.

3.5.2 Policies of major global economies regarding intellectual property rights protection in digital economy

With 5G, artificial intelligence, the Internet of Things, and other technological changes and industrial construction, new product forms, communication methods, and business formats are constantly being created, triggering major and even subversive changes in the Internet industry and bringing more complex issues of infringement, piracy, and copyright authorization. The digital economy era demands more intellectual property rights protection from various countries. In 2002, the APEC member economies—Brunei Darussalam, Hong Kong China, Indonesia, Japan, Republic of Korea, Malaysia, Mexico, New Zealand, Papua New Guinea, Peru, the Philippines, Singapore, Chinese Taipei, Thailand, the United States, Vietnam, and Chile—launched a pioneering initiative: "Statement to Implement APEC Policies on Trade and the Digital Economy", promising to fully implement the "WTO's Agreement on Trade-Related Aspects of Intellectual Property Rights" and ratify and implement the "WIPO Copyright Treaty" and "WIPO Performances and Phonograms Treaty". By using adequate supervisory mechanisms, they are to ensure that their government entities only use genuine software or other products. They should ensure as far as possible that the Internet and e-commerce do not facilitate the trade of counterfeit and copyright infringement products, as well as establish an appropriate management and law enforcement system to reduce such activities.

(1) The United States

The United States has always valued the protection of intellectual property rights. Its intellectual property protection began in the "Copyright Act of 1790" in the 18th century. After revisions and supplements, the "Copyright Act of 1790" was revised in 1976. After more than 200 years of development, the US Federal Government has established many institutions responsible for intellectual property management, like the Patent and Trademark Office, Copyright Office, and Office of the United States Trade Representative. In addition, related bills were further promulgated, and the intellectual property protection system was gradually perfected, as in the "Patent and Trademark Law Amendments Act" of 1980 and the "Federal Trademark Dilution Act" of 1995. In 2004, the US implemented a joint strategic plan and promulgated the "Strategy for Targeting Organized Piracy" (STOP), to jointly protect intellectual property rights with other countries.

In digital economy, the US, as the most advanced Internet technology country, has a large number of patents in various fields. For example, Qualcomm's CMDA (Code Division Multiple Access) has a monopoly in the global market. With the continuous expansion of international trade, in order to maintain its core technological competitiveness and trade interests, the "Tariff Act of 1930" ("Article 337") and the "Trade Act of 1974" ("Article 301") have been enforced. Import and export products are assessed and intellectual property rights are protected.

During his tenure, Obama promulgated policy documents such as the "International Strategy for Cyberspace" to strengthen innovation and intellectual property rights protection in the digital economy era. In 2018, the Trump administration implemented national strategic plans such as the "National Cyber Strategy". While clarifying its vision for the future development of digital economy, it also stressed intellectual property rights protection for digital products. Among them, the "National Cyber Strategy" pointed out that strong intellectual property protection can ensure continued economic growth and innovation in the digital age.

(2) The European Union

Europe, as the birthplace of the earliest capitalist economies, produced early companies in the 17th century. Properties gradually expanded from tangible forms, such as capital, land, and equipment, to intangible forms, such as patents and trademarks. In order to protect the ownership of this type of property, European countries have successively passed patent and trademark laws, and thus began their protection of intellectual property rights. However, during the early stages of legislation, the recognition and protection of intellectual property rights were only applicable domestically. As European integration accelerated, the regional restrictions on intellectual property rights gradually became less useful for new situations, resulting in contradictions between free trade and regional protection within the EU.

In the digital economy era, the number of patents in emerging technologies has increased sharply as technology develops. In order to adapt to this new situation and resolve contradictions, the Western European countries jointly signed the European Patent Convention in 1973, establishing the European Patent Office. European intellectual property protection began to be integrated. In order to adapt to intellectual property protection in the digital economy era, the EU has successively introduced strategic plans such as the "EU 2020 Strategy", the "Single European Act", and the "Digital Agenda for Europe". In May 2011, the EU proposed a new strategy for intellectual property protection, based on intellectual property rights in the digital age. This strategy emphasizes the construction of a European digital library, promoting digitization and online reading of "orphan works". In terms of trademarks, the comprehensive modernization of the EU's trademark system has been carried out by revising the "European Union Trademark Regulation" and the "Trademark Act", making them more effective, efficient, coordinated, and applicable to the digital age. In terms of copyright, the EU is creating a stable copyright management framework that adapts to the digital environment at the European level.

(3) China

China's intellectual property rights system, which has been comprehensively reformed over many years, directly determines the degree of intellectual property protection in China and also helps shape the understanding of intellectual property in Chinese society. The importance of innovation and intellectual property in economic development has become increasingly evident. In recent years, China's R&D expenditure as a proportion of its GDP has continued to rise, reaching 2.11% in 2018, ranking 12th in the world. The United States has a share of 2.74% in the same year. At the same time, social innovation is constantly taking place. Among industrial enterprises with annual revenue of more than ¥20 million, the proportion of R&D activities continues to increase, from 6.4% in 2008 to 27.4% in 2017.[①] If we take into account the fact that industrial enterprises "above designated size" have been statistically adjusted from those with an annual business turnover of ¥5 million to ¥20 million and more since 2011, this change in proportion is even more obvious. Increasing innovation demonstrates the optimization of the innovation environment, as well as the strengthening of intellectual property protection in China. According to statistics from the National Copyright Administration, the size of China's online copyright industry continues to expand, growing from ¥619.1 billion in 2017 to ¥742.3 billion in 2018—a growth rate of 16.6%. The online copyright industry has become a new engine fueling China's economic growth and a pillar of the national economy. China's current digital economy has fully integrated into its industrial transformation and economic structural optimization and upgrade. It is increasingly becoming the mainstream of economic development, an important driving force for new transformations replacing the old.

Since 2005, China has continuously strengthened its crackdown on Internet copyright infringement and piracy. To achieve this, the National Copyright Administration, the Ministry of Public Security, the Ministry of Industry and Information Technology, and the Cyberspace Administration of China jointly launched an Internet-cleansing operation to manage vertical governance in specific fields, striving to cleanse the Internet by rooting out offenders over years and to protect intellectual property rights in the digital economy era. At the same time, by introducing relevant laws and regulations, a legal shield has been erected for intellectual property rights protection. The 18th National Congress of the Communist Party of China was held on November 8, 2012. Since then, laws and regulations on intellectual property rights protection in e-commerce have been promulgated and revised, such as the "Trademark Law", "Foreign Investment Law", and "E-commerce Law". They all play important roles in accelerating the punitive damages system and promoting a new era in China's intellectual property rights protection. With the rapid development of the Internet in recent years, intellectual property rights protection is quickly turning into cyberspace protection, playing a key role

---

① Source: China Science and Technology Database.

especially in e-commerce. As the role of e-commerce becomes increasingly prominent, the "E-commerce Law" is the first such legislation to be implemented in China. It complements and enhances intellectual property rights protection in the global e-commerce system, incorporating it into the industry.

At present, the global intellectual property protection system needs to be improved to adapt to the vast development of digital economy. The "IP Protection in the Data Economy", released by the Information Technology and Innovation Foundation (ITIF) in 2019, pointed out that the existing intellectual property protection system is challenged by many aspects of digital economy, such as incentives for individuals establishing databases, and the balance of the social value of databases. It is also challenged by the non-competitive nature of data, the ownership of data, the ownership of individuals and their data, the ownership of private and personal identification information, mandatory sharing and access, and competition policies.[1] These challenges, coupled with massive data flow that transcends national boundaries, make it necessary for China to cooperate with other economies to overcome international differences in the data intellectual property system, so as to improve and make more consistent data-sharing legislation and regulatory framework, both regionally and globally.

While constructing international intellectual property rules that can adapt to digital economy, China is working hard to transform its digital powers into international institutional powers, so as to protect its interests in future digital economic cooperation. The 2017 McKinsey Global Institute's research report "China's digital economy: A leading global force" found that in the past decade, China has become the global digital economy leader in many fields. In 2016, its e-commerce transactions exceeded 40% of the world's total. It is estimated to have exceeded the sum of those in five countries: the United Kingdom, the United States, Japan, France, and Germany. China's personal consumption-related mobile payment transactions amounted to USD 790 billion, 11 times that of the United States. In the field of financial technology, 9 out of 23 of the world's unlisted "unicorns" are Chinese companies, making up more than 70% of the total valuation of global Fintech (Financial Technology) companies. Among the world's 262 "unicorns", one-third are Chinese companies, accounting for 43% of their total valuation.[2]

3.5.3 Sino-US differences and coordination on the issues of digital intellectual property protection

Since 2018, the trade dispute between China and the United States has been escalating, and one of the excuses the US is using to initiate a "trade war" is intellectual property issues. The US

---

[1] Atkinson R. D. IP Protection in the Data Economy: Getting the Balance Right on 13 Critical Issues. Available at SSRN 3324641, 2019.

[2] Woetzel Jonathan, Seong Jeongmin, Wang Wei Kevin et al. China's digital economy: A leading global force. *China SciTechnology Business*, Issue 11, 2017.

"Special 301 Report"① believed that China had "stolen" the intellectual property rights of the US, and recently included companies such as Huawei in the "Entity List". This further demonstrates that the dispute between technology and intellectual property rights is the source of trade friction between the US and China. Intellectual property plays an important role in the rapid development of the US economy. In the GDP structure of the US, the GDP of intellectual-property-intensive industries is as high as USD 6 trillion, contributing 38.2% to its total GDP. In total US exports, the proportion of intellectual-property-intensive industries is also as high as 52%② (over USD 800 billion), accounting for half of its total exports. Intellectual property rights are related to the core interests of the US in its participation in digital trade governance; intellectual property rights related to digital trade constitute a major component of US digital trade rules. Since Trump came to power, his administration has been more ambitious on this issue than the Obama administration: First, the Trump administration had actively promoted the evolution and upgrading of intellectual property rules in regional trade agreements, signing the US-Mexico-Canada Agreement (USMCA), which stipulates digital trade intellectual property rights as defined in the TPP (Trans-Pacific Partnership Agreement), and proposing a series of expansion accordingly. Second, in order for the US to reap greater profits, the Trump administration had further expanded and adjusted intellectual property rights rules to better apply them at multilateral (WTO) and quasi-multilateral (G20, APEC) levels.

On the issue of digital intellectual property protection, China and the United States have big differences (Chen Chaofan and Liu Hao, 2018③; Zhou Nianli, 2018④; Li Mosi, 2017⑤; Zhou Nianli and Li Yuhao, 2019⑥). On the one hand, although China's laws on intellectual property rights are relatively complete, due to its ineffective online supervision, there is a large number of online pirates selling US audiovisual products, causing huge losses to the US. China's National Security Law stipulates that the source code of an Internet product must be disclosed during assessment, with having an open source code a condition for market access in China. US companies believe that China's forced access to source codes harms their intellectual property rights. Moreover, the US accuses China of compulsory technological transfer and technological acquisition through mergers and acquisitions. This accusation has no reasonable basis and is a distortion of facts.

---

① From USTR (Office of the United States Trade Representative).

② CRS. Digital Trade and US Trade Policy. https://fas.org/sgp /crs/misc/R44565.pdf.

③ Chen Chao & Liu Hao. Global Digital Trade Development Trend, Restrictive Factors and China's Countermeasures. *Theory Journal*, Issue 5, 2018.

④ Zhou Nianli, Chen Huanqi & Wang Tao. A Study of the Main Differences between China and the United States on Digital Trade Governance during Trump's Presidency. *World Economic Studies*, Issue 10, 2018.

⑤ Li Mosi. Digital Trade Rules and New Trends in Negotiations in Super Large Free-Trade Agreements. *Journal of Shanghai Normal University (Philosophy and Social Sciences Edition)*, Issue 1, 2017.

⑥ Zhou Nianli & Li Yuhao. The conflicts, escalation trends and countermeasures between China and the United States on the protection of digital intellectual property rights. *Theory Journal*, Issue 4, 2019.

As an upgraded version of the North American Free Trade Agreement (NAFTA), the US-Mexico-Canada Agreement (USMCA) is the first important trade agreement after the Trump administration took office. Although the withdrawal of the US from the TPP was a decision announced by Trump as soon as he took office, digital trade rules and standards involved in the signed USMCA are higher than those in the TPP. It represents the direction future US trade negotiations will take, and is included in global trade agreements as a "reference". To understand the latest digital intellectual property rules presented in the USMCA, the Sino-US intellectual property dispute is likely to revolve around three areas: lifting bans on "source codes" in infrastructure software other than mass-market software; lifting bans on "algorithms", "codes", and "trade secrets"; strengthening "Internet service providers" to take more responsibility in intellectual property protection.

As an important issue in the trade negotiations between China and the United States, digital intellectual property rights cannot be ignored. If the two countries can resolve their differences and reach a consensus on this issue, it will be conducive to reaching a Sino-US trade agreement. For a long time, the US has attached great importance to the protection of digital intellectual property rights and has many differences with China concerning this. As Sino-US trade relations intensify, China needs to actively respond and consider new US demands on digital intellectual property issues, meet US demands reasonably, reform the market entry and transfer regulations of American enterprises, and actively negotiate and cooperate with the US to resolve their persistent problems on such issues. China should adhere to its principles and not compromise easily. When it comes to negotiable issues, it should uphold the principles of mutual, "win-win" benefits, responding calmly, and negotiating actively. China has been criticized by the US for its "trade bullying" strategy for a long time. By using USMCA and other higher intellectual property protection trade rules, the Trump administration was showing ambitions to protect US digital intellectual property rights, hinting at future conflicts with China. The strengthening of intellectual property rights will play an important role not only in alleviating economic and trade tensions between China and the US, but also in becoming the main engine for China's developing digital economy. This coincides with the reform goals advocated by the 19th National Congress. As a major developing country in digital economy and intellectual property rights, China should take the initiative to speak up on the global governance of digital intellectual property rights. At the same time, it should try its best to meet US demands, basing them on traditional and recent rules of digital intellectual property rights. It should reform and improve its unreasonable foreign investment and technology transfer policies. China must resolve its intellectual property disputes with the US by taking perspectives beyond that of intellectual property rights, turning challenges into opportunities, taking a more active role from her formerly passive stance, and transform itself into an innovation-oriented country.

Section 4 Prospects for Global Governance of Digital Economy

The 11th WTO Ministerial Conference held in December 2017 issued a "Joint Statement on Electronic Commerce", announcing that exploratory work will be carried out on the negotiation of "trade-related electronic commerce" regulations, based clearly on promoting negotiations along international economic and trade rules. In early 2019, at the Davos E-commerce Informal Ministerial Conference, 76 WTO members, including China, the United States, the European Union, and Japan, signed the "Joint Statement on E-commerce", officially launching trade-related e-commerce plurilateral negotiations.① This indicates that digital economy promotion has reached a global consensus. In fact, in recent years, under international multilateral mechanisms like the WTO, the G20, and APEC, digital economy has been a priority issue for trade and investment liberalization, and economic and technological cooperation. Furthermore, the signing and upgrading of many regional and bilateral economic cooperation agreements also regard digital economy as an important negotiation topic.

However, there are still many challenges in global digital economic governance. First, the positions of major economies on this issue are still difficult to reconcile. Judging from e-commerce plurilateral negotiations, the United States' competitive advantage lies in digital products and digital trade. In order to enhance its comparative advantages, the US advocates the liberalization of digital trade, emphasizing the free flow of cross-border data and prohibiting localization of digital infrastructure, while protecting source codes. The EU pays more attention to maintaining fairness and protecting personal privacy in e-commerce activities. In fact, the EU's General Data Protection Regulation (GDPR), launched in 2016 and effected in 2018, has stricter regulations on data protection and privacy. Its purpose is to ensure citizens and residents control over their personal data, and to simplify standard rules within the EU, so as to promote international economic and trade exchanges.② Moreover, the EU has also proposed to include telecommunications issues in e-commerce negotiations to ensure the non-discriminatory governmental supervision of the telecommunications market. Based on TPP/CPTPP clauses, Japan proposes that governments must not restrict specific websites and Internet services and also not violate procedural due process by forcing companies to disclose data and trade secrets and other high standards in digital trade. Russia stresses that governments should first clarify the

---

① Dong Yan & Zhang Lin. Building Rules for the Global Digital Economy. *Guangming Daily*, July 15, 2019.

② Presidency of the Council. Compromise text. Several partial general approaches have been instrumental in converging views in Council on the proposal for a General Data Protection Regulation in its entirety. The text on the Regulation which the Presidency submits for approval as a General Approach appears in annex. 201 pages, June 11, 2015. http://data.consilium.europa.eu/doc/document/ST- 9565-2015-INIT/en/pdf.

existing e-commerce rules under the WTO framework, examine their applicability, and mend loopholes in the system. China advocates to orientate digital economy in the direction of development, and focus on cross-border goods trade and logistics as well as payment and other related services that are traded through the Internet. It recommends that governments should pay attention to challenges faced by developing countries, formulate development cooperation provisions, solve the digital divide, and strengthen technological assistance and capacity building for developing members.

Second, data, as the core resource for developing digital economy, has not yet achieved free global flow. This is mainly reflected in local and industry legislative levels. Local legislation lacks global consensus and discussion, and is still at the stage of "closed-door legislation", in which other entities are forced to comply with relevant requirements through fines, bans, and other penalties.[1] There are also different regulations restricting data flow between industries, which increases the difficulty of data globalization. In the digital economy era where data is productivity, there will be no globalized digital economy without globalized data. Therefore, coordinating differences between countries in free data flow will always be a key issue in the global governance of digital economy.

Third, the relevant parties lack an overall plan for exploring global digital economic governance. A large number of regional rules overlap, and the basis for countries participating in global digital economic governance is not clear. All these issues inhibit the future sustainable development of the global digital economy.

---

[1] Han Bo & Jin Wenkai. Strengthening Transnational Cooperation and Realizing Global Digital Economic Governance. *Economic Information Daily*, August 1, 2019.

Chapter 9 Policy Recommendations for the Development of China's Digital Economy

Section 1 Policy Recommendations for the Development of Digital Technology and Economy

1.1 Develop digital technology vigorously and undertake international technical cooperation

Digital technology is the key force for the sustainable generation and development of digital economy. The vigorous development of digital technology is the key to promoting digital economy. On the one hand, China should take a multi-pronged approach by using economic entities such as the government, scientific research institutions, and enterprises to promote independent innovation of digital technology, taking advantage of policy support, research and development, and commercial applications. Doing this will allow China to overtake other nations in digital technology in the digital economy era. On the other hand, China must actively integrate itself into the world economy, actively encouraging international technical cooperation. It should use the international technology market to attract international investments in digital technology, tracking the international frontier of digital technology and combining practical criticism with learning in order to create a competitive environment for digital technology innovation. China should create a good environment in order to attract outstanding resources for independent digital technology innovation.

1.2 Optimize the configuration of data elements and enhance data security

Data is an important production factor and foundation for the development of digital economy. Realizing the optimal allocation of data elements is an important way to improve the efficiency of digital economy. At the same time, it is necessary to actively respond to severe challenges in data security and privacy protection. First, China must vigorously develop the data market, promote the free flow of data among individuals, companies, industries, and regions, and achieve the best configuration of data elements. Second, China's position should be improved in the global data value chain, transforming data scale advantages into value advantages and striving to improve its position in the global data value chain. Third, China must strengthen data security management by reasonably defining ownership of data property rights and solving related issues involving intellectual property protection and data security to ensure a free and orderly flow of data.

1.3 Establish and improve a market mechanism system compatible with the development of digital economy

As an emerging field, digital economy has started development relatively late. At present, China has not established a complete mechanism system, which limits the expansion scope of its digital economy to a certain extent. Therefore, the government should moderately reduce administrative intervention in digital economy, gradually implementing market-based supervision. It should promote the developing digital economy to adapt to the market, encouraging the role of the market in digital economy. On the other hand, while the government is spearheading major basic and scientific research in related fields, it can also encourage the development of related information technology industries through tax reduction and subsidies, fostering the growth of small and medium-sized enterprises through relevant support and protection policies. It can increase support for technological innovation and innovative enterprises, connecting government and enterprises to create a stable and healthy developing environment for the digital economy market.

1.4 Strengthen the integration of digital economy and traditional industries

To realize the huge potential of digital economy, it is necessary to genuinely apply it in traditional industries. The government should promote the digital transformation of traditional industries through supporting policies and tax reduction or exemption. It must transform relevant digital knowledge into commercial value, giving full play to its huge potential in the market. By responding to the high cost of digital transformation that enterprises generally face, the government should formulate policies to break industry entry barriers and reduce entry costs. At the same time, the government must strengthen support for related companies by constantly changing traditional industrial structures, so as to help traditional industries undertake business model innovation and technological innovation, thus realizing the rapid yet steady development of digital economy.

1.5 Accelerate the construction of digital government, and realize a new model of digitalized management

The rapid development of China's digital economy cannot be separated from effective governmental management. Accelerating the construction of "digital government" is an important foundation for achieving high-quality economic development in China. First, it is necessary to establish an effective overall coordination mechanism by coordinating all activities between the central and local governments like in a game of chess. The government must break down information barriers between all levels and various departments, and perfect the government data-sharing mechanism. It is necessary to push all levels of government to strengthen inter-departmental linkages and ensure the completeness and unity of policy rules. Second, China must openly share government data with the society, promote the openness of information resources by relevant units, increase the diversity of data, and ensure the security of public data through the formulation of sound laws and regulations, so as to construct a social-level data-sharing platform.

1.6 Actively nurture knowledgeable professional talents compatible with digital economy

In response to the talent deficiency facing China in digital economy, the government should attach importance to talents by nurturing human capital in digital economy and increasing investment in related education and scientific research projects, thereby actively promoting creative talents. By perfecting the educational system, it can allow schools to promote training in related digital technologies and create a relatively free environment for innovation, nurturing the students' creative thinking and digital skills. At the same time, it should actively encourage cooperation with the world's top institutions and master the relevant cutting-edge knowledge, promoting theoretical research and application in the field of digital technology. Doing this will accumulate a large number of high-quality talents for digital development, and at the same time improve the flexibility of talent policies, making them more adaptable to the characteristics of developing industries, thereby promoting the high-quality growth of China's digital economy.

Section 2 Policy Recommendations for the Development of Digital Economy Industries

2.1 Promote the digital transformation of traditional industries

For breakthroughs to occur in the industrial fields of digital economy, the digital upgrade of traditional industries needs to intensify. First, the application of new technologies and new platforms must be actively promoted in order to upgrade and transform traditional industries, making the manufacturing industry the main ground for the development of digital economy. Doing this will comprehensively upgrade the traditional manufacturing industries and transform them into intelligent, service-oriented, and green manufacturing, while accelerating the construction of intelligent manufacturing as a new basis of the manufacturing system. Second, various industrial cloud-service platforms and management institutions should be established, and new models such as networked research, intelligent production, and collaborative manufacturing should be vigorously developed. Third, the agricultural industry must form a digital platform on the integrated industrial chain, making full use of information technology to improve agricultural production, operation, management, and service levels, expanding new industries and formats in rural areas. Fourth, it is necessary to promote online and offline integration and innovation to form new models and formats in the service industries. Digital economy must be integrated into the modern service industries, using digital technology to help new business sectors such as e-commerce, finance, education, telemedicine, and intelligent transportation. By developing producer service industries, the transformation and upgrading of service industries will be actively promoted.

2.2 Give free rein to the leadership role of the information software service industry

Digital economy is a massive system, and the information software service industry is a fundamental leading industry driving development in the digital economy era. The information software service industry has always been active in innovation and plays a strong leadership role. Digital technology is also a technology-intensive industry, with urgent needs for capital and talents. Its basic characteristic is dynamic innovation, and it should become an important field in R&D investment. All regions should construct a nationwide exchange-and-transaction platform, introducing basic software R&D to outstanding enterprises and focusing on digital industrialization based on existing resources. They should support existing industries to undertake intelligent upgrade and transformation, introduce new technologies, and give priority to domestic software companies with R&D capabilities to develop big data and artificial intelligence. By providing localized software services and support in terms of empowerment, capital, and talent, they can promote digital industrialization and industrial digitization, thereby revitalizing the local digital economy industries.

2.3 Strengthen policy support and give full play to the main role of enterprises

The implementation of financial funds in industries, technology, talents, and investment attraction should be coordinated, concentrating on the advantageous financial resources to set up special funds for digital economy development, thereby increasing support for digital economy. Also, the construction of information infrastructure should be strengthened, and the informatization of government public services and office systems should be spearheaded. The two-way fusion of government and social data in various regions can be used for innovative applications in order to serve the local digital economy industries and further promote the in-depth integration of local digital technology with real economy, unearthing new data value and application scenarios to help improve the business environment and better serve the digital economy industries. At the same time, as the main body of digital economy, enterprises must closely integrate their practical strengths in order to reach advanced levels of their industries at home and abroad. Through the full use of transforming enterprise and commercial models, they should improve the technical level and quality of their developing enterprises.

2.4 Improve the business environment for digital industry development

Through the proper implementation of guarantee services, regional governments have established inter-departmental collaborative work mechanisms to ensure that digital economy companies will receive comprehensive and personal services that will improve the business environment for digital industry development. By establishing a digital industry public service platform (a virtual digital industrial park), the integration of and access to policy services, industrial finance, entrepreneurship counseling, intellectual property rights, talent services, production capacity sharing, and other resources will provide a unified service portal for the digital industrial park and software development, intelligent manufacturing, e-commerce, and other digital economy-related enterprises, forming an integrated online and offline service system. By precisely implementing policies, increasing policy support for key areas of digital economy and enterprises, and establishing a support mechanism for policy formulation and implementation, the open digital-economy cooperation system and mechanism can be accelerated and improved, thus promoting high-quality development of digital economy.

Section 3 Policy Recommendations for the Development of China's Digital Trade

3.1 Clarify the digital trading system and specifications

As the main form of transactions in the digital economy era, digital trade is a new form of trade. Digital trade, which is deeply integrated with the characteristics of digital economy, differs greatly from traditional trade activities in terms of trade methods and trade objects. However, there is no consensual definition of digital trade in current academic or practical research, and statistical specifications of digital trade have not yet been defined. Therefore, while China is developing its digital trade, the relevant statistical departments need to establish a unified and standardized digital trade statistical system by clarifying statistical specifications for digital trade, clearly differentiating between statistical divisions for various digital trade subdivisions and adapting them to China's developing industries. The construction of a digital trade statistical system will not only help the overall trend of China's digital trade and the development of its industries at the macro level be grasped, so that more precise policies to help its developing digital trade can be implemented, but also clarify the goals and directions for these developing digital enterprises at the micro level to better help coordinate such trade activities as customs clearance, inspection, and quarantine.

3.2 Accelerate the construction of supporting facilities for digital trade

The development of China's digital trade cannot be separated from infrastructure and industry support. First, the development of the logistics and transportation industries needs to be accelerated. Digital trade activities carried out with the help of digital technology have fast operation cycles and high requirements for logistics and transportation. Therefore, the construction of the logistics system should be accelerated to promote the efficiency of transportation and provide a strong backing for the development of digital trade. Second, the development of digital technology R&D industries and digital technology services related to digital trade must be increased, and technological R&D capabilities in related industries to meet the needs of digital trade development must be nurtured. Cross-border services, information, and communications-related industries can be opened further to the outside world, accelerating the integration of digital services, products, and cross-border e-commerce operations into global digital trade activities.

3.3 Improve the regulatory and supervisory system for digital trade

The development of digital trade not only involves domestic regulations and supervision, but also regulation adaptation between different countries and regions. At present, China has not formulated a regulatory system for digital trade, especially digital trade regulations that are in line with international standards. Specifically, digital trade regulations cover many aspects such as cross-border data transmission, taxation, product technical standards, trade barriers, data and intellectual property protection, entry and exit management, etc. One can say that on the one hand, it is a great change from former trade regulations, and on the other, it also involves the establishment of new regulations. China needs to speed up the formulation of the digital trade regulatory system, adapt to the needs of the developing digital trade, and participate in the formulation of international digital trade rules. Similarly, in terms of traditional trade methods, digital trade involves the supervision and coordination of multiple departments such as information, entry and exit, trade, taxation, and the Internet. There are more supervisory links, and the supervisory content is complicated, thus necessitating the coordination of the supervisory authorities between multiple departments. Supervision between various functional departments must be coordinated and the construction of a digital trade supervisory system must be perfected.

3.4 Reasonable policies to guide the balanced development of digital trade

In view of the current imbalance in digital trade between China's various regions and industrial structures, the characteristics of digital trade in terms of trade objects and trade patterns can be combined, with the influence of digital economy on traditional trade practices.

Taking into account trade advantages, location advantages, industrial development advantages, and other characteristics, different policies can be formulated at the national and local levels to guide the balanced development of digital trade. For example, in the current large-scale cross-border e-commerce, as well as between the eastern and southern regions, differentiated policies can be implemented, combined with the original market-size advantage, to help digital trading companies establish a unique competitive edge and help them upgrade their trading methods, while improving the diversification of trade markets and products to enhance their position in the global value chain. As for industries and regions that are underdeveloped, stimulus policies that can help these digital trade industries go out and participate in the global digital trade competition can be introduced. At the same time, policies are needed to support the digital trade transformation of trading companies and increase companies participating in digital trade in these industries and regions.

3.5 Establish a digital trade innovation system

The establishment of a digital trade innovation system is also important for policy measures. Only innovative development can effectively achieve the high-quality development of digital trade. First, a digital trade training system for innovative talents must be established. Digital trade innovation cannot be separated from high-quality creative talents. The training of digital trade innovative talents can be a combination model of schools and enterprises, guided by digital trade innovation needs, targeting the training and nurturing of creative talents in digital trade R&D and management. Second, digital trade innovation policies and regulatory mechanisms must be established. In order to provide innovation incentives for digital trade companies, relevant departments can target different forms of digital trade innovation, introducing different policies and measures to encourage innovation such as digital trade technology innovation, digital product innovation, and digital trade model innovation in enterprises. They can cooperate with relevant departments to supervise digital trade innovation, with timely and precisely adjusted policy measures. Finally, a digital trade innovative business model should be established, with relevant digital trade innovation demonstration parks, using such a digital trade innovative business model as a guide to encourage digital trade companies to make creative attempts, summing up their experience for widespread learning.

Section 4 Policy Recommendations for the Development of International Investment in Digital Economy

4.1 Leverage on "new infrastructure construction" to inject new impetus into digital investment

Combined with China's recent "new infrastructure construction" strategy, we can further upgrade the domestic digital economy's infrastructure, promote the digitalization of industries, and expand the scale of foreign investment in China as well as China's own external digital investment. By implementing the "new infrastructure construction" strategy and vigorously promoting full-speed development of 5G and big data centers, such measures will not only help stimulate overseas investment, but also improve economic efficiency, foster technological innovation, promote industrial digitization and structural upgrading, and further improve the vigor of domestic investment. At the same time, they will accelerate China's external digital investment portfolio layout and inject new impetus into China's long-term economic growth.

4.2 Support micro, small, and medium-sized enterprises and startups to foster innovation

Digital economy is essentially a technological economy, and innovation is the fountainhead of all technologies, especially digital technologies that update themselves quickly and iteratively. Led by Silicon Valley in the United States, a large number of digital technologies are products of startups and micro, small, and medium-sized enterprises. However, most of these companies have insufficient profitability and greater financing constraints. Therefore, the financial and policy support given to such enterprises must help foster China's digital technology innovation and lay a good foundation for the future long-term development of its digital economy. At the same time, technology research and development of such enterprises can also further drive the two-way international investment both externally (in technology acquisition) and internally (in value investment), generating a benign cycle in China's digital economy.

4.3 Strengthen regional cooperation and explore the digital investment potential of the "Belt and Road Initiative"

With the stagnation and regression of globalization, regional cooperation may become the mainstream, and relevant companies also need to pay attention to diversifying their investment areas, and take note of capital attraction as well as investment opportunities in Europe and East Asia. At the same time, we must also be more proficient at discovering the investment value of the "Belt and Road Initiative" countries. For example, India has advantages in financial technology, Israel has strong scientific research capabilities in network information security, and domestic capital can be offered more participatory and cooperative opportunities in these countries.

4.4 Cooperate with international organizations to build a safe digital ecosystem

The central government should actively coordinate and cooperate with international organizations to build a safe digital economy ecosystem, thus ensuring the healthy development of digital economy. With the rapid development of digital economy and the wider expansion of economic digitization, the various risks related to network security have increased sharply, and building a safe digital economy ecology has become a fundamental requirement for the development of the entire national economy and society. As a major country in the world's digital economy, China must strengthen its network security infrastructure, improve digital use, flow, and protection regulations, and prevent potential threats to computer systems, communication networks, digital products, services, and equipment, as well as to its citizens, organizations, and enterprises. China must improve its domestic networking, as well as information and communications security protection framework. Due to the borderless nature of network connections and digital flows, we can learn on the one hand from the advanced experiences of the European Union and other economies, such as the General Data Protection Regulation (GDPR), which took effect in the EU in May 2018. On the other hand, we should also actively cooperate with international organizations and major economies like those in Europe and the United States to negotiate the construction of effective and safe international networks and information dissemination regulations. By developing the domestic digital economy ecology to augment our ability to withstand risks, we will also enhance the potential of China's digital economy for international investment.

4.5 Respond flexibly to changing international economic situations

The recent rise of nationalism and anti-globalization tendencies have further intensified under the Covid-19 pandemic. In particular, economic and trade conflicts between China and the United States, and the crisis of political relations between the two countries may escalate further. This will be a great obstacle for the future development of the digital economies within these two countries. The United States and China are the two giants of the global digital economy. The global digital economy is concentrated in China and the United States in terms of markets, technology, unicorns, and investment opportunities. Moreover, the comparative advantages of the two countries complement each other, and both have strong incentives for transnational investments. However, with the rapid development of China's economy, competition between these two countries has intensified, and Sino-US relations will inevitably cast a dark shadow on the development of China's digital economy. Relatively speaking, there is still enough room for

Chinese investors to participate in the American VC and PE markets, but merger and acquisition activities of US companies may be more affected. In this context, domestic companies that wish to acquire American companies can seek joint mergers and acquisitions there to reduce the impact of non-economic factors. Correspondingly, China also needs to further regulate the entry of foreign investment and strengthen innovation protection under this new pattern of the world economy.

Section 5   Policy Recommendations for the Development of Digital Finance

5.1 Continue promoting the digital transformation of the traditional financial industries and market mechanisms, and reforming monetary policies

With the emergence of private digital financial platforms, traditional industries have suffered greatly, and their markets have been quickly eroded. Affected by the digitalization wave, traditional industries should keep pace with the times and adapt to market demands in order to win over young and middle-aged users. At the same time, the effectiveness of traditional monetary policies will also be greatly reduced. When formulating monetary policies, the government should take into account the increasingly digitalized monetary system and be specific in its targets.

5.2 Provide policy support for developing financial inclusion

The government should actively guide private institutions to provide related services, and gradually standardize the service process and content with state mechanisms. It should prevent abnormal expansion of the risk gap at all times during such vigorous promotion, and provide corresponding legal and regulatory support.

5.3 Continue improving the coordination mechanism to regulate technological development

In terms of departmental set-ups, a supervisory working group of technology experts can be established to guide the creation of data-analysis services. It can review and check the quality of completed data-analysis services, as well as evaluate the subsequent implementation effects. In addition, a liaison system can be established within Fintech companies. The coordinator should maintain real-time communication with the supervisory department, and convey new ideas and policies of the supervisory department to the enterprises in a timely manner. For problems that arise within the enterprises, they can seek expert groups to help in time.① The government should prioritize the practice of regulatory technology in high-risk areas such as the supervision of shadow banking and illegal fund-raising, striving to achieve comprehensive and effective monitoring of risks.

5.4 Formulate relevant systems to promote the development of financial industries

First of all, it is necessary to clarify the responsibilities and obligations of all relevant entities while supervising the development of science and technology. Second, one must develop a data-sharing and confidentiality system by ensuring data interconnection and intercommunication between subjects, while realizing resource-sharing and all-round risk-free monitoring. However, there is a need to take confidentiality measures when sharing data. The original data, analysis results, and conclusions should be managed at different levels.

5.5 Build a learning society

On the one hand, there is a need to encourage practitioners in financial industries to actively learn big data, artificial intelligence, cloud computing, and other related technologies in the digital economy era. These technologies are not only of great help to the field of regulatory technology, but also necessary for many fields and related occupations, greatly benefiting studies in those areas. In particular, financial industry regulators should continue to learn technology. This is the only way they will be qualified to judge and guide innovation. On the other hand, relevant subjects should learn from each other through dynamic learning. The government, regulatory agencies, traditional financial institutions, and financial technology companies should strengthen communication and cooperation, creating a "joint-office" mechanism. At the same time, risks are volatile and unstable, and various departments should continue to pay attention to financial risks.

5.6 Improve financial technology industry standards and safety regulations

At present, financial technology has many serious problems, such as inconsistent technical standards like in facial-recognition payment, and undefined laws and regulations like in big data personal privacy protection. These problems have a relatively negative effect, dampening financial innovation to a certain extent. Therefore, they clearly need to be resolved.

5.7 Strengthen the nurturing and incentives of creative talents

First, it is necessary to establish and improve the incentive and guarantee systems for scientific and technological talents, and formulate a wage system that is compatible with

---

① Guofeng Sun, Dawei Zhao (2018). Challenges and breakdowns in regulatory technology. *China finance*, 21: 19-20.

financial markets, in order to attract, motivate, and nurture talents. Second, relevant departments should establish an evaluation index system for supervising scientific and technological talents. They must certify the financial technology research and application capabilities of practitioners and social personnel, and establish a technological talent reserve mechanism. Finally, colleges and universities must be encouraged to actively integrate superior resources into computer science, economics, and finance, and set up financial technology-related majors. Désirée Klingler (2019) found that a characteristic of global financial centers that helps attract RegTech companies is high-quality education.① Therefore, expanding talent training is conducive to the long-term development of regulatory technology.

Section 6 Policy Recommendations for Digital Economy and the Labor Market

China has entered the fast lane of the developing digital economy. The government, enterprises, and individual workers all face huge opportunities brought about by digital economy, as well as severe challenges. We should actively seize the opportunities presented by the developing digital economy and strive to respond to its impact and challenges, while achieving our own high-quality growth. To this end, we propose relevant public policies and countermeasures on three levels: government, enterprises, and workers.

6.1 The government's public policy choices in response to labor market changes in the digital economy era

6.1.1 Improve governance capabilities, as well as relevant laws and regulations

Governments at all levels should further augment the use of digital technology to enhance their own modern governance capabilities, and continuously improve the precision, science, and predictability of decision-making. The government should study new types of labor relations and reasonable definitions of relations to promote the innovation of legal systems, actively responding to changes in the labor market under the new forms of employment. In terms of employment policies, the government should take precautions, plan ahead for skilled digital talents, and expand their supply. At the same time, it should pay full attention to the unemployment problem as digital economy develops.

6.1.2 Encourage entrepreneurship and innovation, and improve the level of digital technology education and training

In terms of entrepreneurial innovation, the government must actively encourage entrepreneurial behaviors and technological and business innovation. In terms of education and

---

① Klingler D. (2019). RegTech and the Sandbox — Play, Innovate, and Protect!. DOI: 10.1002/9781119362197, Chapter 21.

training, the government must first accelerate professional adjustments in colleges and universities to help develop emerging majors in the digital fields. Secondly, it must actively develop higher vocational education and digital technology education in vocational and technical schools, and cultivate high-skilled applied talents. At the same time, it is necessary to expand channels for continuous education and skills training. We must vigorously promote lifelong digital education to cover the entire career process by developing large-scale online open-course platforms. We should encourage training institutions and some enterprises to jointly construct online modular network courses, so as to improve the overall digital skills of workers.

6.1.3 Strive to narrow the digital divide and income gap

The government should pay attention to the uneven development of digital economy between regions and between urban and rural areas. It should accelerate the construction of information infrastructure in underdeveloped regions, improve the digital skills of rural population and employees, and strive to narrow the digital divide between urban and rural areas and between regions. In order to avoid the expansion of the income gap between different labor groups caused by digital economy development, the government needs to lower the employment threshold for positions related to digital economy, and improve the adaptability of low-skilled workers to digital technology. On the other hand, it is also necessary to adopt income distribution policies and use fiscal and taxation measures to adjust the excessive income gaps between departments and industries, so as to maintain fairness in the labor market.

6.2 Countermeasures for companies responding to changes within the labor market in the digital economy era

6.2.1 Accelerate integration with digital economy, and improve the competitive advantages of the labor market

Companies should regard the development of digital economy as an opportunity to accelerate their transformation and upgrading, and actively apply new digital technologies like big data, artificial intelligence, and the new generation of Internet to technological innovations through digital integration. They should actively improve their traditional R&D, production, and sales. Adjustments should continuously stimulate the creative vitality and innovative spirit of the enterprise to gradually form its own competitive advantages.

6.2.2 Adapt to changes in employment and working methods

Companies must keep track of changes in the labor market, analyze labor dispatch, labor outsourcing, remote work, and other forms of employment. They should expand ways to recruit high-quality talents, improve employment efficiency, reduce employment costs, and choose the most suitable human resources for the company. Business managers must actively adapt to the characteristics of their employees' work style in the digital economy era, create digital work platforms, adopt more flexible working hours and performance-appraisal methods, and improve the performance level of employees by augmenting their sense of identity with the organization.

6.2.3 Create a talent supply chain adaptable to digital economy

Companies should do a good job of human-resource planning for digital talents. They should make full use of digital technology platforms such as big data and the Internet, recruit suitable labor after their digital transformation, and accelerate the accumulation of new digital human capital. Companies should also actively construct an index system for evaluating employee competence in the digital economy era, encouraging employees to participate in digital skills training by linking digital skills with performance compensation. At the same time, they should improve their digital skills and create a continuous supply of digital talents for the company's strategic development chain.

6.3 Strategies for workers responding to changes in the labor market in the digital economy era

6.3.1 Formulate a scientific career progression plan

Workers should fully understand the risks of being replaced in their jobs. They should comprehensively analyze and judge their knowledge and skills reserves, make plans for their career progression on the basis of understanding changes in labor market demand, and prepare for future career changes in advance, so as to realize the transition to digital careers.

6.3.2 Improve one's digital skills

Workers should actively improve their personal digital skills through continuous education and training. At the same time, it is necessary to promote the concept of lifelong learning—continuously learning the knowledge and skills of digital technology through online education network courses and other methods. They should master the ability to use digital platforms for work, and improve their competitive advantages in the labor market through continuous learning.

6.3.3 Seize entrepreneurial opportunities and expand employment forms

As the main body of the job market, workers must grasp the more flexible forms of employment in the digital economy era, and choose the most suitable employment method to participate in social labor in light of actual conditions. Women and workers in remote locations should especially seize employment opportunities brought about by the development of digital economy. They should gain employment through digital platforms to overcome the barriers of time and space, so as to improve the degree of labor participation in digital economy era.

Section 7 Policy Recommendations for Digital Economy and Global Governance

7.1 Respect national sovereignty in digital space

Digital economy has gradually become the core of economic cooperation and even the work and life for people of all nations. Digital security will inevitably become the top priority of national security. At a time when technology cannot yet prevent digital security breaches, the basic prerequisite for the growth of digital economy is realizing the basic security of countries, especially those with relatively backward technology, while they participate in the global digital economy. Therefore, improvements in global digital economy governance should meet the needs of countries by defending their digital security, respecting the national sovereignty of digital space as a prerequisite, and building and developing a secure digital economy environment and infrastructure.

7.2 Accelerate the construction of digital infrastructure to bridge the "digital divide"

While digitalization brings new vitality to the world, it also exacerbates the inequality between different countries, regions, industries, companies, and communities. Only by accelerating the construction of digital infrastructure, ensuring that people can use digital technology equally, and bridging the "digital divide" can digital technology possibly be prevented from breeding new global divisions.

7.3 Promote digital technology exchanges and share the fruits of digital economy

Inclusiveness is the basic attribute of digital economy. Therefore, the vigorous development of digital economy requires in essence the continuous promotion of deep digital economy integration into various industries, as well as the protection of the free and orderly flow of data in cyberspace, and the early formation of a digital market connected to the world. These will provide strong supports for the healthy, sustainable development of the global economy. New digital technologies have greatly reduced the obstacles of space, distance, and information formats in business communication. As we work toward an "Internet of Everything", we should endorse the legacy of outstanding social, economic, and cultural achievements of all humanity in digital form. This will encourage the diversity and progress of human civilization by building digital space into a common home for all.

7.4 Build an efficient cooperation mechanism

At present, there is still a clear lack of overall planning between all cooperating parties seeking global governance of digital economy. This is mainly reflected in two aspects: on the one hand, a complete plan for "global digital economy governance" has not yet been formulated, and there is a lack of systematic links between cooperation projects in various fields and levels. On the other hand, a cooperation mechanism in global digital economy governance has not been perfected and is still unclear, with the operation process and division of labor between various economies and organizations requiring improvement. This not only leads to overall inefficiency between cooperating parties, but also to overlaps and conflicts. Emphasis should be placed on communication and coordination between various cooperation platforms in the future, and the efficiency of planning, design, and organizational operation mechanisms should be continuously improved.

7.5 Encourage the business community to actively participate in cooperation projects on global digital economy governance

Digital economy cooperation projects cannot be separated from the participation of the business community. However, in terms of current project cooperation practices, digital economy cooperation projects have low relevance to the commercial/private sectors, and there are also large gaps in commercial relevance and participation of different cooperation projects. For example, the business community is very interested in projects like the adaptive transformation of enterprises, policy consultation, vocational qualification certification, and employee vocational training programs under the new wave of digital economy. It is not so interested in community projects such as basic education in digital technology, development of unskilled labor, and the integration of women. The main reason is that there are serious communication obstacles in the project implementation process—industrial and commercial departments cannot efficiently transfer the projects they are interested in to their partners in real time, making project participation rates low. Hence, in the future, project planning, communication, and coordination between the business communities and government departments ought to be strengthened, so that industrial and commercial departments can keep abreast of their interested projects, thus boosting their enthusiasm during participation and cooperation.

In general, digital economy is the foundation of future global economic development, and the formulation of global governance rules must involve multiple parties, seeking to maximize consensus while balancing the interests of all parties. This is the only way digital economy can develop benignly, narrowing rather than expanding global rifts, while achieving balanced, orderly, coordinated, and inclusive development on a global scale.